D1442527

John Willis
Theatre World
1986–1987 SEASON

VOLUME 43

CROWN PUBLISHERS, INC.

225 PARK AVENUE SOUTH • NEW YORK, NEW YORK 10003

COPYRIGHT © 1988 BY JOHN WILLIS. ALL RIGHTS RESERVED. MANUFACTURED IN THE U.S.A.
LIBRARY OF CONGRESS CATALOG CARD NO. 73-82953.
ISBN 0-517-56828-4

T O
HAROLD SCHIFF

an eminent and exemplary attorney, whose compassion and generosity have made him an invaluable friend. . . .

CONTENTS

EDITOR: JOHN WILLIS
Assistant Editor: Walter Willison
Assistants: Stanley Reeves, Giovanni Romero, John Sala
Staff Photographers: Bert Andrews, Evan Romero, Michael Viade, Van Williams
Designer: Peggy Goddard

Clockwise from top: Charles Brown, Ray Aranha, Mary Alice, Frankie R. Faison, Courtney B. Vance (with football), Karima Miller, James Earl Jones in "Fences" 1987 Winner of Pulitzer Prize for Drama, "Tony" Award, and citations from the New York Drama Critics Circle, the Drama Desk, and the Outer Critics Circle.

Ron Scherl Photo

THE SEASON IN REVIEW
(June 1, 1986–May 31, 1987)

Good News! It is encouraging to report that after two seasons in the doldrums, the 1986–1987 theatre season showed a modest recovery, and planted the seeds of optimism for what had been mourned as a dying art form. There were 41 new productions on Broadway this season, compared to 33 presented during each of the past two years. Both *Variety* and the League of American Theatres and Producers reported increases in attendance and in gross receipts. Unlike the case in many previous years, summer is becoming a boost to the box office intake. The average paid admission for New York theatres increased less than 2 percent, reportedly less than the inflation rate. The average ticket price was $29.65, and the most expensive ticket remained at $47.50, the 1984 top price.

The sad news is that in spite of an increase in audience for the first time in 5 years, road companies and their gross receipts dropped 5 percent from last season, when they were greater than those for Broadway. There were only 901 playing weeks for road companies compared with last year's 983, when its gross was $235 million. This season's gross was only $223 million. These figures were discouraging, and equally discouraging was the very small number of touring units, caused by a paucity of productions adaptable for the road.

The season began with a surprising number of early openings, unlike prior seasons. However, it garnered only one hit, the 1937 London musical success "Me and My Girl," which was enjoying a long-run revival in England. It opened the new Marriott Hotel's 1,600-seat Marquis Theatre. At the end of the season, "Me and My Girl" received Tony Awards for Leading Actor (the incredible Robert Lindsay) and Actress (Maryann Plunkett) in a Musical, and for its choreographer, Gillian Gregory. The majority of the musicals this season were imported from England, an embarrassment for Broadway's superior musical reputation. Outstanding was "Les Miserables," the 3-hour adaptation of Victor Hugo's 1862 novel. This British import was the recipient of 8 Tonys, including Best Musical, Best Direction of a Musical, Best Featured Actor (Michael Maguire) and Featured Actress (Frances Ruffelle) in a Musical, and Best Original Score, Book, Scenic Design, and Lighting. Another English musical transplant, "Starlight Express," was the costliest and most technically elaborate show ever produced on Broadway, but it received only one Tony . . . for its costumes. The only native-born Tony-nominated musical was "Rags," which closed shortly after opening during the early part of the season. The United States has not spawned a musical hit since "La Cage aux Folles" in 1983.

"Fences" by August Wilson won 4 Tonys, including Best Play, Best Direction of a Play, Best Actor (James Earl Jones), and Best Featured Actress (Mary Alice) in a Play. It had already been honored with this year's Pulitzer Prize, the New York Drama Critics Circle Citation, and a Drama Desk Award, the only play ever to receive all major awards. The last segment of Neil Simon's personal trilogy, "Broadway Bound," was Tony-nominated but received Tonys only for Linda Lavin and John Randolph (Leading Actress/Best Featured Actor in a Play). Other nominated plays were "Les Liaisons Dangereuses" (from London) and "Coastal Disturbances." The Tony for Best Reproduction of a Play or Musical went to Long Wharf Theatre's "All My Sons" with Richard Kiley. The other nominees were Lincoln Center Theater's "The Front Page," and the British imports "Pygmalion" with Peter O'Toole and Amanda Plummer, and "The Life and Adventures of Nicholas Nickleby." The season's only financial success in the play category were "Arsenic and Old Lace" with Jean Stapleton, "Cuba and His Teddy Bear" with Robert DeNiro, and Jackie Mason's solo performance in "The World According to Me," for which he was voted a Special Tony. The televised Tony Awards were produced by Don Mischer for the first time. During the ceremony in the newly refurbished Mark Hellinger Theatre, special tributes were paid to the late actor Robert Preston and to actor-director-writer George Abbott, who was celebrating his 100th birthday on June 25. Angela Lansbury (a 4-time Tony winner) made a beautiful, dignified, and exemplary hostess for the ceremonies.

Other Broadway productions during the year that should be recognized, for one reason or another, include "Blithe Spirit" with Richard Chamberlain, Blythe Danner, and Geraldine Page, in her final characterization; Circle Repertory Theatre's transfer to Broadway of "The Musical Comedy Murders of 1940"; and "You Never Can Tell" with Uta Hagen, Philip Bosco, and Victor Garber. The season included 15 new plays, 8 revivals of plays, 11 new musicals, 2 musical revivals, and 12 theatrical attractions.

Performers worthy of note during the season, and not previously mentioned, are Don Amendolia, Michele Bautier, Susan Beaubian, Annette Bening, Nicola Cavendish, Barbara Cook, Timothy Daly, Lindsay Duncan, Patricia Elliott, Randy Graff,

Faye Grant, Harry Groener, Julie Hagerty, Earle Hyman, Bill Irwin, Larry Kert, Judy Kuhn, Swoosie Kurtz, Bobo Lewis, John Lithgow, John Lynch, John Mahoney, Terrence Mann, Ian McKellen, Mary Tyler Moore, Joe Morton, Greg Mowry, Lonny Price, Lynn Redgrave, Jason Robards, Carole Shelley, Michael Siberry, Jonathan Silverman, Teresa Stratas, Jane Summerhays, Lynne Thigpen, Richard Thomas, Robert Torti, Courtney B. Vance, and Colm Wilkinson.

Broadway again welcomed productions from Off-Broadway and regional theatres, including the multi-prize-winning "Fences," "Cuba and His Teddy Bear," "The Nerd," "Raggedy Ann," and "Safe Sex." The Belasco Theatre housed the New York Shakespeare Festival's successful educational project in which thousands of high school students saw free Shakespeare.

Off-Broadway did not experience a very distinguished season. There was a decline in the number of productions and in long-run hits. Outstanding productions in the Off-Broadway arena include "Groucho: A Life in Revue," "Bittersuite," the visiting Japanese "Médea," "The Early Girl," "Lily Dale," "Lady Day at Emerson's Bar & Grill," "Olympus on My Mind," "Goblin Market," "Stardust," "Steel Magnolias," "Driving Miss Daisy," "Angry Housewives," "Sills & Company," "The Widow Claire," "Brownstone," "The Colored Museum," "The Common Pursuit," "Coastal Disturbances" (which was moved to Broadway), "Raisin in the Sun," "My Gene," "Burn This!," "the dreamer examines his pillow," "On the Verge," "Staggerlee," "The Miracle Worker," "North Shore Fish," "The Knife," "Beirut," "The Perfect Party," and "Shogun Macbeth."

Outstanding Off-Broadway performances were given by Ernest Abuba, Tom Aldredge, Joan Allen, Karen Allen, Blanche Baker, Ina Balin, Lisa Banes, Robin Bartlett, Steve Bassett, Elizabeth Berridge, Don Bloomfield, Eric Bogosian, Philip Bosco, Bob Bowyer, Maureen Brennan, Fran Brill, Matthew Broderick, Ruth Brown, Liz Callaway, Joanne Camp, Semina DeLaurentis, Loretta Devine, Colleen Dewhurst, Ed Dixon, Cara Duff-MacCormick, Pamela Dunlap, Charles S. Dutton, Patricia Elliott, John Ellison, Eno, Christine Estabrook, Alan Feinstein, Frank Ferrante, Frances Fisher, Mary Fogarty, Morgan Freeman, Peter Friedman, June Gable, Boyd Gaines, Julie Garfield, Judy Geeson, Stephen Geoffreys, Tom Gerard, Daniel Gerroll, Anita Gillette, Jason Graae, Ben Harney, Cecilia Hart, Eevin Hartsough, Laura Hicks, Michael Higgins, Patricia Hodges, Avi Hoffman, Tommy Hollis, Katharine Houghton, Dana Ivey, Ernestine Jackson, Ken Jennings, Larry Kert, Juliette Koka, Christine Lahti, Lou Liberatore, Charles Ludlum (his final performances in "The Artificial Jungle"), W. H. Macy, Amy Madigan, John Malkovich, Les Marsden, Margo Martindale, Mary Stuart Masterson, Mary Elizabeth Mastrantonio, Andrew McCarthy, Lonette McKee, S. Epatha Merkerson, Laurie Metcalf, Mark Metcalf, Demi Moore, Kathy Morath, Paulene Myers, Novella Nelson, Cynthia Nixon, John Pankow, Mandy Patinkin, Rosemary Prinz, Keith Reddin, Scott Renderer, Charles Repole, Sarah Rice, Rusty Riegelman, Molly Ringwald, John Rubinstein, Debra Jo Rupp, Camille Saviola, Alan Scarfe, Ron Silver, John Sloman, Rex Smith, Lewis J. Stadlen, Robert Stattel, Fisher Stevens, Ray Stricklyn, Clarice Taylor, Jaime Tirelli, Marisa Tomei, Puli Toro, Allen Toussaint, Joe Urla, Dianne Wiest, and John Wood.

The League of American Theatres and Producers and the American Theatre Wing reached a new agreement and signed a 4-year pact (until 1990) that will give the latter more control over the Tonys, and more income from the television production of its awards ceremony. The administrative committee will continue to decide eligibility and nominations. A revival is now defined as a play or musical that has been presented previously on Broadway or in a New York non-Broadway theatre and which reopens in an eligible theatre more than 3 years after its first production. Plays or musicals determined by the committee to be "classics" will not be eligible in the "Best" category.

RANDOM NOTES: Unions made concessions for 5 of Broadway's "endangered theatres" (Belasco, Lyceum, Ritz, Nederlander, Biltmore) to help them remain active and available. . . . Cut-off date for 1986 Tony eligibility was May 6, 1987. . . . Computerized sets are causing delayed openings and canceled performances. . . . Even with seemingly exorbitant prices for ducats, the first seats to sell out are those at top prices, according to boxoffice personnel. . . . La Mama celebrated a silver anniversary with its founder Ellen Stewart. . . . After maintaining an audience for 19 years, the Light Opera of Manhattan (LOOM) was happily saved from extinction. It is the only year-round operetta company in the U.S., and the only group in the world to have all 13 Gilbert and Sullivan works in its repertoire.

BROADWAY PRODUCTIONS

(June 1, 1986 through May 31, 1987)

MUMMENSCHANZ
The New Show

Presented by ICM Artists Ltd.; General Manager, Larry Kapust; Production Stage Manager, Dino De Maio; Stage Assistants, Lee Dassler, Walter Flohr; Lighting Designer, Beverly Emmons; Press, Marilynn LeVine/P.R. Partners, Meg Gordean, Patricia Robert, Ken Sherber, Darrel Joseph, Allison Dixon. Opened at the Helen Hayes Theatre Tuesday, June 17, 1986.*

CAST

ANDRES BOSSARD
FLORIANA FRASSETTO
BERNIE SCHURCH

Performed with one intermission.

*Closed October 26, 1986 after 152 performances.

Christian Altorfer Photos

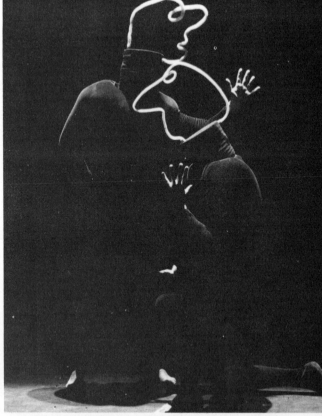

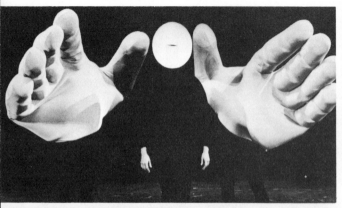

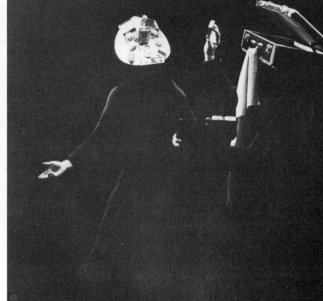

ARSENIC AND OLD LACE

By Joseph Kesselring; Director, Brian Murray; Setting, Marjorie Bradley Kellogg; Costumes, Jeanne Button; Lighting, Pat Collins; Casting, Marjorie Martin; Presented by Elliott Martin, Act III Productions, James M. Nederlander, Burton Kaiser; General Manager, Ralph Roseman; Stage Managers, Elliott Woodruff, Wally Peterson; Hair Design, Paul Huntley; Company Manager, Mitchell Brower; Props, Bob Curry; Wardrobe, Florence Driscoll; Production Assistant, James Struthers; Assistant to Director, Richard Seer; Associate Producer, Marjorie Martin; Press, Jeffrey Richards, C. George Willard, Ben Morse, Susan Lee, Marie-Louise Silva, Ken Mandelbaum, L. Glenn Poppleton III. Opened at the 46th Street Theatre on Thursday, June 26, 1986.*

CAST

Abby Brewster	Jean Stapleton
Rev. Dr. Harper	Gwyllum Evans
Teddy Brewster	MichaelJohn McGann
Officer Brophy	Andrew Gorman
Officer Klein	J. J. Johnston
Martha Brewster	Polly Holliday †1
Elaine Harper	Mary Layne
Mortimer	Tony Roberts †2
Mr. Gibbs	William Preston
Jonathan Brewster	Abe Vigoda †3
Dr. Einstein	William Hickey †4
Officer O'Hara	Kevin McClarnon
Lt. Rooney	Barry Snider
Mr. Witherspoon	Phillip Pruneau

STANDBYS AND UNDERSTUDIES: Timothy Landfield (Mortimer/Teddy), Virginia Downing (Abby/Martha), J. J. Johnston (Jonathan), Phillip Pruneau (Einstein), Karen Trott (Elaine), John Leighton (Gibbs/Harper/Rooney/Witherspoon), Andrew Gorman (O'Hara).

A comedy in 3 acts and 4 scenes. The action takes place in the living room of the Brewster home in Brooklyn during September 1941.

*Closed Jan. 3, 1987 after 221 performances and 14 previews to tour.

†Succeeded by: 1. Marion Ross, 2. Gary Sandy, 3. Jonathan Frid, 4. Larry Storch

Martha Swope Photos

Right: Tony Roberts, Polly Holliday, Jean Stapleton Top: Jean Stapleton, Tony Roberts, Mary Layne, Polly Holliday

Polly Holliday, Jean Stapleton

Jean Stapleton, Phillip Pruneau, Polly Holliday

HONKY TONK NIGHTS

Book and Lyrics, Ralph Allen, David Campbell; Music, Michael Valenti; Direction-Choreography, Ernest O. Flatt; Associate Choreographer, Toni Kaye; Scenery, Robert Cothran; Costumes, Mardi Philips; Lighting, Natasha Katz; Sound, Jack Mann; Musical Direction/Vocal Arrangements, George Broderick; Orchestrations, Jim Tyler; Dance Arrangements, David Kane; Casting, Stuart Howard; Hairstylist, Marc Daniels; Presented by Edward H. Davis and Allen M. Shore in association with Marty Feinberg and Schellie Archbold; Dance Captain, Robin Kersey; Production Supervisor, Jeremiah H. Harris; Props, Dennis Randolph; Wardrobe, Kathleen Gallagher; Magic Consultant, William Veloric; Circus Co-ordinator, Hovey Burgess; Stage Managers, Larry Forde, Mark Rubinsky, Clifford Schwartz; Press, Mark Goldstaub, Kevin P. McAnarney, Dan Kellachan, Phil Butler, Virginia Gillick. Opened in the Biltmore Theatre, Thursday, August 7, 1986.*

CAST

Barney Walker	Joe Morton
Billy Sampson	Ira Hawkins
Armistead Sampson	Danny Strayhorn
Lily Meadows	Teresa Burrell
George Gooseberry	Reginald VelJohnson
Ruby Bush	Yolanda Graves
Ivy Vine	Kyme
Countess Aida	Susan Beaubian
Kitty Stark	Robin Kersey
Montgomery Boyd	M. Demby Cain
Winston Grey	Keith Rozie
Sparks Roberts	Lloyd Culbreath
Patron	Charles Bernard Murray

SAMPSON PHILHARMONIA: George Broderick, Kaman Adilifu, John Gale, Robert Keller, David Krane, Gregory Maker, James Sedlar, Andrew Stein, Quinten White

UNDERSTUDIES: Danny Strayhorn (Barney), Keith Rozie (Billy/George), Lloyd Culbreath (Armistead), Susan Beaubian (Lily), Julia Lema-Jackson (Ruby/Countess/Kitty), Yolanda Graves (Ivy), Charles Bernard Murray (Montgomery/Winston/Sparks)

MUSICAL NUMBERS: The Honky Tonk Nights Rag, Honky Tonk Nights, Hot and Bothered, Roll with the Punches, Lily of the Alley, Choosing a Husband's a Delicate Thing, Little Dark Bird, Withered Irish Rose, Tapaholics, Eggs, A Ticket to the Promised Land, Stomp the Blues Away, I've Had It, The Sampson Beauties, The Reform Song, I Took My Time, The Brothers Vendetto, A Man of Many Parts, Finale

A musical in two acts. The action takes place in Sampson's Music Hall on a winter evening in 1912 in New York City's Hell's Kitchen, and in the Promised Land Saloon in Harlem during the summer of 1922.

*Closed August 9, 1986 after 4 performances and 16 previews.

Bert Andrews Photos

Top Right: Joe Morton

Teresa Burrell Above: Reginald VelJohnson, Susan Beaubian

ME AND MY GIRL

Book and Lyrics, L. Arthur Rose, Douglas Furber; Music, Noel Gay; Book Revision, Stephen Fry; Contributions to revision, Mike Ockrent; Director, Mike Ockrent; Choreography, Gillian Gregory; Sets, Martin Johns; Costumes, Ann Curtis; Lighting, Chris Ellis, Roger Morgan; Musical Direction, Stanley Lebowsky; Sound, Tom Morse; Orchestrations/Dance Arrangements, Chris Walker; Dance Assistant, Karin Baker; Casting, Howard Feuer; Presented by Richard Armitage, Terry Allen Kramer, James M. Nederlander, Stage Promotions Ltd.; General Manager, Ralph Roseman; Company Manager, Robb Lady; Technical Director, Jeremiah Harris; Props, Joseph Harris, Jr., Ted Wondsel; Wardrobe, Linda Berry, Cissy Obidowski; Dance Captain, Tony Parise; Wigs, Tiv Davenport, Antonio Belo; Makeup, Margaret Sunshine; Hairstylist, Paul Huntley; Associate Music Director, Tom Helm; Stage Managers, Steven Zweigbaum, Arturo E. Porazzi, Tracy Crum; Press, Jeffrey Richards, C. George Willard, Ben Morse, Susan Lee, Marie-Louise Silva, Ken Mandelbaum, Audrey Scheiderman. Opened the new Marquis Theatre, Sunday, August 10, 1986.*

CAST

Lady Jaqueline Carstone	Jane Summerhays
Honorable Gerald Bolingbroke	Nick Ullett
Lord Battersby	Eric Hutson
Lady Battersby	Justine Johnston
Stockbrokers	Cleve Asbury, Randy Hills, Barry McNabb
Footman	Larry Hansen
Herbert Parchester	Timothy Jerome
Sir Jasper Tring	Leo Leyden
Maria, Duchess of Dene	Jane Connell
Sir John Tremayne	George S. Irving
Charles Heathersett, Butler	Thomas Toner
Bill Snibson	Robert Lindsay †1
Sally Smith	Maryann Plunkett
Pub Pianist	John Spalla
Mrs. Worthington-Worthington	Gloria Hodes
Lady Diss	Elizabeth Larner
Lady Brighton/Lambeth Tart	Susan Cella
Bob Barking	Kenneth H. Waller
Telegraph Boy	Bill Brassea †2
Mrs. Brown	Elizabeth Larner
Constable	Eric Johnson

ENSEMBLE: Bill Brassea, Jonathan Brody, Frankie Cassady, Susan Cella, Sheri Cowart, Bob Freschi, Ann-Marie Gerard, Larry Hensen, Ida Henry, Randy Hills, Gloria Hodes, K. Craig Innes, Eric Johnson, Michael Hayward-Jones, Barry McNabb, Donna Monroe, Barbara Moroz, Cindy Oakes, William Ryall, John Spalla, Cynthia Thole, Mike Turner, Kenneth H. Waller

UNDERSTUDIES: Larry Hansen (Gerald), Sheri Cowart (Sally), Justine Johnston (Duchess), Eric Hutson (Sir John), Susan Cella (Jaqueline), John Spalla (Parchester), Kenneth H. Waller (Jasper/Battersby/Heathersett), Elizabeth Larner (Lady Battersby), Donna Monroe (Mrs. Brown), Barbara Moroz (Lady Brighten/Lady Diss), Michael Hayward-Jones (Constable), Jonathan Brody (Barking), Swings: Corinne Melancon, Tony Parise

MUSICAL NUMBERS: A Weekend at Hareford, Thinking of No-one But Me, The Family Solicitor, Me and My Girl, An English Gentleman, You Would If You Could, Hold My Hand, Once You Lose Your Heart, Preparation Fugue, The Lambeth Walk, The Sun Has Got His Hat On, Take It on the Chin, Song of Hareford, Love Makes the World Go Round, Leaning on a Lamppost, Finale

A musical in 2 acts and 9 scenes and a prologue. The action takes place in the late 1930's in and around Hareford Hall, Hampshire, Mayfair and Lambeth.

*Still playing May 31, 1987. "Tonys" were awarded Robert Lindsay and Maryann Plunkett (Best Actor and Actress in a Musical), and Gillian Gregory for Best Choreography.

†Succeeded by: 1. Jim Dale, 2. Jamie Torcellini

Alan Berliner, Nathaniel Kramer Photos

Top Right: Leo Leyden, Timothy Jerome, Jane Summerhays, Justine Johnston, Robert Lindsay (seated), Eric Hutson, Nick Ulett, Jane Connell, George S. Irving Below: Summerhays, Lindsay

Maryann Plunkett, Robert Lindsay
(also center above)

9

RAGS

Book, Joseph Stein; Music, Charles Strouse; Lyrics, Stephen Schwartz; Director, Gene Saks; Musical Staging, Ron Field; Presented by Lee Guber, Martin Heinfling, Marvin A. Krauss; Sets, Beni Montresor; Costumes, Florence Klotz; Lighting, Jules Fisher; Sound, Peter Fitzgerald; Musical Direction/Additional Arrangements, Eric Stern; Orchestrations, Michael Starobin; Associate Producer, Madeline Lee Gilford; Production Supervisor, Robert V. Straus; Casting, Meg Simon/Fran Kumin; General Management, Marvin A. Krauss, Gary Gunas, Joey Parnes; Company Manager, Allan Williams; Assistant Director, Bill Molloy; Props, Charles Zuckerman, Alan Steiner; Wardrobe, Joe Busheme, Don Brassington; Wig Master, Andrew Reese; Hairstylists, Jim Jeppi, Annie Miles; Assistant to Mr. Field/Dance Captain, Patti Mariano; Creative Production Coordinator, Paula Kalustian; Stage Managers, Joel Tropper, John Actman; Press, Solters/Roskin/Friedman, Joshua Ellis, Adrian Bryan-Brown, Cindy Valk, Bill Shuttleworth, Jackie Green. Opened Thursday, August 21, 1986 in the Mark Hellinger Theatre*

CAST

Immigrant/Recruiter/Thug/Italian Tenor	Andy Gale
Rebecca Hershkowitz	Teresa Stratas
David Hershkowitz	Josh Blake
Guard/Mr. Rosen/Herschel Cohen	John Aller
Guard/Cigar Boss/Hamlet/Thug	Peter Samuel
American/Rosencrantz/Frankie/Irish Tenor	Michael Cone
American/Mike	Michael Davis
"Big Tim" Sullivan	Rex Everhart
Bella Cohen	Judy Kuhn
Avram Cohen	Dick LaTessa
Anna Blumberg	Evalyn Baron
Jack Blumberg	Mordecai Lawner
Ben	Lonny Price
Recruiter/Editor/Bronstein/Passerby	Stan Rubin
Nathan's Landlady/Gertrude/Violinist's Mother	Irma Rogers
Millie/Morris' Mother/Mrs. Sullivan	Bonnie Schon
Social Worker/Shopper/Ophelia/Tenor's Mother	Joanna Glushak
Rosa/Irish Mother	Audrey Lavine
Esther/Wealthy New Yorker	Joan Finkelstein
Sam/Laertes/Ragman	Gabriel Bare
Saul	Terrence Mann
Rachel Halpern	Marcia Lewis
Mr. Harris	Larry Kert
Wealthy New Yorkers	Bill Hastings, Wendy Kimball, Robert Radford, Catherine Ulissey
Morris	Devon Michaels
Violinist	Marshall Coid
Irish Girl	Wendy Kimball

UNDERSTUDIES: Audrey Lavine (Rebecca), Peter Samuel (Mr. Harris/Saul), Devon Michaels (David), Joanna Glushak (Bella), Stan Rubin (Jack/Avram), John Aller (Ben), Irma Rogers (Anna), Swings: Patti Mariano, Cissy Rebich, Mark Fotopoulos

MUSICAL NUMBERS: I Remember, Greenhorns, Brand New World, Children of the Wind, Penny a Tune, Easy for You, Hard to Be a Prince, Blame It on the Summer Night, What's Wrong with That, For My Mary, Rags, On the Fourth of July, To America, Yankee Boy, Uptown, Wanting, Three Sunny Rooms, The Sound of Love, Democratic Club Dance, Bread and Freedom, Dancing with the Fools, Finale

A musical in 2 acts and 22 scenes. The action takes place during 1910 on the Lower East Side of New York City.

*Closed Aug. 23, 1986 after 4 performances and 18 previews.

Carol Rosegg/Martha Swope Photos

**Top Right: Josh Blake, Teresa Stratas,
Peter Samuel Below: Larry Kert, Teresa Stratas**

**Teresa Stratas, Larry Kert
Above: Dick Latessa, Marcia Lewis**

THE LIFE AND ADVENTURES OF NICHOLAS NICKLEBY

By Charles Dickens; Adapted by David Edgar; Directors, Trevor Nunn, John Caird; Setting, John Napier; Costumes, Andreane Neofitou; Lighting, David Hersey; Music/Lyrics, Stephen Oliver; Sound, T. Richard Fitzgerald; Musical Direction, Donald Johnston; Executive Producer, Nelle Nugent; Presented by The Shubert Organization, Three Knights Ltd., Robert Fox Ltd., and The Royal Shakespeare Company; Assistant Director, Cordelia Monsey; Tour Manager, Michael Hyatt; General Management, Brent Peek Productions, Scott Green; Company Manager, Mario DeMaria; American Design Associate, Randy Drake; Technical Director, Elbert Kuhn; Props, Timothy Abel, Larry Palazzo, Michael Bernstein; Wardrobe, Kevin Woodworth, Irene Ferrari; Hair Supervisor, Dale Brownell; Stage Managers, Zane Weiner, Michael Townsend, Rachael Artingstall, Philip MacDonald, Ian Barber; Press, Fred Nathan, Marc P. Thibodeau, Anne Abrams, Dennis Crowley, Bert Fink, Merle Frimark, Philip Rinaldi. Opened in the Broadhurst Theatre on Sunday, August 24, 1986.*

CAST

The Nickleby Family: Nicholas Nickleby (Michael Siberry), Kate Nickleby (DeNica Fairman), Mrs. Nickleby (Frances Cuka), Ralph Nickleby (John Carlisle)
London: Sir Matthew Pupker (Hubert Rees), Mr. Bonney (Alan Gill), Irate Gentleman (George Raistrick), Furious Man (David Delve), Flunkey (Timothy Kightley), Newman Noggs (David Collings), Hannah (Jane Whittenshaw), Miss LaCreevy (Eve Pearce), William (Jimmy Yuill), Waitresses (Karen Lancaster, Rebecca Saire), Belling (Allan Hendrick), Snawley (Richard Simpson), Snawley Major (Jane Whittenshaw), Snawley Minor (Raymond Platt), Coachman (George Raistrick), Guard (Ian East), Flunkey (Jimmy Gardner), Mantalini (Alan David), Mme. Mantalini (Karen Archer), Miss Knag (Frances Cuka), Milliners (Jane Carr, Ian East, Allan Hendrick, Karen Lancaster, Eve Pearce, Raymond Platt, Alison Rose, Richard Simpson, Jane Whittenshaw), Rich Ladies (Shirley King, Rebecca Saire)
YORKSHIRE: Squeers (David Delve), Mrs. Squeers (Pat Keen), Smike (John Lynch), Phib (Rebecca Saire), Fanny Squeers (Jane Carr), Young Wackford Squeers (Jimmy Yuill), John Browdie (Clive Wood), Tilda Price (Alison Rose), Boys: Timothy Kightley, Jimmy Gardner, Alan Gill, George Raistrick, Alan David, Bryan Torfeh, Karen Lancaster, Simon Templeman, DeNica Fairman, Frances Cuka, Karen Archer, Ian East
LONDON AGAIN: Mr. Crowl (Ian East), Kenwigs (George Raistrick), Mrs. Kenwigs (Shirley King), Morleena Kenwigs (Jane Whittenshaw), Baby Kenwigs (Jane Carr/Alison Rose), Lillyvick (Timothy Kightley), Henrietta Petowker (Karen Lancaster), George (Alan Gill), Cutler (Richard Simpson), Mrs. Cutler (Karen Archer), Mrs. Kenwigs' Sister (Rebecca Saire), Lady Downstairs (Eve Pearce), Miss Green (Frances Cuka), Babysitter (Allan Hendrick), Pugstyles (Roderick Horn), Old Lord (Jimmy Gardner), Young Fiancee (Jane Whittenshaw), Landlord (Richard Simpson), Stable Boy (Alan Gill)
PORTSMOUTH: Vincent Crummles (Tony Jay), Mrs. Crummles (Pat Keen), Master Crummles (Bryan Torfeh), Master Percy Crummles (Raymond Platt), Infant Phenomenon (Alison Rose), Folair (Alan David), Lenville (Roderick Horn), Miss Snevellicci (Jane Carr), Bane (Allan Hendrick), Wagstaff (David Delve), Fluggers (Jimmy Gardner), Blighty (Richard Simpson), Hetherington (Simon Templeman), Pailey (Jimmy Yuill), Miss Ledrock (Rebecca Saire), Miss Belvawney (Jane Whittenshaw), Mrs. Lenville (Shirley King), Miss Bravassa (Karen Archer), Mrs. Grudden (Eve Pearce), Curdle (Hubert Rees), Mrs. Curdle (DeNica Fairman), Snevellicci (John Carlisle), Mrs. Snevellicci (Shirley King)
LONDON AGAIN: Scaley (Jimmy Yuill), Tix (Raymond Platt), Lord Frederick Verisopht (Simon Templeman), Sir Mulberry Hawk (Clive Wood), Pyke (Bryan Torfeh), Pluck (Raymond Platt), Snobb (Richard Simpson), Col. Chowser (Timothy Kightley), Brooker (George Raistrick), Mrs. Witterley (Karen Archer), Alphonse (Allan Hendrick), Witterley (Hubert Rees), Opera Singers (Roderick Horn, Karen Lancaster, Bryan Torfeh), Box-Keeper (Jimmy Gardner), Head Waiter (George Raistrick), Waiters (Alan Gill, Jane Whittenshaw), Charles Cheeryble (Timothy Kightley), Ned Cheeryble (Hubert Rees), Tim Linkinwater (Jimmy Gardner), Man Next Door (Raymond Platt), Keeper (Alan Gill), Angry Fellow (Simon Templeman), Frank Cheeryble (Allan Hendrick), Nurse (Karen Archer), Dr. Lumbey (Roderick Horn), Stout Lady (Pat Keen), Married Women (Ian East, Raymond Platt, Richard Simpson), Arthur Gride (Alan David), Walter Bray (Tony Jay), Madeline Bray (Rebecca Saire), Peg Sliderskew (Jane Carr), Minister (Roderick Horn), Croupier (Timothy Kightley), Casino Proprietor (George Raistrick), Hawk's Rival (David Collings), Westwood (Allan Gill), Capt. Adams (Jimmy Yuill), Umpire (Roderick Horn), Surgeon (Timothy Kightley), Policemen (Simon Templeman, Bryan Torfeh), Mrs. Snawley (Karen Archer), Young Woman (Jane Whittenshaw)
UNDERSTUDIES: All members of the acting company listed, and Colin Campbell, Stephen Finlay, Caroline Ryder, Ruth Trouncer.

Performed in two parts: Part One (4 hours), Part Two (4½ hours).

*Closed Oct. 12, 1986 after 29 performances and 3 previews.

Chris Davies Photos

Top Right: John Lynch (Smike), Michael Siberry (Nicholas Nickleby) Below: Alison Rose, Clive Wood, Rebecca Saire, Jane Carr, Michael Siberry

The Cast

11

CUBA & HIS TEDDY BEAR

By Reinaldo Povod; Director, Bill Hart; Scenery, Donald Eastman; Costumes, Gabriel Berry; Lighting, Anne E. Militello; Presented by Joseph Papp; Associate Producer, Jason Steven Cohen; A New York Shakespeare Festival Production; General Manager, Laurel Ann Wilson; Company Manager, Susan Sampliner; Props, Daniel Telesca, Jr.; Wardrobe, John A. Guiteras; Sound, Gene Ricciardi; Stage Managers, Ruth Kreshka, J. P. Elins; Press, Richard Kornberg, Barbara Carroll, Reva Cooper, Kevin Patterson, Don Anthony Summa. Opened Wednesday, Sept. 16, 1986 in the Longacre Theatre.*

CAST

Cuba	Robert De Niro
Teddy	Ralph Macchio
Jackie	Burt Young
Redlights	Nestor Serrano
Lourdes	Wanda De Jesus
Che	Michael Carmine
Dealer	Paul Calderon

UNDERSTUDIES: Antonio Aponte (Redlights/Dealer), Paul Calderon (Che), Eddie Castrodad (Teddy), Tom Mardirosian (Jackie), Olivia Negron (Lourdes)

A drama in two acts. The action takes place at the present time in the apartment of Cuba in New York's lower eastside.

*Closed Sept. 21, 1986 after a limited engagement of 55 performances.

Martha Swope Photos

Left: Robert De Niro, and below with Ralph Macchio (C), Burt Young (L)

Robert De Niro, Burt Young

Ralph Macchio, Robert De Niro, and above with Burt Young

(standing) Tracy Sallows, Stephen McHattie, Philip Bosco,
Victor Garber, Stefan Gierasch, John David Cullum,
Gordon Sterne, (seated) Lise Hilboldt, Uta Hagen,
Amanda Plummer

YOU NEVER CAN TELL

By George Bernard Shaw; Director, Stephen Porter; Scenery, Thomas Lynch; Lighting, Richard Nelson; Costumes, Martin Pakledinaz; Wigs, Paul Huntley; Presented by Circle in the Square Theatre (Theodore Mann, Artistic Director; Paul Libin, Producing Director); Company Manager, William Conn; Casting, Hughes/Moss; Props, Frank Hauser; Wardrobe, Claire Libin; Hairstylist, James Herrara; Production Assistant, Charles Cissel; Stage Managers, Michael F. Ritchie, Carol Klein; Press, Merle Debuskey, William Schelble. Opened in the Circle in the Square Theatre on Thursday, October 9, 1986.*

CAST

Dolly Clandon .... Amanda Plummer †1
Valentine .... Victor Garber
Parlormaid .... Tracy Sallows
Philip Clandon .... John David Cullum
Mrs. Clandon .... Uta Hagen
Gloria Clandon .... Lise Hilboldt
Mr. Crampton .... Stefan Gierasch
Mr. M'Comas .... Gordon Sterne
Waiter .... Philip Bosco †2
Second Waiter .... Eric Swanson
Mr. Bohun .... Stephen McHattie †3

UNDERSTUDIES: Tom Brennan (Crampton/M'Comas/Waiter), Tracy Sallows (Dolly/Gloria), Eric Swanson (Philip Clandon), Glynis Bell (Mrs. Clandon/Parlormaid), John Hutton (Valentine/Bohun/2nd Waiter)

A comedy in two acts and four scenes. The action takes place in a dentist's office, and the terrace and sitting room of a suite in the Marine Hotel.

†Succeeded by: 1. Susan Diol, 2. John Cullum, 3. Richard Backus

*Closed Jan. 25, 1987 after 125 performances and 23 previews. The original production opened in the Garrick Theatre on Jan. 9, 1905 and ran for 129 performances. In the cast were Arnold Daly, Jeffries Lewis, Mabel Taliaferro and John Findlay.

Martha Swope Photos

Top Right: John David Cullum, Amanda Plummer
Below: Uta Hagen

Victor Garber, Uta Hagen

13

ROWAN ATKINSON AT THE ATKINSON

Written by Richard Curtis, Rowan Atkinson, Ben Elton; Music, Howard Goodall; Director, Mike Ockrent; Musical Director, Steven Margoshes; Design, Will Bowen; Lighting, Mark Henderson; Sound, Tony Meola; Production Supervisor, Mitchell Erickson; Technical Supervisor, Peter Fulbright; Presented by Arthur Cantor, in association with Caroline Hirsch, Peter Wilson, Tony Aljoe; General/Company Manager, Alexander Fraser; Stage Manager, John Handy; Props, Val Medina; Wardrobe, Warren Morrill; Press, Arthur Cantor, Stephen Cole, Jeffrey Richards Associates. Opened in the Brooks Atkinson Theatre on Tuesday, October 14, 1986.*

CAST

Rowan Atkinson

Angus Deayton

An "evening of comedy" presented in two parts.
*Closed Oct. 18, 1986 after 6 performances and 8 previews.

Top: Angus Deayton, Rowan Atkinson

Rowan Atkinson

THE HOUSE OF BLUE LEAVES

By John Guare; Words and Music, John Guare; Director, Jerry Zaks; Sets, Tony Walton; Costumes, Ann Roth; Lighting, Paul Gallo; Sound, Aural Fixation; Hair, J. Roy Helland; Production Manager, Jeffrey Hamlin; Presented by Lincoln Center Theater (Gregory Mosher, Director; Bernard Gersten, Executive Producer); General Manager, Steven C. Callahan; Company Managers, Lynn Landis, Sally Campbell; Wardrobe, Tony Karniewich; Assistant to Director, Steven Clar; Stage Managers, Steven Beckler, Peter J. Downing; Press, Merle Debuskey, Robert W. Larkin, Tracy Gore. Opened in the Plymouth Theatre on Tuesday, October 14, 1986, after playing 177 performances at Lincoln Center.*

CAST

Artie Shaughnessy	John Mahoney
El Dorado Bartenders	Ian Blackman, Brian Evers
Ronnie Shaughnessy	Ben Stiller
Bunny Flingus	Christine Baranski
Bananas Shaughnessy	Swoosie Kurtz
Corrinna Stroller	Faye Grant †
Head Nun	Patricia Falkenhain
Second Nun	Jane Cecil
Little Nun	Debra Cole
M.P.	Ian Blackman
The White Man	Brian Evers
Billy Einhorn	Danny Aiello

UNDERSTUDIES: Brian Evers (Artie/Billy), Peter J. Downing/Debra Cole (Bartenders), Ian Blackman (Ronnie), Melodie Somers (Bunny/Corrinna/2nd Nun), Peter J. Downing (M.P./White Man), Kathleen McKiernan (Bananas/Corrinna/2nd Nun/Little Nun), Jane Cecil (Head Nun).

A comedy in two acts. The action takes place in the El Dorado Bar and Grill, and in an apartment in Sunnyside, Queens, NY on October 4, 1965.

†Succeeded by Julie Hagerty
*Closed March 15, 1987 after 397 performances and 23 previews.

Brigitte Lacombe Photos

Right: John Mahoney, Faye Grant, Patricia Falkenhain, Debra Cole, Jane Cecil
Below: John Mahoney, Christine Baranski

Christine Baranski, John Mahoney and Top Right with Swoosie Kurtz

John Mahoney, Swoosie Kurtz

RAGGEDY ANN

Book, William Gibson; Music and Lyrics, Joe Raposo; Direction/Choreography, Patricia Birch; Sets, Gerry Hariton, Vicki Baral; Costumes, Carrie Robbins; Lighting, Marc B. Weiss; Sound, Abe Jacob; Flying, Foy; Hair/Makeup, Hiram Ortiz; Musical Supervision/Dance Arrangements, Louis St. Louis; Orchestrations, Stan Applebaum; Musical Directors, Ross Allen, Roy Rogosin; Conductor, Ross Allen; Casting, Johnson-Liff; Assistant Choreographer, Helena Andreyko; Presented by Jon Silverman Associates, Kennedy Center, Empire State Institute for the Performing Arts, Donald K. Donald in association with CBS; General Manager, Ralph Roseman; Company Manager, Marion Finkler; Technical Direction, Jeremiah J. Harris Associates; Props, John Lofgren, John Thompson; Wardrobe, Peter J. FitzGerald; Dance Captain, Steve Owsley; Assistant Conductor, Lawrence Yurman; Producing Consultant, Alan Wasser; Stage Managers, Peggy Peterson, Franklin Keysar, Amy Peil; Press, Shirley Herz, Glenna Freedman, Pete Sanders, Peter Cromarty, David Roggensack, Miller Wright, Jillana Devine. Opened in the Nederlander Theatre on Thursday, October 16, 1986.*

CAST

Doctors	Dick Decareau, Joe Barrett, Richard Ryder
Poppa	Bob Morrisey
Marcella	Lisa Rieffel
Raggedy Ann	Ivy Austin
Raggedy Andy	Scott Schafer
Baby Doll	Carolyn Marble
Panda	Michelan Sisti
General D	Leo Murmester
Bat	Gail Benedict
Wolf	Gordon Weiss
Camel with the wrinkled knees	Joel Aroeste
Mommy	Elizabeth Austin

Company: Melinda Buckley, Gregory Butler, Anny DeGange, Susann Fletcher, Michaela Hughes, Steve Owsley, Andrea Wright

UNDERSTUDIES: Joe Barrett (Wolf), Kenneth Boys (Raggedy Andy/Panda/Swing), Melinda Buckley (Bat), Sara Carbone (Marcella), Dick Decareau (Poppa), Anny DeGange (Mommy), Susann Fletcher (Raggedy Ann), Steve Owsley (Doctors), Richard Ryder (Camel), Gordon Weiss (General), Andrea Wright (Baby Doll), Helena Andreyko (Swing)

MUSICAL NUMBERS: Overture, Gingham and Yarn, Carry On, Diagnosis, The Light, Make Believe, Blue, Something in the Air, Delighted, So Beautiful, A Heavenly Chorus, The Shooting Star, The Wedding, Rag Dolly, You'll Love It, A Little Music, Gone, Why Not, What Did I Lose, Somewhere, Welcome to L.A., I Come Riding, Finale

A musical in two acts. The action takes place sometime earlier this century on a New York riverfront.

*Closed Oct. 19, 1986 after 5 performances and 15 previews.

Joan Marcus Photos

Top left: (clockwise from top left) Richard Ryder, Dic Decareau, Joe Barrett, Lisa Rieffel, Ivy Austin

Ivy Austin, Lisa Rieffel

Eduardo Serrano

FLAMENCO PURO

Conceived, Directed and Designed by Claudio Segovia and Hector Orezzoli; Presented by Mel Howard and Donald K. Donald; Associate Producer, Marilynn LeVine; General Management, Elizabeth Ireland McCann; Props, Tim Abel; Wardrobe, Charo, Caballero, Rosalie Lahm; Sound, F. Richard Fitzgerald; Stage Manager, Demetrio Mendez; Press, David Musselman, Mary T. Nealon, P. R. partners, Meg Gordean, Susan Arons, Wayne McWorter, Allison Dixon. Opened in the Mark Hellinger Theatre on Sunday, October 19, 1986.*

COMPANY

DANCERS: Manuela Carrasco, Jose Cortes (El Blencasao), Antonio Montoya (El Farruco), Pilar Montoya (La Faraona), Rosario Montoya (La Farruquita), Eduardo Serrano (El Guito), Angelita Vargas
SINGERS: Juan Jose Amador, Diego Camacho (El Boqueron), Adela Chaqueta, Enrique (El Extremeno), Fernanda de Utrera, Juan Fernandez (El Moreno), Antonio Nunez (El Chocolate)
GUITARISTS: Joaquin Amador, Ramon Amador, Agustin Carbonell (El Bola), Jose Carmona Carmona (El Habichuela), Juan Carmona Carmona (El Habichuela), Jose Miguel Carmona Nino

PROGRAM

PART I: Bulerias, Martinete, Toque, Cana, Alegrias, Romeras, Garrotin, Romance, Farruca, Fandangos, Tarantos
PART II: Tangos, Tientos, Soleares, Seguiriya, Bulerias

*Closed Nov. 30, 1986 after 53 performances, and began its national tour.

Martha Swope Photos

Top Right: Pilar Montoya

Manuela Carrasco

17

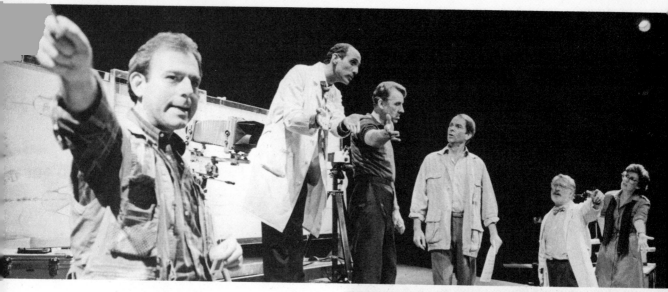

INTO THE LIGHT

Book, Jeff Tambornino; Music, Lee Holdridge; Lyrics, John Forster; Director, Michael Maurer; Choreography, Mary Jane Houdina; Scenery/Projections, Neil Peter Jampolis, Hervig Libowitzky; Costumes, Karen Roston; Lighting, Neil Peter Jampolis; Sound, Jack Mann; Musical Direction, Peter Howard; Orchestrations, Ira Hearshen; Laser Design, Marilyn Lowey; Special Laser Effects, Laser Media; Synthesizer Programing, Jeff Waxman; Casting, Dennis D'Amico; Music Supervisor, Stan Sheldone; Presented by Joseph Z. Nederlander, Richard Kughn, Jerrold Perenchio; General Manager, Darwall Associate, Barbara Darwall, Peter von Mayrhauser, Ken Silverman; Dance Captain/Assistant Choreographer, Ron Chisholm; Technical Supervisor, Arthur Siccardi; Props, Robert Bostwick, Nick Laudino; Wardrobe, James Hodson, Sylvia Westlake; Assistant Conductor, Al Cavaliere; Stage Managers, William Dodds, Steven Shaw, Paul Reid Roman; Production Assistant, Allison Sommers; Press, Judy Jacksina, Marcy Granata, Julianne Waldheim. Opened in the Neil Simon Theatre on Wednesday, October 22, 1986.*

CAST

Friend	Alan Mintz
Mathew Prescott	Danny Gerard
Kate Prescott	Susan Bigelow
James Prescott	Dean Jones
Colonel	Ted Forlow
Major	David Young
Father Frank Girella	William Parry
Peter Vonn	Lenny Wolpe
Nathan Gelb	Peter Walker
Vijay Bannerjee	Mitchell Greenberg
Phyllis Terwilliger	Kathryn McAteer
Paul Cooper	Alan Brasington
Don Cesare	Casper Roos
Archbishop Parisi	Thomas Batten
Signor Bocciarelli	Gordon Stanley
Ensemble	Michael Duran, David Young, Deborah Carlson, Terri Homberg, Valerie DePena

UNDERSTUDIES: Alan Brasington (James Prescott), Ron Chisholm (Friend), Michael Marona (Mathew), Kathryn McAteer (Kate), David Young (Peter/Paul), Gordon Stanley (Father Girella/Archbishop), Michael Duran (Vijay), Deborah Carlson (Phyllis), Ted Forlow (Gelb/Signor Bocciarelli), Peter Walker (Don Cesare), Swings: Cheri Butcher, Ron Chisholm

MUSICAL NUMBERS: Poltergeist, Neat/Not Neat, It Can All Be Explained, The Data, A Talk about Time, Trading Solos, Let There Be light, Wishes, The Three of Us, Rainbow Logic, Fede Fede, To Measure the Darkness, The Testing, The Rose and I, Be There, Into the Light

A musical in 2 acts and 13 scenes, with a prologue and an epilogue. The action takes place at the present time during late summer in Los Alamos, New Mexico.

*Closed Oct. 26, 1986 after 6 performances and 14 previews.

Martha Swope Photos

Top: Lenny Wolpe, Mitchell Greenberg, Alan Brasington, Dean Jones, Peter Walker, Kathryn McAteer Below: (C) Casper Roos, Thomas Batten

Susan Bigelow Above: Lenny Wolpe, Alan Brasington, Dean Jones, Mitchell Greenberg, Danny Gerard, Peter Walker, William Parry, Kathryn McAteer, Thomas Batten, Alan Mintz

A LITTLE LIKE MAGIC

Conceived and Directed by Diane Lynn Dupuy, C.M.; Production Supervisor, Sam Ellis; Visual Arts Effects, Mary C. Thornton; Lighting, Ken Billington; Sound, Lewis Mead; General Manager, Maria Productions; Presented by Famous People Players; Press, Mark Goldstaub, Kevin P. McAnarney, Dan Kellachan, Virginia Gillick. Opened Sunday, October 26, 1986.*

CAST

Darlene Arsenault	Greg Kozak
Michelle Busby	Debbie Lim
Sandra Ciccone	Renato Marulli
Charlene Clarke	Debbie Rossen
Annastasia Danyliw	Mary Thompson
Benny D'Onofrio	Neil Thompson
Any Fitzpatrick	Lenny Turner
Kim Hansen	

Understudies: Debra Camilleri, Alison Pounder, Gary Graham, Ida Colalillo

PROGRAM

A Little Like Magic, Aruba Liberace, Aquarium, The Sorcerer's Apprentice, The Bear and the Bee, Concertino for Carignan, Viva Las Vegas, The Gambler, Theme from "Superman," Music of 007, The Battle Hymn of the Republic, Divertissement, Night on Bald Mountain, Fossils, The Swan, Billie Jean, Part-time Lovers, That's Entertainment, New York New York, 42nd Street, Ease on Down the Road, Don't Rain on My Parade, Send in the Clowns, The Night They Invented Champagne, Get Me to the Church on Time, Oklahoma!, Can-Can, Lullaby of Broadway, Give My Regards to Broadway

The Canadian life-size puppet theatre presented in two parts.

*Closed Dec. 7, 1986 after 49 performances and 11 previews.

Right: Stevie Wonder
Top: Cast

Liberace, Barbra Streisand
Above: Michael Jackson

Elvis Presley

19

SHAKESPEARE ON BROADWAY FOR THE SCHOOLS

A New York Shakespeare Festival Production presented by Joseph Papp; Director, Estelle Parsons; Scenery, Loren Sherman; Costumes, Ruth Morley; Lighting, Victor En Yu Tan; Fight Choreography, B. H. Barry; Casting, Rosemarie Tichler/James Mulkin; Associate Producer, Jason Steven Cohen; Principal Sponsors, New York Newsday/Times Mirror, The Board of Education of the City of New York; General Managers, Laurel Ann Wilson, Bob MacDonald; Manager, Steven H. David; Administrator, Michelle Macau; Assistant Manager, Arthur Leon; Props, Vince Klemmer; Wardrobe, Robert S. Miller, Mark Niedzolkowski; Hairdresser, Ducki Contreras; Stage Manager, Lisa Ledwich; Press, Richard Kornberg, Kevin Patterson, Barbara Carroll, L. Glenn Poppleton III. Opened in the Belasco Theatre on Wednesday, November 12, 1986.*

COMPANY

F. Murray Abraham, Arnold Bankston III, Christian Baskous, Deborah Bremer, Rocky Carroll, Ivonne Coll, Bertila Damas, Keith David, Mariye Inouye, Jeffery Logan, Jordan Lund, Judith Moreland, Rene Moreno, James Puig, Mac Randall, Michael Rivera, Rene R. Rivera, Yukio Tsuji, Ching Valdes-Aran

IN REPERTORY: Macbeth, As You Like It, Romeo and Juliet

*Closed May 31, 1987 after 174 performances in repertory. From July 26 through Aug. 31, 1986 the company performed "Romeo and Juliet" and "As You Like It" in repertory for 32 performances in the parks in all five boroughs of New York City.

Cast not identified

OH COWARD!

Words and Music, Noel Coward; Devised and Directed by Roderick Cook; Settings, Helen Pond, Herbert Senn; Lighting, F. Mitchell Dana; Costumes, David Toser; Hairstylist, Paul Warden; Musical Director, Dennis Buck; Musical Arrangements, Rene Wiegert; Executive Producer, Richard Seader; Presented by Raymond J. Greenwald; General Management, Sylrich Management Co.; Assistant to Mr. Greenwald, Susan Ferrary; Production Assistant, Pearl Berman; Wardrobe, Anne-Marie Walker; Casting, Myers/Techner; Stage Managers, J. Andrew Burgreen, Jim Woolley; Press, Jeffrey Richards, C. George Willard, Ben Morse, Susan Lee, Irene Gandy, Ken Mandelbaum, William Stewart, John Curtis-Michael. Opened in the Helen Hayes Theatre on Monday, November 17, 1986.*

CAST

Roderick Cook
Catherine Cox
Patrick Quinn
Standbys: Marianne Tatum, Dalton Cathey

ACT I: *Introduction:* The Boy Actor, *Oh Coward!:* Poor Little Rich Girl, Zigeuner, Let's Say Goodbye, This Is a Changing World, We Were Dancing, Dance Little Lady, Room with a View, Sail Away, *England:* London Is a Little Bit of All Right, The End of the News, The Stately Homes of England, London Pride, *Family Album:* Auntie Jessie, Uncle Harry, *Music Hall:* Chase Me Charlie, Saturday Night at the Rose and Crown, Island of Bolamazoo, What Ho Mrs. Brisket!, Has Anybody Seen Our Ship?, Men about Town, If Love Were All, *Travel:* Too Early or Too Late, Why Do the Wrong People Travel?, The Passenger's Always Right, Mrs. Worthington
ACT II: Mad Dogs and Englishmen, The Party's Over Now, Dance Little Lady, You Were There, *Theatre:* Three White Feathers, The Star, The Critic, The Elderly Actress, *Love:* Gertie, Loving, I Am No Good at Love, Sex Talk, A Question of Lighting, Mad about the Boy, *Women:* Nina, Mrs. Went-Worth-Brewster, World Weary, Let's Do It (Music, Cole Porter), Where Are the Songs We Sung?, Someday I'll Find You, I'll Follow My Secret Heart, If Love Were All, Play Orchestra Play, I'll See You Again

*Closed Jan. 3, 1987 after 56 performances.

Peter Cunningham Photos

Top: Patrick Quinn, Catherine Cox, Roderick Cook

Roderick Cook, Catherine Cox
Above: Patrick Quinn, Roderick Cook

SMILE

Music, Marvin Hamlisch; Book and Lyrics, Howard Ashman; Based on screenplay by Jerry Belson; Director, Howard Ashman; Musical Staging, Mary Kyte; Scenery, Douglas W. Schmidt; Costumes, William Ivey Long; Lighting, Paul Gallo; Sound, Otts Munderloh; Musical Director, Paul Gemignani; Orchestrations, Sid Ramin, Bill Byers, Dick Hazard, Torrie Zito; Vocal Arrangements, Buster Davis; Presented by Lawrence Gordon, Richard M. Kagan, Sidney L. Shlenker; Associate Producers, Barbara Livitz, Ronald and Barbara Balser; General Management, R. Tyler Gatchell, Peter Neufeld, Nina Lannan; Company Manager, Roger Gindi; Assistant Director, Albert Tavares; Assistant Choreographer, Dance Captain, Liza Gennaro-Evans; Associate Conductor, Ronald Melrose; Props, George Green, Abe Einhorn; Wardrobe, Adelaide Laurino, Rachele Bussanich; Hair Supervisor, Angela Gari; Stylists, Bobby Grayson, Dale Brownell; Casting, Albert Tavares; Stage Managers, Alan Hall, Ruth E. Rinkin, Paul Mills Holmes, Betsy Nicholson; Press, Fred Nathan, Bert Fink, Anne Abrams, Dennis Crowley, Merle Frimark, Marc P. Thibodeau. Opened in the Lunt-Fontanne Theatre on Monday, November 24, 1986.*

CAST

Robin Gibson, Antelope Valley	Anne Marie Bobby
Doria Hudson, Yuba City	Jodi Benson
Sandra-Kay Macaffee, Bakersfield	Veanne Cox
Maria Gonzales, Salinas	Cheryl-Ann Rossi
Shawn Christianson, La Jolla	Tia Riebling
Valerie Sherman, Sacramento	Lauren Goler
Heidi Anderson, Anaheim	Deanna D. Wells
Patti-Lynn Bird, El Centro	Mana Allen
Debralee Davis, Eureka	Andrea Leigh-Smith
Kate Gardner, Fresno	Mia Malm
Linda Lee, San Francisco	Valerie Lau-Kee
Kimberly Lyons, Palo Alto	Julie Tussey
Gina Minelli, San Luis Obispo	Donna Marie Elio
Dana Simpson, Sausalito	Renee Veneziale
Connie-Sue Whipple, Visalia	Cindy Oakes
Cookie Wilson, Carson	Nikki Rene
Joanne Marshal, last year's winner	Mia Malm
Brenda DiCarlo Freelander	Marsha Waterbury
Big Bob Freelander	Jeff McCarthy
Tommy French, choreographer	Michael O'Gorman
Dale Wilson-Shears, foundation chairman	Richard Woods
Ted Farley, M.C.	Dick Patterson
Carol, Brenda's assistant	Ruth Williamson
Tony, a volunteer	Jeffrey Wilkins
Robin's Mom/Judge/Volunteer	Laura Gardner
Photographer/Judge/Volunteer	K. C. Wilson
Little Bob Freelander	Tommy Daggett
Freddy	Andrew Cassese

UNDERSTUDIES: Joyce Nolen (Brenda), Jeffrey Wilkins (Big Bob), Mana Allen (Robin), Susan Dow (Robin/Sandra-Kay), Donna Marie Elio (Doria/Maria), Deanna D. Wells (Doria/Shawn), K. C. Wilson (Farley/Wilson-Shears), Nikki Rene (Maria), Lauren Goler (Shawn), Cindy Oakes (Sandra-Kay), Andrea Leigh-Smith (Valerie), Michael Bologna (Tommy), Swings: Michael Bologna, Susan Dow, Linda Hess, Woody Howard, Joyce Nolen
MUSICAL NUMBERS: Prologue, Orientation/Postcard 1, Disneyland, Shine, Postcard 2, Nerves, Young and American, Until Tomorrow Night, Postcard 3/ Dressing Room, Smile, In Our Hands, Pretty as a Picture

A musical in 2 acts. The action takes place in Santa Rosa Junior College during three days last summer.

*Closed Jan. 3, 1987 after 48 performances and 11 previews.

Martha Swope Photos

Top Left: Michael O'Gorman
Lower Left Center:
Young American Miss Contestants
Above: Anne Marie Bobby, Jodi Benson

Marsha Waterbury, Jeff McCarthy

BROADWAY BOUND

By Neil Simon; Director, Gene Saks; Scenery, David Mitchell; Costumes, Joseph G. Aulisi; Lighting, Tharon Musser; Sound, Tom Morse; Casting, Simon/Kumin; Hair Design, J. Roy Helland; Presented by Emanuel Azenberg; Assistant Director, Bill Molloy; Technical Supervision, Arthur Siccardi, Pete Feller/Theatrical Services; Props, Jan Marasek; Assistant to Producer/Company Manager, Leslie Butler; Consultant, Jose Vega; Company Liaison, Linda Wright; Production Assistant, Katrina Stevens; Wardrobe, Penny Davis; Stage Managers, Peter Lawrence, Henry Velez; Press, Bill Evans, Sandra Manley, Jim Baldassare, Marlene DeSavino. Opened in the Broadhurst Theatre on Thursday, December 4, 1986.*

CAST

Kate	Linda Lavin †1
Ben	John Randolph †2
Eugene	Jonathan Silverman †3
Stanley	Jason Alexander †4
Blanche	Phyllis Newman
Jack	Philip Sterling †5

Radio Voices:

Mrs. Pitkin	Marilyn Cooper
Chubby Waters	MacIntyre Dixon
Announcer	Ed Herlihy

STANDBYS: Carol Locatell (Kate/Blanche), Alan Manson (Ben/Jack), Peter Birkenhead (Eugene/Stanley)

A comedy in two acts. The action takes place in Brighton Beach, Brooklyn, New York, in February of the late 1940's.

†Succeeded by: 1. Elizabeth Franz, 2. Alan Manson, 3. Evan Handler, 4. Mark Nelson, 5. Dick Latessa

*Still playing May 31, 1986. "Tonys" were awarded Linda Lavin for Best Actress in a Play, and John Randolph for Best Featured Actor in a Play.

Martha Swope Photos

Top Left: (rear) Phyllis Newman, Philip Sterling, Jason Alexander, (front) Linda Lavin, Jonathan Silverman, John Randolph Below: Jonathan Silverman, Jason Alexander

Philip Sterling, Linda Lavin

Jonathan Silverman, Linda Lavin

23

WILD HONEY

By Michael Frayn; From the play without a title by Anton Chekhov; Conceived and Directed by Christopher Morahan; Scenery, John Gunter; Costumes, Deirdre Clancy; Lighting, Martin Aronstein; Incidental Music, Dominic Muldowney; Casting, Howard Feuer; Presented by Duncan C. Weldon, Jerome Minskoff, Robert Fryer, Karl Allison, Douglas Urbanski, Jujamcyn Theaters/Richard G. Wolff, Albert and Anita Waxman in association with the National Theatre of Great Britain; General Management, Joseph Harris, Peter T. Kulok, Steven E. Goldstein; Manager, Thomas P. Santopietro; Associate Manager, Russ Lori Rosensweig; Props, Paul Biega; Wardrobe, Karen Lloyd; Technical Supervision, Jeremiah J. Harris; Sound, Valerie L. Spradling, Tom Angelotti; Assistant Director, Christopher Markle; Stage Managers, Bob Borod, Joseph Cappelli, Arthur Gaffin; Press, Fred Nathan, Merle Frimark, Marc P. Thibodeau, Anne Abrams, Dennis Crowley, Bert Fink. Opened in the Virginia Theatre on Thursday, December 18, 1986.*

CAST

Dr. Triletzky, the local doctor	Sullivan Brown
Yakov, servant in Voynitzev household	Timothy Landfield
Maids	Vivienne Avramoff, Kitty Crooks
Anna Petrovna, widow of General Voynitzev	Kathryn Walker
Porfiry Semyonovich Glagolyev, local landowner	Jonathan Moore
Sergey, Anna's stepson	Frank Maraden
Colonel Triletzky, father of the doctor and Sasha, and retired officer	Franklin Cover
Sofya, Sergey's wife	Kim Cattrall
Vasily, another servant	Ron Johnston
Marko, a process server	George Hall
Marya Yerfimovna Grekova, a student	J. Smith-Cameron
Platonov, the local schoolmaster	Ian McKellen
Sasha, his wife	Kate Burton
Gerasim Kuzmich Petrin, wealthy merchant	William Duff-Griffin
Osip, a horsethief	Stephen Mendillo
Peasant	William Cain

STANDBYS AND UNDERSTUDIES: Vivienne Avramoff (Anna/Sofya), Kitty Crooks (Sasha/Grekova), William Cain (Colonel/Glagolyev/Marko/Vasily/Yakov), Timothy Landfield (Dr. Triletzky/Osip), Ron Johnston (Petrin), Guy Paul (Platonov/Sergey)

A comedy in two acts. The action takes place on the Voynitzev family estate in one of the southern provinces of Russia.

*Closed Jan. 11, 1987 after 28 performances and 7 previews.

Frederic Ohringer Photos

Top Right: Franklin Cover, Kim Cattrall, Frank Maradan, Ian McKellen, Jonathan Moore Below: Kate Burton, Ian McKellen

Kathryn Walker, Ian McKellen

J. Smith-Cameron, Ian McKellen

Jackie Mason (also top)

THE WORLD ACCORDING TO ME

Created and Written by Jackie Mason; Supervised by Ron Clark; Scenery and Lighting, Neil Peter Jampolis; Sound, Bruce D. Cameron; Presented by Nick Vanoff; Associate Producer, Jyll Rosenfeld; General Management, Joseph Harris, Ira Bernstein, Peter T. Kulok, Steven E. Goldstein; Manager, Nancy Simmons; Associate Manager, Russ Lori Rosensweig; Technical Supervision, Jeremiah J. Harris; Production Assistant, Gerri Higgins; Stage Manager, Don Myers; Props, Joseph Harris, Jr.; Press, Patt Dale, Zarem Inc. Opened in the Brooks Atkinson Theatre on Monday, December 22, 1986.*

CAST

JACKIE MASON

Presented in two parts, with material selected from U.S. Politics, World Affairs, Hollywood Producers and Celebrities, Dating, Communism, Sex Education, Psychiatry, Hookers, Health Hazards, The Army, The Weather, Gentiles and Jews

*Still playing May 31, 1987. Mr. Mason was the recipient of a 1987 Special "Tony" Award.

Martha Swope Photos

Mary Tyler Moore, Lynn Redgrave

SWEET SUE

By A. R. Gurney, Jr.; Director, John Tillinger; Scenery, Santo Loquasto; Costumes, Jess Goldstein; Lighting, Ken Billington; Background Display, Kodak Duratrans; Casting, Donna Isaacson/John Lyons; Creative Photography, FPG International; General Management, Kingwill & Goossen; Presented by Arthur Whitelaw, Dick Button, Byron Goldman; Associate Producers, Norma and David Langworthy; Company Managers, Marion Finkler, Noel Stern; Props, Trish Avery; Wardrobe, Darthula McQueen; Production Assistant, Ward Oberman; Stage Managers, Ed Aldridge, Noel Stern; Press, David Powers. Opened in The Music Box on Thursday, January 8, 1987 and moved to the Royale Theatre on April 1, 1987.*

CAST

Susan	Mary Tyler Moore
Susan Too	Lynn Redgrave
Jake	John K. Linton
Jake Too	Barry Tubb

Standbys: Karen Grassle, Steven Flynn

A comedy in two acts. The action takes place during the course of a recent summer in various rooms of Susan's house in a suburb of New York City.

*Closed May 31, 1987 after 164 performances and 15 previews.

Martha Swope Photos

Top: Barry Tubb, Mary Tyler Moore, John K. Linton, Lynn Redgrave (also left) Below: John K. Linton, Redgrave, Moore

STEPPING OUT

By Richard Harris; Director, Tommy Tune; Scenery, David Jenkins; Costumes, Neil Spisak; Lighting, Beverly Emmons; Sound, Otts Munderloh; Choreographic Associate, Marge Champion; Directorial Associate, Bruce Lumpkin; Music Supervised/Arranged by Peter Howard; Hair/Makeup, Kelvin R. Trahan; Casting, Lyons/Isaacson; Presented by James M. Nederlander, The Shubert Organization, Jerome Minskoff, Elizabeth I. McCann, Bill Kenwright; Associate Producer, Stanley A. Glickman; General Management, Next Wave/Mary T. Nealon, David Musselman; Wardrobe, Rosalie Lahm; Props, Timothy Abel, Michael Bernstein; Special Effects, Chic Silber; Production Assistant, Larry Reitzer; Assistant Manager, Edward Nelson; Dialect Consultant, Elizabeth Smith; Associate Lighting Designer, Craig Miller; Stage Managers, Bruce Lumpkin, David Wolfe; Press, Judy Jacksina, Marcy Granata, Julianne Waldhelm, Stacey Sena. Opened in the John Golden Theatre on Sunday, January 11, 1987.*

CAST

Mavis	Pamela Sousa
Mrs. Fraser	Victoria Boothby
Lynne	Cherry Jones
Dorothy	Marcell Rosenblatt
Maxine	Carole Shelley
Andy	Janet Eilber
Geoffrey	Don Amendolia
Vera	Meagen Fay
Sylvia	Sheryl Sciro
Rose	Carol Woods

STANDBYS: Candace Tovar (Mavis/Andy), Roo Brown (Mrs. Fraser), Nancy Callman (Maxine/Vera/Sylvia), Susanna Frazer (Lynne/Dorothy), Gwen Shepherd (Rose), David Doty (Geoffrey)

A musical in two acts. The action takes place at the present time in the hall of a North London Church.

*Closed March 15, 1987 after 72 performances and 29 previews.

Martha Swope Photos

Right: Carole Shelley, Sheryl Sciro, Carol Woods
Above: (front) Pamela Sousa, Don Amendolia Top:
Carol Woods, Carole Shelley, Sheryl Sciro, Pamela Sousa, Meagen Fay, Janet Eilber, Cherry Jones, Marcell Rosenblatt

Pamela Sousa

Carole Shelley

Janet Eilber, Don Amendolia

STARDUST

Lyrics by Mitchell Parish; Music, Hoagy Carmichael, Benny Goodman, Duke Ellington, LeRoy Anderson, and others; Based on an idea by Burton L. Litwin and Albert Harris; Conceived and Directed by Albert Harris; Musical Staging; Patrice Soriero; Musical Supervision/Direction/Vocal Arrangements/Orchestrations, James Raitt; Scenery, David Jenkins; Costumes, Mardi Philips; Lighting, Ken Billington; Sound, Gary Harris; Casting, Warren Pincus; Tap Dance, Henry LeTang; Presented by William H. Kessler, Jr., Burton L. Litwin, Martin Rein, Howard Rose, Louise Westergaard in association with Paula Hutter Gilliam; A Theatre Off Park Production; Associate Producer, Richard Jay Smith; General Management, Weiler/Miller Associates; Technical Coordinator, Richard Siegel; Dance Captain, Deborah Graham; Props, Don Zingaro; Wardrobe, Avery Kent; Production Assistant, Brandon Doemling; Hair Design, Dale Brownell; Stage Managers, William Hare, Rachel S. Levine; Press, Henry Luhrman, Terry M. Lilly, Susan Chicoine, Andrew P. Shearer, Anne Holmes. Opened in the Biltmore Theatre on Thursday, February 19, 1987.*

CAST

Michele Bautier	Andre DeShields
Maureen Brennan	Jason Graae
Kim Criswell	Jim Walton

UNDERSTUDIES: Leata Galloway, Deborah Graham, Joel Blum, Vondie Curtis-Hall

MUSICAL NUMBERS: Act I: Carolina Rolling Stone, Riverboat Shuffle, One Morning in May, Sweet Lorraine, Sentimental Gentleman from Georgia, Sophisticated Lady, Dixie after Dark, Stairway to the Stars, Wealthy Shmelthy as Long as You're Healthy, Hands Across the Table, You're So Indiff'rent, It Happens to the Best of Friends, I Would If I Could But I Can't, The Scat Song, Sidewalks of Cuba, Evenin', Deep Purple, Act II: Sophisticated Swing, Midnight at the Onyx, Tell Me Why, Does Your Heart Beat for Me?, Stars Fell on Alabama, Don't Be That Way, Organ Grinder's Swing, Moonlight Serenade, Star Dust, Belle of the Ball, The Syncopated Clock, Take Me in Your Arms, Ciao Ciao Bambino, Sleigh Ride, Volare, Ruby, Forgotten Dreams, Star Dust

*Closed May 17, 1987 after 118 performances. It had previously played 59 sold-out performances Off-Broadway at Theatre Off Park.

Gerry Goodstein, Anita and Steve Shevett Photos

(front) Maureen Brennan, Jim Walton, Kim Criswell (rear) Jason Graae, Michele Bautier, Andre De Shields
Top Left: Andre De Shields, Maureen Brennan Below: Maureen Brennan, Kim Criswell, Michele Bautier

SOUTH PACIFIC

Music, Richard Rodgers; Lyrics, Oscar Hammerstein 2nd; Book, Oscar Hammerstein 2nd, Joshua Logan; Adapted from James A. Michener's "Tales of the South Pacific"; Orchestrations, Robert Russell Bennett; Conductor, Paul Gemignani; Direction/Musical Staging, Gerald Freedman; Sets/Costumes, Desmond Heeley; Lighting, Duane Schuler; Choreography, Janet Watson; Sound, Thomas Maher; Assistant Directors, Raymond Menard, Christian Smith; Technical Director, Rik Kaye; Stage Managers, Stephen Chaiken, Joseph Gasperee, John Knudsen; Props, Karen McDuffee; Press, Susan Woelzl, Joan McDonald; Presented by The New York City Opera (Beverly Sills, General Director). Opened Friday, Feb. 27, 1987 in the New York State Theater.*

CAST

Ngana	Lynn Chen/Allegra Forste
Jerome	Robin Ria/Peter Yarin
Henry	Thomas Ikeda
Ensign Nellie Forbush	Susan Bigelow/Marcia Mitzman
Emile de Becque	Justino Diaz/Stanley Wexler
Bloody Mary	Muriel Costa-Greenspon/Camille Saviola
Bloody Mary's Assistant	Raven Wilkinson
Luther Billis	Tony Roberts
Lt. Joseph Cable, USMC	Richard White/Cris Groenendaal
Capt. George Brackett, USN	James Billings
Cmdr. William Harbison, USN	Daren Kelly/Joseph Culliton
Lt. Buzz Adams	Ralph Bassett
Seabee Tom O'Brien	Terry Lacy
Cpl. Hamilton Steeves, USMC	Ron Hilley
Abner	Charles Mandracchia
Sgt. Kenneth Johnson	Gregory Moore
Radio Operator Bob McCaffrey	Jonathan Guss
Stewpot	John Welch
Professor	Jeff Blumenkrantz
Private Victor Jerome	Andrew Cuk
Private Sven Larsen	Edward Zimmerman
Yeoman Herbert Quale	Frank Ream
Sgt. Jack Waters	Louis Perry
Seabee Richard West	Robert Brubaker
Seabee Morton Wise	William Dyszel
Staff-Sgt. Thomas Hassinger	David Frye
Seabee Joseph Grant	Don Yule
Lt. Genevieve Marshall	Michele McBride
Ensign Lisa Minelli	Ivy Austin
Ensign Connie Walewska	Deborah Darr
Ensign Janet McGregor	Janet Villas
Ensign Bessie Noonan	Paula Hostetter
Ensign Pamela Whitmore	Mary Ann Rydzeski
Ensign Rita Adams	Deanna Wells
Ensign Sue Yaeger	Tina Johnson
Ensign Betty Pitt	Beth Pensiero
Ensign Cora MacRae	Sylvia Rhyne
Ensign Dinah Murphy	Kay Schoenfeld
Liat	Ann Yen/Adrienne Telemaque
Marcel	Henry Ravelo

MUSICAL NUMBERS: Dites-Moi, A Cockeyed Optimist, Twin Soliloquies, Some Enchanted Evening, Bloody Mary, There Is Nothin' Like a Dame, Bali Hai, I'm Gonna Wash That Man Right Out of My Hair, I'm in Love with a Wonderful Guy, This Is How It Feels, Happy Talk, Honey Bun, You've Got to Be Carefully Taught, This Nearly Was Mine, Finale

A musical in two acts. The action takes place on two islands in the South Pacific during World War II.

*Closed Apr. 26, 1987 after 68 performances.

Top Left: Susan Bigelow, Justino Diaz
Below: Marcia Mitzman, Cris Groenendaal

Muriel Costa-Greenspon, Tony Roberts (C)
Above: Stanley Wexler, Marcia Mitzman

COASTAL DISTURBANCES

By Tina Howe; Director, Carole Rothman; Scenery, Bob Shaw; Lighting, Dennis Parichy; Costumes, Susan Hilferty; Sound, Gary Harris; Hair, Antonio Soddu; Production Manager, Michael F. Ritchie; Presented by Circle in the Square Theatre (Theodore Mann, Artistic Director; Paul Libin, Producing Director); The Second Stage Production; Casting, Meg Simon/Fran Kumin; Company Manager, William Conn; Stage Manager, Pamela Edington; Props, Frank Hauser; Wardrobe, Claire Libin; Press, Merle Debuskey, William Schelble. Opened in Circle in the Square Theatre on Wednesday, March 4, 1987.*

CAST

Leo Hart	Timothy Daly†1
Holly Dancer	Annette Bening†2
Winston Took	Jonas Abry†3
Miranda Bigelow	Angela Goethals†4
Ariel Took	Jean De Baer
Faith Bigelow	Heather MacRae
M. J. Adams	Rosemary Murphy
Dr. Hamilton Adams	Addison Powell
Andre Sor	Ronald Guttman

UNDERSTUDIES: Susan Wands (Holly/Faith/Ariel), Don Fischer (Leo), David Cryer (Dr. Adams/Andre), Christopher Cunningham (Winston), Monique Lawrence (Miranda)

A comedy in 2 acts and 10 scenes. The action takes place during the last two weeks of August at the present time on a private beach on Massachusetts' North Shore.

*Still playing May 31, 1987. It was transferred from The Second Stage where it had given 93 performances Off-Broadway.

†Succeeded by: 1. Tim Ryan, 2. Madeleine Potter, 3. Michael Maronna, 4. Jami Lynne Grenham

Susan Cook Photos

Right: Timothy Daly, Annette Bening, Rosemary Murphy, Addison Powell Top: Angela Goethals, Heather MacRae, Jonas Abry, Jean De Baer

Timothy Daly, Annette Bening

Annette Bening, Ronald Guttman

STARLIGHT EXPRESS

Music, Andrew Lloyd Webber; Lyrics, Richard Stilgoe; Director, Trevor Nunn; Choreography, Arlene Phillips; Designer, John Napier; Lighting, David Hersey; Sound, Martin Levan; Musical Director, Paul Bogaev; Musical Direction/ Supervision, David Caddick; Orchestrations, David Cullen, Andrew Lloyd Webber; Casting, Johnson-Liff Associates; Production Adviser, Arthur Cantor; Executive Producer, Gatchell & Neufeld Ltd.; Produced originally on the London stage by The Really Useful Theatre Co.; Presented by Martin Starger and Lord Grade in association with MCA Music Entertainment Group, Stage Promotions (Four)/Strada Holdings, Weintraub Entertainment Group; Concept Album on MCA Compact Discs, HiQ Cassettes and Records; General Management, Gatchell & Neufeld Ltd.; Company Manager, Roger Gindi; Technical Supervisor, Peter Fulbright; Scenic and Bridge Engineer, William M. Mensching; Wardrobe, Adelaide Laurino, David Hemenway; Hairstylist, Wayne Herndon; Hair Supervisor, Leon Gagiardi; Production Assistant, Graham Ingle; Second Director, Dion McHugh; Dance Captain, Denny Shearer; Stunt Coordinator, J. P. Romano; Skating Coach, Michal Fraley; Wigs, Paul Huntley; Stage Managers, Frank Hartenstein, Perry Cline, Randall Whitescarver, Janet Friedman, Michael J. Passaro; Press, Bill Evans, Sandra Manley, Jim Baldassare. Opened in the Gershwin Theatre on Sunday, March 15, 1987.*

CAST

Bobo (A. C. Ciulla), Espresso (Philip Clayton), Weltschaft (Michael Berglund), Turnov (William Frey), Hashamoto (D. Michael Heath), Prince of Wales (Sean McDermott), Greaseball (Robert Torti), Greaseball's Gang (Todd Lester, Sean Grant, Ronald Garza, Angel Vargas, Joey McKneely, Gordon Owens), Rusty (Greg Mowry), Pearl (Reva Rice), Dinah (Jane Krakowski), Ashley (Andrea McArdle), Buffy (Jamie Beth Chandler), Rocky I (Frank Mastrocola), Rocky II (Sean Grant), Rocky III (Ronald Garza), Rocky IV (Angel Vargas), Dustin (Michael Scott Gregory), Flat-Top (Todd Lester), Red Caboose (Berry K. Bernal), Krupp (Joey McKneely), Wrench (Christina Youngman), Joule (Nicole Picard), Volta (Mary Ann Lamb), Purse (Gordon Owens), Electra (Ken Ard), Poppa (Steve Fowler), Belle (Janet Williams Adderley), Voice of the boy (Braden Danner), Voice of the mother (Melanie Vaughan), Starlight Chorus (Paul Binotto, Lon Hoyt, Melanie Vaughan, Mary Windholtz).

STANDBYS/UNDERSTUDIES: Ashley: Jamie Beth Chandler/Amelia Prentice/ Christina Youngman, Belle: Lola Knox/Amelia Prentice, Bobo: Mark Frawley/ Anthony Galde/Ron Morgan/Dwight Toppin, Buffy: Lola Knox/Mary Ann Lamb/ Christine Langner, Dinah: Christine Langner/Nicole Picard, Dustin: Anthony Galde/ D. Michael Heath/Sean McDermott, Electra: Michael-Demby Cain/Philip Clayton/ Gordon Owens/Broderick Wilson, Espresso: Mark Frawley/Ron Morgan/Broderick Wilson, Flat-Top: Mark Frawley/Anthony Galde/Joey McKneely, Greaseball: Mark Frawley/William Frey/Frank Mastrocola, Hashamoto: Mark Frawley/Ron Morgan/ Dwight Toppin, Joule: Lola Knox/Christine Langner/Amelia Prentice, Krupp: Mark Frawley/Anthony Galde/Ron Morgan/Dwight Toppin/Broderick Wilson, Pearl: Lola Knox/Christine Langner, Poppa: Danny Strayhorn/Broderick Wilson, Prince of Wales: Mark Frawley/Ron Morgan/Michael-Demby Cain/Dwight Toppin, Purse: Michael-Demby Cain/ Dwight Toppin/Broderick Wilson, Red Caboose: Mark Frawley/Anthony Galde/ Todd Lester, Rocky I: Michael-Demby Cain/William Frey/Broderick Wilson, Rocky II: Michael-Demby Cain/Dwight Toppin/Broderick Wilson, Rocky III: Michael-Demby Cain, A. C. Ciulla/Dwight Toppin, Volta: Lola Knox/Christine Langner/ Christina Youngman, Weltschaft: Mark Frawley/Anthony Galde/Ron Morgan, Wrench: Lola Knox/Christine Langner/Amelia Prentice

MUSICAL NUMBERS: Rolling Stock, Engine of Love, Lotta Locomotion, Freight, AC/DC, Pumping Iron, Make Up My Heart, Race One, There's Me, Poppa's Blues, Belle, Race Two, Laughing Stock, Starlight Express, Silver Dollar, U.N.C.O.U.P.L.E.D., Wide Smile High Style That's Me, First Final, Right Place Right Time, I Am the Starlight, Final Selection, Only You, Chase, One Rock and Roll Too Many, Light at the End of the Tunnel

A musical in two acts.

*Still playing May 31, 1987. Recipient of 1987 "Tony" for Best Costume Design.

Martha Swope Photos

**Top Right: Robert Torti (C) and counter
clockwise: Mary Ann Lamb, Nicole Picard, Reva
Rice, Lola Knox, Jane Krakowski, Christina
Youngman, Andrea McArdle**

**Greg Mowry, Reva Rice, Jane Krakowski,
Lola Knox, Andrea McArdle**

LES MISERABLES

Music, Claude-Michel Schonberg; Lyrics, Herbert Kretzmer; Original French text by Alain Boubil, Jean-Marc Natel; Additional material, James Fenton; Based on novel by Victor Hugo; Directed and Adapted by Trevor Nunn and John Caird; Orchestral Score, John Cameron; Musical Supervision/Direction, Robert Billig; Sound, Andrew Bruce/Autograph; Executive Producers, Martin McCallum, Richard Jay-Alexander; Designed by John Napier; Lighting, David Hersey; Costumes, Andreane Neofitou; Casting, Johnson-Liff Associates; General Management, Alan Wasser; Presented by Cameron Mackintosh in association with the JFK Center for the Performing Arts (Roger L. Stevens, Chairman); Original London production by Cameron Macintosh and the Royal Shakespeare Co.; Associate Director, Richard Jay-Alexander; Technical Manager, John H. Paull III; Company Managers, Gordon G. Forbes, Beth Riedmann; Dance Captain, Joanna Glushak; Associate Musical Director, Jefrey Silverman; Props, Timothy Abel; Wardrobe, Adelaide Laurino; Wig Master, Jody Thomas; Production Assistant, Paula Williams; Stage Managers, Sam Stickler, Mitchell Lemsky, Fredric Hanson; Press, Fred Nathan, Anne Abrams, Dennis Crowley, Bert Fink, Merle Frimark, Marc Thibodeau. Opened in the Broadway Theatre on Thursday, March 12, 1987.*

CAST

Prologue: 1815 Digne: Jean ValJean (Colm Wilkinson), Javert (Terrence Mann), Chain Gang (Kevin Marcum, Paul Harman, Anthony Crivello, John Dewar, Joseph Kolinski, Leo Murmester, David Bryant, Alex Santoriello, Michael Maguire), Farmer (Jesse Corti), Labourer (Alex Santoriello), Innkeeper (John Norman), Innkeeper's Wife (Susan Goodman), Bishop of Digne (Norman Large), Constables (Marcus Lovett, Steve Shocket). *1823 Montreuil-sur-Mer:* Fantine (Randy Graff), Foreman (Paul Harman), Workers (Jesse Corti, John Dewar), Women Workers (Cindy Benson, Marcie Shaw, Jane Bodle, Joanna Glushak), Factory Girl (Ann Crumb), Sailors (Joseph Kolinski, Kevin Marcum, John Dewar), Whores (Susan Goodman, Joanna Glushak, Jane Bodle, Kelli James, Ann Crumb, Frances Ruffelle, Judy Kuhn, Gretchen Kingsley-Weihe), Old Woman (Cindy Benson), Crone (Marcie Shaw), Pimp (Steve Shocket), Bamatabois (Anthony Crivello), Fauchelevent (Steve Shocket). *1823 Montfermeil:* Young Cosette (Donna Vivino), Mme. Thenardier (Jennifer Butt), Thenardier (Leo Burmester), Young Eponine (Chrissie McDonald), Drinker (Jesse Corti), Young Couple (Alex Santoriello, Gretchen Kingsley-Weihe), Drunk (John Norman), Diners (Norman Large, Joanna Glushak), Other Drinkers (Steve Shocket, Anthony Crivello, Kevin Marcum, Ann Crumb, Susan Goodman), Young Man (Joseph Kolinski), Young Girls (Jane Bodle, Kelli James), Old Couple (Marcie Shaw, John Dewar), Travelers (Paul Harman, Marcus Lovett). *1832 Paris:* Gavroche (Braden Danner), Old Beggar Woman (Susan Goodman), Young Prostitute (Ann Crumb), Pimp (John Norman), Eponine (Frances Ruffelle), Montparnasse (Alex Santoriello), Babet (Marcus Lovett), Brujon (Kevin Marcum), Claquesous (Steve Shockett), Enjolras (Michael Maguire), Marius (David Bryant), Cosette (Judy Kuhn), Combeferre (Paul Harman), Feuilly (Joseph Kolinski), Courfeyrac (Jesse Corti), Joly (John Dewar), Grantaire (Anthony Crivello), Lesgles (Norman Large), Jean Prouvaire (John Norman)

UNDERSTUDIES: Jean ValJean (Kevin Marcum/Paul Harman), Javert (Anthony Crivello/Norman Large), Bishop (Steve Shocket/John Dewar), Fantine (Ann Crumb/Joanna Glushak), Young Cosette (Brandy Brown/Chrissie McDonald), Mme. Thenardier (Cindy Benson/Susan Goodman), Thenardier (John Norman/Norman Large), Young Eponine (Brandy Brown), Gavroche (R. D. Robb/Kelli James), Eponine (Kelli James/Gretchen Kingsley-Weihe/Jane Bodle), Enjolras (Joseph Kolinski/Paul Harman), Swings: Patrick A'Hearn, Diane Della Piazza, Jordan Leeds

MUSICAL NUMBERS: Prologue, Soliloquy, At the End of the Day, I Dreamed a Dream, Lovely Ladies, Who Am I?, Come to Me, Castle on a Cloud, Master of the House, Thenardier Waltz, Look Down, Stars, Red and Black, Do You Hear the People Sing?, In My Life, A Heart Full of Love, One Day More, On My Own, A Little Fall of Rain, Drink with Me to Days Gone By, Bring Him Home, Dog Eats Dog, Soliloquy, Turning, Empty Chairs at Empty Tables, Wedding Chorale, Beggars at the Feast, Finale

A dramatic musical in 2 acts and 4 scenes with a prologue.

*Still playing May 31, 1987. Winner of 1987 "Tonys" for Best Musical, Best Musical Book, Best Musical Score, Best Featured Actor and Actress in a Musical (Michael Maguire, Frances Ruffelle), Best Direction of a Musical, Best Scenic Design, Best Lighting Design

Michael Le Poer/Bob Marshak Photos

Top Left: Colm Wilkinson
Below: Randy Graff

Colm Wilkinson, Terrence Mann
Above: Leo Burmester, Jennifer Butt

John Dewar, Frances Ruffelle, Colm Wilkinson,
David Bryant, Judy Kuhn, Randy Graff Above:
Michael Maguire, David Bryant Top: Wilkinson,
Donna Vivino Below: Wilkinson, Graff, Terrence Mann

Colm Wilkinson, Terrence Mann Above: Judy Kuhn, Wilkinson,
Randy Graff Top: David Bryant, Frances Ruffelle Below:
Leo Burmester

THE NERD

By Larry Shue; Director, Charles Nelson Reilly; Set, John Lee Beatty; Costumes, Deborah Shaw; Lighting, Dennis Parichy; Sound, Timothy Helgeson; Casting, Deborah Brown; Presented by Kevin Dowling, Joan Stein, Melvyn J. Estrin, Susan Rose, Gail Berman, and Lynn Dowling in association with F. Harlan Batrus, Gina Rogak, George A. Schapiro; Associate Producers, Gintare Sileika Everett, Allan Matthews, Yentl Productions; By arrangement with Bruce Hyman and Andre Ptaszynski; Originally produced by Milwaukee Repertroy Theatre Co.; General Management, Proscenium Services and TheatrePop/Kevin Dowling, Joan Stein; Company Manager, Susan Gustafson; Wardrobe, Eileen Miller; Production Assistant, Morgan Fae Kennedy; Monster Costume, Andrew Benepe; Hair Design, Vito Mastrogiovanni; Stage Manager, Daniel R. Bauer; Press, Adrian Bryan-Brown, Josh Ellis, Leo Stern, Jackie Green, Bill Shuttleworth. Opened in the Helen Hayes Theatre on Sunday, March 22, 1987.*

CAST

Willum Cubbert .... Mark Hamill†1
Tansy McGinnis .... Patricia Kalember
Axel Hammond .... Peter Riegert†2
Warnock Waldgrave .... Wayne Tippit
Clelia Waldgrave .... Peggy Cosgrave
Thor Waldgrave ....Timmy Geissler
Rick Steadman ....Robert Joy

UNDERSTUDIES: Daniel Hagen, Josh Saviano

A comedy in two acts and three scenes. The action takes place during November 1981 in Terre Haute, Indiana.

*Still playing May 31, 1987.

†Succeeded by: 1. Gary Berghoff, 2. Jim Borrelli

Marc Bryan-Brown Photos

Top Right: Patricia Kalember, Peter Riegert
Below: Robert Joy

Peter Riegert, Mark Hamill, Patricia Kalember

FENCES

By August Wilson; Director, Lloyd Richards; Set, James D. Sandefur; Costumes, Candice Donnelly; Lighting, Danianne Mizzy; General Manager, Robert Kamlot; Casting, Meg Simon/Fran Kumin; Presented by Carole Shorenstein Hays in association with The Yale Repertory Theatre (Lloyd Richards, Artistic Director/Benjamin Mordecai, Managing Director); Company Manager, Lisa M. Poyer; Props, George Wagner; Wardrobe, John Guiteras; Stage Managers, Martin Gold, Terrence J. Witter; Press, Joshua Ellis, Reva Cooper, Adrian Bryan-Brown, Jackie Green, Bill Shuttleworth, Susanne Tighe. Opened in the 46th Street Theatre on Thursday, March, 26, 1987.*

CAST

Troy Maxson .... James Earl Jones
Jim Bono, Troy's friend .... Ray Aranha
Rose, Troy's wife .... Mary Alice
Lyons, Troy's oldest son .... Charles Brown
Gabriel, Troy's brother .... Frankie R. Faison
Cory, Troy and Rose's son .... Courtney B. Vance
Raynell, Troy's daughter .... Karima Miller

UNDERSTUDIES: Ethel Ayler (Rose), Byron Keith Minns (Cory), Mike Hodge (Bono/Gabriel), Vince Williams (Lyons), Tatyana Ali (Raynell)

A drama in 2 acts and 9 scenes. The action takes place from 1957 to 1965 in the backyard of the Maxson house in an urban neighborhood of a Northern American industrial city.

*Still playing May 31, 1987. Recipient of 1987 Pulitzer Prize for Drama, and adjudged Best Play by the New York Drama Critics Circle, the Outer Critics Circle, and the Drama Desk, and "Tonys" for Best Play, Best Actor (James Earl Jones), Best Featured Actress (Mary Alice), Best Director. It is the only play to ever win all 5 major theatre awards for best play.

Ron Scherl Photos

Right: Courtney B. Vance, James Earl Jones
Top: Charles Brown, James Earl Jones,
Mary Alice, Ray Aranha

James Earl Jones

Mary Alice, James Earl Jones

BLITHE SPIRIT

By Noel Coward; Director, Brian Murray; Set, Finlay James; Costumes, Theoni V. Aldredge; Lighting, Richard Nelson; Music arranged by Marvin Hamlisch; Sound, Jan Nebozenko; General Management, Kingwill & Goosen; Casting, Julie Hughes, Barry Moss; Presented by Karl Allison, Douglas Urbanski, Sandra Moss in association with Jerome Minskoff, Duncan C. Weldon; Production Assistant, Lisa Contadino; Props, Patricia Avery; Wardrobe, James M. Kabel; Hair Stylist, David H. Lawrence; Wigs/Hairstyles, Paul Huntley; Movement Consultant, Rob Marshall; Trance Medium Consultant, David Vass; Song "Always" by Irving Berlin; Stage Managers, Murray Gitlin, T. L. Boston; Press, Joshua Ellis, Adrian Bryan-Brown, Reva Cooper, Jackie Green, Bill Shuttleworth, Susanne Tighe. Opened in the Neil Simon Theatre on Tuesday, March 31, 1987.*

CAST

Edith .... Nicola Cavendish
Ruth .... Judith Ivey
Charles .... Richard Chamberlain
Dr. Bradman .... William LeMassena
Mrs. Bradman .... Patricia Conolly †1
Madame Arcati .... Geraldine Page †2
Elvira .... Blythe Danner

UNDERSTUDIES: Lewis Arlt (Charles/Dr. Bradman), Jennifer Harmon (Ruth/Elvira), Patricia Conolly (Mme. Arcati), leClanche duRand (Edith/Mrs. Bradman)

A comedy in 3 acts and 7 scenes. The action takes place in the late 1930's in Kent, England, in the home of Ruth and Charles Condomine.

*Closed June 28, 1987 after 103 performances and 24 previews.

†Succeeded by: 1. Jennifer Harmon, 2. Patricia Conolly after Miss Page's death on June 13, 1987.

Martha Swope Photos

Geraldine Page, Richard Chamberlain

Top: Judith Ivey, Geraldine Page, Blythe Danner, Richard Chamberlain

THE MIKADO

By Gilbert and Sullivan; As originally presented by Stratford Festival of Canada; Direction/Choreography, Brian Macdonald; Musical Direction/Additional Musical Arrangements, Berthold Carriere; Set and Costumes, Susan Benson; Associate Set Designer, Douglas McLean; Lighting, Michael J. Whitfield; Conductor, Fen Watkin; Presented by Ed and David Mirvish and Brian Macdonald; General Manager, Yale Simpson; General Management, Frank Scardino Associates; Company Manager, Lynn McKay; Technical Director, Jeremy Lach; Wardrobe, Marjorie Fielding; Props, Mark Fisher; Wardrobe, Helen Basson; Wigs, Paul Elliot, Margaret Dreveny; Assistant Director/Choreographer, Kelly Robinson; Assistant Musical Director, Chuck Homewood; Additional Lyrics, John Banks; Wigs, Doreen Freeman; Stage Managers, Pat Thomas, Shirley Third; Press, Max Eisen, Madelon Rosen, Barbara Glenn, Steven Friep, Gino Empry. Opened in the Virginia Theatre on Thursday, April 2, 1987.*

CAST

The Mikado	Avo Kittask
Nanki-Poo, his son	John Keane
Ko-Ko, Lord High Executioner	Eric Donkin
Pooh-Bah (Lord High Everything Else)	Richard McMillan
Pish-Tush (A Noble Lord)	Paul Massel

Three Sisters, wards of Ko-Ko:

Yum-Yum	Marie Baron
Pitti-Sing	Karen Wood
Peep-Bo	Karen Skidmore
Katisha (An Elderly Lady)	Arlene Meadows
Acrobats	David Gonzales, Walter Quigley

CHORUS: Elizabeth Adams, Stephen Beamish, Timothy Cruickshank, Aggie Cekuta Elliot, Glori Gage, Paul Gatchell, Larry Herbert, Debora Joy, David Keeley, Richard March, Janet Martin, David Playfair, Lyndsay Richardson, Gerald Smuin, Joy Thompson-Allen, Marcia Tratt, Jim White, Steve Yorke

UNDERSTUDIES: Janet Martin (Yum-Yum), Stephen Beamish (Pish-Tush), Karen Skidmore (Pitti-Sing), Timothy Cruickshank (Mikado), Stephen Beamish (Pooh-Bah), Jim White (Ko-Ko), Elizabeth Adams (Katisha), Marcia Tratt (Peep-Bo), Richard March/Paul Gatchell (Nanki-Poo)

MUSICAL NUMBERS: If You Want to Know Who We Are, A Wand'ring Minstrel I, Our Great Mikado, Young Man Despair, And Have I Journey'd for a Month, Behold the Lord High Executioner, As Some Day It May Happen, Comes a Train of Little Ladies, Three Little Maids from School, So Please You Sir, Were You Not to Ko-Ko Plighted, I Am So Proud, With Aspect Stern and Gloomy Stride, Braid the Raven Hair, The Sun Whose Rays Are All Ablaze, Brightly Dawns Our Wedding Day, Here's a How-de-do!, Mi-ya-sa-ma-mi-ya-sa-ma, A More Humane Mikado, The Criminal Cried, The Flowers That Bloom in the Spring, Alone and Yet Alive, On a Tree by a River, There Is a Beauty in the Bellow of the Blast, For He's Gone and Married Yum-Yum

An operetta in two acts. The action takes place in the past in Japan.

*Closed May 3, 1987 after 38 performances and 2 previews. It had previously played New York City Center for a limited run of 7 performances (Jan. 13–18, 1987).

Robert C. Ragsdale Photos

Top Right: John Keane, Marie Baron, Paul Massel, Karen Wood Below: Richard McMillan, Eric Donkin, Paul Massel

Karen Wood, Marie Baron, Karen Skidmore

SAFE SEX

By Harvey Fierstein; Director, Eric Concklin; Scenery, John Falabella; Costumes, Nanzi Adzima; Lighting, Craig Miller; Sound, Tom Morse; Music, Ada Janik; Presented by the Shubert Organization and MTM Entertainment Ltd; Associate Producer, Scott Robbe; World Premiere at La Mama E.T.C.; General Manager, Leonard Soloway; Casting, Jimmy Bohr; Assistant General Manager, Brian Dunbar; Company Manager, Sammy Ledbetter; Technical Supervisor, Theatre Service Inc./ Arthur Siccardi, Peter Feller; Props, Jan Marasek; Props, Arthur Hoaglund; Wardrobe, Kathy Powers; Hair/Makeup, John Quaglia; Production Assistant, Richard Jackson; Sculptures, Gretchen Green; Stage Managers, Bob Borod, Glen Gardali; Press, Jim Baldassare, Jim Randolph. Opened in the Lyceum Theatre on Sunday, April 5, 1987.*

CAST

"Manny and Jake"
Manny ....John Mulkeen
Jake .... John Wesley Shipp
"Safe Sex"
Mead .... John Wesley Shipp
Ghee ....Harvey Fierstein
"On Tidy Endings"
Marion .... Anne De Salvo
Jimmy ....Ricky Addison Reed
June ....Billie McBride
Arthur ....Harvey Fierstein

STANDBYS: Stephen Bogardus (Arthur/Ghee/Jake/Manny/Mead), Megan McTavish (June/Marion), Christopher Unger (Jimmy)

Three one-act plays presented with one intermission. The action takes place at the present time.

*Closed April 12, 1987 after 9 performances and 22 previews. It had played 19 performances at LaMama from Jan. 8 to Feb. 1, 1987.

Peter Cunningham Photos

Top Left: John Wesley Shipp, Harvey Fierstein
Below: John Wesley Shipp, John Mulkeen

Billie McBride, Anne De Salvo

Harvey Fierstein, Ricky Addison Reed, Anne De Salvo

THE MUSICAL COMEDY MURDERS OF 1940

Written and Directed by John Bishop; Set, David Potts; Costumes, Jennifer von Mayrhauser; Lighting, Jeff Davis; Original Music, Ted Simons; Sound, Chuck London Media/Stewart Werner; Presented by Bill Wildin; Originally produced by Circle Repertory Co. (Marshall W. Mason, Artistic Director); General Management, George Elmer Productions, Patricia Berry; Technical Supervisor, Technical Services/Arthur Siccardi, Peter Feller; Electrical Supervisor, Brian Lynch; Props, Daniel Telesca, Jr.; Wardrobe, Robert Miller; Hair/Wigs, Claudette Buelow; Hair/Makeup Design, James Sarzotti; Music Consultant, Jack Lee; Dramaturg, Joe Mathewson; Dialect Consultant, Curt Vogelsang; Dramaturg, Joe Mathewson; Stage Managers, Fred Reinglas, Leslie Loeb; Press, Jeffrey Richards, C. George Willard, Ken Mandelbaum, Ben Morse, Irene Gandy, Susan Lee. Opened in the Longacre Theatre on Monday, April 6, 1987.*

CAST

Helsa Wenzel	Lily Knight
Elsa von Grossenknueten	Ruby Holbrook †1
Michael Kelly	Willie C. Carpenter
Patrick O'Reilly	Nicholas Wyman †2
Ken de la Maize	Michael Ayr
Nikki Crandall	Dorothy Cantwell
Eddie McCuen	Kelly Connell
Marjorie Baverstock	Pamela Dunlap
Roger Hopewell	Richard Seff
Bernice Roth	Bobo Lewis †3

UNDERSTUDIES: Matthew Gottlieb (Ken/Roger/Patrick), Mark Enis (Kelly/McCuen), Susan Bruce (Nikki/Helsa), Elizabeth Perry (Elsa/Marjorie/Bernice)

A comedy in two acts. The action takes place on an estate in Chappaqua, NY, in December 1940.

*Closed Aug. 2, 1987 after 136 performances and 6 previews. It was transferred from Off-Broadway's Circle Repertory Theatre where it had played 107 performances.

†Succeeded by: 1. Sasha von Schoeler, 2. Bill Faberbakke, 3. Avril Gentles

Martha Swope/Carol Rosegg Photos

Top: Richard Seff, Nicholas Wyman, Dorothy Cantwell, Kelly Connell, Bobo Lewis

Nicholas Wyman, Lily Knight

Barbara Cook, John Beal
Right: Barbara Cook, Wally Harper

BARBARA COOK:
A Concert for the Theatre

Music arranged and conducted by Wally Harper; Scenery, John Falabella; Costumes, Joseph G. Aulisi; Lighting, Richard Winkler; Sound, Fred Miller; Keyboard Coordinator, John Clifton; Presented by Jerry Kravat, The Shubert Organization, Emanuel Azenberg; Associate Producer, Perry B. Granoff; Original Songs, Wally Harper (Music), David Zippel (Lyrics); General Manager, Leonard Soloway; Company Manager, Bruce Birkenhead; Assistant Conductor, Mack Schlefer; Assistant General Manager, Sammy Ledbetter; Technical Supervision, Theatrical Services/Arthur Siccardi, Peter Feller; Props, Jan Marasek; Wardrobe, John Quaglia; Production Assistant, Michael Marshall; Stage Managers, Martin Herzer, Jane E. Cooper; Press, Bill Evans, Sandra Manley, Jim Baldassare, Becky Flora, Jim Randolph. Opened in the Ambassador Theatre on Wednesday, April 15, 1987.*

A solo performance presented in two parts.

*Closed April 26, 1987 after 13 performances and 13 previews.

Mike Martin Photos

Barbara Cook

A MONTH OF SUNDAYS

By Bob Larbey; Director, Gene Saks; Set, Marjorie Bradley Kellogg; Costumes, Joseph G. Aulisi; Lighting, Tharon Musser; Sound, Brian Lynch; Casting, Simon and Kumin; Presented by Emanuel Azenberg, Jerome Minskoff, Jujamcyn Theaters/ Richard G. Wolff; Assistant Director, Bill Molloy; General Manager, Leonard Soloway; Manager, Brian Dunbar; Technical Supervisors, Theatrical Services/ Arthur Siccardi, Peter Feller; Props, Jan Marasek; Wardrobe, Roberta Christy; Production Assistant, Katrina Stevens; Stage Managers, William Buxton, Steven Shaw; Press, Bill Evans, Sandra Manley, Jim Baldassare, Becky Flora, Jim Randolph. Opened in the Ritz Theatre on Thursday, April 16, 1987.*

CAST

Cooper	Jason Robards
Nurse Wilson	Felicity LaFortune
Mrs. Baker	Lynne Thigpen
Aylott	Salem Ludwig
Julia	Patricia Elliott
Peter	Richard Portnow

STANDBYS: James Cahill (Aylott/Cooper), L. Scott Caldwell (Mrs. Baker), Alma Cuervo (Julia/Nurse Wilson), Curt Karibalis (Peter)

A comedy in two acts. The action takes place in Cooper's room in a rest and retirement home in Westchester County, New York, on the first Sunday in April and the first Sunday in May of the present time.

*Closed April 18, 1987 after 4 performances and 19 previews.

Martha Swope Photos

Right: Salem Ludwig, Jason Robards
Top: Felicity LaFortune, Jason Robards,
Lynne Thigpen

Richard Portnow, Jason Robards, Patricia Elliott

ALL MY SONS

By Arthur Miller; Director, Arvin Brown; Set, Hugh Landwehr; Costumes, Bill Walker; Lighting, Ronald Wallace; Casting, Deborah Brown; Presented by Jay H. Fuchs, Steven Warnick in association with Charles Patsos; A Long Wharf Theatre production; General Management, Darwall Associates; Company Manager, Michael Gill; Production Supervisor, Arthur Siccardi; Props, Robert Bostwick; Wardrobe, James Hodson; Stage Managers, Zoya Wyeth, Stacey Fleischer; Press, Shirley Herz, Peter Cromarty, Pete Sanders, Glenna Freedman, David Roggensack, Miller Wright, Jillana Devine. Opened in the John Golden Theatre on Wednesday, April 22, 1987.*

CAST

Dr. Jim Bayliss	Dan Desmond
Joe Keller	Richard Kiley
Frank Lubey	Stephen Root
Sue Bayliss	Kit Flanagan
Lydia Lubey	Dawn Didawick
Chris Keller	Jamey Sheridan
Bert	Michael Maronna
Kate Keller	Joyce Ebert
Ann Deever	Jayne Atkinson
George Deever	Christopher Curry

STANDBYS: Rex Robbins (Joe), Rose Arrick (Kate), Tracy Griswold (Chris/George/Bayliss/Frank), Wendy Barrie-Wilson (Ann/Lydia/Sue)

A drama in three acts, presented with one intermission. The action takes place at the end of summer 1946, in the back yard of the Keller home on the outskirts of an American town.

*Closed May 17, 1987 after 29 performances and 6 previews. Recipient of a 1987 "Tony" for Best Revival of a Play or Musical. Original production opened Wednesday, Jan. 29, 1947 in the Coronet Theatre and ran for 328 performances. In the cast were Ed Begley, Arthur Kennedy, Beth Merrill, Lois Wheeler and Karl Malden.

T. Charles Erickson Photos

Left: Jamey Sheridan, Richard Kiley
Top: Joyce Ebert, Richard Kiley

Richard Kiley, Jayne Atkinson, Jamey Sheridan, Joyce Ebert

Thami Cele, Bongani Hlophe, Solomzi Bisholo,
Bheki Mqadi, Bhoyi Ngema

ASINAMALI!

Written and Directed by Mbongeni Ngema; Production Supervisor, Makalo Mofokeng; Lighting, Wesley France; presented by Kenneth Waissman, Robert A. Buckley, Jane Harmon, Nina Keneally, Edward L. Schuman with Harry Belafonte, Hamilton Fish 3rd, Miriam Makeba, Duma Nolovu, Paul Simon; General Management, Waissman and Buckley Associates/Karen Leahy; Production Assistant, Angela Foster; Stage Managers, Bruce Hoover, Judith Binus; Press, Jeffrey Richards, C. George Willard, Ben Morse, Ken Mandelbaum, Susan Lee, Irene Gandy, Carolee Fisher. Opened in the Jack Lawrence Theatre on Thursday, April 23, 1987.*

CAST

Solomzi Bhisholo
Thami Cele
Bongani Hlophe
Bheki Mqadi
Bhoyi Ngema
Mbongeni Ngema

The play is set in a prison cell at Leeuwkop Prison outside Johannesburg, South Africa, and performed without intermission.

*Closed May 17, 1987 after 29 performances and 9 previews.

Pamela Frank Photos

Bheki Mqadi, Bongani Hlophe, Solomzi Bisholo,
Bhoyi Ngema, Thami Cele

PYGMALION

By George Bernard Shaw; Director, Val May; Scenery, Douglas Heap; Costumes, Terence Emery; Lighting, Martin Aronstein; Presented by The Shubert Organization, Jerome Minskoff and Duncan C. Weldon; General Management, Joseph Harris, Peter T. Kulok, Steven E. Goldstein; Technical Supervision, Jeremiah J. Harris; Props, Joseph Harris, Jr.; Manager, Kathleen Lowe; Wardrobe, Jennifer Bryan; Production Assistant, Gerri Higgins; Stage Managers, Martin Gold, John Vivian, Meryl Jacobs; Press, Fred Nathan, Merle Frimark, Anne Abrams, Dennis Crowley, Bert Fink, Marc P. Thibodeau. Opened in the Plymouth Theatre on Sunday, April 26, 1987.*

CAST

Mrs. Eynsford-Hill	Mary Peach
Clara Eynsford-Hill	Kirstie Pooley
Tart	Selena Carey-Jones
Sarcastic Bystander	Ivar Brogger
Freddy Eynsford-Hill	Osmund Bullock
Eliza Doolittle	Amanda Plummer
Colonel Pickering	Lionel Jeffries
Professor Higgins	Peter O'Toole
Mrs. Pearce	Dora Bryan
Alfred Doolittle	John Mills
Mrs. Higgins	Joyce Redman
Parlormaid	Selena Carey-Jones
Teamaid	Wendy Makkena

BYSTANDERS: Lucy Martin, Wendy Makkena, Robertson Dean, Angela Thornton, Richard Neilson, Edward Conery

UNDERSTUDIES: Ivar Brogger (Higgins), Kirstie Pooley (Eliza), Edward Conery (Sarcastic Bystander/Doolittle), Richard Neilson (Pickering), Lucy Martin (Mrs. Pearce/Mrs. Eynsford-Hill), Angela Thornton (Mrs. Higgins/Mrs. Eynsford-Hill), Robertson Dean (Freddy), Wendy Makkena (Tart/Parlormaid), Selena Carey-Jones (Clara/Bystander), Meryl Jacobs (Teamaid)

A comedy in 3 acts and 5 scenes. The action takes place in London in 1912.

*Closed Aug. 2, 1987 after 113 performances and 15 previews. The original production opened with Mrs. Patrick Campbell in the Park Theatre on Oct. 12, 1914 and ran for 72 performances. The longest-running revival (181 performances) was in 1946 with Gertrude Lawrence and Raymond Massey at the Barrymore Theatre.

Martha Swope Photos

**Kirstie Pooley, Osmund Bullock, Mary Peach, Amanda Plummer, Joyce Redman, Peter O'Toole Top
Left: Amanda Plummer, Peter O'Toole, Lionel Jeffries Below: John Mills, Peter O'Toole**

LES LIAISONS DANGEREUSES

By Christopher Hampton; From novel by Choderlos de Lacios; Director, Howard Davies; Design, Bob Crowley; Lighting, Chris Parry in association with Beverly Emmons; Sound, Otts Munderloh in association with John A. Leonard; Music, Ilona Sekacz; Fight Direction, Malcolm Ranson; The Royal Shakespeare Company production presented by James M. Nederlander, The Shubert Organization, Jerome Minskoff, Elizabeth I. McCann, Stephen Graham in association with Jonathan Farkas; Associate Producer, Sylvia Brennick; General Management, Next Wave/Mary T. Nealon, David Musselman; Props, Timothy Abel, Michael Bernstein; Wardrobe, Felicity Jones, Rosalie Lahm; Hair, Leon Gagliardi, Manuel Rodriguez; Production Assistant, Mary-Susan Gregson; Wigs, Jane Edmonds; Stage Managers, Susie Cordon, Jane Tamlyn, Paul Mills Holmes; Press, Joshua Ellis, Adrian Bryan-Brown, Jim Sapp, Reva Cooper, Jackie Green, Bill Shuttleworth, Susanne Tighe. Opened in the Music Box on Thursday, April 30, 1987.*

CAST

Major-domo	Barry Heins
La Marquise de Merteuil	Lindsay Duncan
Madame de Volanges	Kristin Milward
Cecile Volanges	Beatie Edney
Le Vicomte de Valmont	Alan Rickman
Azolan, Valmont's valet	Hugh Simon
Madame de Rosemonde	Jean Anderson
La Presidente de Tourvel	Suzanne Burden
Emile, a courtesan	Lucy Aston
Le Chevalier Danceny	Hilton McRae
Harpsichord	Michael Dansicker

UNDERSTUDIES: Lucy Aston (Mme. de Tourvel/Cecile), Cissy Collins (Mme. de Rosemonde/Mme. de Volanges/Emilie), Barry Heins (Danceny/Azolan), Kristin Milward (Marquise de Merteuil), Hugh Simon (Valmont)

A comedy in two acts. The action takes place in various salons and bedrooms in a number of hotels and chateaux in and around Paris and in the Bois de Vincennes, one autumn and winter in the 1780's.

*Closed Sept. 6, 1987 after 148 performances and 9 previews.

Martha Swope, Steve MacMillan, Dee Conway Photos

Lindsay Duncan, Beatie Edney
Above: Alan Rickman, Lindsay Duncan

Lindsay Duncan, Alan Rickman
Top Left: The Cast

SLEIGHT OF HAND

By John Pielmeier; Director, Walton Jones; Settings, Loren Sherman; Lighting, Richard Nelson; Costumes, William Ivey Long; Magic Consultant, Charles Reynolds; Sound, Jan Nebozenko; Special Effects, Jauchem & Meeh; Fight Staging, B. H. Barry; Casting, Simon & Kumin; Title Song recorded by Carly Simon; Presented by Suzanne J. Schwartz in association with Jennifer Manocherian; Associate Producers, Alison Clarkson, Douglas B. Leeds; General Management, Brent Peek Productions/Scott Green/Douglas Gerlach; Company Manager, Marshall B. Purdy; Assistant Director, Michael Greif; Technical Director, Elbert Kuhn; Props, John Lofgren, Michelle L. Hout; Wardrobe, Peter J. FitzGerald; Production Associate, Martin Teitel; Production Assistant, Ann Harada; Stage Managers, Franklin Keysar, R. Nelson Barbee; Press, Zarem Inc./Patt Dale. Opened in the Cort Theatre on Sunday, May 3, 1987.*

Harry Groener

CAST

Paul .... Harry Groener
Sharon .... Priscilla Shanks †
Dancer .... Jeffrey DeMunn
Understudy: Stephen Rowe

A "suspense thriller" in two acts. The action takes place at the present time in a New York City loft apartment on Christmas Eve, and on the stage of an empty Broadway theatre later that night.

*Closed May 9, 1987 after 9 performances and 31 previews.

†Played by Cecilia Peck in previews.

Martha Swope Photos

Priscilla Shanks, Harry Groener

Jeffrey DeMunn

LINCOLN CENTER THEATER

Second Season

Director, Gregory Mosher; Executive Producer, Bernard Gersten; General Manager, Steven C. Callahan; Company Manager, Lynn Landis; Production Manager, Jeff Hamlin; Casting, Risa Bramon, Billy Hopkins; Press, Merle Debuskey, Robert W. Larkin, Tracy Gore

(Mitzi E. Newhouse Theater/Lincoln Center) Thursday, Oct. 23–Nov. 2, 1986 (5 performances and 19 previews). Lincoln Center Theater and American Music Theater Festival present:

THE TRANSPOSED HEADS adapted from Thomas Mann's novella by Julie Taymor, Sidney Goldfarb; Director, Julie Taymor; Book & Lyrics, Sidney Goldfarb; Music, Elliot Goldenthal; Music Director, Richard Martinez; Conductor, Joshua Rosenblum; Choreography, Margo Sappington, Julie Taymor and the company; Indian Choreography, Swati Gupte Bhise, Rajika Puri; Scenic Design based on concept by Alexander Okun; Costumes, Carol Oditz; Lighting, Marcia Madeira; Sound, Tom Gould; Lightscapes, Caterina Bertolotto; Puppets & Masks, Julie Taymor; Casting, Myers/Tecshner; Props, Elizabeth Fischer; Stage Manager, Renee Lutz

CAST: Yamil Borges (Sita), Scott Burkholder (Shridaman), Richard Hester, Stephen Kaplin, Barbara Pollitt (Puppeteers), Rajika Puri (Narrator), Byron Utley (Nanda), Erin Cressida Wilson (Puppeteer/Assistant to Miss Taymor)

"A tale of passion" presented in two acts.

THE FRONT PAGE

By Ben Hecht and Charles MacArthur; Director, Jerry Zaks; Set, Tony Walton; Costumes, Willa Kim; Lighting, Paul Gallo; Sound, Otts Munderloh; Production Manager, Jeff Hamlin; General Manager, Steven C. Callahan; Props, James Gallagher, C. J. Simpson; Production Supervisor, Joseph Busheme; Wardrobe, Donald L. Brassington; Hairdresser, Joan E. Weiss; Stage Managers, George Darveris, Chet Leaming; Opened in the Vivian Beaumont Theater on Sunday, November 23, 1986.*

CAST

McCue, *City Press*	Trey Wilson
Endicott, *Post*	Bernie McInerney
Schwartz, *Daily News*	Lee Wilkof
Murphy, *Journal*	Ed Lauter
Wilson, *American*	Charles Stransky
Kruger, *Journal of Commerce*	Ronn Carroll
Hildy Johnson, *Herald Examiner*	Richard Thomas
A Woman	Amanda Carlin
Frank, a deputy	Philip LeStrange
Bensinger, *Tribune*	Jeff Weiss
Woodenshoes Eichorn	Jack Wallace †
Diamond Louis	Raymond Serra
Jennie	Mary Catherine Wright
Mollie Malloy	Deirdre O'Connell
Sheriff Hartman	Richard B. Shull
Peggy Grant	Julie Hagerty
Mrs. Grant	Beverly May
The Mayor	Jerome Dempsey
Mr. Pincus	Bill McCutcheon
Earl Williams	Paul Stolarsky
Walter Burns	John Lithgow
Tony	Patrick Garner
Carl, a deputy	Michael Rothhaar
Policemen	Richard Peterson, Patrick Garner

UNDERSTUDIES: Amanda Carlin (Peggy/Molly), Anita Dangler (Mrs. Grant/Jenny), Patrick Garner (Earl/Pincus/Carl/Frank), Philip LeStrange (Murphy/McCue/Wilson/Endicott), Richard Peterson (Kruger/Bensinger/Schwartz/Tony), Michael Rothhaar (Hildy/Diamond Luis/Woodenshoes/Policeman)

A comedy classic in three acts performed with one intermission. The action takes place in the press room of the Criminal Courts Building, Chicago, Illinois.

†Succeeded by Tom Brennan

*Closed Jan. 11, 1987 after 57 performances and 27 previews. Original production opened in the Times Square Theatre on Aug. 14, 1928 with Lee Tracy and Osgood Perkins.

Brigitte Lacombe Photos

Top Right: Richard Thomas, John Lithgow
(also below)

John Lithgow, Richard Thomas, Julie Hagerty

LINCOLN CENTER THEATRE (cont.)

WOZA AFRIKA: A FESTIVAL OF SOUTH AFRICAN THEATER

(Mitzi Newhouse Theater) Wednesday, September 10–14, 1986 (9 performances)
ASINAMALI! by Mbongeni Ngema; Directed by the author. CAST: Solomzi Bisholo, Thami Cele, Bongani Hlophe, Makalo Mofokeng, Bheki Nqadi, Bhoyi Ngema. Performed without intermission. The action takes place in a South African Jail.
Wednesday, September 17–21, 1986 (9 performances).
BOPHA! by Percy Mtwa; Directed by the author. CAST: Aubrey Moalosi Molefe, Aubrey Radebe, Sidney Khumalo, Small Ndaba. A drama performed without intermission, portraying the brutality of life in South Africa.
Wednesday, September 24–28, 1986 (9 performances).
CHILDREN OF ASAZI by Matsemela Manaka; Directed by the author. CAST: Peter Boroko, Ali Hlongwane, Job Kubatsi, Simon Mosikili, Themla Pooe, Soentjie Thapeli. A drama performed without intermission, and with:
GANGSTERS by Maishe Maponya who directed. CAST: George Lamola, Nomathemba Nomvume Mdini, Anthony "Speedo" Wilson, Simon Mosikili.
Wednesday, October 1–5, 1986 (9 performances)
BORN IN THE RSA by Playwright-Director, Barney Simon; Conceived by Barney Simon and cast. CAST: Vanessa Cooke, Melanie Dobbs, Timmy Kwebulana, Neil McCarthy, Geina Mhlophe, Fiona Ramsay, Thoko Ntshinga, Terry Norton. The play depicts the brutality of the apartheid system and reveals the resilience of the people.
(Mitzi E. Newhouse Theater/Lincoln Center) Sunday, Dec. 14, 1986–Jan. 4, 1987 (22 performances and 28 previews).
BODIES, REST, AND MOTION by Roger Hedden; Director, Billy Hopkins; Set, Thomas Lynch, Costumes, Isis Mussenden; Lighting, James F. Ingalls; Sound, Bruce Ellman; Assistant Director, Neel Keller; Props, Ira Belgrade; Wardrobe, Helen Toth, Jean Kennedy; Production Assistant, Wendy Bach; Stage Managers, Susan Selig, Nicholas Dunn CAST: W. H. Macy (Nick), Christina Moore (Carol), Laurie Metcalf (Beth), Andrew McCarthy (Sid), Larry Bryggman (Mr. August/Man Shopping for a TV), Carol Schneider (Elizabeth), Lois Smith (Mrs. Dotson), Larry Bryggman, Lois Smith (Newlyweds), Understudies: Marcus Olson (Nick/Sid), Dani Klein (Carol/Beth/Elizabeth)
A comedy in two acts.
(Mitzi E. Newhouse Theater/Lincoln Center) Sunday, Feb. 8–March 8, 1987 (33 performances and 22 previews)
DANGER: MEMORY! by Arthur Miller; Director, Gregory Mosher; Sets, Michael Merritt; Costumes, Nan Cibula; Lighting, Kevin Rigdon; Wardrobe, Helen Toth; Props, Ira Belgrade, C. J. Simpson; Stage Managers, George Darveris, Neel Keller CAST: *I Can't Remember Anything* with Geraldine Fitzgerald (Leonora), Mason Adams (Leo) and *Clara* with James Tolkan (Det. Lt. Fine), Victor Argo (Tierney), Kenneth McMillan (Albert Kroll), Karron Graves (Clara)
Understudies: Vince O'Brien (Leo/Kroll), Victor Argo (Fine)

Two one-act plays performed with an intermission.

Ben Halley, Jr., Earle Hyman
Above: Geraldine Fitzgerald, Mason Adams

DEATH AND THE KING'S HORSEMAN

Written and Directed by Wole Soyinka; Set, David Gropman; Costumes, Judy Dearing; Lighting, Pat Collins; Sound, John Kilgore; Production Manager, Jeff Hamlin; General Manager, Steven C. Callahan; Presented by Lincon Center Theater (Gregory Mosher, Director; Bernard Gersten, Producer); Company Manager, Lynn Landis; Dance Assistant, Normadien Gibson; Assistant to Director, Aisha Coley; Production Supervisor, Joseph Busheme; Wardrobe, Don Brassington; Makeup/Wigs, Linda Rice; Hairstylist, Leigh Lee; Production Assistant, Wendy Bach; Props, George T. Green; Stage Managers, Clinton Turner Davis, Bonnie Panson; Press, Merle Debuskey, Robert Larkin. Opened in the Vivian Beaumont Theater on Sunday, March 1, 1987*

CAST

Olohun-iyo, the Praise Singer	Ben Halley, Jr.
Elesin, Horseman of the King	Earle Hyman
Iyaloja, "Mother" of the Market	Trazana Beverley
Ekeji-Oja, "Deputy" of the Market	Celestine Heard
The Bride	Sylvia Best
Simon Pilkings, District Officer	Alan Coates
Jane Pilking, his wife	Jill Larson
Sergeant Amusa	Ernest Perry, Jr.
Joseph, Houseboy to the Pilkinges	Abdoulaye N'Gom
The Resident	Dillon Evans
Aide de Camp	Graeme Malcolm
H.R.H. The Prince	Roderick McLachlan
His Consort	Erika Petersen
Conductor	Robert Cenedella
Olunde, eldest son of Elesin	Eriq LaSalle
Constables	Kenneth Arch Johnson, Munir Salaam
Drummers	Kimati Dinizulu, Yomi Obileye, Tunji Oyelana, Edwina Lee Tyler

ENSEMBLE: Naimani Asante-Rich, Sylvia Best, John K. Blandford, Marilyn Buchanan, Gregory Ince, Kenneth Arch Johnson, Marcya A. Joseph, Nanama Amankwaa Moore, Abdoulaye N'Gom, Munir Salaam, Phyllis Yvonne Stickney, Wilhelmina T. Taylor, Karen Thornton, Byron Utley, Vanessa Williams
UNDERSTUDIES: Arthur French (Elesin), Byron Utley (Olohun-iyo/Olunde), Phyllis Yvonne Stickney (Iyaloja/Ekeji-Oja), Roderick McLachlan (Pilkings), Erika Petersen (Jane)

A drama in two acts and five scenes. The action takes place in Nigeria in 1944.

*Closed Apr. 5, 1987 after 31 performances and 20 previews.

Brigitte Lacombe Photos

Top: Aubrey Radebe, Sydney Khumalo, Aubrey Moalosi Molefe in "Bopha" Below: Christina Moore, Laurie Metcalf, Andrew McCarthy in "Bodies, Rest, and Motion"

THE REGARD OF FLIGHT
and
The Clown Bagatelles

Written by Bill Irwin; In collaboration with the company and Nancy Harrington; Original Music, Doug Skinner; Set, Douglas O. Stein; Lighting, Robert W. Rosentel; Premiered at the American Place Theatre; Production Supervisor, Joseph Busheme; Wardrobe, Don Brassington; Stage Managers, Nancy Harrington, Scott Allison. Opened in the Vivian Beaumont Theater on Sunday, April 12, 1987.*

CAST

Bill Irwin
M. C. O'Connor
Doug Skinner

An "entertainment" performed without intermission.

*Closed April 26, 1987 after a limited engagement of 17 performances and 4 previews

Martha Swope Photos

Bill Irwin in "Regard of Flight"
Left: Thoko Ntshinga, Vanessa Cooke, Gcine Mhlophe in "Born in the R.S.A." Below: James Tolkan, Kenneth McMillan in "Clara"

THE COMEDY OF ERRORS

By William Shakespeare; Director, Robert Woodruff; Sets, David Gropman; Costumes, Susan Hilferty; Lighting, Paul Gallo; Music, Douglas Wieselman, Thaddeus Spae; Sound, John Kilgore; Musical Direction/Arrangements, Douglas Wieselman; Props, Robert Hancox, William Muller, Edward Rausenberger; Production Supervisor, Joseph Busheme; Wardrobe, Don Brassington; Production Assistant, David Torrey Wells; Stage Managers, George Darveris, Chet Leaming. Opened in the Vivian Beaumont Theater on Sunday, May 31, 1987.*

CAST

The Janitor	Avner Eisenberg
Duke of Ephesus	Karla Burns
Egeon, a merchant of Syracuse	Daniel Mankin
Antipholus of Ephesus	Howard Jay Patterson
Antipholus of Syracuse	Paul Magid
Dromio of Ephesus	Randy Nelson
Dromio of Syracuse	Sam Williams
Balthasar, a merchant	Mark Sackett
Angelo, a goldsmith/merchant	Alec Willows
Doctor Pinch, the conjurer	Avner Eisenberg, Timothy Daniel Furst
First Merchant	Raz
Emilia, Abbess at Espesus	Ethyl Eichelberger
Adriana, wife of Antipholus of Ephesus	Sophie Hayden
Luciana, her sister	Gina Leishman
Luce, her maid	Karla Burns
Courtesan	Ethyl Eichelberger
William Shakespeare	Timothy Daniel Furst

CITIZENS OF EPHESUS: Steven Bernstein, Karla Burns, Bud Chase, Ethyl Eichelberger, Danny Frankel, Timothy Daniel Furst, Sophie Hayden, Gina Leishman, Paul Magid, Daniel Mankin, Derique McGee, Randy Nelson, Wendy Parkman, Howard Jay Patterson, Raz, Rosalinda Rojas, Mark Sackett, Douglas Wieselman, Sam Williams, Alec Willows.

A comedy in two acts. The action takes place during the past in Ephesus.

*Closed July 26, 1987 after 65 performances and 22 previews.

Brigitte Lacombe Photos

Raz, Sam Williams, Paul Magid, Karla Burns, Ethyl Eichelberger in "Comedy of Errors"

BIG RIVER

Music and Lyrics, Roger Miller; Book, William Hauptman; Adapted from "The Adventures of Huckleberry Finn" by Mark Twain; Scenery, Heidi Landesman; Costumes, Patricia McGourty; Lighting, Richard Riddell; Sound, Otts Munderloh; Musical Supervision, Danny Troob; Orchestrations, Steven Margoshes, Danny Troob; Dance/Incidental Music, John Richard Lewis; Musical Direction/Vocal Arrangements, Linda Twine; Staged by Des McAnuff; Choreography, Janet Watson; Stage Movements/Fights, B. H. Barry; Casting, Stanley Sable/Jason LaPadura; General Management, David Strong Warner; Sound Effects, John Kilgore; Hairstylist, Angela Gari; Presented by Rocco Landesman, Heidi Landesman, Rick Steiner, M. Anthony Fisher, Dodger Productions; Associate Producers, Arthur Katz, Emily Landau, Fred Mayerson, TM Productions; Company Managers, Sandra Carlson, Jill Hurwitz; Assistant Conductor, Kenneth Kosek; Props, Richard Patria, Michael Fedigan; Wardrobe, Joseph Busheme; Production Assistant, Chris Fielder; Associate Scenic Designer, Bob Shaw; Hairstylists, Chris Calabrese, Howard Leonard, Raymond Burns, Jung-Sin Kim; Stage Managers, Frank Hartenstein, Peter Glazer, Marianne Cane, Neal Jones, Steven Adler, John Ehrlich, James Dawson; Press, Solters/Roskin/Friedman, Joshua Ellis, Adrian Bryan-Brown, Jim Sapp, Cindy Valk, Reva Cooper, Jackie Green, Bill Shuttleworth, Susanne Tighe. Opened in the Eugene O'Neill Theatre on Thursday, April 25, 1985.*

CAST

Mark Twain	Gordon Connell †1
Huckleberry Finn	Daniel Jenkins †2
Widow Douglas/Sally Phelps	Susan Browning
Miss Watson/Harmonia Player	Evalyn Baron †3
Jim	Ron Richardson †4
Tom Sawyer	John Short †5
Ben Rogers/Hank/Young Fool	William Youmans †6
Jo Harper/Joanna Wilkes	Andi Henig
Simon	Aramis Estevez
Dick/Andy/Hiredhand	Michael Brian †7
Pap Finn/Sheriff Bell	John Goodman †8
Judge Thatcher/Harvey Wilkes/Silas Phelps	Ralph Byers
The King	Bob Gunton †9
The Duke	Rene Auberjonois †10
Lafe/Counselor Robinson/Hiredhand	Reathel Bean †11
Mary Jane Wilkes	Patti Cohenour †12
Susan Wilkes	Peggy Harmon
Bill, a servant	Franz Jones
Alice, a slave	Carol Dennis †13
Alice's Daughter	Jennifer Leigh Warren

UNDERSTUDIES: Huck (Romain Fruge/Skip Lackey), Jim (Elmore James/Jimmy Lockett), King/Preacher (Robert Serva/William McClary), Duke/Teacher (William McClary/Larry Raiken), Ensemble: Romaine Fruge, Peggy Harmon, Linda Kerns, Skip Lackey, Jimmy Lockett, William McClary, Yvonne Over, Robert Serva

MUSICAL NUMBERS: Do Ya Wanna Go to Heaven?, The Boys, Waitin' for the Light to Shine, Guv'ment, Hand for the Hog, I Huckleberry Me, Muddy Water, The Crossing, River in the Rain, When the Sun Goes Down in the South, The Royal Nonesuch, Worlds Apart, Arkansas, How Blest We Are, You Oughta Be Here with Me, Leavin's Not the Only Way to Go, Free at Last

A musical in two acts. The action takes place along the Mississippi River Valley sometime in the 1840's.

*Closed Sept. 20, 1987 after 1005 performances and 50 previews. Received 1985 "Tonys" for Best Musical Book, Score, Director, Scenic Design, Lighting Design, and Featured Actor in a Musical (Ron Richardson).

†Succeeded by: 1. Robert Sevra during vacation, 2. Martin Moran, Romaine Fruge, Brian L. Green, Jon Ehrlich, 3. Karen Looze, 4. Larry Riley, George Merritt, 5. Clint Allen, Roger Bart, 6. Patrick Breen, Russ Jolly, Neal Jones, 7. Adam Bryant, 8. Leo Burmester, John Connolly, Roger Miller, Graham Pollock, 9. Michael McCarty, 10. Brent Spiner, Ken Jenkins, Stephen Mellor, Ken Jenkins, 11. Gary Holcombe, Larry Raiken, 12. Karla DeVito, Marin Mazzie, 13. Carol Woods, Kecia Lewis-Evans

Martha Swope Photos

Top Right: George Merritt, Jon Ehrlich

George Merritt, Brian L. Green

CATS

Based on "Old Possum's Book of Practical Cats" by T. S. Eliot; Additional Lyrics, Trevor Nunn, Richard Stilgoe; Music, Andrew Lloyd Webber; Director, Trevor Nunn; Associate Director/Choreographer, Gillian Lynne; Presented by Cameron Mackintosh, The Really Useful Company, David Geffen, The Shubert Organization; Executive Producers, R. Tyler Gatchell, Jr., Peter Neufeld; Design, John Napier; Lighting, David Hersey; Sound, Martin Levan; Musical Director, Jack Gaughan; Production Musical Director, David Caddick, Stanley Lebowsky; Casting, Johnson/Liff; Orchestrations, David Cullen, Andrew Lloyd Webber; Original Cast Album, Geffen Records; Company Manager, James G. Mennen; Production Supervisor, David Taylor; Dance Supervisors, T. Michael Reed, Richard Stafford; Assistant Choreographer, Jo-Anne Robinson; Dance Captain, Greg Minahan; Associate Musical Director, Bill Grossman; Assistant Conductor, Arthur M. Greene; Production Assistant, Nancy Hall Bell; Technical Supervisors, Theatre Services/Arthur Siccardi, Peter Feller; Props, George Green, Jr., Merlyn Davis, George Green III; Wardrobe, Adelaide Laurino, Rachele Bussanich; Hairstylists, Leon Gagliardi, Frank Paul, Geordie Sheffer, Michael Wasula; Wigs, Paul Huntley; Makeup, Candace Carell; Stage Managers, Jeff Lee, Sally J. Jacobs, Sherry Cohen; Press, Fred Nathan, Dennis Crowley, Anne Abrams, Bert Fink, Merle Frimark, Marc P. Thibodeau, Philip Rinaldi. Opened in the Winter Garden Theatre on Thursday, October 7, 1982.*

CAST

Alonzo	Brian Sutherland †1
Bustopher Jones/Asparagus/Growltiger	Gregg Edelman †2
Bombalurina	Marlene Danielle
Carbucketty	Steven Gelfer †3
Cassandra	Jessica Northrup †4
Coricopat/Mungojerrie	Joe Antony Cavise †5
Demeter	Jane Bodle †6
Etcetera/Rumpleteazer	Paige Dana
Grizabella	Laurie Beechman
Jellylorum/Griddlebone	Bonnie Simmons
Jennyanydots	Anna McNeely
Mistoffolees	Barry K. Bernal †7
Munkustrap	Claude R. Tessier †8
Old Deuteronomy	Clent Bowers
Plato/Macavity/Rumpus Cat	Jamie Patterson
Pouncival	Robert Montano
Rum Tum Tugger	Rick Sparks †9
Sillabub	Denise DiRenzo †10
Skimbleshanks	Robert Burnett
Tantomile	Sundy Leigh Leake
Tumblebrutus	Jay Poindexter
Victoria	Claudia Shell
Cats Chorus	Jay Aubrey Jones, Susan Powers, Brenda Pressley, Joel Robertson

STANDBYS & UNDERSTUDIES: Alonzo (Brian Andrews/Jack Magradey/Greg Minahan), Bustopher/Asparagus/Growltiger (Joel Robertson), Bombalurina (Karen Curlee/Julietta Marcelli/Rebecca Timms), Carbucketty (Brian Andrews/Steven Hack/Marc Hunter/Jack Magradey/Greg Minahan), Cassandra (Karen Curlee/Rebecca Timms/Lily-Lee Wong), Coricopat/Mungojerrie (Steven Hack/Marc Hunter/Jack Magradey/Greg Minahan), Demeter (Karen Curlee/Teresa DeZarn/Julietta Marcelli/Rebecca Timms), Etcetera/Rumpleteazer (Dodie Pettit/Lily-Lee Wong), Grizabella (Karen Curlee/Teresa DeZarn/Brenda Pressley), Jellylorum/Griddlebone (Dodie Pettit/Susan Powers), Jennyanydots (Dodie Pettit/Susan Powers), Mistoffelees (Johnny Anzalone/Robert Montano), Munkustrap (Jack Magradey/Greg Minahan/Scott Taylor), Old Deuteronomy (Jay Aubrey Jones), Plato/Macavity/Rumpus Cat (Brian Andrews/Greg Minahan/Scott Taylor), Pouncival (Brian Andrews/Steven Hack), Rum Tum Tugger (Marc Hunter/Jack Magradey/Greg Minahan/Jamie Patterson/Scott Taylor), Sillibub (Dodie Pettit/Lily-Lee Wong), Skimbleshanks (Marc Hunter/ Jack Magradey/Greg Minahan), Tantomile (Karen Curlee/Rebecca Timms/Lily-Lee Wong), Tumblebrutus (Brian Andrews/Steven Hack/Greg Minahan), Victoria (Paige Dana/Dodie Pettit/Lily-Lee Wong)

MUSICAL NUMBERS: Jellicle Songs for Jellicle Cats, The Naming of the Cats, The Invitation to the Jellicle Ball, The Old Gumbie Cat, The Rum Tum Tugger, Grizabella the Glamour Cat, Bustopher Jones, Mungojerrie and Rumpleteazer, Old Deuteronomy, The Awefull Battle of the Pekes and Pollicles, The Marching Songs of the Pollicle Dogs, The Jellicle Ball, Memory, The Moments of Happiness, Gus the Theatre Cat, Growltiger's Last Stand, Skimbleshanks, Macavity, Mr. Mistoffelees, The Journey to the Heaviside Layer, The Ad-Dressing of Cats

A musical in two acts and twelve scenes.

Right Center: Laurie Beechman

*Still playing May 31, 1987. Winner of 1983 "Tonys" for Best Musical, Best Book, Best Score, Best Direction, Best Supporting Musical Actress (Betty Buckley as Grizabella), Best Costumes, Best Lighting. For original production, see THEATRE WORLD, Vol. 39.

†Succeeded by: 1. Scott Taylor, 2. Bill Carmichael, 3. Ray Roderick, 4. Roberta Stiehm, Julietta Marcelli, 5. Johnny Anzalone, 6. Patricia Ruck, 7. Don Johanson, 8. Mark Fotopoulos, Rob Marshall, 9. Steve Yudson, 10. Teresa DeZarn

Martha Swope Photos

A CHORUS LINE

Conceived, Choreographed and Directed by Michael Bennett; Book, James Kirkwood, Nicholas Dante; Music, Marvin Hamlisch; Lyrics, Edward Kleban; Co-Choreographer, Bob Avian; A New York Shakespeare Festival production presented by Joseph Papp in association with Plum Productions; Musical Direction/Vocal Arrangements, Don Pippin; Orchestrations, Bill Byers, Hershy Kay, Jonathan Tunick; Setting, Robin Wagner; Costumes, Theoni V. Aldredge; Lighting, Tharon Musser; Sound, Abe Jacob; Music Directed by Jerry Goldberg; Music Coordinator, Robert Thomas; Associate Producer, Bernard Gersten; Original Cast Album by Columbia Records; Assistant to Choreographers, Baayork Lee; Company Manager, Susan Sampliner; Dance Captain, Troy Garza; Wardrobe, Alyce Gilbert; Stage Managers, Tom Porter, Ronald Stafford, Morris Freed, Robert Amirante; Press, Merle Debuskey, William Schelble, Richard Kornberg. Opened in the Shubert Theatre on Friday, July 25, 1975.*

CAST

Roy	Tommy Re
Kristine	Kerry Casserly
Sheila	Susan Danielle †1
Mike	Mark Bove
Val	DeLyse Lively-Mekka
Butch	Michael-Pierre Dean
Larry	J. Richard Hart
Maggie	Pam Klinger
Richie	Gordon Owens †2
Tricia	Robin Lyon
Tom	Frank Kliegel
Zach	Eivind Harum
Mark	Gib Jones †3
Cassie	Wanda Richert †4
Judy	Angelique Ilo †5
Lois	Cynthia Fleming †6
Don	Michael Danek
Bebe	Tracy Shayne
Connie	Sachi Shimizu
Diana	Roxann Cabalero †7
Al	Kevin Neil McCready
Frank	Fraser Ellis
Greg	Bradley Jones
Bobby	Ron Kurowski
Paul	Wayne Meledandri
Vicki	Trish Ramish †8
Ed	Morris Freed
Jarad	Troy Garza
Linda	Laureen Valuch Piper †9
Douglas	Gary Chryst
Herman	Robert Amirante
Hilary	Karen Curlee †10

UNDERSTUDIES: Robert Amirante (Greg/Zach), Gary Chryst (Paul/Larry), Michael Danek (Zach), Michael-Pierre Dean (Richie), Fraser Ellis (Mark/Bobby/Don), Cynthia Fleming (Cassie/Sheila/Judy/Kristine/Bebe), Laurie Gamache (Cassie/Sheila/Judy/Kristine/Bebe), Troy Garza (Mike/Greg/Paul/Larry/Al), J. Richard Hart (Mike), Frank Kliegel (Don/Zach/Bobby), Cindi Klinger (Judy/Sheila), Robin Lyon (Bebe/Diana/Val/Maggie), Laureen Valuch Piper (Sheila/Val), Trish Ramish (Val), Tommy Re (Greg/Al/Larry/Mike), Tracy Shayne (Diana/Maggie/Connie), Dorothy Tancredi (Maggie/Bebe/Diana)

MUSICAL NUMBERS: I Hope I Get It, I Can Do That, And . . ., At the Ballet, Sing!, Hello 12 Hello 13 Hello Love, Nothing, Dance 10 Looks 3, The Music and the Mirror, One, The Tap Combination, What I Did for Love, Finale

A musical performed without intermission. The action takes place in 1975 during an audition in the theatre.

*Still playing May 31, 1987. Cited as Best 1975 Musical by NY Drama Critics Circle, winner of 1976 Pulitzer Prize, and 1976 "Tonys" for Best Musical, Best Book, Best Score, Best Direction, Best Lighting, Best Choreography, Best Musical Actress (Donna McKechnie), Best Featured Actor and Actress in a Musical (Sammy Williams, Kelly Bishop), and a Special Theatre World Award was presented to each member of the creative staff and original cast. See THEATRE WORLD Vol. 31. On Thursday, Sept. 29, 1983 it became the longest running show in Broadway history.

†Succeeded by: 1. Cynthia Fleming, 2. Bruce Anthony Davis, 3. Andrew Grose, 4. Angelique Ilo, Donna McKechnie, Laurie Gamache, 5. Trish Ramish, 6. Cindi Klinger, 7. Mercedes Perez, 8. Lauren Valuch Piper, 9. Laurie Gamache, 10. Dorothy Tancredi

Martha Swope Photos

**Top Left: DeLyse Lively-Mekka, Andrew Grose,
Wayne Meledandri, Mercedes Perez**

**Gay Marshall (center)
Above: Donna McKechnie**

42nd STREET

Music, Harry Warren; Lyrics, Al Dubin; Book, Michael Stewart, Mark Bramble; Based on novel by Bradford Ropes; Directed and Choreographed by Gower Champion; Scenery, Robin Wagner; Costumes, Theoni V. Aldredge; Lighting, Tharon Musser; Musical Direction/Dance Arrangements, Donald Johnston; Orchestrations, Philip J. Lang; Vocal Arrangements, John Lesko; Sound, Richard Fitzgerald; Hairstylist, Ted Azar; Casting, Julie Hughes/Barry Moss; Dance Assistants, Karin Baker, Randy Skinner; General Manager, Leo K. Cohen; Dance Captain, Lizzie Moran; Props, Leo Herbert; Wardrobe, Gene Wilson, Shelly Friedman; Assistant Musical Director, Bernie Leighton; Company Manager, Marcia Goldberg; Stage Managers, Jack Timmers, Harold Goldfaden, Michael Pule, Dennis Angulo; Press, Joshua Ellis, Adrian Bryan-Brown, Jackie Green, Leo Stern, Bill Shuttleworth, Susanne Tighe. Opened in the Winter Garden Theatre on Monday, August 25, 1980; moved to the Majestic Theatre on Monday, March 30, 1981, and to the St. James Theatre on Tuesday, April 7, 1987.*

CAST

Andy Lee	Danny Carroll
Oscar	Robert Colston
Mac/Thug/Doctor	Stan Page
Annie	Beth Leavel
Maggie Jones	Marie Lillo †1
Bert Barry	Joseph Bova
Billy Lawlor	Lee Roy Reams
Peggy Sawyer	Clare Leach
Lorraine	Neva Leigh
Phyllis	Jeri Kansas
Julian Marsh	Barry Nelson †2
Dorothy Brock	Dolores Gray †3
Abner Dillon	Don Crabtree
Pat Denning	Steve Elmore
Thugs	Stan Page, Ron Schwinn
Doctor	Stan Page

ENSEMBLE: Susan Banks, Carole Banninger, Dennis Batutis, Paula Joy Belis, Kelly Crafton, Ronny DeVito, Rob Draper, Barndt Edward, Judy Ehrlich, David Fredericks, Cathy Greco, Christine Jacobsen, Suzie Jary, Jeri Kansas, Billye Kersey, Neva Leigh, Bobby Longbottom, Chris Lucas, Maureen Mellon, Ken Mitchell, Bill Nabel, Don Percassi, Rosemary Rado, Anne Rutter, Linda Sabatelli, Jeanna Schweppe, David Schwing, Ron Schwinn, Pamela S. Scott, J. Thomas Smith, Karen Sorensen, Susanne Leslie Sullivan, Vickie Taylor, Mary Chris Wall.

UNDERSTUDIES: Connie Day (Dorothy/Maggie), Karen Sorensen (Dorothy), Steve Elmore/Stan Page (Julian), Vickie Taylor/Debra Ann Draper (Peggy), Rob Draper/Dennis Angulo (Billy), Bill Nabel/Ron Schwinn (Bert/Mac), Don Percassi/Ron Schwinn (Andy), Stan Page (Abner), Stan Page/Brandt Edwards (Pat), Billye Kersey/Linda Sabatelli (Annie), Bernie Leighton (Oscar), Lizzie Moran/Debra Ann Draper (Phyllis/Lorraine), Ensemble: Debra Ann Draper, Lizzie Moran, Brenda Pipik, Dennis Angulo, John Salvatore.

MUSICAL NUMBERS: Audition, Young and Healthy, Shadow Waltz, Go into Your Dance, You're Getting to Be a Habit with Me, Getting Out of Town, Dames, I Know Now, We're in the Money, Sunny Side to Every Situation, Lullaby of Broadway, About a Quarter to Nine, Overture, Shuffle Off to Buffalo, 42nd Street.

A musical in 2 acts and 16 scenes. The action takes place during 1933 in New York City and Philadelphia.

*Still playing May 31, 1987. Recipient of 1981 "Tonys" for Best Musical, Best Choreography. For original production, see THEATRE WORLD Vol. 37.

†Succeeded by: 1. Denise Lor, Bobo Lewis, 2. Jamie Ross, 3. Elizabeth Allen

Martha Swope Photos

Top Left: Lee Roy Reams (center) and chorus

Moving from the St. James to the Majestic

I'M NOT RAPPAPORT

By Herb Gardner; Director, Daniel Sullivan; Set, Tony Walton; Costumes, Robert Morgan; Lighting, Pat Collins; Fight Staged by B. H. Barry; Presented by James Walsh, Lewis Allen, Martin Heinfling; General Manager, James Walsh; Company Manager, Stanley D. Silver; Technical Coordinator, Robert Scales; Wardrobe, Mary Eno; Makeup, Chris Bingham, Suzanne Kruck, Michael Laudati; Stage Managers, Thomas A. Kelly, Charles Kindl; Press, Jeffrey Richards, C. George Willard, Ben Morse, Irene Gandy, Susan Lee, Ken Mandelbaum. Opened in the Booth Theatre on Tuesday, November 19, 1985.*

CAST

Nat	Judd Hirsch †1
Midge	Cleavon Little †2
Danforth	Gregg Almquist †3
Laurie	Liann Pattison †4
Gilley	Jace Alexander †5
Clara	Cheryl Giannini †6
The Cowboy	Steve Ryan †7

STANDBYS & UNDERSTUDIES: Sidney Armus (Nat), William Hall, Jr. (Midge), Elaine Bromka (Clara/Laurie), Richard Buckley (Gilley), Chip Mitchell (Danforth/Cowboy)

A comedy in 2 acts and 4 scenes. The action takes place on a bench near a path at the edge of the lake in Central Park in New York City early in October of 1982.

*Still playing May 31, 1987. Winner of 1986 "Tonys" for Best Play, Best Leading Actor in a Play (Judd Hirsch), Best Lighting Design.

†Succeeded by: 1. Hal Linden, Jack Klugman, Judd Hirsch, 2. Ossie Davis, Cleavon Little, 3. Richard E. Council, Gregg Almquist, Daniel Ziskie, 4. Jane Fleiss, Elaine Bromka, 5. Josh Pais, 6. Mercedes Ruehl, Marcia Rodd, Christine Estabrook, Cheryl Giannini, 7. James Rebhorn, Richard E. Council

Martha Swope Photos

Christine Estabrook, Hal Linden
Top: Jack Klugman, Ossie Davis

LA CAGE AUX FOLLES

Music and Lyrics, Jerry Herman; Book, Harvey Fierstein; Based on the play of same title by Jean Poiret; Director, Arthur Laurents; Choreography, Scott Salmon; Presented by Allan Carr with Kenneth D. Greenblatt, Stewart F. Lane, James M. Nederlander, Martin Richards and Barry Brown, Fritz Holt, Marvin A. Krauss; Produced in association with Jonathan Farkas, John Pomerantz, Martin Heinfling; Settings, David Mitchell; Costumes, Theoni V. Aldredge; Lighting, Jules Fisher; Musical Director/Vocal Arranger, Donald Pippin; Sound, Peter J. Fitzgerald; Hairstylist/Makeup, Ted Azar; Orchestrations, Jim Tyler; Dance Music Arrangements, G. Harrell; Assistant Choreographer, Richard Balestrino; Music Coordinator, John Monaco; Casting, Stuart Howard; Original Cast Album on RCA Records and Cassettes; General Management, Marvin A. Krauss Associates/Gary Gunas, Joey Parnes; Company Manager, Nina Skriloff; Dance Captain, Dennis Callahan; Props, Charles Zuckerman, Jack Cennamo; Wardrobe, Gayle Patton, Irene Bunis; Assistant Conductor, Rudolph Bennett; Production Assistant, Trey Hunt; Stage Managers, David Caine, Jay Adler, Allan Sobeck; Press, Shirley Herz, Peter Cromarty, Pete Sanders, Glenna Freedman, David Roggensack, Miller Wright. Opened in the Palace Theatre on Sunday August 21, 1983.*

CAST

Georges	Steeve Arlen †1
Les Cagelles:	
Chantal	Frank DiPasquale
Monique	Dennis Callahan
Dermah	Kyle White †2
Nicole	Eric Underwood
Hanna	David Engel
Mercedes	David Evans
Bitelle	Lynn Faro
Lo Singh	Eric Lamp
Odette	Dan O'Grady
Angelique	Shannon Lee Jones
Phaedra	David Scala
Clo-Clo	Sam Singhaus
Francis	Robert Brubach
Jacob	Darrell Carey †3
Albin	Walter Charles †4
Jean-Michel	John Weiner
Anne	Juliette Kurth
Jacqueline	Elizabeth Parrish
Renaud	Jack Davison †5
Mme. Renaud	Sydney Anderson
Paulette	Betsy Craig †6
Hercule	Jack Neubeck †7
Etienne	Jay Pierce
Babette	Marie Santell
Colette	Pamela Cecil
Tabarro	Mark Waldrop
Pepe	David Jackson †8
Edouard Dindon	Jay Garner
Mme. Dindon	Merle Louise †9

STANDBYS & UNDERSTUDIES: Tom Urich (Georges), Mace Barrett (Albin/Dindon), David Jackson (Jacob), Drew Geraci (Jean-Michel/Hercule/Tabarro/Chantel/Hanna/Mercedes/Dermah), Jan Leigh Herndon (Anne/Mme. Renaud/Paulette/Babette/Colette/Angelique), Suzanne Ishee (Mme. Dindon), Sydney Anderson (Jacqueline), Frank DiPasquale (Francis), David Klatt (Etienne/Photographer/Pepe/Phaedra), Rex Hays (M. Renaud)
MUSICAL NUMBERS: We Are What We Are, A Little More Mascara, With Anne on My Arm, The Promenade, Song on the Sand, La Cage aux Folles, I Am What I Am, Masculinity, Look over There, Cocktail Counterpoint, The Best of Times, Finale

A musical in two acts. The action takes place during summer in St. Tropez, France, at the present time.

*Still playing May 31, 1987. Winner of 1984 "Tonys" for Best Musical, Musical Book, Musical Score, Outstanding Actor in a Musical (George Hearn as Albin), Outstanding Direction, Costumes.

†Succeeded by: 1. Peter Marshall, 2. Keith Allen, 3. David Jackson, 4. Keene Curtis, 5. Mace Barrett, 6. Suzanne Ishee, 7. Rex Hays, 8. David Klatt, 9. Darcy Pulliam

Martha Swope Photos

Top Right: Peter Marshall, Keene Curtis

Les Cagelles
Above: Keene Curtis

55

THE MYSTERY OF EDWIN DROOD

On Nov. 16, 1986 the title was changed to DROOD; Book, Music and Lyrics, Rupert Holmes; Suggested by Charles Dickens' unfinished novel *The Mystery of Edwin Drood;* Director, Wilford Leach; Choreography, Graciela Daniele; A New York Shakespeare Festival production presented by Joseph Papp; Scenery, Bob Shaw; Costumes, Lindsay W. Davis; Lighting, Paul Gallo; Sound, Tom Morse; Magic Lantern Projections, James Cochrane; Hair/Wigs, Paul Huntley; Musical Supervision, Michael Starobin; Musical Director/Conductor, Edward Strauss; Orchestrations, Rupert Holmes; Associate Producer, Jason Steven Cohen; General Managers, Laurel Ann Wilson, Bob MacDonald; Company Manager, David Conte; Dance Captain, Rob Marshall; Props, Walter Bullard; Wardrobe, Daniel Eaton, Mindy Eng; Hairdressers, Sonia Rivera, Thelma Pollard; Production Assistant, Connie Drew; Stage Managers, James Harker, Pamela Singer, Michele Pigliavento; Press, Richard Kornberg, Kevin Patterson, Barbara Carroll, L. Glenn Poppleton III. Opened in the Imperial Theatre on Monday, December 2, 1985.*

CAST

Mayor Thomas Sapsea/William Cartwright/Your Chairman	George Rose
Stage Manager/Barkeep/James Throttle	Peter McRobbie
John Jasper/Clive Paget	Howard McGillin
Rev. Crisparkle/Cedric Moncrieffe	George N. Martin
Edwin Drood/Alice Nutting	Betty Buckley †1
Rosa Bud/Deirdre Peregrine	Patti Cohenour †2
Wendy/Isabel Yearsley	Judy Kuhn †3
Beatrice/Florence Gill	Donna Murphy †4
Helena Landless/Janet Conover	Jana Schneider †5
Neville Landless/Victor Grinstead	John Herrera
Durdles/Nick Cricker	George Dempsey †6
Deputy/Master Nick Cricker/Statue/Satyr	Stephen Glavin †7
Princess Puffer/Angela Prysock	Cleo Laine †8
Shade of Jasper/Harry Sayle	Nicholas Gunn
Shade of Drood/Montague Pruitt	Brad Miskell

Clients of Princess Puffer:

Alan Eliot/Julian	Herndon Lackey
Christopher Lyon	Rob Marshall †9

†Succubae:

Gwendolyn Pynn	Francine Landes †10
Sarah Cook	Karen Giombetti †11

Servants:

Philip Bax/Bazzard	Joe Grifasi †12
Violet Balfour	Susan Goodman †13
Horace/Brian Pankhurst	Charles Goff
Dick Datchery	????????????

STANDBYS & UNDERSTUDIES: David Cromwell (Chairman), Charles Goff (Chairman), Peter McRobbie/Charles Goff (Crisparkle), Paige O'Hara/Lorraine Goodman (Edwin Drood), Herndon Lackey/Rick Negron (John Jasper), Lorraine Goodman/Paige O'Hara (Rosa Bud), Mary Robin Roth (Princess Puffer/Helena Landless), Herndon Lackey/John DeLuca (Neville), Joe Pichette (Durdles/Horace), Steve Clemente/Robert Radford (Deputy), Rick Negron/Brad Miskell (Satyr), Joe Pichette/Nicholas Gunn (Bazzard), Charles Goff (Stage Manager), Michele Pigliavento (Beatrice/Wendy), Swings: John DeLuca, Michele Pigliavento, Rick Negron

MUSICAL NUMBERS: There You Are, A Man Could Go Quite Mad, Two Kinsmen, Moonfall, The Wages of Sin, Jasper's Vision, Ceylon, Both Sides of the Coin, Perfect Strangers, No Good Can Come from Bad, The Name of Love, Settling Up the Score, Off to the Races, Don't Quit While You're Ahead, The Garden Path to Hell, The Solution

A musical in two acts.

*Closed May 16, 1987 after 608 performances and 24 previews. Prior to its Broadway debut it had given 24 performances in Central Park's Delacorte Theater. It was the recipient of 1986 "Tonys" for Best Musical, Leading Actor in a Musical (George Rose), Best Book of a Musical, Best Original Score, Best Direction of a Musical.

†Succeeded by: 1, Donna Murphy, 2. Karen Culliver, 3. Lorraine Goodman, 4. Mary Robin Roth, 5. Alison Fraser, 6. Tony Azito, 7. Brad Miskell, Steve Clemente, 8. Loretta Swit, Karen Morrow, 9. Robert Radford, 10. Catherine Ulissey, 11. Camille de Ganon, 12. David Cromwell, 13. Mary Robin Roth

Martha Swope Photos

Left Center: Karen Morrow
Top: (center) George Rose

(center) Karen Morrow, George Rose, Howard McGillin

OH! CALCUTTA!

Devised by Kenneth Tynan; Conceived and Directed by Jacques Levy; Presented by Hillard Elkins, Norman Kean; Production Supervisor, Ron Nash; Authors and Composers, Robert Benton, David Newman, Jules Feiffer, Dan Greenburg, Lenore Kandel, John Lennon, Jacques Levy, Leonard Melfi, Sam Shepard, Clovis Trouille, Kenneth Tynan, Sherman Yellen; Music and Lyrics, Robert Dennis, Peter Schickle, Stanley Walden, Jacques Levy; Choreography, Margo Sappington; Musical Director, Stanley Walden; Music Conductor, Tim Weil; Scenery/Lighting, Harry Silverglat Darrow; Costumes, Kenneth M. Yount; Sound, Sander Hacker; Assistant to Director, Nancy Tribush; Projected Media Design, Gardner Compton; Live Action Film, Ron Merk; Company Manager, Doris J. Buberl; Producer, Norman Kean; Production Associates, Karen Nagle, Nancy Arrigo; Assistant General Manager, Tobias Beckwith; Assistant Musical Conductor, Dan Carter; Wardrobe, Mark Bridges; Stage Managers, Maria DiDia, Ron Nash; Press, Les Schecter, Timothy Fisher. Opened at the Eden Theatre on Friday, June 17, 1969, and at the Edison Theatre on Friday, September 24, 1976.*

CAST

Cheryl Hartley	Michael A. Clarke †2
Jodi Johnson	David Heisey
Vivian Paxton †1	Charles Klausmeyer †3
Deborah Robertson	James E. Mosiej

MUSICAL NUMBERS & SKITS: Taking Off the Robe, Will Answer All Sincere Replies, Playin', Jack and Jill, The Paintings of Clovis Trouille, Delicious Indignities, Was It Good for You Too?, Suite for Five Letters, One on One, Rock Garden, Spread Your Love Around, Four in Hand, Coming Together Going Together

An "erotic musical" in two acts and twelve scenes.

*Still playing May 31, 1987. For original production, see THEATRE WORLD Volume 33.

†Succeeded by: 1, Danielle P. Connell, 2. William Thomas, 3. Louis Silvers. Cheryl Hartley has celebrated her tenth year with the production, and holds the record for the longest run by a performer in the same show.

Martha Swope Photos

Top Left: Cheryl Hartley Below: Deborah Robertson, Michael Clarke, James Mosiej, Cheryl Hartley, Charles Klausmeyer, Nannette Bevelander, Jodi Johnson, David Heisey

PRODUCTIONS FROM PAST SEASONS THAT CLOSED DURING THIS SEASON

Title	Opened	Closed	Performances
Benefactors	12/22/85	6/29/86	217
Biloxi Blues	3/28/85	6/29/86	524
Penn & Teller	4/18/85	1/4/87	666
Song and Dance	9/18/85	11/8/86	474
Sweet Charity	4/27/86	3/15/87	368

OFF-BROADWAY PRODUCTIONS FROM PAST SEASONS THAT PLAYED THROUGH THIS SEASON

BEEHIVE

Created and Directed by Larry Gallagher; Musical Direction/Arrangements, Skip Brevis; Choreography, Leslie Dockery; Scenic/Lighting Design, John Hickey; Costumes, David Dille; Hair/Makeup, J. Stanley Crowe; Vocal Adaptation, Claudia Brevis; Sound, Lewis Mead; Presented by Betty Lee Hunt, Maria Cristina Pucci and Charles Allen; Associate Producer, Gideon Rothschild; General Management, Leonard A. Mulhern, James Hannah; Production Assistants, Joe McGuire, Tom Roberts; Associate Conductor, Peter Grant; Wardrobe, Mary Lou Rios; Dance Captain, B. J. Jefferson; Stage Manager, Brian Kaufman; Press, Betty Lee Hunt, Maria Cristina Pucci, James Sapp. Opened in Top of the Gate (Village Gate) on Tuesday March 11, 1986.*

CAST

Pattie Darcy †1
Alison Fraser †2
Jasmine Guy †3
Adriane Lenox †4
Gina Taylor †5
Laura Theodore †6

UNDERSTUDIES: Andrea Petty, Jenny Douglas, Bertilla Baker, Andrea Frierson

MUSICAL NUMBERS: Overture, The Name Game, My Boyfriend's Back, Sweet Talkin' Guy, One Fine Day, I Sold My Heart to the Junkman, Academy Award, Will You Still Love Me Tomorrow, Give Him a Great Big Kiss, Remember Walking in the Sand, I Can Never Go Home Again, Where Did Our Love Go?, Come See about Me, I Hear a Symphony, It's My Party, I'm Sorry, Rockin' Around the Christmas Tree, I Dream about Frankie, She's a Fool, You Don't Own Me, Judy's Turn to Cry, Where the Boys Are, The Beehive Dance, The Beat Goes On, Downtown, To Sir with Love, Wishin' and Hopin', Don't Sleep in the Subway, You Don't Have to Say You Love Me, Beehive Boogie, A Fool in Love, River Deep Mountain High, Proud Mary, Society's Child, Respect, A Natural Woman, Do Right Woman, Piece of My Heart, Try Just a Little Bit Harder, Me and Bobby McGee, Ball and Chain, Mark Your Own Kind of Music

A musical revue in two acts. A nostalgic tribute to the girl groups and the great female singers of the 1960's.

*Closed Aug. 23, 1987 after 600 performances.

†Succeeded by: 1. Julee Cruise, 2. B. J. Jefferson, 3. Debbie Lyons, 4. Carol Maillard, Adriane Lenox, 5. Cookie Watkins, 6. Jessie Richards

Gerry Goodstein Photos

Right: Carol Maillard, Jasmine Guy, Gina Taylor
Top: Alison Fraser, Patti Darcy (seated), Jasmine Guy

Debbie Lyons, Adriane Lenox, Cookie Watkins,
Jessie Janet Richards, Julee Cruise, B. J. Jefferson

Jasmine Guy, Cookie Watkins, Alison Fraser,
Adriane Lenox, Laura Theodore, Patti Darcy

THE FANTASTICKS

Book and Lyrics, Tom Jones; Music, Harvey Schmidt; Suggested by Edmund Rostand's play "Les Romanesques"; Presented by Lore Noto; Director, Word Baker; Original Musical Direction/Arrangements, Julian Stein; Designed by Ed Wittstein; Associate Producers, Sheldon Baron, Dorothy Olim, Robert Alan Gold; Assistant Producers, Bill Mills, Thad Noto; Original Cast Album by MGM or Polydor Records; Production Assistant, John Krug; Stage Managers, Geoffrey Brown, James Cook, Jim Charles, Paul Blankenship; Press, Tony Noto. Opened in the Sullivan Street Playhouse on Tuesday, May 3, 1960.*

CAST

The Narrator	George Lee Andrews †1
The Girl	Jennifer Lee Andrews †2
The Boy	Bill Perlach †3
The Boy's Father	George Riddle †4
The Girl's Father	William Tost
The Old Actor	Bryan Hull †5
The Man Who Dies/Indian	Robert R. Oliver †6
The Mute	Paul Blankenship †7
At the piano	Dorothy Martin
At the harp	Elizabeth Etters

UNDERSTUDIES: Kim Moore (Narrator/Boy), Marti Morris (The Girl), William Tost (The Boy's Father), Jim Charles (Narrator/Boy)

MUSICAL NUMBERS: Overture, Try to Remember, Much More, Metaphor, Never Say No, It Depends on What You Pay, Soon It's Gonna Rain, Rape Ballet, Happy Ending, This Plum Is Too Ripe, I Can See It, Plant a Radish, Round and Round, They Were You

*The world's longest running musical was still playing May 31, 1987. Performed in two acts.

†Succeeded by: 1. Lance Brodie, David Brummel, Dennis Parlato, Michael Licata, 2. Martin Morris, Virginia Gregory, Liz Bruzzese, Lorrie Harrison, 3. Paul Blankenship, Jim Charles, Kim Moore, 4. Henry Quinn, Lowry Miller, Gene Jones, Ron Lee Savin, 5. Des Philpot, Bryan Hull, 6. George Curley, John Thomas Waite, 7. Tom Brittingham, Paul Blankenship, Jim Charles

(front) John T. Waite, Lorrie Harrison, Bill Perlach, Brian Hull **(back)** William Tost, George Lee Andrews, Kim Moore, Ron Lee Savin Top Right: George Lee Andrews, Lorrie Harrison

Mark Mitchell, Barbara Walsh, Craig
Wells, Roxie Lucas Top: Wells, Walsh

FORBIDDEN BROADWAY

Concept and Lyrics by Gerard Alessandrini; Director, Mr. Alessandrini; Presented by Playkill Productions; Executive Producer, Sella Palsson; Costumes, Chet Ferris; Choreography, Roxie Lucas; General Manager, Elizabeth Hermann; Music Supervisor, Fred Barton; Production Assistant, Ron Drummond; Stage Manager, Jerry James; Press, Becky Flora. Opened at Palsson's Supper Club on Friday, January 15, 1982 and still playing May 31, 1987.

CAST

Roxie Lucas
Mark Martino†1
Mark Mitchell†2
Barbara Walsh
Craig Wells

A musical satire in two acts.

†Succeeded by: 1. Ron Bohmer, Gerard Alessandrini, Merwin Foard, 2. Philip Fortenberry

Henry Grossman Photos

Top: Roxie Lucas

LITTLE SHOP OF HORRORS

Book and Lyrics, Howard Ashman; Music, Alan Menken; Director, Howard Ashman; Musical Staging, Edie Cowan; Setting, Edward T. Gianfrancesco; Lighting, Craig Evans; Costumes, Sally Lesser; Sound, Otts Munderloh; Puppets, Martin P. Robinson; Vocal Arrangements/Musical Supervision, Robert Billig; Orchestrations, Robby Merkin; Originally produced by the WPA Theatre (Kyle Renick, Artistic Director); Original cast album by Geffen Records; Presented by The WPA Theatre, David Geffen, Cameron Mackintosh and the Shubert Organization; Based on film by Roger Corman with Screenplay by Charles Griffith; General Manager, Albert Poland; Company Manager, Nancy Nagel Gibbs; Dance Captain, Deborah Dotson; Makeup and Wigs, Lenora Brown; Props, Matt Silver; Wardrobe, Craig Aspden, James Durso; Casting, Albert Tavares; Puppeteers, Matt Silver, James Durso, Craig Aspden, Michael Verbil; Stage Managers, Donna Fletcher, Donna A. Drake; Press, Milly Schoenbaum, Meg Bloom. Opened in the Orpheum Theatre on Tuesday, July 27, 1982.*

CAST

Chiffon	Melodee Savage †1
Crystal	Tena Wilson
Ronnette	Deborah Dotson †2
Mushnik	Fyvush Finkel
Audrey	Marsha Skaggs †3
Seymour	Andrew Hill Newman
Derelict	William Szymanski †4
Orin/Bernstein/Snip/Luce/Everyone Else	Ken Land
Audrey II:	
Manipulation	Lynn Hippen
Voice	Ron Taylor

STANDBYS: Mimi Bessette (Audrey), Michael Pace (Seymour/Orin/Snip/Luce/Audrey II Voice), Arn Weiner (Mushnik), William Szymanski (Derelict/Audrey II Manipulation), Deborah Dotson (Chiffon/Crystal/Ronnette)
MUSICAL NUMBERS: Prologue, Little Shop of Horrors, Skid Row, Downtown, Da—Doo, Grow for Me, Don't It Go to Show Ya Never Know, Somewhere That's Green, Closed for Renovations, Dentist!, Mushnik and Son, Feed Me (Git It), Now (It's Just the Gas), Call Back in the Morning, Suddenly Seymour, Suppertime, The Meek Shall Inherit, Finale (Don't Feed the Plants)

A musical in two acts.

*Still playing May 31, 1987. Recipient of 1983 citation from NY Drama Critics Circle as Best Musical of the 1982–1983 season.

†Succeeded by: 1. B. J. Jefferson, 2. Sheila Kay Davis, 3. Katherine Meloche, 4. Lynn Hippen

Peter Cunningham Photos

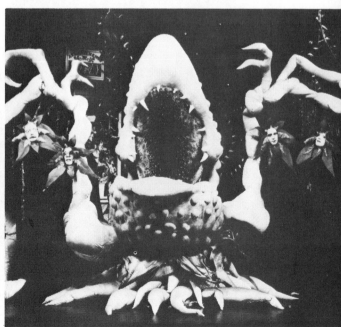

Audrey II, Katherine Meloche
Top Right: Andrew Hill Newman, Meloche

Top: Audrey II

NUNSENSE

Written and Directed by Dan Goggin; Musical Staging/Choreography, Felton Smith; Set, Barry Axtell; Lighting, Susan A. White; Musical Direction/Arrangements, Michael Rice; Presented by The Nunsense Theatrical Company and Joseph Hoesl, Bill Crowder; Associate Producer, Jay Cardwell; Originally presented by the Baldwin Theatre; General Management, Roger Alan Gindi; Company Manager, Danielle Fenton; Wardrobe, Nicole Hill; Technical Supervisor, Ted Kent Wallace; Tap Sequence composed by Paul Lewis; Slide Production, Kathryn Decker; Ventriloquist Consultant, Todd Stockman; Stage Managers, Trey Hunt, Nancy Hillner, Susan Gordon-Clark; Press, Shirley Herz, Pete Sanders, Peter Cromarty, Glenna Freedman, Gary Lawrence. Opened in the Cherry Lane Theatre on Tuesday, December 3, 1985. Moved to the Sheridan Square Playhouse/Circle Repertory Theatre on Monday, February 27, 1986, and to the Douglas Fairbanks Theatre Monday, September 8, 1986.*

CAST

Sister Mary Cardelia .... Marilyn Farina †1
Sister Mary Hubert .... Vicki Belmonte †2
Sister Robert Anne .... Christine Anderson
Sister Mary Amnesia .... Semina DeLaurentis †3
Sister Mary Leo .... Suzi Winson
Understudies: Susan Gordon-Clark, Nancy Hillner, Julie J. Hafner, Karen Ziemba

MUSICAL NUMBERS: Nunsense Is Habit-Forming, A Difficult Transition, Benedicite, The Biggest Ain't the Best, Playing Second Fiddle, So You Want to Be a Nun, Turn Up the Spotlight, Lilacs Bring Back Memories, Tackle That Temptation with a Time Step, Growing Up Catholic, We've Got to Clean out the Freezer, Just a Coupl'a Sisters, Soup's On (The Dying Nun Ballet), I Just Want to Be a Star, The Drive In, I Could've Gone to Nashville, Gloria in Excelsis Deo, Holier Than Thou

A musical comedy in two acts. The action takes place at the present time in Mt. Saint Helen's School auditorium.

†Succeeded by: 1. Travis Hudson, 2. Edwina Lewis, 3. Nancy Hillner, Susan Gordon-Clark

*Still playing May 31, 1987.

Adam Newman Photos

clockwise from top: Marilyn Farina, Edwina Lewis, Suzi Winson, Susan Gordon-Clark,
Christine Anderson Top Left: Edwina Lewis, Marilyn Farina

VAMPIRE LESBIANS OF SODOM
and SLEEPING BEAUTY or COMA

By Charles Busch; Director, Kenneth Elliott; Choreography, Jeff Veazey; Scenery, B. T. Whitehill; Costumes, John Glaser; Lighting, Vivien Leone; Casting, Stuart Howard; Wigs, Elizabeth Katherine Carr; Presented by Theatre-in-Limbo, Kenneth Elliott, Gerald A. Davis; Company Manager, Terry Byrne; Assistant to the Director, Jim Griffith; Wardrobe, Bob Locke; Production Assistant, Sandy Fischler; Stage Managers, Elizabeth Katherine Carr, Robert Carey; Press, Shirley Herz, Pete Sanders, Peter Cromarty, Glenna Freedman, David Roggensack, Miller Wright, Jillana Devine. Opened in the Provincetown Playhouse on Wednesday, June 19, 1985.*

CAST

"Sleeping Beauty" or "Coma"

Miss Thick .... Andy Halliday †1
Enid Wetwhistle .... Meghan Robinson †2
Sebastian Lore .... Kenneth Elliott †3
Fauna Alexander ....Charles Busch †4
Ian McKenzie .... Tom Aulino †5
Anthea Arlo .... Theresa Marlowe †6
Barry Posner ....Robert Carey
Craig Prince .... Arnie Kolodner †7

The action takes place in and around London in the 1960's.

"Vampire Lesbians of Sodom"

Ali, a guard/P.J. a chorus boy ....Robert Carey
Hujar, a guard/Zack, chorus boy .... Arnie Kolodner
Virgin Sacrifice/Madeleine Astarte .... Charles Busch †4
The Succubus/La Condesa, silent screen vamp .... Meghan Robinson †2
King Carlisle, silent movie idol .... Kenneth Elliott †3
Etienne, butler/Danny, a chorus boy .... Andy Halliday †1
Renee Vain, starlet/Tracy, singer .... Theresa Marlowe †6
Oatsie Carewe, gossip columnist .... Tom Aulino †5

UNDERSTUDIES: Dee Ann McDavid (Ms. London/Ms. Baker), Mark Hamilton (Messrs. Hartney/Gutterson/Carey/Brown/Wintle), Chuck Brown (Mr. Drake)

Performed with three scenes: Sodom in days of old, Hollywood in 1920 in La Condesa's mansion, and in a Las Vegas rehearsal hall today.

*Still playing May 31, 1987.

†Succeeded by: 1. Chuck Brown, 2. Becky London, 3. Ralph Buckley, 4. David Drake, 5. Wilder Gutterson, 6. Beata Baker, 7. Ed Wintle

Adam Newman Photos

Top: David Drake, Theresa Marlowe
Right: Ed Wintle

Brick Hartney, David Drake, Becky London
Above: Wilder Gutterson, Chuck Brown

OFF-BROADWAY PRODUCTIONS

(William Redfield Theatre) Tuesday, June 3–15, 1986 (14 performances). Circus Theatricals (Jack Stehlin, Artistic Director) with Sheane Productions present:
GRAVITY SHOES by John Bunzel; Director, Richard Ziman; Press, Edie Frampton. CAST: Christian Baskous, Jason Brill, Edythe Frampton Anthony Fusco, Jack Stehlin, Robert-Michael Tomlinson. No other credits submitted.

(Westbeth Theatre Center) Tuesday, June 3–15, 1986 (12 performances). The Invisible Performance Workshop (Malka Percal, Producer) presents:
MUD by Maria Irene Fornes; Director, Shela Xoregos; Design, Bill Layton; Lighting, Lori Dawson CAST: Stephanie Berry, Mansoor Najeeullah, Stanley Earl Harrison. No other credits submitted.

(INTAR Hispanic American Arts Center) Wednesday, June 4–29, 1986 (28 performances). International Arts Relations (Max Ferra, Artistic Director; Dennis Ferguson-Acosta, Managing Director) present:
BURNING PATIENCE by Antonio Skarmeta; Director, Paul Zimet; Scenery, Christopher Barreca; Lighting, Arden Fingerhut; Costumes, David Navarro Velasquez. CAST: Gregorio Rosenblum, Monique Cintron, Angel David, Lola Pashalinski and recorded voices of Phil Lee, Gregorio Rosenblum, Stanley Stairs, Paul Zimet.

(Actors Playhouse) Monday, June 9,–29, 1986 (28 performances) Gup-Mitchell Productions, Mack Gilbert, Diane Mitchell present:
ELECTRIC MAN by Mark Eisenstein; Director, James Karr; Design, Andrew Bush; Stage Manager, Michael Makman. CAST: Philip Bruns, Steve Potfora, Jerry Terheyden

(Lamb's Theatre) Monday, June 9–Sept. 28, 1986 (118 performances and 24 previews). Moved to Actors Playhouse July 8, 1986. Thomas Viertel, Steven Baruch, Richard Frankel, Jeffrey Joseph present:
SILLS & COMPANY with Severn Darden, MacIntyre Dixon, Paul Dooley, Garry Goodrow, Gerrit Graham, Bruce Jarchow, Mina Kolb, Maggie Roswell, Rachel Sills; Director, Paul Sills; Artistic Consultant, Art Wolff; Musical Director, David Evans; Set, Carol Sills; Lighting, Malcolm Sturchio; Costume Consultant, Deborah Shaw; Sound, Chuck London Media/Stewart Werner; Technical Coordinator, Thomas A. Shilhanek; General Management, Richard Frankel Productions; Stage Manager, Denise Yaney; Press, Cindy Valk, Joshua Ellis, Adrian Bryan-Brown, Jim Sapp, Bill Suttleworth, Jackie Green, Solters/Roskin/Friedman.

Top Right: Rachel Sills, Mina Kolb, Maggie Roswell
Below: Garry Goodrow, Paul Dooley, MacIntyre Dixon
in "Sills & Company" *(Harry Benson)*

(Jan Hus Playhouse) Monday, June 9–23, 1986 (12 performances). Robert Nicholas presents:
HOW I SURVIVED HIGH SCHOOL with Music by Glen Slater; Book, E. Taubenslag, Bob/Alec Nemser, Charles Jones; Director, Michael Taubenslag; Choreography, Tammy Thomas; Musical Direction/Arrangement, Michael Bergman; Sets/Costumes, Jeffrey Allen; Stage Manager, Rosanne Limoncelli. CAST: Joe Buffington, Scott Fried, Nancy Pothier, Orlando Powers, Eileen Tepper, Torri Whitehead.
MUSICAL NUMBERS: High School, Shy Couple, Phone Calls, I'm Leaving, Wondering, Prom Date, By Myself, V. D., Lonely, Please Don't Tell My Father, Where, Afraid of Rejection, Child Abuse, Hi Grandma, The Note, Living a Dream, Numbers, Friendship, Song of Youth, Virgin, View from the Hill, Life.
   A musical in two acts.

(Pearl Theatre) Wednesday, June 18–29, 1986 (12 performances). Robert Schaffer and Counterpane Productions (Robert Schaffer/David Waggett, Directors) presents:
BLOOD by Donald S. Olson; Director, David Waggett; Setting, Paul Steinberg; Costumes, Jennifer Hance; Lighting, David Gritzner. CAST: Todd Michael Lewis, Susan Jones Mannino, Hue Sabri, Fredda Hardy, Katherine Shepard.

(Theatre of the Riverside Church) Friday, June 13–29, 1986 (12 performances). Theatre of the Riverside Church (David K. Manion, Artistic Director) presents:
THE TEXAS DREAM BAR JAMBOREE with Book, Lyrics and Music by Robert Brittan; Director, Howard Rossen; Lighting, Deborah Constantine; Set, David Seavey; Costumes, Karen Perry; Musical Arrangements, Dean Powell; Stage Manager, Alice Farrell. CAST: Melanie Backer, Harry Bennett, Michael Oberlander, Ann Peck, Ric Stoneback

(Astor Place Theatre) Tuesday, June 24–October 26, 1986 (144 performances). Nicholas Benton, Stanley Flink, Norma and David Langworthy, Craig MacDonald, Nathan Weiss, in association with Playwrights Horizons present:
THE PERFECT PARTY by A. R. Gurney, Jr.; Director, John Tillinger; Set, Steven Rubin; Costumes, Jane Greenwood; Lighting, Dan Kotlowitz; Sound, Gary Harris; Casting, Amy Introcaso; General Management/,Brent Peek Productions/Scott Green; Company Manager, Marshall B. Purdy; Props, David Birn; Wardrobe, Lyle Jones; Stage Managers, Suzanne Fry, Doug Flinchum; Press, Bob Ullman; Originally presented at Playwrights Horizons for 110 performances. CAST: John Cunningham (Tony), Charlotte Moore (Lois), Debra Mooney succeeded by Margo Skinner (Sally), Stephen Pearlman succeeded by George Guidall (Wes), June Gable succeeded by Julia Newton, Marilyn cooper (Wilma), Understudies: David Cryer, Julia Newton. A comedy in two acts.

Debra Mooney, Stephen Pearlman, Charlotte Moore,
June Gable, John Cunningham in "The Perfect Party"
(Peter Cunningham)

(Theater 890) Thursday, June 26–October 12, 1986 (124 performances). Lou Kramer, Ken Waissman, Robert A. Buckley in association with Louis W. Scheeder, Michael Lonergan, Roadworks Productions present:
TODAY, I AM A FOUNTAIN PEN by Israel Horovitz; Director, Stephen Zuckerman; Based on "A Good Place to Come From" by Morley Torgov; Setting, James Fenhagen; Costumes, Mimi Maxmen; Lighting, Curt Ostermann; Sound, Aural Fixation; Casting, Darlene Kaplan; First produced by American Jewish Theatre; Genersl Management, Waissman & Buckley; Associate General Manager, Karen Leahy; Wardrobe, Suzanne Bradshaw; Props, Beth Kushnick, Leah Menken; Production Associate, Julianne Waldheim; Hairstylist, Vito Mastrogiovanni; Stage Managers, Michael S. Mantel, Joseph D. Giardina; Press, Jeffrey Richards, Patt Dale, Ken Mandelbaum. CAST: Danny Gerard succeeded by Jonathan Goch, Josh Blake (Irving Yanover), Stan Lachow (Emil Ilchak), Sol Frieder (Ardenshensky/Ukrainian Priest), Dana Keeler (Mrs. Ilchak), Marcia Jean Kurtz (Esther Yanover), Barbara Garrick (Annie Ilchak), Sam Schacht (Moses Yanover), Grant Shaud (Pete Lisanti), Understudies: Brian Koh (Irving), Joseph Giardina (Emil/Pete), Cordelia Richards (Annie), Christine Jansen (Mrs. Ilchak/Esther). The action takes place in the home of the Yanover family in Sault Ste. Marie, Ontario, Canada, in the early 1940's during the early stages of the war in Europe.

(St. Clement's Church) Friday, June 27–July 19, 1986 (12 performances and 3 previews). Moved to Actors Outlet for 12 additional performances (Wednesday, January 28,–February 14, 1987. Soupstone Project presents:
THE DELUSION OF ANGELS by Don Rifkin; Director, Neile Weissman; Assistant Director, Avril Hordyk; Set and Lighting, Randall Etheredge; Stage Managers, James St. Pierre, Andrea Nugit; Press, Max Fleischman. CAST: Michael Ornstein (Michael Moorehead), James Selby (Evan Buckman), Kathryn Layng (Sharon Glass), Richard M. Hughes/John Anthony Lack (George Brandon)

Marcia Jean Kurtz, Sam Schacht, Sol Frieder
in "Today I Am a Fountain Pen" *(Martha Swope)*

(Apple Corps Theatre) Wednesday, July 9–August 17, 1986 (30 performances). Three one-act plays by Agatha Christie, presented by The Apple Corps Theatre (John Raymond, Artistic Director).
RULE OF THREE Director, John Raymond; Scenery, Larry Brodsky; Lighting, Deborah Constantine; Costumes, Maryann D. Smith; Sound, Neal Arluck; Technical Director, Alex LaBianca; Stage Manager, Kara Sheridan; Press, Aviva Cohen. CAST: *"The Patient"*—Keith Williams (Lansen), Judith Scarpone (Nurse), Allan Stevens (Dr. Ginsberg), Earle Edgerton (Inspector Cray), Sean O'Sullivan (Bryan Wingfield), Rica Martens (Emmeline Ross), Richard Voigts (William Ross), Janet Kingsley (Brenda Jackson), Lois Raebeck (The Patient), *"The Rats"*—Judith Scarpone (Sandra Grey), Janet Kingsley (Jennifer Brice), Allan Stevens (David Forrester), Keith Williams (Alec Hanbury), *"Afternoon at the Seaside."*—Allan Stevens (Bob Wheeler), Judith Scarpone (Noreen Somers), Sean O'Sullivan (Arthur Somers), Earle Edgerton (George Crum), Rica Martens (Mrs. Crum), Richard Voigts (Beach Attendant), Lois Raebeck (Mrs. Gunner), Keith Williams (Percy Gunner), Janet Kingsley (The Beauty), Richard Voigts (Inspector Foley)

(Judith Anderson Theatre) Friday, July 11–27, 1986 (18 performances and 19 previews). PACT (Gregory T. Brennan, Peter J. Brennan) present:
OUT! by Lawrence Kelly; Director, Max Charruyer; Set, John-Michael Deegan; Costumes, Sarah Conly; Lighting, John Conway; Stage Managers, Mercedes Leonard, David Munnell; Press, Shirley Herz, Peter Cromarty, Glenna Freedman, Pete Sanders. CAST: Michael Countryman (Joe Jackson), Rick Tolliver (Hap Felsch), Terry Hempleman (Lefty Williams), Richard Tabor (Buck Weaver), Paul Christie (Chick Gandil), Arnie Mazer (Swede Risberg), Steven Stahl (Eddie Cicotte), John A. O'Hern (Fred McMullin). A drama in 2 acts and 10 scenes. The action takes place in the Fall of 1919 in Chicago.

(Lamb's Theatre) Tuesday, July 15, 1986–January 10, 1987 (207 performances). Harve Brosten and Mainstage Peoductions, in association with "Murray the Furrier" present:
OLYMPUS ON MY MIND with Book & Lyrics by Barry Harman; Suggested by "Amphitryon" by Heinrich von Kleist; Music, Grant Sturiale; Director, Barry Harman; Choreography, Pamela Sousa; Set, Christopher Stapleton; Costumes, Steven Jones; Lighting, Fabian Yeager; Production Consultant, Jay S. Bulmash; Assistant Director, Edward Marshall; General Management, Horner/Stuart Enterprises; Company Manager, Evan Sanders; Assistant Choreographer, Laurent Giroux; Dance Captain, Peter Kapetan; Music Coordinator, John Monaco; Wardrobe, Sahra Henrickson; Hairstylist, Gene Condemi; Furs, Christie Brothers; Stage Managers, Joseph A. Onorato, Paul Kassel; Press, Henry Luhrman, Terry M. Lilly, Andrew P. Shearer, Susan Chicoine. CAST: Peter Kapetan (Tom), Andy Spangler succeeded by Danny Weathers (Dick), Keith Bennett succeeded by David Andrew White (Horace), Elizabeth Austin succeeded by Rusty Riegelman (Delores), Martin Vidnovic succeeded by Tom Wopat (Jupiter/Jove/Zeus), Jason Graae succeeded by John Scherer (Mercury), Peggy Hewett succeeded by Naz Edwards (Charis), Emily Zacharias succeeded by Susan Powell (Alcmene), Lewis J. Stadlen succeeded by Charles Repole (Sosia), George Spelvin (Amphitryon), Understudies: Paul Kassel, Nancy Johnston, Bruce Moore.
MUSICAL NUMBERS: Welcome to Greece, Heaven on Earth, The Gods on Tap, Surprise!, Wait'Til It Dawns, I Know My Wife, It Was Me, Back So Soon?, Wonderful, At Liberty in Thebes, Jupiter Slept Here, Back to the Play, Don't Bring Her Flowers, General's Pandemonium, Olympus Is a Lonely Town, A Star Is Born, Final Sequence. A musical in two acts.

Lewis J. Stadlen, Peggy Hewett, Jason Graae
Above: Susan Powell, Charles Repole, Tom Wopat
in "Olympus on My Mind" *(Anita & Steve Shevett)*

(INTAR Stage 2) Friday, August 15–September 14, 1986 (28 performances)
THE DIXIE DEWDROP by R. Santinelli and Patrick Sky; Director, Thomas J. Carroll; Scenery, Aron Tager; Lighting, Deborah Constantine; Sound, Aural Fixation; Presented by Thomas J. Carroll; Stage Manager, Pamela Edington; Press, Bruce Cohen/Kathleen von Schmid
CAST: Ralph P. Martin (Uncle Dave Macon), Gilles Malkine (Newt Pomeroy)
  A country musical performed without intermission.

(Samuel Beckett Theatre) Wednesday, August 27–November 30, 1986 (104 performances). The Harold Clurman Theatre (Jack Garfein, Artistic Director) presents:
KRAPP'S LAST TAPE by Samuel Beckett; Director, Samuel Beckett; Set/Lighting, Bud Thorpe; Costumes, Teresita Garcia Suro; General Manager, Judy Novgrod; Company Manager, Larry Staroff; Technical Director, Doug Rogers; Production Assistant, Lynn Johnson; Stage Manager, Bud Thorpe; Press, Joe Wolhandler Associates
CAST: Rick Cluchey (Krapp), Bud Thorpe (Sound Operator). This one-act play was preceded by the American premiere of two 1984 films written and directed by Samuel Beckett: "Quad" and "Nacht und Traume."

(The Little Theatre at the Lamb's) Tuesday, August 12–23, 1986 (12 performances)
A THEATRE HISTORY by Sam Johnson; Music, Brian Lohmann; Director, Anthony DiPietro; Musical Direction, Peter Blue; Set, Miguel Lopez; Lighting, Glenn Wade; Costumes, Sandy Jeronimo; Graphics, Rob Waters; Stage Manager, Wanda Buncamper
CAST: Neal Bishop, Robert Bowen, Julia Karlson, Francesca Casale, Frank Deal, Kevin Dwyer, Abby Gibson, Dana Hickox, Melinda McDonough, Judy Malloy, Kevin Nagle, Brian Sullivan, Guy Waid, John David Westfall
  Presented in 2 acts and 9 scenes. "All performances broadcast live on W.N.S.S.

Rick Cluchey in "Krapp's Last Tape"
Top: Gilles Malkine, Ralph P. Martin
in "The Dixie Dewdrop" *(Carol Rosegg)*

Lonette McKee as "Lady Day at Emerson's
Bar & Grill" *(Martha Swope)*

(Westbeth Theatre Center) Wednesday, September 3–14, 1986 (12 performances). Sarah Lindemann and Westmoreland Productions present:
PERFECT FOR BLUE by Alan Walter; Director, Jordan Simon; Lighting, Laszlo Reichardt; Stage Manager, Jenny Peek. No other credits submitted.
CAST: Leslye Anderson, Elaine Barrow, Alan Boyce, Clyde Fulton, Stacie Linardos, Jane Krakowski, Carol Mayhew, Stephen O'Dwyer, Hudson Olumb, Robert Whaley

(Westside Arts Theatre/Upstairs) Wednesday, September 3, 1986–May 17, 1987 (281 performances and 9 previews). Lady Day at Emerson's Company presents the Vineyard Theatre production of:
LADY DAY AT EMERSON'S BAR & GRILL by Lanie Robertson; Director, Andre Ernotte; Musical Direction/Arrangements, Danny Holgate; Set, William Barclay; Lighting, Phil Monat; Costumes, Muriel Stockdale; Sound, Phil Lee; Associate Producer, Kenneth Polokoff; General Manager, Leonard A. Mulhern; Associate General Manager, James Hannah; Stand-by Musical Director, Neal Tate; Production Coordinator, Susan Wilder; Wardrobe, Janie McIntosh; Props, Lane Hurwitz; Stage Manager, Crystal Huntington; Press, Bruce Cohen/Kathleen von Schmid
CAST: Lonette McKee succeeded by S. Epatha Merkerson (Billie Holiday), Danny Holgate (Piano), Rudy Stevenson (Buck Wilson), David Jackson (Frankie Lee Jones/Bass), Bambi Herrera (Pepe)
  Performed without intermission. The scene is midnight on a Friday night in March 1959, four months before Billie Holiday's death, in a South Philadelphia bar.

(Minetta Lane Theatre) Sunday, September 7, 1986–January 11, 1987 (137 performances and 15 previews). M Square Entertainment Inc., Mitchell Maxwell, Alan J. Schuster, Marvin R. Meit and Alice Field present:
ANGRY HOUSEWIVES with Book by A. M. Collins; Music & Lyrics, Chad Henry; Director, Mitchell Maxwell; Musical Staging/Choreography, Wayne Cilento; General Manager, Alan J. Schuster; Assistant, Victoria Maxwell; Company Manager, Margay Whitlock; Dance Captain, Vicki Lewis; Props, Linda Borman; Wardrobe, Cheryl Woronoff; Assistant Choreographer, Lisa Mordente; Stage Managers, Clayton Phillips, Elisabeth Farwell; Press, Shirley Herz, Peter Cromarty, Glenna Freedman, Pete Sanders, Gary Lawrence.
CAST: Michael Manasseri (Tim), Carolyn Casanave (Bev), Lorna Patterson (Wendy), Vicki Lewis (Jetta), Camille Saviola (Carol), Nicholas Wyman (Larry), Michael Lembeck (Wallace), Lee Wilkof (Lewd), Mary Munger (Understudy)
SCENES & MUSICAL NUMBERS: Think Positive, Betty Jean, It's Gonna Be Fun, Generic Woman, Not at Home, Betsy Moberly, Cold Cruel Dark, First Kid on the Block, Love-O-Meter, Saturday Night, Nobody Loves Me, Stalling for Time, Eat Your@*#@*!@#! Cornflakes, Finale
  A musical in 2 acts and 9 scenes.

(Rutherford House) Thursday, September 11–October 26, 1986 (49 performances). Murder A La Carte presents:
MURDER AT RUTHERFORD HOUSE by Tom Chiodo, Peter DePietro; Directed by authors; Musical Director/Original Music/Pianist, James Followell; Costumes, Kip Kirkendall; Harpist, Peris Alban; Assistant Director/Stage Manager, Tony Hamill; Business Manager, Fran Rodin; Press, Hunt/Pucci Associates.
CAST: Irma St. Paul succeeded by Jean Marie Evans (Hermione Rutherford), Quentin Crisp succeeded by Geoffrey Garland, Frank Vohs, Phillip Astor, Thomas Chiodo (Quentin Hotchkiss), Patricia Michael (Lady Millicent Rutherford), Beth Broderick (Camille Rutherford), Lee H. Doyle succeeded by Geoffrey Garland, Frank Vohs (Oswald Rutherford), Sharon McNight succeeded by Shelley Wald (Baroness Greta von Keepsemfrumfloppen), William Simington (Wendle Weedle), Mark Ritter (Cameron Worthleston), Andrea Davis succeeded by Shelley Wald (Sarah Rutherford), Carleton Carpenter succeeded by Colin Fox, George Himes, Ian Thomson (Chadwick Sterling)
  A murder mystery performed during dinner at the present time in Rutherford House, New York City.

(Stage Art Theatre) September 15-16-17, 1986 (3 performances). Women Who Do Commercials presents:
SIX WOMEN ON STAGE by Fredricka Weber; Directed by the author. CAST: Cynthia Burke, Dena Dietrich, Judy Gwyll, Fayn LeVeille, Nancy Reddon, Sally Shermerhorn, Deidre Westervelt, Kenneth French. A comedy-drama in two acts. The action takes place at the present time.

Top Right: Michael Manasseri, Michael Lembeck, Camille Saviola, Vicki Lewis, Lorna Patterson, Carolyn Casanave, Nicholas Wyman, Lee Wilkof in "Angry Housewives" *(Carol Rosegg)* **Below: Lee Doyle, Sharon McNight, William Simington, Patricia Michael, Carleton Carpenter in "Murder at Rutherford House"**
(Robert Sengstacke)

"Six Women on Stage"

Black-Eyed Susan, Everett Quinton
in "The Artificial Jungle"
(Anita & Steve Shevett)

(One Sheridan Square) Sunday, September 21, 1986–February 1, 1987 (112 performances and 50 previews). The Ridiculous Theatrical Company (Charles Ludlam, Artistic Director) presents:
THE ARTIFICIAL JUNGLE by Charles Ludlam who directed; Original Music, Peter Golub; Set, Jack Kelly; Costumes, Everett Quinton; Lighting, Richard Currie; General Manager, Steven Samuels; Hairstylist, Ethyl Eichelberger; Sound, Edward McGowan; Stage Manager, Mike Taylor
CAST: Charles Ludlam (Chester Nurdiger), Philip Campanaro (Frankie Spinelli), Black-Eyed Susan (Roxanne Nurdiger), Ethyl Eichelberger (Mrs. Nurdiger), Everett Quinton (Zachary Slade)
  A "suspense thriller" in two acts. The action takes place at 966 Rivington Street in lower Manhattan, New York City, at the present time.

(47th Street Theatre) Sunday, Sept. 21–Oct. 26, 1986 (21 performances and 6 previews) Double Image Theatre (Helen Waren Mayer, Founder/Executive Director; Max Mayer, Artistic Director; Leslie Urdang, Managing Director) presents:
THE RETURN OF PINOCCHIO by Richard Nelson; Director Max Mayer; Sets, Kate Edmunds; Costumes, Candice Donnelly; Lighting, Jennifer Tipton; Sound, Janet Kalas; Technical Director, Carle Atwater; Wardrobe, Lisa Cavanaugh; Props, O'Hara Fleming; Slides, David Prittie; Stage Managers, William H. Lang, Monroe Head, Sibbie Sullivan; Press, Fred Nathan, Dennis Crowley
CAST: Dan Moran (Lucio), Joe Urla (Pinocchio), Mary-Louise Gemmill (Lucio's Wife), Daniel DeRaey (Leone), Marylouise Burke (Mama), Jean Bacharach (Silia), Marcell Rosenblatt (Rosina), Rob Morrow (Carlo), Carles Cleveland (Soldier), Phil Kaufmann (Understudy)
    Performed without intermission.

(Theatre Guinevere) Monday, Sept. 22–Oct. 12, 1986 (16 performances). Stage Three presents:
NOT SHOWING by James Ryan; Director, Joe Gilford; Set, Scott Bradley; Lighting, Greg MacPherson; Costumes, Rusty Smith; Sound, Sarah Ackerman; Stage Manager, Melissa L. Burdick; Press, Shirley Herz, Peter Cromarty
CAST: Ashley Gardner (Dee), W. T. Martin (Red), Christina Moore (May), Jordan Roberts (Billie)

(Audrey Wood Playhouse) Tuesday, September 23–November 2, 1986 (57 performances and 9 previews). Jack and Richard Lawrence present:
CONFESSIONS OF A NIGHTINGALE based on Charlotte Chandler's "The Ultimate Seduction"; Adapted by Charlotte Chandler, Ray Stricklyn; Director, John Tillinger; Set/Costume, Richard Lawrence; Lighting, Natasha Katz; General Manager, Jack Lawrence; Technical Director, Tom Shilhanek; Stage Manager, Doug Laidlaw; Press, Shirley Herz, David Roggensack, Peter Cromarty, Pete Sanders, Glenna Freedman
CAST: Ray Stricklyn as Tennessee Williams. Performed with one intermission.

Ashley Gardner, Christina Moore in "Not Showing" *(Carol Rosegg)*
Top: Joe Urla in "The Return of Pinocchio" *(Adam Newman)*

(Judith Anderson Theatre) Thursday, September 25, 1986-Juli Reding Hutner presents:
A SCENT OF ALMONDS by Marjorie Osterman; Director, Langdon Brown; Sets, Tom Schwinn; Costumes, Joseph Cigliano; Lighting, Jackie Manassee; Stage Manager, Tracy Brigden; Press, Patricia Krawtiz
CAST: Heather Osterman (Young Deborah Mayer), Mel Cobb (Fred Miller), Carlotta Schoch (Mature Deborah), Robin Howard (Emma), Matt Conley (Robert Mayer), Peg Daloia (Fraulein Bauer).
    No other credits submitted.

(Royal Court Repertory Theater) Sunday, Sept. 28, 1986–May 10, 1987 (120 performances). Leo Productions presents:
THE ACTORS by Ward Morehouse III; Director, Phyllis Craig; Set, RCR Productions; Sound, Roger Hammer; Stage Manager, Joann C. Stekler; Press, Philip Leshin
CAST: John Messenger succeeded by Jack Aranson (Jack McClain), Ralph Douglas (Louis Kleper), Richard Waring (Jim O'Brien), Mel Silverman (Lee Fremont), France Poeta (Jack McClain, Jr.), Phyllis Craig (Irene Lawrence)
    A play in 2 acts and 5 scenes. The action takes place in 1981 in the Actors' Club Lounge off Times Square in New York City.

(47th Street Theatre) Tuesday, Sept. 30–Nov. 23, 1986 (43 performances). Double Image Theatre (Helen Waren Mayer, Founder/Executive Director; Max Mayer, Artistic Director) presents:
the dreamer examines his pillow by John Patrick Shanley; Director, Max Mayer; Sets, Adrianne Lobel; Costumes, Dunya Ramicova; Lighting, James F. Ingalls; Sound, Janet Kalas; Stage Managers, William H. Lang, Monroe Head, Sibbie Sullivan; Press, Fred Nathan Co./Dennis Crowley
CAST: Scott Renderer (Tommy), Anne O'Sullivan (Donna), Graham Beckel (Dad)
    A drama performed without intermission.

Ray Stricklyn as Tennessee Williams in "Confessions of a Nightingale"
(Adam Newman)

(South Street Theatre) Thursday, October 2–26, 1986 (12 performances). Robert E. Richardson presents:
BACK IN THE BIG TIME with Book by Abe Kroll; Lyrics & Music, Johnny Brandon; Director, Bernard Johnson; Choreography, Henry LeTang; Musical Staging, Henry LeTang, Bernard Johnson; Assistant Choreographer, Ellie LeTang; Musical Direction/Orchestrations, Barry Levitt; Costumes, Bernard Johnson; Scenery, Don Jensen; Lighting, Kenneth Tabachnik; Dance Music Arrangements, Mitch Kerper; Stage Manager, Bill McComb; Press, David Rothenberg
CAST: Jeffrey Adams, Ruth Adams, Shaun Baker-Jones, Louie Baldonieri, Adam Bryant, Rashamella Cumbo, Luther Fontaine, Germaine Goodson, Marc Heller, Deborah Mitchell, Michael Mitorotondo, Bernard Pollock, Nancy Salo, Jimmy W. Tate, and Mable Lee

(Lamb's Theatre) Monday, Oct. 6–Nov. 15, 1986 (43 performances and 5 previews). The Lamb's Theatre Co. (Carolyn Rossi Copeland, Producing Director; Pamela Perrell, Associate Director) presents:
THE CHINA FISH by David McFadzean; Director, Susan Gregg; Sets/Lighting, Dale F. Jordan; Costumes, Ellen Ryba; Production Assistant, David Baronov; Sound, Alan Kerr; Props, Neal Bishop; Stage Managers, Steve Zorthian, Denise Nations; Press, G. Theodore Killmer
CAST: Sally Prager (Val), Leon Russom (The Man), Leesa Bryte (Lydia), Clarke Gordon (Gus), Mary Armstrong (Jenise), Paul Collins (Bud)
A drama in two acts. The action takes place during 1975 in Southern Indiana.

**Sally Prager, Leon Russom
in "The China Fish"** *(Carol Rosegg)*
**Left Center: Vondie Curtis-Hall, Adam Wade, Brian
Wesley Thomas, Tico Wells in "The War Party"**
(Bert Andrews)

(Theatre Four) Tuesday, Oct. 7–Nov. 30, 1986 (32 performances and 16 previews) The Negro Ensemble Company presents:
THE WAR PARTY by Leslie Lee; Director, Douglas Turner Ward; Set, Charles H. McClennahan; Sound, Harrison Williams; Lighting, Shirley Prendergast; Costumes, Judy Dearing; Stage Managers, Ed DeShea, Lisa Blackwell; Press, Howard Atlee; Managing Director, Leon B. Denmark; General Manager, Larry K. Walden
CAST: Carla Brothers (Kathy Robbins), Vondie Curtis-Hall (Roosevelt Gwynne), Kathryn Hunter (Sookie Jenkins), Larry Sharp (David Hansen), Carmen Mathis (Cora Henry), Roberta Pikser, (Dorothy Robbins), Kirk Taylor (Joey Robbins), Brian Wesley Thomas (Maddog), Tico Wells (Outlaw), Adam Wade (Stan Younger), Rome Neal, Kevin Rock (Diamond Streeters)
A drama in two acts. The action takes place in 1978 in Philadelphia, Pennsylvania.

(Classic Stage Company) Wednesday, Oct. 8–Nov. 1, 1986 (26 performances). CSC Repertory (Carol Ostrow, Producing Director; Jennifer Ober, General Manager) presents:
THE MAIDS by Jean Genet; Translation, Bernard Frechtman; Director, David Kaplan; Set, Rick Butler; Costumes, Marcy Grace Froehlich; Lighting, Ken Tabachnick; Sound, Gary Harris; Production Manager, Brett Buckwalter; Dramaturg, Todd London; Stage Managers, William H. Lang, Liz Small; Press, Dara Hershman
CAST: Marceline Hugot (Claire), Etain O'Malley (Solange), Deborah Offner (Madame)
Performed without an intermission. The action takes place at midnight in Paris, between the wars.

**Marceline Hugot, Deborah Offner, Etain O'Malley
in "The Maids"** *(Paula Court)*

(Lucille Lortel Theatre) Wednesday, Oct. 8, 1986–May 3, 1987 (254 performances and 16 previews). Louis C. Blau with Dennis D. Hennessy, Stockton Briggle, Richard Carrothers present:

GROUCHO: A LIFE IN REVUE by Arthur Marx, Robert Fisher; Director, Arthur Marx; Executive Producer, Jon Wilner; Co-Producers, Nancy and Ronnie Horowitz; Associate Producer, Howard Pechet; Scenery, Michael Hotopp; Costumes, Baker Smith; Lighting, Richard Winkler; Sound, Tony Meola; Musical Director, Brian Hurley; Assistant Director, David Storey; Casting, Stuart Howard; General Management, Elizabeth I. McCann, Mary T. Nealon, David Musselman; Technical Advisors, Paul Allen, John Hodge; Wardrobe, Diane Thorson; Production Coordinator, Donn G. Miller; Assistant Manager, Edward Nelson; Stage Managers, Robert T. Bennett, Daniel R. Bauer; Press, Shirley Herz, Peter Cromarty, Pete Sanders, Glenna Freedman, David Roggensack

CAST: Frank Ferrante (Groucho), Les Marsden (Chico/Harpo), Faith Prince (The Girls), Rusty Magee (Understudy)

Act I: Groucho's Memories of the Early Years. Act II: Groucho's Memories of the Later Years

Les Marsden, Faith Prince, Frank Ferrante (also top left) (*Martha Swope*)

(Playhouse 91) Tuesday, October 14–26, 1986 (8 performances). Artists Ensemble Productions and Russell Barnard present:
TIGERS WILD by John Rechy; Director, Michael Ewing; Sets, Nancy Thun; Costumes, Kathleen Blake; Lighting, Jan Kroeze; Sound, Brian Ronan; Casting, Darlene Kaplan; General Manager, Waissman & Buckley; Company Manager, Stephen Arnold; Wardrobe, Steve Jordan; Stage Managers, Giles F. Colahan, John Allee; Press, Jeffrey Richards Associates
CAST: Cordelia Richards (Shell), Frank Whaley (Cob), Leonard P. Salazar (Manny), Michael David Morrison (Jerry), Gary Matanky (Stuart), Lynn Chausow (Violet Fever), Peter Zapp (Pipe), Understudies: John Allee (Cob/Manny/Jerry), Hannah O'Regan (Shell/Violet Fever), Clifford Fetters (Stuart/Pipe)
  A drama in two acts. The action takes place at the present time during two days of summer in El Paso, Texas.

(Westbeth Theatre Center) Thursday, Oct. 16–Nov. 2, 1986 (12 performances and 7 previews). Coola Woola Productions presents:
ANNIE WOBBLER by Arnold Wesker; Director, Gerald Chapman; Scenery, Venustiano Borromeo; Costumes, Dana John Raso/Dada Leeds; Lighting, Richard Latta; Sound, John Cacciatore; Props, Ed Clein; Wigs, Paul Huntley; Makeup, Colelloworks; General Management, David Lawlor, Thom Shovestull; Stage Manager, Roger Hatch; Press, Shirley Herz, Peter Cromarty
CAST: Sloane Bosniak as Annie, Anna and Annabella

Peter Zapp, Lynn Chausow
in "Tigers Wild" *(Peter Cunningham)*

(Samuel Beckett Theatre) Friday, Oct. 17,–Nov. 2, 1986 (12 performances). Alice Adler presents:
CICERO by Sam Segal; Director, Vince Tauro; Costumes, Marti Ladd; Lighting, Tina Ann Byers; Sets, Alex Polner; Technical Director/Stage Manager, Gary Dunn; General Manager, Sidney E. Adler; Original Music, Katherine Bel Geddes; Consultants, D. R. Shackleton Bailey, Neil Canavan; Press, Howard Atlee
CAST: Hal Robinson (Cicero), Jeanette Aguilar (Tullia), Neil Carpenter (Octavian), Dino Scopas (Tiro), Neil Canavan (Lictor/Masseur/Servant), Charles Matheny (Mark Antony), Patti Munter (Servant), Andrea Arora (Musician/Servant), Katherine Bel Geddes (Musician), Karen Cummings (Neaera), Nelson Avidon (Ventidius), Leo Ferstenberg (Lepidus), Craig Barnett (Dolabella), Richard Willis (Atticus), Steve Parris (Piso)
  A drama in 2 acts and 16 scenes. The action takes place in and around Rome in 43 A.D., in the aftermath of Julius Caesar's murder.

(Unitarian Church of All Souls) Friday, Oct. 17–Nov. 2, 1986 (16 performances). All Souls Players present:
TWO BLIND MICE by Samuel Spewack; Director, Roy B. Steinberg; Costumes, Virginia Wood; Sets/Lights, Tran Wm. Rhodes; Producers, Charlotte Dennis Kagen, Howard Van Der Meulen; Wardrobe, Gio Scarlata; Technical Director, Keith Burns; Stage Managers, Marlene Greene, Toby Sanders
CAST: Joseph Aronica (Simon), Richard Briggs (Brenner), Joseph Clifton, Jr. (Sgt./Visitor), Frank Elmore (Tommy Thurston), Jeff Garrett (Ens. Jamison), Charmaine Gordon (Crystal Hower), Edward D. Griffith (Dr. McGill), Barbara Guarino (Karen Norwood), David Manchester (Cmdr. Jellicoe), Patricia Mertens (Letitia Turnbull), John Nicholson (Lt. Robbins), Jonathan Powers (Mr. Murray), Carolyn Rapier (Miss Johnson), Toby Sanders (Mailman/Asst. Stage Manager), Nicholas Saunders (Senator Kruger), Steve Steiner/Terry Lee Swarts (Maj. Groh), Robert Trumbull (Mr. Threadwaite)
  A comedy in three acts. The action takes place in the spring of 1949 in the Office of Herbs and Standards in Washington, D.C.

Katherine Bel Geddes, Jeanette Aquilar, Karen
Cummings in "Cicero" *(Martha Swope)*

(Promenade Theatre) Sunday, Oct. 19, 1986–August 23, 1987 (352 performances and 19 previews). John A. McQuiggan in association with Hart Entertainment Group (John N. Hart, Jr./Hugh J. Hubbard/Amy Freitag/Barbara Cartwright) and Douglas M. Lawson presents:

THE COMMON PURSUIT by Simon Gray; Directors, Simon Gray, Michael McGuire, Settings, David Jenkins; Costumes, David Murin; Production Manager, Laura Heller; Associate Producers, Lois Deutschman, James Peck, Harold Reed, Sharon Scruggs; General Management, New Roads Productions (John A. McQuiggan, Ruth Rosenberg), Musical Director, Ray Leslee; Fight Choreography, Richard Raether; Hairstylist, Paul Huntley; Production Assistant/Management Associate, Jill Larmett; Wardrobe, Eileen Miller; Casting, David Tochterman; Stage Manager, Lois Griffing; Press, Henry Luhrman, Terry M. Lilly, Andrew P. Shearer, Susan Chicoine CAST: Kristoffer Tabori succeeded by Charles Shaw Robinson, Daniel Gerroll, Patrick O'Connell (Stuart Thorne), Judy Geeson succeeded by Lisa Eichhorn, Mary Dierson (Marigold Watson), Michael Countryman succeeded by Reed Birney (Martin Musgrove), Peter Friedman succeeded by Mark Nelson, Robertson Dean (Humphry Taylor), Nathan Lane succeeded by Bill Buell, Nathan Lane (Nick Finchling), Dylan Baker succeeded by Wayne Alexander, Jack Coleman, Patrick O'Connell, Charles Shaw Robinson (Peter Whetworth), Understudies: Robertson Dean, Sharon Scruggs

A play in 2 acts and 4 scenes. The action takes place in England over a period of twenty years.

(Anita & Steve Shevett)
Below: Peter Friedman, Nathan Lane, Dylan Baker, Michael Countryman Top Right: Judy Geeson, Kristoffer Tabori

Daniel Gerroll, Lisa Eichhorn

(from top) Nathan Lane, Michael Countryman, Kristoffer Tabori, Judy Geeson

(Harold Clurman Theatre) Wednesday, Oct. 22–Nov. 9, 1986 (28 performances and 3 previews). Legacy Productions in association with Elmer Mann and David Jenny presents:

AN ACUTE OBSESSION by Barbara Feldman, Eric Rosse; Director, Gardner Compton; Set/Lighting, Michael Lincoln; Original Music, Michael Carey, Eric Rosse; General Management, Craig S. Dorfman; Technical Director, John Guertz; Stage Manager, Lee Bloomrosen; Press, Shirley Herz, Pete Sanders, Peter Cromarty, Glenna Freedman, David Roggensack, Miller Wright, Jillana Devine
CAST: Eric Rosse (Alex), Michael Carey (Max), Kate Merrick (Kate/Maya), Ben Frank (Ben/David), Christian Andrews (Chris/Peter), Dianne Paglia (Dianne/Tenant)
   A play in two acts. The action takes place at the present time in Alex's loft.

Top Right: Christian Andrews, Kate Merrick
in "An Acute Obsession" *(Arthur Coleman)*

(Judith Anderson Theatre) Tuesday, Oct. 28–Nov. 23, 1986 (43 performances). Gary Wertheim presents:
TRIANGLES by June Bingham; Director, Aaron Frankel; Set/Lighting, Daniel A. Saks; Company Manager, Craig Noble; Costumes/Wardrobe, Beverly Bullock; Stage Managers, Linda Carol Young, Michael Schiralli; Press, Shirley Herz, Peter Cromarty, Pete Sanders, Glenna Freedman, David Roggensack, Miller Wright
CAST: Kathleen Butler (Eleanor), Linda Cameron (Anna), Diane Warren (Alice), Maggi-Meg Reed (Lucy), Redman Maxfield (Franklin), Abetha Aayer (Sara), Ian O'Connell (Butler/Louis), Michael Schiralli (Corpsman/Valet)
   A play in two acts. The action takes place in the Franklin D. Roosevelts' homes in Washington and in New York from 1917 to 1945.

Right Center: Kathleen Butler, Redman Maxfield,
Abetha Aayer in "Triangles" *(Carol Rosegg)*

(Second Avenue Theatre) Wednesday, Oct. 29, 1986–Jan. 4, 1987 (78 performances and 8 previews). Heide Mintzer, George Grec, Frank Laraia, David Singer in association with Gary H. Herman present:
HAVE I GOT A GIRL FOR YOU! with Book by Joel Greenhouse, Penny Rockwell; Music & Lyrics, Dick Gallagher; Based loosely on Frankenstein story by Mary Shelley; Director, Bruce Hopkins; Choreography, Felton Smith; Set, Harry Darrow; Costumes, Kenneth M. Yount; Lighting, Jeffrey Schissler; Musical Director/Conductor, Michael Rice; Sound, James K. Morris; Illusions, Ben Robinson; Wigs, Michael DeCesare; Associate Producer, Robert DeRothschild; General Management, Maria Di Dia; Company Manager, Thom Shovestull; Production Assistant, John L. Bryson, Jr.; Wardrobe, Nancy Lawson; Stage Managers, Gary Zabinski, Russell Halley; Press, Shirley Herz, Pete Sanders, Peter Cromarty, Glenna Freedman, David Roggensack
CAST: Gregory Jbara (Monster), Walter Hudson (Baron von Frankenstein), Semina DeLaurentis (Nurse Mary Phillips), Angelina Fiordellisi (Elke, her maid), J. P. Dougherty (Dr. Pretorius), Dennis Parlato (Igor), Ritamarie Kelly (Little Peasant Girl/Little Blind Girl), Chorus: Barry Finkel, Alain Freulon, Daniel Guzman, Heidi Joyce, Ritamarie Kelly, Erica Paulson, Russell Halley (understudy)
MUSICAL NUMBERS: The Peasants Song, Don't Open the Door, Always for Science, Hollywood, Girlfriends for Life, The Monster's Song, I Love Me, Have I Got a Girl for You, Mary's Lament, The Opera, Something, Finale
   A musical in 2 acts and 10 scenes. The action takes place a long time ago in a Bavarian forest just east of Hollywood.

J. P. Dougherty, Semina DeLaurentis, Walter Hudson
in "Have I Got a Girl for You!" *(Adam Newman)*

(Quaigh Theatre) Monday, Oct. 27–Nov. 30, 1986 (16 performances). The Quaigh Theatre (Will Lieberson, Artistic Director) presents:
A BOY IN NEW YORK CALLS HIS MOM IN L.A. by John Ford Noonan; Director, Pat McNamara; Lighting/Sound, George Jacobs; Stage Manager, Winifred Powers
CAST: Jim Rosin (Norman St. Clair)
   Performed without intermission. The action takes place at the present time in the third floor rear apartment of a brownstone on New York's upper Westside.

Right: Jim Rosin

(Theatre Off Park) Wednesday, Oct. 29, 1986–Jan. 4, 1987 (50 performances and 9 previews before moving to Broadway) Theatre Off Park (Bertha Lewis, Producing Director/Albert Harris, Artistic Director/James Randolph, Managing Director) presents:
STARDUST based on an idea by Burton Litwin and Albert Harris; Director, Albert Harris; Choreography, Patrice Soriero; Musical Direction/Arrangements/Orchestrations, James Raitt; Lyrics, Mitchell Parish; Music, Hoagy Carmichael, Glenn Miller, Benny Goodman, Duke Ellington, LeRoy Anderson, and others; Scenery, David Jenkins; Costumes, Mardi Philips; Lighting, Ken Billington; Sound, Gary Harris; Casting, Warren Pincus; General Management, Whitbell Productions; Technical Director, David H. Tasso; Props, Lisa Finney; Wardrobe, Pat Sullivan; Dance Captain, Jim Walton; Assistant Director, Charlie Eisenberg; Stage Managers, William Hare, Susi Mara; Press, Michael Alpert, David Rothenberg
CAST: Michele Bautier, Maureen Brennan, Kim Criswell, Andre DeShields, Jason Graae, Jim Walton
For Musical Numbers, see Broadway production.

Left: Jim Walton, Kim Criswell
Above: Maureen Brennan, Jason Graae
in "Stardust" *(Gerry Goodstein)*

(Town Hall) Wednesday, Oct. 29–Dec. 22, 1986 (48 performances). International Artistic Productions and Ralph Mercado present:
L'CHAIM TO LIFE in Yiddish and in English by Martin Buber, Martin Hamar, Yitzhok Perlov, Neil Steinberg, Leybele Schwartz, Ben Zion Witler, Sholom Secunda, Eber Lobato, Mordechai Gebirtig, Aaron Lebedeff, Mariano Mores, Max Perlman, Jacob Jacobs, Joseph Rumshinsky, Chaim Tauber, Ben Bonus, and additional music by Eber Lobato; Direction/Lighting, Neil Steinberg; Choreography/Costumes, Eber Lobato; Sets, Ari Roussimoff; Musical Direction, Renee Solomon; Sound, David Smith; Dance Captain, Mary MacLeod; Stage Manager, Sandy Levitt; Press, Max Eisen, Madelon Rosen, Maria Somma
CAST: Jackie Jacobs, Leon Liebgold, Mina Bern, Gerri-Ann Frank, Ari Roussimoff, Helen Frank, Michael Fritzke, Trish Kane, Eric Kaufman, Mary MacLeod, Mary Ann Marek, Alec Timerman, Jesse Webb
   A musical revue in 2 acts and 7 scenes, performed alternately in Yiddish and English.

Jackie Jacob, Mina Bern in "L'Chaim to Life"
(Martha Swope)

Richard Lupino, Gordon Gould, Tony Tanner,
Sarah Rice, Chip Cornelius in "Swan Song"
(Henry Grossman)

(Our Studios) Thursday, Oct. 30–Nov. 16, 1986 (12 performances and 2 previews). The Cab Theatre Company presents:
FEMALE TRANSPORT by Steve Gooch; Director, Joan Sitomer; Set, Rick Lahti; Lighting, Nicole Werner; Costumes, Sunni Farrington; Sound, Danny McCleary, Kimberly Otto; Combat Choreography, Vince Donvito; Dramaturg, Regan Kramer; Production Coordinator, Judy Sternlight; Stage Managers, Michele Costantini, Susan Lewis; Press, Mary Mac
CAST: Joann Carollo, Sunni Farrington, Cynthia Forgays, Mary Mac, Brian Mac-Ready, Sherry Mandel, Jessica Rausch, Brian Glover, Michael Pollard, Brian Smiga

(Masur Theatre) Friday, Oct. 31–Nov. 22, 1986 (16 performances). The Swan Song Company by arrangement with The York Theatre Company presents:
SWAN SONG by John Greenwood, Jonathan Levi; Based on novel by Edmund Crispin; Music, Gioacchino Rossini; Director, Tony Tanner; Set, Mina Albergo; Costumes, A. Christina Giannini; Lighting, Raymond J. Dooley; Musical Director, Erica Kaplan; Wardrobe, Amy Rabinowitz, Jennifer Arnold; Technical Director, Michael Tardi; Stage Managers, Michael A. Clarke, Ken Saltzman; Press, Becky Flora
CAST: Erica Kaplan (Fiona), Mark Chamberlin (George Peacock), Brent Barrett (Colin Langley), Ann Marie Lee (Judith Haynes), Chip Cornelius (Adam Dalton), Jo Ann Cunningham (Joan Davis), Michael Tartel (Bruno Sododori), Ron Randell (Wilkes), Tony Tanner (Prof. Gervase Fen), Sarah Rice (Elizabeth Dalton), Adam Redfield (Hodgkins), Richard Lupino (Insp. Mudge), Gordon Gould (Dr. Rashmole), Jack Eddleman (Edwin/Charles Shorthouse)
   A "Mystery with Music" in 2 acts and 5 scenes. The action takes place on the stage of the Cambridge Arts Theatre in England.

(Riverwest Theatre) Saturday, Nov. 1–Dec. 21, 1986 (45 performances and 3 previews). CHS Productions in association with Riverwest Theatre and Leonard Kaplan presents:
PAGEANT with Book & Lyrics by Bill Russell, Frank Kelly; Music, Albert Evans; Choreography, Tony Parise, Bobby Longbottom; Musical Direction/Supervision, Glen Kelly; Set, Leo Meyer; Costumes, Frank Krenz; Lighting, Richard Latta; Costume Adviser, Suzy Benzinger; Sound, David Lawson, Deena Kaye; Hair/Makeup, Suzy Mazzarese; Props, Robert Brubach; Casting, Joseph Abaldo; Conceived and Directed by Bobby Longbottom; Stage Managers, Robert Kellogg, Pat Trott, Paul A. Kochman; Press, FLT/Francine Trevens
CAST: Rex Carlton (Miss Industrial Northeast), Bill Fabris (Miss Bible Belt), Russell Giesenschlag (Miss Texas), Edward Marona (Miss Deep South), John Salvatore (Miss West Coast), Dick Scanlan (Miss Great Plains), Lawrence Raiken (Frankie Cavalier)
MUSICAL NUMBERS: Natural Born Female, Something Extra, One Smile at a Time, Don't Be Afraid, More Than a Woman, Pageant Days, Nightie Night, We're on Our Way, It's Gotta Be Venus, Beauty Work, Goodbye, A Pretty Life
   A musical in two acts. The action takes place at the 1987 Miss Glamouresse Pageant.

Larry Raiken (with mike), and clockwise from bottom
left: Bill Fabris, Rex Carlton, Russell Giesenschlag, Dick
Scanlan, John Salvatore, Edward Marona in "Pageant"
(Adam Newman)

Paulene Myers in "Mama"

(Ernie Martin Studio Theatre) Saturday, Nov 1–17, 1986 (12 performances and one preview) Ben-Am-My Productions presents:
MAMA written by Paulene Myers; Originally staged by Terrence Shank and Paulene Myers; Costumes, Charles Berliner, Grant Kilpatrick; Lighting, Terrence Shank, Arthur Seidelman; Production Consultant, Bruce Franchini
CAST: Paulene Myers in a portrait of five black women who lived in the 18th, 19th and 20th Centuries. Performed with one intermission.

David Groh, Ina Balin
in "Face to Face"

(American Folk Theatre) Sunday, Nov. 2–23, 1986 (16 performances). The Working Theater (Robert Owens Scott, Artistic Director) presents:
MAN WITH A RAINCOAT by William Wise; Director, Stephen Rosenfield; Production Manager, Johnny Kline; Scenery, Michael C. Smith; Lighting, Whitney Quesenbery; Sound, Edward Cosla; Music, Skip Kennon; Costumes, Stephanie Kerley; Technical Director, Jim Murphy; Stage Managers, Susan D. Greenbaum, Melinda Metz, Barbara Bruno; Press, Bruce Cohen, Kathleen von Schmid
CAST: Robert Acaro (Charlie), Janet Aspers (Nurse/Go-Go Dancer), Maggie Burke (Helen), J. Kenneth Campbell (Frank Walker), Mary Daciuk (Adrian), Greg Giordano (Cop), Michael Grodenchik (Wankowski), Earl Hagan, Jr. (Rudy), Jonathan Lipnick (Mayor Jeffries/Man in bar), Frank Lowe (Mr. Bricker), Spartan McClure (Burt), Bill Mitchelson (Reporter/Man in bar), Robin Polk (Peggy/Go-Go Dancer), Barbara Ramsey (Mrs. Bricker), Marisa Redanty (Fran), Joel Simon (Larry), Nelson Simon (Young Doctor), Ron Stetson (Parker), Wendelle Weill (Nora Hartline), Daniel Whitner (Monroe)
    A mystery in two acts. The action takes place in an American city from October 1956 to October 1981.

(Players Theatre) Tuesday, Nov. 4–29, 1986 (28 performances). Judith Rubin presents the Quaigh Theatre production of:
FACE TO FACE by Alexander Gelman; Translation from Russian by Zora Essman; Director, Will Lieberson; Designed by Donald L. Brooks; Casting, Slater/Willet; Assistant to Producer, John Dwyer; Stage Managers, Nancy Rutter, Julia Hoban; Press, David Rothenberg, Marjorie Waxman
CAST: David Groh (Andrei), Ina Balin (Natasha)
    A drama in two acts. The action takes place at the present time in a major city of the Soviet Union.

Top Left: Daniel Whitner, Joel Simon, Earl
Hagen, Jr., J. Kenneth Campbell in "Man
with a Raincoat" *(Carol Rosegg)*

(The Triplex) Friday, Nov. 4–Dec. 7, 1986 (22 performances and 9 previews). H.A.U. Yiddish National Theatre presents:
THE STRANGER'S RETURN by Miriam Kressyn, Michael Fried; Director, Michael Fried; Set, Roger Mooney; Costumes, A. Christina Giannini; Lighting, Norman Coates; Original Music, Elliott Finkel; Yiddish Lyrics, Miriam Kressyn; Dance, Kenston Ames; English Lyrics, Maggie Bloomfield; Technical Director, Bonnie Burnhan; Wardrobe, Michael Quarry; Hairstylist, Tomo N' Tomo; Stage Manager, Jane Sanders; Press, Hale & Husted/Al Husted, Alan Hale, Darrel Joseph, Jeffrey Seller
CAST: Bruce Adler (Alexander Taylor), David Eichenbaum (Peretz), Ibi Kaufman (Grace Taylor), Shifra Lerer (Nana Thomas), Michael Michalovic (David Ben-Ari), Bradford Minkoff (William Taylor), Moultrie Patten (Butler), Herschel Rosen (Shamus), Dawn Spare (Katherine Clark), Raquel Yossiffon (Margaret Taylor), Ruth Barlas (Understudy)
    A comedy-drama in three acts with one intermission. The action takes place in the Taylor home in New York City from 1938 to 1946.

(R.A.P.P. Arts Center) Thursday, Nov. 6–23, 1986 (16 performances)
EDWARD II by Bertolt Brecht; Director, R. Jeffrey Cohen; Design, Alexis Cohen; Lighting, Ed Durkee; Producer, Joe Holloway; Music/Sound, Bob Muller; Press, David Rothenberg
CAST: Stephen R. Tracy (Edward II), Jeffrey Becker, Jessica Black, Melody Cooper, Brenda Foley, Rebecca Godson, Paul Kerry, Ron King, Sandra Laub, Allison Rutledge-Parisi, Jim Pratzon, Marty Rudoy, Laurence C. Schwartz, Ann Shea, Steve Tracy

Steven Tracy, Jim Pratzon in "Edward II" *(Herbert Migdoll)*
Above: Shifra Lerer, Bruce Adler in "The Stranger's Return"
(Martha Swope)

(Baldwin Theatre) Friday, Nov. 7–23, 1986 (12 performances and 5 previews).
Baldwin Theatre (Anita Sorel, Artistic Director; Marty Kovach, Managing Director) presents:
MIRACLE OF THE MONTH by T. Wayne Moore; Director, Marty Kovach; Set, Anthony Fanning; Costumes, Paul Tazewell; Lighting, David Finley; Stage Manager, Victoria Visiko
CAST: Judith Moore, Jennie Moreau, Cameron Arnett

**Left: Jennie Moreau, Cameron Arnett
in "Miracle of the Month"**

(Samuel Beckett Theatre) Friday, Nov. 7, 1986–Feb. 15, 1987 (112 performances).
J. R. Productions presents:
LILY DALE by Horton Foote; Director, William Alderson; Set, Johnny Kline; Lighting, John Hastings; Costumes, Deborah Shaw; Wig/Hair Design, Paul Huntley; General Management, Darwall Associates; Company Manager, Ken Silverman; Wardrobe, Nicole Hill; Production Assistant, Laura Shelton; Stage Managers, Laura Kraveta, Laura Young; Press, Burnham-Callaghan/Gary Murphy
CAST: Don Bloomfield (Horace Robedaux), Jane Welch (Mrs. Coons), Molly Ringwald succeeded by Mary Stuart Masterson (Lily Dale Robedaux), Julie Heberlein (Corella Davenport), Greg Zittel (Pete Davenport), Johnny Kline (Will Kidder), Cullen Johnson (Albert), Standbys: Kathleen Gibbons (Lily), Matthew Penn (Horace/Will), Sara Croft (Corella/Mrs. Coons), Cullen Johnson (Pete)
   A play in 2 acts and 4 scenes. The action takes place in 1909 on a train from Harrison, Texas, and in the home of Pete Davenport in Houston, Texas.

**Above: Molly Ringwald, and Right Center
with Don Bloomfield** (Carol Rosegg)

**Molly Ringwald, Don Bloomfield
in "Lily Dale"** (Carol Rosegg)

(Classic Stage Company) Sunday, Nov. 9–Dec. 6, 1986 (27 performances). CSC Repertory (Carol Ostrow, Producing Director; Jennifer Ober, General Manager) present:

THE SKIN OF OUR TEETH by Thornton Wilder; Director, Carey Perloff; Sets, Loy Arcenas; Costumes, Candice Donnelly; Lighting, Anne Militello; Sound, Tom Gould; Composer, Wayne Horvitz; Casting, Soble/LaPadura; Production Manager, Brett Buckwalter: Masks, Rebecca Kravetz; Props, Mimi Cohen; Wardrobe, Hunter Sloan; Stage Managers, William H. Lang, Liz Small; Press, Dara Hershman
CAST: Ron Orbach (Announcer/Stage Manager), Park Overall (Sabina), Novella Nelson (Mrs. Antrobus), Renaud Knapp (Dinosaur), Melissa Salack (Mammoth), John Aaron Beall (Telegraph Boy), Lisa Goodman (Gladys), Peter Francis-James (Henry), Steve Coats (Mr. Antrobus), Sandford Stokes (Doctor/Conveneer), George McGrath (Moses/Broadcast Official/Tremayne), Joanne Bowling (Homer), Alexandra Rhodie (Miss E. Muse), Kathy Karl (Miss T. Muse), Shawn Powers (Miss M. Muse/Conveneer/Ivy), Elaine Hausman (Fortune Teller), Aaron Kjenaas, Anthony L. Ejarque (Conveneers)
A play in two acts. The action takes place at the present time in various New Jersey locations

Lisa Goodman, Steve Coats, Novella Nelson,
Peter Francis-James in "The Skin of Our Teeth"
(Paula Court)

clockwise from bottom left: Ralph Marrero, Frank Torren, Bina Sharif, Francisco Rivela, Roger Rignack, Anna Larreta, Elizabeth Ruiz in "The Red Madonna" *(Carol Rosegg)*

(INTAR Theatre) Wednesday, Nov. 12–Dec. 14, 1986 (36 performances)
THE RED MADONNA or A Damsel for a Gorilla by Arrabal; Translated by Lynne Alvarez; Director, Arrabal; Set, David Peterson; Lighting, John Gisondi, Costumes, Donna Zakowska; Sound, Gary Harris; Masks/Puppets, Ralph Lee; Casting, Janet L. Murphy; Production Manager, Robert L. Anderson; Artistic Director/Founder INTAR, Max Ferra; Hair/Makeup, Jacques Olivier; Production Assistant, Dana Rappaport; Stage Manager, T. J. Carroll; Press, Bruce Cohen, Kathleen von Schmid
CAST: Elizabeth Ruiz (Aurora), Francisco Rivela (Father), Frank Torren (Nemesio), Bina Sharif (Torcuata), Roger Rignack (Lenica), Ralph Marrero (Sailor), Anna Larreta (Hildegart)
A drama performed without intermission. The action takes place "in a country whose name I don't wish to remember," during the first third of the 20th Century.

(270 Lafayette Street) Thursday, Nov. 13–Dec. 13, 1986 (28 performances and 2 previews). En Garde Arts (Michael Engler, Artistic Director; Anne Hamburger, Producer) presents:
TERMINAL BAR by Paul Selig; Director, Michael Engler; Set, Philipp Jung; Lighting, Heather Carson; Costumes, Michael Krass; Sound, David Cremlin; Assistant Director, Ethan Goldman; Technical Director, George Zegarsky; Props, Hayley N. Schwartz; Stage Managers, Lesley Lynne Moore, Jeni Crockett; Press, G. Theodore Killmer
CAST: Jayne Haynes (Holly), Roxanne Rogers (Martinelle), Fisher Stevens (Dwayne), Kevin O'Rourke (Radio Announcer's Voice)
A black comedy in two acts with a prologue. The action takes place in an abandoned club in New York City's red-light district in the near future.

Fisher Stevens, Jayne Haynes
in "Terminal Bar" *(Barry Swimar)*

(24 Bond Street) Friday, November 14–22, 1986 (4 performances)
THE AMERICAN MIME THEATRE (Founder/Director, Paul J. Curtis; Managing Director, Jean Barbour) presents: Dreams, The Lovers, The Scarecrow, Hurly-Burly, Evolution, Sludge, Six, The Unitaur
CAST: Jean Varbour, Charles Barney, Joseph Citta, Paul J. Curtis, Dale Fuller, Jill Jeffrey, Rafael Risemberg, Mr. Bones

Below and Right: American Mime Theatre
(Tim Lee, Tom Yee, Jim Moore)

(Hartley House Theater) Friday, Nov. 14–Dec. 13, 1986 (14 performances and 1 preview). Playwrights Preview Productions presents:
CHILI QUEEN by Jim Lehrer; Director, Frances Hill; Producers, Baba Paul, Marnie Winston; Set, Reagan Cook; Lighting, Pat Dingan; Costumes, Richard Curtis; Sound/Music, Joe Gallant; Assistant Directors, Stuart Laurence, Ellen White; Stage Manager, Elaine O'Donnell
CAST: Fred Burrell, Jane Chamberlin, Paul Doherty, Rick J. Porter
  A serio-comic play set in a fast food chili franchise in a small Texas town.

(Greenwich House) Friday, Nov. 14–Dec. 7, 1986 (16 performances). SoHo Repertory Theatre (Artistic Directors, Jerry Engelbach, Marlene Swartz; Business Manager, Laurie J. Greenwald; Dramaturg, Victor Gluck) presents:
THE RAGGED TROUSERED PHILANTHROPISTS by Stephen Lowe; Based on novel by Robert Tressell; Director, Julian Webber; Set, David Nelson; Costumes, Patricia Adshead; Lights, Nancy Collings; Musical Director, Frank Lindquist; Technical Director, Darren Lee Cole; Stage Managers, Alice Perlmutter, Margaret Durkin; Press, Bruce Cohen, Kathleen von Schmid
CAST: Steven Hofvendahl (Bob Cross/Rev. Belcher/Holy Man/Brigand), Michael Wetmore (Frank Owen/Sign Writer/Didlum/Food Supplier/Brigand), Ellen Mareneck (Bert White/Apprentice/Elsie/Mrs. Sweater), Time Winters (Joe Philpott/Rushton/Brigand), Ray Collins (Will Easton/Linden/Grinder/Brigand), George Taylor (Harlow/Lettum/Brigand)
  A play in two acts. The action takes place in London in 1906.

Michael Wetmore, Ellen Mareneck, Ray Collins, George Taylor, Time Winters in "Ragged Trousered Philanthropist" *(Gerry Goodstein)*

79

(New Performance Space) Saturday, Nov. 15–23, 1986 (6 performances). Incognito Mars Productions presents:
FOUR FACES OF LEE by Lee Bollinger; Director, Martha Schmoyer Lo Monaco; Designer, Mara Williams; Producer, Marty Davey; Illustrator, Charles Harker; Assistant to Producer, Lora McLaughlin; Stage Manager, Bonita Silverman
CAST: Charles E. Gerber, Claudia Hommel, Ann Timmons, Marty Davey
No other details submitted.

(Folksbiene Playhouse) Saturday, Nov. 15, 1986–March 15, 1987 (54 performances). The Folksbiene Playhouse (Managing Director, Ben Schechter) presents:
THE FLOWERING PEACH by Clifford Odets; Director, Roger Sullivan; Translated/Adapted into Yiddish by Miriam Kressyn; Original Music, Ira Taxin; Set, Brian P. Kelly; Lighting, Tracy Dedrickson; Costumes, Ben Gutierrez-Soto; Props, Kathryn Markey, Rebecca Waron; Hair/Makeup, Georgianna Fischer; Stage Management/Movement, Jodi Klosner; Press, Max Eisen, Madelon Rosen
CAST: Norman Kruger (Noah), Zypora Spaisman (Esther), Richard Silver (Yaphet), I. W. Firestone (Shem), Daniel Chiel (Ham), Paula Teitelbaum (Leah), Miriam Gordon (Rachel), Paula Newman/Sarit Gerval (Zehava)
 A play in two acts. The action takes place in a Bible land in the beginning.

Top Left: Zipora Spaisman, Sol Frieder,
I. W. Firestone Below: Paula Teitelbaum,
Miriam Gordon, Zipora Spaisman, Sarit Gervai
in "The Flowering Peach"

(Triplex) Tuesday, November 18–30, 1986 (14 performances). IPA (Robert LoBianco/Jedediah Wheeler, Directors) presents:
LE CIRQUE IMAGINAIRE devised and performed by Victoria Chaplin and Jean Baptiste Thierree; Company Manager, Alicia Adams; Production Manager, Susan Resnick; Artistic Adviser, David Gothard; Staff: Giovanni Consentino, Marie Germaine Fath, Antonio Magrina, Jose Magrina; Press, Susan Bloch Company/Ellen Zeisler, Peter Carzasty, Alison Sherman
 Performed with one intermission

Victoria Chaplin
in "Le Cirque Imaginaire"

(Vineyard Theatre) Wednesday, Nov. 19–Dec. 21, 1986 (30 performances). Vineyard Theatre (Artistic Director, Douglas Aibel; Executive Director, Barbara Zinn Krieger; Managing Director, Gary P. Steuer) presents:
HOW TO SAY GOODBYE by Mary Gallagher; Director, Liz Diamond; Set, William Barclay; Lighting, Phil Monat; Costumes, Janna Gjesdal; Sound, Phil Lee; Production Coordinator, Susan Wilder; Technical Director, Peter Barbieri; Props, Lane Hurwitz; Stage Managers, Richard Costabile, Tyrone Henderson; Press, Bruce Cohen, Kathleen von Schmid
CAST: Cheryl McFadden (Casey Staiger), Kathryn Rossetter (Jana Sklar), Christine Jansen (Phyllis Castellano), D. W. Moffett (Marty Staiger), Jason Ruggiero (Conor Staiger)
   A play in two acts. The action takes place in Cleveland, Ohio, in the present (1980), and in the past (1972–79).

**Top Left: D. W. Moffett, Jason Ruggiero,
Cheryl McFadden in "How to Say Goodbye"**
(Carol Rosegg)

(Lee Strasberg Theatre Institute) Friday, Nov. 21–Dec. 15, 1986 (16 performances). The Lee Strasberg Creative Center presents:
MODIGLIANI by Dennis McIntyre; Director, Louis Rackoff; Scenery, Gary Dartt; Costumes, Madeline Cohen; Lighting, Richard Dandrea; Fight Coordinator, J. Allen Suddeth; Stage Manager, Elizabeth R. Rogers; Press, Monica M. Hayes
CAST: Priscilla Corbin, Bill Ferrell, David Gideon, Peter Johl, James Paradise, Gregory Paslawsky, Chris Strang
No other details submitted.

(Courtyard Playhouse) Tuesday, Nov. 28–Dec. 21, 1986 (13 performances). The Actors Collective (Warren Manzi, Artistic Director) presents:
CORK by Samm-Art Williams; Director, Warren Manzi; Scenery, Dan Gray; Costumes, Dara Norman; Dramaturg, Janice Paran; Movement, Denise Dalfo; Choreographer, Horace Turnbull; Stage Managers, Evan A. Georges, Lark Hackshaw; Press, Dolph Browning
CAST: Bernard J. Lunon (Randy Madison), Geoffrey C. Ewing (William Henry Lane), Regina Lorraine Davis (Lois), Paul Hart (Paul), Elain Graham (Cork), Nan-Lynn Nelson (Topsy/Wanda/Beatrice), W. MacGregor King (Mr. Bingham), Lois Raebeck (Mrs. Bingham), Hank Wagner (Homer), Melissa Meg Davis (Essie), Tim Zay (Al Jolson)
   A play in two acts. The action takes place at the present time, backstage of a West End theatre in London, England.

**Nan-Lynn Nelson, Elain Graham, Geoffrey Ewing
in "Cork"** *(Arthur L. Cohen)*

**Boyd Gaines
in "The Double Bass"**
(Jessica Katz)

(47th Street Theatre) Friday, Nov. 28–Dec. 29, 1986 (21 performances). Double Image Theatre (Helen Waren Mayer, Founder/Executive Director; Max Mayer, Artistic Director; Leslie Urdang, Managing Director) presents:
THE DOUBLE BASS by Patrick Suskind; Translated by Harry Newman and Eric Overmyer; Director, Kent Paul; Set, William Barclay; Lighting, Phil Monat; Costumes, Jared Aswegan; Sound, Tom Gould; Props, Nancy Greenstein; Stage Managers, Louis D. Pietig, Siobhan Sullivan; Press, Fred Nathan Co./Dennis Crowley
CAST: Boyd Gaines as the Double Bassist. The action takes place at the present time in his apartment in Germany.

(Circle in the Square/Downtown) Wednesday, Nov. 26, 1986–April 26, 1987 (150 performances and 24 previews). Circle in the Square Theatre (Theodore Mann, Artistic Director/Paul Libin, Producing Director) presents:

THE WIDOW CLAIRE by Horton Foote; Director, Michael Lindsay-Hogg; Set, Eugene Lee; Costumes, Van Broughton Ramsey; Lighting, Natasha Katz; Hair/Makeup, Hiram Ortiz; Dance Sequences, Margie Castleman; Fight Sequences, B. H. Barry; Company Manager, Susan Elrod; Casting, Hughes/Moss; Wardrobe, Susan Freel; Production Assistant, Daniel Henning; Stage Managers, Carol Klein, Julie Swenson; Press, Merle Debusky, Leo Stern

CAST: Matthew Broderick succeeded by Eric Stoltz (Horace Robedaux), Anthony Weaver (Archie), Joel Anderson succeeded by Horton Foote, Jr. (Felix), Spartan McClure (Spence), William Youmans (Ed Cordray), Hallie Foote (Widow Claire), John Daman (Buddy), Sarah Michelle Gellar (Molly), Patrick James Clarke succeeded by Joel Anderson (Val), Dan Butler (Roger), Understudies: Ned Bridges (Horace/Archie/Spence/Ed), Kevin O'Meara (Roger/Val/Felix), Julie Swenson (Widow), Sky Berdahl (Buddy), Angela Goethals (Molly)

A play without intermission. The action takes place in 1911 in Harrison, Texas, at the home of Widow Claire.

Top Right: Hallie Foote, Matthew Broderick
(Deborah Feingold)

John Daman, Sarah M. Gellar, Hallie Foote,
Matthew Broderick *(Deborah Feingold)*

Hallie Foote, Eric Stoltz
(Susan Cook)

(Riverwest Theatre) Monday, December 1–21, 1986 (16 performances and 12 previews). Riverwest Theatre (Nat Habib, June Summers, Joe Cahalan) and Acorn Productions (Jane Myers, Pamela Moller, Brooke Palamce) present:
THE FOX by Allan Miller; Adapted from novella by D. H. Lawrence; Director, Constance Grappo; Set, Byron Taylor; Costumes, Vicki Davis; Lighting, Peggy Eisenhauer; Sound, David Lawson; Technical Director, Rick Morganelli; Production Assistant, Madelein Elancry; Stage Managers, Paul A. Kochman, Margaret Giovinco, Dana Rappaport; Press, FLT/Francine Trevens
CAST: Pamela Moller (Jill Banford), Brooke Palance (Nellie March), Stephen Caffrey (Henry Grenfel)
   A drama in 2 acts and 6 scenes. The action takes place in 1918 on the old Bailey Farm in England.

(Nat Horne Theatre) Wednesday, December 3–20, 1986 (15 performances and 2 previews)
THE MAGICIAN conceived and produced by Peter Samelson; Director, Annegret M. M. Reimer; Lighting, Nadine Charlsen; Costumes, Gail Cooper-Hecht, Robert Locke; Original Synthesizer Music, Mundaka; Company Manager, Chris Dunlop; Press, G. Theodore Killmer
CAST: Peter Samelson in two acts: The Magic Without, The Magic Within

**Top Right: Brooke Palance, Stephen Caffrey
in "The Fox"** *(Doug Hay)* **Below: Peter
Samelson in "The Magician"**

(R. A. P. P. Arts Center) Thrusday, December 4–21, 1986 (12 performances and 4 previews) The Theatre Project at R.A.P.P. presents:
THE THREE SISTERS by Anton Chekhov; New Translation/Adaptation, Elaine Devlin, Gail Mishkovich; Director, Elaine Devlin; Producer, Joe Holloway; Design, Alexis Siroc; Lighting, Ed Durkee; Assistant Director, Meg Anderson; Company Manager, Evelyn Nunlee; Stage Manager, Lori Fein; Press, David Rothenberg
CAST: Susan Furey-Lloyd (Olga), Ellen Boggs (Masha), Maude Mitchell (Irina), Jeffrey Becker (Tusenbach), Steven R. Tracy (Solyony), Eve Sorel (Anfisa), Clay Dickinson (Ferapont), Ron King (Vershinin), Laurence C. Schwartz (Andrei), Robert Mason (Kulygin), Allison Rutledge-Parisi (Natasha)
   A drama in two acts.

(Actors' Space) Thursday, December 4–14, 1986 (8 performances). The Actors' Space (Alan Langdon, Artistic Director) presents:
CHICKS by Grace McKeaney; Director, Ralph Stenwall; with June Ballinger as Mary Margaret Phallon.
   The action takes place at the present time in a kindergarten classroom in a public school somewhere in the Midwest.
THE GRAND CANYON by Sandra Fenichel Asher; Director, Brian Meister; Technical Director, Bob Briggs; Lighting, Peggy Lei Mueller; Costumes, Elizabeth Kate Shelton; Stage Managers, Sharon Rush, Lee Milinazzo; Managing Director, James L. Homan
CAST: Kat Singleton (Mildred), Barbara Wilder (Anna), Karen Braga (Sleeping Beauty), Bijou Clinger (Understudy)
   A play in two acts. The action takes place at the present time on a Sunday in a room in the psychiatric ward of a general hospital.

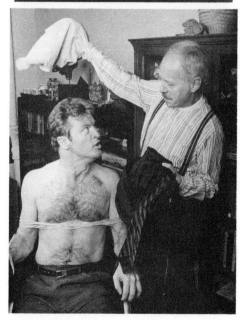

(Quaigh Theatre) Friday, Dec. 5, 1986–April 26, 1987 (98 performances)
DOWN AN ALLEY FILLED WITH CATS by Warwick Moss; Director, Peter Askin; Producer, Melanie Webber; Set, Roy Hine; Lighting, Nancy Collings; Sound, George Jacobs; Stage Managers, Nancy Sorel, Winifred Powers; Press, FLT/Francine Trevins
CAST: Theo Barnes (Timmothy Timmony), Stewart Finlay-McLennan (Simon Mathews)
   A drama in two acts. The action takes place during the winter of 1986 in Timmothy Timmony's bookshop in a forgotten corner of the city of Sydney, Australia.

**Stewart Finlay-McLennan, Theo Barnes in "Down an Alley
Filled with Cats"** *(Adam Newman)*

Kristine Nielsen, Sigourney Weaver
in "The Merchant of Venice" *(Paula Court)*

(Lamb's Club Little Theatre) Saturday, Dec. 6, 1986–Jan. 3, 1987 (32 performances and 5 previews). Lamb's Theatre Company (Carolyn Rossi Copeland, Producing Director; Pamela Perrell, Associate Director) presents:
THE GIFTS OF THE MAGI based on the classic O. Henry stories; Book & Lyrics, Mark St. Germain; Music & Lyrics, Randy Courts; Set, Michael C. Smith; Costumes, Hope Hanafin; Lighting, Heather Carson; Choreography, Piper Pickrell; Musical Direction/Original Incidental Music, Steven M. Alper; Director, Carolyn Rossi Copeland; Props, Jim Murphy; Stage Managers, Steve Zorthian, Melissa L. Burdick; Press, G. Theodore Killmer
CAST: Jeff Etjen (Him), Sarah Knapp (Her), Ken Jennings (Willy), John David Westfall (Jim), Cissy Rebich (Della), Clint Vriezelaar (Soapy)
MUSICAL NUMBERS: Star of the Night, The Gifts of the Magi, Jim and Della, Christmas Is to Blame, How Much to Buy My Dream, The Restaurant, Once More, Bum Luck, Greed, Pockets, The Same Girl, The Gift of Christmas
   Performed without intermission. The action takes place in New York City, December 23–25, 1905.

Ken Jennings, Clint Vriezelaar, John David Westfall,
Cissy Rebich, Jeff Etjen, Sarah Knapp in "The Gifts
of the Magi" *(Carol Rosegg)*

(American Folk Theater) Thursday, Dec. 11, 1986–Jan. 11, 1987 (26 performances). American Folk Theater (Artistic Director, Dick Gaffield) by special arrangement with Arthur Shafman presents The Adaptors (Founders: Tony Brown, Kari Margolis) in:
AUTOBAHN written and directed by Tony Brown, Kari Margolis; Original Compositions/Arrangements, Neil Alexander, Charles Haynes; Costumes, Kari Margolis; Lighting, Peter Anderson; Sound, Kyle Chepulis; Videos, Tony Brown, Kari Margolis; Press, G. Theodore Killmer
CAST: Ed Alletto, Erica Babad, Tony Brown, Frandu, Jeannie Kranich, Beth Margolis, Kari Margolis, Joan Merwyn, Nob Modaff, Larry Picard
SCENES: American Safari, The Homecoming, The Survivors, Stereophonic Fantasy, Cardboard Ladies, The Microphone, Not For All the Rice in China, Electric Lady Video, The Hairdryer, Let's Bring Back WWI, The Executive Suite, Breakfast
   Performed without an intermission.

The Adaptors in "Autobahn"
(Tony Brown)

(CSC Rep. Theatre) Sunday, Dec. 14, 1986–Jan. 18, 1987 (33 performances). CSC Repertory Ltd. (Carol Ostrow, Producing Director; Jennifer Ober, General Manager) presents:
THE MERCHANT OF VENICE by William Shakespeare; Director, James Simpson; Scenery, Loy Arcenas; Costumes, Claudia Brown; Lighting, Anne Militello; Composer, Richard Porterfield; Casting, Soble/LaPadura; Assistant Director, Karen E. White; Props, Mimi Cohen; Wardrobe, Hunter Sloan; Stage Managers, William H. Lang, Liz Small; Press, Dara Hershman
CAST: Anthony W. Ejarque (Boat Boy/Understudy), John Aaron Beall (Leonardo/Understudy), Reg E. Cathey (Prince of Morocco/Salerio/Old Gobbo), Tom Ericson (Musician), Michael Hammond (Bassanio), Michael Jung (Musician), Kathy Karl (Koken), Aaron Kjenaas (Boat Boy/Understudy), Renaud Knapp (Koken/Understudy), George McGrath (Antonio), Dan Moran (Solanio/Launcelot Gobbo/Arragon), Kristine Nielsen (Nerissa), Shawn M. Powers (Understudy), Alexandra Rhodie (Jessica), Melissa Salack (Understudy), John Seitz (Shylock), Rocco Sisto (Duke of Venice/Balthazar/Tubal), Sandford Stokes (Jailer/Boat Boy/Understudy), Victor Talmadge (Gratiano), Sigourney Weaver (Portia), John Wojda (Lorenzo)

   Performed with two intermissions.

(John Houseman Theatre) Thursday, Dec. 25, 1986–Feb. 8, 1987 (31 performances and 16 previews) Eric Krebs presents:

THE RISE OF DAVID LEVINSKY based on novel by Abraham Cahan; Book & Lyrics, Isaiah Sheffer; Music, Bobby Paul; Director, Sue Lawless; Musical Director, Lanny Meyers; Set, Kenneth Foy; Costumes, Mimi Maxmen; Lighting, Phil Monat; Casting, Joseph Abaldo; General Management, Whitbell Productions; Hairstylist, Bruce Geller; Dance Captain, Lynne Wintersteller; Wardrobe, Claire Fuller; Technical Director, Mark Porter; Stage Managers, Donald Christy, Anita Ross, David Kenner, Wendy Baila; Press, Max Eisen, Maria Somma

CAST: Larry Kert (Levinsky), Avi Hoffman (David), Bruce Adler (Gitelson), Judith Cohen (Mrs. Noodleman), Arthur Howard (Bender), W. M. Hunt (Huntington), Jean Kauffman (Matilda), Jack Kenny (Chaiken), Rende Rae Norman (Ruchel), Larry Raiken (Maximum Max), Eleanor Reissa (Dora), David Vosburgh (Moscowitz), Lynne Wintersteller (Sadie)

MUSICAL NUMBERS: Who Is This Man?, 500 Pages, Grand Street, In America, The Boarder, The Transformation, Sharp, Two of a Kind, Little Did I Know, Hard Times, Credit Face, 500 Garments, The Garment Trade, Some Incredible Guy, Just Like Me, Be Flexible, A Married Man, Little Did We Know, Bittersweet, Survival of the Fittest, A View from the Top

A musical in 2 acts and 24 scenes. The action takes place from 1883 to 1910 in Manhattan, New York City.

Top Left: Avi Hoffman, Larry Kert
in "The Rise of David Levinsky"
(Gerry Goodstein)

(American Theatre of Actors) Wednesday, January 7–24, 1987 (8 performances)
RIME ICE by Melba LaRose; Director, Melba LaRose; Composer/Pianist, Paul Serrato; Costumes/Sound, Theresa Purcell; Lighting, Stephen Petrilli
CAST: Russ Hatfield (Billy), Christina Gillespie (Fleur)
The action takes place in 1979 in Manhattan, New York City.

(South Street Theatre) Wednesday, Jan. 14–Feb. 1, 1987 (15 performances). Phoenix Arts presents:
TASTER'S CHOICE by Christopher Blake; Director, Gregory Dale; Costumes, Lauren Gibson; Set, Diann Duthie; Lighting, David A. Finn; Stage Manager, Laura Gewurz; Press, Annette B. Stover
CAST: James Jenner (Ross Sandusky), Anna Scott (Karoline Thun), Lee Beltzer (Bernard Tartainville), Florence Fox (Mathilda Sanders), Tom McMorrow, Jr. (Harry St. James), Fay Cooper (Charlotte Smithey), James Davies (Bellboy)

Russ Hatfield, Christina Gillespie
in "Rime Ice"

Stephen Rowe, Joan MacIntosh in "Whispers"
(Carol Rosegg)

(Open Space Theatre) Wednesday, Jan. 14–Feb. 15, 1987 (35 performances). The Open Space Theatre Experiment (Lynn Michaels, Artistic Director) presents:
WHISPERS by Crispin Larangeira; Director, Nancy Gabor; Sets, Harry Baum; Lighting, Richard Dorfman; Costumes, Barbara Weiss; Dramaturg, Beate Hein Bennett; Technical Director, Michael Schutte; Stage Managers, Maureen Palmer, Leslie Ball; Press, Bruce Cohen, Kathleen von Schmid
CAST: Stephen Rowe (Neftaly Aidad Savaty), Joan MacIntosh (Jana Latvis)
A play in three scenes performed without intermission. The action takes place during late autumn of 1966 on a mountain in Magadan Province, Russia.

(StageArts Theater) Thursday, Jan. 15–Feb. 1, 1987 (13 performances and 2 previews) StageArts Theater Company (Nell Robinson, Ruth Ann Norris, Artistic Directors) present:
BETTER LIVING by James van Maanen; Director, Robin Swados; Set, Daniel Conway; Lighting, Robert Bessoir; Costumes, Sheila Kehoe; Technical Director, Alan Moyer; Stage Managers, Steven H. Wildern, Cher Ledwith; Press, Shirley Herz Associates/Pete Sanders
CAST: Richard Bowne (Don), Charles Major (Will), Tom Gerard (Marsh), Gordon MacDonald (Scott)
  A play in two acts. The action takes place at the present time over a six month period in a large two-story house in a middle class section of East Hollywood, California.

(T.O.M.I. Theatre) Wednesday, Jan. 21–March 22, 1987. Moved to Samuel Beckett Theatre March 7, 1987 (38 performances) The Threshold Theater Company (Artistic Directors, Pamela Billig, Eugene Brogyanyi; Producing Director, David Edelman) presents:
WICKED PHILANTHROPY by Denis Diderot; Translated by Gabriel John Brogyanyi; Director, Pamela Caren Billig; Dance Consultant, Catherine Turocy; Costumes, Anita D. Ellis; Set, Eugene Brogyanyi; Lighting, Ron Burns; Casting, Alan Coleridge; Music, Mozart, Haydn, Gluck; Stage Manager, D. C. Rosenberg; Press, Jeffrey Richards Associates/Ben Morse
CAST: Eleanor Ruth (Mme. de Chepy), Richie Allan (Picard), Jennifer Campbell (Mlle. Beaulieu), Patricia Natale (Mme.de Vertillac), Richard Pruitt (M. Hardouin), Betsy Mohler (Mme. Bertrand), Conrad L. Osborne (M. des Renardeaux), Kevin O'Keefe (M. de Crancey), Kelly Roman (Mlle. Henriette de Vertillac), Gabriel Barre (M. de Surmont), David Edelman (M. Poultier), Sam Riddle (Binbin), Rose Mackey succeeded by Barbara Herbst (Mme. de Malves).
  A comedy in two acts. The action takes place around 1780 in Paris at the house of Madame de Malves.

Tom Gerard, Richard Bowne
in "Better Living" *(Carol Rosegg)*
Left Center: Richard Pruitt, Patricia Natale
in "Wicked Philanthropy" *(Carol Rosegg)*

(Theatre Guinevere) Thursday, Jan. 22–Feb. 8, 1987 (15 performances). Amtex Productions (Karmyn Lott, Producer) presents:
WE SHALL by Karmyn Lott; Director, Anderson Johnson; Set, James Wolk; Costumes, Katherine Roberson; Lighting, Howell Binkley; Musical Director, Cliff Terry; Stage Manager, Judith Chew; Press, Howard Atlee
CAST: Jeffrey Harmon (Ezekel Witherspoon), Pa Sean Wilson (Glenda Ann Russell), Timothy F. Murray (Dr. Ward/Sam Junior), James Foster (Rev. Arnold), Nicole Powell (Gwen Johnson), Michael Gaines (Sam Russell, Sr.), Consuelo Hill (Lena Russell)
MUSICAL NUMBERS: Let the Church Say Amen, Woke Up This Morning, These Blessings, I'm on My Way, Whose Side Are You On?, Ain't Gonna Let Nobody, Why the King of Love Is Dead, Never Turn Back, We Shall
  A play with music in two acts. The action takes place in Levelland, Texas, in February of 1968, and in March and April of 1968.

(Courtyard Theatre) Saturday, Jan. 24–Feb. 15, 1987 (14 performances and 2 previews). The Actors Collective (Warren Manzi, Artistic Director) presents:
BETWEEN TIME AND TIMBUKTU by Kurt Vonnegut, Jr. for television; Adapted for the stage; Conceived and Directed by Warren Manzi; Set, Ziska Childs; Costumes, Randall Ouzts; Dramaturg, Janice Paran; Choreographer, Denise Dalfo; Sound, Dara Norman; Lighting, Laura Perlman; Producers, Cathy Russell, William Carrigan; Stage Manager, Evan A. Georges; Press, Dolph Browning
CAST: Nina Tremblay (Miss Blast-Off), Mark Carson (Host), Michael Worth (Photographer), Lois Raeback (Mrs. Stevenson), Perry Pirkkanen (Stony), Graham Roberts (Harrison), Honor Mosher (Wanda June), Douglas Simes (Walter), Brian Corrigan (Bud), G. Gordon Cronce (Tex), Richard Spore (Sandy), Marc Lutsky (Dr. Denton), W. MacGregor King (Bokonon), Renee Tuzun (Ballerina), Tim Zay (Dr. Proteus), Dara Norman (General), Dancers: Patricia Chin, Deborah Tobias, Lorien House, Horace Turnbull, Ensemble: Daniel Bello, Meryl Goodfader, Wells Fischer, Christopher Pickart, Christine Schneider, Julianne Endler
  A play in two acts.

(West Bank Cafe) Tuesday, January 27–31, 1987 (5 limited performances)
BUDDHA by Katharine Houghton; Director, Rand Foerster. CAST: William Cain (The Man), Katharine Houghton (The Woman). The first act of a trilogy THE HOODED EYE performed without intermission.
Second play in the trilogy: ON THE SHADY SIDE by Katharine Houghton; Director, Linda Lees; Lighting, Karl Hamann; Production Assistant, Laura Makay.
CAST: Tracy Thorne (Daughter), Katharine Houghton (Mother). Performed Tuesday, March 31–April 4, 1987 (5 performances)
Third play: THE RIGHT NUMBER by Katharine Houghton; Director, Rand Foerster; Production Assistants, Katharyn Pinder, Cece Donoghue. CAST: Patrick Tovatt (The Brother), Katharine Houghton (The Sister). Performed Tuesday, May 19–23, 1987 (4 performances only).

William Cain, Katharine Houghton
in "Buddha" *(Len Tavares)*

(New York Academy of Art) Wednesday, January 28–29, 1987 (2 performances). Mission Theater Company presents:
THE STONES OF VENICE or John Ruskin's Honeymoon by Steven Katz; Director, Mark Plesent; Assistant Director, Elizabeth Cohen; Lighting, Chris Oldcorn; Costumes, Daryl Kerrigan; Sound/Stage Manager, Mark Wlordarkiewicz
CAST: Joyce Leigh Bowden (Effie Grey Ruskin), Christopher Combes (John Ruskin), Ed Vincent (Michelangelo), Skeletons: William Brown, Spence Waugh, Mark Wlordarkiewicz

(Greenwich House) Friday, Jan. 30–Feb. 22, 1987 (15 performances). SoHo Rep (Jerry Engelbach, Marlene Swartz, Artistic Directors) present:
SERGEANT OLA AND HIS FOLLOWERS by David Lan; Director, Tazewell Thompson; Sets, Dale Jordan; Costumes, Eiko Yamaguchi; Lighting, David Noling; Music/Sound, Deena Kaye; Props, Steve Rosse, Terry Foster; Stage Manager, Deborah A. Friedman; Press, Bruce Cohen, Kathleen von Schmid
CAST: Mark Kenneth Smaltz (Gau), Helmar Augustus Cooper (Pioba), Karen Jackson (Moro), Ladonna Mabry (Joana), Roy MacArthur (Scovill), Jonathan Peck (Ola), Brian Evaret Chandler (Mamba), Leon Addison Brown (Swansi), Charles Watts (Makis), Jaison Walker (Don), Dennis Green (Yim)
  A comedy in two acts. The action takes place in 1945 in Papua, New Guinea.

(St. Clement's Theatre) Thursday, Feb. 5–April 4, 1987 (68 performances). Music-Theatre Group (Lyn Austin, Producing Director) and the John F. Kennedy Center present:
THE HUNGER ARTIST a work in progress based on the writings of Franz Kafka; Conceived & Directed by Martha Clarke; Created with the Company; Set/Costumes, Robert Israel; Lighting, Paul Gallo; Illusions, Ben Robinson; Composer, Richard Peaslee; Adapted by Richard Greenberg; Stage Manager, Steven Ehrenberg, Elizabeth Sherman; Wardrobe, George Erdman; Press, Shirley Herz Associates/Peter Cromarty
COMPANY: Rob Besserer, Brenda Currin, Anthony Holland, Jill Jaffe, David Jon, Bill Ruyle, Paola Styron

Mark Smaltz, Karen Lois Jackson, Jonathan Earl Peck in "Sgt. Ola & His Followers" *(Gerry Goodstein)*

Below: Rob Besserer, Anthony Holland, David
Jon in "The Hunger Artist" *(Carol Rosegg)*

Ruth Jaroslow, Mitch Kreindel, Kurt Fuller,
Laura Esterman, Hy Anzell in "Kvetch"
(Martha Swope)

(Theatre Four) Friday, Feb. 6–March 15, 1987 (37 performances). CMD Productions presents:
CAST ME DOWN by J. Howard Holland; Director, Susan Watson Turner; Producers, Lucy Holland, Susan Watson Turner; Set, Lisa L. Watson; Costumes, Ali Turns; Lighting, Kathy Perkins; Sound, Richard V. Turner; Assistant to Producers, Peter Wilson; Stage Manager, P. J. Wilson; Press, Howard Atlee
CAST: Marcus Naylor (T. Thomas Fortune), Eldon Bullock (Booker T. Washington), Howard J. Garner (Emmet Scott), Shannon Baker (Samuel Chapman Armstrong), Leo V. Finnie III (Thomas Ferris)
  A play in 3 acts and 15 scenes with one intermission.

(Westside Arts Theatre) Tuesday, Feb. 10–March 15, 1987 (31 performances and 9 previews).
KVETCH written and directed by Steven Berkoff; Set, Don Llewellyn; Costumes, Ruth A. Brown; Lighting, Jason Kantrowitz; Production Coordinator, Bernard Block; General Manager, Bunni Roberts; Company Manager, Florie Seery; Technical Director, Lew Harrison; Stage Manager, Jason Fogelson; Press, Max Eisen, Madelon Rosen
CAST: Laura Esterman (Donna), Kurt Fuller (Frank), Ruth Jaroslow (Mother-in-law), Mitch Kreindel (Hal), Hy Anzell (George)
  A comedy in two acts.

(Nat Horne Theatre) Wednesday, Feb. 18–March 15, 1987 (20 performances and 2 previews). Shelter West Company (Judith Joseph, Artistic Director) presents:
TOPOKANA MARTYRS' DAY by Jonathan Falla; Director, Judith Joseph; Assistant Director, Laura Henry; Lighting, David Tasso; Sound, Kenn Dovel; Costumes, Rachel Kusnetz; Set, Merel Ray; Stage Manager, Mike Montgomery; Press, Bruce Cohen, Kathleen von Schmid
CAST: Dee Dee Friedman (Ibis), Ray Iannicelli (Apoo), Robert Jetter (Julius), William Lucas (Ramilies), and radio voices of Howard Wesson, Jane Sharp, Victor Castelli, Kenn Dovel
  A play in 2 acts. The action takes place somewhere in East Africa during 1980–81.

(Playhouse 91) Thursday, Feb. 19–April 26, 1987 (57 performances) Robert Klein and Overture Productions present:
WOMEN BEWARE WOMEN by Thomas Middleton and Howard Barker; Director, Sharon Gans; Design, Wolfgang Roth; Costumes, Ruth Morley; Lighting, Jeff Davis; Choreography, William Burdick; General Management, Frank Scardino Associates; Company Manager, Jim Brandeberry; Props, Jay Hendricks; Wardrobe, Lena Carling; Production Assistants, Mary Mournier, Andre San Million; Stage Managers, John Handy, William Castleman
CAST: Florence Winston (Leantio's Mother), Neil Maffin succeeded by Graves Kiely (Leantio), Caroline Beck (Bianca), John Heffernan (Guardiano), Marcus Powell (Fabritio), Sally Kirkland (Livia), Roy Steinberg (Hippolito), Katell Pleven (Isabella), Barry Jon Lynch (Ward), Judson Camp (Sordido), Chet London (Duke of Florence), William Newman (Cardinal), Graves Kiely succeeded by William Castleman (Messenger), Lynn Elliott (Citizen/Servant), Dede Lowe (Citizen/Servant)
   A comedy in 2 acts and 15 scenes. The action takes place in Florence, Italy, during the 17th Century and today.

(All Souls Church Theatre) Friday, Feb. 20–March 8, 1987 (16 performances). The All Souls Players (Producers, Tran Wm. Rhodes/Howard Van Der Meulen) present:
NEW GIRL IN TOWN based on the play "Anna Christie" by Eugene O'Neill; Book, George Abbott; Music & Lyrics, Bob Merrill; Director, Jeffery K. Neill; Musical Director, Wendell Kindberg; Settings, Robert Edmonds; Costumes, Sue Ellen Rohrer; Lighting, David Bean; Assistant to Director, Suzanne Kaszynski; Dance Captain, Cindy Stroud; Wardrobe, Mary Jane Gocher, Rochelle Moskowitz; Props, Julia A. Parisi; Stage Managers, Linda Panzner, Julie Polk, Scott Will
CAST: Joan Baker (Marthy), Jim Bumgardner (Alderman), Gloria Boucher (Katie/Little Girl), Debra Cardona (Ivy/Mrs. Dowling), Victor H. Ephrussi (Seaman/1st Mate/Svenson), Siobhan Fallon (Flo), Kathleen Gray (Anna Christopherson), Kevin T. Halpin (Oscar), Billy Hipkins (Pete), Pia Holm (Pearl), John Horvath (Mat Burke), Herbert Jasmine (Politician), Robert Laconi (Smith/Sailor), Lawrence Motsll (Larry/Mosher), P. J. Nelson (Lily), Tom Reiter (Johnson/Waiter/Krimp/Henry), Steven Riddle (Bernie/Bass), Laurie Sheppard (Rose/Mrs. Hammacher), Sally Sherwood (Violet/Mrs. Smith), Cindy Stroud (Moll), William Walters (Chris Christopherson)
MUSICAL NUMBERS: Roll Yer Socks Up, Anna Lilla, Sunshine Girl, On the Farm, Flings, It's Good to Be Alive, Look at 'er, Yer My Friend Aintcha?, Did You Close Your Eyes?, At the Check Apron Ball, There Ain't No Flies on Me, Ven I Valse, If That Was Love, Red Light Ballet, Chess and Checkers
   A musical in 2 acts and 17 scenes.

**Top Left: William Newman, Caroline Beck, Chet London
in "Women Beware Women"** *(Peter Cunningham)*
**Below: John Horvath, Kathleen Gray
in "New Girl in Town"** *(Sue Ellen Rohrer)*

(John Houseman Theatre) Saturday, Feb. 21–May 3, 1987 (72 performances). The Acting Company (Producing Artistic Director, John Houseman; Artistic Director, Michael Kahn; Executive Producer, Margot Harley; Associate Artistic Director, Gerald Gutierrez) in association with Everett King presents:
ON THE VERGE or The Geography of Yearning by Eric Overmyer; Director, Garland Wright; Set, John Arnone; Lighting, James F. Ingalls; Costumes, Ann Hould-Ward; Music, John McKinney; Sound, Bruce D. Cameron; Hair/Makeup, Patrik D. Moreton; Director's Assistant, Sari Ketter; Production Assistant, Fran Schwartz; Stage Managers, Robin Rumpf, Roy Harris
CAST: Lisa Banes (Mary), Patricia Hodges (Fanny), Laura Hicks (Alexandra), Tom Robbins (Grover/Alphonse/Gorge Troll/Yeti/Gus/Mme. Nhu/Mr. Coffee/Nicky Paradise), Understudies: Becky Borczon, Barry Heins
   A comedy in two acts. The play begins in 1888, in Terra Incognita.

(Triplex Theatre II) Monday Feb. 23–March 28, 1987 (16 performances). Theatre for a New Audience (Jeffrey Horowitz, Producing Director) presents:
TWELFTH NIGHT by William Shakespeare; Director, Mary B. Robinson; Original Music, Ray Leslee; Sets, Steven Saklad; Costumes, Gene Lakin; Lighting, Frances Aronson; Associate Producer, Richard Hester; Stage Manager, Renee Lutz; Press, Richard Hester
CAST: Martha Burns (Viola), Kim Staunton (Olivia), David Schramm (Malvolio), Herb Foster (Feste), Ivar Brogger (Sir Andrew), Richard Poe (Sir Toby), Angela Pietropinto (Maria), Raul Aranas, Victor Bevine, Reg E. Cathey, Michael Laswell, Lance Lewman

**Patricia Hodges, Lisa Banes, Laura Hicks
in "On the Verge"** *(Tony Triolo)*

(Kaufman Theater) Tuesday, Feb. 24–March 29, 1987 (39 performances). Martin R. Kaufman presents:
GAY DIVORCE with Music & Lyrics by Cole Porter; Book, Dwight Taylor, Kenneth Webb, Samuel Hoffenstein; Book Adaptation, Robert Brittan; Director, Robert Brink; Choreography, Helen Butleroff; Scenery, James Morgan, Costumes, Patricia Adshead; Lighting, Jeffrey Schissler; Musical Direction/Arrangements, David Schaefer; General Management, Marshall B. Purdy; Company Manager, Richard Biederman; Wardrobe, Michael Hannah; Props, Joey Loggia, John Geurts; Hairstylist, Robert W. Cybula; Stage Managers, Nadine Charlsen, Josette Amato
CAST: Paul V. Ames (Teddy Egbert), Ray DeMattis (Robert), Debra Dickinson (Mimi Pratt), Leonard Drum (Waiter), Diane J. Findlay (Hortense Howard), Christine Gradl (Gladys), Kristie Hannum (Iris), Richard Lupino (Octavius Pratt), Steven Minning (Porter), Joaquin Romaguera (Rudolfo), Peggy Taphorn (Doris), Gina Trano (Vivian), Oliver Woodall (Guy Holden), Karen Ziemba (Barbara Wyndham)
MUSICAL NUMBERS: After You Who, Please Don't Make Me Be Good, Salt Air, Why Shouldn't I, Pets, A Weekend Affair, Night and Day, How's Your Romance, My Cozy Little Corner in the Ritz, I'm in Love Again, I've Got You on My Mind, You Do Something to Me, I Love Only You, Mr. & Mrs. Fitch, You're in Love
  A musical in two acts with a prologue. The action takes place in the 1930's.

Debra Dickinson, Joaquin Romaguera, Oliver Woodall
in "Gay Divorce" *(Henry Grossman)* Top Right: Helen
Shumaker in "Mona Rogers in Person" *(Carol Rosegg)*

(Cherry Lane Theatre) Thursday, Feb. 26–April 4, 1987 (36 performances) The Hart Entertainment Group and Pamela Koslow present:
MONA ROGERS IN PERSON by Philip-Dimitri Galas; Director, Lynne Taylor-Corbett; Lighting, Mimi Jordan Sherin; General Management, Amy L. Freitag; Associate Producers, Jane Holzer, Jon Kane; Production Assistant, Anna DiStefano; Stage Manager, Lynn Moffat; Press, Shirley Herz Associates, Glenna Freedman, Peter Cromarty, Pete Sanders, David Roggensack, Miller Wright, Jillana Devine
CAST: Helen Shumaker as Mona Rogers

(Theater for the New City) Thursday, Feb. 26–March 22, 1987 (12 performances and 4 previews). Theater for the New City (Bartenieff/Field) presents:
CARRYING SCHOOL CHILDREN by Thomas Babe; Director, David Briggs; Set, James Tilton; Lighting, Peter A. West; Costumes, Daphne Stevens-Pascucci; Sound/Musical Composition/All Instruments & Vocals, Michael Brennan; Technical Director, Steven Stiler; Props, John Paino, Beth Savage; Wardrobe, Kim M. Petrozinno; Stage Managers, Daniel S. Lewin, Margaret Bodriguian; Press, Shirley Herz Associates/Pete Sanders
CAST: Fisher Stevens (Schyler Blue), Jodie Markell (Vita Truman), Scott Hitchcock (Buck Morgan), Nealla Spano (Mrs. Truman), Rush Pearson (Gorbo), Ron Eldard (Amos Spicer), Brian Zipin (Zolch Needa), Craig Zakarian (The Cadet), Paul Marcasso (Zeph Needa), Pamela Sutton (Crystal), Space Children: Rick-Anthony English, Eben Davidson, Kyla Maull, Dash Mihok, Ivan Schonfeld
  A play in two acts.

**Right: Fisher Stevens, Jodie Markell
in "Carrying School Children"** *(Adam Newman)*

(American Folk Theatre) Friday, Feb. 27–March 15, 1987 (14 performances). I Comici Confidanti (Michael Wright, Artistic Director) presents:
WHORES OF HEAVEN with Music & Lyrics by Michael Wright; Additional Lyrics, Luisa Inez Newton, David Wells, Niccolo Machiavelli; Libretto, David Wells, Luisa Inez Newton; Based on the improvisations of I Comici Confidanti on La Mandragola and other writings of Niccolo Machiavelli; Director/Choreographer, Kim Johnson; Producer, Michael Manganiello; Scenery, Jan Harvey; Costumes, Jeffrey Wallach; Orchestrations, Martin Erskine, Michael Wright; Lighting, Susan Roth; Stage Manager, Jay Kane; Press, Bruce Cohen, Kathleen von Schmid
CAST: Suzanne Parke (Arlecchino), John Dolphin (Liguro), David Carr (Siro), Dana Morosini (Raffaella), Duffy Hudson (Nicia Calfucci), Katie Geissinger (Isabella), Pam Sabrin (Sostrata), Ron Golding (Callimaco), David Wells (Father Timoteo), Cindy Foster Jones (La Cantarella)
  A comedy with song in 2 acts and 9 scenes, with prologue and epilogue. The action takes place at the point in space and time where 16th Century Florence and a mid-summer street fair in Little Italy (New York City) are most apt to intersect.

David Wells, Christopher LeBlanc, Duffy Hudson,
John Dolphin in "Whores of Heaven" *(Carol Rosegg)*

(Second Avenue Theatre) Friday, Feb. 27–June 28, 1987 (118 performance and 32 previews). John H. Williams, Ruth Mieszkuc, The Program Development Company, and the Encore A Partnership present:
STAGGERLEE with Music & Lyrics by Allen Toussaint; Book/Additional Lyrics, Vernel Bagneris; Director, Vernel Bagneris; Choreography, Pepsi Bethel; Musical Coordinator/Conductor, Allen Toussaint; Scenery, Akira Yoshimura; Costumes, JoAnn Clevenger; Lighting, Allen Lee Hughes; Sound, Paul Garrity; Associate Producer, Kirk D'Amico; General Manager, Fred Walker; Company Manager, Mary Ellyn Devery; Technical Supervisor, Michael S. Egna; Wardrobe, Joy Becker; Masks, Mike Stark; Hairstylist, Anderson Phillips; Stage Managers, Duane F. Mazey, Kenneth Hanson, Ronald Woodall; Press, Milly Schoenbaum
CAST: Adam Wade (Staggerlee), Juanita Brooks (Zelita), Ruth Brown (Elenora), Marva Hicks (June), Reginald VelJohnson (Tiny), Carol Sutton (Bertha Ann), Angeles Echols (Dolores), Christie Gaudet (Andrea), Alfred Bruce Bradley (Peat), Kevin Ramsey (Piano Player/Policeman), Bernard J. Marsh (Bone), Leon Williams (Silk), Allen Toussaint (Piano/Conductor), Understudies: Yvonne Talton Kersey (Elenora), Claire Bathe (June), Angeles Echols (Zelita), Ron Wyche (Staggerlee/Silk/Bone/Policeman/Piano Player), Kenneth Hanson (Peat/Bone)
MUSICAL NUMBERS: Iko Iko, Night People, Staggerlee, Discontented Blues, With You in Mind, Big Chief, Mardi Gras Time, A Pimp Like That, You Knew I Was No Good, Lover of Love, Saved by Grace, Happy Time, Victims of Darkness, Devil's Disguise, One Monkey Don't Stop No Show, Ruler of My Heart, Going Down Slowly, Lighting a Candle, Knocking Myself Out, We're Gonna Do It Good, Let's Live It Up

A musical in two acts. The action takes place in the late 1950's at a local corner bar in the deep South.

Top Right: Ruth Brown, Allen Toussaint in "Staggerlee" *(Martha Swope)* **Below: Shirley Knight in "The Depot"** *(Paula Allen)*

(Art & Work Ensemble Theatre) Monday, March 2–April 4, 1987 (19 performances). Fischetti Productions and Art & Work Ensemble Theatre present:
HALF THE BATTLE written and performed by Deborah Baber about Susan B. Anthony.

(Interart Theatre) Tuesday, March 3–27, 1987 (16 performances). Women's Interart Center in association with the Center for Defense Information present:
THE DEPOT by Eve Ensler; Director, Joanne Woodward; Scenic Designer, Nina Jordan; Lighting and Set Adapter, Larry Decle; Press, David Rothenberg
CAST: Shirley Knight (A Mother), Robin Erbert or Peter Gregory (A Soldier)
Perfomed without intermission. The action takes place at a missile sight located near any large city in the United States.

Right: Mia Dillon, Reed Birney in "Lady Moonsong, Mr. Monsoon" *(Carol Rosegg)*

(Westbeth Theatre Center) Saturday, March 7–29, 1987 (21 performances). Practical Cats Theatre Company (Artistic Director, Alice Eve Cohen; Managing Director, Polly Kahn) presents:
LADY MOONSONG, MR. MONSOON by Alice Eve Cohen; Music composed by Miss Cohen; Director, David Saint; Choreography, Paul Thompson; Sets, Alexander Okun; Costumes, Madeline Cohen; Lighting, Donald Holder; Casting, Jeff Solis; Stage Managers, Jane Grey, Billy Barnes; Press, Bruce Cohen, Kathleen von Schmid
CAST: Mia Dillon (Lady Moonsong), Reed Birney (Mr. Monsoon), George Ashiotis (Fish), Rick Lawless (Apprentice), Ennis Dexter Locke (Guard), Steven Silverstein (Musician)

(INTAR) Wednesday, March 11–April 5, 1987 (28 performances). INTAR Hispanic American Arts Center (Max Ferra, Artistic Director; Dennis Ferguson-Acosta, Managing Director) and the New York Shakespeare Festival (Joseph Papp, Producer) present:
ROOSTERS by Milcha Sanchez-Scott; Director, Jackson Phippin; Set, Loy Arcenas; Lighting, John Gisondi; Costumes, C. L. Hundley; Sound, Janet Kalas; Fight Direction, Nels Hennum; Dialect Consultant, Tim Monich; Associate Producer, Jason Steven Cohen; Fight Captain, Albert Farrar; Production Assistants, Carlos Jimenez, Jenny Peek; Stage Manager, Michele Steckler; Press, Bruce Cohen, Kathleen von Schmid
CAST: Joaquim DeAlmeida (Gallo), Jonathan Del Arco (Hector), Sara Erde (Angela), Suzanne Costallos (Juana), Ilka Tanya Payan (Chata), Albert Farrar (Adan)
A play in two acts. The action takes place at the present time somewhere in the Southwest.

Sara Erde, Jonathan Del Arco in "Roosters" *(Carol Rosegg)*

(Ernie Martin Studio Theatre) Friday, March 13–29, 1987 (15 performances). The American Boys Company presents:
THE AMERICAN BOYS . . . or The Gamecocks by Joshua Danese; Director, Angela Foster; Producer, Alison Zimet; Original Music, Mr. Foote & J. D. Edwards; Performed by Mr. Foote and the Punch Band; Set, Michael Kostroff; Lighting, Elaine O'Donnell; Assistant Director, Michael Fife; Stage Managers, Paula Gray, Stuart Leigh; Press, FLT/Francine Trevens
CAST: Joshua Danese (Isaiah), David Schachter (Harold), Michael Kostroff (Robin), John Ryker O'Hara (Justin), Nancy Sorel (Debra), Mary Cushman (Sharon), Suzanne O'Rourke (Mimi), Tess Curtis (Courtney, Understudies: Stuart Leigh, Peggy O'Toole
   A comedy in two acts. The action takes place at the present time in and around campus and off-campus of a major university.

Top Right: Mary Cushman, Suzanne O'Rourke,
Michael Kostroff in "The American Boys"
(David Zimet) **Below: Erika Naj, Jonathan**
Goldstein, Richard Long in "Angel City"
(Carol Rosegg)

(Ohio Theatre) Friday, March 13–April 12, 1987 (16 performances each in repertory). Project III Ensemble Theatre presents:
ANGEL CITY by Sam Shepard; Director, David Petrarca; Costumes, Cathy Zuber
CAST: Jonathan Goldstein, Carlo Novi, Richard Long, Steven Haworth, Erika Naj, Bill Fichner

Sunday, March 15,–April 12, 1987 (16 performances).
BLISS by Mikhail Bulgakov; Director, Charles Otte; English translation, Mirra Ginsburg; Set, Tom Kamm; Costumes, Susan Lyall; Production Manager, Robert Lyons; Original Music, Charles Notte/Carlo Novi; Stage Manager, Kenneth Smith; Press, Bruce Cohen, Kathleen von Schmid
CAST: Jonathan Baker, Christine Carter, Sal Candido, Carissa Channing, Will Kepper, Neil Larson, Franca Barchiesi, Elizabeth Gee, Carlo Novi, Evan Press, Amy Rhodes, Robin Siemens, John Siemens, Christopher Shaw, Jeffrey Steefel

(The Kittredge Club) Saturday, March 14–22, 1987 (6 performances) The Maxine B. Production of:
THE NEW ODD COUPLE by Neil Simon; Director, Ray Bonett; Scenic Designer, Claus Oleson; Stage Manager, John O'Hare
CAST: Laine Valentino (Sylvie), Pitty Jennings (Mickey), Kate Stillwell (Renee), Jeanie Columbo (Vera), Marianne Mangan (Olive Madison), Sharon O'Neal (Florence Ungar), Don Striano (Manolo Costazuela), Randy Schein (Jesus Costazuela)
   A comedy in 2 acts and 4 scenes. The action takes place at the present time in Olive Madison's Riverside Drive apartment in New York City.

(Morse Center Theatre) March 19–29, 1987 (12 performances). The Actors' Space (Alan Langdon, Artistic Director) presents:
THE TWO GENTLEMEN OF VERONA by William Shakespeare; Director, Alan Langdon; Sets, Robert Briggs; Costumes, Elizabeth Kate Shelton; Lighting, Peggy Lei Mueller; Original Music, Paul Sullivan; Stage Manager, Linda Carol Young
CAST: Richard Glockner (Valentine), Dan Baum (Proteus), David McCullough (Antonio/Outlaw), Miles Herter (Panthino/Eglamoure), Richard Maynard (Speed), Ernie Shaheen (Launce), Kathryn Dickinson (Julia), Joan Rosenfels (Lucetta), Lisa Altomare (Hostess), Elizabeth Browning (Silvia), Lee Milinazzo (Ursula/ Understudy), Paul Garrett (Thurio), Harold Shepard (Duke), Tony DeMarco, Christopher Innvar (Henchmen), Michael Schaefer (Crab/Outlaw)
   Performed with one intermission. The action takes place during the 1950's in Verona and Milan, Italy.

(Theatre 890) Thursday, March 19–April 5, 1987 (3 performances and 10 previews). The Shubert Organization (Gerald Schoenfeld, Chairman; Bernard B. Jacobs, President) presents:
STANDUP SHAKESPEARE conceived by Ray Leslee, Kenneth Walsh; Music, Ray Leslee; Words, William Shakespeare; Staged by Mike Nichols; Setting, John Arnone; Lighting, Mitchell Bogard; Costumes, Cynthia O'Neal; Sound, Barbara U. Schwartz; Musical Direction/Orchestrations/Arrangements, Ray Leslee; Vocal Arrangements, Thomas Young; General Manager, Albert Poland; Company Manager, Bruce Klinger; Production Assistants, Paul King, Ingrid Veninger; Makeup/Hair, Manuel Rodriguez; Stage Managers, Zane Weiner, Frank DiFilia; Press, Bill Evans, Sandra Manley, Jim Randolph
CAST: Taborah Johnson, Kenneth Welsh, Thomas Young, and the Band: Jack Bashkow, Marshall Coid, Dean Johnson, Ray Leslee
   Performed without intermission.

Right Center: Kathryn Dickinson, Daniel Baum,
Elizabeth Browning, Lee Milinazzo in "Two Gentlemen
of Verona" *(Rebecca Lesher)*

Taborah Johnson, Thomas Young, Kenneth Welsh
in "Standup Shakespeare" *(Peter Cunningham)*

(Shakespeare Center) Thursday, March 19–April 5, 1987 (12 performances). The Classic Theatre (Nicholas John Stathis, Executive Director; Adda C. Gogoris, Associate Producer) presents:
THE JEW OF MALTA by Christopher Marlowe; Director, Maurice Edwards; Set, Peter R. Reuche; Lighting, Clay Shirky; Fight Sequences, Joseph Travers; Costumes, Deirdre E. Donohue; Music/Sound, Daniel Hart; Assistant Directors, Christine MacDonald, Tobi Kanter; Technical Director, David von Salis; Props/Sound, Debbie Gantert; Stage Manager, Lynn Vaag; Press, Bruce Cohen, Kathleen von Schmid
CAST: Michael Graves (Machiavelli/Ferneze), Owen S. Rackleff (Barabas), Brenda Lynn Bynum (Abigail, his daughter), Charles Geyer (Ithamore/1st Jew/Carpenter), Dan Lutzky (Selim-Calymath/Friar Jacomo), Greg Houston (Callipine/Friar Bernadine), Joseph Travers (Don Lodowick), Robert Tyrone (Don Mathias/2nd Merchant), Hans Goldfuss (Martin Del Bosco/Merchant/Bashaw), Richard Dahlia (Pilia-Broza/Jew/Carpenter), Frances Peter (Katherine/Abbess), Lillian Richards (Bellamira), Katherine Mayfield (Sonia/1st Nun), Stanley Winston (Jew/Slave Marketeer/Carpenter), Taso Stavrakis (Knight/Slave/Messenger), Jeff Robins (Officer, Tobi Kanter (Nun)
Performed with one intermission. The action takes place in Malta circa 1931.

(Theatre Four) Thursday, March 19–April 5, 1987 (15 performances). RTTR Limited Partnership presents the Loaves and Fish Theater Company (Artistic Director, Douglas Farren; Managing Director, Charles duMas) production of:
RETURN TO THE RIVER by Charles duMas; Director, Douglas Farren; Set, B. B. Burnham; Lighting, Dominick Balletta; Sound, Jo Farrell; Costumes, Marcia Belton; Original Music, John McCallum; Company Manager, Seret Scott; Wardrobe, Mary Doyle, Lynn Nonnenmacher; Technical Director, Norman Carlberg; Stage Manager, Dominick Balletta; Press, Howard Atlee
CAST: Michael Haney (Mike Neal), W. Allen Taylor (Al Gilroy), Joe Viviani (Fred Knight), Gail O'Blenis Dukes (Angela Manley), Nikki Barthen (Sarah Myers), Dan Kelley (Coffee Dan), Jonathan Peck (Odabi)
A play in two acts. The action takes place at the present time in the offices of CRT Corporation, a large oil company in California.

Brenda Lynn Bynum, Owen S. Rackleff in "The Jew of Malta" *(Robert Feiner)* Left Center: **Michael Morrison, Marisa Tomei in "Beirut"** *(Carol Rosegg)*

(18th Street Playhouse) Sunday, March 22–April 15, 1987 (10 performances and 6 previews). Bridge Arts (Gibson Glass, Producing Artistic Director; Tim Habeger, Artistic Director) presents:
FIRE IN THE BASEMENT by Pavel Kohout; Director, Tim Habeger; Set, Geoffrey D. Freeman; Stage Manager, Timothy Joseph; Press, FLT/Francine Trevens; Costumes, NYC Fire Department
CAST: Tarn Magnuson (Engl), Amy Denis (Jartchi), Ian Schneiderman (Vodicka), Michael Juzwak (Hurnik), Stephen Falat (Janik), Bert Goldstein (Tvrznik)
A "black comedy" performed without intermission.

(Nat Horne Theatre) Monday, March 23–April 12, 1987 (19 performances and 7 previews). Manhattan Class Company (Executive Directors, Robert LuPone, Bernard Telsey) present:
CLASS 1 ACTS: Producers, Will Cantler, Pat Skipper; Associate Producer, Christopher A. Smith; Production Managers, Laura Kravets, Laura Young; Casting, Bernard Telsey, Laurel Smith; Technical Director, Tony Georgan; Scenery, Betsy Doyle; Lighting, John Hastings; Costumes, Ashley Fraser, Baden; Sound, Elliott Forrest; Stage Managers, Maria Schlanger, Georgett Lewis, Lillian Butler, Maria Kliavkoff; Press, G. Theodore Killmer
EVENING A: *Language as Communication* by John Angell Grant; Director, Brian Mertes; with Pat Skipper (The Man). *Tuba Solo* by Michael Lynch; Director, Pam Pepper; with Brenda Curtis (Maggie), James Doerr (Lewis). *Beirut* by Alan Bowne; Director, Jimmy Bohr; with Michael David Morrison (Torch), Marisa Tomei (Blue), Terry Rabine (Patrol).
EVENING B: *Where Have All the Virgins Gone?* by Anna Theresa Cascio; Director, Kevin Kelley; with Jaclyn Ross (A Woman). *A Capella Hardcore* by Erik Ehn; Director, Janet Herzenberg; Music, Chris Kowanko; Choreography, Karen MacIntyre; with Ken Marks (Average), Simon Brooking (Below Average), Kathryn Hunter (B. B.), Mark Hymen (Ott), Kathleen McCall (Sheila), Kent Adams (Tay-O), Robin Robson (Walt). *Lurker* by Don Nigro; Director, Roy B. Steinberg; with Mary B. Ward (Lil), Robert LuPone (Marston). *Sister Gloria's Pentecostal Baby* by Michael Lynch; Director, Will Cantler; with Gary B. Sauer (Jimmy Fawcett), John Conley (Sgt. Phillips), James Mathers (Garvin Fawcett), Christine Jones (Gloria Fawcett)

(Greenwich House) March 27–April 19, 1987 (16 performances). SoHo Repertory Theatre (Artistic Directors, Jerry Engelbach, Marlene Swartz) presents:
THE MOCK DOCTOR or The Dumb Lady Cured adapted from Moliere's "The Doctor in spite of Himself" by Henry Fielding, and **EURYDICE** by Henry Fielding; Direction/Music, Anthony Bowles; Sets, Joseph A. Varga; Costumes, Michael S. Schler; Lighting, David Noling; Choreography, Gillian Gregory; Stage Manager, Andrea Nugit; Press, Bruce Cohen, Kathleen von Schmid
CAST: *The Mock Doctor:* Mark Kenneth Smaltz (Gregory), Anna Lank (Dorcas), Dane Knell (Robert), Steve Sterner (Harry), Jim Bracchitta (James), Nicholas Saunders (Sir Jasper), Dee Ann McDavid (Nurse), Denise Dillard (Charlotte), Martin Moran (Leander), Dane Knell (Davy/Hellebore). *Eurydice* with Jim Bracchita (Author), Nicholas Saunders (Critic), Steve Sterner (Capt. Weazel), Martin Moran (Spindle), Denise Dillard (Eurydice), Kane Knell (Pluto), Dee Ann McDavid (Proserpine), Tory Alexander (Orpheus), Mark Kenneth Smaltz (Charon), Anna Lank (Dancing Devil)

Cast of "A Capella Hardcore"
(Carol Rosegg)

(Baldwin Theatre) Sunday, March 29–April 26, 1987 The Baldwin Theatre (Anita Sorel, Artistic Director) presents:
DAY SIX by Martin Halpern; Director, Louis D. Pietig; Scenery, Barry Axtell; Lighting, Donald Edmund Thomas; Costumes, Elsa Ward; Sound, Jeffrey Allgeier; Stage Managers, Cindy Weissler, Michele Hayes, Felicia Shpall
CAST: Len Cariou (David Porter), Heather Summerhayes (Eleanor Manning)

(Astor Place Theatre) Wednesday, April 1–19, 1987 (14 performances and 9 previews). ERB Productions (Melvyn J. Estrin/Susan R. Rose/Gail Berman), Joan Stein, The Seco Production Company (P. L. Seidman, Gary D. Cohn), John Roach present:
TENT MEETING by Rebecca Wackler, Larry Larson, Levi Lee; Director, Norman Rene; Set, Andrew Jackness; Costumes, Walker Hicklin; Lighting, Paul Gallo; Sound, James M. Bay; Associate Producers, Judie Amsterdam, Elysa Lazar; General Management, Gail Berman, Susan Rose, Joan Stein; Company Manager, Helen V. Meier; Hairstylist, Emmanuel Rodriguez; Wardrobe, Hartsel Taylor; Props, Melissa Badger; Production Assistant, Judith Verno; Casting, Deborah Brown; Stage Managers, Jerry Bihm, Tina Smith; Press, Henry Luhrman, Terry M. Lilly, Andrew P. Shearer, Susan Chicoine, Anne Holmes
CAST: Levi Lee (Reverend Ed), Larry Larson (Darrell), Rebecca Wackler (Becky Ann), Tina Smith (Understudy for Becky Ann)
 A play in two acts. The action takes place in 1946 outside a laboratory at the University of Arkansas; in Moose Jaw Saskatchewan; and on the road in between

Larry Larson, Levi Lee, Rebecca Wackler
in "Tent Meeting" *(Peter Cunningham)*

Left Center: Nealla Spano, Paul Collins, Kevin
Spacey, Joanne Camp in "As It Is in Heaven"
(Bob Marshak)

(Perry Street Theatre) Wednesday, April 1–25, 1987 (10 performances and 11 previews). New York Theatre Workshop (Artistic Director, Jean Passanante) presents:
AS IT IS IN HEAVEN by Joe Sutton; Director, Mark Lutwak; Set, Richard Hoover; Costumes, Walker Hicklin; Lighting, John Gisondi; Composer, Wayne Horvitz; Casting, Ellen Novack; Production Assistants, Maria Gillen, David Fuhrer; Technical Director, John Paul Guerts; Props, John Sullivan; Stage Manager, Virginia Addison; Press, Milly Schoenbaum, Brian Drutman
CAST: Joanne Camp (Liz Barfield), Kevin Spacey (Mitch Pikus), Paul Collins (Dick Wisner), Nealla Spano (Lee Enfield), Alan Scarfe (Jack Bross), Stephen Harrison (Rev. "Rat" Patterson)
 A play in seven scenes with one intermission. The action takes place the year before presidential election year in a guest lodge on a mountaintop estate somewhere in the Rocky Mountains.

(CSC Repertory Theatre) Friday, April 3–18, 1987 (14 performances). Musical Theatre Works (Artistic Director, Anthony J. Stimac; Associate Artistic Director, Mark Herko) presents:
ABYSSINIA with Music by Ted Kociolek; Lyrics, James Racheff; Book, James Racheff, Ted Kociolek; Based on novel "Marked by Fire" by Joyce Carol Thomas; Director, Tazewell Thompson; Casting, Mark Herko; Scenery, Evelyn Sakash; Lighting, Clarke W. Thornton; Costume Consultant, Amanda Klein; Musical Supervision/Choral Arrangements, Daryl Waters; Choreography Consultant, Julie Arenal; Stage Manager, Greta Minsky; Press, Bruce Cohen, Kathleen von Schmid
CAST: Jennifer Leigh Warren (Abyssinia Jackson), Tina Fabrique (Mother Vera), Cheryl Freeman (Patience Jackson), Lehman Beneby (Minister), Karen Jackson (Trembling Sally), Zelda Pulliam (Lilly Noreen), LaDonna Mabry (Selma), Connie Fredericks (Mavis), Bambi Jones (Corine), Jaison Walker (Marcus), Clyde Jones (Leon), Roderick Cloud (Jesse), Stanley Earl Harrison (Brother Samuels), Zelda Pulliam (Mother Samuels)
MUSICAL NUMBERS: Rise and Fly, Song of the Field, Abyssinia, Lift Up Your Voice!, Song of Mother Samuels, Recipe, There Has to Be a Reason, The Sound of a Ragtime Band, I Have Seen the Wind, Blackberry Wine, Cry, Lightnin' Bug, Abby's Lament, Pickin' Up the Pieces, Get Thee Behind Me Satan, Sister of Healing, Honey and Lemon, Finale
 A musical in 2 acts and 15 scenes. The action takes place some time in the past in rural Oklahoma.

Tina Fabrique, Jennifer Lee Warren, Karen Jackson
in "Abyssinia" *(Rita Katz)*

(Duo Theatre) Friday, April 3–26, 1987 (12 performances). Duo Theatre (Manuel Martin, Jr., Executive/Artistic Director) presents:
SALON with Book & Lyrics by Michael Alasa; Music, David Welch; Directors, Michael Alasa, Christopher Markle; Set, Dain Marcus; Costumes, Natalie Barth Walker; Lighting, Joanna Schielke; Assistant Director/Stage Manager, Mary Lisa Kinney; Musical Director, Joe Baker
CAST: Jody Walker-Lichtig (Athenais Longet), Jacqueline Bertrand (Kitty), Lynne Charnay (Misia Sert), Juliette Koka (Coco Chanel), Mark Lotito (Francisco Goya), Nila Greco (Marie-Laure), Luciano Valerio (Jean Cocteau), Blanca Camacho (Clothilde/Marie-Antoinette), Catherine Lippencott (Reporter), Missy Baldino (Marie-Antoinette 2), Ovidio Vargas (Servant/Sailor)
MUSICAL NUMBERS: Paris, Can-Can, An Adventure, What Remains, Details, Seek and Ye Shall Find, Images, Nature of Art, Don't Let Go of His Arm, Paris about to Fall, Joie de Vivre, Come the Revolution, Salon, Bibi Paco, Always, Final Arrangements, New York Is about to Fall, Where Do We Go from Here?, In Between the Lines, Something to Remember You By, Finale

(The Duplex) Sunday, April 5, 1987—and still playing at press time. Next Wave Management (David Musselman/Mary T. Nealon) in association with Laric Entertainment presents:
BITTERSUITE with Music by Elliot Weiss; Lyrics, Michael Champagne; Director, Mr. Champagne; Costumes, Judy Dearing; Musical Direction, Elliot Weiss; Associate Musical Director, Steve Flaherty; Executive Producer, Next Wave Management; Company Manager, Edward J. Nelson; Sound/Lighting, Clay Coury, Matt Burman, Linda Wallen; Stage Manager, Mary-Susan Gregson; Press, Henry Luhrman, Terry M. Lilly, Susan Chicoine, Andrew P. Shearer, Anne Holmes
CAST: Claudine Cassan-Jellison, Joy Franz, John Jellison, Joseph Neal
MUSICAL NUMBERS: The Bittersuite, The Life That Jack Built, You're Not Getting Older, Our Favorite Restaurant, John's Song, Soap Opera, The Recipe, Ice Cream, Win and Lose, Fathers and Sons, Mama Don't Cry, Snap Back, The Cliche Waltz, The Apology, Narcissism Rag, Dungeons and Dragons, Twentieth Reunion, I'll Be There, How Little We've Learned, World without End, Flight of the Phoenix
  "Songs of Experience" in two acts.

Left: John Jellison, Joy Franz, Joseph Neal, Claudine Cassan-Jellison in "Bittersuite"
(Peter Cunningham) **Top: Juliette Koka in "Salon"**

(Harold Clurman Theatre) Tuesday, April 7–26, 1987 (16 performances). Cactus Theatre and Patrick Johnson present:
HENHOUSE by Bo Brinkman; Director, Linda Nerine; Scenery, Greg Mercurio; Music, Carmen Yates, Tony Fortuna; Costumes, Debra Trout; Lighting, Dennis M. Size; Set, Daniel Conway; Technical Director, Mark Porter; Company Manager, Henry Wyatt; Props, Lindsay Stevens; Stage Manager, Sonya Smith; Press, Pieter O'Brien
CAST: Jen Jones (Evelyn), Jayne Chamberlin (Annalee), Betty Pelzer (Gaither), Eric Uhler (Wayne), Stan Tracy (Rev. Birk), Nickie Feliciano (Pedro), Vincent Procida (Henry), Frank Vohs (Ham)
    A drama in 2 acts and 7 scenes. The action takes place in Southeast Texas in the living room of an old run-down wood frame house on the edge of an oil refinery district.

(Theater for the New City) Wednesday, April 8–26, 1987 (12 performances). Theater for the New City (Artistic/Managing Director, George Bartenieff; Executive Artistic Director, Crystal Field; Executive Director, Harvey Seifter) presents:
THE HEART THAT EATS ITSELF by Rosalyn Drexler; Director, John Vaccaro; Costumes, Gabriel Berry; Set, Abe Lubelski; Lighting, Jeffrey Nash; Music, John Braden; Props, Noel MacFetrich; Musical Direction, Zecca; Stage Managers, Danny Dragon, Jo Ann Cutrera, Christopher DeSanto; Press, Shirley Herz, Pete Sanders, Peter Cromarty, Glenna Freedman, David Roggensack
CAST: John Barilla (Baker/Doctor/Clown), George Bartenieff (Franz Kafka), Tom Cayler (Hunger Artist), Richard Ellis (Camill Czeck), Crystal Field (Dora/Emma), Don Harrington (Impressario), Alexa Hunter (Old Woman/Nurse/Clown/Showgirl), Jill Kotler (Rose/Clown/Showgirl), Michael Sollenberger (Max/Butcher/Clown/Overseer), Tom Todoroff (Accountant/Clown/Attendant), David Joe Wirth (Georg von Schonerer)
    The action takes place in the early 1920's in Kierling and Prague.

Tom Cayler, Don Harrington in "The Heart That Eats Itself"
(Adam Newman)

(Lamb's Theatre) Saturday, April 11–July 19, 1987 (103 performances and 12 previews). Nancy E. Diamond in association with Hieronymus Foundation, and Universal Artists Management presents:

FUNNY FEET conceived by Bob Bowyer; Creative Supervision, Art Wolff; Direction/Choreography, Bob Bowyer; General Management, Joseph Harris Associates; Dance Captain, Irene Cho; Wardrobe, Valerie Gladstone, Dawn Walnut; Scenery/Costumes, Lindsay W. Davis; Lighting, Arden Fingerhut; Sound, Bruce Ellman; Casting, Dube/Zakin; Associate Producers, Andrea Pullman, Pearl Tisman Minsky; Stage Managers, Vincent Paul, Elizabeth Heeden; Press, Shirley Herz, Glenna Freedman, Peter Cromarty, Pete Sanders, David Roggensack, Miller Wright, Jillana Devine

CAST: Wilton Anderson, Matthew Baker, Bob Bowyer, Veronica Castonguay, Sandra Chinn, Irene Cho, Martha Connerton, Amy Flodd, Zane Rankin, D. Kevin Rhind

MUSICAL NUMBERS: Black Cockroach Pas de Deux, Jacques and Jeannine, Baby Bobby's Backyard, La Stampa de Feeta, Les Jazz Chics, Duet for Mating Organisms, Molotov Brothers, Remembrance Waltz, Pas de Trois pour la Psychologie Contemporaine, The Buttercups, Smile, Faux Pas de Trois, The Big Ballet in the Sky
Performed without intermission.

Zane Rankin (above), Bob Bowyer
Right: D. Kevin Rhind, Veronica Castonguay
in "Funny Feet" *(Martha Swope)*

(No Smoking Playhouse) Wednesday, April 15–May 9, 1987 (16 performances).
ON EXTENDED WINGS by Sara Brooks; Adapted from a memoir by Diane Ackerman; Director, John Camera; Sets/Lighting, David Tasso; Sound/Music, Kenn Dovel; Costume Consultant, Sis Obidowski; General Management, Whitbell/Gail Bell; Stage Manager, Joanna Mulkern; Press, Bruce Cohen, Kathleen von Schmid
CAST: Norma Jean Giffin (Diane), Neil Lyons (Brad), Richard Willis (Tom), Jeff Vaughn (Martin)

A play in two acts. The action takes place over a period of one year, in and around the flight offices of Ithaca Airport (New York) and Williamsburg/Jamestown Airport (Virgina) . . . and in the sky.

Neil Lyons, Norma Jean Giffin
in "On Extended Wings" *(Carol Rosegg)*

Jeff Vaughn, Norma Jean Giffin
in "On Extended Wings" *(Carol Rosegg)*

(Actors Outlet Theatre) Thursday, April 16–May 9, 1987 (16 performances). Actors Outlet Theatre (Artistic Director, Ken Lowstetter; Executive Director, Eleanor Segan) presents:
BLACK MEDEA: A Tangle of Serpents by Ernest Ferlita; Director, Ken Lowstetter; Producer, Eleanor Segan; Musical Designer/Assistant Director, Bonnie Devlin; Choreography, Mari Nobles Da Silva; Costumes, Ellen Ryba; Set/Lighting, Eric Veenstra; Technical Director, Randall Etheredge; Stage Manager, Julianne Flynn; Press, FLT/Francine Trevens, Billy Lope
CAST: Daniel Barton (Pierre LaGuerre), Lee Beltzer (Croydon), Stephanie Berry (Hunsi), David Jeffreys (Jerome), Monica Parks (Hunsi), Essene R (Madeleine), Cheryl Ann Scott (Hunsi), Brenda Thomas (Tante Emilie), Bells & Drums: Bonnie Devlin, Batcha Cates, Donna Allegro, Robin Loeb
   A play in two acts. The action takes place in 1810 in the French Quarter of New Orleans, Louisiana.

(Courtyard Theatre) Saturday, April 18–May 10, 1987 (15 performances and 3 previews). The Actors Collective (Warren Manzi, Artistic Director) presents:
PERFECT CRIME by Warren Manzi; Director, Jeffrey Hyatt; Producers, Marc Lutsky, Perry Pirkkanen; Set, Chris Pickart; Sound, Phil Lee, Scott G. Miller; Lighting, John Sellars; Costume Design, Barbara Blackwood; Stage Managers, Tim Pritchard, Max Koltuv; Fight Choreography, G. Gordon Cronce; Press, Dolph Browning
CAST: Cathy Russell (Margaret Thorne), Perry Pirkkanen (Inspector James Ascher), G. Gordon Cronce (W. Harrison Brent), Marc Lutsky (Lionel McAuley), W. MacGregor King (David Breuer)
   A mystery in 2 acts and 7 scenes. The action takes place at the present time in and around the living room of the Brent home in Windsor Locks, Connecticut, an out-of-the-way wealthy community.

**Cheryl Ann Scott, Stephanie Berry, Essene R
in "Black Medea"** (*Adam Newman*)

**Laurie Metcalf, Austin Pendleton
in "Educating Rita"** (*Martha Swope*)

(18th Street Theatre) Monday, April 20–May 13, 1987 (16 performances). Bridge Arts (Producing Artistic Director, Gibson Glass; Artistic Director, Tim Habeger) presents:
TRANSFORMATIONAL COUNTRY DANCES by Penelope Prentice; Director, Gibson Glass; Costumes, Judy Hugentobler; Set, Geoffery Freeman; Stage Manager, Wesley Richmond; Press, FLT/Francine Trevens
CAST: Mim Solberg (Manya), William Charlton (Kevin), Julianne Ramaker (Maryanna), Ron Tomme (Dominic), Mary McTigue (Miriam), Stephen Falat (Harry), Lauren Joseph (Tara), Alec Nemser (Gregory)
   A play in 2 acts and 7 scenes. The action takes place at the present time in Dominic and Maryanna's country home

(Westside Arts Theatre) Wednesday, April 22–July 19, 1987 (85 performances and 16 previews). Raymond L. Gaspard presents the Steppenwolf Theatre Company production of:
EDUCATING RITA by Willy Russell; Director, Jeff Perry; Associate Producer, Marc Sferrazza; Production Supervisor, Sam Ellis; Set/Lighting, Kevin Rigdon; Costumes, Erin Quigley; Original Music, Ray Leslee; Technical Director, Benno Schoeberth; Managing Director, Clover Swann; Sound/Stage Manager, Jeffrey Webb; Press, Robert Ganshaw
CAST: Austin Pendleton succeeded by Milo O'Shea (Frank), Laurie Metcalf succeeded by Kitty Sullivan (Rita)
   A comedy in two acts. The action takes place at the present time in a first-floor room in a university in the north of England.

(INTAR Theatre) Thursday, April 23–May 17, 1987 (16 performances). The City Troupe (Artistic Director, Time Vode) presents:
READY OR NOT with Music/Lyrics/Book by Michael Smit; Director, Tim Vode; Set, Stephen Caldwell; Lighting, Dennis W. Moyes; Costumes, C. Jane Epperson; Casting, Mark B. Simon; Choreography, Keith Michael; Musical Direction/Arrangements, Paul L. Johnson; Technical Director, Michael J. Kondrat; Props, Myrna Duarte; Stage Managers, Charlie Siedenburg, Donna Jo Fuller, John Oliver; Press, Cynthia Kirk
CAST: Michael DeVries (Robert Dennison), Mark Roland (Steven Dennison), Pamela McLernon (Jenny), Colleen Fitzpatrick (Lauren Harper), Melinda Tanner (Maggie Potter), Alie Smith (Mary Ellen), Charles Hettinger (Frank Dekker), Nick Locilento (George Dekker), Suzanne Hevner (Tina Dekker), Robert Tiffany (Cab Schneider), Gail Titunik (Mrs. Schneider), Ensemble: Kirsten Lind, Greg Hellems, Marianne Ferrari, Jody Abrahams, Gail Titunik, Robert Tiffany, Suzanne Hevner, Nick Locilento
MUSICAL NUMBERS: Watery Blue, They're Going Sailing, A Way of Showing I Love You, Does He Think of Her, The Arrangement, Daddy, Prayer Chain, The Samba, Quartet, From Here to Here, Villains of History, Gradfather Clock in the Hall, It Didn't Used to Be This Way, Am I Nuts, The Lake, State Fair, Lord We Thank Thee, Aeronautics Revelation, Ready or Not, I Have to Tell You, Take the Boat, I Knew I Could Fly, The Fog, Jenny, Finale
A dramatic musical in 2 acts. The action takes place in the early 1950's in Maisonville, a small town near the Great Lakes.

(Musical Theatre Works) Thursday, April 23–May 17, 1987 (16 performances). Solstice Productions presents:
A CHASTE MAID IN CHEAPSIDE by Thomas Middleton; Director, Dennis Thread; Music, Robert Casel; Costumes, Chelsea Harriman; Movement, Lynn Krigbaum; Dramaturg/Set, Greg Tishar; Stage Manager, Lynne Harris
CAST: Jody Catlin, Paul Edwards, Eddie L. Furs, Sheila Gordon, Helen Halsey, Charles Michael Howard, Susan Jeffers, Robert Johnson, Dale Keever, Nancy Lipner, Mark Lowe, Paul Mantell, Nancy McDonald, Morton Milder, Michael Proft, Linda Shirley, Douglas Simes

Michael DeVries, Pamela McLernon, Mark Roland
in "Ready or Not" *(Cynthia Kirk)*

(All Soul's Church Theatre) Friday, April 24,–May 10, 1987 (15 performances). The All Souls Players presents:
THE LITTLE SHOW AND FRIENDS: The Intimate Revues of Dietz & Schwartz; Words, Howard Dietz; Music, Arthur Schwartz; Sketches, Howard Dietz/Charles Sherman, Moss Hart, George S. Kaufman, Kaufman/Dietz, William Miles/Donald Blackwell; Director, David McNitt; Choreography, Linda Panzer; Musical Directors, Joyce Hitchcock/David Lahm; Costumes, Virginia Wood; Lighting, David Bean; Conceived and Produced by Tran William Rhodes; Stage Managers, Douglas Gettel, Robbie Coppola, Michael McCurry; Dance Captain, John Corker; Technical Director, David Bean
CAST: Patricia Berg, Jim Bumgardner, John Corker, Beth Crook, Siobhan Fallon, Nathan Gibson, Clay Guthrie, Marion Markham, Jeff Paul, Jeff Shonert, John Sullivan, Alphie Thorn, Ellen Zachos, Madeline Zeiberg
MUSICAL NUMBERS & SKETCHES: It Better Be Good, Prologue to "The Little Show," Right at the Start of It, New Sun in the Sky, Alone Together, The Pride of the Claghornes, I See Your Face Before Me, Confession, Thief in the Night, Better Luck Next Time, Don't Go Away Monsieur, To Remember You By, On the American Plan, Triplets, Hoops, Lucky Seven, I Love Louisa, Haunted Heart, First Prize at the Fair, Blue Grass, Miserable with You, In Marbled Halls, Smokin' Reefers, I Guess I'll Have to Change My Plan, Lost in a Crowd, Mother Told Me So, By Myself, The Still Alarm, A Shine on Your Shoes, Sing a Lament, High and Low, Dancing in the Dark, Right at the End of It, That's Entertainment
Presented in two acts.

(American Folk Theater) Friday, April 24–May 31, 1987 (16 performances). American Folk Theater (Dick Gaffield, Artistic Director) presents:
BIRTH RITES by Elaine Jackson; Director, June Pyskacek; Set, Felix Cochren; Costumes, Natalie Barth Walker; Lighting, Peter Anderson; Sound, Steven Menasche; Technical Director, Darren Cole; Stage Managers, Tom Jarus, Edwin Todd; Press, G. Theodore Killmer
CAST: Eva Lopez (Perez), Arlene Roman (Guerra), Lola Loui (Louise), Jennifer Joseph (Ruth), Alta Withers (Johnson), Shelley Delaney (Dr. Rubin), John Bakos (Dr. Jessup), Suzen Murakoshi (Wong), Gladys D. McQueen (Beaucour)
A play in 2 acts and 5 scenes. The action takes place at the present time in a New York City hospital.

Eva Lopez, Arlene Roman, Alta Withers
in "Birth Rites" *(Terrance Carney)*

(CSC THEATRE) Friday, April 24–May 9, 1987 (16 performances). Musical Theatre Works (Artistic Director, Anthony J. Stimac; Associate Artistic Director, Mark Herko) presents:
STARMITES with Music & Lyrics by Barry Keating; Book, Stuart Ross, Barry Keating; Director, Mark Herko; Scenery, Evelyn Sakash; Lighting, Clarke W. Thornton; Costumes, Amanda J. Klein; Musical Direction/Arrangements, Dianne Adams; Choreography, Edmond Kresley; Stage Manager, Sheila Bam; Press, Bruce Cohen, Kathleen von Schmid
CAST: Liz Larsen (Eleanor Fairchild), Sharon McNight (Her Mother), George Spelvin (Shak Graa), Steve Watkins (Space Punk), Victor Cook (Herbie Harrison), Bennett Cale (Ack Ack Ackerman), Keith Crowningshield (Dismo Dittersdorf), Gabriel Barre (Trinkulus), Mary Law (Shotzi), Kristine Nevins (Ballbraka), Norma Jean Sitton (Canibelle), Sarah Knapp (Maligna), Sharon McNight (Diva), Liz Larsen (Bizarbara, her daughter)
MUSICAL NUMBERS: Superhero Girl, Starmites, Trink's Narration, Afraid of the Dark, Lullaby, Cry of the Banshee, Hard to Be a Diva, Love Song, Festival Dance of Pleasure and Pulchritude, Bizarbara's Wedding, Milady, Beauty Within, The Cruelty Stomp, Reach Right Down, Immolation, Finale
 A musical in 2 acts and 9 scenes with a prologue and epilogue.

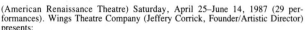

Top Right: Steve Watkins, Liz Larsen
in "Starmites" *(Rita Katz)*

(American Renaissance Theatre) Saturday, April 25–June 14, 1987 (29 performances). Wings Theatre Company (Jeffery Corrick, Founder/Artistic Director) presents:
THE CASTING OF KEVIN CHRISTIAN by Stephen Holt; Director, Michael Hillyer; Sets, Cecil B. Songco, Phyllis Wilson; Costumes, Natalie Barth Walker; Lighting, Jeffery Corrick; Fight Director, Rick Sordelet; Stage Managers, Susan Wigal, Sara Heza, Joseph Flaccamio; Press, Bruce Cohen, Kathleen von Schmid
CAST: Pete Benson (Kevin Mark Christian), Stephen Holt (Jack Marron, Jr.), Ellaxis Smith (Delores Wilson)
 The action takes place during the present summer in an inconveniently located Off-Off-Broadway theatre in New York City.

Left: Stephen Holt, Pete Hans Benson
in "The Casting of Kevin Christian"
(Carol Rosegg)

(Lamb's Little Theatre) Wednesday, April 29–June 13, 1987 (40 performances and 6 previews). Lamb's Theatre Company (Carolyn Rossi Copeland, Producing Director; Pamela Perrell, Associate Director) presents:
THE WONDERFUL ICE CREAM SUIT by Ray Bradbury; Director, Sonya Baehr; Set, Bob Phillips; Choreography, Luis Perez; Costumes, Susan Branch; Lighting, Jean Redmann; General Manager, Joel Ruark; Stage Managers, Luke Sickle, Denise Nations; Press, G. Theodore Killmer
CAST: Andres Rieloff (Manulo), Emilio Del Pazo (Villanazul), Anthony Ruiz (Vamenos), Philip Carrubba (Martinez), Yvonne Martin (Celia Obregon), Cliff Batuello (Gomez), Luis Perez (Dominguez), Ian D. Shupeck (Mr. Shumway), Neal M. Bishop (Leo), Denise Nations (Ruby Escuadrillo), Jon Lerner (Toro Ruiz)
 Performed without intermission. The action takes place in New York City on an evening in early summer of 1975.

Cast of "The Wonderful Ice Cream Suit"
(Carol Rosegg)

(StageArts Theater) Wednesday, April 29–May 24, 1987 (20 performances). StageArts Theater Company (Artistic Directors, Nell Robinson, Ruth Ann Norris) presents:
COWBOY based on an idea by Ronnie Claire Edwards; Book, Jess Gregg; Music & Lyrics, Richard Riddle; Director, Robert Bridges; Choreography, Dennis Dennehy; Musical Direction, Wendell Kindberg; Musical Staging, Robert Bridges, Dennis Dennehy; Sets/Lighting, Tom Hennes; Costumes, Barbara A. Bell; Orchestrations, Christopher Bankey; Casting, Joseph Abaldo; Production Supervisor, Mary E. Lawson; Technical Director, Alan Moyer; Stage Managers, Dennis Cameron, Cher Ledwith; Press, Shirley Herz, Pete Sanders, Peter Cromarty, Glenna Freedman, David Roggensack, Miller Wright, Jillana Devine
CAST: George Ball (Kid Russell), Richard Bowne (Pretty Freddy/Brother Van), Lee Chew (Teddy Blue), Carolyn DeLany (Mamie Cooper), Dennis Edenfield (Sheriff), Barry Finkel (Smitty), Joyce Fleming (Ruby), Madelyn Griffith-Haynie (Trixie), Mary Kilpatrick (Flo), Ilene Kristen (Dynamite), Audrey Lavine (Widow), Ken Lundie (Bullnose), Michael Mann (Ensemble), Craig Oldfather (Slim), Steven Riddle (Con Price), Judith Tillman (Dan's Mrs.), Mary Wing-Porter (Lou)
MUSICAL NUMBERS: Hunker Down Cowboy, Loud and Tacky, It Seems to Me, The Dutchman's Pants, I'll Dream Your Dream, Oh Oh Cowboy, The Horse, You Look Like My Valley, Hey Kid, Light Doesn't Last That Long, Pass the Bread and Butter Brother Van, The Blue Hen's Chick, The Card Game, Singin' to 'Em, Goin' East, Charles, Montana, She's a Shame, Finale
  A musical in two acts. The action takes place in Montana and points east at the turn of the Century.

Top Left: Ilene Kristen, Carolyn Delany, George Ball in "Cowboy" *(Carol Rosegg)*

Thursday, April 30–May 23, 1987 (8 performances and 3 previews in repertory with "Birth Rites").
TERRITORIAL RITES by Kerry Kennedy; Director, William Roudebush; Scenery, Felix Cochren; Costumes, Annette Dieli; Lighting, Peter Anderson; Sound, Steven Menasche; Technical Director, Darren Cole; Stage Managers, Jessica Christie, Edwin Todd; Press, G. Theodore Killmer
CAST: Michael O'Neill (Michael), Laura Carney (Maura), Shelia Russell (Rachel)
  A play in two acts. The action takes place at the present time in a rather cool April on the outskirts of a university town in the southwest.

(Samuel Beckett Theatre) Saturday, May 2–24, 1987 (21 performances). The Vartan Company in association with Pamela Phillips presents:
MISS JULIE by August Strindberg; Translated by Michael Meyer; Director, Maria Mazer; Set, Philip Hanson; Lighting, Whitney Quesenbery; Sound, Phil Lee; Costumes, Heidi Hollmann; Technical Director, Scott Dixon; Wardrobe, Jennifer Mellett; Stage Managers, Susan D. Greenbaum, Douglas James Hamilton; Press, Shirley Herz Associates/David Roggensack
CAST: Diane Tarleton (Christine), Shan Sullivan (Jean), Caroline Arnold (Julie), Douglas James Hamilton (Peasant/Standby for Jean)
  Performed without intermission. The action takes place in Sweden on a midsummer's night of 1888.

(Raft Theatre) Monday, May 4–21, 1987 (16 performances). Raft Theatre (Martin Zurla, Artistic Director; Terry Kester, Producing Director) presents:
PAS DE DEUX written and directed by Lee Gundersheimer; Assistant Director, Paige Matheson; Scenery/Costumes, James Scott
CAST: Jennifer Ashe, Carol Caver, Brett Fadem, Julie Follansbee, Marisa Miller, Tom Nielson, Leonie Norton, Guy Waid

Shelia Russell, Michael O'Neill, Laura Carney in "Territorial Rites" *(Terrance Carney)*

(INTAR Stage 2) Sunday, May 10–June 14, 1987 (27 performances). The Working Theatre (Bill Mitchelson, Artistic Director; Cynthia Allen, Coordinating Producer) presents:

WORKING ONE-ACTS 1987: Directors, William Alderson, Joanna Beckson, Richard Bly, Lee Costello, John Pynchon Holms, Kent Paul, Stephen Rosenfield, Gabrielle Roth, Robert Owens Scott, Peter Zapp; Settings, Bob Barnett; Lighting, Spencer Mosse; Sound, Edward Cosla; Costumes, Debra Stein; Technical Director, Jim Slater; Stage Managers, Wendy Davidson, Reagan Fletcher, Joseph Whelan, Carl Condra; Wardrobe, Carole Etkin, Stacey Woods; Press, Bruce Cohen, Kathleen von Schmid
EVENING A: *Breakdown* by Bill Bozzone; with Nelson Simon (Kenny), Jonathan Lipnick (Sid). *Comrades* by Elizabeth Diggs; with Laralu Smith (Nina), Janet Aspers (Karen), Ron Stetson (Policeman), Kate Redway (Tape Interview). *How Women Break Bad News* by John Bishop; with Robin Polk (Muriel), Johnny Kline (Richard). *Asleep on the Wind* by Ellen Byron; with Danielle DuClos (Rootie DeJaun), Earl Hagan, Jr. (Beau DeJaun). *Deep Sleepers* by Charles Leipart; with Robin Polk (Loraine Fuller), Ron Stetson (Wally Tuttle), Mary Daciuk (Mother), Robert Arcaro (Father)
EVENING B: *The Great Labor Day Classic* by Israel Horovitz; with Janet Aspers (Mary Peas), Nicola Sheara succeeded by Mary Jay (Rebecca Coon), Joseph Daly (Eben Coon), Greg Giordano (August Day), Kristina Loggia (Doreen Duffy), Earl Hagan, Jr. (Spike Coffin). *Montana* by David Kranes; with Marisa Redanty succeeded by Lea Floden (Autumn Jennings), Spring Aspers (Gayle Radford), Janet Aspers (Mrs. T. Radford). *MacTerrance Moldoon's Dress Rehearsal* by John Heller; with Johnny Kline (Treves), Robert Arcaro (Balmoral), Bill Corsair (Stagehand), Honour Molloy (Laurie), Jackie Reingold (MacTerrance Moldoon). *Walking Papers* by Michael Stephens; with Honour Molloy (Woman), Ron Stetson (Man). *San Antonio Sunset* by William Holtzman; with Dennis Green (Mr. Johnson), Bill Mitchelson (Mr. Stone), Earl Hagan, Jr. (Hotel Clerk)

Right: Earl Hagan, Jr., Nicola Sheara, Greg Giordano, Joseph Daly, Janet Aspers, Kristina Loggia in "The Great Labor Day Classic" Above: Ron Stetson, Robin Polk in "Deep Sleepers" *(Carol Rosegg Photos)*

Greg Germann, Beth Dixon Above: Beth Dixon, Debra Monk in "A Narrow Bed" *(Bob Marshak Photos)*

(Actors' Space) Wednesday, May 13–18, 1987 (8 performances). The Actors' Space (Alan Langdon, Artistic Director) presents:
HOME STEADERS by Nina Shengold; Director, Kevin Thompson; Set, Robert Briggs; Costumes, Virginia Johnson; Lighting, Peggy Lei Mueller; Stage Manager, Marcy Drogan; Press, Jan Malthaner
CAST: Bram Lewis (Neal), Scott Klavan (Jack), Elizabeth Browning (Edra), Jennifer Hetrick (Jake), Lee Milinazzo (Laurel)

(45th Street Theatre) Thursday, May 14–30, 1987 (14 performances and 2 previews). Primary Stages Company (Artistic Director, Casey Childs; Associate Artistic Director, Janet Reed) presents:
HIDDEN PARTS by Lynne Alvarez; Director, Susan Gregg; Production Manager, Herbert H. O'Dell; Assistant Director, Marilyn McIntyre; Scenery/Lighting, Dale F. Jordan; Costumes, Cynthia Flynt; Technical Director, Al Ksen; Sound, Paul Radelat; Stage Managers, Douglas Green, Tony Luna; Press, Anne Einhorn, Sara Maxwell
CAST: Leon Russom (Thomas), Joan Grant (Cynthia), Christopher Fields (Justin), Cara Buono (Daria)
A drama in two acts. The action takes place during five days at the present time, around a cornfield on a farm in the Midwest.

(Perry Street Theatre) Thursday, May 14–30, 1987 (10 performances and 11 previews). New York Theatre Workshop (Jean Passanante, Artistic Director; Nancy Kassak Diekmann, Managing Director) presents:
A NARROW BED by Ellen McLaughlin; Director, Sarah Ream; Set, Kate Edmunds; Costumes, Michael Krass; Lighting, John Gisondi; Music Composed/Arranged by John Miller; Technical Director, Peter Duhaime; Production Assistant, Anne Terrail; Props, John Sullivan; Associate Artistic Director, Tony Kushner; Casting Coordinator/Company Manager, Jenny Schneider; Production Manager, David N. Feight; Stage Manager, Virginia Addison; Press, Milly Schoenbaum
CAST: Christopher McCann (Willie), Debra Monk (Lucy), Beth Dixon (Megan), Greg Germann (John), Kate McKillip (Connie Tate)
A drama in two acts. The action takes place at the present time, late winter, in Alvington, New York, a tiny rural town upstate.

(John Houseman Theatre) Monday, May 11–16, 1987 (Limited 8 performances). The Acting Company (John Houseman, Producing Director; Michael Kahn, Artistic Director) present:
MUCH ADO ABOUT NOTHING by William Shakespeare; Director, Gerald Gutierrez; Choreography, Theodore Pappas; Set, Douglas Stein; Costumes, Ann Hould-Ward; Lighting, Pat Collins; Original Music/Musical Direction, Bruce Pomahac; Repertory Director, Rob Bundy; Stage Managers, Mark Baltazar, Lisa Rollins; Press, Fred Nathan Co./Marc P. Thibodeau
CAST: Terrence Caza (Don Pedro), Joseph Houghton (Don John/Watchman), Michael McKenzie (Claudio), Philip Goodwin (Benedick), Kevin McGuire (Leonato), Ralph Zito (Antonio/Verges), Douglas Krizner (Conrade/Friar/Watchman), Matt Bradford Sullivan (Borachio), Joel Miller (Dogberry/Guest), Melissa Gallagher (Hero), Alison Stair Neet (Beatrice), Constance Crawford (Margaret), Wendy Brennan (Ursula)

The action takes place in Cuba during the 1930's.

Friday & Saturday, May 8–9, 1987 (2 limited performances)
THE GILDED AGE: from the novel by Mark Twain and Charles Dudley Warner; A Co-production with Hartford Stage Co.; Adapted by Constance Congdon; Director, Mark Lamos; Set, Marjorie Bradley Kellogg; Costumes, Jess Goldstein; Music, Mel Marvin; Sound, David Budries; Wigs, Paul Huntley
CAST: Wendy Brennan, Craig Bryant, Terrence Caza, Constance Crawford, Melissa Gallagher, Philip Goodwin, Joseph Houghton, Douglas Krizner, Kevin McGuire, Michael McKenzie, Joel Miller, Alison Stair Neet, Matt Bradford Sullivan, Ralph Zito

Alison Stair Neet, Philip Goodwin and above with the cast of "Much Ado About Nothing"
(Diane Gorodnitzki)

(Cherry Lane Theatre) Tuesday, May 12—Turner/Ross Productions in association with Gene S. Jones presents:
ENO written by Daniel Lappin and Eno Rosenn; Set/Costumes, Yael Pardes; Lighting, Zeev Navon; Original Score, Nir Brandt; Sound, Stan Mark; General Manager, Albert Poland; Company Manager, Peter Bogyo; Wardrobe, Kathe Mull; Stage Manager, Chris Kelly; Press, Burnham-Callaghan Associates/David Lotz
CAST: Eno Rosenn in a one-man show

(South Street Theatre) Wednesday, May 13–June 7, 1987 (20 performances). Kindred Productions presents:
LOVEPLAY a new translation by Lawrence Leibowitz of Arthur Schnitzler's "Liebelei"; Director, Susan Einhorn; Set, Dan Hubp; Lighting, David A. Finn; Costumes, Muriel Stockdale; Sound, Phil Lee; Composer, Stephen Hoffman; Associate Producer, Barbara J. Hodgen; Wardrobe, Paula Gray; Stage Managers, Dan Weir, Laura Gewurz; Press, Bruce Cohen, Kathleen von Schmid
CAST: Lawrence Prescott (Theodore), John Hickok (Fritz), Katherine Hiler (Mitzi), Sarah Hornby (Christine Weiring), Joel Leffert (Gentleman), Cynthia Crumlish (Mrs. Binder), Victor Raider-Wexler (Herr Weiring)

A play in three acts with one intermission. The action takes place in Fritz's apartment and in Christine's home.

Sarah Hornby, John Hickok in "Loveplay"
(Carol Rosegg) Above: Eno

(Minetta Lane Theatre) Friday, May 15–August 23, 1987 (120 performances). McSquare Entertainment (Mitchell Maxwell/Alan J. Schuster/Marvin R. Meit) and Margo Lion present Music-Theatre Group's production of:
THE GARDEN OF EARTHLY DELIGHTS conceived and directed by Martha Clarke; Created in collaboration with Robert Barnett, Felix Blaska, Robert Faust, Marie Fourcaut, Margie Gillis, Paola Styron; Music, Richard Peaslee in collaboration with Eugene Friesen, Bill Ruyle, Steven Silverstein; Lighting, Paul Gallo; Costumes, Jane Greenwood; Flying, Foy; Consultant, Peter Beagle; Production Associate, Warren Trepp; General Managers, M Square Entertainment/Alan J. Schuster/ Victoria Maxwell; Stage Managers, Steven Ehrenberg, David Carriere; Press, Shirley Herz, Peter Cromarty
CAST: Rob Besserer, Felix Blaska, Martha Clarke, Marie Fourcaut, Margie Gillis, Raymond Kurshal, Matthias Naegele, Bill Ruyle, Steven Silverstein, Paola Styron
 Performed without intermission in four scenes: Eden, The Garden, The Seven Sins, Hell.

Martha Clarke, Bill Ruyle, Margie Gillis (top)
Left: Felix Blaska, Margie Gillis, Marie Fourcaut (top)
in "The Garden of Earthly Delights" *(Carol Rosegg)*

Rob Faust in "The Garden of Earthly
Delights" *(Carol Rosegg)*

(Apple Corps Theatre) Tuesday, May 19–June 28, 1987 (42 performances). Mabou Mines (Managing Director, Marion Koltun) presents:
IT'S A MAN'S WORLD by Greg Mehrten; Director, David Schweizer; Set, Philipp Jung; Lighting, Pat Dignan; Costumes, Michael Kaplan; Sound, L. B. Dallas; Videography, Paul Clay; Assistant Director, Randee Trabitz; Technical Director, Anthony Gerber; Production Manager, Tom Andrews; Wardrobe, Leslie Werthamer; Company Manager, Byeager Blackwell; Stage Manager, Derrick McQueen; Press, Ellen Jacobs
CAST: Roger Guenveur Smith (Roy Rivertree), Greg Mehrten (Joey Fontina), Paul Schmidt (Harry Atwater), Ruth Maleczech (Eileen Mandel), Rhonda Aldrich (Cheryl Spring), Dan Froot (Peter), Tom Cayler (Jon Waterson)
 A play in two acts. The action takes place during days and nights of 1974 in Los Angeles and Palm Springs, California.

(Actor's Outlet Theatre) Wednesday, May 20–June 13, 1987 (16 performances).
Actors Outlet (Artistic Director, Ken Lowstetter; Executive Director, Eleanor Segan) presents:
DISPATCHES FROM HELL by Melvin I. Cooperman; Director, Stuart Warmflash; Sets/Lighting, Randy Etheredge; Costumes, Kerney Young; Sound, Kenn Dovel; Props, Jane Ray; Wardrobe, Julianne Flynn; Stage Managers, Maryanne Mognoni, Julianne Flynn, Billy Lope; Press, FLT/Francine Trevens, Michael Calkins, Loren Segan
CAST: Panel I: *Die Judenbank* (The Yellow Bench) with George Cambus (Waremann), Rhoda Chimacoff (Frau Dunkel), Marcella Markham (Frau Wechsel), Tibor Feldman (Kanenlauf), Panel II: *Burostuck* (Office Play) with Joanne Dorian (Elsa Eichen), Jeffrey Bingham (Richard Mittler), Michael Wilding (Wilhelmfrett), Panel III: *Der Hanswurstzauberer* (The Clown-Magician) with Kenn Dovel (Voice of Ringmaster), William Kiehl (Hans Weisgau), Jacqueline Kroschell (Greta Weisgau), Jonathan Fried (Jugendfuhrer Kollner), George McGrath (Jakob)
A Holocaust Triptych performed with one intermission.

(Vineyard Theatre) Thursday, May 21–June 21, 1987 (30 performances). Vineyard Theatre (Douglas Aibel, Artistic Director; Barbara Zinn Kreiger, Executive Director; Gary P. Steuer, Managing Director) presents:
SONGS ON A SHIPWRECKED SOFA by James Milton, Polly Pen; Based on poems by Mervyn Peake; Additional Material, James Milton; Music, Polly Pen; Director, Andre Ernotte; Set, William Barclay; Lighting, Phil Monat; Costumes, Muriel Stockdale; Musical Direction, Stephen Milbank; Orchestrations, John McKinney; Choreography, Ara Fitzgerald; Sound, Phil Lee; Production Coordinator, Susan Wilder; Stage Manager, Roy Harris; Press, Bruce Cohen/Kathleen von Schmid
CAST: Alma Cuervo (Mother), Francisco McGregor (Father), Stephen Geoffreys (Son), Ann Talman (Daughter)
MUSICAL NUMBERS: O'er Seas That Have No Beaches, Pygmies Palms and Pirates, The Sunlight, I Float, Our Ears, Dear Children, The Darkness, It Is Most Best, O Here It Is! And There It Is!, Shrink, Lean Sideways on the Wind, The Men in Bowler Hats, O Love! O Death! O Ecstacy!, I Cannot Give the Reasons, The Trouble with Geraniums, And I Thought You Beside Me, All Flowers That Die, I Have My Price, Leave the Stronger and the Lesser Things to Me, The Threads Remain, Out of the Overlapping, All Flowers That Die
A musical in two acts.

**Jacqueline Kroschell, George McGrath
in "Dispatches from Hell"** *(Adam Newman)*

**Stephen Geoffreys, Alma Cuervo, Francisco McGregor,
Ann Talman in "Songs on a Shipwrecked Sofa"**
(Carol Rosegg)

(The New Theatre) Tuesday, May 26–June 28, 1987 (29 performances). The New Theatre presents:
THE SILO by Tom White; Director, Dennis Schneider; Set, Matt Aston; Lighting, Judith M. Daitsman; Sound/Music, Tom McGrath; Costume Coordinator, Kim Austin; Props, Carol Ann Landry; Hairstylist, Margo Mullis; Stage Manager/Sound, Dorothy Burton; Press, Bruce Cohen/Kathleen von Schmid
CAST: Patrick Roche (Witt Holcomb), David Hawes (Tom Blackmore), Susan Aston (Judy Holcomb), Alex Johnson (Sheriff), Charles Abraham (Rev. Williams), Stephanie Thompson (Paulette Holcomb), Patti Chambers (Linda Perkins), Scott LaChance (Chip McAlister), Barbara Brandon (Maureen Holcomb)
A drama in two acts.

(Grace & St. Paul's Church) Thursday, May 28–June 20, 1987 (12 performances). Grace Repertory (Artistic Director, Michele Harper; Executive Director, Rod McLucas) presents:
THE MISER by Moliere; U.S. premiere of a new translation by Albert Bermel; Director, Daniel Wilson; Music, Galuppi, Vivaldi, Rameau; Technical Director, William Raulerson; Set, William Engel; Costumes, Sue Jane Stoker; Stage Managers, John Belcastro, Nina Sciacca; Press, Randall Fostvedt
CAST: Lisa Griffith (Elise), Ryan Reid (Valere), Steve Hofvendahl (Cleante), Fred Sanders (La Fleche), Kevin O'Connor (Harpagon), John Belcastro (Simon), Michele Harper (Frosine), Rod McLucas (Maitre Jacques), Kathleen Ireton (Mariane), William Raulerson (Commissioner), Alfred Cherry (Anselme)
Performed without intermission.

(Cubiculo) Friday, May 29–June 28, 1987 (28 performances). The Open Space Experiment (Lynn Michaels, Artistic Director) presents:
THE LEADER/THE BALD SOPRANO by Eugene Ionesco; Director, Joseph Chaikin; Associate Director, Nancy Gabor; Sets, Watoku Ueno; Lighting, Beverly Emmons; Costumes, Mary Brecht; Sound, Gary Harris; Dramaturg, Bill Coco; Stage Managers, T. J. Carroll, Lillian Butler; Press, Bruce Cohen/Kathleen von Schmid
CAST: *The Leader:* Yolande Bavan (The Announcer), Geoffrey C. Ewing (Young Lover), Judith Cohen (Girl Friend), Sam Tsoutsouvas (Fan 1), John Turturro (Fan 2), Jayne Haynes (The Leader) *The Bald Soprano:* John Turturro (Mr. Smith), Jayne Haynes (Mrs. Smith), Sam Tsoutsouvas (Mr. Martin), Judith Cohen (Mrs. Martin), Yolande Bavan (Mary), Geoffrey C. Ewing (Fire Chief)

Top Right: John Turturro, Jayne Haynes
in "The Bald Soprano" Below: Jayne Haynes,
John Turturro, Judith Cohen, Sam Tsoutsouvas
in "The Bald Soprano" *(Carol Rosegg Photos)*

(Theatre Guinevere) Friday, May 29–June 14, 1987 (14 performances and 3 previews). The Classic Theatre presents:
SIX CANDLES by Joseph S. King; Director, Maurice Edwards; Producer, Nicholas John Stathis; Set/Costumes, Peter R. Feuche; Lighting, Sonya Smith; Sound/Music, George Jacobs; Associate Producer, Adda S. Gogoris; Stage Managers, Donald Moore, Andrea Abrahams, Press, FLT/Francine Travens
CAST: Hal Blankenship (Millard "Mike" Helmsley), Daniel Pollack (Marvin Kupferman), Albert Sinkys (Charles Coleman), Pamela H. Osowski (Julia Coleman), Barry Dunleavey (Rev. Stahlmeister), Vincent Harta (Harry Webber), Dan Lutzky (Felix Greenstein)
A drama in three acts with one intermission. The action takes place in the late 1970's in New York City, and in Elmwood, Long Island, N.Y.

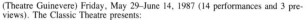

Right: Albert Sinkys (front), Hal Blankenship,
Daniel Pollack, Pam Osowski in "Six Candles"
(Adam Newman)

Mark Nichols, Nell Balaban
in "Some Summer Night"
(Anita Shevett)

(Ernie Martin Studio Theater) Friday, May 29–June 28, 1987 (23 performances and 12 previews). SSN Company presents:
SOME SUMMER NIGHT written and directed by Steve Josephson; Music, Joel Adlen; Lyrics, Joel Adlen/Steve Josephson; Co-producer, Mark Nichols; Associate Producer, Anne P. Goodman; General Manager, Lourdes Babauta; Set, Dean Dalton; Lighting, Sharon Brown; Costumes, Costumes West; Props, Marguerite MacIntyre; Masks, Michael Schaefer; Stage Manager, Kate Broderick; Press, FLT/Francine Trevens, Michael Calkins
CAST: Spencer Beglarian (Theseus Killington), Andrew Dawson (Lysander Lovelorn), Mark Nichols (Demetrius Killington), Jim Boerlin (Egeus Upham), Sheila Mart (Hippolyta Heartstop), Nell Balaban (Hermia Upham), Marguerite MacIntyre (Helena Troy), Ron Keith (Oberon Fairly), Julie Gibson (Titania Fairly), Steve Josephson (Robin Goodfellow), Alicia Gold (Peaseblossom Hummingtree), Scarlett O'Hara (Mustardseed), Tony Kish (Peter Quince), Jay Rubenstein (Nick Bottom), Mary Lilygren (Stine Snout), Kim Crumley (Snug), Gregg Washington (Robin Starveling), Lauren Cloud (Card Girl)
The action takes place some summer night on Theseus' estate outside London.

OFF-BROADWAY COMPANIES

AMAS REPERTORY THEATRE

Eighteenth Year

Founder/Artistic Director, Rosetta LeNoire; Associate Artistic Director, Billie Allen; Administrator/Business Manager, Gary Halcott; Administrator, Jerry Lapidus; Press, Fred Nathan Company, Dennis Crowley, Merle Frimark

Thursday, Oct. 23–Nov. 16, 1986 (16 performances).

HOT SAKE WITH A PINCH OF SALT with Book & Lyrics by Carol Baker, Lana Stein; Music, Jerome I. Goldstein; Based on "A Majority of One" by Leonard Spigelglass; Setting/Production Design, Frank J. Boros; Lighting, Kenneth J. Lapham; Costumes, Howard Behar; Technical Director, Beau Kennedy; Wardrobe, Elle von Schair, Howard Behar; Musical Director/Arranger, Neal Tate; Choreographer; Director, William Martin; Stage Managers, Jay McManigal, James Balfour, Bruce Greenwood

CAST: Wendy Baila (Alice Black), Jim Donahoe (Mr. Putnam), Laurie Katzman (Mrs. Jacoby), Alvin K. U. Lum (Mr. Asano), Gary Kenji Masuoka (Houseboy/Ensemble), Mary Rocco (Essie/Ensemble), Steve Steiner (Jerry Black), Ann Yen (Ayako/Ensemble), Ensemble: Anne allgood, Carle E. Atwater, Gordon Kupperstein; Marzetta Tate, Kirby Wahl

MUSICAL NUMBERS: Fridays, Pictures of You, Here We Go Again, How Do You Do, Another Martini, Trust No One, How Was Your Day?, I Found a Friend, Moon Watching, Let the Flowers Find Me, Mama's Advice, All or Nothing Woman, Sake, What Good Does Loneliness Do?, The Embassy Sidestep, El Tango de la Embasada, You Who Have Taught Me to Love, A Nice Man Like That

A musical in 2 acts and 15 scenes. The action takes place at the Brooklyn home of Mrs. Jacoby, aboard ship on the Pacific Ocean, and in the homes of Mr. Asano, and the Blacks in Tokyo, Japan in 1959.

Thursday, Feb. 12–March 8, 1987 (16 performances)

DAZY with Concept and Lyrics by Norman Simon; Book, Allan Knee; Music, Lowell E. Mark; Technical Director, Larry Smith; Wardrobe, Frances Botta; Hairstylist, Teddy Jenkins; Dance Captain, Teresa Wolf; Casting, Lynda Watson; Dramaturg, Jack Zetlin; Stage Managers, Jay McManigal, Robyn C. Hardy

CAST: Leah Hocking (Dazy), Jack Landron (Charlie), Tom Flagg (Eddie), Peter Gunther (Frank), Joie Gallo (Dorothy), Ensemble: Leslie Bates, Philip Carrubba, Norman Golden, Peter Lind Harris, Denise LeDonne, Richie McCall, Ken McMullen, Sel Vitella, LaTonya Welch, Teresa Wolf, Wendy Worth

UNDERSTUDIES: Leslie Bates, Philip Carruba, Peter Lind Harris, Richie McCall, LaTonya Welch, Wendy Worth

MUSICAL NUMBERS: Streets, You Can Own the Whole World, Two for a Quarter Three for a Dime, It Takes Time, Rockaway Beach, Better Get a Grip, Telephones, Where Did the World Go?, In the Rainbow of My Mind, Love Got in the Way, Who Am I?, Layin' in the Sand, Some of It's Good, The Other Side of Time, A Mother's Love Song

A musical in 2 acts and 19 scenes. The action takes place in New York City at the present time and twenty years earlier.

Thursday, April 9–May 3, 1987 (16 performances)

PRIME TIME with Lyrics & Music by Johnny Brandon; Book, R. A. Shiomi; Musical Direction, Joyce Brown; Directed & Staged by Marvin Gordon; Lighting, David Segal; Costumes/Set, Vicki Davis; Technical Director, Larry Smith; Associate Choreographer, Loretta Abbott; Wardrobe, Frances Botta; Assistant Musical Director, Donna Yvette Brown; Assistant to Director, John Yohannon

CAST: Elly Barbour (Dr. Amy Klein), George Constant (Parker), Marcia Dadds (Suzanne), Kevin John Gee (John Kobayashi), Valerie Lau-Kee (Vicki Lee), Eric Riley (Phil Short), Eddie Simon (James Wilson), Helena-Joyce Wright (Della), Peter Yoshida (Charley Kobayashi), Ensemble: Debra Dauria, Rommel Hyacinth, Jun Nagara, Eddie Simon, Patricia Ward

MUSICAL NUMBERS: The Six O'Clock News, Prime Time, A Blond in Bed, Make Way for One More Dream, It's a Jungle Out There, Health Club Rap, Inside the Inside of Another Person's Mind, Somethin' 'Bout Love, A Very Good Night, Get Off My Back, A Reason for Living, Nobody Ever Hears What I've Got to Say, You Blow Hot and Cold, Leading My Own Parade

A musical in 2 acts and 17 scenes. The action takes place at the present time in New York City.

**Top Right: Laurie Katzman, Ann Yen
in "Hot Sake" (JWL) Below: Leah Hocking,
Tom Flagg, Joie Gallo in "Dazy" (Stephen
Shaffer) Lower Center: Valerie Lau-Kee,
Kevin Gee, Marcia Dadds in "Prime Time"
(Gil Johnson)**

**Eric Riley, Valerie Lau-Kee, Kevin Gee, Peter Yoshida in "Prime Time"
(Gil Johnson)**

AMERICAN JEWISH THEATRE

Twelfth Season

Artistic Director, .Stanley Brechner; Managing Director, Leda Gelles; Production Associate, Evanne Christian; Technical Director, F. R. Swagerty, Jr.; Production Coordinator/Sound Engineer, Abby Farber; Development, Norman Golden; Costumes, Don Newcomb; Props, Leah Menken; Literary Manager, Peter Gordon; Stage Managers, Diane Hartgagen, Tom Stokes; Press, Jeffrey Richards Associates/Ken Mandelbaum

(92 Street Y) Saturday, Nov. 1–Dec. 14, 1986 (33 performances)
PASSOVER by Lloyd Gold; Director, Louis W. Scheeder; Set, Daniel Proett; Lighting, Mitchell Bogard; Casting, Deborah Brown
CAST: Jadrien Steele (A. J. Overby), Devon Michaels (Buddy Ashkenazy), Sophie Hayden (Lucy Ashkenazy), Ava Haddad (Stella Ashkenazy), Victor Raider-Wexler succeeded by Matthew Lewis (Kurt Eisenberg), David S. Howard succeeded by Mark Goldbaum (Jack Pinsky), Doug Wert (Ray Sparks), Marc Epstein (Jerry Ashkenazy).

A comedy in two acts. The action takes place on a day in Spring during 1965 in a small town in northwest Georgia.

Saturday, Jan. 3–Feb. 22, 1987 (45 performances)
PANACHE! by Ron Mark; Director, Stanley Brechner; Set, Daniel Proett; Lighting, Victor En Yu Tan; Sound, Deena Kaye; Fight Choreographer, Richard Raether
CAST: Sam Gray (Shmulke Coldwater), Richard Parnell Habersham (Blinky Escobar), Steven Gilborn (Hobby Coldwater), Sol Frieder (Yekel Coldwater), Yusef Bulos (Boris Koromorsky), Ann Sachs (Jenny Appleton), Rebecca Schull (Ruth Epstein), Understudy: Norman Golden

A comedy in two acts. The action takes place in Chicago during the winter of 1978.
Saturday, March 7–April 26, 1987 (38 performances)
I LOVE YOU, I LOVE YOU NOT by Wendy Kesselman; Director, Ben Levit; Scenery, Nancy Thun; Lighting, Beverly Emmons; Sound, Deena Kaye; Technical Director, Walter Ulasinski
CAST: Rita Karin (Nana), Daria Maazel (Daisy)

A play performed without intermission. The action take place at the present time in a country house.

Saturday, May 9–June 28, 1987 (17 performances and 28 previews)
SONG FOR A SATURDAY titled changed to **BAR MITZVAH BOY** with Book by Jack Rosenthal; Music, Jule Styne; Lyrics, Don Black; American adaptation, Martin Gottfried; Director, Robert Kalfin; Choreography, Larry Hayden; Scenery, Eugene Gurlitz; Costumes, Gail Cooper-Hecht; Lighting, Brian MacDevitt; Assistant Director, Andrew Glant-Linden; Music Consultant, Eric Stern; Pianist, Lorraine Wolf; Hair Design, Butch Leonard; Musical Director/Vocal Arranger, Buster Davis; Technical Director, Alan Sporing, Walter Ulasinski; Stage Manager, Sandra M. Franck; Production Manager, Stephen Lisner; Wardrobe, Cynthia Izzo; Production Assistants, Donald Hill, Sarah Galbraith
CAST: Mary Gutzi (Eliot's mother), Mary Stout (Lucille), Michael Callan (Eliot's father), Michael Cone (Solly), Eleanor Reissa (Eliot's sister Lesley), Daniel Marcus (Harold), Reuben Schafer (Grandfather), Peter Smith (Eliot Green), Larry Keith (Rabbi Kaplan), Kimberly Stern (Denise)
MUSICAL NUMBERS: Always Me, The Cohens Are Coming, Why, If Only a Little Bit Sticks, I'm Grown Up, This Time Tomorrow, The Harolds of the World, We've Done Alright, Simcha, You Wouldn't Be You, Kill Me, Why Did I Do It, Only Myself to Blame, That's Grown Up, Hamakom, I've Just Begun

A play with music in 2 acts and 17 scenes. The action takes place in 1946.

Gerry Goodstein Photos
Right: Rita Karin, Daria Maazel in "I Love You"
Top: Sophie Hayden, Victor Raider-Wexler in "Passover" Below: Rebecca Schull, Sam Gray in "Panache!"

Sam Gray, Ann Sachs in "Panache!"   **Peter Smith, Eleanor Reissa in "Bar Mitzvah Boy"**   **Peter Smith, Larry Keith, Reuben Schafer in "Bar Mitzvah Boy"**

AMERICAN PLACE THEATRE

Twenty-third Season

Director, Wynn Handman; Associate Director, Julia Miles; Business Manager, Joanna Vedder; Literary Manager, Chris Breyer; Production Manager, Alfred Miller; Press, Fred Nathan Co., Merle Frimark, Marc P. Thibodeau

Friday, Oct. 17–Nov. 2, 1986 (21 performances)

NEON PSALMS by Thomas Strelich; Director, Richard Hamburger; Set, Christopher Barecca; Lighting, Stephen Strawbridge; Costumes, Connie Singer; Sound, Aural Fixation; Wardrobe, Agatha Kallmann; Casting, Jeffrey Passero; Stage Managers, Rebecca Green, Mary Fran Loftus

CAST: Tom Aldredge (Luton Mears), Scotty Bloch (Patina Mears), Cara Duff-MacCormick (Barbara Mears), Kelly Connell (Ray)

A drama in 2 acts and 4 scenes. The action takes place in and around an isolated trailer near Boron, California, site of the world's largest open pit borax mine, at the present time.

Friday, Nov. 14, 1986–May 10, 1987 (193 performances)

A GIRL'S GUIDE TO CHAOS by Cynthia Heimel; Director, Wynn Handman; Set, Brian Martin; Costumes, Deborah Shaw; Lighting, Brian MacDevitt; Casting, Paul Garten; Assistant to Director, Ingrid Roberg; Props/Wardrobe, Marcella Zambelli; Stage Managers, Rebecca Green, Joseph S. Kubala

CAST: Debra Jo Rupp (Cynthia), Mary Portser (Cleo), Rita Jenrette (Rita), Eric Booth succeeded by Peter Neptune (Jake/Other Men), Celeste Mancinelli (Lurene), F. D. Herrick (The Physicist), Understudies: Joseph S. Kubala, Lynn Watson

A comedy performed without intermission. The action takes place at the present time.

Monday, February 9–20, 1987 (7 performances)

THE SNICKER FACTOR conceived and directed by Suzanne Bennett, Liz Diamond; Music composed and directed by Adrienne Torf; Writers, Billy Aronson, William Boardman, Cynthia Cooper, Holly Hughes, LaVonne Mueller, Michael Quinn, Jack Shannon, Y. York; Lighting, Nicole Werner; Assistant Director, Maurya Wickstrom; Production Assistants, Rachael Nadel, Elissa Bassler; Technical Consultant, Nancy Harrington; Stage Manager, Greta Minsky

CAST: Edward Baran, Alma Cuervo, Nancy Giles, Anderson Matthews, Joseph C. Phillips

SKETCHES & SONGS: Snicker Factor Theme, Hostage-cises, Great WWII Love Song, Race Relations, Bureau of Presidential Clarification, Coupla White Couples, Powerful Women, Richard Dungeon, Crazy Caspar, Ron-Anon, You're On Your Own, A Right-to-Life Dirge, Science Series, Where's Mr. Wizard When We Really Need Him?, Bureau of Presidential Clarification, Oh I Am a Liberal, All the Way Safe, Hottip, Self-Dep, The Ballad of Bob Dole, Hu Watt, Shuttle Our Troubles Away

"An Evening of Political Satire" performed without intermission.

Martha Holmes Photos

Right: Cara Duff-MacCormick, Scotty Bloch, Tom Aldredge in "Neon Psalms"

Alma Cuervo

Edward Baran

Anderson Matthews

Nancy Giles

Mary Portser, Debra Jo Rupp, Rita Jenrette, also above with Peter Neptune, Celeste Mancinelli in "A Girl's Guide to Chaos"

Kelly Connell, Cara Duff-MacCormick in "Neon Psalms"

CIRCLE REPERTORY COMPANY

Eighteenth Season

Artistic Director, Marshall W. Mason; Managing Director, Suzanne M. Sato; Associate Artistic Director, B. Rodney Marriott; General Manager, Tim Hawkins; Production Manager, Shannon Curran; Props, Alice Maguire; Wardrobe, Jamie Haskins; Stage Managers, Fred Reinglas, Jody Boese, Vincent DonVito; Press, Burnham-Callaghan Associates, Jacqueline Burnham, Edward Callaghan, Gary Murphy

(Circle Repertory Theatre) Wednesday, September 10–November 14, 1986 (39 performances in repertory with "The Early Girl")

IN THIS FALLEN CITY by Bryan Williams; Director, Marshall W. Mason; Set, David Potts; Costumes, Jennifer von Mayrhauser; Lighting, Dennis Parichy; Sound, Chuck London Media/Stewart Werner

CAST: Danton Stone (Paul Forrest), Michael Higgins (Abner Abelson)

A drama in two acts. The action takes place at the present time on Saturday and Sunday afternoons, in a small house in a run-down neighborhood of an American city.

Thursday, October 9–November 30, 1986 (48 performances in repertory with "In This Fallen City.")

THE EARLY GIRL by Caroline Kava; Director, Munson Hicks; Set, John Lee Beatty; Costumes, Jennifer von Mayrhauser; Lighting, Dennis Parichy; Sound, Chuck London Media/Stewart Werner; Stage Managers, Denise Yaney, Nancy Caterino

CAST: Lily Knight (Pat), Robin Bartlett (Jean), Demi Moore (Lily), Roxann Cabalero (George), Pamela Dunlap (Lana), Sharon Schlarth (Laurel), Tisha Roth (Sally)

A comedy in two acts. The action takes place "a few years ago" in a house of prostitution in a mining town out West.

Thursday, December 11, 1986–March 22, 1987 (85 performances and 32 previews). It was transferred to Broadway's Longacre Theatre on April 1, 1987.

THE MUSICAL COMEDY MURDERS OF 1940 written and directed by John Bishop; Original Music, Ted Simons; Set, David Potts; Costumes, Jennifer von Mayrhauser; Lighting, Mal Sturchio, Dennis Parichy; Hair/Makeup, Joan Weiss; Assistant Director, Lee Costello; Wardrobe, Elizabeth-Ann English, Nitza Wilon; Assistant Stage Manager, Reed A. Clark

CAST: Michael Ayr (Ken de la Maize), Dorothy Cantwell (Nikki Crandall), Willie C. Carpenter (Michael Kelly), Kelly Connell (Eddie McCuen), Pamela Dunlap (Marjorie Baverstock), Ruby Holbrook (Elsa von Grossenknueten), Lily Knight (Helsa Wenzel), Bobo Lewis (Bernice Roth), Richard Seff (Roger Hopewell), Nicholas Wyman (Patrick O'Reilly)

A comedy mystery in two acts. The action takes place on an estate in Chappaqua, NY, in December of 1940.

(Theatre 890) Wednesday, February 18–March 8, 1987 (22 limited performances)

BURN THIS! by Lanford Wilson; Director, Marshall W. Mason; Set, John Lee Beatty; Costumes, Laura Crow; Lighting, Dennis Parichy; Sound, Bill Ballard; Fight Direction, Randy Kovitz; Dramaturg, Jack Viertel; Sound, Chuck London Media/Stewart Werner; Presented in association with Center Theatre Group/Mark Taper Forum (Gordon Davidson, Artistic Director); Wardrobe, Miriam Nieves, Nancy Caterino; Stage Managers, Mary Michele Miner, Paul Knox

CAST: Joan Allen (Anna Mann), Jonathan Hogan (Burton), Lou Liberatore (Larry), John Malkovich (Pale)

A play in 2 acts and 7 scenes. The action takes place in a loft in a converted cast iron building in lower Manhattan, New York City.

Wednesday, April 15–June 5, 1987 (37 performances)

AS IS by William Hoffman; Director, Michael Warren Powell; Based on original direction by Marshall W. Mason; Set, David Potts; Lighting, Dennis Parichy; Costumes, Susan Lyall, Michael Warren Powell; Props, Gary Cowling, Dana Gee; Wardrobe, Reed A. Clark; Interim Artistic Director, Tanya Berezin; Associate Artistic Director, B. Rodney Marriott

CAST: Steve Bassett (Rich), Claris Erickson (Hospice Worker/Business Partner/Nurse), Alan Feinstein (Saul), Steven Gregan (Chet), June Stein (Lily), Francis Guinan (Barney/Brother), Rob Gomes (Clone/Pat/Orderly), Robert Myers (Clone)

A drama performed without intermission. The action takes place at the present time in New York City.

Thursday, May 21–June 14, 1987 (37 performances)

ROAD SHOW by Murray Schisgal; Director, Mel Shapiro; Set, David Potts; Lighting, Dennis Parichy; Costumes, Laura Crow; Sound, Chuck London Media/Stewart Werner; Choreography, Candace Tovar; Stage Managers, Kate Stewart, Jamie Haskins

CAST: Anita Gillette (Bianca Broude), David Groh (Andy Broude), Jonathan Hadary (Robert Lester), Trish Hawkins (Evelyn Lester)

A comedy performed without intermission. The action takes place on an early September afternoon of the present, in a small town in Indiana.

Top Left: Lily Knight, Demi Moore, Pamela Dunlap and Below: Lily Knight, Roxann Cabalero, Pamela Dunlap, Demi Moore, Sharon Schlarth (standing), Robin Bartlett in "The Early Girl" *(Carol Rosegg Photos)*

Michael Higgins, Danton Stone in "In This Fallen City" *(Gerry Goodstein)*

Richard Seff, Bobo Lewis, Nicholas Wyman, Dorothy Cantwell, Kelly Connell, Ruby Holbrook in "The Musical Comedy Murders of 1940" *(Adam Newman)* **Left Center: Joan Allen, John Malkovich in "Burn This"** *(Jay Thompson)* **Top: Alan Feinstein, June Stein, Steve Bassett, Steve Gregan in "As Is"** *(Gerry Goodstein)* **Top Right: (front) Anita Gillette, Jonathan Hadary, (back) David Groh, Trish Hawkins in "Road Show"** *(Gerry Goodstein)*

Melissa Johnson, Jase Draper in "Take Me Along"

EQUITY LIBRARY THEATRE

Forty-fourth Season

Managing Director, George Wojtasik; Production Manager, Randy Becker; Business Manager, Helen S. Burton; Development, Lisa Salomon; Assistant to Mr. Wojtasik, Paul Gerard Wiley; Production Coordinator, Pamela Hamilton; Technical Director, Steven Sitler; Assistant Production Manager, Mathew J. Williams; Costumer, Ken Brown; Staff Musician, Edward Reichert; Sound/Audio, Hal Schuler; Press, Lewis Harmon

(Master Theatre) Thursday, Sept. 25–Oct. 12, 1986 (24 performances and 2 previews)

RELATIVE VALUES by Noel Coward; Director, William Hopkins; Scenery, Michael E. Daughtry; Costumes, Vicki Davis; Lighting, Richard Latta; Stage Managers, Craig Butler, Rachel Levine, Jodi Katzman

CAST: P. L. Carling (Admiral Hayling), Ann Ducati (Moxie), Mark Hofmaier (Don Lucas), Marla Johnson (Miranda), Helen Marcy (Lady Hayling), Rica Martens (Felicity), Dennis Pfister (Peter), Bernadette Quigley (Alice), Mitchell Sugarman (Nigel), Ronald Wendschuh (Crestwell)

A comedy in 3 acts and 5 scenes. The action takes place during early July of 1951 in the library of Marshwood House, East Kent, England.

Thursday, Oct. 30–Nov. 23, 1986 (30 performances and 2 previews)

THE PAJAMA GAME with Music & Lyrics by Richard Adler, Jerry Ross; Book, George Abbott, Richard Bissell; Director, Bill Herndon; Choreography, Edie Cowan; Musical Direction, Francis P. Minarik; Scenery, Robert Klingelhoefer; Lighting, Edward R. F. Matthews; Costumes, Susan Branch; Props, Page. P. Billingham; Stage Managers, John F. Sullivan, Maureen Palmer, Ernie Jewell

CAST: Connie Baker (Gladys), Jeff Blumenkrantz (2nd Helper), Richard Chiffy (Ensemble), Norma Crawford (Mabel), John Deyle (Hasler), Felicia Farone (Ensemble), Ann Fleuchaus (Babe), Nanette Gordon (Carmen), Ashley Wade Hancock, Jr. (Charley), Phil LaDuca (Max), Terry LaGarde (Ensemble), Daniel Marcus (Prez), Lee Mathis (Ensemble), Casey Nicholaw (Ensemble), Laura Patinkin (Brenda), Michael E. Piontek (Sid), Jack Poggi (Pop), Rick Porter (Hines), Susie Purdy (Ensemble), Bronwyn Rucker (Poopsie), Tom Russell (Ensemble), Jessica Sheridan (Mae), Darius Keith Williams (Ensemble), Kathleen Yates (Ensemble)

MUSICAL NUMBERS: The Pajama Game, Racing with the Clock, A New Town Is a Blue Town, I'm Not at All in Love, I'll Never Be Jealous Again, Hey There, Her Is, Sleep-Tite, Once-a-Year Day, Small Talk, There Once Was a Man, Steam Heat, Think of the Time I Save, Hernando's Hideaway, Jealousy Ballet, 7½ Cents, Finale

A musical in 2 acts and 18 scenes.

Thursday, Dec. 4–21, 1986 (24 performances and 2 previews)

NIGHT WATCH by Lucille Fletcher; Director, Licia Colombi; Scenery, Jim Chesnutt; Costumes, Lauren Press; Lighting, Robert Bessoir; Stage Managers, Lee Copenhaver, Elli Agosto, Kim Wilson

CAST: Richard Dahlia (Sam Hoke), Herbert DuVal (Curtis Appleby), Alison Edwards (Blanche), Kevin Hagan (Lt. Walker), Walter Hook (John Wheeler), Edward Joseph (Vanelli), Estelle Kemler (Helga), Marlena Lustik (Elaine Wheeler), Mary McTigue (Dr. Tracey Lake)

A mystery thriller in 2 acts and 4 scenes. The action takes place in 1960 in a New York City townhouse located in the East 30's.

Thursday, Jan. 8–Feb. 1, 1987 (30 performances and 2 previews)

TAKE ME ALONG based on the play "Ah, Wilderness!" by Eugene O'Neill; Music & Lyrics, Bob Merrill; Book, Joseph Stein, Robert Russell; Direction/Choreography, Richard Casper; Musical Direction, Jonathan D. Cole; Scenery, Pepper Ross; Lighting, Benjamin L. White; Costumes, Cecilia A. Friederichs; Hair/Wigs, Hari-Kari; Wardrobe, Rebecca Weinstein; Props, Shari Ann Fischer, Pamela Hamilton; Stage Managers, Alice Perlmutter, Kenneth R. Saltzman, Andrea Wilk, Marc Todd

CAST: Jody Abrahams (Ensemble), Tony Carlin (Wint), Alisa Carroll (Mildred), Philip Carrubba (Ensemble), Jase Draper (Richard), Mary Gant (Essie), Melissa Johnson (Muriel), Dan Kael (Ensemble), Evan Matthews (Bartender), Kathryn McAteer (Lily), William McCauley (Sid), Benjamin Moore (Ensemble), Jeanette Palmer (Belle), Nicholas Saunders (David Macomber), Michele Scirpo (Ensemble), Mary Beth Shepard (Ensemble), Ken Shepski (Ensemble), Tom Souhrada (Arthur), Cyndy Taylor (Ensemble), Richard Voigts (Nat), Christopher Zunner (Ensemble)

MUSICAL NUMBERS: Opening, Oh Please, I Would Die, Sid Ol' Kid, Staying Young, I Get Embarrassed, We're Home, Take Me Along, Pleasant Beach House, That's How It Starts, If Jesus Don't Love Ya, Slight Detail, Green Snake, Nine O'Clock, But Yours, Finale

A musical in 2 acts and 17 scenes.

Ned Snyder Photos
Lower Left Center: Mary McTigue, Alison Edwards, Marlena Lustik, Walter Hook in "Night Watch" Above: Connie Baker, Darius Keith Williams in "The Pajama Game" Top: Mitchell Sugarman, Marla Johnson, P. L. Carling, Dennis Phister, Rica Martens (seated) Ann Ducati, Helen Marcy (seated), Mark Hofmaier in "Relative Values"

Thursday, Feb. 12–March 1, 1987 (24 performances and 2 previews)
THE LITTLE FOXES by Lillian Hellman; Director, Thomas Edward West; Scenery, Anthony Hume; Costumes, Julie Doyle; Lighting, Deborah Constantine; Sound, J. Bloomrosen; Wardrobe, Maureen Frey; Props, Mary Barto, Mercedes Olea; Stage Managers, J. Bloomrosen, Craig Palanker, Mary Barto, Mercedes Olea
CAST: Joy Moss (Addie), Ken Threet (Cal), Mary Ed Porter (Birdie Hubbard), Gordon G. Jones (Oscar Hubbard), James Davies (Leo Hubbard), Juanita Walsh (Regina Giddens), Ed Easton (William Marshall), Frederick Walters (Benjamin Hubbard), Gillian Ruth Hemstead (Alexandra Giddens), Ward Asquith (Horace Giddens)
A drama in three acts. The action takes place in the spring of 1900 in the living room of the Giddens house in a small town in the South.

Thursday, March 12–April 5, 1987 (30 performances and 2 previews)
TOO MANY GIRLS with Music by Richard Rodgers; Lyrics, Lorenz Hart; Book, George Marion, Jr.; Director, Stephen G. Hults; Scenery, Pepper Ross; Lighting, Stephen Petrilli; Costumes, Arnold S. Levine; Musical Direction, Jay Dias; Choreographer, Larry Hayden; Dance Captain, Harrison McEldowney; Assistant Musical Director, Douglas Besterman; Stage Managers, Sandra M. Franck, Lori Lundquist, Thomas M. Shea, Josh Sherer, Valerie J. Roux
CAST: Bryan Batt (Al), Timothy Scott Bennett (Pokey), Keith Bernardo (Lister), Leslie Castay (Ruth), Kelly Crafton (Sylvia), Carol Dilley (Eileen), Trisha Forgione (Joanie), Amy Fortgang (Nancy), David Gebel (Beverly), Carolyn German (Frannie), Teri Gibson (Tallulah-Lou), Chan Harris (Manuelito), Pamela Khoury (Peppy), Lynne Kolber (Connie), Renee Laverdiere (Mimi), Harrison McEldowney (Tewks/Randy), Kimberly Nazarian (Sheila), William Reynolds (Harvey), Richard Waterhouse (Clint), Robert A. Woronoff (Jo-Jo)
MUSICAL NUMBERS: Heroes in the Fall, Tempt Me Not, What a Prince, Pottawatomie, 'Cause We Got Cake, Love Never Went to College, Spic and Spanish, You're Nearer, I Like to Recognize the Tune, Look Out, Sweethearts of the Team, She Could Shake the Maracas, I Didn't Know What Time It Was, Too Many Girls, Give It Back to The Indians, Finale
A musical in 2 acts and 12 scenes. The action takes place in 1939 in New England and in New Mexico at Pottawatomie College.

Thursday, April 16–May 3, 1987 (24 performances and 2 previews)
MISALLIANCE by George Bernard Shaw; Director, Geoffrey Hitch; Scenery, David Weller; Costumes, Bruce Goodrich; Lighting, David Noling; Sound, Paul Garrity; Dialect Consultant, Jon Sperry; Props, Darsell Brittingham, David Weller; Stage Managers, Connie Drew, Darsell Beatrice Brittingham, Valerie Roux
CAST: Lori Bezahler (Hypatia), Mark Diekmann (Gunner), Craig Dudley (Joey Percival), Max Gulack (Mr. Tarleton), Elizabeth C. Loftus (Lina), Aaron Lustig (Bentley Summerhays), Patricia Mertens (Mrs. Tarleton), Don Sobolik (Lord Summerhays), John C. Talbot (Johnny Tarleton)
A comedy presented in two acts. The action takes place on a beautiful Saturday in May of 1909 in the solarium of the country house of John Tarleton in Hindhead, England.

Thursday, May 14–June 7, 1987 (30 performances and 2 previews)
WISH YOU WERE HERE based on Arthur Kober's play "Having a Wonderful Time"; Book, Mr. Kober, Joshua Logan; Music & Lyrics, Harold Rome; Director, Don Price; Musical Staging/Choreography, Bob Rizzo; Musical Director, Randall Kramer; Scenery, Barry Axtell; Lighting, Susan A. White; Costumes, Kathleen Egan; Sound, Hal Schuler; Associate Musical Director, Edward Reichart; Dance Captain, Eileen Griffin; Stage Managers, Michael A. Clarke, Barbara Lynn Rice, Gaye Kendall, Mark Poppleton, Margi Kerns
CAST: Janetta Betz (Miriam), Mark Chmiel (Schmutz), Tracy Darin (Alex), David Edwards (Herman), Jack Eldon (Sid), Leslie Esser (Sonia), Larry Francer (Itchy), Eileen Griffin (Irma), Sean Hopkins (Pinky), Michael Kalthoff (Phil), Carlos Lopez (Eli), Charles Mandracchia (Harry "Muscles" Green), Alicia Miller (Mildred), Kari Nicolaisen (Fay), Barbara Rhayne-Gordon (Shirley), Tia Riebling (Teddy), Steven M. Schultz (Marvin), Jeff Shonert (Lou), Doug Tompos (Chick), Wendy Waring (Gussie)
MUSICAL NUMBERS: Camp Karefree, There's Nothing Nicer Than People, Social Director, Shopping Around, Bright College Days, Mix and Mingle, Could Be, Tripping the Light Fantastic, Where Did the Night Go, Certain Individuals, They Won't Know Me, Summer Afternoon, Don Jose, Everybody Loves Everybody, Wish You Were Here, Relax, Flattery, Finale
A musical in 2 acts and 15 scenes. The action takes place in a summer of the early 1950's at Camp Karefree, a summer camp for adults located in the heart of the Catskill Mountains.

Right Lower Center: Craig Dudley, Aaron Lustig in "Misalliance" Above: Bryan Batt, Carol Dilley, Robert Woronoff (kneeling), Teri Gibson in "Too Many Girls" Top: Gillian Hemstead, Juanita Walsh in "The Little Foxes" (*Ned Snyder*)

Carlos Lopez, Tracy Darin, Jack Eldon, Doug Tompos, Steven Schultz, Michael Kalthoff, Mark Chmiel in "Wish You Were Here"

ENSEMBLE STUDIO THEATRE

Fifteenth Season

Artistic Director, Curt Dempster; Managing Director, Erik Murkoff; Producing Director, John McCormack; Literary Manager, D. S. Moynihan; Casting, Risa Bramon, Billy Hopkins; Production Manager, Jim D'Asaro; Production Coordinator, Dante Alencastre; Technical Director, David Mead; Development, Lucy Mayer Harrop; Business Manager, Brian D. Berk; Marketing, Scott W. Brennan; Press, Bruce Cohen, Kathleen von Schmid

(Ensemble Studio Theatre) Monday, Dec. 1, 1986–Jan. 4, 1987 (31 performances)
DREAM OF A BLACKLISTED ACTOR by Conrad Bromberg; Director, Jack Gelber; Set, Steve Saklad; Costumes, Deborah Shaw; Sound, Bruce Ellman; Production Assistants, Geraldine Estrada, Tom Polley; Wardrobe, Beth McCormack; Stage Managers, Diane Ward, Georgette Lewis
CAST: Ryan Cutrona (Kiehl), Ned Eisenberg (Joe), Rose Gregorio (Cookie), Michael Kaufman (Mr. Warren), Joseph McKenna (Mr. Bennett), Frederica Meister (Grace), Barry Primus (Ed), Victor Raider-Wexler (Al), Sam Schacht (Charlie), Jodi Thelen (Teresa)

A drama in two acts: The Dream and The Nightmare.
Tuesday, December 12–20, 1986 (12 performances)
MAMA DRAMA written by Leslie Ayvasian, Cherie Burns, Donna Daley, Christine Farrell, Marianna Houston, Rita Nachtmann, Ann Sachs; Director, Pamela Berlin; Set/Costumes, Philipp Jung; Lighting, Jackie Manassee; Sound, Bruce Ellman; Stage Manager, Carol Anne Clark
VIGNETTES ON MOTHERHOOD: A Man Plants a Seed, Office Visit, I Started with the Diaphragm, The Lie, Sophia Loren, Streetfair, A Baby Cries, My Mother Had a Baby, D.O.A., Sherry, Getta Job, Stepping In, "Soo-Soo," Bargain Baby, Traditions, Dimwit, Morphine, Talking to Great Grandma, From Europe to Asia, Crowning Point, Tales of My Mother, Aunt Grace, She's Coming from Korea, Labor Party. Performed by Leslie Ayvazian, Christine Farrell, Rita Nachtman, Anne O'Sullivan, Ann Sachs

Performed without an intermission.
Original Music and Lyrics by the Roche Sisters were added, and the production re-opened on Thursday, April 2–April 19, 1987 (16 performances).
Tuesday, Feb. 10–March 1, 1987 (18 performances)
CLEVELAND AND HALF-WAY BACK by Leslie Lyles; Director, James Hammerstein; Set, Richard Harmon; Lighting, Tina Ann Byers; Sound, Bruce Ellman; Costumes, David Woolard; Production Coordinator, Karen S. Friedman; Production Assistants, Geraldine Estrada, Elaine Leone, Meredith Muncy, Pam Wheeler; Stage Managers, Jane Sanders, Peggy Pierce
CAST: Julie Garfield (Betty), Bruce MacVittie (Anthony), Rebecca Nelson (Buffy), Cynthia Nixon (Piper), Lola Pashalinski (Mama), Keith Reddin (Jeffery)

A drama in two acts. The action takes place at the present time.
Wednesday, May 6–June 15, 1987 (48 performances with each program presented 16 times)
MARATHON '87: Tenth annual festival of new one-act plays. Producer, John McCormack; Associate Producer, Jamie Mendlovitz; Production Manager, James D'Asaro; Technical Director, David Mead; Props, Kate Dale; Wardrobe, G. Gary Winley; Production Assistant, Eric Zeisler; Stage Managers, Jeffrey L. Pearl, Judith Ann Chew, Stephen Vallillo, Ken Saltzman
EVENING A: *The One about the Guy in the Bar* by Ernest Thompson; Director, Curt Dempster; with Jim Murtaugh (Boston), Frank Girardeau (Other Guy), Jude Ciccolella (Bartender), Ann Stoney (Other Woman), Deborah Snyderman (Beautiful Girl), Tom Verica (Young Man). *The Author's Voice* by Richard Greenberg; Director, Evan Yionoulis; with Patricia Clarkson (Portia), Kevin Bacon (Todd), David Pierce (Gene). *The Last Outpost at the Edge of the World* by Stuart Spencer; Director, Shirley Kaplan; with Bruce MacVittie (Batcho), Campbell Scott (Gus), Chris Kowanko (Phil). *A Million Dollar Glass of Water* by Anthony McKay; Director, Joel Bernstein; with Marilyn Rockafellow (Margie), Pirie MacDonald (Hugh)
EVENING B: Scenery, Lewis Folden; Costumes, Michael S. Schler; Lighting, Greg MacPherson; Stage Managers, Robert Cohen, Michael Griffith, Susan Selig, Denise Laffer, Joanna Ward, Patricia H. Sutherland; Props, Susan Kappel; Production Assistant, Sean Noonan. *Lady of Fadima* by Edward Allan Baker; Director, Risa Bramon; with Victor Slezak (Billy), Billie Neal (Val), Lucinda Jenney (Terri), Voices: James Murtaugh, Mary Joy. *Dinah Washington Is Dead* by Kermit Frazier; Director, Fred Tyson; with Venida Evans (Sarah), Darnell Williams (Richard). *A Ripe Banana* by Jennifer Lombard; Director, W. H. Macy; with Barbara Andres (Margaret), Jane Hoffman (Kitty), Grant Shaud (Thomas). *AfterSchool Special* by Keith Reddin; Director, Billy Hopkins; with Boyd Gaines (Sam), Janet Zarish (Beth), Macaulay Culkin (Sammy), Robert Stanton (Visitor). *All For Charity* by John Patrick Shanley; Director, Willie Reale; with Miguel Correa (William), Tracy Thorne (Lana)
EVENING C: Scenery, Lewis Folden, Bonny Ann Whitehouse; Costumes, Bruce Goodrich; Lighting, Greg MacPherson; Stage Managers, Susan Selig, Darsell Brittingham, Jane Sanders, Tom Roberts, Suzanne Renaud; Props, Bridget Kelley; Production assistant, Sharon Miripolsky; Wardrobe, G. Gary Winley. *Real to Reel* by Frank D. Gilroy; Director, Curt Dempster; with Doris Belack (Sophie Brill), David Gautreaux (Gordon Rideout), Sam Schacht (Man's Voice). *April Snow* by Romulus Linney; Director, David Margulies; with Thomas Gibson (Bill), Sarah Jessica Parker (Millicent), Joe Ponazecki (Lucien), Sam Schacht (Thomas), Lois Smith (Grady), Harris Yulin (Gordon). *Bad Blood* by Peter Maloney; Director, Mr. Maloney; with Kristin Griffith (Rooney McCallum), Pat McLemore (Hattie Fairchild). *Waking Women* by Cassandra Medley; Director, Irving Vincent; with Ebony Jo-Ann (Ms. Edie), Darsell Beatrice Brittingham (Stage Manager)

Carol Rosegg Photos
Top Left: Barry Primus, Jodi Thelen in "Dream of a Blacklisted Actor"
Below: Anne O'Sullivan, Leslie Ayvazian, Ann Sachs in "Mama Drama"

Patricia Clarkson, Kevin Bacon in "The Author's Voice"
Pirie MacDonald, Marilyn Rockafellow in "A Million Dollar Glass of Water" Above: Cynthia Nixon, Keith Reddin in "Cleveland Half-way Back" (Valerie Ross)

HUDSON GUILD THEATRE

Twelfth Season

Producing Director, Geoffrey Sherman; Associate Director, James Abar; Literary Manager, Steven Ramay; Production Manager/Technical Director, John B. Morean; Business Manager, Laura L. Fowler; Stage Manager, John M. Atherlay; Press, Jeffrey Reichards Associates, E. George Willard, Ben Morse, Irene Gandy, Ken Mandelbaum, L. Glenn Poppleton III, Marie-Louise Silva

Wednesday, Oct. 15–Nov. 9, 1986 (28 performances)

INSIGNIFICANCE by Terry Johnson; Director, Geoffrey Sherman; Set/Lights, Paul Wonsek; Costumes, Pamela Scofield; Sound, Marc. C. Stager; Makeup/Hairstylist, J. Stanley Crowe; Production Assistant, Lynette Fox; Props, Erin deWard
CAST: Yusef Bulos (The Professor), Lou Bedford (The Senator), Polly Draper (The Actress), Keith Langsdale (The Ballplayer)

A comedy-drama in two acts. The action takes place in 1953 in a hotel room in New York City.

Thursday, Dec. 11, 1986–Jan. 4, 1987 (28 performances)

PANTOMIME by Derek Walcott; Director, Kay Matschullat; Set, Rosario Provenza; Lighting, Robert Wierzel; Musical Staging, Edward Love; Musical Direction, Deborah R. Lapidus; Costumes, Pamela Peterson; Sound, Tom Gould; Special Effect, Carter Burwell; Masks, Rodney Gordon; Wardrobe, Samantha Merceante; Production Assistant, Lynette Fox
CAST: Edmond Genest (Harry Trewe), Charles S. Dutton (Jackson Phillip)

A drama in two acts. The action takes place outside a guest house on the island of Tobago, West Indies at the present time.

Wednesday, Feb. 4–March 8, 1987 (36 performances)

MOMS by Alice Childress; Director, Walter Dallas; Original Music & Lyrics, Nathan Woodard, Alice Childress; Additional Music/Arrangements, Grenoldo Frazier; Musical Staging, Andy Torres; Set, Rosario Provenza; Costumes, Judy E. Dearing; Lighting, Robert Wierzel; Sound, Aural Fixation; Production Assistant, Alvin Schuh; Props, Janet Smith; Wardrobe, Sara Phillips
CAST: Grenoldo Frazier (Luther: Mom's piano player/manager/friends), S. Epatha Merkerson (Adele: Dresser/Secretary/Housekeeper/Various Friends), Clarice Taylor (Moms Mabley as herself, her mother, father, friends and enemies), Understudy: Darlene Bel Grayson (Adele)

The action takes place in 1970. . . . before and after, and presented in two acts.

Tuesday, Feb. 10–26, 1987. "Black History Festival '87" with performances of "The Road," "Hot Sauce," "The Chosen"/"Telebrain," "Road to the Kingdom,", "Hang in There!," "Fried Chicken & Invisibility," "The Last Passion Play," "To Die for Grenada," "Sepia Tone," and "Wild Milk"

Wednesday, April 1–26, 1987 (28 performances)

CRACKWALKER by Judith Thompson; Directors, James Abar, Judith Thompson; Set/Lighting, Paul Wonsek; Sound, Aural Fixation; Costumes, Karen Hummel; Technical Director, Gordon W. Brown; Production Assistants, Alvin Schuh, Allan Issac; Props, Janet Smith; Wardrobe, Carol Ogsbury
CAST: Elizabeth Berridge (Theresa), Frances Fisher (Sandy), Matt Craven (Joe), Joe Mantello (Alan), Graham Greene (The Man)

A drama in two acts. The action takes place at the present time.

Wednesday, May 27–July 5, 1987 (27 performances and 14 previews)

NO WAY TO TREAT A LADY with Book, Music & Lyrics by Douglas J. Cohen; Based on novel by William Goldman; Director, Jack Hofsiss; Choreography, Christopher Chadman; Conductor/Musical Direction/Dance Music Arrangements, Uel Wade; Orchestrations, Danny Troob; Set, David Jenkins; Lighting, Beverly Emmons; Costumes, Michael Kaplan; Sound, Aural Fixation; Fight Choreography, John Curless; Assistant Director/Dramaturg, Robert Jess Roth; Assistant Choreographer, Linda Haberman; Wigs/Makeup, Bobby Miller; Production Assistant, Paul Hutchison; Wardrobe, Anita Adsit; Props, Janet Smith; Assistant to Director, Lisa Edelstein
CAST: Stephen Bogardus (Christopher "Kit" Gill), Peter Slutsker (Morris Brummell), June Gable (Mother), Liz Callaway (Sarah Stone)
MUSICAL NUMBERS: Five More Minutes, A Very Funny Thing, So Far So Good, Safer in My Arms, I've Been a Bad Boy, The First Move, I Hear Humming, Killer on the Line, The Next Move, Whose Hands, You're Getting Warmer, Front Page News, Female Encounters, Once More from the Top, One of the Beautiful People, Still, Sarah's Touch, I've Noticed a Change, A Close Call

A musical in two acts. The action takes place at the present time in New York City.

Bob Marshak Photos
**Top Left: Edmond Genest, Charles S. Dutton
in "Pantomime" Below: Grenoldo Frazier, Clarice
Taylor, S. Epatha Merkerson in "Moms"
Lower Center: Liz Callaway, Peter Slutsker,
Stephen Bogardus in "No Way to Treat a Lady"
Bottom: (L) Joe Mantello, Elizabeth Berridge,
Frances Fisher, Matt Craven in "Crackwalker"
(R) Lou Bedford, Keith Langsdale in
"Insignificance"** *(Adam Newman)*

113

JEWISH REPERTORY THEATRE

Thirteenth Season

Artistic Director, Ran Avni; Associate Director, Edward M. Cohen; Casting, Stephanie Klapper; Company Manager, Eric Schussel; Press, Shirley Herz Associates/Pete Sanders

Saturday, Nov. 1–30, 1986 (27 performances)
ROOTS by Arnold Wesker; Director, Edward M. Cohen; Set, Geoffrey Hall; Costumes, Karen Hummel; Lighting, Dan Kinsley; Sound, Laura Lampel; Dialogue Consultant, Elizabeth Smith; Production Assistant/Wardrobe, Julianne Flynn; Stage Managers, Gay Smerek, Christopher Merrill
CAST: Gloria Barret (Mrs. Bryant), Roger DeKoven (Stan Mann), Brian Drillinger (Frankie), Bonnie Gallup (Jenny), Dermot McNamara (Mr. Bryant), Christopher Merrill (Mr. Healey), Elaine Rinehart (Pearl), Fred Sanders (Jimmy), Nealla Spano (Beatie)
   A play in three acts. The action takes place in Norfolk, a farming community in England, in 1959.
   Thursday, Jan. 22–Feb. 5, 1987 (27 performances)

THE SQUARE ROOT OF THREE by Michael Golder; Director, Steven Robman; Set, Marjorie Bradley Kellogg; Costumes, Jennifer von Mayrhauser; Lighting, Donald Holder; Sound, Laura Lampel; Production Assistant/Wardrobe, Julianne Flynn; Stage Managers, D. C. Rosenberg, Geraldine Teagarden
CAST: Larry Block (Elliot Atlas), Dominic Chianese (Lucky Mankiewitz), Brian Drillinger (Danny Atlas), Bonnie Gallup (Pauline Atlas), Sylvia Kauders (Rita Atlas)
   A comedy in two acts. The action takes place in a town north of Boston, near the New Hampshire border, at the present time.
   Tuesday, March 3–22, 1987 (27 performances)
OUR OWN FAMILY plays by JRT playwrights in residence; Sets, Ray Recht; Costumes, Edi Giguere; Lighting, Dan Kinsley; Sound, Phil Lee; Company Manager, Eric Schussel; Producer, Edward M. Cohen; Wardrobe, Julianne Flynn; Stage Managers, Geraldine Teagarden, Mary E. Tiefenbrunn, Barbara A. Bruno
CAST: "Zimmer" by Donald Margulies; Director, Michael Arabian; with Joe Urla as Zimmer. "The Renovation" by Susan Sandler; Director, Susan Einhorn; with Beth McDonald (Sylvie), Jennifer Blanc (Caroline). "The Converts" by Michael Taav; Director, William Partlan; with Michael Albert Mantel (Jack), John Diehl (Joe). "Scrabble" by David Rush; Director, Lynn Polan; with Dolores Sutton (Ruth), Victor Raider-Wexler (Jerry), Maury Cooper (Sid)
   Presented with one intermission.
   Wednesday, April 29–May 24, 1987 (27 performances)

WAVING GOODBYE by Bob Morris; Director, Robin Saex; Set, Jeffrey Schneider; Costumes, Karen Hummel; Lighting, Dan Kinsley; Sound, Phil Lee; Assistant Director, Christopher Smith; Wardrobe, Julianne Flynn; Production Assistant, Megan Spooner; Stage Manager, Mary Tiefenbrunn
CAST: Robert Dorfman (David), Michael Ornstein (Jonathan), Viola Harris (Mom), Bernie Passeltiner (Dad), Debbie silver (Nancy)
   A comedy in two acts.

Adam Newman Photos
Right: Victor Raider-Wexler, Maury Cooper in "Scrabble"
Above: Bonnie Gallup, Larry Block in "Square Root of 3"
Top: Gloria Barret, Nealla Spano in "Roots"

**Michael Ornstein, Robert Dorfman
in "Waving Goodbye"**

**Jennifer Blanc, Beth McDonald
in "The Renovation"**

Joe Urla in "Zimmer"

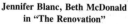

114

LA MAMA

Twenty-fifth Year

(La Mama) Thursday, Nov. 13–Dec. 14, 1986 (16 performances). La Mama E.T.C. presents:
ETIQUETTE with Book & Lyrics by William M. Hoffman; Director, John Vaccaro; Music & Lyrics, John Braden; Choreography, Michael Lichtefeld; Set, Neil Peter Jampolis; Costumer, Gabriel Berry; Lighting, Jeffrey Nash; Musical Supervision/Piano Arrangements, Michael Dansicker; Synthesizer Orchestrations/Programming, Jeff Waxman; Stage Manager, Christopher de Santo; Press, Jim Baldassare
CAST: Lia Alex, Willi Burke, Carroll Carter, Lynn Eldredge, Louisa Flaningam, Jamie Hanes, Marian Haraldson, Don Harrington, Alexa Hunter, Jill Kotler, Tom McClary, Richard Walker
   A comedy in seven scenes.
   Wednesday, Nov. 12–Dec. 21, 1986 (30 performances). La Mama E.T.C. (Executive Director, Wickham Boyle; Business Manager, James W. Moore) presents:
THE ARCHITECT AND THE EMPEROR OF ASSYRIA by Fernando Arrabal; Direction/Music, Tom O'Horgan; Set, Bill Stabile; Costumes, Joseph G. Aulisi; Lighting, Beverly Emmons; Sound, David Adams; Masks, Barbara Sexton; Translation by Everard d'Harnoncourt, Adele Shank; Stage Manager, Houstoun Demere; Press, Jim Baldassare
CAST: Miles Mason/Alexi Mylonas (Emperors), Ray Contreras/Jonathan Walker (Architects), M. A. Whiteside (Mother's Voice)
   Monday, Dec. 29, 1986–March 22, 1987 (47 performances). La Mama E.T.C. presents:
FRAGMENTS OF A GREEK TRILOGY conceived and directed by Andrei Serban; Composed by Elizabeth Swados; Set, Jun Maeda; Lighting, Carol Mullins; Costumes, Sharon Lynch; Musical Direction, Onni Johnson; Wardrobe, Mary-Ann Monforton; Masks, Martine Vermeulen; Production Assistant, Margaret Schultz; Stage Manager, Richard Jakiel; Press, Jim Baldassare
CAST: Bruce Adgate, Du-Yee Chang, Sheila Dabney, Keith David, Sussan Deihim, Jon DeVries, William Duff-Griffin, Karen Evans-Knadel, Maureen Fleming, Mohammad Ghaffari, Neal Harris, Paul Harris, James Anders Jabir, Onni Johnson, Jane Lind, Dan Nutu, Aneza Papdopoulos, Tony Scheitinger, Priscilla Smith, Joseph Sokolsky, Frances Ellen Thorpe, Valois, Lou Zeldis, Gabriel Cohen-DeVries, James Sheffield Dewees, Rainah Golden Chang Faulk
   Scenes from Medea, Electra, and The Trojan Women.
   Thursday, Jan. 8–Feb. 1, 1987 (19 performances). La Mama E.T.C. presents:
SAFE SEX by Harvey Fierstein; Director, Eric Concklin; Music, Ada Janik; Sets, Jun Maeda; Lighting, Craig Miller; Costumes, Nanzi Adzima; Sculptures, Gretchen Green; Casting, Jimmy Bohr; Synthesizer/Conductor, Ada Janik; Sound, Guy Sherman/Aural Fixation; Production Assistant, Richard Jackson; Press, Jim Baldassare
CAST: *Manny and Jake* with John Mulkeen (Manny), John Bolger (Jake). *Safe Sex* with John Bolger (Mead), Harvey Fierstein (Ghee), *On Tidy Endings* with Anne DeSalvo (Marion), Ricky Addison Reed (Jimmy), Billie McBride (June), Harvey Fierstein (Arthur)
   Three one-acts with one intermission. The action takes place at the present time.

Carol Rosegg/Martha Swope Photos
Right: Valois (C), Du Yee Chang (R)
Above: Jane Lind (C) in "The Trojan Women"

**Ray Contreras, Alexi Mylonas
in "The Architect and the Emperor"**

**John Bolger, Harvey Fierstein in "Safe Sex"
Top: Marian Haraldson in "Etiquette"**

MANHATTAN THEATRE CLUB

Fifteenth Season

Artistic Director, Lynne Meadow; Managing Director, Barry Grove; General Manager, Victoria Bailey; Artistic Associates, Jonathan Alper (Plays), Michael Bush (Administration); Literary Manager, Molly Fowler; Casting, Donna Isaacson; Development, Janet M. Harris; Marketing/Press, Helene Davis, Carol R. Fineman, Leisha DeHart; Business Manager, Michael P. Naumann; Production Manager, Michael R. Moody; Technical Director, Betsy Tanner; Props, Shelley Barclay; Wardrobe, MaryAnn D. Smith

(City Center Theater) Thursday, Oct. 30–Dec. 7, 1986 (46 performances)
THE HANDS OF ITS ENEMY by Mark Medoff; Director, Kenneth Frankel; Sets, John Lee Beatty; Costumes, Jennifer von Mayrhauser; Lighting, Pat Collins; Sound, Aural Fixation; Dramaturg, Molly Fowler; Props, Merrill Rauch; Wardrobe, Zorba Soteras; Production Assistant, Andrew Rosen; Stage Managers, John Vivian, Tammy Taylor
CAST: Lucy Deakins (Amanda Yerby), Jeffrey DeMunn (Howard Bellman), Dann Florek (Skip Donner), Phyllis Frelich (Marieta Yerby), Jane Kaczmarek (Diane Newburry), Joyce Reehling (Elma Pafko), Robert Steinberg (Mel Katzman), Tammy Taylor (Assistant Stage Manager), Ralph Williams (T. O. Finn), Standbys: Carole Addabbo (Marieta), David Berman (Mel/Howard/Skip), Patrice Colihan (Amanda/Stage Manager), Judith Yerby (Diane/Elma/T. O. Finn)
A drama in two acts. The action takes place at the present time in a university resident theatre in the Southwest.

Thursday, Dec. 18, 1986–Jan. 25, 1987 (46 performances)
BLOODY POETRY by Howard Brenton; Sets, John Lee Beatty; Costumes, Dunya Ramicova; Lighting, Dennis Parichy; Sound, Scott Lehrer; Assistant Director, Michael Breault; Vocal Coach, Elizabeth Smith; Wigs, Bruce Geller; Wardrobe, Zorba Soteras; Props, Carol Silverman; Production Assistant, Erica Simpson; Stage Managers, Peggy Peterson, Daniel S. Lewin
CAST: Thomas Gibson (Percy Bysshe Shelley), Laila Robins (Mary Shelley), Jayne Atkinson (Claire Clairmont), Daniel Gerroll (George, the Lord Byron), Keith Reddin (Dr. William Polidori), Denise Stephenson (Harriet Westbrook/Her Ghost)
A drama in two acts. The action takes place between the summers of 1816 and 1822 in Switzerland, England and Italy.

Thursday, Feb. 12–March 22, 1987 (46 performances)
HUNTING COCKROACHES by Janusz Glowacki; Translation, Jadwiga Kosicka; Director, Arthur Penn; Set, Heidi Landesman; Costumes, Rita Ryack; Lighting, Richard Nelson; Sound, Stan Metelits; Dramaturg, Jack Temchin; Vocal Coach, Tim Monich; Props, Carol Silverman; Production Assistant, Tina Koubek; Stage Managers, Susie Cordon, Laura deBuys
CAST: Dianne Wiest (She), Ron Silver (He), Reathel Bean (Immigration Officer), David Berman (Rysio), Martin Shakar (Czesio), Paul Greco (Bum), Paul Sparer (Mr. Thompson), Joan Copeland (Mrs. Thompson), Larry Block (Censor), Standby: Paul Greco (Rysio), David Berman (Jan)
A comedy in two acts. The action takes place at the present time in an apartment in Manhattan's Lower East Side.

Gerry Goodstein Photos
**Left: Dianne Wiest, Ron Silver in "Hunting
Cockroaches" Above: Laila Robins, Thomas Gibson
in "Bloody Poetry" Top: Phyllis Frelich, Robert
Steinberg, Jeffrey DeMunn in "The Hands of Its
Enemy"**

**Dianne Wiest, Ron Silver
in "Hunting Cockroaches"**

**Alan Ruck, Amy Madigan, Belita Moreno,
Lanny Flaherty in "The Lucky Spot"**

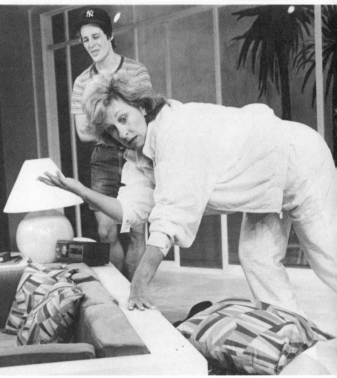

Mary Stuart Masterson, Amy Madigan
in "The Lucky Spot"

Tim Guinee, Christina Pickles,
in "Death of a Buick"

F. Murray Abraham, Kathy Bates in "Frankie and
Johnny in the Clair de Lune"

Thursday, April 9–May 17, 1987 (46 performances)
THE LUCKY SPOT by Beth Henley; Director, Stephen Tobolowsky; Set, John Lee Beatty; Costumes, Jennifer von Mayrhauser; Lighting, Dennis Parichy; Sound, Scott Lehrer; Fight Staging, B. H. Barry; Wigs, Paul Huntley; Props, Carol Silverman; Wardrobe, Bridget Kelley; Hairstylist, Vito Mastorgiovanni; Production Assistant, Jill Cordle; Stage Managers, Peggy Peterson, Jim Fontaine
CAST: Mary Stuart Masterson (Cassidy Smith), Alan Ruck (Turnip Moss), Ray Baker (Reed Hooker), Lanny Flaherty (Whitt Carmichael), Belita Moreno (Lacey Rollins), Amy Madigan (Sue Jack Tiller Hooker), John Wylie (Sam)
A comedy in two acts. The action takes place on Christmas Eve of 1934 in The Lucky Spot Dance Hall in Pigeon, Louisiana.
(Stage II) Tuesday, April 21–May 3, 1987 (46 performances)
DEATH OF A BUICK by John Bunzel; Director, Jonathan Alper; Set, Philipp Jung; Costumes, C. L. Hundley; Lighting, Arden Fingerhut; Sound, James M. Bay; Fight Coordinator, Jack Stehlin; Props, Charles Eisenberg; Props, Elizabeth Cohen; Wardrobe, Hilarie Blumenthal; Production Assistant, Margaret Bodriguian; Stage Managers, Daniel S. Lewin, Anita Ross
CAST: Brian Evers (Dad), Tim Guinee (Benji), Scott Plank (Jack), Christina Pickles (Mom), Brian Cousins (Arnie/Voice of newscaster)
A comedy in 2 acts and 8 scenes. The action takes place during Christmas of 1979 in and around the Masters' house in Pacific Palisades, California.
Thursday, May 28–July 5, 1987 (46 performances)
CLAPTRAP by Ken Friedman; Director, David Trainer; Set, David Potts; Costumes, David Murin; Lighting, Ken Billington; Sound, Kim Kruger; Props, Jill Cordle; Production Assistant, Emily Ehrenfeld; Stage Managers, James Harker, Allison Sommers
CAST: Cherry Jones (Sara Littlefield), Joel Polis (Sam Krulik), Fran Brill (Sybil Swensen), Nathan Lane (Harvey Wheatcraft), Tresa Hughes (Cynthia Littlefield), Standby: Jonathan Freeman (Sam/Harvey)
A farce in two acts. The action takes place at the present time in New York City in not the best of neighborhoods.
(Space II) Tuesday, June 2–21, 1987 (24 performances)
FRANKIE AND JOHNNY IN THE CLAIR DE LUNE by Terrence McNally; Director, Paul Benedict; Set, James Noone; Costumes, David Woolard; Lighting, David Noling; Sound, John Gromada; Props, Carol Silverman; Wardrobe, Elizabeth Cohen; Production Assistant, Jan Carr; Stage Managers, Evelyn J. Plummer, Craig Palanker
CAST: Kathy Bates (Frankie), F. Murray Abraham (Johnny)
A drama in two acts. The action takes place at the present time in Frankie's one-room apartment in a walk-up tenement in the West 70's of Manhattan, New York City.

Left Center: Nathan Lane, Cherry Jones, Joel
Polis, Tresa Hughes in "Claptrap"
Gerry Goodstein Photos

MANHATTAN PUNCH LINE

Eighth Season

Artistic Director, Steve Kaplan; Executive Director, Craig Bowley; Development, Kristine Niven; Production Manager, Kate Hancock; Administrative Assistant, Elyse Barbell; Press, Bruce Cohen, Kathleen von Schmid

(Judith Anderson Theatre) Saturday, Nov. 29–Dec. 31, 1986 (26 performances)
EPIC PROPORTIONS by Larry Coen, David Crane; Director, Paul Lazarus; Set, William Barclay; Stage Combat, Kent Shelton; Costumes, Mary L. Hayes; Casting, Herman/Lison; Lighting, Curt Osterman; Sound, Otts Munderloh/David Gotwald; Technical Director, John Geurts; Assistant Director, Gary Clare; Stage Manager, Tamara K. Heeschen
CAST: Humbert Allen Astredo (Narrator/DeWitt), Robert Blumenfeld (Octavium/Shel/Egyptian), Michael Heintzman (Benny), Mic Murphy (Phil), Patricia Norcia (Conspirator 3/Queen of the Nile/Cochette), Paul O'Brien (Conspirator 2/Jack/General 2), Louise Roberts (Louise), Mark Kenneth Smaltz (Conspirator 1/General 1/Queen's Attendant)
A comedy in two acts.
Friday, Jan. 9–Feb. 22, 1987 (44 performances)
FESTIVAL OF ONE-ACT COMEDIES with Sets by Jane Clark, Christopher Stapleton, Kurt Rauchenberger; Costumes, Michael S. Schler (Program A), Lillian Pan (Program B); Sound, James Reichert; Lighting, Mark DiQuinzio; Production Manager, Kate Hancock; Artistic Associate, Kathrin King Segal; Casting, Ronnie Yeskel; Stage Managers, Kate Hancock, Tamara K. Heeschen (Program A), Elain Zofrea (Program B)

PROGRAM A: *Child's Play* by Peter Manos; Director, Lee Costello; with Toby Wherry (Joe), Mary Testa (Amy), Bill Cohen (Claude), Christina Haag (Jenny), Willie Reale (Principal). *The Moaner* by Susan Sandler; Director, Pamela Berlin; with Susan Greenhill (Annabelle), Lisa Sokolov (Voice). *The Deep End* by Neil Cuthbert; Director, Charles Karchmer; with Robert Trebor (Husband), Ronnie Farer (Wife), Michael Patterson (Ice Cream Man). *Words Words Words* by David Ives; Director, Fred Sanders; with Warren Keith (Milton), Christopher Fields (Swift), Helen Greenberg (Kafka). *Almost Romance* by Howard Morris; Director, Robin Saex; with Fisher Stevens (Harry), Helen Slater (Nicole), Robert Tyler (Roger), Paul Cono Marcazzo (The Kid).
PROGRAM B: *In the Park* by M. B. Valle; Director, Jason Buzas; with Julie Cutrer (Beatrice), J. David Rozsa (William). *The Greenhouse Keeper Died over the Weekend* by Terri Wagener; Director, Gavin Cameron-Webb; with Oliver Platt (Bubba), Thomas Mills Wood (Andrew), Terri Hawkes (Baby), Jo Anderson (Sarah). *The Tablecloth of Turin* by Ron Carlson; Director, Jason Buzas; with Ron Lee Savin (Leonard Christofferson). *If Walls Could Talk* by Laurence Klavan; Director, Steve Kaplan; with Christopher Fields (Gilbert Wall), Roberta Wallach (Arlene Wall), Irving Burton (Gaggy), Leo Postrel (Jack), Victor Raider-Wexler (Gus), Ronald Hunter (Ike), Lee Kheel (The Woman), Sally-Jane Heit (Madge), Shirl Bernheim (Aunt), J. David Rozsa (Boy), Oliver Platt (The Man)
Both programs performed with one intermission.
Friday, April 25–May 24, 1987 (23 performances)

SECOND AVENUE by Allan Knee; Director, Steve Kaplan; Set, Richard Harmon; Lighting, Mark DiQuinzio; Costumes, David Loveless; Sound, Robert Passaretti; Production Manager, Brandon Doemling; Choreography, Marcia Milgrom Dodge; Casting, Jeffrey Passero; Assistant Director, Jennifer Hill; Technical Director, H. Shep Pamplin; Props, Charlie Eisenberg; Musical Director/Composer/Lyricist, Barry Kleinbort; Stage Managers, Jeffrey M. Markowitz, Howard Morris
CAST: Nelson Avidon (New Man), Buzz Bovshow (Manager/Husband), Ned Eisenberg (Shlomo Bachman), Julie Garfield (The Woman), John Hallow (Mr. Moshkovitch), Max Jacobs (Simon), David Lipman (Moishe), Ralph Pochoda (Elias), Maxine Taylor-Morgan (Mrs. Weinblatt/Shirley), Gerry Vichi (Morris), Roberta Wallach (Fanny)
A play in two acts. The action takes place in 1908 on the Lower East Side of Manhattan, New York City.
Saturday, May 30–July 12, 1987 (31 performances)
BIGFOOT STOLE MY WIFE a program of six short comedies by Ron Carlson; Director, Jason Buzas; Set, Bobby Berg; Lighting, Brian MacDevitt; Costumes, Mimi Maxmen; Sound, Daryl Bornstein; Production Manager, Brandon Doemling; Casting, Jay Binder & Jack Bowden; Wardrobe, Mary Alyce Vienneau; Original Music, Mark Hardwick, John Foley, John Schimmel; Stage Managers, Jonathan D. Secor, Jodi Lustig
Program: *Bigfoot Stole My Wife* with Ray Dooley (Man), *Baby Born with 2000 Year Old Bracelet* with Hansford Rowe (Obstetrician), *I Ate My Best Friend's Brain* with Thomas Nahrwold, *The Tablecloth of Turin* with Eddie Jones (Leonard Christofferson), *I Am . . .* with David Jaffe (Special Guest), *Phenomena* with Darren McGavin (Derec Ferris). Presented with one intermission.

Carol Rosegg Photos
**Top Right: Robert Tyler, Helen Slater
in "Almost Romance" Below: Darren McGavin
in "Bigfoot Stole My Wife" (*Linda Alaniz*)
Lower Center: Ned Eisenberg, Julie Garfield
in "Second Avenue"**

**Mic Murphy, Mark Kenneth Smaltz, Michael
Heintzman in "Epic Proportions"**

MEAT AND POTATOES COMPANY

Eleventh Season

Artistic Director, Neal Weaver; Administrative Director, Diane Pekunka; Lighting Designer, David L. Arrow; Treasurer, Terri Musto

(Alvina Krause Theatre) Thursday, June 12–July 13, 1986 (20 performances).

VIEUX CARRE by Tennessee Williams; Direction/Set, Neal Weaver; Lighting, David L. Arrow, Kathleen Lassiter; Stage Manager, Dan Erickson
CAST: Charles Deitz (The Writer), Jan Meredith (Mrs. Wire), Jacquetta LaMay (Nursie), Laura Neal (Jane Sparks), David Scott Taylor (Nightingale), Babette Glass (Mary Maude), Michael Dellafemina (Blake/Tye McCool/T. Hamilton Biggs/Photographer/Intern), Dan Erickson (Policeman/Sky/Intern)

A drama in 2 acts and 6 scenes. The action takes place in an old house in the Vieux Carre District of New Orleans in the winter and spring of 1939.

Wednesday, July 30–Aug. 24, 1986 (20 performances).

THE SOUND OF MURDER by William Fairchild; Director, Charles Pekunka; Set, Neal Weaver; Lighting, David L. Arrow; Stage Manager, Lisa Contadino
CAST: Vernon Morris (Charles Norbury), Barbara Leto (Anne Norbury), Cliff Weissman (Peter Marriott), Amy Rowe succeeded by Barbara Callander (Miss Forbes), Ronald Willoughby (Insp. Davidson), Jeffrey Livingston (Constable Nash)

A mystery in 3 acts and 6 scenes. The action takes place in the living-room of the Willows, the Norbury's cottage in Surrey.

Thursday, Sept. 4–Oct. 5, 1986 (20 performances)

MISALLIANCE by George Bernard Shaw; Design/Direction, Neal Weaver; Costumes, Georgea Pace; Lighting, Janet Herzenberg; Stage Manager, Pat Pankhurst
CAST: Ray Ivey (Johnny Tarleton), Samuel D. Cohen succeeded by Aaron Kjenaas (Bentley Summerhays), Cecile Andrea Lee (Hypatia Tarleton), Joan Shepard (Mrs. Tarleton), Henry J. Quinn (Lord Summerhays), Donald Pace (Tarleton), Jeffrey Livingston (Aviator), Kathleen Monteleone (Passenger), Owen Thompson (Gunner)

A comedy in two acts. The action occurs in the hall of Mr. Tarleton's house, on the slope of Hindhead, in Surrey, England on May 31, 1909.

Thursday, Oct. 23, 1986–Mar. 15, 1987 (104 performances).

INITIATION RITES by Neal Weaver; Design/Direction, Neal Weaver; Assistant, Barbara Callander; Fight Staging, Vernon Morris; Stage Manager, Leslie C. Nemet
CAST: Robert Bruno, succeeded by Frank Uzzolino, Aris Tompulis, John A. C. Kennedy, Brian McDaniel (Harvey), Gregory Paul Jackson, succeeded by Frank Uzzolino, Paul Jordan (Rocky), Chuck Schneider succeeded by Matt Durkan, Steven Poortenga (Reggie), Sean Hagerty succeeded by Douglas Herdt, Paul Jordan (Brew), Thomas Lasley succeeded by Nick Pelino, Steven Poortenga, Sam Inglese, Jr., (Tommy), John A. C. Kennedy succeeded by Matthew Hoffman, Chris Burmester (Santelli), David M. Mullins succeeded by Mark Edward Lang, Dennis Dooley (G. D.), Charles Reynolds succeeded by Matthew Hoffman (Bobby)

A play in 2 acts and 5 scenes. The action occurs in the livingroom of Tri-U's cabin on Logan Lake in a Southeastern state at the present time.

Thursday, April 16–May 17, 1987 (20 performances).

MILESTONES by Arnold Bennett and Edward Knoblock; Director, Neal Weaver; Lighting, Janet Herzenberg; Stage Manager, Leslie C. Nemet
CAST: Ruby Payne (Mrs. Rhead), Wendy C. H. Peace (Rose Sibley), Kathleen Huber (Gertrude Rhead), Leslie C. Nemet (Thompson), Mark Edward Lang (Ned Pym), Stephen O'Dwyer (John Rhead), Ronald Willoughby (Samuel Sibley), Barbara Leto Hilson (Emily Rhead), Aaron Kjenaas (Arthur Preece), Tessa M. Mills (Nancy Sibley), Simon Allen (Webster), Matthew Hoffman (Gerald Pym), Lynn Weaver (Muriel Pym), Greg Martin (Richard Sibley)

A play in three acts. The action takes place in the drawing room of the Rhead residence in Kensington Gore, London, on December 29, 1860, in June 1885, and June 1912.

Thursday, May 28–June 28, 1987 (20 performances)

SAILOR BEWARE! by Philip King and Falkland Cary; Design/Direction, Vernon Morris; Lighting, David L. Arrow; Stage Manager, Tony Spano
CAST: Barbara Callander (Edie Hornett), Tessa M. Mills (Emma Hornett), Kate Britton (Florrie Lack), Ronald Willoughby (Henry Hornett), Julian Stone (Albert Tufnell), Simon Allen (Carnoustie Bligh), Kim McCarthy (Daphne Pink), Lynn Marie Booth (Shirley Hornett), Henry Traeger (Rev. Oliver Purefoy)

A play in 2 acts and 4 scenes. The action takes place in the living room of the Hornett's residence in a small inland town in England on the day before the daughter's wedding, and on the wedding day.

in repertory with:

Sunday, May 31–June 30, 1987 (19 performances)

THE TRONZINI RISTORANTE MURDERS by Si Isenberg; Director, Sally Darling; Stage Manager, Uriel Menson, Clare Whalen
CAST: Peter Reznikoff (Justin), Charles Fatone (J. P. Gabriel), Kathleen Huber (Mavis Kelly), Michael J. Carter (Clark Wakefield), Barbara J. Hilson (Jacqueline Morris), Greg A. Martin (Bunyip Taylor), Julie Goldsmith Gilbert (Millicent Bingham), Muriel Gould (Lorraine Stevenson), Philip Wentworth (Helmut Krieg), Patricia L. Sexton (Mavis Kelly)

A play in 2 acts and 3 scenes. The action takes place in a private room in Tronzini's Ristorante on the east side of Manhattan, New York

Herb Fogelson Photos
**Top Right: (back) Robert Bruno, Gregory Paul Jackson,
Sean Haggerty, (seated) Nick Pelino, Jr., Charles
Reynolds, David M. Mullins, (on floor) Matt Durkan,
John A. C. Kennedy in "Initiation Rites" Below:
Kathleen Huber, Charles Fatone in "Tronzini Murders"**

NEW FEDERAL THEATRE

Woodie King, Jr., Producer

(Louis Abrons Arts for Living Center) Sunday, July 13–August 3, 1986 (24 performances).

THE SOVEREIGN STATE OF BOOGEDY BOOGEDY by Lonnie Carter; Director, Dennis Zacek; Set, Bob Edmonds; Lighting, William H. Grant III, Costumes; Judy Dearing; Sound, Galen G. Ramsey; Company Manager, Linda Herring; Production Manager, Clarence L. Taylor; Production Assistant, Phil Lane Williams; Technical Director, Casandra Scott; Wardrobe, Harriet Foy; Stage Manager, Jesse Wooden, Jr.; Press, Max Eisen, Madelon Rosen. CAST: Reggie Montgomery (Abed-Nego), Helmar Augustus Cooper (Shadrach), Robert Jason (Meshach), Angela Sargeant (Danielle), Andre DeShields (Nebuchadnezzar), Brian Thomas (Fourth Man). The action takes place in a courtroom in the Sovereign State of Boogedy Boogedy, and is performed without intermission.

(Harry DeJur Playhouse) Friday, Oct. 10–Nov. 2, 1986 (20 performances)

LILLIAN WALD: AT HOME ON HENRY STREET by Clare Coss; Director, Bryna Wortman; Set, Richard Harmon; Lighting, Jackie Manassee; Costume, Gail Cooper-Hecht; Sound, Linda Burns; Hairstylist, Patrik D. Moreton; Company Manager, Linda Herring; Technical Director, Casandra Scott; Wardrobe, Illeana Peyron; Props, Myrna Duarte; Stage Manager, Karen Moore; Press, Max Eisen, Madelon Rosen

CAST: Patricia Elliott as Lillian Wald on May 8, 1916 in her sitting room/office at the Henry Street Settlement House.

(Louis Abrons Arts for Living Center) Thursday, Nov. 13–Dec. 7, 1986 (24 performances)

TIME OUT OF TIME by Clifford Mason; Director, Al Freeman, Jr.; Set, Charles McClennahan; Lighting, James Worley; Costumes, Judy Dearing; Sound, Dennis Ogburn; Company Manager, Linda Herring; Technical Director, James Worley; Wardrobe, Harriet Foy; Props, Linda Stewart, Ileana Peyron; Stage Manager, Gwendolyn Gilliam; Press, Max Eisen, Madelon Rosen

CAST: Hazelle Goodman (Enid), Monica Williams (Esme), Donald Lee Taylor (Clebert), Clifford Mason (Hugh), Hazel Medina (Mavis), Helmar Augustus Cooper (Percy), Vaughn Dwight Morrison (Basil), Thomas Anderson (Clive), Petronia Paley (Fae), Thomas Pinnock (Rasta)

A drama in 3 acts and 5 scenes. The action takes place in 1960 just before Jamaica's independence.

(Henry DeJur Playhouse) Thursday, February 12–22, 1986 (10 performances). National Black Touring Circuit presents:

HATS a one-woman show in two acts with Saundra Dunson Franks as Harriet Tubman. Musical Compositions and Arrangements, Joseph W. Jennings; Vocal Artist, Bernadine Mitchell; Slides, William Kantz Collection

(Louis Abrons Arts for Living Center) Thursday, Feb. 12–March 15, 1987 (30 performances)

BOOGIE WOOGIE AND BOOKER T by Wesley Brown; Director, A. Dean Irby; Set, Charles H. McClennahan; Musical Director, John McCallum; Costumes, Judy Dearing; Lighting, Victor En Yu Tan; Sound, Jacqui Casto; Company Manager, Linda Herring; Wardrobe, Marcia Belton; Props, Linda Stewart; Stage Manager, Jesse Wooden, Jr.; Press, Max Eisen, Madelon Rosen

CAST: Ruben S. Hudson (Thaddeus Stewart), John McCallum (Butterfingers McCann), Cortez Nance, Jr. (William Monroe Trotter), LaTanya Richardson (Ida B. Wells), Marie Thomas (Mary Church Terrell), Nick Smith (W. E. B. DuBois), Charles Dumas (Booker T. Washington)

A play in 2 acts and 4 scenes. The action takes place in New York City in January 1904.

(Harry DeJur Henry Street Settlement Playhouse) Thursday, April 16–May 3, 1987 (27 performances)

THE MEETING by Jeff Stetson; Director, Judyann Elder; Company Manager, Linda Herring; Stage Manager, Michael Schaefer; Press, Max Eisen, Madelon Rosen

CAST: Dick Anthony Williams (Malcolm X), Taurean Blacque (Rashad), Felton Perry (Dr. Martin Luther King, Jr.)

A drama performed without intermission. The action takes place in a hotel room in Harlem, New York City, on February 14, 1965 . . . one week before the assassination of Malcolm X.

Bert Andrews Photos
**Center Lower Right: Ruben Hudson, Marie Thomas
in "Boogie Woogie and Booker T" Above: Patricia
Elliott in "Lillian Wald, at Home on Henry Street"
Top: Helmar Augustus Cooper, Robert Jason, Reggie
Montgomery in "Sovereign State of Boogedy"**

**Dick Anthony Williams, Taurean Blacque,
Felton Perry in "The Meeting"**

TNT/THE NEW THEATRE OF BROOKLYN

Artistic Director, Deborah J. Pope
Third Season

(465 Dean Street) Thursday, Oct. 23,–Nov. 16, 1986 (20 performances)
SPACE WALK by Alan Mokler; Director, Peter Wallace; Original Music, Brad Garton; Set, Rosario Provenza; Lighting, Mary Louise Geiger; Costumes, Catherine Zuber; Sound, Brad Garton; Technical Director, David Raphel; Props, Edward J. Magalong; Stage Managers, C. A. Clark, Jill Clark
CAST: Paul Zimet (Joe), Nancy Mayans (Dora/Melinda), Jen Jones (Grandma/Mama), Todd Oleson (Lee/Doctor/Engineer), Stacie Linardos (Sunbather/Elsie/Miss G), Albert Ownes (Mike/H. Cassidy), Voices: Lawrence Baldine, Jill Griggs
   Performed without intermission. The action takes place at the present time.
   Thursday, December 4–14, 1986 (10 performances). The Second Stage presents:
AN EVENING OF SHOLOM ALEICHEM translated by Joseph Singer; Director, Richard Maltby, Jr.; Lighting, Fred Jason Hancock; Costumes, Pegi Goodman; Music, Raphael Crystal; Technical Director, Patrick Mathieu
CAST: Murray Horwitz as Sholom Aleichem
   Stories by the Yiddish writer presented in two parts.
   Thursday, Feb. 19–March 15, 1987 (20 performances)
DONKEYS' YEARS by Michael Frayn; Director, Steve Stettler; Set, Lewis Folden; Lighting, Victor En Yu Tan; Costumes, Eiko Yamaguchi; Sound, Tom Gould; Assistant Director, David Newman; Dramaturg, Janice Paran; Choreographer, Lynn Britt; Production Manager, Julie Nessen; Technical Director, Jess M. Klarnet; Props, Sue Jane Stoker; Wardrobe, Patricia Spanneda; Stage Managers, Nicholas Dunn, Kim McNutt; Press, Reva Cooper
CAST: Regina Baff (Lady Drive), John Henry Cox (Buckle), Rob Comes (Taylor), Davis Hall (Rev. Sainsbury), Neil Hunt (Headingley), Frank Lowe (Birkett), James Maxwell (Snell), Allan Stevens (Tate), Rudolph Willrich (Quine)
   A comedy in three acts. The action takes place in one of the lesser colleges, at one of the older universities of England.
   April, 23–May 17, 1987 (20 performances)
THE ART OF WAR by George F. Walker; Director, Stephen Katz; Set, Lewis Folden; Lighting, Fred Jason Hancock; Costumes, Arnall Downs; Sound, Gary Harris; Assistant Director, Erin Sanders; Production Manager, Sandy Fischler; Technical Director, Richard Morganelli; Props, Mimi Cohen; Stage Managers, David Dunn Bauer, Kim McNutt, Kate Dale
CAST: John Perkins (General John Hackman), Michael Kemmerling (Brownie Brown, Hackman's Aide), K. C. Wilson (Tyrone M. Power), Rudy Goldschmidt (Jamie McLean), June Gable (Karla Mendez, Hackman's guest), Amy Griscom Epstein (Heather Masterson)
   A play in two acts. The action takes place in and around a large summer estate in Maine.

Regina Baff, James Maxwell, Frank Lowe in "Donkey's Years"
Top Right: Stacie Linardos, Paul Zimet in "Space Walk"
Below: Michael Kemmerling, John Perkins, June Gable in "The Art of War" (*Jessica Katz Photos*)

NEW YORK SHAKESPEARE FESTIVAL

Producer, Joseph Papp; General Manager, Laurel Ann Wilson; Company Manager, David Conte; Plays/Musicals Department, Gail Merrifield; Literary Manager, Bill Hart; Casting, Rosemarie Tichler; Art Director, Paul Davis; Production Manager, Andrew Mihok; Technical Director, Mervyn Haines, Jr.; Costume Shopmaster, Milo Morrow; Audio Master, Gene Ricciardi; Prop Master, James Gill; Press, Richard Kornberg, Barbara Carroll, Kevin Patterson

(Public/Newman Theater) Wednesday, June 4–July 27, 1986 (68 performances).
VIENNA: LUSTHAUS conceived and directed by Martha Clarke; Composer, Richard Peaslee, with the aid of Bach, Friesen, and Strauss; Text, Charles Mee, Jr.; Sets/Costumes, Robert Israel; Lighting, Paul Gallo; Production and Stage Manager, Steven Ehrenberg; Presented by Music-Theatre Group/Lenox Arts Center (Lyn Austin, Producing Director) with Robert DeRothschild; Associate Producer for NYSFestival, Jason Steven Cohen; Associate Producing Directors for MTG/LAC, Diane Wondisford, Mark Jones; Wardrobe, George Erdman, Kathy Lee Cawley; Production Assistants, Blair Breard, Dan Kester; Stage Manager, Elizabeth Sherman. CAST: Rob Besserer, Timothy Doyle, Marie Fourcaut, Lotte Goslar, Laura Innes, Robert Langdon-Lloyd, Rick Merrill, Gianfranco Paoluzi, Amy Spencer, Paola Styron, Lila York

(Delacorte Theater/Central Park) Friday, June 20–July 20, 1986 (26 performances). Presented by the New York Shakespeare Festival (Joseph Papp, Producer) with the cooperation of the City of New York, and in association with New York Telephone.
TWELFTH NIGHT by William Shakespeare; Director, Wilford Leach; Scenery, Bob Shaw; Costumes, Lindsay W. Davis; Lighting, Stephen Strawbridge; Fight Direction, B. H. Barry; Music, Rupert Holmes; Associate Producer, Jason Steven Cohen; Speech Consultant, Elizabeth Himelstein; Technical Director, Peter R. Feuche; Props, John Masterson; Wardrobe, Carol Gant; Wigs, James Herrera; General Manager, Laurel Ann Wilson; Stage Manager, Ginny Martino, Alan Traynor; Press, Richard Kornberg, Bruce Campbell, Kevin Patterson, Pat Krawitz, Reva Cooper, Don Anthony Summa. CAST: Tony Azito (Singer/Clown), Kim Greist (Viola), Jordan Lund (Sea Captain), Renardo Johnson (Sailor), Thomas Gibson (Orsino), Michael David Morrison (Curio), Tim Guinee (Valentine), Kevin Black (Officer), Jeff Bender (Attendant of Duke), Marco St. John (Antonio), Perry Lang (Sebastian), William Duff-Griffin (Sir Toby Belch), Meagen Fay (Maria), Peter MacNicol (Sir Andrew Aguecheek), Kathleen Layman (Olivia), F. Murray Abraham (Malvolio), James Lancaster (Fabian), Michael Gerald (Olivia's Servant/Priest), Ashley Crow, Kathleen McNenny (Ladies attending Olivia), UNDERSTUDIES: Jeff Bender (Sebastian/Fabian/Valentine), Kevin Black (Aguecheek/Sailor), Ashley Crow (Olivia/Maria), Renardo Johnson (Feste/Priest/Servant), Kathleen McNenny (Viola), Marco St. John (Malvolio), Jordan Lund (Sir Toby), Michael Gerald (Antonio/Captain/Curio), Michael David Morrison (Orsino)
   Performed with one intermission

Martha Swope Photos
**Left: Gianfranco Paoluzi, Paola Styron
in "Vienna:Lusthaus" Top: Rob Besserer,
Paola Styron in "Vienna:Lusthaus"**

F. Murray Abraham, Tony Azito, Peter MacNicol
in "Twelfth Night" *(George Joseph)*

Mikijiro Hira as "Medea"
(Maurizio Buscarino)

(Public and Delacorte Theaters) Tuesday, August 6–31, 1986. Tenth anniversary of FESTIVAL LATINO IN NEW YORK presenting over 30 attractions of theater, music and dance, as well as a film festival representing countries throughout Latin America, the Carribean, Spain, Italy and cities across the U.S. Produced by Joseph Papp; Associate Producer, Jason Steven Cohen; Directors, Oscar Ciccone, Cecilia Vega, Special Consultant, Fernando Torres; Assistant to Directors, Melia Bensussen; Technical Director, Jose R. Fernandez; Costumes Supervisors, Tony Powell, Bruce Brumage, Carol Grant; Production Assistants, Marguerite MacIntyre, Diana Londono; Stage Managers, Kristina Kinet, Pat Sosnow, Buzz Cohen, Roylan Diaz, Erie Nord, Ginny Martino, Vincente Castro; Press, Reva Cooper, Michelle Macau, Julio Marzan.

(Delacorte Theater/Central Park) Wednesday, September 3–8, 1986 (6 performances)

MEDEA by Euripides; Director, Yukio Ninagawa; Produced by Toho Company Ltd.; Scenario, Mutsuo Takahashi; Art Direction/Costumes, Jusaburo Tsujimura; Scenery, Setsu Asakura; Lighting, Sumio Yoshii; Sound, Akira Honma; Choreography, Kinnosuke Hanayagi; Producer, Tadao Nakane; Associate Producer for NYSF, Jason Steven Cohen; Executive Assistant (Toho/NY), Lucille Carra; Assistant Producers, Ko Takahashi, Michiyo Tomitsuka; Sponsored by Hitachi; Stage Managers, Takayuki Yamada, Hideyasu Murai

CAST: Mikijiro Hira (Medea), Masane Tsukayama (Jason), Ryunosuke Kaneda (Creon), Hatsuo Yamaya (Nurse), Kazuhisa Seshimo (Tutor), Ryuzaburo Otomo (Aegus), Takayuki Sugo (Messenger), Ken Osawa, Tatsuya Miura (Sons of Medea), Fujiro Higashi, Takuzo Kaneda (Soldiers), Chorus: Kazunaga Tsuji, Goro Daimon, Tatsumi Aoyama, Susumu Kakuma, Hirofumi Yamabi, Eiichi Seike, Chihiro Ito, Masahiko Nakata, Tsukasa Nakagoshi, Keita Oishi, Hiroki Okawa, Kazuhiro Kikuchi, Toru Takagi, Kunihiro Iida, Sho Shinohara, Kurokazu Aoyama

Performed in two acts by an all-male cast in Japanese without translations.

(Public/Susan Stein Shiva Theater) Tuesday, Oct. 7, 1986–July 19, 1987 (324 performances). Moved Apr. 29, 1987 to Public/Newman Theater.

THE COLORED MUSEUM by George C. Wolfe; Director, L. Kenneth Richardson; Scenery, Brian Martin; Costumes, Nancy L. Konrady; Lighting, Victor En Yu Tan, William H. Grant III; Sound, Rob Gorton; Composer/Arranger, Kysia Bostic; Musical Direction/Vocal Arrangements, Daryl Waters; Choreographer, Hope Clarke; Slide Projections, Anton Nelessen; Associate Producer, Jason Steven Cohen; Wigs, James Herrera; Props, Frances Smith, Evan Canary; Wardrobe, Odel Perry, Bruce Brumage; Stage Managers, Kenneth Johnson, Roylan Diaz

CAST: Loretta Devine, Tommy Hollis, Reggie Montgomery, Vickilyn Reynolds, Danitra Vance, Jonea Thomas alternating with Colette Baptiste

EXHIBITS IN THE COLORED MUSEUM: Git on Board, Cooking with Aunt Ethel, The Photo Session, Soldier with a Secret, The Gospel according to Miss Roj, The Hairpiece, The Last Mama-on-the-Couch Play, Symbiosis, Lala's Opening, Permutations, The Party. Performed without intermission.

(Public/Martinson Hall) Friday, Jan. 16–March 22, 1987 (77 performances)

MY GENE by Barbara Gelb; Director, Andre Ernotte; Associate Producer, Jason Steven Cohen; Costumes, Muriel Stockdale; Lighting, Phil Monat; Production Assistant, Diana Schmidt; Props, Mary Kay Carter, Anne Doherty, Colin Gregory, Jean Paradis; Stage Manager, Buzz Cohen

CAST: Colleen Dewhurst as Carlotta Monterey O'Neill, widow of Eugene O'Neill.

Performed with one intermission. The action takes place during November of 1968 in a room in St. Luke's Hospital in New York City.

Colleen Dewhurst in "My Gene"
Above: Loretta Devine, Reggie Montgomery
in "The Colored Museum"

Top: Teatro Belli in "Pranza di Familia"
Left: Danitra Vance, Vickilyn Reynolds
in "The Colored Museum"

Eric Bogosian in "Talk Radio" Left: Mary Elizabeth Mastrantonio, Mar
Patinkin in "The Knife" Below: John C. McGinley, Eric Bogosian,
Robyn Peterson, Michael Wincott in "Talk Radio"
Martha Swope Photos

NEW YORK SHAKESPEARE FESTIVAL
(cont.)

(Public/Newman Theater) Thursday, Feb. 12–April 15, 1987 (60 performances).
THE KNIFE with Music by Nick Bicat; Book, David Hare; Lyrics, Rim Rose Price;
Director, David Hare; Choreography, Graciela Daniele; Scenery, Hayden Griffin;
Costumes, Jane Greenwood; Lighting, Tharon Musser; Sound, Otts Munderloh;
Orchestrations, Chris Walker; Musical Director, Michael Starobin; Associate Producer, Jason Steven Cohen; Production Assistant, Christie Wagner; Associate Conductor, Scott Frankel; Props, Frances Smith; Wardrobe, Vicki Jo DeRocker; Stage Managers, Karen Armstrong, Alan R. Traynor
CAST: Mandy Patinkin (Peter), Cass Morgan (Angela), Michael Willson (Lifeboat Collector), Wade Raley (Johnny), William Parry (Ralph), Tim Shew (Jeremy), Mary Elizabeth Mastrantonio (Jenny), Mary Gordon Murray (Roxanne/Nurse), Mary Testa (Sally), Louis Padilla (1st Waiter), Reuben Gaumes (Kitchen Boy/Choir Boy), Shelly Paul (Chloe), Devon Michaels (Richard), Lisa Vroman (Citizens Advice Bureau), Louise Flaningam (Citizens Advice Bureau/Michael's Wife), Ronn Carroll (G. P./Michael), Olivia Virgil Harper (Therapist), Kevin Gray (English Surgeon), Mary Gutzi (Mariachi Singer), Dennis Parlato (Dr. Bauer), Hansford Rowe (Andrew), Jeremy Cummins, Roshi Handwerger (Choir Boys)
A musical in two acts. The action takes place at the present time in Winchester, England.
(Public/Martinson Hall) Tuesday, May 12–
TALK RADIO by Eric Bogosian; Based on an original idea by Tad Savinar; Director, Frederick Zollo; Visuals, Tad Savinar; Scenery, David Jenkins; Costumes, Pilar Limosner; Lighting, Jan Kroeze; Props, Frances Smith; Wardrobe, Ira Rosenbaum; Stage Managers, Alan R. Traynor, Pat Sosnow
CAST: Zach Grenier (Sid Greenberg), Peter Onorati (Bernie), John C. McGinley (Stu Noonan), Robyn Peterson (Linda MacArthur), Eric Bogosian (Barry Champlain), Mark Metcalf (Dan Woodruf), Michael Wincott (Kent), Linda Atkinson (Dr. Susan Fleming), William DeAcutis, Callers' Voices: Linda Atkinson, William DeAcutis, Susan Gabriel, Zach Grenier, Michele M. Mariana, Peter Onorati, Michael Wincott
Performed without intermission. The action takes place in Studio B of radio station WTLK in Cleveland, Ohio, at 7:45 P.M.

**Eric Bogosian, Robyn Peterson, John McGinley,
Mark Metcalf in "Talk Radio"**

PAN ASIAN REPERTORY THEATRE

Tenth Season

Artistic/Producing Director, Tisa Chang; Managing Director, Elizabeth A. Hyslop; Marketing, Maggie Browne; Development, Ed Schmidt; Production Manager, Dominick Balletta; Wardrobe, Neeke Lisa Brice; Technical Director, Doug Ward; Press, G. Theodore Killmer

(Playhouse 46) Tuesday, Oct. 7–Nov. 1, 1986 (24 performances)

THE IMPOSTOR by Sha Yexin, Li Shoucheng, Yao Mingde; Director, Ron Nakahara; Special Consultant, William Sun; Lighting, Victor En Yu Tan; Costumes, Linda Taoka; Stage Manager, Patrice Thomas

CAST: Kati Kuroda (Theatre Director Zhao), Mary Lum (Division Head Qian), Norris M. Shimabuku (Section Head Sun), Keenan Shimizu (Li Xiaozhang), Hamilton Fong (Security Officer/Farm Youth), Dalton Leong (Security Officer/Farm Youth/Judge), Mary Lee-Aranas (Zhou Minghua), Tom Matsusaka (Secretary Wu), Donald Li (Farm Director Zheng), Bea Soong (Juanjuan/Assessor), Ben Lin (Venerable Comrade Zhang/Man on telephone)

A satire from China in two acts.

Tuesday, Nov. 18–Dec. 20, 1986 (30 performances)

SHOGUN MACBETH by William Shakespeare; Adapted and Directed by John R. Briggs; Lighting, Tina Charney; Set, Atsushi Moriyasu; Costumes, Eiko Yamaguchi; Military Armour/Macbeth's Helmet, Robin Murray; Movement, Sachiyo Ito; Fight Director, David Leong; Special Creation, Stanley Allan Sherman; Stage Managers, Dominick Balletta, Arthur C. Catricala

CAST: Lori Tanaka (Kuroko/Soldier/Fleance/Momo Macduff), Shigeko Suga (Kuroko/Soldier/Gentlewoman/Jiro Kaja), Tom Matsusaka (Biwa Hoshi), Allan Tung (Yojo of Evil Samurai), Toshi Toda (Yojo of Death), Ako (Yojo with Spider Face), Donald Li (Duncan), Mel Duane Gionson (Malcolm), Michael G. Chin (Donalbain), Dalton Leong (Shoko/Young Siward), Ron Nakahara (Angus), Christen Villamor (Soldier/Taro Kaja/Young Macduff), Kati Kuroda (Ross), Ernest Abuba (Macbeth), Raul Aranas (Banquo), Freda Foh Shen (Fujin Macbeth), Norris M. Shimabuku (Macduff), Natsuko Ohama (Fujin Macduff)

A tragedy performed in two acts.

Tuesday, April 28–May 23, 1986 (24 performances)

WHA . . . I, WHAI, A LONG LONG TIME AGO by Che Inhoon; Translation, Hui-jin Pak with additional phrases by Oh-kon Cho; Director, Tisa Chang; Set, Alex Polner; Lighting, Victor En Yu Tan; Costumes, Eiko Yamaguchi; Masks, Rebecca Kravitz; Sound, Joseph Tornabene; Choreographer, Du-Yee Chang; Stage Manager, Dominick Balletta

CAST: Ginny Yang (Wife), Du-Yee Chang (Husband), Mary Lum (Kaetong's Mother), Hae Ryen Kim (Old Woman/Villager), Jung Nam Lee (Policeman), Steve Park (Villager)

A tragedy in four acts. The action takes place in a Korean mountain village a long long time ago.

Carol Rosegg/Martha Swope Photos
**Right: Ernest Abuba, Freda Foh Shen
in "Shogun Macbeth" Top: Norris Shimabuku,
Kati Kuroda, Keenan Shimizu, Tom Matsusaka,
Mary Lum in "The Impostor (If I Were Real)"**

**Du Yee Chang, Ginny Yang
in "Wha . . . I, Whai"**

**Mary Lum, Ginny Yang
in "Wha . . . I, Whai"**

Greg Germann, Jim Fyfe, Adam Redfield
in "Coup d'Etat" *(Susan Cook)*

PLAYWRIGHTS HORIZONS

Sixteenth Season

Artistic Director, Andre Bishop; Executive Director, Paul S. Daniels; Production Manager, Carl Mulert; Development, Ruth Cohen; Business Manager, Donna M. Gearhardt; Casting, Amy Introcaso; Props, Tom Zofrea; Technical Director, Albert Webster; Wardrobe, Laurie Buehler; Press, Bob Ullman

Tuesday, September 16–October 12, 1986 (32 performances and 5 readings). **FIFTH ANNUAL YOUNG PLAYWRIGHTS FESTIVAL** presented by the Foundation of the Dramatists Guild. Sets, Rick Dennis; Costumes, Michael Krass; Lighting, Ann G. Wrightson; Sound, James M. Bay; Production Manager, Carl Mulert; Producing Director, Melissa Davis; Stage Managers, Melissa Davis, Anne Marie Kuehling, Johnna Murray; Associate Director, Sheri M. Goldhirsch; Program Coordinator, Richard Wolcott; Props, Elain Zofrea; Wardrobe, Jennifer Smith, Ulrike Steinle; Production Assistants, Kelly Hewitt, Jennifer Smith

COUP D'ETAT by Carolyn Jones (age 18); Director, Art Wolff. CAST: Susan Greenhill (Mama), Evan Handler (Juan), Shawn Elliott (Papa), Tom Mardirosian (King), Shawn Elliott (Enrico), Ted Sod (Abdul), Susan Greenhill (Stephanie), Larry Block (Yuri Brushnik), Jim Fyfe (Troy LeFlame), Greg Germann (Julio Fernandez). The action takes place at the present time on the island of St. Passis.

A DELICATE SITUATION by Eve Goldfarb (Age 17); Director, Mary B. Robinson. CAST: Kelly Wolf (Amelia), Evan Handler (Derek), Susan Greenhill (Susan), Fran Brill (Lydia), Nicholas Kallsen (Chuck). The action takes place at the present time in two Manhattan apartments.

REMEDIAL ENGLISH by Evan Smith (Age 18); Director, Ron Lagomarsino. CAST: Greg Germann (Vincent), Anne Pitoniak (Sister Beatrice), Nicholas Kallsen (Rob), Shawn Elliott (Coach), Jim Fyfe (Chris), Adam Redfield (David). The action takes place at the present time in Cabrini Catholic Academy, a private high school for boys, and in Vincent's living room.

Friday, October 31–November 30, 1986 (19 performances and 14 previews). **HIGHEST STANDARD OF LIVING** by Keith Reddin; Director, Don Scardino; Set, John Arnone; Costumes, David C. Woolard; Lighting, Joshua Dachs; Sound, Scott Lehrer; Production Manager, Carl Mulert; Wardrobe, Virginia Patton, Ulrike Steinle; Props, Elaine Zofrea; Dialect Consultant, Timothy Monich; Stage Managers, Fredric H. Orner, Amanda Mengden

CAST: Steven Culp (Bob), Timothy Carhart (Vlad/Jack), Kevin Skousen (Man on Ferry/Yuri/Gary), Leslie Lyles (Ludmilla), Lola Pashalinski (Tatiana/Jean/Adele), James Murtaugh (Tom/Larry), Sloane Shelton (Mother/Helen), Clement Fowler (Sergei/Don), Peter Crombie (Dmitri/Doug), Robert Stanton (Rodger/Waiter/Man at bus stop/Eskimo Pie Man), Children: Phillip Daniels, David Jon, Robert Meltzer, Meredith Muller, Caryn Osofsky, Shiah Schwartz, Christopher Spellman.

A play in two acts. The action takes place in Moscow and in New York City.

Steven Culp, James Murtaugh in "Highest Standard of Living" *(Gerry Goodstein Photo)*

Henry Stram, Alan Scarfe, David Chandler
in "Black Sea Follies" *(Clemens Kalischer)*

Philip Coccioletti, Boyd Gaines, Mary Joy,
Patricia Clarkson, Lenny Von Dohlen, Paul
Collins, Amanda Carlin in "The Maderati"
(Henry Grossman)

Friday November 28, 1986–January 11, 1987 (31 performances and 19 previews).
Playwrights Horizons and Music-Theatre Group (Lyn Austin, Producing Director)
present.
BLACK SEA FOLLIES by Paul Schmidt; Conceived and Directed by Stanley
Silverman; Music, Dmitri Shostakovich and other Russians; Music adapted by Mr.
Silverman; Russian lyrics translated by Mr. Schmidt; Additional Material, Mr.
Silverman; Sets, James Noone; Costumes, Jim Buff; Lighting, Ken Tabachnick;
Music Coordinated by Mark Bennett; Dances, Liz Lerman; Production Assistants,
Nina Mankin, Anthony Phelan; Wardrobe, Ulrike Steinle; Hairstylist, Tom Munoz;
Stage Managers, Roy Harris, Anne Marie Kuehling
CAST: David Chandler (Shostakovich), Alan Scarfe (Stalin), Henry Stram (Misha),
Carmen Pelton (Katerina Lvovna), David Dusing (Seryozha), Robert Osborne (Ste-
panych), Martha Caplin (Violin), Carol Zeavin (Violin), Sarah Clarke (Viola),
Matthias Naegele, Elena Ivanina (Piano)
A play in two acts. It is the early 1970's in Moscow. A young ensemble of Soviet
musicians has asked Dmitri Shostakovich to coach them in his late chamber music. It
is the music of these pieces that reawakens Shostakovich's memories of the Stalin
years.
Friday, January 30–March 1, 1987 (12 performances and 22 previews)
THE MADERATI by Richard Greenberg; Director, Michael Engler; Set, Philipp
Jung; Costumes, Candice Donnelly; Lighting, Michael Orris Watson; Sound, Lia
Vollack; Production Manager, Carl Mulert; Production Assistant, Christopher Ashle-
y; Wardrobe, Virginia Patton; Props, Neal Carpenter; Hairstylist, Thomas Brac-
coneri; Stage Managers, Melissa Davis, Leslie Loeb.
CAST: Mary Joy (Rena deButts), Boyd Gaines (Chuck deButts), Patricia Clarkson
(Dewy Overlander), Lenny von Dohlen (Ritt Overlander), Paul Collins (Martin
Royale), David Pierce (Keene Esterhazy), Anna Levine (Cuddles Molotov), Amanda
Carlin (Charlotte Ebbinger), Philip Coccioletti (Danton Young)
A play in two acts. The action takes place at the present time on Sunday in several
apartments in Manhattan, New York City.
Tuesday, March 31,–June 7, 1987 (80 performances)
DRIVING MISS DAISY by Alfred Uhry; Director, Ron Lagomarsino; Set, Thomas
Lynch; Costumes, Michael Krass; Lighting, Ken Tabachnick; Incidental Music,
Robert Waldman; Production Manager, Carl Mulert; Stage Managers, Anne Marie
Kuehling, Elaine Zofrea
CAST: Dana Ivey (Daisy Werthan), Ray Gill (Boolie Werthan), Morgan Freeman
(Hoke Coleburn)
Performed without intermission. The action takes place in Atlanta, Georgia, from
1948 to 1973.
Friday, April 24–May 31, 1987 (22 performances and 22 previews)
THREE POSTCARDS by Craig Lucas, Craig Carnelia; Director, Norman Rene;
Choreography, Linda Kostalik-Boussom; Set, Loy Arcenas; Costumes, Walker
Hicklin; Lighting, Debra J. Kletter; Sound, Bruce D. Cameron; Musical Theatre
Program Director, Ira Weitzman; Props, Paul Warren; Wardrobe, Jennifer Smith;
Stage Managers, M. A. Howard, Thomas S. Spital
CAST: Craig Carnelia (Bill), Brad O'Hare (Waiter), Jane Galloway (Big Jane),
Maureen Silliman (Little Jane), Karen Trott (K. C.)
A comedy performed without intermission. The action takes place at the present
time in a restaurant.

Right Center: Dana Ivey, Morgan Freeman in "Driving Miss Daisy"
(Bob Marshak)

Karen Trott, Brad O'Hare, Jane Galloway, Maureen
Silliman, Craig Carnelia in "Three Postcards"
(Gerry Goodstein)

PEARL THEATRE COMPANY

Fourth Season

Artistic Director, Shepard Sobel; General Manager, John Hedges; Artistic Associate, Joanne Camp; Dramaturg, Dale Ramsey; Producing Consultant, Tarquin Jay Bromley

(Pearl Theatre) Thursday, Dec. 18, 1986–Jan. 17, 1987 (20 performances)

PERICLES by William Shakespeare; Director, Joel Bernstein; Set, Robert Joel Schwartz; Lighting, Douglas O'Flaherty; Costumes, Murrey Nelson; Sound, T. J. Bromley/Celia Hollander; Assistant Director, Tarquin Jay Bromley; Movement, Michelle Boston; Stage Managers, Laura Rathgeb, Gino Montesinos

CAST: James Nugent (Gower/Helicanus), Stuart Lerch (Antiochus/Cleon), Patrick Turner (Pericles/Leonine), Robin Leslie Brown (Antiochus' Daughter/Marina), David Brazda (Thaliard/Lysimachus), Laura Margolis (Thaisa/Bawd/Others), Robin Westphal (Dionyza/Lychorida), Daniel Region (Simonides/Boult), Pinkney Mikell (Cerimon/Pandar)

Performed with one intermission.

Thursday, Jan. 22–Feb. 21, 1987 (20 performances)

THE RIVALS by Richard Brinsley Sheridan; Director, Shepard Sobel; Set, Robert Joel Schwartz; Lighting, Douglas J. O'Flaherty; Speech Consultant, Robert Neff Williams; Costumes, Barbara Forbes; Sound, T. J. Bromley; Movement, Alice Teirstein; Stage Manager, Elli Agosto

CAST: Joanne Camp, Frank Geraci, Michael Hill, Stuart Lerch, Anna Minot, James Nugent, Rose Stockton, Patrick Turner, Joseph Warren, Robin Westphal

Thursday, Feb. 26–March 28, 1987 (20 performances)

ANDROMACHE by Jean Racine; Translated by Earle Edgerton; Director, Allan Carlsen; Set, Robert Joel Schwartz; Lighting, Douglas O'Flaherty; Costumes, P. Chelsea Harriman; Sound, Tarquin Jay Bromley; Assistant Director, Donnah Welby; Technical Director, Stephen Petrilli; Stage Managers, Mary-Susan Gregson, Fred Hahn

CAST: Robert Emmet (Orestes), Michael John McGuinness (Pylades), Stuart Lerch (Pyrrhus), Christian Kauffmann (Phoenix), Eliza Ventura (Andromache), Joanne Camp (Hermione), Robin Leslie Brown (Cleone), Bonnie K. Allison Gould (Cephissa)

Performed with one intermission.

Thursday, April 2–26, 1987 (16 performances)

DEEP SWIMMER by Dale Ramsey; Freely adapted from "The Wild Duck" by Henrik Ibsen; Director, Shepard Sobel; Set, Robert Joel Schwartz; Costumes, Murrey Nelson; Lighting, Douglas O'Flaherty; Sound, Kenn Dovel; Technical Director, Stephen Petrilli; Assistant Director, Daniel Region; Production Assistant, Barry Buickel; Stage Manager, Lee J. Copenhaver

CAST: Frank Geraci (Capt. Ecker), W. Benson Terry (Nick Peters), James Nugent (Senator Tom Carpenter), Jane C. Hamilton (Louisa Wheeler), Pinkney Mikell (Harley Ecker), Joel Bernstein (Grayson Wheeler), Herman Petras (Harris Randolph Wheeler), Lee Roy Giles (Dr. Collins), Laura Margolis (Jeanie Ecker), Laura Rathgeb (Letty Ecker)

A drama in two acts. The action takes place during May of 1958 in Richmond, Virginia.

Carol Rosegg/Martha Swope Photos
Right: Anna Minot, Joseph Warren in "The Rivals"
Top: Patrick Turner, Joanne Camp in "The Rivals"

Pinkney Mikell, Laura Margolis, Joel Bernstein in "Deep Swimmer"

Joanne Camp, Stuart Lerch in "Andromache"

PUERTO RICAN TRAVELING THEATRE

Twentieth Season

Artistic Director, Miriam Colon Edgar; Managing Director, Patricia Baldwin; Community Coordinator, Julio E. Martinez; Development, Vera Ryan; Props, Annalee Van Kleeck; Wardrobe/Props, Amy Meisner; Design Supervisor, Janice Davis; Press, Max Eisen, Madelon Rosen, Maria Somma, Barbara Glenn
  (Summer Tour of City Parks) Friday, August 8–31, 1986 (23 performances)
LADY WITH A VIEW with Music and Lyrics by Fernando Rivas; Book Translation, Manuel Ramos Otero; Director, Max Ferra; Musical Director, Fernando Rivas; Set, James D. Sandefur; Costumes, David Navarro Velasquez; Sound, Manuel Gonzalez; Stage Manager, Douglas R. Bergman; Staging/Choreography, Poli Rogers; Technical Director, Mark Preuss
CAST: Anthony Laguerre/Reuben Gaumes (Johnny), Linda Reyes/Nina Laboy (Josefa), James Callun (Joe), Edward Rodriguez (Harry), Milton Demel (Chief), Nina Laboy/Linda Reyes (Mary)
MUSICAL NUMBERS: Overture, Lady Liberty, Johnny's Rap A, You Gotta Be Strong, Life Is Not So Bad, Josefa's Plea, My Country, The Manhattan Song, We're Gonna Sue You, The River Flows, What's It Gonna Be, Finale
  The action takes place at the present time, at or near the Statue of Liberty.
  Wednesday, January 14,–February 22, 1987 (42 performances)
A LITTLE SOMETHING TO EASE THE PAIN by Rene R. Aloma; Director, Mario Ernesto Sanchez; Set, Rolando Moreno; Lighting, Rachel Budin; Costumes, Kay Panthaky; Musicalization, Raul Reyes-Roque; Producer, Miriam Colon Edgar; Stage Manager, Sandra M. Bloom
CAST: Jorge Luis Ramos (Carlos), Jorge Rios (Father Ephraim), Jeannette Mirabal (Amelia), Carmen Rosario (Delia), Graciela Lecube/Graciela Mas (Dona Cacha), Laura E. Delano (Ana), Rita Ben-Or/Cari Gorostiza (Clara), Ruben Pla (Nelson), Arcadio Ruiz Castellano (Paco/Julio)
  A drama in two acts. The action takes place during a week of July 1979 in a church, and in the house of the Rabel family in Santiago, Cuba.
  Thursday, March 19–April 19, 1987 (42 performances)
A ROSE OF TWO AROMAS by Emilio Carballido; English Translation, Margaret Peden; Director, Vicente Castro, Scenery, Janice Davis; Lighting, Rachel Budin; Costumes, Gail Brassard; Sound, Gary Harris; Technical Director, Ed Bartosik; Stage Manager, Leslie Moore
CAST: Sully Diaz (Marlene), Irene De Bari (Gabriela)
  A comedy in six scenes. The action takes place in a city, anywhere in the world, at the present time.
  Wednesday, May 13–June 28, 1987 (56 performances)
BODEGA by Federico Fraguada; Spanish Translation, Freddy Valle; Director, Alba Oms; Producer, Miriam Colon Edgar; Scenery, Carl A. Baldasso; Lighting, Rachel Budin; Costumes, Sue Ellen Rohrer; Sound, Gary Harris; Fight Director, Thomas Schall; Stage Manager, T. J. Carroll
CAST: Puli Toro (Elena Toro), Jaime Tirelli (Maximo Toro), Regina Baro (Norma Toro), Antonio Aponte (Rafy Lopez), Olga Molina-Tobin (Dona Luz), Donald Silva (Michael Peterson), Bodega Customers: Rudy Fort, Jaime Rodriguez, John Rivera
  A tragedy in two acts. The action takes place at the present time in a bodega in the South Bronx of New York City

Right: Graciela LeCube, Jorge Luis Ramos
Above: Jorge Luis Ramos, Ruben Pla, Arcadio Ruiz Castellano
in "A Little Something to Ease the Pain" Top:
"Lady with a View"

Jaime Tirelli, Regina Baro, Puli Toro
in "Bodega" (*Peter Krupenye*)

Sully Diaz, Irene De Bari
in "A Rose of Two Aromas"

Kim Yancey, Starletta DuPois, John Fiedler,
James Pickens (back), Richard Habersham,
Olivia Cole in "A Raisin in the Sun"

Ernestine Jackson, Ben Harney, Rex Smith,
Liz Callaway, Kimberly Farr in "Brownstone"

ROUNDABOUT THEATRE

Twenty-first Season

Artistic Director, Gene Feist; Executive Director, Todd Haimes; General Manager, Ellen Richard; Development, Vicki Reiss; Marketing, Michael P. Lynch; Subscriptions, Martin S. Herstein; Literary Manager/Artistic Associate, Eileen Cowel; Assistant to Executive Director, Margaret L. Wolff; Casting Associate/Internship Coordinator, Mitzi Metzl-Pazer; Assistant General Manager, Ellen Scrimger Gordon; Production Manager, Robert N. Chase; Wardrobe, Tad Webb; Musical Director/Sound Design, Philip Campanella; Stage Managers, Matthew T. Mundinger, Kathy J. Faul; Press, Joshua Ellis, Adrian Bryan-Brown, Jim Sapp, Cindy Valk, Bill Shuttleworth, Jackie Green, Solters/Roskin/Friedman

Wednesday, July 23–September 21, 1986 (70 performances)

A RAISIN IN THE SUN by Lorraine Hansberry; Director, Harold Scott; Set, Thomas Cariello; Costumes, Judy Dearing; Lighting, Shirley Prendergast; Sound, Rick Menke; Casting, David Tochterman; Presented in collaboration with Robert Nemiroff; Props, Hunter Nesbitt Spence, Patricia Bobo; Wigs, Susan Holster; Hairstylist, Walter Thomas; African Dance staged by Loretta Abbott

CAST: Olivia Cole (Lena Younger), Vondie Curtis-Hall (Joseph Asagai), Starletta DuPois (Ruth Younger), John Fiedler (Karl Lindner), Richard Habersham (Travis), Stephen Henderson (Bobo), Kimble Joyner (Travis), Joseph C. Phillips (George Murchison), James Pickens, Jr. (Walter Lee Younger), Kim Yancy (Beneatha Younger), Jacob Moultrie (Moving Man), Ron O. J. Parson (Moving Man)

A drama in three acts. The action takes place in the early 1950's in the Youngers' apartment in Chicago's Southside over a period of three weeks.

Wednesday, October 8–December 6, 1986 (69 performances)

BROWNSTONE with Music & Lyrics by Peter Larson, Josh Rubins; Book, Josh Rubins, Andrew Cadiff; Director, Andrew Cadiff; Set, Loren Sherman; Costumes, Ann Emonts; Lighting, Richard Nelson; Musical Director, Don Jones; Orchestrations, Harold Wheeler; Additional Musical Staging, Don Bondi; Sound, Peter Fitzgerald; Assistant Conductor, Larry Esposito; Props, Terry Foster

CAST: Liz Callaway (Claudia), Rex Smith (Stuart), Ben Harney (Howard), Ernestine Jackson (Mary), Kimberly Farr (Joan). MUSICAL NUMBERS: Someone's Moving In, Fiction Writer, I Just Want to Know, There She Goes, We Should Talk, Camouflage, Thanks a Lot, Neighbors Above Neighbors Below, I Wasn't Home for Christmas, What Do People Do?, Not Today, The Water through the Trees, You Still Don't Know, Babies on the Brain, Almost There, Don't Tell Me Everything, One of Them, Spring Cleaning, Fiction Writer Duet, He Didn't Leave It Here, It Isn't the End of the World, See That Lady There, Since You Stayed Here, We Came Along Too Late, Hi There Joan, It's a Funny Thing, Nevertheless, Someone's Moving Out

A musical in 2 acts and 4 scenes with an epilogue. The action takes place at the present time during the course of one year, from autumn to autumn, in and around a brownstone apartment building in New York City.

Thursday, December 11, 1986–February 8, 1987 (69 performances)

A MAN FOR ALL SEASONS by Robert Bolt; Director, Paul Giovanni; Set, Daniel Ettinger; Costumes, Abigail Murray; Lighting, Dawn Chiang; Production Assistant, James Fontaine; Stage Manager, Franklin Keysar; Speech Consultant, Elizabeth Himelstein

CAST: Philip Bosco (Sir Thomas More), Charles Keating (Common Man), Campbell Scott (Master Richard Rich), George Guidall (Duke of Norfolk), Maria Tucci (Lady Alice More), Diane Venora (Lady Margaret More), Robert Stattel (Thomas Cromwell), Ted van Griethuysen (Signor Chapuys), Chip Davis (Chapuys' Attendant), Patrick O'Connell (William Roper), J. Kenneth Campbell (Henry VIII), Evelyn Senter (A Woman), Ron Randell (Cardinal Wolsey/Thomas Cranmer), Jo Jones (Attendant)

A drama in 2 acts and 16 scenes. The action takes place in England during the 16th Century.

Wednesday, February 18–April 12, 1987 (63 performances)

THE MIRACLE WORKER by William Gibson; Director, Vivian Matalon; Set/Lighting, Neil Peter Jampolis; Costumes, Sigrid Insull; Fight Coordinator, B. H. Barry; Technical Adviser, Dr. Alana Zambone; Assistant to Mr. Matalon, Judy Goldman; Production Assistant, Jill Merzon; Props, Matthew Mundinger, Randy Noojin; Animal Handler, Lane Haverly

CAST: Frank Hamilton (Doctor), Laurie Kennedy (Kate), Jack Ryland (Keller), Eevin Hartsough (Helen), Tracy Yanger (Martha), Anthony Alexander (Percy), Elizabeth Owens (Aunt Ev), Victor Slezak (James), John Niespolo (Anagnos), Karen Allen (Annie Sullivan), Kim Hamilton (Viney), Moose (Belle)

A drama in three acts. The action takes place in 1887 in the Keller homestead in Tuscumbia, Alabama; also briefly in the Perkins Institution for the Blind in Boston.

Wednesday, April 29–June 28, 1987 (69 performances)

ROSENCRANTZ AND GUILDENSTERN ARE DEAD by Tom Stoppard; Director, Robert Carsen; Set, Peter David Gould; Costumes, Andrew B. Marlay; Lighting, Robert Jared; Original Music, Peter Golub; Movement/Fights, Carryer & Bailey; Assistant to Mr. Carsen, Resa Alboher; Production Assistants, Amy Holderness, Susan Wilbur; Props, Keith Michl; Masks, Marechel Brown; Production Manager, Ray Swagerty

CAST: Stephen Lang (Rosencrantz), John Rubinstein (Guildenstern), John Wood (The Player), William Russo (Alfred), David Purdham (Hamlet), Barbara Garrick (Ophelia), Stephen Newman (Claudius), Delphi Harrington (Gertrude), Ron Randell (Polonius), James Sheerin (Courtier), Daniel Southern (Soldier/Pirate/Horatio), Barbara Garrick, James Sheerin (Pirates), Ken Forman, Joshua Worby (Musicians). Tragedians: David Barbee, John Aaron Beall, Frandu, Robert Prichard

A comedy in three acts.

Martha Swope Photos

John Rubinstein, Stephen Lang, John Wood in "Rosencrantz and Guildenstern Are Dead" Top:
(L) Diane Venora, Philip Bosco, Maria Tucci, (top) J. Kenneth Campbell in "A Man for All Seasons"
(R) Eevin Hartsough, Karen Allen in "The Miracle Worker"

SECOND STAGE

Eighth Year

Artistic Directors, Robyn Goodman, Carole Rothman; Managing Director, Rosa I. Vega; Marketing, Carol Bixler; Development, Sarah Kelley; Dramaturg, Anne Cattaneo; Casting, Meg Simon/Fran Kumin; Sound, Gary Harris; Artistic Associate, Andrew Jackness; Production Supervisor, James B. Simpson; Technical Director, Michael S. Russell; Production Assistant, Janet Marie Sanders; Press, Richard Kornberg

(Second Stage Theatre) Tuesday, Oct. 21, 1986–Jan. 1, 1987 (45 performances and 28 previews before moving to Broadway)
COASTAL DISTURBANCES by Tina Howe; Director, Carole Rothman; Set, Tony Straiges; Lighting, Dennis Parichy; Costumes, Susan Hilferty; Hairstylist, Antonio Soddu; Props, Charlie Eisenberg, Melissa L. Burdick; Wardrobe, Rachel Kusnetz, Jose M. Rivera; Stage Managers, Pamela Edington, Ken Simmons
CAST: Annette Bening (Holly Dancer), Timothy Daly (Leo Hart), Heather MacRae (Faith Bigelow), Rachel Mathieu (Miranda Bigelow), Joanne Camp (Ariel Took), Jonas Abry (Winston Took), Addison Powell (Dr. Hamilton Adams), Rosemary Murphy (M. J. Adams), Ronald Guttman (Andre Sor)
   A comedy in 2 acts and 11 scenes. The action takes place during the last two weeks in August of the present time on a private beach on Massachusetts' North Shore.
   Thursday, Jan. 15–Feb. 22, 1987 (18 performances and 19 previews)
DIVISION STREET by Steve Tesich; Director, Risa Bramon; Set, Bill Stabile; Lighting, Greg MacPherson; Costumes, Deborah Shaw; Assistant Director, Jackie Reingold; Props, Wendy Bach, Ira Belgrade; Recording/Original Music, Michael Bramon, Susan Feingold/Turnstyle Productions; Wardrobe, Jimmell G. S. Mardome; Stage Managers, Denise Laffer, Craig Butler
CAST: Saul Rubinek (Chris), Novella Nelson (Mrs. Bruchkinski), Olek Krupa (Yovan), Kathleen Wilhoite (Nadja), John Spencer (Roger), Cecilia Hart (Dianah)
   A comedy in 2 acts. The action takes place at the present time in Chicago, Illinois.
   Wednesday, April 15–June 7, 1987 (32 performances and 20 previews)
LITTLE MURDERS by Jules Feiffer; Director, John Tillinger; Set, Andrew Jackness; Lighting, Natasha Katz; Costumes, Candice Donnelly; Technical Director, Jason Townley; Props, JoAnne Basinger, Myrna Duarte; Wardrobe, Christina Heath; Stage Managers, Neal Ann Stephens, David Lawrence Folender
CAST: Frances Sternhagen (Marjorie Newquist), Fisher Stevens succeeded by Patrick Breen (Kenny Newquist), MacIntyre Dixon (Carol Newquist), Christine Lahti (Patsy Newquist), Graham Beckel (Alfred Chamberlain), Mike Nussbaum (Judge/Henry Dupas/Miles Practice)
   A comedy in 2 acts and 5 scenes. The action takes place in the recent past in the Newquist apartment.

Susan Cook Photos
Right: Kathleen Wilhoite, Saul Rubinek
Top: Novella Nelson, Olek Krupa
in "Division Street"

Timothy Daly, Annette Bening, Rosemary Murphy,
Addison Powell in "Coastal Disturbances"

Christine Lahti, Graham Beckel
in "Little Murders"

STARET . . . THE DIRECTOR COMPANY

Artistic/Producing Director, Michael Parva; Artistic/Managing Director, Victoria Lanman Chesshire; Resident Master Director, Stephen Zuckerman; Associate Producer, Nelson Taxel; Production Manager, Sandy Fischler; Production/Business Manager, Jim Bumgardner; Literary Manager, Michael Norton

(Space 603) Monday, June 9–19, 1986 (9 performances)
SAVAGE/LOVE by Sam Shepard and Joseph Chaikin and
TALK TO ME LIKE THE RAIN AND LET ME LISTEN by Tennessee Williams; Director, Jon Larson; Sets, Bill Clarke; Lighting, Danianne Mizzy; Costumes, Carol Squadra; Composer, Margo Hennebach; Sound, Lia Vollack; Casting, Brian Chavanne; Stage Managers, Jim Bumgardner, Liz Small
Savage/Love: Flynn-Lawson (Woman), Peter Strong (Man). Nineteen common poems of real and imagined moments in the spell of love.
Talk to me Like the Rain . . .. Wanda Bimson (Woman), George Gerdes (Man), Colleen Flynn-Lawson, Peter Strong (Children's Voices).
 The action takes place at the present time in a furnished room west of Eighth Avenue in mid-town Manhattan, New York City.
 Monday, June 23–July 3, 1986 (9 performances)
LONG ISLAND DREAMER by Paul Selig, Kim D. Sherman, with
MOON CITY by Paul Selig; Director, Tim Sanford; Assistant Director, Shelley Mason; Set, Bill Clarke; Lighting, Danianne Mizzy; Costumes, Carol Squadra; Musical Director, Jonathan Werking; Casting, Brian Chavanne; Stage Manager, Betsy Spanbock
CAST: *Long Island Dreamer* with Nancy Mayans (Amana del Ray), McElhiney (Engineer), Suzan Postel, Lovette George, Susie Goddard (Backup Singers). *Moon City* with Michael Tighe (Cubby Huckaby), Marcella Lowery (Velveeta), Anita Keal (Mama), Cynthia Darlow (Nancy Huckaby), Spartan McClure (Georgie Lane), Winnie Holzman (Lila deBolt).
 Monday, July 7–17, 1986 (9 performances)
THE MISANTHROPE by Moliere; Translated by Richard Wilbur; Director, Todd London; Assistant Director, Constance McCord; Set, Bill Clarke; Costumes, Carol Squadra; Lighting, Danianne Mizzy; Sound, Jac Rubenstein; Production Manager, James Dawson; Stage Manager, Jane I. Roth
CAST: J. C. Cutler (Alceste), John Bolger (Philinte), James Lally (Oronte), Trace Ellis (Celimene), Laura San Giacomo (Basque), Stephanie Correa (Eliante), Eric Swanson (Clitandre), Nate Harvey (Acaste), Brian Poteat (Guard/Dubois), Donna Snow (Arsinoe)
 Performed with one intermission. The action takes place at the present time in the gallery of Celimene's Paris home.
 (Judith Anderson Theatre) Monday, August 11–28, 1986 (16 performances). Staret . . . The Directors Company & TRG Repertory Company (Artistic Director, Marvin Kahan) present:
SHOTS AT FATE by Steven Braunstein; Director, Michael Parva, Set, Harry Lines; Sound, Andrew Bargieri; Lighting, Victor En Yu Tan; Costumes, Eiko Yamaguchi; Casting, Brian Chavanne; Assistant Director, Christopher M. Lillja; Stage Manager, Sandy Fischler; Press, FLT/Francine Trevens
CAST: Donna Snow (Flosie), George Dickerson (Gardner Bean), David Staller (Kip Osgood), Liliana Komorowska (Roberta)
 A murder mystery in 2 acts and 4 scenes. The action takes place at the present time.
 (South Street Theater) Sunday, Nov. 9–23, 1986 (16 performances). Staret . . . The Directors Company and TRG Repertory Company present:
MY PAPA'S WINE by Ron Mark; Director, Peter Frisch; Set, Dennis Kralovec; Lighting, Victor En Yu Tan; Costumes, Jeffrey Ullman; Sound, Laura Lampell; Props, Janet E. Smith; Production Manager, Sandy Fischler; Assistant Director, Jane I. Roth; Stage Manager, Adam Kushner; Press, FLT/Francine Trevens
CAST: Stan Lachow (Joe Buffone), David Youse (Toulouse "Toby"), Walt Gorney (Papa), Zohra Lampert (Annie), Ted Marcoux (Ricky), Jesse Doran (Bud Devito), Matthew Lewis (Jacob Cox), Laura San Giacomo (Tracy Devito)
 A play in 2 acts and 10 scenes. The action takes place in the late 1950's in Chicago Heights, Illinois.

**Top Right: George Dickerson, Donna Snow
in "Shots at Fate"**

**Stan Lachow, Walt Gorney (standing), David J.
Youse, Zohra Lampert in "My Papa's Wine"**
(Mel Nudelman)

133

WPA THEATRE

Tenth Season

Workshop of the Players Art Foundation; Artistic Director, Kyle Renick; Managing Director, Wendy Bustard; Casting/Literary Adviser, Darlene Kaplan; Resident Designer, Edward T. Gianfrancesco; Lighting, Craig Evans, Production Manager/Technical Director, Gordon W. Brown

(Chelsea Playhouse) Thursday, Oct. 23–Nov. 16, 1986 (34 performances)

ALTERATIONS by Leigh Curran; Director, Austin Pendleton; Costumes, Don Newcomb; Stage Manager, David Lawrence Folender; Press, Milly Schoenbaum; Props, Leah Menken

CAST: Gretchen Cryer (Erica), Jane Hoffman (Biesel), Mary Kane (Adrianna), Cynthia Nixon (Phoebe), Wayne Tippit (Peter)

A drama performed without intermission. The action takes place at the present time in Erica's apartment.

Wednesday, Dec. 31, 1986–Feb. 15, 1987 (49 performances)

NORTH SHORE FISH by Israel Horovitz; Director, Stephen Zuckerman; Costumes, Mimi Maxmen; Sound, Aural Fixation; Production Assistant, Chip Hellman; Fights, Nels Hennum; Props, Catherine Policella; Stage Manager, David Lawrence Folender; Press, Jeffrey Richards Associates/Ben Morse

CAST: John Pankow (Alfred Martino), Christine Estabrook (Florence Rizzo), Mary Klug (Arlyne Flynn), Cordelia Richards ((Ruthie), Thomas G. Waites (Salvatore Morella), Michelle M. Faith (Josephine Evangelista), Elizabeth Kemp (Maureen Vega), Laura San Giacomo (Marlena), Wendle Malick (Catherine Shimma)

A drama in two acts. The action takes place in Gloucester, Massachusetts, in a frozen-fish processing plant.

Wednesday, March 11–April 19, 1987 (29 performances)

STEEL MAGNOLIAS by Robert Hartling; Director, Pamela Berlin; Sound, Otts Munderloh; Hair, Bobby Grayson; Production Assistant, Norman Eric Lazarus; Stage Manager, Paul Mills Holmes; Press, Jeffrey Richards Associates/Ken Mandelbaum

CAST: Margo Martindale (Truvy), Constance Shulman (Annelle), Kate Wilkinson (Clairee), Blanche Baker (Shelby), Rosemary Prinz (M'Lynn), Mary Fogarty (Ouiser)

A drama in 2 acts and 4 scenes. The action takes place at the present time in Truvy's Beauty Salon in Chinquapin, Louisiana.

Wednesday, June 3,–28, 1987 (15 performances and 13 previews)

COPPERHEAD by Erik Brogger; Director, Mary B. Robinson; Casting, Patricia Hoag; Sound, Aural Fixation; Props, Janet Smith; Production Assistant, Melissa L. Stephenson; Stage Manager, Crystal Huntington; Press, Jeffrey Richards Associates/Ken Mandelbaum

CAST: Dave Florek (Oliver Wright), Kathleen Nolan (Lucille), Campbell Scott (Parker Smith), William Cain (Rev. Paul Raeder), William Wise (Calvin)

A drama in 2 acts and 8 scenes. The action takes place at the present time in Central Pennsylvania.

Martha Swope Photos
Right: Kate Wilkinson, Constance Shulman, Mary Fogarty, Blanche Baker, Margo Martindale in "Steel Magnolias"
Top: Michelle Faith, Laura San Giacomo, Elizabeth Kemp, Thomas Waites, Christine Estabrook in "North Shore Fish"

Wayne Tippit, Cynthia Nixon, Gretchen Cryer in "Alterations"

William Wise, William Cain, Campbell Scott, Kathleen Nolan in "Copperhead"

YORK THEATRE COMPANY

Eighteenth Year

Producing Director, Janet Hayes Walker; Managing Director, Molly Pickering Grose; Scenic Designer, James Morgan; Sound Design, Dirk Kuyk; Technical Director, Jim Jensen; Casting, Judy Henderson; Press, Keith Sherman
  (Church of the Heavenly Rest) Friday, Oct. 24–Nov. 16, 1986 (16 performances)
TAKING STEPS by Alan Ayckbourn; Director, Alex Dmitriev; Costumes, Muriel Stockdale; Lighting, Brian MacDevitt; Wardrobe, Robert Swasey; Stage Managers, Nereida Ortiz, Nicole Rosen
CAST: Fran Brill (Elizabeth), Michael Zaslow (Mark, her brother), Sam Robards (Tristram, a solicitor), Rudolph Willrich (Roland, Elizabeth's husband), Skip Hinnant (Leslie, a builder), Marguerite Kelly (Kitty, Mark's fiancee)
  A comedy in two acts. The action takes place at the present time in February in The Pines, a Victorian mansion.
  Friday, Jan. 16–Feb. 7, 1987 (20 performances)
MARRY ME A LITTLE conceived and developed by Craig Lucas, Norman Rene; Songs, Stephen Sondheim; Director, Stephen Lloyd Helper; Choreographer, Liza Gennaro-Evans; Musical Director, Sand Lawn; Costumes, Holly Hynes; Lighting, Mary Jo Dondlinger; Technical Director, Jason Townley; Assistant Musical Director, Connie Meng; Program Coordinator, Kate Grinnell; Associate Technical Director, Sally Smith; Stage Managers, Mary E. Lawson, Nicole Rosen
CAST: Liz Callaway (Woman), John Hellison (Man)
Musical Numbers: Two Fairy Tales, Saturday Night, What More Do I Need?, The Girls of Summer, Silly People, Uptown/Downtown, Can That Boy Fox Trot?, All Things Bright and Beautiful, Bang!, Who Could Be Blue/Little White House, Your Eyes Are Blue, So Many People, A Moment with You, Marry Me a Little, Pour le Sport, It Wasn't Meant to Happen, Happily Ever After, There Won't Be Trumpets
  A musical performed without intermission. The action takes place at the present time in Brooklyn on a Saturday night in early fall.
  (Mazur Theatre) Thursday, Feb. 19–March 1, 1987 (12 performances)
BILLY BISHOP GOES TO WAR written and composed by John Gray in collaboration with Eric Peterson; Director, William S. Morris; Set, James M. Youmans; Costumes, Robert W. Swasey; Lighting, Rachel Bikel; Musical Director, T. O. Sterrett; Stage Managers, Jonathan D. Secor, Valerie J. Roux
CAST: T. O. Sterrett (Narrator/Pianist), Robin Haynes (Billy Bishop/Etc.)
  Thursday, March 24–April 11, 1987 (20 performances)
THE APPLE TREE with Book/Music/Lyrics by Sheldon Harnick and Jerry Bock; Additional Material, Jerome Coopersmith; Based on stories by Mark Twain, Frank R. Stockton, Jules Feiffer; Direction/Musical Staging, Robert Nigro; Conductor/Pianist/Musical Director, David Krane; Costumes, John Glaser; Lighting, Mary Jo Dondlinger; Technical Director, Jason Townley; Associate Musical Director, Paul Ford; Hair/Wigs, Elizabeth Katherine Carr; Stage Managers, Victor Lukas, Karol Siegel, Ralph David Westfall
CAST: "The Diary of Adam and Eve" on a Saturday in Eden: John Sloman (Adam), Kathy Morath (Eve), Rufus Bonds, Jr. (Snake). *Musical Numbers:* Here in Eden, Feelings, Eve, Friends, The Apple Tree, Beautiful World, It's a Fish, Go to Sleep, What Makes Me Love Him. "The Lady or the Tiger" takes place Now and Then at some bar, and a semi-Barbaric Kingdom. Rufus Bonds, Jr. (M.C./Snake), Lyle Garrett (King Arik), Kathy Morath (Princess Barbara), John Sloman (Capt. Sanjar), Kimberly Harris (Nadjira), Semi-Barbarians: Jonathan Courie, Ron LaRosa, William Selby, Kevin Wallace, Wendy Cross, Siobhan Marshall, Jane Wasser. *Musical Numbers:* I'll Tell You a Truth, Make Way, Forbidden Love, The Apple Tree, I've Got What You Want, Tiger Tiger, Which Door?. "Passionella" in Gotham and Tinseltown during "Those Fabulous Fifties" with Rufus Bonds, Jr. (Narrator/Snake), Kathy Morath (Ella/Passionella), Ron LaRosa (Fallible), Kevin Wallace (Producer), John Sloman (Flip, The Prince Charming), and Jonathan Courie, Wendy Cross, Lyle Garrett, Kimberly Harris, Siobhan Marshall, William Selby, Jane Wasser. *Musical Numbers:* Oh to Be a Movie Star, Gorgeous, Who Is She?, Wealth, You Are Not Real
  A musical performed with two intermissions.
  Thursday, April 23–May 3, 1987 (12 performances)
SHYLOCK based on "The Merchant of Venice" by William Shakespeare; Musical adaptation by Ed Dixon; Director, Lloyd Battista; Musical Director, Kathleen Rubbicco; Scenery, Daniel Ettinger; Lighting, Marcia Madeira; Technical Director, Jason Townley; Assistant Director, Helen Lee Henderson; Props, Deborah Scott; Stage Managers, Victor Lukas, Karol Siegel
CAST: Dennis Parlato (Antonio), Charles Pistone (Bassanio), Joel Fredrickson (Lorenzo), Ed Dixon (Shylock), Ann Brown (Jessica), Lisa Vroman (Portia), Brooks Almy (Nerissa), Leslie Quinn (Standby)
  The action takes place in the Piazza di San Marco in 15th Century Venice. Performed with one intermission.

Carol Rosegg Photos
**Top: Fran Brill, Rudolph Willrich, Sam Robards
in "Taking Steps" Below: Liz Callaway, John
Jellison in "Marry Me a Little"**

**Ed Dixon, Lisa Vroman, Dennis Parlato
in "Shylock" Above: John Sloman, Kathy
Morath in "The Apple Tree"**

NATIONAL TOURING COMPANIES
(Failure to meet deadline necessitated omissions)

ARSENIC AND OLD LACE

By Joseph Kesselring; Director, Brian Murray; Presented by Elliot Martin, Act III Productions, James M. Nederlander, Burton Kaiser; Set, Marjorie Bradley Kellogg; Costumes, Jeanne Button; Lighting, Pat Collins; Associate Producer/Casting, Marjorie Martin; General Management/William Court Cohen, Ralph Roseman, Charlotte Wilcox; Company Manager, Mitchell Brower; Wigs, Paul Huntley; Hairstylist, Patrick D. Moreton; Props, Bob Curry; Wardrobe, Florence Driscoll; Production Assistant, Katharyn Pinder; Stage Managers, Elliott Woodruff, Wally Peterson; Press, Jeffrey Richards, Susan Lee, C. George Willard, John Curtis-Michael, Jennifer Avery. Opened Tuesday, Jan. 6, 1987 in Louisville's Kentucky Centre for the Arts, and closed June 28, 1987 in Los Angeles' Wilshire Theatre.*

CAST

Abby Brewster	Jean Stapleton
Rev. Dr. Harper	John Eames
Teddy Brewster	MichaelJohn McGann
Officer Brophy	Andrew Gorman
Officer Klein	William Metzo
Martha Brewster	Marion Ross
Elaine Harper	Mary Layne
Mortimer Brewster	Gary Sandy
Mr. Gibbs	Paul Rosson
Jonathan Brewster	Jonathan Frid
Dr. Einstein	Larry Storch
Officer O'Hara	Kevin McClarnon
Lieutenant Rooney	George Bamford
Mr. Witherspoon	Phillip Pruneau

STANDBYS & UNDERSTUDIES: Andrew Gorman (Mortimer/O'Hara), Peg Small (Abby/Martha), William Metzo (Jonathan), Phillip Pruneau (Einstein/Harper/Gibbs), Kevin McClarnon (Teddy), Charlotte Maier (Elaine), Rick Tolliver (Brophy/Klein/Rooney), John Eames (Witherspoon).

A comedy in three acts.

*For original Broadway production, see THEATRE WORLD Volume 1.

Jean Stapleton, Gary Sandy, Mary Layne, Marion Ross Top: Jean Stapleton (standing), Marion Ross
(Martha Swope Photos)

BILOXI BLUES

By Neil Simon; Director, Gene Saks; Set, David Mitchell; Costumes, Ann Roth; Lighting, Tharon Musser; Presented by Emanuel Azenberg; Assistant Director, Bill Molloy; Sound, Tom Morse; Casting, Meg Simon/Fran Kumin; General Manager, Robert Kamlot; Technical Supervision, Theatrical Services; Props, Jan Marasek; Company Manager, Noel Gilmore; Consultant, Jose Vega; Props, Brian DeVerna; Wardrobe, Kathleen Sullivan; Stage Managers, Frank Marino, Greg Johnson, Linnea Sundsten; Press, Bill Evans, Sandra Manley, Jim Baldassare, Marlene DeSavino. Opened in the Fox Theatre in Atlanta, Ga., on Tuesday, May 27, 1986, and closed at the Kentucky Arts Center in Louisville on May 25, 1987. For original Broadway production, see THEATRE WORLD Volume 41.

CAST

Roy Selridge	John Younger
Joseph Wykowski	David Warshofsky †1
Don Carney	John C. MacKenzie
Eugene Morris Jerome	William Ragsdale †2
Arnold Epstein	Andrew Polk
Sgt. Merwin J. Toomey	John Finn †3
James Hennessey	Michael McNeill
Rowena	Kathy Danzer †4
Daisy Hannigan	Marita Geraghty †5

UNDERSTUDIES: David Nackman/Michael McNeill (Eugene), David Nackman (Epstein), Milton Elliott (Selridge/Wykowski/Hennessey), Michael McNeill (Carney), Kenneth Kay (Toomey), Linnea Sundsten (Rowena), Kelly Baker (Daisy)

A comedy in 2 acts and 14 scenes. The action takes place in Biloxi and Gulfport, Mississippi in 1943.

†Succeeded by: 1. Scott McClelland, 2. Geoffrey Nauffts, 3. Kenneth Kay, 4. Pat Nesbit, 5. Amy Ryan

Martha Swope Photos
Right: Andrew Polk, Kenneth Ray
Top: Kenneth Ray, Geoffrey Nauffts, Andrew Polk,
John Younger, Scott McClelland, John C. McKenzie

Amy Ryan, Geoffrey Nauffts

Pat Nesbit, Geoffrey Nauffts

CABARET

Book, Joe Masteroff; Based on John Van Druten's play "I Am a Camera" and stories by Christopher Isherwood; Music, John Kander; Lyrics, Fred Ebb; Director, Harold Prince; Dances/Cabaret numbers, Ron Field; Scenery, David Chapman; Based on original design by Boris Aronson; Costumes, Patricia Zipprodt; Lighting, Marc B. Weiss; Sound, Otts Munderloh; Assistant Director, Ruth Mitchell; Assistant Choreographer, Bonnie Walker; Orchestrator, Don Walker; Presented by Barry and Fran Weissler; Additional Orchestrations, Michael Gibson; Associate Producer, Alecia Parker; Musical Supervisor, Don Pippin; Musical Director, Don Chan; Musical Coordinator, John Monaco; General Management, Kevmar Productions; Company Manager, Robert H. Wallner; Stage Managers, William Dodds, Robert Kellogg, Bonnie Walker; Press, Fred Nathan Associates Merle Frimark. Opened Saturday, February 28, 1987 in the Playhouse Theatre, Wilmington, Delaware, and still touring May 31, 1987. For original Broadway production, see THEATRE WORLD Volume 23.

CAST

Master of Ceremonies	Joel Grey
Clifford Bradshaw	Gregg Edelman
Ernst Ludwig	David Staller
Customs Officer/Maitre d'	David Vosburgh
Fraulein Schneider	Regina Resnik
Herr Schultz	Werner Klemperer
Telephone Girl	Ruth Gottschall
Sally Bowles	Alyson Reed
Max	Jon Vandertholen
Bobby/Gorilla	Michelan Sisti
Victor	Lars Rosager
First Waiter	Stan Chandler
Two Ladies	Ruth Gottschall, Sharon Lawrence
German Sailors	Jim Wolfe, Mark Dovey, Gregory Schanuel
Girl Orchestra	Sheila Cooper, Barbara Merjan, Panchali Null, Eve Potfora
Kit Kat Girls	Laurie Crochet, Noreen Evans, Caitlin Larsen, Sharon Lawrence, Mary Rotella

ENSEMBLE: Stan Chandler, Laurie Crochet, Bill Derifield, Mark Dovey, Noreen Evans, Karen Fraction, Laurie Franks, Ruth Gottschall, Caitlin Larsen, Sharon Lawrence, Mary Munger, Panchali Null, Steve Potfora, Lars Rosager, Mary Rotella, Gregory Schanuel, Michelan Sisti, Jon Vandertholen, David Vosburgh, Jim Wolfe

STANDBYS & UNDERSTUDIES: Michelan Sisti (M.C.), Mary Munger (Sally), Laurie Franks (Schneider), David Vosburgh (Schultz), Jon Vandertholen (Cliff/Ernst), Caitlin Larsen (Kost), Swings: Candy Cook, Aurelio Padron

MUSICAL NUMBERS: Willkommen, So What?, Don't Tell Mama, Telephone Song, Perfectly Marvelous, Two Ladies, It Couldn't Please Me More, Tomorrow Belongs to Me, Don't Go, The Money Song, Married, If You Could See Her, What Would You Do?, I Don't Care Much, Cabaret

A musical in two acts. The action takes place in Berlin, Germany, before the start of the Third Reich in 1929–30.

Joan Marcus/Bob Marshak Photos

Joel Grey

Joel Grey
Above: Alyson Reed

CAMELOT

Book and Lyrics, Alan Jay Lerner; Based on "The Once and Future King" by T. H. White; Music, Frederick Loewe; Staged and Directed by Richard Harris; Presented by King Arthur Productions; Scenery, Tom Barnes; Lighting, Norman Coates; Sound, Christopher "Kit" Bond; Fight Direction, B. H. Barry; Assistant Director, Dianne Trulock; Choreographer/Dance Captain, Norb Joerder; Additional Costumes, Michael Bottari, Ronald Case; Musical Director, Terry James; General Manager, Richard Martini; Tour Direction, NAMCO Booking; Company Manager, Patricia Crowe; Assistant Musical Director, John Visser; Props, Glenn Belfer; Wardrobe, Donna Peck, Ann Bruskiewitz; Stage Managers, Christopher "Kit" Bond, Allen McMullen, Mary Johansen; Press, Deborah Hime, Elizabeth Lipsey, Judy McCoy. Opened in Minneapolis, Mn, on June 4, 1985 and closed Dec. 7, 1986 in Hershey, Pa. For original Broadway production, see THEATRE WORLD Volume 17.

CAST

Arthur	Richard Harris
Sir Sagramore	Gregg Busch †1
Merlyn/King Pellinore	James Valentine
Merlyn Sprites	Norb Joerder, Mark Hoebee, Andre Noujaim
Guenevere	Martha Travers †2
Sir Dinadan	Patrick Godfrey †3
Nimue/Lady Sibyl	Marcia Brushingham
Nymphs	Diane DiLascio, Judith Laxer, Kelly Sanderbeck
Lancelot du Lac	Chip Huddleston †4
Mordred	Andy McAvin †5
Tom of Warwick/Young Arthur	William Thomas Bookmyer
Musician/Sir Castor	Dean G. Watts
Lady Anne	Mary Gaebler †6
Lady Margaret	Julie Ann Fogt †7
Sir Lionel	William James †8
Jester	S. Chris Pender †9
Squire Dap.Turquine	Robert Ousley
Horrid	Sean Sable Beleveder
Herald	John Nicoletti †10
Sir Bliant/Forest Merlyn	John Deyle †11
Lord Chancellor	Martin Van Treuren
Court Dancer	Norb Joerder
Wenches	Tarry Caruso, Rebecca Hoodwin

UNDERSTUDIES: J. C. Sheets (Arthur), Barbara Scanlon (Guenevere), Michael Scott (Lancelot), Martin Van Treuren (Merlyn), Robert Oursley (Pellinore), Mark Hoebee (Mordred), Tracey Moore (Nimue), Debbie Birch (Lady Anne), Wallace Sherertz (Sir Dinadan), Andre Noujaim (Sir Sagramore), Paul Dobie (Lord Chancellor)

MUSICAL NUMBERS: Guenevere, Where Are the Simple Joys of Maidenhood, I Wonder What the King Is Doing Tonight, Camelot, Follow Me, Madrigal, C'Est Moi, The Lusty Month of May, Take Me to the Fair, How to Handle a Woman, The Jousts, Before I Gaze at You Again, If Ever I Would Leave You, The Seven Deadly Virtues, Fie on Goodness, What Do the Simple Folk Do?, I Loved You Once in Silence

A musical in 2 acts and 16 scenes, with a prologue.

†Succeeded by: 1. William Solo, 2. Elizabeth Williams, 3. Dennis Skerik, 4. Bob Cuccioli, 5. Chris Pender, 6. Tracey Moore, 7. Lady Sanderbeck, 8. J. C. Sheets, 9. Frank Maio, 10. Andre Noujaim, 11. Wallace K. Sherertz

Richard Harris, Elizabeth Williams
Top Right: Richard Harris

Bob Cuccioli, Elizabeth Williams

CATS

For original creative credits and musical numbers, see Broadway Calendar. Company Manager, Barbara Nunn; Production Supervisor, David Taylor; General Management, Gatchell & Neufeld; Dance Supervisors, Richard Stafford, T. Michael Reed; Musical Director, David Caddick; Dance Captains, Niki Harris, Suzanne Viverito; Associate Musical Director, Tony Geralis, Jack Gaughan; Assistant Company Manager, Mark Johnson; Props, George Green, Jr., John Alfredo, Sr., Paul Bach; Wardrobe, Adelaide Laurino, Linda Lee; Hairstylists, Christine Domenech Cantrell, Carol Shurley, Henri Coultas; Stage Managers, Jake Bell, Dan Hild, Marybeth Abel; Press, Fred Nathan Company, Dennis Crowley, Anne Abrams, Bert Fink, Merle Frimark, Marc Thibodeau. Opened in Boston's Shubert Theatre on Wednesday, Dec. 21, 1983, and still touring May 31, 1987.

CAST

Alonzo/Rumpus Cat	Fred Anderson †1
Bustopher/Asparagus/Growltiger	Bill Carmichael †2
Bombalurina	Cindi Klinger †3
Cassandra	Kim Noor
Coricopat	Bob Amore †4
Demeter	Diana Kavilis
Grizabella	Janene Lovullo
Jellylorum/Griddlebone	Jennifer Butt †5
Jennyanydots	Sally Ann Swarm
Mistoffelees	Mark Esposito †6
Mungojerrie	Todd Lester †7
Munkustrap	Scott Dainton †8
Old Deuteronomy	Calvin E. Remsberg
Plato/Macavity	Russell Warfield †9
Pouncival	Brian Jay †10
Rum Tum Tugger	Paul Mack †11
Rumpleteazer	Kelli Ann McNally †12
Sillabub	Joanne Baum
Skimbleshanks	Danny Rounds †13
Tantomile	Patricia Forestier
Tumblebrutus	Tony Jaeger
Victoria	Susan Zaguirre
Cats Chorus	R. F. Daley, Kirsti Carnahan, Raissa Katona, Skip Harris

†Succeeded by: 1. Ken Nagy, 2. Frank Mastrone, 3. Nora Brennan, 4. Eric Kaufman, 5. Jessica Molaskey, 6. Roger Kachel, 7. Bill Brassea, 8. Joe Locarro, 9. Fred Anderson, 10. Daniel Jamison, 11. Douglas Graham, 12. Andrea Karas, 13, Eric Scott Kincaid

Martha Swope Photos

Leslie Ellis

CATS

Musical Director, Jay Alger; Dance Supervisor, Richard Stafford; Production Musical Director, David Caddick; Company Manager, Brian Liddicoat; Assistant, Jeffrey Capitola; Dance Captain, James Walski; Associate Musical Director, Edward G. Robinson; Production Assistant, Gregg Victor; Props, George Green, Jr., Alan Price, Joseph Poc; Wardrobe, Adelaide Laurino, Robert Daily, Jose Tellez Ponce; Hairstylists, Raul Arzola, Charmaine Henninger; Stage Managers, Scott Glenn, William Kirk, Nancy Ann Adler; Press, Fred Nathan Co./Jim Kerber, Anne Abrams, Dennis Crowley, Bert Fink, Merle Frimark, Marc Thibodeau. Opened Thursday, August 7, 1986 in the West Point (NY) Theatre, and still touring May 31, 1987.

CAST

Alonzo/Rumpus Cat	Jeff Siebert
Bustopher Jones/Asparagus/Growltiger	Richard Poole
Bombalurina	Andrea Gibbs Muldoon
Cassandra	Aimee Turner
Demeter	Deborah Geneviere
Grizabella	Leslie Ellis
Jellylorum/Griddlebone	Joanna Beck
Jennyanydots	Cathy Susan Pyles
Mistoffelees	Randy Slovacek
Mungojerrie	Michael O'Steen
Munkustrap	Randy Clements
Old Deuteronomy	Larry Small
Plato/Macavity	David Roberts
Pouncival	Matt Zarley
Rumpleteazer	Beth Swearingen
Rum Tum Tugger	Andy Spangler
Sillabub	Nikki Rene
Skimbleshanks	Jonathan Cerullo
Tumblebrutus	Anthony Bova
Victoria	Joann M. Hunter
Cats Chorus	Arminae Azarian, Austin Jetton, Peter Marinos, Jacqueline Reilly

STANDBYS & UNDERSTUDIES: Alonzo (Urban Sanchez/Jay Tramel/James Walski), Bombalurina (Lisa Dawn Cave/Jill B. Gounder), Bustopher (Brian B. K. Kennelly/Peter Marinos), Demeter (Arminae Azarian/Karen Longwell/Beth Swearingen), Grizabella (Arminae Azarian/,Karen Longwell), Jellylorum (Karen Longwell/Jacqueline Reilly), Jennyanydots (Arminae Azarian/Jacqueline Reilly), Mistoffelees (Marty Benn/Michael O'Steen/Matt Zarley), Mungojerrie (Brian B. K. Kennelly/Urban Sanchez/Matt Zarley), Munkustrap (Brian B. K. Kennelly/Urban Sanchez), Old Deuteronomy (Austin Jetton), Plato/Macavity (Jay Tramel/James Walski), Pouncival (Marty Benn/James Walski), Rum Tum Tugger (Brian B. K. Kennelly, Urban Sanchez), Tumblebrutus (Marty Benn/Jay Tramel/James Walski), Victoria (Lisa Dawn Cave/Jill B. Gounder)

Martha Swope Photos

Calvin E. Remsberg

CATS

Musical Director, Janet Glazener Roma; Executive Producers, Tyler Gatchell, Jr., Peter Neufeld; Casting, Johnson-Liff and Zerman; Orchestrations, Stanley Lebowsky; Choreography reproduced by T. Michael Reed, Richard Stafford; Direction reproduced by David Taylor; Associate Production Musical Director, Jack Gaughan; Company Managers, Abbie Strassler, Michael Sanfilippo; Dance Captain, Leigh Webster; Associate Musical Director, Michael Huffman; Stage Managers, B. J. Allen, Scott Faris, L. A. Lavin, Michael McEowen; Press, Fred Nathan Co./Philip Rinaldi, Anne Abrams, Dennis Crowley, Bert Fink, Merle Frimark, Marc Thibodeau. Opened in the Shubert Theatre in Los Angeles, Ca., and still touring May 31, 1987. For original Broadway production, see THEATRE WORLD Volume 39.

CAST

Alonzo/Rumpus Cat	Derryl Yeager †1
Bustopher/Asparagus/Growltiger	Reece Holland †2
Bombalurina	Edyie Fleming †3
Cassandra	Leigh Webster †4
Coricopat	Marc C. Oka
Demeter	April Ortiz †5
Grizabella	Kim Criswell †6
Jellylorum/Griddlebone	Linden Waddell †7
Jennyanydots	Marsha Mercant †8
Mistoffelees	Jamie Torcellini †9
Mungojerrie	Don Johanson †10
Munkustrap	Mark Morales †11
Old Deuteronomy	George Anthony Bell †12
Plato/Macavity	Jeff Adkins †13
Pouncival	Phineas Newborn III †14
Rum Tum Tugger	Gregory Donaldson †15
Rumpleteazer	Kristi Lynes †16
Sillabub	Susan Carr George †17
Skimbleshanks	Thom Keeling †18
Tantomile	Andrea Gibbs Muldoon
Tumblebrutus	David Reitman †19
Victoria	J. Kathleen Lamb
Cats Chorus	Richard Bigelow, Jean Kauffman, Bryan John Landrine, Terry Mason

†Succeeded by: 1. General McArthur Hambrick, 2. Jeffrey Clonts, 3. Wendy Walter, 4. Paula-Marie Benedetti, 5. Helen Frank, Patricia Everett, 6. Donna Lee Marshall, 7. Lindsay Dyett, 8. Robin Boudreau, 9. Eddie Buffum, 10. Jack Noseworthy, 11. Dan McCoy, 12. Richard Nickol. 13. T. Michael Dalton, David Reitman, 14. Marc C. Oka, 15. Steven Bland, 16. Nancy Melius, 17. Leslie Trayer, 18. Kevin Winkler, 19. Robert Torres

Martha Swope Photos

Top Right: Jeffrey Clonts, Dan McCoy

Kevin Winkler

Jeffrey Clonts, Lindsay Dyett

DREAMGIRLS

Book/Lyrics, Tom Eyen; Music, Henry Krieger; Direction/Choreography, Michael Bennett; Co-Choreographer, Michael Peters; Production Supervisor, Bob Avian; Scenery, Robin Wagner; Costumes, Theoni V. Aldredge; Lighting, Tharon Musser; Sound, Otts Munderloh; Musical Supervision/Orchestrations, Harold Wheeler; Musical Coordinator, Yolanda Segovia; Musical Director, Randy Booth; Vocal Arrangements, Cleavant Derricks; Hairstylist, Ted Azar; Casting, Johnson-Liff; Presented by Marvin A. Krauss, Irving Siders; General Management, Marvin A. Krauss, Joey Parnes, Gary Gunas; Company Manager, Allan Williams; Technical Coordinator, Arthur Siccardi; Props, Charles Zuckerman, Alan Steiner, Gregory Martin, Joe Schwarz; Wardrobe, Alyce Gilbert, Walter Douglas, Marilyn Knotts; Wig Master, Michael Robinson; Dance Captain, Brenda Braxton; Vocal Coordinator, Rhetta Hughes; Stage Managers, Peter B. Mumford, Thomas A. Bartlett, Robert Gould; Press, Norman Zagier. Opened in the Providence (R.I.) Performing Arts Center on Tuesday, Oct. 8, 1985, and closed June 21, 1987 in the Fox Theatre, Atlanta, Ga. For original Broadway production, see *THEATRE WORLD* Volume 38.

CAST

The Stepp Sisters	Rhetta Hughes, LueCinda Ramseur [1], R. LaChanze Sapp, Lauren Velez [2]
Charlene	Yvette Louise Cason
Joanne	Lynda McConnell
Marty	Larry Stewart [3]
Curtis Taylor, Jr.	Weyman Thompson [4]
Deena Jones	Alisa Gyse
The M.C.	Vernon Spencer
Tiny Joe Dixon	Roy L. Jones [5]
Lorrell Robinson	Arnetia Walker
C. C. White	Lawrence Clayton [6]
Effie Melody White	Sharon Brown [7]
Little Albert & The True Tones	Robert Clater, Germaine Edwards, Robert Fowler [8], Kevin Morrow [9], Harold Perrineau, Jr.
James Thunder Early	Herbert L. Rawlings, Jr.
Edna Burke	Fuschia Walker
James Early Band	Robert Clater, Germaine Edwards, Robert Fowler, Kevyn Morrow, Steve Marder [10], Harold Perrineau, Jr.
Wayne	Milton Craig Nealy
Dave & Sweethearts	Paul Binotto [11], Shirley Tripp, Lauren Velez
Frank, a press agent	Tim Cassidy
Dwight, a TV director	Steve Marder [10]
TV Stage Manager	Paul Binotto [11]
Michelle Morris	LueCinda Ramseur [12]
Jerry, nightclub owner/Guard	Roy L. Jones
Carl, a piano player	Robert Fowler
The Five Tuxedos	Robert Clater, Germaine Edwards, Robert Fowler, Kevyn Morrow, Harold Perrineau, Jr.
Les Style	Yvette Louise Cason, Rhetta Hughes, Lynda McConnell, R. LaChanze Sapp
Film Executives	Paul Binotto, Robert Fowler, Kevyn Morrow
Mr. Morgan	Vernon Spencer

ENSEMBLE: Psul Binotto, Yvette Louise Cason, Tim Cassidy, Robert Clater, Germaine Edwards, Robert Fowler, Rhetta Hughes, Roy. L. Jones, Steve Marder, Lynda McConnell, Kevyn Morrow, Milton Craig Nealy, Harold Perrineau, Jr., R. LaChanze Sapp, Vernon Spencer, Shirley Tripp, Lauren Velez, Fuschia Walker. Swings: Brenda Braxton, B. J. Jefferson[13], Phillip Gilmore, Darryl Eric Tribble

MUSICAL NUMBERS: I'm Looking for Something, Goin' Downtown, Takin' the Long Way Home, Move! You're Steppin' on My Heart, Fake Your Way to the Top, Cadillac Car, Steppin' to the Bad Side, Party Party, I Want You Baby, Family, Dreamgirls, Press Conference, Only the Beginning, Heavy, It's All Over, And I Am Telling You I'm Not Going, Love Love You Baby, I Am Changing, One More Picture Please, When I First Saw You, Got to Be Good Times, Ain't No Party, I Meant You No Harm, Quintette, The Rap, I Miss You Old Friend, One Night Only, I'm Somebody, Faith in Myself, Hard to Say Goodbye

A musical in 2 acts and 20 scenes. The action takes place during the 1960's and early 1970's.

†Succeeded by: 1. Susan Beaubian, 2. Lorraine Velez, 3. Roy L. Jones, 4. Obba Babatunde, Weyman Thompson, 5. Nat Morris, Leonard Piggee, 6. Kevyn Morrow, 7. Lillias White, 8. Matthew Dickens, Bobby Daye, 9. David Thome, 10. Stephen Terrell, 11. Evan Pappas, Stephen Bourneuf, 12. Susan Beaubian, 13. Graciela Simpson

Martha Swope Photos

Top Right: Sharon Brown, Alisa Gyse, Arnetia Walker
Below: Susan Beaubian, Alisa Gyse, Sharon Brown, Arnetia Walker

Weyman Thompson (c) Above: Arnetia Walker, Alisa Gyse, LueCinda RamSeur

DOUBLES

By David Wiltse; Director, Morton DaCosta; Set/Costumes, Robert Fletcher; Lighting, Craig Miller; General Manager, Gary Gunas; Presented by Marvin A. Krauss, Irving Siders, PACE Theatrical Group Inc.; Company Manager, L. Liberatore; Technical Supervisor, Eddie Collins; Props, Patrick Harmeson; Wardrobe, Arlene Konowitz, Sydney Smith; Production Associate, Rod Kaats; Sound Effects, Robert Kerzman; Stage Managers, Joseph Donovan, Amy Richards; Tour Direction, Roadworks; Press, Molly Smith. Opened in Wilmington, Del., Playhouse on Tuesday, October 7, 1986 and closed Feb. 25, 1987 in Eckard Hall, Clearwater, Florida. For original Broadway production, see THEATRE WORLD Volume 41.

CAST

Guy	Peter Flint
Lennie	Gabe Kaplan
George	Martin Milner
Arnie	Peter Shuman
Heather	Jill Jones
Chuck	Gavin Troster
Tennis Player	Kenny Morris

UNDERSTUDIES: Bob Adrian (Lennie/George/Chuck), Kenny Morris (Arnie/George), Gavin Troster (Guy), Amy Richards (Heather)

A comedy in two acts. The action takes place at the present time in the men's locker room of the Norwalk Racquet Club, Norwalk, Connecticut.

Martha Swope Photos

Kathleen McCall, Peter Flint, Peter Shuman,
Gabe Kaplan in "Doubles"

Robert Nichols, Lenny Wolpe, Mitchell Greenberg,
Mickey Rooney Above: Jennifer Lee Andrews, Rooney,
Bob Walton Top: Michael Dantuono

A FUNNY THING HAPPENED ON THE WAY TO THE FORUM

Music & Lyrics, Stephen Sondheim; Book, Larry Gelbart, Burt Shevelove; Director, George Martin; Choreographer, Ethel Martin; Music Director, Sherman Frank; Scenery, Michael Bottari, Ronald Case; Lighting, Richard Winkler; Costumes, Gail Cooper-Hecht; General Manager, Robert V. Straus; Sound, Abe Jacob; Consultant, Madeline Lee Gilford; Casting, Jeffrey Dunn; Presented by Guber/Gross/Young Productions; Company Manager, Mitzi Harder; Dance Captain, Danielle DeCrette; Associate Conductor/Keyboards, Howard Levitsky; Technical Supervisor, Steve Cochrane; Props, Greg Kermery; Wardrobe, Michele Nezwazky; Hairstylist, Howard Leonard; Stage Managers, Joel Tropper, John Actman, Hank Brunjes; Press, Mark Goldstaub, Daniel J. P. Kellachan, Kevin P. McAnarney, Virginia Gillick, Peter Morris. Opened Monday, March 2, 1987 in New Haven's (Ct.) Shubert Theatre, and still touring May 31, 1987. For original Broadway production, see *THEATRE WORLD* Volume 18.

CAST

Prologus	Mickey Rooney
Proteans	James Darrah, Steven Gelfer, Reed Jones
Senex	Robert Nichols
Domina, his wife	Marsha Bagwell
Hero, his son	Bob Walton
Hysterium, slave to Senex and Domina	Lenny Wolpe
Lycus, a dealer in courtesans	Mitchell Greenberg
Pseudolus, slave to Hero	Mickey Rooney
Tintinnabula	Zoie Lam
Panacea	Karen Byers
The Geminae	Lori Ellen Mello, Renee Robertson
Vibrata	Victoria Dillard
Gymnasia	Lesley Durnin
Philia	Jennifer Lee Andrews
Erronius	Frank Nastasi
Miles Gloriosus, a warrior	Michael Dantuono

STANDBYS & UNDERSTUDIES: Steve Blanchard (Miles/Proteans), Hank Brunjes (Proteans), Danielle DeCrette (Courtesans/Domina), Karen Byers (Philia), Steven Gelfer (Pseudolus/Senex), Reed Jones (Hysterium/Lycus/Erronius), James Darrah (Hero)

MUSICAL NUMBERS: Comedy Tonight, Love I Hear, Free, The House of Marcus Lycus, Lovely, Pretty Little Picture, Everybody Ought to Have a Maid, I'm Calm, Impossible, Bring Me My Bride, That Dirty Old Man, That'll Show Him, Funeral, Finale

A musical in two acts. The action is continuous, and takes place 200 years before the Christian era on a day in Spring on a street in Rome in front of the houses of Erronius, Senex and Lycus.

Martha Swope Photos

GREATER TUNA

By Jaston Williams, Joe Sears, Ed Howard; Director, Ed Howard; Scenery, Kevin Rupnik; Costumes, Linda Fisher; Lighting, Judy Rasmuson; General Management, Robinwood Enterprises/Cheryl Fluehr, Joe Watson; Tour Marketing Directing Director, Sheron Leonard; Presented by Charles H. Duggan; Stage Managers, T. L. Boston, Sam Sexton; Press, Smyth/Katzen (Molly Smyth). Opened in the Tower Theatre, Houston, Texas, on Tuesday, October 7, 1986, and still touring May 31, 1987. For original New York production, see *THEATRE WORLD* Volume 39.

CAST

JOE SEARS playing Thurston Wheelis, Bertha Bumiller, Leonard Childres, Elmer Watkins, Aunt Pearl Burras, R. R. Snavely, The Reverend Spikes, Sheriff Givens, Hank Bumiller, Yippy
JASTON WILLIAMS playing Arles Struvie, Didi Snavely, Harold Dean Lattimer, Petey Fisk, Little Jody Bumiller, Stanley Bumiller, Charlene Bumiller, Chad Hartford, Phinas Blye, Vera Carp

A comedy in 2 acts and 12 scenes. The action takes place on a late-summer day of the present time in Tuna, the third-smallest town in Texas.

Joe Sears, Jaston Williams in "Greater Tuna"
(Ken Howard)

Judy Kaye (c) Above: Frank Gorshin (c)
Top: Imogene Coca, Frank Gorshin, Judy Kaye

ON THE 20th CENTURY

Book & Lyrics, Betty Comden, Adolph Green; Music, Cy Coleman; Based on play by Ben Hecht, Charles MacArthur, Bruce Millholland; Director, Jeffrey B. Moss; Choreography, Barbara Siman; Musical Director/Conductor, Kay Cameron; Scenery, James Morgan; Costumes, Martin Pakledinaz; Lighting, Richard Winkler; Assistant Conductor, Rita Mosley; Presented by Jerry Kravat Entertainment; Sound, Lewis Mead; General Manager, Maria Di Dia; Company Manager, Steven Schnepp; Dance Captain, Michael Radigan; Technical Director, Richard Warwinsky; Props, Joe Burns; Wardrobe, Patricia Britton; Production Assistant, Jose Smith; Stage Managers, Clifford Schwartz, Roger Franklin, Mark T. Menard; Press, Kevin P. McAnarney, Mark Goldstaub, Dan Kellachan, Virginia Gillick. Opened in Miami's Coconut Grove Playhouse on Friday, October 10, 1986, and closed in Scranton, Pa., on March 5, 1987. For original Broadway production, see *THEATRE WORLD* Volume 34.

CAST

Rodney/Lead Actor	Gary Barker
Owen O'Malley	King Donovan
Oliver Webb	David Green
Conductor Flanagan/Congressman Lockwood/Dr. Johnson	Glenn Mure
Letitia Primrose	Imogene Coca
Oscar Jaffee	Frank Gorshin
Anita	Susan Shofner
Max Jacobs	Mark Basile
Imelda Thornston	Alexana Ryer
Maxwell Finch/Nigel/Attendant	Michael Radigan
Lily Garland	Judy Kaye
Bruce Granit	Keith Curran
Agnes	Peggy Bayer
Nurse	Wysandria Woolsey

ENSEMBLE: Gary Barker, Mark Basile, Peggy Bayer, Bruce Daniels, Cheryl Hodges, Michael Radigan, Susan Shofner, Wysandria Woolsey

UNDERSTUDIES: Wysandria Woolsey (Letitia), Mark Basile (Bruce), Gary Barker (Oliver), Alexana Ryer (Lily), Bruce Daniels (O'Malley/Conductor/Doctor/Congressman), David Green (Oscar)

MUSICAL NUMBERS: Stranded Again, On the 20th Century, I Rise Again, Indian Maiden's Lament, Veronique, I Have Written a Play, Together, Never, Our Private World, Repent, Mine, I've Got It All, Five Zeros, Sign Lily Sign, She's a Nut, Max Jacobs, Babette, The Legacy, Lily-Oscar, Finale

A musical in two acts. The action takes place on board the 20th Century between Chicago's Union Station and New York City's Grand Central Station.

Tom Elliott Photos

I'M NOT RAPPAPORT

By Herb Gardner; Director, Daniel Sullivan; Set, Tony Walton; Costumes, Robert Morgan; Lighting, Pat Collins; Fights Staging, B. H. Barry; Presented by James Walsh, Lewis Allen, Martin Heinfling; General Manager, James Walsh; Company Manager, Hans Hortig; Casting, Pat McCorkle; Props, Edward "Buddy" Horton; Wardrobe, Jenna Krempel; Makeup, Joseph Laudati, Joseph Tomasini; Stage Managers, Warren Crane, Dennis Robert Fox; Press, Jeffrey Richards, Irene Gandy, Susan E. Lee, C. George Willard. Opened in the Colonial Theatre, Boston, Ma., on Friday, Nov. 28, 1986, and closed in the Henry Fonda Theatre, Los Angeles, Ca., on July 12, 1987. For original Broadway production, see *THEATRE WORLD* Volume 42.

CAST

Nat	Judd Hirsch
Midge	Cleavon Little
Danforth	Richmond Hoxie
Laurie	Catherine Christianson
Gilley	Kevin M. Moccia
Clara	Cheryl Giannini
The Cowboy	Tom Stechschulte

UNDERSTUDIES: David S. Howard (Nat), David Downing (Midge), Lauren Klein (Clara/Laurie), Dennis Robert Fox (Gilley), Tom Stechschulte (Danforth), Kevin Carrigan (Cowboy)

A comedy in two acts and 4 scenes. The action takes place during early October 1982 on a bench near a path at the edge of the lake in Central Park, New York City.

Martha Swope Photos

Judd Hirsch, Cleavon Little

PIPPIN

Book, Roger O. Hirson; Music & Lyrics, Stephen Schwartz; Director, Ben Vereen; Choreography/Musical Staging, Kathryn Doby; Scenery, Tony Walton; Costumes, Patricia Zipprodt; Lighting, Ken Billington; Sound, Abe Jacob; Musical Director, David Loeb; Presented by Tom Mallow, James Janek; General Management, American Theatre Productions/Jay Brooks, George MacPerson, Jan Mallow; Company Manager, Alan Ross Kosher; Props, Devon Query; Wardrobe, C. Smolens; Wigs, Mundi M. S. Lawrey; Hairstylist, Paul Germano; Stage Managers, Mark S. Krause, Charles Collins, Scott Fless; Press, Max Eisen, Maria Somma, Madelon Rosen, Glenn Eisen. Opened Tuesday, July 8, 1986 in Dallas, Tx., and closed in the Van Wezel Theatre, Sarasota, Fl., Nov. 9, 1986. For original Broadway production, see THEATRE WORLD Volume 29.

CAST

Leading Player	Ben Vereen
Pippin	Sam Scalamoni
Charles	Ed Dixon
Lewis	Michael Kubala
Fastrada	Ginger Prince
Musician	Robert Ashford
The Head	Charles Edward Hall
Berthe	Betty Ann Grove
Beggar	Tony Lillo
Peasant	Jeffery C. Ferguson
Noble	Greg Schanuel
Field Marshall	Charles Edward Hall
Catherine	Rende Rea Norman
Theo	Jeb Handwerger

UNDERSTUDIES: Michael Kubala (Pippin), Judith Laxer (Fastrada), Jeffery C. Ferguson (Leading Player), Charles Edward Hall (Charles), Rende Rae Norman (Berthe), Kimberly Duddy (Catherine), Rosh Handwerger (Theo), Swings: Kimberly Duddy, Scott Fless

MUSICAL NUMBERS: Magic to Do, Corner of the Sky, Welcome Home, War Is a Science, Glory, Simple Joys, No Time at All, With You, Spread a Little Sunshine, Morning Glow, On the Right Track, Kind of Woman, Extraordinary, Love Song, Finale

A musical in eight scenes performed without intermission. The action takes place in 780 A.D. and thereabouts, in the Holy Roman Empire and thereabouts.

Martha Swope Photos

Ben Vereen, Sam Scalamoni Above: Judith Laxer, Ben Vereen, Dominique Decaudain

A RAISIN IN THE SUN

By Lorraine Hansberry; Director, Harold Scott; Set, Thomas Cariello; Costumes, Judy Dearing; Lighting, Shirley Prendergast; Sound, Rick Menke, Philip Campanella; Casting, David Tochterman; General Manager, Ellen Richard; Presented by Roundabout Theatre Co. (Gene Feist/Todd Haimes) in association with Robert Nemiroff; Production Manager, Robert N. Chase; Wardrobe, Tad Webb; Props, Hunter Nesbitt Spence; Musical Director, Philip Campanella; Stage Managers, Gary M. Zabinski, Scott Rodabaugh; Press, Joshua Ellis, Adrian Bryan-Brown, Jim Sapp, Cindy Valk, Jackie Green, Bill Shuttleworth. Opened in the Eisenhower Theater, Kennedy Center, Washington, DC., on Wednesday, November 12, 1986, and closed in the Wilshire Theatre, Los Angeles, on April 26, 1987.

CAST

Ruth Younger	Starletta DuPois
Travis Younger	Kimble Joyner
Walter Lee Younger	Delroy Lindo
Beneatha Younger	Kim Yancey
Lena Younger (mother)	Esther Rolle
Joseph Asagai	Lou Ferguson
George Murchison	Joseph C. Phillips
Bobo	Stephen Henderson
Karl Lindner	John Fiedler
Moving Men	Ron O. J. Parson, Charles Watts

UNDERSTUDIES: Louise Mike (Mama), Ron O. J. Parson (Walter Lee/Bobo), Jennifer Trott (Ruth/Beneatha), Charles Watts (Asagai/Murchison), Richard Habersham (Travis), Scott Rodabaugh (Karl)

A drama in three acts. The action takes place over a period of three weeks in the early 1950's in the Youngers' apartment in Chicago's Southside.

Starletta DuPois (seated), Esther Rolle
(Joan Marcus)

Lucie Arnaz, Laurence Luckinbill
Above: Arthur Tracy, Mary Louise Wilson

SOCIAL SECURITY

By Andrew Bergman; Director, Peter Lawrence; Scenery, Tony Walton; Costumes, Ann Roth; Lighting, Marilyn Rennagel; Presented by Zev Bufman and Pace Theatrical Group (Allen Becker/Sidney Shlenker/Miles Wilkin); General Management, Leonard Soloway, Brian Dunbar; Company Manager, L. Liberatore; Props, R. Bruce Martin; Wardrobe, Pat White; Production Associate, Rod Kaats; Casting, Simon/Kumin; Hair Design, J. Roy Helland; Sound, Otts Munderloh; Stage Managers, John Brigleb, Linnea Sundsten; Press, Smyth/Katzen (Molly Smyth). Opened in the Royal Poinciana Playhouse, Palm Beach, Fl., on March 3, 1987, and closed in San Francisco's Curran Theatre on July 19, 1987. For original Broadway production, see *THEATRE WORLD* Volume 42.

CAST

David Kahn	Laurence Luckinbill
Barbara Kahn	Lucie Arnaz
Trudy Heyman	Evalyn Baron
Martin Heyman	Robert Ott Boyle
Sophie Greengrass	Mary Louise Wilson
Maurice Koenig	Arthur Tracy

STANDBYS: Donna Haley (Barbara/Trudy), Ken Kliban (David/Martin), Irma St. Paule (Sophie), Ben Kapen (Maurice)

A comedy in 2 acts and 3 scenes. The action takes place at the present time in the Eastside apartment of Barbara and David Kahn in New York City.

Cathy Blaivas Photos

SINGIN' IN THE RAIN

Based on the MGM film; Screenplay and Adaptation, Betty Comden, Adolph Green; Songs, Nacio Herb Brown, Arthur Freed; Director, Lawrence Kasha; Choreography, Peter Gennaro; Presented by Marvin A. Krauss, Irving Siders and Pace Theatrical Group by arrangement with Maurice Rosenfield, Lois F. Rosenfield and Cindy Pritzker; Scenery, Peter Wolf Concepts; Costumes, Robert Fletcher; Lighting, Thomas Skelton; Sound, Sound Associates; Original Dance/Vocal Arrangements, Stanley Lebowsky; Additional Arrangements, Wally Harper; Music Director, Raymond Allen; Orchestrations, Larry Wilcox; Rain System, Showtech; Film Sequences, Gordon Willis, Lawrence Kasha; Casting, Slater/Willett; General Manager, Gary Gunas; Music Coordinator, John Monaco; Production Supervisor, Thomas P. Carr; Company Manager, Connie Weinstein; Technical Supervisor, Ed Collins; Props, Tim Anderson, Steven Callahan; Wardrobe, Barrett Hong; Dance Captain, Dan Mojica; Assistant Musical Director, Sheilah Walker; Assistant Choreographer, Liza Gennaro-Evans; Production Associate, Rod Kaats; Production Assistants, John Rainwater, Greg Weiss; Stage Managers, David Hansen, Joseph Godwin, Joe Deer; Press, Shirley Herz Associates, Smyth/Katzen. Opened in the Dallas (Tx) Music Hall on Tuesday, June 10, 1986, and closed in the Tennessee Performing Arts Center, Nashville, on June 7, 1987. For original Broadway production, see *THEATRE WORLD* Volume 42.

CAST

Dora Bailey	Lou Williford
Zelda Zanders	Valerie Dowd
Olga Mara	Jennifer Hammond
Mary Margaret	Deborah Bartlett
R. F. Simpson	Elek Hartman
Roscoe Dexter	Alan Sues
Cosmo Brown	Brad Moranz
Lina Lamont	Jennifer Smith
Don Lockwood	Donn Simione
Young Don/Assistant Director	Frank Kosik
Young Cosmo	Rick Conant
Villain/Diction Teacher	Gerry Burkhardt
Lady in Waiting in film	Holly K. Watts
Rod	Steve Goodwillie
Kathy Selden	Cynthia Ferrer
Policemen/Sid Phillips	Darryl Ferrera
Butler	Jim Kirby
1st Assistant Director	George Giatrakis
Production Singer	Campbell Martin
Miss Dinsmore	Holly K. Watts

ENSEMBLE: Kelli Barclay-Boelsterli, Deborah Bartlett, Beverly Anne Britton, Gerry Burkhardt, Newton Cole, Rick Conant, Valerie Dowd,, Rick Ferrera, George Giatrakis, Steve Goodwillie, Jennifer Hammond, Andrea Hopkins, Jim Kirby, Frank Kosik, Dana Lewis, Campbell Martin, Ann Neiman, Mark T. Owens, Erin Robbins, James Van Treuren, Holly K. Watts, Lou Williford

UNDERSTUDIES: Frank Kosik (Don), Deborah Bartlett (Kathy), Rick Conant (Cosmo), Valerie Dowd (Lina), James Van Treuren (Simpson), Mark T. Owens (Singer), Lou Williford (Phoebe), Holly K. Watts (Dora), Rick Ferraro (Sid), Gerry Burkhardt (Roscoe), Swings: Andrea Cohen, Joe Deer, Dan Mojica

MUSICAL NUMBERS: Fit as a Fiddle, You Stepped Out of a Dream, All I Do Is Dream of You, Make 'Em Laugh, Beautiful Girl, You Are My Lucky Star, You Were Meant for Me, Moses, Good Mornin', Singin' in the Rain, Would You, What's Wrong with Me?, Broadway Melody, Finale

A musical in 2 acts and 23 scenes. The action takes place in Hollywood in the 1920's.

Martha Swope Photos

Right Center: Darryl Ferrera, Donn Simione

Donn Simione, Cynthia Ferrer, Brad Moranz

STOP THE WORLD. . . . I WANT TO GET OFF

Book/Music/Lyrics, Leslie Bricusse, Anthony Newley; Musical Director, Tom Fay; Choreography, Philip Burton, Lynn Taylor-Corbett; Musical Supervisor/Arranger, Ian Fraser; Set, David Chapman; Costumes, Carol Oditz; Sound, T. Richard Fitzgerald; Presented by Barry and Fran Weissler, Pace Theatrical Group; General Management, National Artists Management/Alecia Parker; Company Manager, Michael Gill; Props, Howard Walker; Wardrobe, Curtis Hay; Hairstylist, Caterina Fiordellisi; Makeup, Sonia Kashuk; Dance Captain, Teresa Tracy; Assistant Conductor, Mark Lipman; Stage Managers, Michael McEowen, Bill Vosburgh, Teresa Tracy; Press, Fred Nathan, Marc P. Thibodeau, Anne Abrams, Bert Fink, Dennis Crowley, Merle Frimark, Philip Rinaldi, Smyth/Katzen (Janet Spencer). Opened Tuesday, September 23, 1986 in Houston (Tx) Music Hall, and closed in the Embassy Theatre, Fort Wayne, In., on Feb. 18, 1987. For original Broadway production (with Anthony Newley), see *THEATRE WORLD* Volume 19.

CAST

Anthony Newley (Little Chap)	Stacey Logan
Beth Blatt	Janet Metz
Danette Cuming	Suzie Plaksin (Evie/Anya/Ilse)
Madeleine Doherty	Jill Powell
Diana Georger (Jane)	Karyn Quackenbush
Chikae Ishikawa	Joey Rigol
Kathy Leonardo	Teresa Tracy

UNDERSTUDIES: Danette Cuming, Teresa Tracy

MUSICAL NUMBERS: Once in a Lifetime, A.B.C. Song, Typically English, Lumbered, Welcome to Sludgepool, Gonna Build a Mountain, Meilinki Meilchick, Family Fugue, Typische Deutsche, Nag Nag Nag, All-American, Mumbo Jumbo, Welcome to Sunvale, Someone Nice Like You, What Kind of Fool Am I?

A musical in two acts.

John Reilly Photos

Anthony Newley, Karyn Quackenbush, Suzie Plaksin, Diana Georger, Joey Rigol *(John Reilly)*

SWEET BIRD OF YOUTH

By Tennessee Williams; Director, Michael Blakemore; Sets, Michael Annals; Costumes, Carrie Robbins; Lighting, Martin Aronstein; Set Consultant, Michael Vale; Music, Barrington Pheloung; Sound, Jan Nebozenko; Casting, Hughes/Moss; Presented by Center Theatre Group/Ahmanson Theatre (Robert Fryer, Artistic Director), Duncan C. Weldon, Jerome Minskoff, Karl Allison, Douglas Urbanski; Production Manager, Ralph Beaumont; Technical Director, Robert Routolo; Props, Steve Rapollo; Wardrobe, Eddie Doods; Stage Managers, George Rondo, Robert Schear, Charles Douglass; Press, Joshua Ellis, Adrian Bryan-Brown, Solters/Roskin/Friedman. Opened in the Denver Center for the Performing Arts on Wednesday, Nov. 19, 1986 and closed in the Ahmanson Theatre, Los Angeles, on Jan. 25, 1987. For original Broadway production, see *THEATRE WORLD* Volume 15.

CAST

Chance Wayne	Mark Soper
The Princess Kosmonopolis	Lauren Bacall
Fly	Mansoor Najee-Ullah
George Scudder	Joseph McCaren
State Trooper	Ed Trotta
Boss Finley	Henderson Forsythe
Tom Junior	Howard Sherman
Charles	Hugh L. Hurd
Aunt Nonnie	Georgia Southcotte
Heavenly Finley	Donna Bullock
Jackie	Jimmy Justice
Stuff	Peter Strong
Miss Lucy	Carol Goodheart
The Heckler	James Cahill
Page	Charles Douglass
Violet	Sharon Ullrick
Edna	Alexandra Nelson
Scotty	Lee Chew
Bud	Robertson Carricart
Hatcher	Saylor Creswell
Man #1	Hugh A. Rose
Man #2	David Lee Taylor
Doctor	Alex Paul
Drum Majorette	Laurane Sheehan

UNDERSTUDIES: Peter Strong (Chance), James Cahill (Boss), Sharon Ullrick (Miss Lucy), Alexandra Nelson (Heavenly), Ed Trotta (Junior/Heckler), Saylor Creswell (Scudder), Hugh A. Rose (Hatcher/Doctor), David Lee Taylor (Stuff/Scotty/Bud), Laurane Sheehan (Violet/Edna), Mansoor Najee-Ullah (Charles), Charles Douglass (Fly), Alex Paul (Page/Trooper)

A drama in 2 acts and 5 scenes. The action takes place at the present time somewhere on the Gulf Coast.

Martha Swope Photos

Mark Soper, Lauren Bacall

TANGO ARGENTINO

Conceived and Directed by Claudio Segovia, Hector Orezzoli; Choreographic Conception, Claudio Segovia, Juan Carlos Copes; Musical Directors, Luis Stazo, Jose Libertella, Osvaldo Berlingieri; Scenery/Costumes, Hector Orezzoli, Claudio Segovia; Lighting, Claudio Segovia; Executive Producer, Norman Rothstein; Presented by Mel Howard, Donald K. Donald; Company Managers, Stephen Arnold, Lola Leon; Wardrobe, Dolores Gamba; Makeup/Hair, Jean-Luc DonVito; Stage Managers, David Coffman, Otto von Bruening; Press, Marilynn LeVine-P.R. Partners/Meg Gordean, Leslie Anderson, Wayne McWorter. Opened in Sundome Center, Phoenix, Az, on Thursday, March 5, 1987, and closed at Kennedy Center, Washington, D.C., on July 18, 1987.

COMPANY

DANCERS: Cecilia Narova, Juan Carlos Copes and Maria Nieves, Nelida and Nelson, Gloria and Eduardo, Virulazo and Elvira, The Dinzels, Monica and Luciano, Miguel Angel Zotto and Milena Plebs, Carlos Borquez and Ines

SINGERS: Raul Lavie, Alba Solis, Jovita Luna, Elba Beron

Presented in two parts.

Scott W. Aszkenas, Martha Swope Photos

Nelida and Nelson, Maria Nieves and Juan
Carlos Copes, Gloria and Eduardo (*Beatriz Schiller*)

THE TAP DANCE KID

Book, Charles Blackwell; Music, Henry Krieger; Lyrics, Robert Lorick; Based on novel "Nobody's Family Is Going to Change" by Louise Fitzhugh; Director, Jerry Zaks; Choreography, Danny Daniels; Musical Supervisor/Orchestra and Vocal Arrangements, Harold Wheeler; Scenery, Michael Hotopp, Paul dePass; Costumes, William Ivey Long; Lighting, Harrison Clend; Music Consultant, Don Jones; Dance Music Arrangement, Peter Howard; Associate Choreographer, D. J. Giagni; Scenic Photography, Mark Feldstein; Wigs, Paul Huntley; General Management, American Theatre Productions; Company Manager, Alan Ross Kosher; Presented by Zev Bufman Theatre Partnership Ltd.; Props, Chet Perry II, Jack Montgomery; Wardrobe, Barbara Hladsky, Margaret Danz; Hairstylist, Brent Dillon; Assistant Conductor, Robert Webb; Dance Captain, J. J. Jepson; Stage Managers, Ed Fitzgerald, J. Marvin Crosland, Ara Marx; Press, Smyth/Katzen (Molly Smyth). Opened at Purdue University, Lafayette, In., on Saturday, Oct. 4, 1986, and closed in Mechanic Theatre, Baltimore, Md., on Jan. 4, 1987. For original Broadway production, see *THEATRE WORLD* Volume 40.

CAST

Willie	Dule Hill
Emma	Martine Allard
Ginnie	Monica Pege
William	Chuck Cooper
Dipsey	Eugene Fleming
Carole	Theresa Hayes
Mona	Patrice McConachie
Dulcie	Dawnn J. Lewis
Daddy Bates	Harold Nicholas
Winslow	Mark Santoro
Richie	Ron Bastine

DANCERS & NEW YORKERS: Ron Bastine, Alain Freulon, Frantz Hall, J. J. Jepson, Mark DiNoia, Mark Santoro, Janice Lorraine, Patrice McConachie, Kim Meyer, Maryellen Scilla, Amy O'Brien, Horace Turnbull, Dawnn J. Lewis

STANDBYS & UNDERSTUDIES: Jeff Bates (Dipsey), Shawana Kemp (Emma), Donny Burks (William), Hassoun Tatum (Willie), Frantz Hall (Daddy/Dipsey/Richie), Theresa Hayes (Ginnie), Janice Lorraine (Mona/Carole/Dulcie), Ron Bastine (Winslow), Swings: Ara Marx, Gary Sullivan

MUSICAL NUMBERS: Dipsey's Comin' Over, High Heels, Something Better Something More, Four Strikes Against Me, Class Act, They Never Hear What I Say, Dancing Is Everything, Crosstown, Fabulous Feet, I Could Get Used to Him, Man in the Moon, Like Him, My Luck Is Changing, Someday, Dipsey's Vaudeville, I Remember How It Was, Lullabye, Tap Tap, Dance If It Makes You Happy, William's Song, Finale

A musical in 2 acts and 15 scenes. The action takes place at the present time in New York City.

Eugene Fleming (c) Above: Harold Nicholas,
Dule Hill

PROFESSIONAL REGIONAL COMPANIES

(Failure to meet deadline necessitated omissions)

ACT/A CONTEMPORARY THEATRE

Seattle, Washington
Twenty-second Season

Producing Director, Gregory A. Falls; Administrative Manager, Susan Trapnell Moritz; Producing Manager, Phil Schermer; Resident Director, Jeff Steitzer; Songworks Director, David Hunter Koch; Production Manager, James Verdery; Marketing, Polly Conley; Development, Sarah S. Coyle; Operations, Janet Upjohn; Directors, Gregory A. Falls, Anne-Denise Ford, Rita Giomi; Sets, Shelly Henze Schermer, Bill Forrester, Scott Weldin, Michael Olich; Costumes, Sally Richardson, Sarah Campbell, Laura Crow, Rose Pederson, Celeste Cleveland, Nanrose Buchman; Lighting, Phil Schermer, Rick Paulson, James Verdery, Jody Briggs; Stage Managers, James Verdery, Jorie Wackerman; Press, Michael Sande

PRODUCTIONS & CASTS
ON THE RAZZLE by Tom Stoppard; with Mark Drusch, Judy Ford Taylor, Tony Soper, Suzanne Irving, John Aulward, Jill C. Klein, Dan Daily, R. Hamilton Wright, Rex McDowell, Jo Vetter, Dianne Benjamin Hill, David Mong, David Pichette, Edward R. Williams, Casey Trupin
PAINTING CHURCHES by Tina Howe; with Eve Roberts, John MacKay, Stephanie Kallos
TALES FROM HOLLYWOOD by Christopher Hampton; with Laurence Ballard, Russell J. Reed, Rex McDowell, Ray Fry, Tony Mockus, Jo Leffingwell, Mary Petzold, David S. Klein, B. J. Douglas, Laurel Anne White, Stephanie Kallos, Peter Silbert, Susan Finque, Rod Pilloud
BRIGHTON BEACH MEMOIRS by Neil Simon; with Andy McCutcheon, Lois Smith, Catherine Wolf, Shana Bestock, Tara Herivel, Peter Killy, David Margulies
THE JAIL DIARY OF ALBIE SACHS by David Edgar; with R. Hamilton Wright, Tom Hammond, David S. Klein, Frank Corrado, John Gilbert, William Earl, Ray I, Rick Tutor, Peter Silbert
LITTLE SHOP OF HORRORS by Howard Ashman, Alan Menken; with Doris Hayes, Michelle Blackmon, Kyra Hider, Ron Lee Savin, Jan Maxwell, William Weir, David Silverman, William Szymanski, James M. Caddell
A CHRISTMAS CAROL by Charles Dickens; with Richard Farrell, Allen Nause, Rex Rabold, Scott Kaiser, Todd Moore, Tom Hammond, Gretchen V. O'Connell, Jayne Muirhead, Geoffrey Weyrick, David S. Klein, Jeanne Paulson, Christopher Marks, Daniel Milder, Cameron Dokey, Diane Weyrick, John Pribyl, Tatum Nolan, Sarah Baskin, Jeff Sellers, Malcolm Lowe

Chris Bennion Photos

William Weir, Jan Maxwell, David Silverman
in "Little Shop of Horrors" Top: Eve Roberts,
John MacKay in "Painting Churches"

ALASKA REPERTORY THEATRE

Anchorage, Alaska
June 12, 1986–January 25, 1987

Artistic Director, Robert J. Farley; Managing Director, Alice Chebba; Technical Director, Dennis G. Booth; Marketing, Patricia Eckert; Development, James Murphy, Assistant to the Directors, Suzanne Launer; Stage Manager, Michael Paul; Sound, Bruce Crouch; Lighting, Lauren MacKenzie Miller; Press, Jill McGuire

PRODUCTIONS & CASTS
EL GRANDE DE COCA-COLA by Ron House, John Neville-Andrews, Alan Sherman, Diz White, Sally Willis; Director, Walton Jones; Set, Connie Lutz; Costumes, Cathy McFarland; Choreography, Susan Rosenstock. CAST: D. B. Novaki, F. J. Pratt, Eleanor Reissa, Tracy Shaffer, Guy Strobel
THE RAINMAKER by N. Richard Nash; Director, Robert J. Farley; Set, Karen Gjelsteen; Costumes, Sally Richardson. CAST: Sid Conrad, Stephen Pelinski, Andy McCutcheon, Betsy Scott, James Hotchkiss, Ron Evans, D. B. Novak
I'M NOT RAPPAPORT by Herb Gardner; Director, Andrew Traister; Set, William Bloodgood; Costumes, Jenniver Svensno. CAST: Robert Ellenstein, David Downing, Michael Cadigan, Susan Diol, James Morrison, Andy McCutcheon, Susan Barnes
SLEUTH by Anthony Shaffer; Director, Clayton Corzatte; Set, Keith Brumley; Costumes, Sally Richardson. CAST: Philip Pleasants, Larry Paulsen, Phillip Farrar, Harold K. Newman, Roger Purnell
THE FOREIGNER by Larry Shue; Director, David McClendon; Set, Jennifer Lupton; Costumes, Jayna Orchard. CAST: Bill Buell, Thomas Oleniacz, Julianna McCarthy, Jay Louden, Harriet Hall, Gary McGurk, John Cameron Mitchell

Chris Arend, Jim Lavrakes Photos

Julianna McCarthy, Bill Buell
in "The Foreigner"

ALLIANCE THEATRE COMPANY

Atlanta, Georgia
Eighteenth Season

Artistic Director, Robert J. Farley; Managing Director, Edith H. Love; Interim Associate Artistic Director, Timothy Near; Literary Manager, Sandra Deer; Casting, Adam Muzzy; General Manager, William B. Duncan; Assistant Manager, Steven Martin; Production Manager, Billings Lapierre; Marketing, Kim Resnik; Development, Betty Blondeau-Russell; Press, Ruthie Ervin; Props, Mark Edlund; Sound, Brian Kettler; Stage Managers, Dale C. Lawrence, Kathy E. Richardson, Patricia Munford, Ed Rosendahl

PRODUCTIONS & CASTS

THE GOSPEL AT COLONUS by Lee Breuer, Bob Telson; Director, Lee Breuer; Musical Direction, Bob Telson; Set, Alison Yerxa; Costumes, Ghretta Hynd; Lights, Julie Archer; Stage Manager, Adrienne Neye; with Morgan Freeman (Messenger), Clarence Fountain and the Five Blind Boys of Alabama (Oedipus), Mary Alice (Antigone), Rev. Earl Miller (Theseus), Jevetta Steele (Ismene), Robert Earl Jones (Creon), Kevin Davis (Polyneices), Chorus and Choir

OUR TOWN by Thornton Wilder; Director, David Kerry Heefner; Set, Paul Wonsek; Costumes, Patricia Adshead; Lights, Marilyn Rennagel; with Tom Key (Stage Manager), Kurt Knudson (Dr. Gibbs), Dorothy Lancaster (Mrs. Gibbs), Beth Fowler (Mrs. Webb), Keith Noble (Joe/Si), Bruce Evers (Howie), Kevin Black (George Gibbs), Katie Kolesky (Rebecca), Nancy Hume (Emily Webb), Michael Jolluck (Wally), Wade Benson (Prof. Willard), Page Johnson (Editor Webb), Pat Hurley (Simon), Roberta Illg (Mrs. Soames), Frank Groseclose (Constable), Neal Williams (Carter), Ernest L. Dixon (Joe), Peter Thomasson (Sam), Ginnie Randall, Alice Heffernan-Sneed, Haynes Brooke, Lynn Todd Craig.

A FUNNY THING HAPPENED ON THE WAY TO THE FORUM by Stephen Sondheim, Larry Gelbart, Burt Shevelove; Director, Edward Stone; Choreography, D. J. Giagni; Musical Direction, Michael Fauss; Set, Mark Morton; Costumes, Susan Hirschfeld; Lights, Jason Kantrowitz; with David Schramm (Prologus), Rick Kerby (Mercury), Bryan C. Jones (Mars), David Pevsner (Mo), Michael Connolly (Senex), Lulu Downs (Domina), Philip Astor (Hysterium), Don Goodspeed (Hero), David Schramm (Pseudolus), Ken Prymus (Lycus), Felicia Hernandez (Tintinabula), Valerie Kassel, Jr./Sharlene Ross (The Geminae), Victoria Tabaca (Vibrata), Megan McFarland (Gymnasia), Glory Crampton (Philia), Frank Groseclose (Erronius), Jonathan Simmons (Miles Gloriosus), Joan Crocker, Jonathan Davis

THE FOREIGNER by Larry Shue; Director, Ron Lagomarsino; Set, Lowell Detweiler; Costumes, Pierre DeRagon; Lights, Spencer Mosse; with Michael Connolly (Froggy LeSueur), Jeff Brooks (Charlie Baker), Mary Wickes (Betty Meeks), David Head (Rev. Lee), Heather Lee (Catherin), Al Hamacher (Owen), Adam Redfield (Ellard), Joan Croker, Jonathan Davis, Timothy Egan, Bruce Young

AN AMERICAN DOLL'S HOUSE by Kathleen Nolan; Based on play by Henrik Ibsen; Director, Timothy Near; Set, Mark Morton; Lights, Paulie Jenkins; Costumes, Pierre DeRagon; with Michelle Shay (Nora Helmer), Christopher Broughton (Ian Helmer), Toi Campbell (Emmy Helmer), Sullivan H. Walker (Torvald Helmer), Lorraine Touissaint (Christine Lind), Tucker Smallwood (Krogstad), Michael O'Neill (Dr. Rank), Ginnie Randall (Anne Marie), Timothy Egan, Marguerite Hannah, Tess Malis, Andre Wiggins

Top Right: Al Hamacher, Jeff Brooks
in "The Foreigner" Below: Michael
Connolly, Lulu Downs, Philip Astor
in "A Funny Thing Happened . . ."

Jack Gwaltney, Tom Key in "Orphans"

THE PASSION OF DRACULA by Robert Hall, David Richmond; From novel by Bram Stoker; Director, Skip Foster; Set/Lights, Victor Becker; Costumes, Kathleen Blake; with Al Hamacher (Dr. Seward), Lance Davis (Jameson), Joan Croker (Medical Assistant), Alison Edwards (Dr. Helga Van Zandt), Ken Strong (Prof. Van Helsing), Simon Reynolds (Lord Godalming), Richard Levine (Renfield), Bernadette Wilson (Wilhelmina Murray), Tom Key (Jonathan Harker), Kim Coates (Count Dracula), Joan Croker, Christopher Ekholm, Jeff Portell.

ANNULLA, AN AUTOBIOGRAPHY by Emily Mann; Director, Timothy Near; Set/Costumes, Jeff Struckman; Lighting, Liz Lee; with Jacqueline Bertrand (Annulla), Jennifer Weldon (Voice).

ORPHANS by Lyle Kessler; Director, Skip Foster; Set, Michelle Bellavance; Costumes, Pierre DeRagon; Lights, Peter Shinn; with Tom Key (Treat), Jack Gwaltney (Phillip), Edmond Genest (Harold).

BLESS by Cindy Lou Johnson; *World Premiere;* Director, Paul Lazarus; Set, William Barclay; Costumes, Susan Mickey; with Jo Henderson (Mo), Pirie MacDonald (Ches), Greg Germann (Carl).

AMAZING GRACE by Sandra Deer; *World Premiere;* Director, Dan Bonnell, Set, James Wolk; Costumes, Pierre DeRagon; Lights, William B. Duncan; with Bette Henritze (Grace Tanner), C. duMas (Josh Shepard), Jayne Bentzen (Maggie Ames), Haynes Brooke (Troy).

DON QUIXOTE adapted by Sandra Deer from novel by Miguel de Cervantes; *World Premiere;* Director, Skip Foster; Set, Charles Caldwell; Costumes, Pierre DeRagon; Lights, Marilyn Rennagel; with Lynn Brown (Maria/Company), Al Hamacher (Sancho Panza/Company), Christian Hesler (Barber/Company), Jon Ludwig (Rosinante/Company), Theresa O'Shea (Housekeeper/Company), John Purcell (Curate/Company), Kelvin R. Shepard (Jock/Company), Ken Strong (Don Quixote/Company), Kee Strong (Dapple/Company), Suzanne Ventulett (Dulcinea/Company)

CHARLOTTE'S WEB adapted by Joseph Robinette from book by E. B. White; Director, Munson Hicks; Set, Mark Morton; Costumes, Susan Mickey; Lights, Paulie Jenkins; with John Ammerman (Narrator/Announcer/Photographer/Reporter), Lynn Brown (Charlotte), Lynn Todd Craig (The Lamb/Mrs. Zuckerman), Christian Hesler (The Sheep/Uncle/Judge), Pat Hurley (Gander/Lurvy), Michael Keck (Avery Arable/Zuckerman), Jon Ludwig (Templeton/Arable), Theresa O'Shea (Goose/Mrs. Arable/Judge), Ken Strong (Wilbur), Suzanne Ventulett (Fern Arable)

ALLEY THEATRE

Houston, Texas
Fortieth Season

Artistic/Executive Director, Pat Brown; Managing Director, Michael Tiknis; Associate Artistic Director, George Anderson; Assistant to Mr. Brown, Trent Jenkins; Resident Director, Beth Sanford; Young Company/Staff Director, James Martin; Literary Manager, Robert Strane; Production Manager, Bettye Fitzpatrick; Assistant, Carol L. Hickle; Resident Lighting, Pamela A. Gray; Resident Sets, Charles S. Kading; Resident Costumes, Howard Tsvi Kaplan; Resident Sound, Art Yelton; Wardrobe, Laura K. Wortham; Technical Director, Barry Griffith; Props, Tim Miller; Marketing, Carl Davis; Company/Operations Manager, Chris Kawolsky; Stage Managers, Cathy A. Fank, Robert S. Garber, M. Pat Hodge, Melinda Lamoreux, Richard Earl Laster, Mark Tynan; Press, Julie Devane

RESIDENT ACTING COMPANY: Timothy Arrington, James Belcher, Jeff Bennett, Jim Bernhard, Charlene Bigham, Bonnie Black, Lillian Evans, Bettye Fitzpatrick, Michael R. Gill, Robert Graham, Sarah Hill, Annalee Jefferies, Tom Klunis, Charles Kroh, Marietta Marich, Jim McQueen, Sally Parrish, Wyman Pendleton, Cynthia Rider, Charles Sanders, Brandon Smith, Greg Kean Williams

PRODUCTIONS & GUEST ARTISTS

Another Part of the Forest: Rosemary Prinz, Jackie Teamer, James Jeter, Kenneth Foster, Harold Suggs, Cynthia Rider, Dennis Wells. *Counting the Ways:* Patricia Kilgarriff. *The Death of Bessie Smith:* John McCurry, Trish Hawkins, Albert Farrar, John Ottavino. *Trelawny of the 'Wells':* Marjorie Carroll, Stephanie Shine, Gloria Biegler, Michael McCarrell, Mary McCormick. *The Marriage of Bette and Boo:* Marilyn McIntyre, Judith Helton, Adam LeFevre, Bob Marich, Iggie Wolfington, Leigh Selting. *Glengarry Glen Ross:* John Newton, Michael M. Ryan, James Harper. *The Normal Heart:* Donald Berman, John Gould Rubin, Suzy Hunt. *The Immigrant/A Hamilton County Album:* Jonathan Hadary, Robert Cornthwaite, Robin Groves. *The Middle Ages:* Joe Barrett. *The Common Pursuit:* Richard Bekins, Arthur Hanket. *A Lie of the Mind:* The Red Clay Ramblers

Carl Davis Photos

Right: Robert Cornthwaite, Robin Groves, Jonathan Hadary, Sally Parrish in "The Immigrant" Top: James Harper, John Newton, Robert Graham, Michael M. Ryan in "Glengarry Glen Ross"

**Melanie Chartoff, Jeff Keller
in "Sunday in the Park with George"**

AMERICAN CONSERVATORY THEATRE

San Francisco, California
Twenty-first Season

Artistic Director, Edward Hastings; Managing Director, John Sullivan; Resident Director, Joy Carlin; Communications, Dennis Powers; Costumes, Beaver Bauer, Robert Fletcher, Fritha Knudsen, Robert Morgan; Sets, Robert Blackman, Ralph Funicello, Jesse Hollis, Michael Olich, Richard Seger; Lighting, Derek Duarte; Production Coordinator, Cynthia McCain; Musical Director, John Johnson; Props, Oliver C. Olsen; General Manager, Dianne M. Prichard; Company Manager, Mary Garrett; Stage Managers, James Haire, Eugene Barcone, Duncan W. Graham, Alice Elliott Smith, Karen Van Zandt; Press, Ralph Hoskins

COMPANY: Tony Amendola, Joseph Bird, Peter Bradbury, Kate Brickley, Richard Butterfield, Joy Carlin, Nancy Carlin, Peter Donat, Drew Eshelman, Gina Ferrall, Timothy Greer, Lawrence Hecht, Ruth Kobart, Barry Kraft, Kimberley LaMarque, Delores Mitchell, Robin Goodrin Nordli, Liam O'Brien, Frank Ottiwell, William Patterson, Stephen Rockwell, Ken Ruta, Ken Sonkin, Lannyl Stephens, Howard Swain, Bernard Vash, Joe Vincent, Sydney Walker, J. Steven White

GUEST ARTISTS: Jeff Keller, Melanie Chartoff, Ann Weldon, Charles S. Dutton

PRODUCTIONS: *Sunday in the Park with George* by Stephen Sondheim, James Lapine; *The Doctor's Dilemma* by George Bernard Shaw; *The Floating Light Bulb* by Woody Allen; *The Real Thing* by Tom Stoppard; *The Seagull* by Anton Chekhov; *Ma Rainey's Black Bottom* by August Wilson; *Faustus in Hell* by Nagle Jackson

Larry Merkle Photos

AMERICAN MUSICAL THEATRE

New London, Connecticut
Second Season

Producer, Charles S. Peckham; Associate Producer/Technical Director, Daniel C. Mores; Musical Director, Glen Clugston; Lighting, Greg MacPherson; Stage Managers, John Brigleb, Regan Morse, Deborah L. Moignard; Development, Marion H. Bigelow; Company Manager, Arthur A. Pignataro; Wardrobe, Celeste Gisommi, Lynn Poirot, Kathy Williams; Props, Chrissy Mitchell, James Warykas, Hazel Tal, Lynn Hill; Scenic Artists, Suzy Abbott, Daniel Truth, Elaine Mills, Donna Wieters, Kathleen Fillion, Nancy Gibson, Bernice M. Rosenthal; Assistant Conductor, Stephen Hinnenkamp; Make-up/Hair, James Stidfole, Wayne Beebe, John Driscoll, Alan Mitchell, Mae Awad; Production Manager, Victor Panciera; Press, Evelyn R. Warner/The Communications Group
RESIDENT COMPANY: Gary Allen Baillargeon, Michael Boss, Susan Lee Daniels, John Driscoll, Eva Engman, Holly Evers, Rob Francis, Celeste Furman, Rosejean Goddard, Rich Grohocki, Dalton Helms, Kathy Hershey, Walter Hughes, Billy Jay, Mitch Kartalia, Molly M. Loughlin, Patrick Dennis Loughlin, Kathleen Marshall, Franklin D. May, Jr., Michael Novin, James Boyd Parker, Eddie Simon, John Tobin, Patricia Uguccioni, Wendy Waring, Elizabeth Gray Williams, John M. Weltberger, Kathleen Yates, Ryan Zemanek, Douglas Bjorn, Paul Dobie, Donald J. Hall, Betsy Heart, Rita M. Herbert, Steve Hill, Mary Norris, Stephen Reed, Carol Ann Robey, Ashley Aimetti, Paul Andre Levesque, David Loring, Sage Morse, Arthur A. Pignataro, Paul Sardinha, Clement Blais, Kelly Farrell, Jo Ann Kijak, Paul H. Knipler, Charles C. G. Lapointe, Sue Lawrence, Susan J. Matula, Evy O'Rourke, Elizabeth Stratton, Lisa Hockman, Julie Schroll, Pat Shaw, Marilyn Kay Huelsman, May Awad, Wayne Beebe, Jill Davis, Linda Fouche, Diane LeFrancois, Carroll Mailhot, Roger Preston Smith, Susan Jerome

PRODUCTIONS & CASTS

CAMELOT with Book & Lyrics by Alan Jay Lerner; Music, Frederic Lowe; Director, Jack Allison; Choreographer, Thom Warren; Sets, Ernest Allen Smith. CAST: David Dunbar (Arthur), Lisa Vroman (Guenevere), Davis Gaines (Lancelot), Ralston Hill (Pellinore), James Hindman (Merlyn), Charles Michael Wright (Mordred), Joseph Billone (Sir Dinadan)
THE PAJAMA GAME with Music & Lyrics by Richard Adler, Jerry Ross; Book, George Abbott, Richard Bissell; Director, Jerry Heymann; Choreographer, Leo Muller; Sets, Leo Meyer. CAST: Larry Small (Sid), Kathleen Marsh (Babe), Alex Molina (Hines), Dorothy Kiara (Gladys), Eleanor Glockner (Mabel), Terry Runnels (Prez), Leonard Drum (Hassler)
CAROUSEL with Music by Richard Rodgers; Book & Lyrics, Oscar Hammerstein; Director/Choreographer, Jack Eddleman; Co-Choreographer, Stephanie Hall; Sets, Leo Meyer. CAST: Walter Willison (Billy Bigelow), Judith McCauley (Julie Jordan), Marsha Bagwell (Nettie Fowler), Barbara Marineau (Carrie Pipperidge), Kevin Dearinger (Enoch Snow), Rosejean Goddard (Mrs. Mullin); Andrew Hammond (Jigger), Jennifer Henson (Louise), Stephanie Hall (Hannah), Jack Eddleman (Starkeeper)
FIDDLER ON THE ROOF with Book by Joseph Stein; Music, Jerry Bock; Lyrics, Sheldon Harnick; Director, Leslie B. Cutler; Choreographer, Leo Muller; Sets, Leo Meyer. CAST: Lew Resseguie (Tevye), Mary Ellen Ashley (Golde), Jean Baker (Tzeitel), Eva Engman (Hodel), Holly Evers (Chava), Mitch Kartalia (Motel), Merwin Foard (Perchik), Peter Johl (Lazar), Leslie B. Cutler (Rabbi), Leo Muller (Fiddler)
BABES IN ARMS with Music by Richard Rodgers; Lyrics, Lorenz Hart; Book, George Oppenheimer, Based on original book by Rodgers & Hart; Director, Ginger Rogers; Choreographer, Randy Skinner; Sets, Linda E. Hacker; Lighting, Clarke W. Thornton; Dance Assistant, Debra Draper; In association with Valentine Productions/Producers, Robert Kennedy, III, Michael Lipton, Sandy Lucot. CAST: Heidi Albrecht (Jennifer), Carleton Carpenter (Lee), Jack Doule (Barney), Dwight Lee Edwards (John-Henry), Merwin Foard (Steve), Susan Long (Bunny), Kim Morgan (Terry), Jen Nelson (Phyllis), Wendy Oliver (Libby), Denise Roberts (Margaret), Hansford Rowe (Seymour), Christopher Scott (Matt), Randy Skinner (Valentine), Bob Walton (Gus), Karen Ziemba (Susie)

A. Vincent Scarano Photos

Top Right: Walter Willison, Rosejean Goddard in "Carousel" Below: Lisa Vroman as Guinevere in "Camelot"

A performance of "The Merchant of Venice"

AMERICAN PLAYERS THEATRE

Spring Green, Wisconsin
Seventh Season

Artistic Director, Randall Duk Kim; Literary Director, Anne Occhiogrosso; Managing Director, Charles Bright; Lighting, Dan Brovarney; Composer/Assistant Music Director, Douglas Brown; Marketing, Kevin Clark; Costumes, Bud Hill, Pierre DeRagon; Movement, Jerry Gardner; Props, William Gleave; Business Manager, Monica Jaehnig; Development, John Ramer; Production Manager, Dennis Richards; Music Director/Composer, Tim Schirmer; Directors, Charles J. Bright, Sue Klemp, Anne Occhiogrosso, Fred Ollerman, Sandra Reigel-Ernst, Theodore Swetz; Stage Managers, Colleen D. Lewis, Rhoda F. Nathan
COMPANY: Paul Bentzen, David Cecsarini, Sarah Day, Lee Elmer Ernst, Oksana Fedunyszyn, John Fionte, Steven A. Helmeke, Stephen Hemming, Jonathan Herold, David B. Heuvelman II, Joel Hooks, Terry Kerr, Randall Duk Kim, Art Manke, Rod McFall, Alexandra Mitchell, Charles Noel, Anne Occhiogrosso, William Schlaht, Laurie Shaman, Brad Sherwood, Karl Stoll, Theodore Swetz, Brad Waller, Thomas Winslow
PRODUCTIONS: Hamlet, The Merry Wives of Windsor, The Merchant of Venice, The Comedy of Errors, One-act Comedies by Anton Chekhov: The Bear, The Proposal, On the Harmfulness of Tobacco, The Wedding, The Anniversary, Swan Song

Zane Williams Photos

AMERICAN REPERTORY THEATRE

Cambridge, Massachusetts
Eighth Season

Artistic Director, Robert Brustein; Managing Director, Robert J. Orchard; Literary Director, Jonathan Marks; Production Manager, Jonathan Miller; Marketing, Henry Lussier; Technical Directors, Jeff Muskovin; Donald Soule; Stage Managers, Abbie H. Katz, Anne S. King; Resident Directors, Andrei Serban, David Wheeler; Senior Actor, Jeremy Geidt; Press, Jan Geidt, Nancy Sherlock

PRODUCTIONS & CASTS

TONIGHT WE IMPROVISE by Luigi Pirandello; Director, Robert Brustein; Video Sequences, Frederick Wiseman; Set/Costumes, Michael H. Yeargan; Lighting, Stephen Strawbridge. CAST: John Bottoms, Thomas Derrah, Elizabeth Franz, Pamela Gien, Richard Grusin, Harriet Harris, Isabell Monk, Harry S. Murphy, Nestor Serrano, Lynn Torgrove, James Andreassi, Benjamin Evett, Rima Miller, Dean Norris

END OF THE WORLD WITH SYMPOSIUM TO FOLLOW by Arthur Kopit; Director, Richard Foreman; Set, Michael H. Yeargan; Costumes, Lindsay W. Davis; Lighting, Stephen Strawbridge. CAST: John Bottoms, Jeremy Geidt, Pamela Gien, Richard Grusin, Ken Howard, Ted Kazanoff, Isabell Monk, Harry S. Murphy, Matthew Dundas, Alison Taylor, Pamela Woodruff

SWEET TABLE AT THE RICHELIEU by Ronald Ribman; *World Premiere;* Director, Andrei Serban; Set/Costumes, John Conklin; Lighting, Howell Binkley. CAST: Lucinda Childs, Thomas Derrah, Elizabeth Franz, Jeremy Geidt, Pamela Gien, Harriet Harris, Ken Howard, Isabell Monk, Harry S. Murphy, Nestor Serrano, Sandra Shipley, Lynn Torgrove, James Andreassi

THE DAY ROOM by Don DeLillo; Original Director, Michael Bloom; Restaged by David Wheeler; Set, Loy Arcenas; Costumes, Karen Eister; Lighting, Randle Riddell. CAST: John Bottoms, Thomas Derrah, Jeremy Geidt, Pamela Gien, Richard Grusin, Harriet Harris, Isabell Monk, Harry S. Murphy, Nestor Serrano

THE GOOD WOMAN OF SETZUAN by Bertolt Brecht; Translation, Eric Bentley; Director, Andrei Serban; Music, Elizabeth Swados; Sets, Jeff Muskovin; Costumes, Catherine Zuber; Lighting, Howell Binkley; Movement, Thom Molinaro; Associate Director, Charles Otte. CAST: Joseph Costa, Thomas Derrah, Alvin Epstein, Pamela Gien, Thom Molinaro, Isabell Monk, Harry S. Murphy, Sandra Shipley, Priscilla Smith, James Andreassi, Nina Bernstein

ARCHANGELS DON'T PLAY PINBALL by Dario Fo; *American Premiere;* Directors, Dario Fo, Franca Rame; Translation, Ron Jenkins; Set/Costumes, Dario Fo; Lighting, Frank Butler; Assistant Director, Arturo Corso. CAST: John Bottoms, Peter Gerety, Richard Grusin, Harriet Harris, Geoff Hoyle, Benjamin Evett, Rima Miller, Dean Norris, Alison Taylor

THE CANNIBAL MASQUE/A SERPENT'S EGG by Ronald Ribman; *World Premiere;* Director, David Wheeler; Set, Loy Arcenas; Costumes, Christine Joly de Lotbiniere; Lighting, Frank Butler; Original Music, Karl Lundeburg; Stage Manager, Laurence J. Geddes. CAST: *The Cannibal Masque:* John Bottoms, Richard Grusin, Jane Loranger, Ed Schloth. *A Serpent's Egg:* Jeremy Geidt, Harry S. Murphy

MRS. SORKEN PRESENTS by Christopher Durang; Three one-acts; *World Premiere;* Directors, R. J. Cutler, Wesley Savick; Set, Loy Arcenas; Costumes, Karen Eister; Lighting, Frank Butler; Music, Richard Peaslee; Music Director, Paul Brusiloff. CAST: Thomas Derrah, Elizabeth Franz, Pamela Gien, Harriet Harris, Isabell Monk, Sandra Shipley, James Andreassi, Nina Bernstein, Dean Norris, Alison Taylor

Richard Feldman Photos

**Ken Howard, Jeremy Geidt
in "End of the World. . . ."**

ARENA STAGE

Washington, D.C.
Thirty-sixth Season

Producing Director, Zelda Fichandler; Managing Director, William Stewart; Associate Producing Director, Douglas C. Wager; Production Coordinator, Guy Bergquist; Producing Associate, James C. Nicola; Literary Manager/Dramaturg, Lloyd Rose; Technical Director, David M. Glenn; Marketing, Patricia Nicholson; Development, Elspeth Udvarhelyi; Press, Beth Hauptle; Stage Directors, James C. Nicola, Douglas C. Wager, Garland Wright, Yuri Lyubimov, Les Waters, Mel Shapiro, Zelda Fichandler; Sets, Thomas Lynch, George Tsypin, John Arnone, David Borosky, Annie Smart, Karl Eigsti, Douglas Stein; Costumes, Gregg Barnes, Marjorie Slaiman, Annie Smart; Lighting, Allen Lee Hughes, Frances Aronson, Nancy Schertler; Stage Managers, Robin Rumpf, Pat Cochran, Maxine Krasowski Bertone, Martha Knight, Wendy Streeter

RESIDENT COMPANY: Stanley Anderson, Richard Bauer, Casey Biggs, Ralph Cosham, Terrence Currier, Randy Danson, Heather Ehlers, Mark Hammer, Tom Hewitt, Tana Hicken, John Leonard, Thomas Anthony Quinn, Cary Anne Spear, Kim Staunton, Henry Strozier, Robert Westenberg, Halo Wines, Maggie Winn-Jones

GUEST ARTISTS: Jason Adams, Kerry Armstrong, Erika Bogren, Beverly Brigham Bowman, Helen Carey, Veronica Castang, Marissa Copeland, Michael Chaban, Brigid Cleary, Leticia Copeland, Marissa Copeland, Steven Dawn, Richard Dix, Kevin Donovan, Morgan Duncan, Elizabeth Duvall, John Finn, Frances Foster, Adam Freedman, Kate Fuglei, John Gegenhuber, Joe Glenn, June Hansen, Bus Havenstein, Terry Hinz, Mart Hulswit, W. Blair Larsen, Katherine Leask, Leah Lipsky, Marty Lodge, April Lynn Lutz, Walt MacPherson, Christopher McHale, Randle Mell, Jason Minor, Christina Moore, Scott Morgan, Greg Pake, Ralph Pripstein, David Proval, Lillian Rozin, Joanne Schmoll, Vivienne Shub, Donna Snow, Kevin Tighe, Paul Walker, Kathleen Weber, Ellis E. Williams

PRODUCTIONS: *The Marriage of Bette and Boo* by Christopher Durang, *Measure for Measure* by William Shakespeare, *The Piggy Bank* by Eugene Labiche and A. Delacour, *Glengarry Glen Ross* by David Mamet, *Heartbreak House* by George Bernard Shaw, *The Crucible* by Arthur Miller, and U.S. PREMIERES of *Crime and Punishment* by Fyodor Dostoevsky adapted by Yuri Lyubimov and Yuri Karyakin, *Ourselves Alone* by Anne Devlin

Joan Marcus Photos

AMERICAN STAGE COMPANY

Teaneck, New Jersey
Second Season

Artistic Director, Paul Sorvino; Executive Producer, Theodore Rawlins; Executive Director, James R. Singer; Associate Producer, Jamie Milestone; Business Manager, Robert A. Lusko; Technical Director, Garrit Lydecker; Sets, Lewis Folden, James Morgan, Alexander Okun, Daniel Ettinger; Costumes, Gail Cooper-Hecht, Barbara Forbes, Joan V. Evans; Lighting, Michael Prosceo, Peter J. Monahan, Stuart Duke, Donald Holder; Stage Managers, John W. Calder III, Robert Vandergriff, Nereida Ortiz; Press, Libby McNeill Seymour

PRODUCTIONS & CASTS

THE RAINMAKER by N. Richard Nash; Director, Paul Sorvino. CAST: G. Denny French (H. C. Curry), Dan Diggles (Noah Curry), Daniel Quinn (Jim Curry), Karen Sederholm (Lizzie Curry), Joseph McKenna (File), Eddie R. White (Sheriff), Gary Sandy (Bill Starbuck)

VILLA SERENA by Rick Johnston; *World Premiere;* Director, Paul Shyre. CAST: Lisa Emery (Nancy), Anthony Call (McShane), Marge Redmond (Sister), Lyn Greene (Jane), Jack Betts (Donald), Frank B. McGowen (Mr. Jenner), Mary Orr (Virginia)

THE DIARY OF ANNE FRANK dramatized by Frances Goodrich, Albert Hackett; Director, Rick Lombardo. CAST: Louis Albini, Eve Annenberg, Clement Fowler, Tony M. Gillan, Michael Gilpin, Zohra Lampert, Nicholas Levitin, Linda Selman, Amanda Sorvino, Isabelle Werenfels

SOME ENCHANTED EVENING: The Songs of Rodgers and Hammerstein; Conceived and Directed by Jeffrey B. Moss. CAST: Ernestine Jackson, Ken Jennings, Marcia King, Liz Larsen, Kurt Peterson

OTHER PEOPLE'S MONEY by Jerry Sterner; *World Premiere;* Director, John Ferraro, CAST: Keith Langsdale (William Coles), Henderson Forsythe (Andrew Jorgenson), Stanja Lowe (Bea Sullivan), David Schramm (Lawrence Garfinkle), Katherine Cortez (Kate Sullivan), Ben Sweetwood (Arthur)

Emmett Francois Photos

ARIZONA THEATRE COMPANY

Tucson/Phoenix, Arizona

Artistic Director, Gary Gisselman; Resident Director, Walter Schoen; Associate Artistic Director, Ken Ruta; Costumes, Bobbi Culbert; Production Manager, Don Hooper; Managing Director, Richard Bryant; General Manager, Nancy Thomas; Development, Barbara R. Levy; Company Manager, Becky Schwartz; Sound, Jeff Ladman; Wardrobe, Maggi Shaw; Props, Vick L. Dittemore; Press, Gary Bacal.

PRODUCTIONS & CASTS

THE HOUSE OF BLUE LEAVES with Jerry Mayer (Artie), Ernie Sandidge (Ronnie), Julee Cruise (Bunny), Wendy Lehr (Bananas), Janelle Sperow (Corinna), Francesca Jarvis (Head Nun), Sherilyn Forrester (2nd Nun), Lee Wilson (Little Nun), Michael Grady (Policeman), Tony DeBruno (White Man), Don West (Billy Einhorn)

A DELICATE BALANCE with Patricia Fraser (Agnes), Allen Hamilton (Tobias), Lois Markle (Claire), Helen Backlin (Edna), Tom McGreevey (Harry), Susan Powell (Julia)

THE MARRIAGE OF BETTE AND BOO with Jane Murray (Bette), Kate Williamson (Margaret), Don West (Paul), Rita Rehn (Joan), Kerry Noonan (Emily), Leon Martell (Boo), Tony DeBruno (Karl), Wendy Lehr (Soot), Benjamin Stewart (Father Donnally/Doctor), Stephen Hamilton (Matt)

THE MATCHMAKER with Benjamin Stewart (Horace Vandergelder), Leon Martell (Ambrose Kemper), Don West (Joe), Kate Williamson (Gertrude), Tony DeBruno (Cornelius Hackl), Kerry Noonan (Ermengarde), Paul Ballantyne (Malachi), Wendy Lehr (Dolly Levi), Ernie Sandidge (Barnaby), Rita Rehn (Minnie Fay), Jane Murray (Irene Molloy), Roberto Guajardo (Rudolph), Don West (Cabman), Michael Grady (August), Charlotte Adams (Cook), Kate Williamson (Miss Flora Van Huysen)

GLENGARRY GLEN ROSS with Paul C. Thomas (Shelly Levene), Don West (John Williamson), W. Francis Walters (Dave Moss), Robert Ernst (George Aaronow), Stephen G. Yoakam (Richard Roma), Tony DeBruno (James Link), Bill Pearlman (Baylen)

YOU CAN'T TAKE IT WITH YOU with Wendy Lehr (Penelope), Kerry Noonan (Essie), Veronica Henson-Phillips (Rheba), Bain Boehlke (Paul Sycamore), Don Doyle (DePinna), Gary Briggle (Ed), Bruce Nelson (Donald), Paul Ballantyne (Martin Vanderhof), Jane Murray (Alice), Roberto Guajardo (Henderson), Jay Louden (Tony), Benjamin Stewart (Boris), Suzi List (Gay Wellington), Ray Roberts (Kirby), Julianna McCarthy (Mrs. Kirby), Stella Clancy (Olga), Sidney Dawson, David Yarborough, Roberto Guajardo (G-Men)

Tim Fuller Photos

Mark Johnson, David Landon in "Glengarry Glen Ross" (Arkansas Rep) Top: Jane Murray, Paul Ballantyne in "You Can't Take It with You" (Arizona Theatre Co.)

ARKANSAS REPERTORY THEATRE

Little Rock, Arkansas
Tenth Season

Founding Artistic Director, Cliff Fannin Baker; Managing Director, Andrew C. Gaupp; Associate Director, Cathey Crowell Sawyer; Business Manager, Lynn Frazier; Production Manager, Terry Sneed; Technical Director/Sets, Mike Nichols; Lighting, Kathy Gray; Costumes, Mark Hughes; Stage Manager, Lisa K. Martley; Marketing/Press, Aurora Huston

PRODUCTIONS & CASTS

GLENGARRY GLEN ROSS by David Mamet; Director, Cliff Fannin Baker; with David Landon (Shelly Levene), Mark Johnson (John Williamson), David Alexander (Dave Moss), Scott Edmonds (George Aaronow), Bob Ginnaven (Richard Roma), Joe McCullough (James Lingk), J. C. Mullins (Baylen)

THE LAST MEETING OF THE KNIGHTS OF THE WHITE MAGNOLIA by Preston Jones; Director, Cathey Crowell Sawyer; with Nate Bynum (Ramsey-Eyes), Leonard Schlientz (Rufe Phelps), Terry Sneed (Olin Potts), Jack Wann (Red Grover), David Landon (L. D. Alexander), Mark Johnson (Skip Hampton), Scott Edmonds (Col. Kinkaid), Joe McCullough (Lonnie Roy McNeil), Brent Blair (Milo Crawford)

BRIGHTON BEACH MEMOIRS by Neil Simon; Director, Cliff Fannin Baker; with Steve Wilkerson (Eugene), Cathey Crowell Sawyer (Blanche Morton), Sara Van Horn (Kate Jerome), Janie Hesterly (Laurie Morton), Julianne Griffin (Nora Morton), Felix Eckhard (Stanley Jerome), David Alexander (Jack Jerome)

THE REAL THING by Tom Stoppard; Director, Terry Sneed; with Mark Johnson (Max), Ouida White (Charlotte), Ray Collins (Henry), Christina Wellford (Annie), Peter White (Billy), Julianne Griffin (Debbie), Brent Blair (Brodie)

PUMP BOYS AND DINNETTES by John Foley, Mark Hardwick, Debra Monk, Cass Morgan, John Schimmel, Jim Wann; Director, Cliff Fannin Baker; Musical Director, Terry Sneed; with Mark Johnson (Jim), Bill Holloway (Jackson), Bruce Drive (Eddie), Terry Sneed (L.M.), Julianne Griffin (Prudie), Vivian Morrison (Rhetta)

Barry Arthur Photos

Liz Larsen, Ernestine Jackson, Kurt Peterson, Ken Jennings, Marcia King in "Some Enchanted Evening" (American Stage Co.) Above: Robert Westenberg, Randy Danson in "The Crucible" (Arena Stage)

155

ASOLO STATE THEATER

Sarasota, Florida
Twenty-eighth Season

Chief Executive Officer, Gil Lazier; Acting Executive Director, Donald P. Creason; Resident Director, Robert G. Miller; Artistic Director, John Ulmer; Resident Director/Literary Manager, John Gulley; Sets, Bennet Averyt, John Ezell, Jeffrey Dean, Keven Lock, Joseph Tilford; Costumes, Catherine King; Lighting, Martin Petlock; Production Coordinator, Victor Meyrich; Technical Director, David Ferguson; Stage Managers, Marian Wallace, Stephanie Moss, Juanita Munford, John Toia; Press, Edith N. Anson.
COMPANY: Linda Cook, Sheridan Crist, Ann Ducati, Suzanne Gordner, Douglas Jones, Bill Levis, Carolyn Michel, Karl Redcoff, Eric Tavares, Isa Thomas, Peter Gregory Thomson, Bradford Wallace, Karen Bair, Donna A. DeLonay, Nancy Hartman, Michael Lariscy, Mary Launder, David B. Levine, Lynne Perkins, Parry B. Stewart, Laurel Casey, Art Dohany, Jeff Herbst, Elizabeth Cook Herron, Michael Laird, Beth Lane, Kyndal May, Robb Pruitt, Christine Sloane, Richard Smolenski, Alex C. Thayer, Jill Ann Womack
Bill Cudlipp, Kay Daphne, Karl Redcoff, Eric Tavares, Isa Thomas, Bradford Wallace, Mel Cobb, Warren Frost, Michael Guido, Bob Horen, Douglas Jones, Gretchen Lord, Jeffrey Marcus, Sheridan Crist, Donald May, Annie Murray, Christine Sloane, Alex C. Thayer, Suzanne Grodner, Nancy Johnston, Sharon E. Scott, Cynthia Sophiea, Elizabeth Cook Herron, Donald Christopher, Judith Granite, Michael Alan Gregory, Douglas Jones, Darrie Lawrence, Susan Jones Mannino, Joe Palmieri, Jeff Herbst, Michael Laird, Doug Brown, Robert G. Bubon, Kit Crawford, Rick DeFuria, Christopher Dolman, Robert Mason Ham, Eva Patton, Natalie Picow, Alisa L. Pritchett, Russell Reidinger, Mary Lee Richey, Amy Schoemaker, Jeanne Waters, Ricky Wright
GUEST ARTISTS: Roger Rees, Judith Haskell, David Brunetti
PRODUCTIONS: Tartuffe, How the Other Half Loves, The Foreigner, A Christmas Carol, The Rainmaker, Who's Afraid of Virginia Woolf?, Orphans, Deathtrap, Betrayal, Nunsense, Our Town, The Perfect Party

Gary W. Sweetman Photos

Right: Annie Murray, Eric Tavares in "Who's Afraid of Virginia Woolf" Top: Sharon Scott, Cynthia Sophiea, Suzanne Grodner, Nancy Johnston, Elizabeth Herron in "Nunsense"

Carol Schultz, Peg Small in " 'night, Mother" Above: Bernard Engel, Frances Peter, Sally Parrish in "Morning's at Seven"

BARTER THEATRE

Abingdon, Virginia
Fifty-fourth Season

Artistic Director/Producer, Rex Partington; Business Manager, Pearl Hayter; Directors, Ken Costigan, Byron Grant, Geoffrey Hitch, William Van Keyser, Rex Partington, Steve Umberger; Sets, Gary Aday, Dan Ettinger, Jim Stauder; Costumes, Karen Brewster, Barbara Forbes, Martha Hally, Sigrid Insull, Dorothy Marshall, Lisa Michaels; Stage Managers, Champe Leary, Tony Partington, James Wood
PRODUCTIONS & CASTS
I OUGHT TO BE IN PICTURES by Neil Simon; with Lorraine Morgan, June Daniel White, Larry Sharp
BILLY BISHOP GOES TO WAR by John Gray, Eric Peterson; with Ross Bickell, Byron Grant
THE FOREIGNER by Larry Shue; with Jonathan Bustle, Aaron Lustig, Angus MacLachlan, Barbara McCulloh, Sally Parrish, Graham Smith, John Woodson
MORNING'S AT SEVEN by Paul Osborn; with Bernerd Engel, Katie Grant, Cleo Holladay, George Hosmer, Frank Lowe, Sarah Melici, Sally Parrish, Frances Peter, Stratton Walling
TEN LITTLE INDIANS by Agatha Christie; with Ray Collins, Bernerd Engel, John Fitzgibbon, Stephen Gabis, Katie Grant, George Hosmer, Leonard Kelly-Young, Frank Lowe, Richard Major, Sarah Melici, Sally Parrish
BEDROOM FARCE by Alan Ayckbourn; with John Fitzgibbon, Stephen Gabis, Cleo Holladay, Nicole Orth-Pallavicini, Rex Partington, Barbara McCulloh, Larry Sharp
'NIGHT, MOTHER by Marsha Norman; with Carol Schultz, Peg Small
I DO! I DO! by Tom Jones, Harvey Schmidt; with Schery Collins, Joleen Foder, Joseph Proctor
VANITIES by Jack Heifner; with Barbara McCulloh, Kathy Morath, Lesley Vogel

BEEF AND BOARDS DINNER THEATRE

Indianapolis, Indiana
Fourteenth Season

Artistic Director, Douglas E. Stark; Managing Director, Robert D. Zehr; Musical Directors, Richard Laughlin, Lori Mechem; Stage Manager/Technical Director, Edward Stockman; Sets/Lighting, Michael Layton; Costumes, Livingston; Choreographers, Kathleen Marshall, Millie Garvey; Scenic Artist, Amy Stark; Set Construction, Sean Brown; Press, Mayla Alexander; Stage Directors, Douglas E. Stark, Robert D. Zehr.

PRODUCTIONS & CASTS

THEY'RE PLAYING OUR SONG with Book by Neil Simon; Music, Marvin Hamlisch; Lyrics, Carole Bayer Sager; CAST: Bruce Adler (Vernon Gersch), Isabell Farrell (Sonia Walsk), Ruth Anne Farrelly, Mark Knowles, Laura A. Lamun, Casey Nicolaw (Alter Egos)

LITTLE SHOP OF HORRORS with Book and Lyrics by Howard Ashman; Music, Alan Menken; CAST: Bruce Adler (Seymour), Maggy Gorrill (Audrey), Jack Sevier (Mushnik), Brian Horton (Orin/Bernstein/Snip/Luce/Everyone Else), Tracie D. Siegel (Chiffon), Kimberly Harris (Crystal), Faye Richie (Ronnette), Steve Rivers (Audrey II Manipulation), Myron E. El (Audrey II Voice)

A CHORUS LINE with Book by James Kirkwood & Nicholas Dante; Music, Marvin Hamlisch; Lyrics, Edward Kleban; CAST: Doug Holmes (Zack), Laurie Gamache (Cassie), Stephen Bourneuf (Al), William Alan Coats (Mike), Phillip H. Colglazier (Paul), Tina Dockstader (Judy), Julie Graves (Kristine), Ned Hannah (Mark), Ron J. Hutchins (Richie), Kimberly Nazarian (Diana), Laurie Sheppard (BeBe), Dean Stroop (Larry), Teresa Wolf (Sheila), Carol Lynn Worcell (Val/Cassie), Michael Worcell (Bobby)

THE KING AND I with Music by Richard Rodgers; Book and Lyrics, Oscar Hammerstein 2nd; CAST: William Kiehl (The King), Cynthia Meryl (Anna Leonowens), Doug Holmes (Interpreter/Sir Edward Ramsay), Donald Sherrill (Kralahome), Marcia O'Brien (Lady Thiang), Ron Gibbs (Lun Tha), Carole March (Tuptim), Michael Johnson (Louis Leonowens), Michael Shelton (Prince Chululongkorn), Julie Graves, Tina Dockstader, Ryan Baber, Jay Clator, Michelle Rollings, Melissa Schott, Michelle Miller, Michelle Schott, Becka Vargas

SUGAR BABIES with Sketches by Ralph G. Allen; Music, Jimmy McHugh; Lyrics, Dorothy Fields, Al Dubin; Additional Music & Lyrics, Arthur Malvin, Jay Livingston, Ray Evans; CAST: Whit Reichert, Jack Milo, Wendy Clay, Millie Garvey, Brian Horton, Kimberly Dean, Brian Hulse, Julie Graves, Rhonda Kasper, Wendy Smith, Bonnie Swanson

THE ODD COUPLE by Neil Simon; CAST: Douglas Edward Stark (Oscar Madison), Doug Holmes (Felix Unger), Brian Horton (Vinnie), Dick Laughlin/David Appleford (Roy), Jack Milo (Speed), Dan Scharbrough (Murray), Julie Graves (Cecily), Kelly Meadows (Gwendolyn)

D. Todd Moore Photos

Cynthia Meryl, William Kiehl in "The King and I"
Top: Laurie Gamache, Doug Holmes
in "A Chorus Line"

**Dea Lawrence, Maggie Marshall in "The Women" Above:
Anthony Newfield, Craig Wroe in "The Normal Heart"**

CALDWELL THEATRE COMPANY

Boca Raton, Florida

Artistic/Managing Director, Michael Hall; Resident Set Designer, Frank Bennett; Costumes, Bridget Bartlett; Lighting, Mary Jo Dondlinger; Hairstylist, Don Barnes; Company Manager, Patricia Burdett; Marketing, Kathy Walton; Technical Director, Chip Latimer; Stage Managers, Elisabeth Farwell, Bob Carter; Press, Joe Gillie

PRODUCTIONS & CASTS

THE BOYS IN THE BAND by Mart Crowley and
THE NORMAL HEART by Larry Kramer in rotating repertory; with Arnold Bankston, Barbara Bradshaw, Richard Brandon, Louis Cutolo, Thomas Disney, Rick Ferguson, Byron Gentle, Joe Gillie, Mart McChesney, Anthony Newfield, Robert Slacum, Craig Wroe

BENEFACTORS by Michael Frayn; with Maggie Marshall, Anthony Newfield, Dea Lawrence, Craig Wroe

BEYOND THERAPY by Christopher Durang; with Dea Lawrence, Craig Wroe, Jeffrey Alan Simpson, Becky London, Jeffrey Blair Cornell, Stephen Tyler

THE CHERRY ORCHARD by Anton Chekhov; with Glynis Bell, K. Lype O'Dell, Nick Stannard, William Preston, Annie Stafford, Diana Henderson, Jeffrey Blair Cornell, Ronald Wendschuh, Dea Lawrence, Todd Axton Ellis, Ken Melvin, Craig Wroe, Maggie Marshall

THE WOMEN by Clare Boothe Luce; with Rae Randall, Heidi White, Glynis Bell, Annie Stafford, Maggie Marshall, Jackalyn Carpenter, Mona Jones, Dea Lawrence, Fran Barnes, Alison Takcos, Christine Florio, Darci Oseicki, Geraldine O'Mahoney, Virginia Velenchik, Stephanie Ward, Leigh Bennett, Donna Kimball

RUMBLE SEAT REVUE: a musical cabaret with Kay Brady, Joe Gillie, Susan Hatfield, Jean Bolduc, Linda Kay, Rupert Ziawinski

Joyce Brock Photos

157

CENTER THEATRE GROUP

AHMANSON THEATRE

Los Angeles, California
Twentieth Season

Artistic Director, Rober Fryer; General Manager, Drew Murphy; Manager, Tom Jordan; Executive Associate, Joyce Zaccaro; Administrative Assistant, John Traub; Management Assistant, David Cipriano; Production Manager, Ralph Beaumont; Technical Director, Robert Routolo; Props, Steve Rapollo; Sound, Thomas Angelotti; Wardrobe, Eddie Dodds; Press, James Hansen, Rick Miramontez, Ken Werther, Michael Cooper

PRODUCTIONS & CASTS
THE LIFE AND ADVENTURES OF NICHOLAS NICKLEBY by Charles Dickens; Adapted by David Edgar. See *Broadway Calendar*.
WILD HONEY by Michael Frayn; Adapted from Anton Chekhov. See *Broadway Calendar*.
SWEET BIRD OF YOUTH by Tennessee Williams; Director, Michael Blakemore; Set, Michael Annals; Costumes, Carrie Robbins; Lighting, Martin Aronstein; Set Consultant, Michael Vale; Music, Barrington Pheloung; Sound, Jan Nebozenko; Casting, Hughes Moss; Stage Managers, George Rondo, Robert Schear, Charles Douglas. CAST: Lauren Bacall (Princess Kosmonopolis), Henderson Forsythe (Boss Finley), Mark Soper (Chance Wayne), Carol Goodheart (Miss Lucy), Donna Bullock (Heavenly), Howard Sherman (Tom Junior), Georgia Southcotte (Aunt Nonnie), James Cahill (Heckler), Joseph McCarren (George Scudder), Saylor Cresswell (Hatcher), Peter Strong (Stuff), Lee Chew (Scotty), Robertson Carricart (Bud), Sharon Ullrick (Violet), Alexandra Nelson (Edna), Hugh L. Hurd (Charles), Mansoor Nanjee-Ullah (Fly), Charles Douglass (Page), Ed Trotta (State Trooper), Hugh A. Rose (Man 1), David Lee Taylor (Man 2), Alex Paul (Doctor), Laurane Sheehan (Drum Majorette), Jimmy Justice (Jackie).
LIGHT UP THE SKY by Moss Hart; Director, Ellis Rabb; Set, Douglas W. Schmidt; Costumes, Ann Roth; Lighting, James Tilton; Casting, Slater/Willett; Stage Managers, Barbara-Mae Phillips, Martin Herzer, Catherine Cooper. CAST: Peter Falk (Sidney Black), Robert Morse (Sidney Black), Barry Nelson (Owen Turner), Fritz Weaver (Carleton Fitzgerald), Carrie Nye (Irene Livingston), Deborah Rush (Frances Black), Steven Culp (Peter Sloan), Patricia Kilgarriff (Miss Lowell), Burt Edwards (Tyler Rayburn), Bill McCutcheon (William H. Gallagher), Richard Fancy (Shriner), David Bailey (Shriner), Tim Loughrin (Sven/Shriner)
SOCIAL SECURITY by Andrew Bergman. See *National Touring Companies.*

**Top Right: Barry Nelson, Steven Culp, Patricia
Kilgarriff in "Light Up the Sky" Below: Deborah
Rush, Nancy Marchand in "Light Up the Sky"**
(Jim McHugh)

CENTER THEATRE GROUP

MARK TAPER FORUM

Los Angeles, California
Twentieth Season

Artistic Director/Producer, Gordon Davidson; Executive Managing Director, William P. Wingate; General Manager, Stephen J. Albert; Associate Producer, Madeline Puzo; Resident Director, Robert Egan; Dramaturg, Jack Viertel; Literary Manager, Jessica Teich; Casting, Amy Lieberman; Technical Director, Robert Routolo; Production Administrator, Don Winton; Production Supervisor, Frank Bayer; Artist-in-residence, Victoria Ann-Lewis; Press, Nancy Hereford, Ken Werther, Phyllis Moberly, Carol Ball Oken, Elizabeth Sanchez-Franklin, Jeffrey Partridge

PRODUCTIONS & CASTS
ASINAMALI! by Mbongeni Ngema; Director, Mr. Ngema; Lighting, Mannie Manim. CAST: Solomzi Bisholo, Thami Cele, Bongani Hlophe, Bheki Mqadi, Bhoyi Ngema
THE IMMIGRANT—A HAMILTON COUNTY ALBUM by Mark Harelik; *West Coast Premiere;* Conceived by Mark Harelik, Randal Myler; Director, Randal Myler; Set, Kevin Rupnik; Costumes, Andrew V. Yelusich; Lighting, Martin Aronstein; Original Sound/Recording, Dru P. Allard; Projections, Jeffrey Karoff; Dramaturg, Jack Viertel; Stage Manager, James T. McDermott. CAST: Ann Guilbert, Terri Hanauer, Mark Harelik, Guy Raymond
GHETTO by Joshua Sobol; *English Language Premiere;* Director, Gordon Davidson; Adaptor, Jack Viertel; Literal Translation, Kathleen Komar; Orchestrations/Arrangements/Original Music, Gary William Friedman; English Lyrics, Sheldon Harnick, Jim Friedman; Choreography, Larry Hyman; Music Adviser, Giora Feidman; Set, Douglas Stein; Costumes, Julie Weiss; Lighting, Paulie Jenkins; Stage Manager, Al Franklin. CAST: Daniel Gerard Albert, Lee Arenberg, Stuart Brotman, Jimmy Bruno, Ron Campbell, Barry Dennen, Peter Elbling, Louis Fanucchi, Giora Feidman, Alan Feinstein, Robert Fredrickson, Naomi Goldberg, Harvey Gold, Zinovy Goro, Harry Groener, Paul Haber, Lisa Harrison, David Kagen, Jill C. Klein, Ezra Kliger, Seth Kurland, Jeremy Lawrence, Dinah Lenney, Ron Marasco, Andrea Marcovicci, Joel Polis, Ron Rifkin, Scott Segall, Timothy Smith, David Spielberg, Saul Phillip Stein, Gary Dean Sweeney, David Wohl, D. Paul Yeuell
BURN THIS! by Lanford Wilson; *World Premiere;* Director, Marshall W. Mason; Set, John Lee Beatty; Costumes, Laura Crow; Lighting, Dennis Parichy; Fight Direction, Randy Kovitz; Dramaturg, Jack Viertel; Stage Manager, Mary Michele Miner. CAST: Joan Allen, Jonathan Hogan, Lou Liberatore, John Malkovich
ROZA *(West Coast Premiere)* Book/Lyrics, Julian More; Music, Gilbert Becaud; Based on "La Vie Devant Soi" by Romain Gary; Director, Harold Prince; Choreography, Patricia Birch; Musical Direction/Vocal and Dance Arrangements, Louis St. Louis; Orchestrations, Michael Gibson; Set, Alexander Okun; Costumes, Florence Klotz; Lighting, Ken Billington; Stage Manager, Jonathan Barlow Lee. CAST: Neal Ben-Ari, Yamil Borges, Georgia Brown, Monique Cintron, David Chan, Al DeCristo, Thuli Dumakude, Bob Gunton, Ira Hawkins, Edward Jacobowitz, Thom Keane, Marcia Lewis, Michele Mais, Jerry Matz, Mandla Msomi, Brian Noodt, Alex Paez, Stephen Rosenberg

**Carrie Nye, Steven Culp, Peter Falk
in "Light Up the Sky"**

LOOT by Joe Orton in repertory with
ENTERTAINING MR. SLOANE by Joe Orton; Director, John Tillinger; Sets, John Lee Beatty; Costumes, Bill Walker; Lighting, Martin Aronstein; Stage Manager, James T. McDermott. CAST: Julian Barnes, Barbara Bryne, Maxwell Caulfield, Gwyllym Evans, Meagan Fay, Peter Frechette, Joseph Maher, Richard Venture, Zoaunne LeRoy

TAPER, TOO
THE DREAM COAST by John Steppling; *World Premiere;* Directors, John Steppling, Robert Egan; Sets, John Iacovelli; Costumes/Hair, Nicole Morin; Lights, Paulie Jenkins; Original Music/Sound, Daniel Birnbaum; Dramaturg, Jack Viertel; Stage Manager, James T. McDermott. CAST: Priscilla Cohen, Michael Collins, Bob Glaudini, Robert Hummer, Lee Kissman, Alan Mandell, John Pappas, Tina Preston, Elizabeth Ruscio
THE GAME OF LOVE AND CHANCE by Marivaux; English Version, Adrienne Schizzano Mandel, Oscar Mandel; Director, Brian Kulick; Set/Costumes, Mark Wendland; Lights, Liz Stillwell; Dramaturg, Jack Viertel; Stage Manager, Chip Washabaugh. CAST: Shuko Akune, Dana Acelrod, Ron Campbell, Gerald Papasian, Dana Stevens, Harold J. Surratt, Blair Underwood
LARGO DESOLATO by Vaclav Havel; English Version, Tom Stoppard; Director, Richard Jordan; Set, Jon Iacovelli; Costumes, Shigeru Yaji; Lights, Brian Gale; Sound, John Gottlieb; Stage Manager, Mary K. Klinger. CAST: John Apicella, Robin Gammell, Virginia Madsen, Dakin Matthews, Douglas Roberts, Margot Rose, John Santacrose, Ted Sorel, Aarin Teich, Laurie Walters
AUNT DAN AND LEMON by Wallace Shawn; Director, Robert Egan; Set/Costumes, Mark Wendland; Lights, Paulie Jenkins; Original Music/Sound, N. D. Birnbaum; Stage Manager, Tracy B. Cohen. CAST: Jeff Allin, Kathy Bates, Cynthia Carle, John de Lancie, George de la Pena, Judy Geeson, Elizabeth McGovern
IMPROVISATIONAL THEATRE PROJECT: *One Thousand Cranes* by Colin Thomas; Director, Peter C. Brosius; Choreography/Movement, Gary Mascaro; Sound/Original Music/Lyrics, Michael Silversher; Sets, Richard Hoover; Costumes, Nicole Morin; Administrator, Barbara Leonard; Production Manager, Sarah McArthur; Stage Manager, Chip Washabaugh. CAST: John Allee, Rosie Lee Hooks, Karen Maruyama, Miho
SUNDAYS AT THE ITCHEY FOOT: *Rogues' Gallery* conceived and directed by Jack Viertel; Musical Director/Vocal Arrangements, David Anglin; with Lois Foraker, Gregory Itzin, Marnie Mosiman, David Anglin (piano). *A Christmas Memory* by Truman Capote; Adaptor, Madeline Puzo; Director, Michael Peretzian; with Mary Carver, Michael Tulin, David Johnson. *With Alice in Wonderland* based on "Alice's Adventures in Wonderland" by Lewis Carroll; Adapted by James R. Winker, Diana Maddox; Director, Raye Birk; performed by James R. Winker. *The Good War* by Studs Terkel; Adapted by Robert Egan, Brian Kulick; Conceived/Directed by Gordon Hunt; Musical Director, Billy Barnes; with Helen Hunt, Michael Lembeck, Haunani Minn, Brian Mitchell, B. J. Ward

Right: Gretchen Corbett, John Glover
in "The Traveler" Top: Brian
Noodt, Georgia Brown in "Roza"

Joan Allen, Lou Liberatore
in "Burn This"

Harry Groener, Andrea Marcovicci, Alan Feinstein
in "Ghetto"

159

CAPITAL REPERTORY COMPANY

Albany, New York

Producing Directors, Bruce Bouchard, Peter H. Clough; Business Manager, Barbara H. Smith; Marketing Director, Hilde Schuster; Development Director, Christopher Lino; Literary Manager, Robert Meikeins; Stage Manager, Patricia Frey

PRODUCTIONS & CASTS

DUSKY SALLY by Granville Burgess; *World Premiere;* Direction/Set, Jack Chandler; Lighting, Jane Reisman; Costumes, Randy Barcelo; Sound, Andrew G. Luft, Crispin Catricala. CAST: Erica Gimpel, Pirie MacDonald, L. Peter Callender, Katherine Leask, Richard Maynard

COMMUNITY PROPERTY by Dalene Young; *World Premiere;* Director, Peter H. Clough; Set, Leslie Taylor; Costumes, Heidi Hollman; Lighting, Jackie Manassee. CAST: Anne Newhall, John Shepard, Frank Biancamano, Anna Berger

A VIEW FROM THE BRIDGE by Arthur Miller; Director, Tony Giordano; Set, Hugh Landwehr; Costumes, Mary Ann Powell; Lighting, Dennis Parichy. CAST: Michael Fischetti, Diane Martella, Jennifer Van Dyck, Lawrence Palmisano, Rafael Ferrer, Sully Boyar, Jon Cavaluzzo, Michael Twain

THE MYSTERY OF IRMA VEP by Charles Ludlam; Director, Bruce Bouchard; Set, Rick Dennis; Costumes, Martha Hally; Lighting, Jackie Manassee; Makeup, Bruce Spaulding Fuller. CAST: Michael Arkin, Michael J. Hume

JUPITER AND ELSEWHERE by Gram Slaton; *World Premiere;* Director, Tom Bloom; Set, Robert Thayer; Costumes, Lynda L. Salsbury; Lighting, Lary Opitz; Sound, Kevin Bartlett. CAST: Russ Jolly, Arch Johnson, Doug Wert, Stephanie Saft, Nesba Crenshaw, Michael Heintzman, Vincent Lamberti

BRIGHTON BEACH MEMOIRS by Neil Simon; Director, Lynn Polan; Set, Leslie Taylor; Costumes, Lynda L. Salsbury; Lighting, Andi Lyons. CAST: Rick Lawless, Herbert Rubens, Laura Gardner, Todd Merrill, Anne Gartlan, Ava Haddad, Lori Andresky

Skip Dickstein Photos

**Right: Russ Jolly, Stephanie Saft
in "Jupiter and Elsewhere" Top:
Michael J. Hume, Michael Arkin
in "The Mystery of Irma Vep"**

CLARENCE BROWN THEATRE COMPANY

University of Tennessee
Knoxville, Tennessee

Directors, Lucien Douglas, Wandalie Henshaw, Philip Kerr; Sets, Robert Cothran, Gary Decker, Leonard Harman; Costumes, Bill Black, Marianne Custer, Steven Graver, Sara Irwin; Lighting, Gary Decker, L. J. DeCuir; Sound, G. Scott Corliss; Composers/Music, James Brimer, Paul Jones; Stage Managers, Phebe A. Day, Reggie Law, Page Phillips; Fight Choreographer, Erik Fredericksen

PRODUCTIONS & CASTS

THE TAMING OF THE SHREW by William Shakespeare; with Richard Bowden (Gremio), Robert Hock (Baptista), Monique Morgan (Bianca), Rusty Mowery (Lucentio), Barry Mulholland (Petruchio), Scott Treadway (Hortensio), Lynn Watson (Kate)

PRESENT LAUGHTER by Noel Coward; with Veronica Castang (Monica), Keytha Graves (Daphne), Joanne Hamlin (Lady Saltburn), Mary Jeffries (Miss Erikson), Philip Kerr (Garry), Otto Konrad (Roland), Rita Litton (Joanna), Barry Mulholland (Hugo), Carol Schultz (Liz), Douglas Stender (Morris), Scott Treadway (Fred)

THE HARMFUL EFFECTS OF TOBACCO by Anton Chekov; with Robert Blackburn (Stephan/Ivan/Luka/Vassily), Keytha Graves (Natalia/Helena), Barry Mulholland (Ivan/Grigory/Nikita)

MACBETH by William Shakespeare; with Zack Allen (Seyton/Murderer), David Brian Alley (Menteith), Arnie Burton (Malcolm), Jeanne Love Ferguson (Gentlewoman), Philip Kerr (Macbeth), Alison Lyons (Lady Macduff), Monique Morgan (Lady Macbeth), Rusty Mowery (Donalbain/Fleance), Barry Mulholland (Macduff), Dennis E. Perkins (Witch/Young Siward), David Poirier (Captain/Lennox/Siward), Robbie Robinson (Macduff's son), Brian Semple (Witch/Angus/Murderer), David Snizek (Banquo), Jim Stubbs (Witch/Ross), Ian Thomson (Duncan/Porter/Murderer/Doctor), Greg Amsler, Vernon Bass, Greg Bell, Moses Collins, Jim Conn, Theron Hudgins, Hadley Panzer, Roland Poles, Mark Rowe

Eric L. Smith Photos

**Philip Kerr, David Snizek
in "Macbeth"**

**Carol Schultz, Philip Kerr
in "Present Laughter"**

CLEVELAND PLAY HOUSE

Cleveland, Ohio
Seventy-first Season

Resident Artistic Director, William Rhys; Managing Director, Dean R. Gladden; Associate Artistic Director, Evie McElroy; Business Manager, Nelson Isekeit; Production Manager, Thomas M. Salzman; Company Manager, Angela Pohlman; Musical Director, David Gooding; Dramaturg, Wayne S. Turney; Scenic Design, Richard Gould, Keith Henery; Costumes, Estelle Painter; Props, James A. Guy; Stage Managers, Michael Stanley, Deborah A. Gosney, Richard Lundy; Press/Marketing, Amy Dwyer Corvey
RESIDENT ACTING ENSEMBLE: Catherine Albers, Sharon Bicknell, Marla Fries, Dawn Gray, Jeffrey Guyton, Richard Halverson, Mark Heffernan, Allen Leatherman, Morgan Lund, Rebecca Manning, Andrew May, Evie McElroy, Carlyle B. Owens, Robert C. Rhys, Charles Robinson, Valerie Robinson, Dudley Swetland, Ann Tsuji, Wayne S. Turney, Pamela Tucker-White
GUEST ARTISTS: *Actors:* Robert Grey, David O. Frazier, Jill Larson, Alan Coates, Roger Robinson, Erick Avari, Bill Lewis, James P. Kisicki, Terry Alexander, Richard Oberlin, David Gooding, Tom Fulton, Thomas Kopache, Joseph Pecchio, Paula Duesing, John Buck, Jr., Jon Farris, Robert Frank, Roland Kausen, Phil Bunch, Dennis Bailey, Debby Duffy Young, Ann Mortifee, Rex Nockengust, Mary Michenfelder, Molly McGrath Cornwell, Jean Zarzour. *Directors:* Kay Matschullat, George Ferencz, Marion Andre, Donald Ewer, Joseph J. Garry, Jr., Jack Lee (Musical Director). *Designers:* D. Glen Vanderbilt, Charles Berliner, Bill Stabile, Blu, Kirk Bookman. *Choreographer:* April Shawhan
PRODUCTIONS: *The Praying Mantis* by Alejandro Sieveking, translated by Charles Philip Thomas; *Buried Child* by Sam Shepard; *A Christmas Carol* adapted by Doris Baizley from Charles Dickens; *Orphans* by Lyle Kessler; *The 1940's Radio Hour* by Walton Jones; *Mensch Meier* by Franz Xavier Kroetz/translated by Roger Downey; *Three Sisters* translated by Lanford Wilson from Anton Chekhov; *Cotton Patch Gospel* by Tom Key, Russell Treyz with Music and Lyrics by Harry Chapin; *Noises Off* by Michael Frayn; *World Premieres* of *"To Die for Granada"* by Derek Walcott; *The Arabian Knight* by Joseph J. Garry, Jr., David O. Frazier, based on lyrics, music and poetry by Ann Mortifee.

Robert C. Ragsdale Photos

Sharon Bicknell, Dudley Swetland, Richard Halverson, Evie McElroy in "Noises Off"

COCONUT GROVE PLAYHOUSE

Coconut Grove, Florida

Producing Artistic Director, Arnold Mittelman; Marketing/Sales, Kathleen Bateson Glass; General Manager, Jordan Bock; Production/Financial Analysis, Marsha Hardy Grasselli; Development, Lee Kline; Administrative Coordinator, Terri Schermer; Business Manager, Rudy Volenec; Technical Director, Howard Beals; Props, Steven Lambert; Costumes, Ellis Tillman; Wardrobe, Melanie Batman; Sound, Richard Camuso; Stage Managers, Rafael Blanco, Robin Gray, Steve Neal, Joseph Barry, David M. Flasck, James McGill; Press, Lee Zimmerman, Ida Mattia-Thompson, Cal Kaufman

PRODUCTIONS & CASTS
WAIT UNTIL DARK by Frederick Knott; Director, George Keathley; Set, David Trimble. CAST: Thom Christopher (Harry), Richard McWilliams (Mike), Tom Kouchalakos (Carlino/Patrolman), Lois Nettleton (Susy), Dennis Jones (Sam), Daheli Hall (Gloria), James McGill (Patrolman)
NUNSENSE by Dan Goggin; Director, Mr. Goggin; Choreography, Felton Smith; Musical Direction, Dan Strickland; Scenery, Barry Axtel. CAST: Helen Baldassare (Sister Mary Amnesia), Kaye Ballard (Sister Mary Regina), Michaela Hughes (Sister Mary Leo), Marcia Lewis (Sister Mary Hubert), Jaye P. Morgan (Sister Robert Anne)
THE HOSTAGE by Brendan Behan; Director, Arnold Mittelman; Musical Direction, Bruce W. Coyle; Scenery, David Trimble. CAST: Philip Astor (Mulleady), Roxann Cabalero (Teresa), David M. Glasck (Russian Sailor), Brick Hartney (Rio Rita), Ralston Hill (Monsewer), Myvanwy Jenn (Miss Gilchrist), Anthony Jones (Princess Grace), Ann MacMillan (Ropeen), Sheila MacRae (Meg Dillon), Anthony Newfield (IRA Officer), Darci Osiecky (Colette), Gerald Owens (Volunteer), Fred J. Scollay (Pat), Ann Serrano (Bobo), Derek D. Smith (Leslie), Elizabeth Tercek (Violinist)
ORCHIDS AND PANTHERS by Alfonso Vallejo; *World Premiere* of English Language version; Director, Arnold Mittelman; Scenery/Lighting/Costumes, Fred Kolo; Music Composed/Adapted/Performed by Simon Salz; Assistant to Director, Darby Hayes. CAST: Jeff Ware (Sergio Brandone), Dion Anderson (Berto Leone), Olivia Negron (Tina Leone Dillon), John Shepard (Tony Dillon), Judith Delgado (Julia Leone)
COCONUTS! with Music/Lyrics by Michael Brown/Lesley Davison; Sketches, William Brown; Director, Frank Wagner; Musical Director, Ray Coussins; Set, Howard Beals. CAST: Cyrilla Baer, Christopher Bishop, Julie Prosser
ON THE 20th CENTURY with Book and Lyrics by Betty Comden, Adolph Green; Music, Cy Coleman; Director, Jeffrey B. Moss; Musical Director/Conductor, Kay Cameron; Choreography, Barbara Siman; Set, Jim Morgan; Costumes, Martin Pakledinaz; Stage Manager, Clifford Schwartz. CAST: Judy Kaye (Lily Garland), Frank Gorshin (Oscar Jaffee), Imogene Coca (Letitia Primrose), King Donovan (Owen O'Malley), Keith Curran (Bruce Granitt), David Green (Oliver Webb), Gary Barker (Lead Actor), Mark Basile (Max Jacobs), Peggy Bayer (Anita), Jean Kauffman (Agnes), Glenn Mure (Conductor/Doctor/Senator), Michael Radigan (Maxwell Finch), Alexana Ryer (Imelda Thornton), Bruce Daniels, Cissy Rebich, Susan Shofner, Monte Ralstin

Tom Elliott Photos

Olivia Negron, John Shepard, Dion Anderson, Judith Delgado, Jeff Ware in "Orchids and Panthers"
Above: Marcia Lewis, Michaela Hughes, Jaye P. Morgan, Kaye Ballard, Helen Baldassare in "Nunsense"

DELAWARE THEATRE COMPANY

Wilmington, Delaware
Eighth Season

Artistic Director, Cleveland Morris; Managing Director, Dennis Luzak; Business Managers, Ray Barto, Barbara James; Development, Ann G. Schenck; Marketing, Mary L. Haynes; Operations Managers, Roberta G. Adams, Janet Beeson; Assistant Artistic Director, Danny Peak; Costumes, Marla Jurglanis; Lighting, Bruce K. Morriss; Props, Donna DeAngelo; Sound, Alan Gardner; Stage Managers, Patricia Christian, Paul Taylor

PRODUCTIONS & CASTS

OUR TOWN by Thornton Wilder; Director, Cleveland Morris. CAST: Michael M. Thompson (Stage Manager), Greg Tigani (Dr. Gibbs), David Wright (Joe Crowell), Clay Warnick (Howie), Rebecca Taylor (Mrs. Gibbs), Sarah Burke (Mrs. Webb), Berry Cooper (George Gibbs), Allison Hedges (Rebecca), Joey Del Pesco (Wally), Leah Doyle (Emily), Bill Van Hunter (Mr. Webb), Krystov Lindquist (Simon), Terry Reamer (Mrs. Soames), Joe McCain (Constable), David Wright (Si), Charles J. Conway (Sam), Robert L. Jones (Prof. Willard/Joe Staddard), Bob Balick, Eugenia Barto, Reita Bewley, Michael Burton, Cori Casarino, Richard Chinman, Genevieve Conway, Chris Erickson, Sue Erickson, Della L. Johnson, Doris S. Johnson, Patricia Lake, Wendy Lofting, Dorothy Magner, Marjorie A. Miller, Danny Peak, Mary Rafferty, Danielle Ragazzo, Lauren Ragazzo, Patricia Rutter, Betty Stapleford, Trina Tjersland, Carolin Whalen, Suzanne Winkler.
CHRISTMAS MYSTERIES: *The Second Shepherds Play* (Anonymous) and *Why the Lord Come to Sand Mountain* by Romulus Linney; Director, Cleveland Morris. CAST: Anderson Matthews (1st Shepherd/St. Peter), Ian Schneiderman (2nd Shepherd/Jack), Paul Mulder (3rd Shepherd/14 Children), Rory Kelly (Mak/The Lord), Kathryn Gay Wilson (Gill/Sang Picker), Martha M. Holmes (Mary/Jean), Martin L. Willeford (Angel), Andy Zimmerman (Prosper Valley Farm).
THE TOOTH OF CRIME by Sam Shepard; Director, William Woodman; Original Music, John Spahr, Lachlan Macleay. CAST: P. J. Benjamin (Hoss), Diane Rieck (Becky Lou), Jon Krupp (Starman), Bill Jacob (Galactic Jack), Lachlan Macleay (Cheyenne), Greg Petroff (Doc/Ref), Laurence Overmire (Crow).
THE MIDDLE AGES by A. R. Gurney, Jr.; Director, Derek Wolshonak; Music Supervisor, James Weber. CAST: John Abajian (Barney), Kay Walbye (Eleanor), Richard Voigts (Charles), Maxine Taylor-Morris (Myra)
ELEEMOSYNARY by Lee Blessing; Director, Jamie Brown; Original Music, Leon Odenz. Cast: Judith Klein (Echo), Anna Minot (Dorothea), Marion McCorry (Artie)

Richard Carter Photos

P. J. Benjamin, Laurence Overmire in "Tooth of Crime"

Kay Walbye, John Abajian in "The Middle Ages"

DENVER CENTER THEATRE COMPANY

Denver, Colorado
Eighth Season

Artistic Director, Donovan Marley; Executive Director, Sarah Lawless; Producing Director, Barbara E. Sellers; Associate Artistic Director, Peter Hackett; Associate Artistic Director, Richard L. Hay; Casting, Randal Myler; Technical Director, Dan McNeil; Props, Jaylene Graham; Costumes, Janet S. Morris; Wardrobe, Charlene M. White; Sound, John E. Pryor; Administrative Director, Karen Knudsen; Stage Managers, Lyle Raper, Paul Jefferson, Joseph F. Martin, D. Adams, Christopher C. Ewing, Jessica Evans; Press, Ken Novice
ACTING COMPANY: Roderick Aird, Stephen Anderson, Jim Baker, Jeff Baumgartner, Benny Bell, Tamra Benham, Shell M. Benjamin, Candy Ann Brown, Jack Casperson, David Cleveland, James Coyle, Tupper Cullum, Randy Davis, Craig Diffenderfer, Kay Doubleday, Suzzanne Douglas, Ann Duquesnay, Allison Easter, John Eisner, Richard Elmore, Robert Eustace, Lynnda Ferguson, Al Gallegos, Frank Georgianna, Kevin Gray, Paula Gruskiewicz, Ann Guilbert, Mark Harelik, Wiley Harker, Wendelin Harston, Leslie Hendrix, A. Ashley Hill, Chandler Holland, Jamie Horton, Byron Jennings, David E. Kazanjian, Danis Kovanda, Sandra Ellis Lafferty, James J. Lawless, Wendy Lawless, Eloise Laws, Silvia Lester, Peter Lohnes, Scotch Ellis Loring, Warren "Juba" Lucas, Michael X. Martin, Anna Miller, Gloria Jean Morrison, James Newcomb, Caitlin O'Connell, Art Andre Palmer, Dougald Park, Miles Phillips, Raymond C. A. Purl, Guy Raymond, Mick Regan, M. W. Reid, Archie Smith, Caroline Smith, Judith T. Smith, John Stewart, Vanessa Townsell, Stephen West, Jennifer Dorr White, Ronnie Whittaker, Eyan Williams, Fredye Jo Williams, Michael Winters, Jeff Wittman, Hitomi Yoshimura, Deanar Ali Young, L. Martina Young, Taylor Young
PRODUCTIONS: *South Pacific* by Richard Rodgers, Oscar Hammerstein 2nd, Joshua Logan; Director, Donovan Marley; Musical Director, Bruce K. Sevy; Choreography, Donald McKayle; Set, Richard L. Hay; Costumes, Jeannie Davidson; Lighting, Wendy Heffner. *Man and Superman* by George Bernard Shaw; Director, Dakin Matthews; Set, Ralph Funicello; Costumes, Andrew V. Yelusich; Lighting, Michael W. Vennerstrom. *Don Juan in Hell* by George Bernard Shaw; Director, Anne McNaughton; Set, Ralph Funicello; Costumes, Andrew V. Yelusich; Lighting, Michael W. Vennerstrom. *World Premiere* of *Goodnight, Texas* by Terry Dodd; Director, Bruce K. Sevy; Set, Pavel M. Dobrusky; Lighting, Wendy Heffner. *World Premiere* of *The World of Mirth* by Murphy Guyer; Director, Peter Hackett; Set/Costumes, Pavel M. Dobrusky; Lighting, Wendy Heffner. *House of Flowers* by Harold Arlen, Truman Capote; Direction/Choreography, Donald McKayle; Musical Direction, Bruce K. Sevy; Scenery, Richard L. Hay; Costumes, Andrew V. Yelusich; Lighting, Michael W. Vennerstrom. *The Playboy of the Western World* by John Millington Synge; Director, Donovan Marley; Set, Kevin Rupnik; Costumes, Andrew V. Yelusich; Lighting, Wendy Heffner. *World Premiere* of *Rachel's Fate* by Larry Ketron; Director, Murphy Guyer; Set/Costumes, John Dexter; Lighting, Michael W. Vennerstrom. *Coriolanus* by William Shakespeare; Director, Laird Williamson; Set, Laird Williamson, Andrew V. Yelusich; Costumes, Andrew V. Yelusich; Lighting, Wendy Heffner; Incidental Music, Larry Delinger; Fight Director, Matt McKenzie. *Orphans* by Lyle Kessler; Director, Frank Georgianna; Set, Kent Dorsey; Costumes, Janet S. Morris; Lighting, Michael W. Vannerstrom. *World Premiere* of *Shooting Stars* by Molly Newman; Director, Randal Myler; Set, Richard L. Hay; Costumes, Janet S. Morris; Lighting, Wendy Heffner. *World Premiere* of *Lost Highway;* The Music and Legend of Hank Williams by Randal Myler and Mark Harelik; Director, Randal Myler; Set, Richard L. Hay; Costumes, Andrew V. Yelusich; Lighting, Charles MacLeod

T. Charles Erickson Photos

Leslie Hendrix, Caitlin O'Connell
in "Goodnight, Texas" Above: Byron Jennings as "Coriolanus"

DETROIT REPERTORY THEATRE

Detroit, Michigan
Twenty-ninth Season

Artistic Director, Bruce E. Millan; Executive Director, Robert Williams; Marketing, Reuben Yabuku; Development, Dee Andrus; Literary Manager, Barbara Busby; Costumer, B. J. Essen; Music Director, Kelly Smith; Sets, Bruce Millan, Peter Knox; Stage Managers, Dee Andrus, William Boswell; Lighting, Kenneth R. Hewitt, Jr.; Sound, Reuben Yabuku; Graphics, Barbara Weinberg-Barefield

PRODUCTIONS & CASTS

HEART OF A DOG by Mikhail Bulgakov; Adapted by Frank Galati; Director, Bruce E. Millan. CAST: John W. Puchalski, William Boswell, Charles A. Jackson, Dee Andrus, Kimberly S. Newberry, Robert Vogue, Bill Sinischo
DAYS AND NIGHTS WITHIN by Ellen McLaughlin; Director, Dee Andrus. CAST: Henrietta Hermelin, Robert Grossman
WAITING FOR GODOT by Samuel Beckett; Director, Barbara Busby. CAST: Darius L. Dudley, Jay Johnson, Mack Palmer, Robert Rucker, Robert Skrok
TIME CAPSULE by Paul Simpson; *World Premiere;* Director, Bruce E. Millan. CAST: Council Cargle, Fran L. Washington

Bruce E. Millan Photos

DOWNSTAIRS CABARET THEATRE

Rochester, New York

Producing Director, Jerry Algozer; Managing Director, Nick Fici; Production Manager, Cynthia Sweetland; Production Assistant, Lana Momano; Stage Manager, Tom Vazzana

Opened Friday, October 19, 1986 and still playing May 31, 1987.
NUNSENSE with Book, Music and Lyrics by Dan Goggin; Direction and Musical Staging, Jerry Algozer; Musical Director, Corinne Aquilina; Set Design, Cynthia Sweetland; Lighting Design, David Wiggall; Habitual Designs, Lana Momano; Stage Manager, Tom Vazzana
CAST: Cayla Allen (Sister Mary Leo), Paula Betlem (Sister Robert Anne), Phyl Contestable (Sister Mary Regina), Jane Strauss (Sister Mary Amnesia), Terri White (Sister Mary Hubert)

Kurt Gerber Photo

Derek D. Smith, Laura Hicks
in "Romeo and Juliet"

Robert Vogue, Dee Andrus, John Puchalski,
Kimberly Newberry, William Boswell in
"Heart of a Dog" Left Center: Paula Betlem,
Terri White, Phyl Contestable, Cayla Allen, Jane Strauss
in "Nunsense"

FOLGER SHAKESPEARE THEATRE

Washington, D.C.
Seventeenth Season

Artistic Director, Michael Kahn; Managing Director, Mary Ann de Barbieri; Business Manager, Elizabeth Hamilton; Development, Julie Duke; Production Manager, James Irwin; Technical Director, Tom Whittington; Dramaturg, Genie Barton

PRODUCTIONS AND CASTS

TWELFTH NIGHT by William Shakespeare; Director, Gavin Cameron-Webb; Set, Russell Metheny; Costumes, Gail Brassard; Lighting, Allen Lee Hughes; Fight Director, Michael Tolaydo; Stage Manager, Debra Acquavelva. CAST: Edward Gero, Kryztov Lindquist, Clay Warnick, Sybil Lines, Grady Smith, Emery Battis, Catherine Flye, Richard Hart, Michael W. Howell, Marilyn Caskey, Floyd King, Michael Tolaydo, Michael Kramer, Jim Beard, Orlagh Cassidy, Howard Bass, Lucy Fasano, Susan Manus
ROMEO AND JULIET by William Shakespeare; Director, Michael Kahn; Set, Derek McLane; Costumes, Ann Hould-Ward; Lighting, Nancy Schertler; Fight Director, David Leong; Vocal Consultant, Elizabeth Smith; Choreographer, Virginia Freeman; Composer, Bruce Adolphe; Stage Manager, Liza C. Stein. CAST: Emery Battis, Francelle Stewart Dorn, Laura Hicks, Pat Carroll, Edward Gero, Brian Reddy, Jeff Peters, Richard Pilcher, Alan Woodward, Paul Valley, Hilary Kacser, Bob Hungerford, Catherine Flye, Derek D. Smith, Anthony Powell, Michael Donahue, Michael Wiggins, Barry Boys, Gary Sloan, Richard Ganoung, Floyd King, Chris Brown, Andrew Reilly, Peggy Beasley, Sue Burford, Leah Godbold, Arthur Morton
MANDRAGOLA by Niccolo Machiavelli; Adapted and Directed by Peter Maloney; *Premiere;* Set, Joel Fontaine; Costumes, Martha Kelly; Lighting, James Irwin; Music, Norman L. Berman; Stage Manager, B. Laurie Hunt. CAST: Edward Gero, Floyd King, Brian Reddy, Jack Koenig, Howard Samuelsohn, Catherine Wolf, Tracy Kolis
THE WINTER'S TALE by William Shakespeare; Director, Michael Kahn; Set, Robert Edward Darling; Costumes, Jane Greenwood; Lighting, Nancy Schertler; Composer, Lee Hoiby; Choreographer, Roberta Gasbarre; Musical Director, Sam McClung; Stage Manager, Catherine Carney Hart. CAST: Ray Virta, Tom Tammi, Pamela Nyberg, Roberto Conte, Aaron Zielski, Emery Battis, Francelle Stewart Dorn, Robert Hock, Richard Ganoung, Bill Grimmette, Gillian Doyle, Leah Maddrie, Jeff Peters, Paul Valley, Andrew Reilly, Rosalyn Coleman, Brigitta DePree, Chris Brown, Arthur Morton, Craig Stephen Wallace, Anthony Powell, Floyd King, Brian Reddy, David Manis, Linda Maurel
LOVE'S LABOUR'S LOST by William Shakespeare; Director, Paul Giovanni; Set, Robert Klingelhoefer; Costumes, Jess Goldstein; Lighting, Dawn Chiang; Songs/Incidental Music, Bruce Adolphe; Choreography, Roberta Gasbarre; Stage Manager, B. Laurie Hunt. CAST: Edward Gero, Gary Sloan, Anthony Powell, Richard Ganoung, Floyd King, Bill Grimmette, Ted Van Griethuysen, Alan Nebelthau, Emery Battis, Brian Reddy, Todd Jamieson, Ronna Kress, Paul Valley, Mary Walworth, Leah Maddrie, Christina Haag, Pamela Nyberg, Franchelle Stewart Dorn, Keith Johnson, Deanne Meek

GLOBE PLAYHOUSE

Shakespeare Society of America
Los Angeles, California

Co-Founders/Producing Directors, R. Thad Taylor, Jay Uhley

THE PURITAINE or The Widdow of Watling Street by William Shakespeare. Director, Mark Ringer; Costumes, Libby Jacobs; Stage Manager, Lauren Shpall. CAST: Tom Ashworth, Martin Brumer, Jeffrey Bryan, Dean Cleverdon, Mitch Englander, Lisa Fineberg, Eddie Frierson, Kurt Hansen, Richard LaFond, Paul Maley, Deborah Seidel, Ralph Redpath, Debra Sirwa, Pat Sturges, Brad Thornton, Biff Wiff, Dana White, R. Scott Williams, Mark Ringer.

HAMLET by William Shakespeare; Director, David Ralphe; Costumes, Casandra Carpenter; Fight Movement, Gregory Michaels; Original Music, Dominic Messinger; Set, Walter Flinge; Wardrobe/Props, Mary Munsie; Stage Manager, Sam de Francisco. CAST: Lane Davies (Hamlet), Michael Santiago, Louise Sorel, Oren Curtis, John Allen Nelson, Louise Robbins, J. D. Hall, Jonathan Roberts, Carl Moebus, Steve Munsie, Joseph Reale, Richard Livingston, Richard Fullerton, Steve Stuart, Sam DeFracisco, Richard M. Tyson, David Fritz, Michael Ross-Oddo, Carol Ashley, Michele King, Judy Levitt

JULIUS CAESAR by William Shakespeare; Director, Delbert Spain; Costumes, Valeria Watson; Lights/Sound, Anthony Potter; Original Music, Russel Filippo; Stage Manager, Teresa Trout. CAST: Armand Asselin, Walt Beaver (Julius Caesar), Jeanne Bascom, William Birney, Linda Blakely, Jeffrey Bryan, Henry Capanna, Sam Clay, Gregory Clemens, Jeffrey Concklin, David Davies, Allen Douglas, Anthony Embeck, Stan Fidel, Jack Frankel, Katherine Henryk, Joel Hoffman, Bill Hollis, Ron Kologie, Anthony Krueger, Benjamin Mouton, Rick Nardi, Janet Newberry, Richard Osborn, Jose Payo, Gary Allan Poe, Grady Schneider, Jacqueline Stehr, Ken Strong (Caesar), David Tate, John Terence, Ed Thomas, Marci Thompson, Vance Valencia

CYMBELINE by William Shakespeare; Director, Sami Kamal; Costumes, Linda Reed, Valerie O'Brien; Music, Carl Orff; Lighting, Tony Potter; Choreographer/Stage Manager, Tracey Collins. CAST: Theresa Ambronn, Herman O. Arbeit, Gareth St. John Provan, Tom Sullivan, Julian Ayrs, Kathryn Bikle, Dana Craig, C. Thomas Cunliffe, Andre Diamond, Larry Eisenberg, Clayton James, Colleen Marie Jordan, Vsevolod Krawczeniuk, John Michalski, Jared Moses, Pat Mullins, Richard Nardi, Jenny Redding, Ashley Rout, Angie Synodis, Brian F. Swisher, John Tays, Philip Winterbottom, Tracy Wise

THE RAIGNE OF KING EDWARD III by William Shakespeare; Director/Designer, Dick Dotterer; Costumes, Stephen Bishop; Composer, Mark Binder; Lighting, Tom Petipas; Sound, Rick Larimore; Choreographer, Jody Kielbasa; Assistant Director, Gary Spenser; Stage Managers, Barry Pool, Kevin Crump, Patrick Carlok. CAST: Neil Adams, Tenley Albright, Julian Ayrs, James Bangley, Gary Bell, James Buchanan, Georges Bujold, Victoria Cockrell, Tony Colletti, Gary Lynn Collier, Joel Cone, Marnie Crossen, Edward Dloughy, Eric Curant, Michael Dunn, David Everhart, Don Ericson, Richard German, Corey Hansen, Nevin Harrison, Joel Hoffman, Dak Kelly, Robert Kincaid, David Leach, Brian Patrick McBride, Jeff McVey, Mark Odell, Elizabeth O'Reilly, Martita Palmer, Gregory Quinn, Ashley Rout, Ann Sarnelli, James P. Slingluff, Bill Timoney, Larry Tomashoff, Juliana Venini, Cary Vhugen, Barry Vincent, F. A. West

THE LONDON PRODIGALL by William Shakespeare; Director, Todd Mandel; Costumes, Libby Jacobs; Lights, Kent Inasy; Set, Chez Cherry; Stage Managers, Vicki Berthelot. CAST: Gillian Bagwell, David Ellenstein, Susan Falcon, Tom Hamil, Timothy Juliano, Mat Kirkwood, Chuck Kovacic, Jerry Neill, Stacy Renee, Dale Reynolds, Stuart Rogers, Craig Stout

HENRY VIII in repertory with

CROMWELL by William Shakespeare; Director, Phoebe Wray; Costumes, Neal San Teguns; Lighting, Steven Howell; Sound, Dena Paponis; Choreography, Kit van Zandt; Masks, Randall Wright; Stage Manager, Christian Dahlberg. CAST: Kenyon Austin, Jerry Beal, Debra Brannan, Robert Britton, Paul Carter, Claudia M. Cupp, David Davidson, Peter E. Girard, Michael Jerome, Loring Leeds, Paul Lueken, David Mack, Dan Martin, Mark Martsolf, Lizzie Maxwell, Chris McDonald, Richard Osborn, Garret Smith, Stanley J. Sturing, Ann Bonnie Sarnelli, Richard Roemer, Kit van Zandt, Gary Weissbrot, Randall Wright

SIR JOHN OLDCASTLE by William Shakespeare; Director, R. Thad Taylor; Assistant Director, Greg Owens; Lighting, Anthony Potter; Costumes, Debra Dresser; Stage Manager, Mary Lynn Gill. CAST: Philip Benichou, Charles Gill, Pat Johnson, Paul Chung, Ray Jarris, Dan Dolin, Phyllis Deon Upton, Tom DeMirani, Bill Butts, Stephen Burhoe, David Graf, Agim Coma, Gregory Alexander, Mary Lynn Gill, Georges Bujold, Jon Mullich, Curt Siebert, Rowan Sutherland, Albert-Manes Motil, Edward Howes, Paul Barchelor, Archie Lee Simpson, Nick Scott, Joel Cone, Lisa Andresen, Curtis Laseter, James Bangley

Top Right: Richard German, Roscoe Vest, Ty Warren in "Sir John Oldcastle"

THE MERCHANT OF VENICE by William Shakespeare; Director, Delbert Spain; Costumes, Patricia L. Davis; Technical Director, Tony Potter; Stage Manager, Melissa Harred. CAST: Michael Lucie, Ed Thomas, Clark Jarrett, Brent Christensen, Jeffrey Concklin, Macall Dunahee, Bruce Cromer, David Graf, Barbara Silliman, Janet Newberry, Paul Boardman, Dominic Hoffman, Michael Robinson, Gary Heilsberg, Marci Thompson, Danny Shock, Gary Bonart, Mark Westlund, Aaron Heyman, Delbert Spain

PERICLES, PRINCE OF TYRE by William Shakespeare; Director, Tom Ashworth; Technical Director, Tony Potter. CAST: Jeffrey Bryan, Dana Craig, Christien Cunningham, Matthew Phillip Davis, Joyce Greene, Carol Jones, Eric Menyuk, Cameron Milzer, Timothy Polzin, Mark Ringer, Archie Lee Simpson, Joe Tomko

A YORKSHIRE TRAGEDY by William Shakespeare; Director, R. Thad Taylor; Fights, Hugh Bowles; Costumes, Valerie T. O'Brien; Stage Manager, Jamie Badewa. CAST: James Bangley, Hugh Bowles, Jason Culp, David Graf, Douglas Langworthy, Guy A. Mastroianni, MernaLyn, Brian O'Halloran, Andrea Peatman, Lance Peatman, Robin Scholer, Gali Zisman

KING LEAR by William Shakespeare; Director, Walt Beaver; Music, Ted Nichols; Assistant Director, Elizabeth O'Reilly. CAST: Walt Beaver (King Lear), Kaaren Lee Brown, Dana Charette, David Davies, Larry Eisenberg, Joyce E. Greene, Richard Livingston, Michael Mallory, John Michalski, Cedric Minkin, Janet Newberry, Dennis Nichols, Carl Smith, Ken Strong

Ronny Graham, Kim Hunter in "Jokers"
Above: "A House in the Woods"
Goodspeed Opera House/Diane Sobolewski

GOODSPEED OPERA HOUSE

East Haddum, Connecticut
Twenty-fourth Season

Executive Director, Michael P. Price; Associate Producer/Casting, Warren Pincus; Associate Artistic Director, Dan Siretta; Producing Associate, Sue Frost; Musical Director, Lynn Crigler; Scenery, James Leonard Joy; Lighting, Craig Miller; Assistant Musical Director, Patrick Vaccariello; Music Research Consultant, Alfred Simon; Stage Manager, Michael Brunner; Marketing, Joseph P. Gagliardi; Development, Syd Slater; Company Manager, Jeffrey Capitola; Technical Director, Ted Zuse; Wardrobe, John Riccucci; Props, Jennifer L. Baker; Press, Kay McGrath, Mindy Keskinen, Max Eisen, Madelon Rosen

PRODUCTIONS & CASTS

FANNY with Book by S. N. Behrman, Joshua Logan; Music and Lyrics, Harold Rome; Director, Thomas Gruenewald; Choreography Edie Cowan; Costumes, John Carver Sullivan; Lighting, Curt Ostermann; Production Manager, Anthony M. Forman; Producer, Michael P. Price. CAST: Peggy Bayer, Deborah Bendixen, Joseph Bowerman, Devin Carnicelli, Charlie Costanzo, Leonard John Crofoot, Karen Culliver, John Dorrin, Gary Gage, Dale Hensley, Andy Hostettler, Marilyn Hudgins, David Hurst, Richard Korthaze, Genette Lane, Andrea Leigh-Smith, Lee Lobenhofer, Chester Ludgin, Judith McLane, Gary Moss, Barry Phillips, Michele Scirpo

CARNIVAL! with Music and Lyrics by Bob Merrill; Book, Michael Stewart; Director, Thomas Gruenewald; Choreography, D. J. Giagni; Costumes, Oleksa. CAST: Robert Frisch (Paul), Scott Jarvis (Jacquot), Alix Korey (Rosalie), Mark Martino (Marco), Ann Talman (Lili), Raymond Thorne (Schlegel), Bobby Clark (Gaston), Teri Gibson (Olga), Christopher Harrison (Jean-Claude), Lester Holmes (Francois), Nancy Hughes (Greta), Darrell Miller (Leon), Gary Moss (Bruno), Vince Trani (Grobert/Dr. Glass), Tara Tyrrell (Gladys), Patricia Ward (Gloria)

ONE TOUCH OF VENUS with Music by Kurt Weill; Book, S. J. Perelman, Ogden Nash; Lyrics, Ogden Nash; Director, Ben Levit; Choreography, Rodney Griffin; Costumes, Marjorie McCown; Technical Director, Daniel Renn; Producer, Michael P. Price. CAST: Karen Cantor (Gloria), Nick Corley (Stanley), Semina De Laurentis (Molly), Dale O'Brien (Taxi), Lynnette Perry (Venus), Michael Piontek (Rodney), Irma Rogers (Mrs. Kramer), Richard Sabellico (Whitelaw), Helen Anne Barcay, Peggy Bayer, Diana Brownstone, Mamie Duncan-Gibbs, Christine Hunter, Genette Lane, Paul Laureano, Gerry McIntyre, Christopher Nilsson, Daniel Pelzig, Jeff Siebert, Kyle Whyte

GOODSPEED AT NORMA TERRIS THEATRE/CHESTER

A HOUSE IN THE WOODS with Book and Lyrics by Ellen Weston; Music, Marvin Laird; Directed/Staged by Michael Leeds; Choreography, William Fleet Lively; Producer, Sue Frost; Scenery, Evelyn Sakash; Costumes, John Carver Sullivan; Lighting, Curt Ostermann; Technical Director, Daniel Renn; Stage Manager, Michael Brunner. CAST: Patti Allison (Eulah), Marsha Bagwell (Riba), Sonia Bailey (Mary), Richard H. Blake (Lester), Jeffery Brocklin (Deputy), Victor Cook (Granville), Lisa Felcoski (Anabel), Caryn Lyn Jones (Bessy), T. J. Meyers (Councilman Coombs), Michael Piontek (Michael), James J. Stein, Jr. (Sheriff), Tracy Katz (Jessy), Trey Parker (John Quincy), David Lee Cowles (Cowcatcher/Preacher/Trustee), Troy Britton Johnson (Switcher/Mailman/Western Union Boy), Eric Kaufman (Boxcar/Doctor/Trustee), Jeffrey Alan Walker (Engine/Fireman/Trustee)

JOKERS with Music, Lyrics and Book by Hugo Peretti, Luigi Creatore, George David Weiss; Based on play "The Gin Game" by D. L. Coburn; Directed and Staged by Martin Charnin; Scenery, James Leonard Joy; Costumes, Ann Hould-Ward; Lighting, Judy Rasmusson; Choreography, Linda Haberman; Musical Direction/Vocal Arrangements, Paul Trueblood; Orchestrations, Larry Wilcox; Dance Arrangements, Michael Skloff; Stage Manager, Dale Kaufman. CAST: Kim Hunter (Fonsia Dorsey), Ronny Graham (Weller Martin), Stephani Hardy (Lady), Gerry McIntyre (Ace), Nick Corley (Cowboy), Ric Stoneback (Squeezer), Stephanie McConlough (Little Tiger), Eddie Korbich (Duck), Tracey Brian (Kicker), Sasha Charnin (Puppyfoot)

KALEIDOSCOPE with Book and Lyrics by Mary Bracken Phillips; Music, Jan Mullaney, Mary Bracken Phillips; Director, Munson Hicks; Musical Staging, Terry Rieser; Musical Direction/Arrangements, Jeff Waxman; Scenery, Timothy Jozwick; Costumes, Mardi Philips; Lighting, Judy Rasmuson; Producer, Sue Frost; Stage Manager, Ruth Feldman. CAST: Mary Bracken Phillips (Paula), P. J. Benjamin (Jonathan), Louisa Flaningam (Susan), Gibby Brand (Harding), Standbys: Patricia Kies, Robert Alton

Diane Sobolewski Photos
Top Right: Ann Talman, Robert Frisch, Scott Jarvis Below: Mark Martino, Alix Korey in "Carnival" Lower Right Center: Michael Piontek, Lynnette Perry in "One Touch of Venus"

Mamie Duncan-Gibbs, Christine Hunter, Peggy Bayer, Semina De Laurentis in "One Touch of Venus"

GUTHRIE THEATER

Minneapolis, Minnesota
Twenty-fourth Season

Artistic Director, Garland Wright; Associate Artistic Director, Stephen Kanee; Executive Director, Edward A. Martenson; Dramaturg/Literary Manager, Mark Bly; Stage Directors, Kazimierz Braun, Lee Breuer, Howard Dallin, William Gaskill, Derek Goldby, Stephen Kanee, Patrick Mason, Richard Ooms, Stan Wojewodski, Jr.; Sets, Jack Barkla, Deirdre Clancy, Jon Conklin, Hugh Landwehr, Eugene Lee; Costumes, Deirdre Clancy, Jack Edwards, Ghretta Hynd, Donna Kress, John Pennoyer; Lighting, Julie Archer, Andrei Both, Dawn Chiang, Pat Collins, John Custer, Marcus Dillard, James F. Ingalls, Suane Schuller; Composers, David Bishop, Roberta Carlson, Robert Dennis, Bob Telson, Hiram Titus; Movement, Maria Cheng, Loyce Houlton, Marsha L. Wiest-Hines; Music Directors, Matt Barber, Cliff Walinski; Playwright, Eric Overmyer; Sound, Tom Bolstad; Vocal Coaches, Julia Carey, Elizabeth Smith

ACTING COMPANY: Matthew Austin, Jackie Banks, Lisbeth Bartlett, Mark Benninghofen, Sandra Bogan, Robert Breuler, David Anthony Brinkley, Bobby Butler, Sam Butler, James Carter, J. T. Clinkscales, Peggy Cowles, Stephen D'Ambrose, Paul Drake, Don R. Fallbeck, J. J. Farley, Mary Beth Fisher, Sarah Fleming, Clarence Fountain, Peter Francis-James, Morgan Freeman, Nathaniel Fuller, Arthur Hanket, Richard Hicks, Tara Hugo, Richard S. Iglewski, Martin Jacox, Carolyn Johnson-White, Robert Earl Jones, Richard Levine, John Lewin, Ann MacMillan, John Malloy, Earl F. Miller, Kathryn Nash, Mary O'Brady, Ben Odon, Richard Ooms, Greg Ostrin, Patti Perkins, Pamela Poitier, Faye M. Price, John Prosky, James Richards, Richard Riehle, Willie Rogers, Ken Ruta, Hardic Seay, Laura-Jean Schwartau, Roger Guenveur Smith, Fred Steele, Janice Steele, J. D. Steele, Jevetta Andra Steele, Stephen Temperley, Peter Thoemke, Peter Toran, Patrick Tull, John C. Vennema, Tom Villard, Neil Vipond, Jeff Wade, Joseph Watson, Brenda Wehle, Amelia White, Claudia Wilkens, Carl Williams, Jr., Sally Wingert, Stephen Yoakam

PRODUCTIONS: Saint Joan, The Merry Wives of Windsor, The Birthday Party, On the Verge or The Geography of Yearning, Rhinoceros, A Christmas Carol, Double Infidelities, The Gospel at Colonus

Joe Giannetti Photos

Tara Hugo, Mark Benninghofen
in "St. Joan"

Richard S. Iglewski,
Mary Beth Fisher
in "Merry Wives of Windsor"

HARTFORD STAGE COMPANY

Hartford, Connecticut
Twenty-fourth Season

Artistic Director, Mark Lamos; Managing Director, David Hawkanson; Resident Playwright/Literary Manager, Constance Congdon; Dramaturg, Greg Leaming; Business Manager, Karen Price; Development, Deborah Hornblow; Production Manager, Candice Chirgotis; Technical Director, Jim Keller; Costumer, Martha Christian; Props, Sandy Struth; Press, Howard Sherman

PRODUCTIONS & CASTS

THE GILDED AGE adapted by Constance Congdon from the novel by Mark Twain and Charles Dudley Warner; Director, Mark Lamos; Set, Marjorie Bradley Kellogg; Costumes, Jess Goldstein; Lighting, Pat Collins; Music Composed and Adapted by Mel Marvin; Sound, David Budries; Wigs, Paul Huntley; Stage Managers, Katherine M. Goodrich, Diana Bronson. CAST: Wendy Brennan, Craig Bryant, Terrence Caza, Constance Crawford, Melissa Gallagher, Philip Goodwin, Joseph Houghton, Douglas Krizner, Kevin McGuire, Joel Miller, Alison Stair Neet, M. Bradford Sullivan, Ralph Zito

A DOLL HOUSE by Henrik Ibsen; World Premiere of new translation by Irene B. Berman with English text by Gerry Bamman; Director, Emily Mann; Set, Andrew Jackness; Costumes, Dunya Ramicova; Sound, David Budries; Wigs, Paul Huntley; Choreography, Ara Fitzgerald; Stage Manager, Alice Dewey. CAST: Mary McDonnell (Nora), Justin Pyrke-Fairchild (Messenger), Gerry Bamman (Torvald), Diane Dreux (Helene), Janet Zarish (Mrs. Linde), David Strathairn (Nils), Mark Lamos (Dr. Rank), Margot Stevenson (Anne Marie), William A. Friedle, Jumper Lark, Meagan E. Seitz Smith (Helmer Children)

CHILDREN by A. R. Gurney, Jr. Director, Jackson Phippin; Set, Hugh Landwehr; Costumes, Sam Fleming; Lighting, Pat Collins; Sound, David Budries; Wigs, Paul Huntley; Stage Manager, Katherine M. Goodrich. CAST: Cara Duff-MacCormick (Barbara), Jake Turner (Randy), Scotty Bloch (Mother), Cynthia Mace (Jane), Tom Zemon (Pokey)

THE PAINFUL ADVENTURES OF PERICLES, PRINCE OF TYRE by William Shakespeare, George Wilkins; Director, Mark Lamos; Set/Costumes, John Conklin; Lighting, Robert Wierzel; Sound, David Budries; Dramaturg, Greg Huntley; Wigs, Paul Huntley; Stage Manager, Alice Dewey. CAST: Edward Zang (Gower), Jack Wetherall (Pericles), Mario Arrambide, Lindsay Barnes, Angela Bassett, Darryl Croxton, William Denis, Victoria Gadsden, Bruce Gooch, Mark Loftis, Jodi Long, Howie Muir, Lazaro Perez, Al Rodriguez, Amelia White, John Wojda, Tom Zemon

THE STICK WIFE by Darrah Cloud; Director, Roberta Levitow; Set/Costumes, Michael H. Yeargan; Lighting, Robert Wierzel; Sound, David Budries; Stage Manager, Katherine M. Goodrich. CAST: Lois Smith (Jessie Bliss), Ken Jenkins (Ed Bliss), Jessie K. Jones (Marguerite Pullet), Luke Reilly (Tom Pullet), Phyllis Somerville (Betty Connor), Earl Hindman (Big Albert Connor)

MOROCCO by Allan Havis; Director, Mark Lamos; Set/Costumes, Michael H. Yeargan; Lighting, Robert Wierzel; Sound, David Budries; Stage Managers, Alice Dewey, Katherine M. Goodrich. CAST: Keir Dullea (Kempler), Paul Butler (Colonel), Gordana Rashovich (Mrs. Kempler), Robert Krakovshi (Waiter)

T. Charles Erickson Photos

Gerry Bamman, Mark Lamos, Mary McDonnell
in "A Doll House" Above: Earl Hindman,
Lois Smith, Luke Reilly in "Stick Wife"

HAWAII PERFORMING ARTS COMPANY

Honolulu, Hawaii

General Manager, Dwight T. Martin; Artistic Associate, Mark Medoff; Director of Communications and Marketing, Susannah E. Rake.

PRODUCTIONS & CASTS

GLENGARRY GLEN ROSS by David Mamet; with Dick Villard (Shelly Levene), David Johnson (John Williamson), Les Crandall (George Aaronow), Kirk Mathews (Dave Moss), Bob Fimiani (Richard Roma), Larry Fukumoto (James Lingk), Dennis Carroll (Baylen).

TORCH SONG TRILOGY by Harvey Fierstein; with Tony Curry (Arnold), Robert Brooks (Ed Reiss), Angela Gray (Laurel), Ross Levy (Alan), Jeffrey Vause (David), Gloria Spangler (Mrs. Beckoff), Annie MacLachlan (Lady Blue).

THE MISS FIRECRACKER CONTEST by Beth Henley; with Sheryl Moore (Carnelle Scott), Barbara Lea Weaver (Popeye Jackson), Nancy Puehlman (Elaine Rutledge), Dion Donahue (Delmont Williams), Richard Brill (Mac Sam), Denise Berry (Tessy Mahoney).

THE HOMAGE THAT FOLLOWED by Mark Medoff; *World Premiere;* with Kenton Holden (Archie Landrum), Devon Darrow Guard (Lucy Samuel), Joyce Maltby (Kaybee Samuel), Gray Gleason (Gilbert Tellez), Bill Ogilivie (Joseph Smith).

THE MADWOMAN OF CHAILLOT by Jean Giraudoux; with Jim Tharp (President), Robert Henry (Prospector), Larry Fukumoto (Baron), Walt Robertson (Ragpicker), Nancy Jill Sundberg (Irma), Brian Stermer (Pierre), Mary Kirkham (Countess Aurelia), Edna Lee Leib (Mme. Constance), Alexandra Kernell (Mlle. Gabrielle), Junne Barnes (Mme. Josephine).

MASTER HAROLD. . . and the boys by Athol Fugard; with Jeff Bowman (Willie), Sam Wellington (Sam), Daniel A. Kelin II (Hallie).

Tony Curry, Robert Brooks
in "Torch Song Trilogy"

Devon Darrow Guard,
Kenton Holden,
Joyce Maltby in "The Homage
That Followed"

HUNTINGTON THEATRE COMPANY

Boston, Massachusetts
Fifth Season

Producing Director, Peter Altman; Managing Director, Michael Maso; Business Manager, Mary Kiely; Company Manager, Edwin Light; Marketing/Public Relations, Virginia Louloudes; Press, Elaine Davies; Production Manager, Roger Meeker.

PRODUCTIONS & CASTS

JOE TURNER'S COME AND GONE by August Wilson; Director, Lloyd Richards; Set, Scott Bradley; Costumes, Pamela Peterson; Lighting, Michael Giannitti. CAST: Mel Winkler (Seth Holly), L. Scott Caldwell (Bertha Holly), Ed Hall (Bynum Walker), Raynor Scheine (Rutherford Selig), Bo Rucker (Jeremy Furlow), Delroy Lindo (Herald Loomis), Deidre Kerr/Jayne Skinner (Zonia Loomis), Kimberleigh Burroughs (Mattie Campbell), William Graves/Carlton Knight (Reuben Mercer), Kimberly Scott (Molly Cunningham), Angela Bassett (Martha Pentecost/Evangelist)

HEARTBREAK HOUSE by George Bernard Shaw; Director, Edward Gilbert; Set, John Conklin; Costumes, Robert Morgan; Lighting, Nicholas Cernovich. CAST: Marilyn Caskey (Ellie Dunn), Joyce Worsley (Nurse Guiness), Jonathan Farwell (Captain Shotover), Etain O'Malley (Lady Ariadne Utterword), Tanny McDonald (Hesione Hushabye), Louis Turenne (Mazzini Dunn), Jack Ryland (Hector Hushabye), William Denis (Boss Mangan), Munson Hicks (Randall Utterword), Joseph Costa (Billy Dunn)

AWAKE AND SING! by Clifford Odets; Director, Ben Levit; Set, James Leonard Joy; Costumes, Mariann Verheyen; Lighting, Frances Aronson. CAST: George Axler (Myron Berger), Lydia Bruce (Bessie Berger), Carl Don (Jacob), Marie Marshall (Hennie Berger), Jace Alexander (Ralph Berger), Joseph Costa (Schlosser), Gary Sloan (Moe Axelrod), Roger Serbagi (Uncle Morty), David Brizzolara (Sam Feinschreiber)

JUMPERS by Tom Stoppard; Director, Jacques Cartier; Set, Karl Eigsti; Costumes, John Falabella; Lighting, Toshiro Ogawa. CAST: Jonathan Farwell (George), Marianne Tatum (Dorothy), Munson Hicks (Archie), Ross Bickell (Bones), Joseph Costa (Crouch), Paula Plum (Secretary), James Bodge (Clegthorpe), Ross Clay, Michael Costa, Thomas J. Devine, Mark Pagani, Michael Pereira, Seth Riskin, Adam Rogers (Jumpers)

DIARY OF A SCOUNDREL by Alexander Ostrovsky; Adaptation, Larry Carpenter from a translation by Roberta Reeder; Director, Larry Carpenter; Set, James Leonard Joy; Costumes, Lindsay Davis; Lighting, Marcia Madeira. CAST: Jim McDonnell (Egor Dmitrich Glumov), Tamara Daniel (Glafira Klimovna Glumova), Louis Turenne (Nils Fedoseich Mamaev), Etain O'Malley (Kleopatra Lvovna Mamaeva), Humbert Allen Astredo (Krutitsky), Ron Frazier (Ivan Ivanovich Gorodulin), Jane Cronin (Sofia Ignatevna Turusina), Kathryn Meisle (Mashenka), Walter Hudson (Egor Vassilich Kurchaev), Michael Connolly (Golutvin), Avril Gentles (Manefa), Alice White (Matresha), Ingrid Sonnichsen (Lubinka), Michael Pereira (Mamaev's Servant), James Bodge (Grigory), Matthew Frederick (Krutitsky's Servant)

Gerry Goodstein Photos

Marianne Tatum, Jonathan Farwell in "Jumpers"
Above: Gary Sloan, David Brizzolara, Marie
Marshall in "Awake and Sing!"

ILLINOIS THEATRE CENTER

Park Forest, Illinois

Producing Director, Steve S. Billig; Managing Director, Etel Billig; Sets, Jonathan Roark; Costumes, Henriette Swearingen; Lighting, Richard Peterson

PRODUCTIONS & CASTS

NUTS by Tom Topor; Director, Steve S. Billig. CAST: Patty Rust, Micky Vinson, Tom Sandri, Dan McGrew, Richard H. Lynch, Etel Billig, William A. Miles, Judith McLaughlin

A DAY IN THE DEATH OF JOE EGG by Peter Nichols; Director, Peter Forster. CAST: Jim Ortlieb, Coleen Bade, Pamela Livingstone, David Massie, Etel Billig, Elizabeth Branch

MAN OF LA MANCHA with Book by Dale Wasserman; Music, Mitch Leigh; Lyrics, Joe Darion; Director, Steve S. Billig. CAST: Tom Sandri, Shelley Crosby, R. Scott Brigham, Herb Nottelmann, Cinda Moak-Forsyth, Richard H. Lynch, Rosiland Hurwitz, Steve S. Billig, Mark Donaway, Bernard Rice, Shole Milos, Anthony Cesaretti

A SENSE OF HUMOR by Ernest Thompson; Director, Steve S. Billig. CAST: John R. Tobinski, Catherine Goedert, Don McGrew, Etel Billig

KUNI-LEML with Book by Nahma Sandrow; Music, Raphael Crystal; Lyrics, Richard Engquist; Director, Maureen Kelly. CAST: Catherine Lord, Dan Le Monnier, Karen Wheeler, Anthony Cesaretti, David Rice, Steve S. Billig, Shole Milos, Richard H. Lynch

LITTLE FOOTSTEPS by Ted Tally; Director, Steve S. Billig. CAST: Patty Rust, Mark Bedard, Don McGrew, Etel Billig

HIGH KICKERS Written and Directed by Steve S. Billig. CAST: Judy McLaughlin, Carmen Severino, Diane Fishbein, Danny Musha, Lynne Magnavite, Cinda Moak-Forsyth, Kerry Egglesfield, Etel Billig, Jonathan Roark

Lloyd De Grane Photos

Elizabeth Branch, Coleen Bade, Jim Ortlieb
in "A Day in the Death of Joe Egg"

INTIMAN THEATRE COMPANY

Seattle, Washington

Managing Director, Peter Davis; Artistic Director, Elizabeth Huddle
RESIDENT COMPANY: Mark Anders, John Aylward, Kurt Beattie, Suzanne Bouchard, Megan Cole, Mark Conley, Clayton Corzatte, Barbara Dirickson, Nick Erickson, Tamu Gray, Mark Jenkins, Byron Jennings, Jo Leffingwell, Susan Ludlow, Glenn Mazen, Rikki Ricard
GUEST ARTISTS: Directors, Richard Allan Edwards, Warner Shook
PRODUCTIONS: *Man and Superman* by George Bernard Shaw, *Don Juan in Hell* by George Bernard Shaw, *The Little Foxes* by Lillian Hellman, *The Sea Horse* by Edward J. Moore, *A Doll's House* by Henrik Ibsen, *Private Lives* by Noel Coward

LONG ISLAND STAGE

Rockville Centre, New York

Artistic Director, Clinton J. Atkinson; Managing Director, Ralph J. Stalter, Jr.; Executive Director, Sally Cohen; Production Coordinator, Tom Pavelka; Press, Doris Meadows; Development, Norma Ackerman; Box Office, Jerry Smith-Niles, Carol Harvey, Angie Myers; Stage Manager, David Wahl; Directors, Norman Hall, Michael Breault, Clinton J. Atkinson; Casting, Michael Doyle Fender; Lighting, John Hickey; Sets, Daniel Conway, Daniel Ettinger, Dale F. Jordan; Costumes, Don Newcomb, Claudia Stephens, Sharon Sobel

PRODUCTIONS & CASTS

TARTUFFE by Moliere; Translation, Richard Wilbur; CAST: Peter Bartlett, K. T. Baumann, Robert Burke, David Cohn, Sally Dunn, Mary Pat Gleason, Dennis Helfend, Jim Hillgartner, Anna Lank, Conan McCarty, Jerry Smith-Niles, Scott Whipple

PAINTING CHURCHES by Tina Howe; CAST: Lili Flanders, Russell Nype, Anne Shropshire

DEATH DEFYING ACTS by Doug Haverty *(World Premiere);* CAST: Pamela Burrell, Marilyn Chris, John C. Vennema, John Wylie, Mark Zeisler, Chris Collet

ARMS AND THE MAN by George Bernard Shaw; CAST: Peter Bartlett, Harry Bennett, Debora Fuchs, Jim Hillgartner, John Jellison, Mike Kopelow, Julie Kurnitz, Celia Schaefer

TRUE WEST by Sam Shepard; CAST: Bruce Altman, Trip Hamilton, Jim Hillgartner, Rose Marie Himes

PEG O'MY HEART by J. Hartley Manners; CAST: Peter Bartlett, Jim Hillgartner, Mark Basile, Robert Curtis-Brown, Clay Guthrie, Jane Hoppe, Judith Moore, Andrea Shane, Shelley Williams

Brian Ballweg Photos

Anne Shropshire, Russell Nype in "Painting
Churches" Above: Marilyn Chris, Pamela
Burrell in "Death Defying Acts"

JOHN F. KENNEDY CENTER FOR THE PERFORMING ARTS

Washington, DC

Chairman, Roger L. Stevens; Artistic Director, Marta Istomin; Development, Richard W. Bauer; General Manager, Alan C. Wasser; Press, Laura Longley, Tiki Davies

PRODUCTIONS & CASTS

(Eisenhower Theater)

THE CAINE MUTINY COURT-MARTIAL by Herman Wouk; Director, Charlton Heston; Set, Saul Radomsky; Lighting, Martin Aronstein; Props, William Hauser; Wardrobe, Louise Allen; Company Manager, Max Woodward; Stage Managers, Joe Cappelli, Arthur P. Gaffin. CAST: Charlton Heston (Queeg), Ben Cross (Greenwald), John Corey (Maryk), Stephen Macht (Challee), Robert Rockwell Blakely), William Wright (Keefer), Karl Wiedergott (Urban), Michael Thoma (Keith), Frank Aletter (Southard), Joe George (Lundeen), Vincent Marzello (Bird), Bryan Burch-Worch (Stenographer), Loren Lester (Orderly), Members of the Court: Tony Campisi, Paul Laramore, Robert Legionaire, Mark McIntire, Henry Sutton, Ben Wilson

(Terrace Theater)

AJAX adapted from Sophocles by Robert Auletta, and
THE BOB HOPE WAR ZONE SPECIAL by George Trow; Director, Peter Sellars; Sets, George Tsypin; Costumes, Dunya Ramicova; Lighting, James F. Ingalls; Sound, Bruce Odland; Stage Manager, Keri Muir; Presented by American National Theater (Peter Sellars, Director; Elizabeth LeCompte, Timothy S. Mayer, Associate Directors). CAST: Charles Brown, Ben Halley, Jr., Mark Lutz, Warren Manzi, Khin-Kyaw Maung, Aleta Mitchell, Howie Seago, Lauren Tom, Samm-Art Williams

(Opera House)

CAROUSEL by Richard Rodgers, Oscar Hammerstein II; Director, James Hammerstein; Choreography, Peter Martins; Scenery, Michael Yeargan; Costumes, Jane Greenwood; Lighting, Thomas Skelton; Music Director, John Mauceri; Sound, Tony Meola; Company Manager, Beth Riedman; Production Manager, John H. Paull II; Stage Managers, John J. Bonanni, Bill Braden, Fredric Hanson. CAST: Faith Prince (Carrie), Katharine Buffaloe (Julie), Judith Roberts (Mrs. Mullin), Tom Wopat (Billy), Michael Howell Deane (Policeman), Frank Borgman (David), Judith Farris (Nettie), Michael DeVries (Enoch), John Spencer (Jigger), Mark McVey (Captain), Harry Nordyke (Heavenly Friend), Milo O'Shea (Starkeeper), Barbara Britton (Louise), Tom Condon (Carnival Boy), John Curtis-Michael (Enoch, Jr.), Suzanna Guzman (Principal)

(Eisenhower Theater)

SHOUT UP A MORNING with Music by Julian and Nathaniel Adderley; Lyrics, Diane Charlotte Lampert; Book, Paul Avila Mayer, George W. George; Based on libretto and Lyrics by Peter Farrow; Director, Des McAnuff; Choreography, Dianne Ruth McIntyre; Musical Direction/Vocal Arrangements, Charles H. Coleman; Sets, John Arnone; Costumes, Susan Denison; Lighting, Richard Riddell; Sound, John Kilgore; Stage Managers, Bonnie Panson, Chris Fielder, Linda Fane. CAST: Nick LaTour, Stuart K. Robinson, Leila Danette, Edwin Battle, Charlaine Woodard, Aja Graydon, Michael Leslie, Ellia English, Rolita White, Lisa Willoughby, Tony Floyd, Cheryl Freeman, DeMarco Boone, Demitri Maurice Corbin, Andrea Griffith, Leah Maddrie, George Morton III, Ronn K. Smith, Mary Bond Davis, Leilani Jones, Stewart F. Wilson-Turner, Michael Edward-Stevens, George McDaniel, William Youmans, Michael Champion, Gordon Paddison, Thomas Mills Wood, Jeff Sugarman, Reed C. Martin

(Theater Lab)

TWO FIGURES IN DENSE VIOLET LIGHT directed by Peter Sellars; Performed by Richard Thomas and David Warrilow. Program: *Ohio Impromptu* by Samuel Beckett, *Tsunemasa* translated from a Noh play by Ezra Pound, *Angel Surrounded by Paysans* by Wallace Stevens.

(Eisenhower Theater)

QUEENIE PIE adapted from an original story by Duke Ellington; Music, Duke Ellington; Production Coordinator, Mercer Ellington; Libretto, George C. Wolfe; Lyrics, George David Weiss, Duke Ellington; Musical Adaptation/Development, Maurice Peress; Direction and Choreography, Garth Fagan; Set, David Mitchell, Romare Bearden; Costumes, Eduardo Sicangco; Lighting, Ken Billington; Sound, Jerry L. O'Brate; Music Director, Maurice Peress; Wigs/Makeup, Dennis Bergevin, Jeffrey Frank; Company Manager, Harriet D. Kittner; Stage Managers, Deborah Clelland, Carol S. Cleveland. CAST: Teresa Burrell, Larry Marshall, Patty Holley, Wendell Pierce, Ken Prymus, Marion J. Caffey, Tina Fabrique, Milt Grayson, Andre Montgomery, Denise Morgan, Melodee Savage, Ennis Smith, Lillias White, Laurie Williamson

(Eisenhower Theater)

A RAISIN IN THE SUN by Lorraine Hansberry; Director, Harold Scott; General Manager, Ellen Richard. CAST: Esther Rolle, DelRoy Lindo, Starletta DuPois, Lou Ferguson, Stephen Henderson, Kimble Joyner, Joseph C. Phillips, Kim Yancey, John Fiedler

**Right Center: George Grizzard, Marilyn Cooper,
Stephen Pearlman in "The Perfect Party" Above:
Larry Marshall, Teresa Burrell in "Queenie Pie"
Top: Charlton Heston, Ben Cross in "The Caine Mutiny Court-Martial"**

(Eisenhower Theater)
THE PERFECT PARTY by A. R. Gurney, Jr.; Director, John Tillinger; Set, Steven Rubin; Costumes, Jane Greenwood; Lighting, Mark Stanley; Production Supervisor, Steven McCorkle; Company Manager, Max Woodward; Stage Managers, Barbara Mae Phillips, Les Kniskern. CAST: George Grizzard (Tony), Elizabeth Ashley (Lois), Margo Skinner (Sally), Stephen Pearlman (Wes), Marilyn Cooper (Wilma)

(Opera House)
LES MISERABLES see Broadway Calendar.

(Eisenhower Theater)
CITIZEN TOM PAINE by Howard Fast; Director, James Simpson; Set, James Sandefur; Costumes, Dunya Ramicova; Lighting, James F. Ingalls; Sound, Charles Cohen; Stage Manager, Mary Porter Hall. CAST: Richard Thomas (Tom Paine), Gary Brownlee, Terence Cranendonk, Kristin Flanders, Zach Grenier, Allison Janney, Daniel Jenkins, Nicholas Kepros, Brian McCue, Stephen Pelinski, Michael Sgouros, Tom Teti, Damian Young

(Eisenhower Theater)
OPERA COMIQUE written and directed by Nagle Jackson; Set, Ben Edwards; Costumes, Jane Greenwood; Lighting, Thomas R. Skelton; Stage Managers, Beverley Randolph, Clifford Schwartz. CAST: Anne Jackson (Odile), Richard B. Shull (M. de la Corniche), Charlotte Moore, (Mme. de la Corniche), Randall Edwards (La Tartine), Susan Diol (Viviane), Charles Keating (Georges Bizet), Ian Stuart (Ernest Guiraud), Eli Wallach (M. Paul Vigneron), Anthony Fusco (Hector Vigneron), Brian Bedford (Charles Gounod), Scott Miller, William Denis, June Ballinger, Elizabeth Dennehy

Joan Marcus Photos

169

LONG WHARF THEATRE

New Haven, Connecticut
Twenty-second Season

Artistic Director, Arvin Brown; Executive Director, M. Edgar Rosenblum; Literary Consultant, John Tillinger; Associate Artistic Director, Kenneth Frankel; General Manager, John K. Conte; Development, Kathryn Champlin; Lighting, Ronald Wallace; Technical Director, Gary Field; Props, David Fletcher, Brian Gerrity; Wardrobe, Margaret L. Normand, Maggie Morgan; Press, David Mayhew, David Shimchick

PRODUCTIONS & CASTS

ALL MY SONS by Arthur Miller; Director, Arvin Brown; Set, Hugh Landwehr; Costumes, Bill Walker; Stage Manager, Anne Keefe. CAST: Dan Desmond (Dr. Bayliss), Ralph Waite (Joe Keller), Stephen Root (Frank Lubey), Carol Androsky (Sue Bayliss), Dawn Didawick (Lydia Lubey), Jamey Sheridan (Chris Keller), Nicholas Tamarkind (Bert), Joyce Ebert (Kate Keller), Frances McDormand (Ann Deever), Christopher Curry (George Deever).
CAMILLE by Pam Gems; *American Premiere;* Director, Ron Daniels; Set, Ming Cho Lee; Costumes, Jess Goldstein; Dance/Movement, Wesley Fata; Wigs/Hairstyles, Paul Huntley; Stage Manager, Beverly J. Andreozzi. CAST: Ramy Zada (Armand), Sascha von Schoeler (Prudence), Kit Lefever (Clemence), Janet Hubert (Sophie), William Swetland (M. le Duc), David Pierce (Count Druftheim), Kathleen Turner (Marguerite Gautier), Gina Gershon (Janine/Olympe), Brendan Bloom/Mark Gentile (Jean-Paul), Christie McGinn (Yvette), Rex Robbins (Marquis de Saint-Brieux), David Jaffe (M. de Sancerre/Russian Prince), Jono Gero (Pierre/Appraiser), David Shimchick, Nick Sandys (Footmen), James Gemmell (Pianist).
SELF DEFENSE by Joe Cacaci; *World Premiere;* Director, Arvin Brown; Set, Marjorie Bradley Kellogg; Costumes, Bill Walker; Stage Manager, Anne Keefe. CAST: Steven Marcus (Ronnie), Michael Wikes (Mickey), Lewis Black (Eddie), Kevin O'Rourke (Edgar), Lee Wallace (Phil), Kevin DeCapri (Mark), Brian Smiar (Gerald), Jose Santana (Julio), Julia Newton (Deborah).
DALLIANCE a new version of Arthur Schnitzler's "Liebelei" by Tom Stoppard; Director, Kenneth Frankel; Set, John Conklin; Costumes, David Murin; Lighting, Pat Collins; Orchestrations, Brent Paul Evans; Stage Manager, Beverly J. Andreozzi. CAST: Kerry Armstrong (Christine), Barbara Bryne (Frau Binder), Catherine Butterfield (A Soprano), George Guidall (Herr Weiring), Lucinda Jenney (Mizi), Seth Jones (Servant/Tenor), Scott Kanoff (Stage Manager), Campbell Scott (Fritz), Ian Stuart (A Gentleman), Stanley Tucci (Theodore), James Abbruscato, Richard Grasso, Brian Gerrity, William Nesta, Ron Papale, Stephen Skridulis, Michael Yardley.
THE TENDER LAND with Music by Aaron Copland; Libretto, Horace Everett; Transcribed for chamber ensemble by Murry Sidlin; Director, Arvin Brown; Musical Direction, Murry Sidlin; Choreography, David Bell; Set, Michael H. Yeargan; Costumes, David Murin; Stage Manager, Anne Keefe. CAST: Jamie Louise Baer (Laurie), Dan Entriken (Mr. Splinters), Helen Frank (Party Guest), Vaughn Fritts (Mr. Jenks), Paul Geraci (Guest), Kristen Hurst-Hyde (Ma Moss), James Javore (Top), Bruce Kramer (Grampa), Tony Lillo (Guest), Stephanie Samaras (Mrs. Splinters), Craig Schulman (Martin), Sally Stevens (Mrs. Jenks), Ed Tyler (Guest), April Beth Armstrong/Rebecca Hanson (Beth).
PROGRESS by Doug Lucie; *American Premiere;* Director, John Tillinger; Set, David Jenkins; Costumes, Jess Goldstein; Stage Manager, Robin Kevrick. CAST: Lisa Banes (Ronee), David Purdham (Will), Tony Shalhoub (Mark), Brita Youngblood (Ange), Don Harvey (Lenny), Stephen Bogardus (Bruce), Jack Gilpin (Oliver), David Hunt (Martin).
PAINTING CHURCHES by Tina Howe; Director, David Trainer; Costumes, David Murin; Set, James Noone; Lighting, Mimi Jordan Sherin; Stage Manager, Robin Kevrick. CAST: Dorothea Hammond (Fanny Church), William Swetland (Gardner Church), Ann McDonough (Margaret Church).
DUSE DIED IN PITTSBURGH by Paul Vincent; Director, Josephine R. Abady; Set, Hugh Landwehr; Stage Manager, Ellen Schafroth. CAST: Joyce Ebert (Kate), Laurie Kennedy (Betsy).
MEN IN THE KITCHEN by Loren-Paul Caplin; Director, Kenneth Frankel; Set, Hugh Landwehr; Lighting, Steven Rust; Sound, Brent Paul Evans; Stage Manager, Robin Kevrick. CAST: Michael Zaslow (Johnathon), Josh Mostel (C.K.), Ron Frazier (Hilly), Mark Metcalf (Zack), Barbara Garrick (Theresa), Kelly Wolf (Melody).
THE TRAVELLING SQUIRREL by Robert Lord; Director, John Tillinger; Script Development, Margaret Van Sant; Set, Hugh Landwehr; Lighting, Steven Rust; Stage Manager, Ellen Schafroth. CAST: John Driver (Bart), Priscilla Shanks (Jane), Breon Gorman (Julie), Dennis Bailey (Terry), Brian Starcher (Daryl), Nicholas Martin (Wally), Joyce Reehling (Sarah).
WHEN IT'S OVER by Eduardo Machado, Geraldine Sherman; Director, Margaret Van Sant; Stage Manager, Ellen Schafroth. CAST: Glynnis O'Connor (Eva), Matthew Penn (Kurt), John Shepard (Peter), George Taylor, Jennifer Williams, Jan Leslie Harding, Tom Spackman, Kevin Donovan, Ginger Donelson, Shelley Stenhouse, James Sterling

T. Charles Erickson Photos

Top Right: Kathleen Turner, Ramy Zada in "Camille"
Below: Brian Smiar, Michael Wikes in "Self Defense"

Tony Shalhoub, Jack Gilpin in "Progress" Above:
Craig Schulman, Jamie Louise Baer, James Javore
in "The Tender Land"

LOS ANGELES THEATRE CENTER

Los Angeles, California
Third Season

Artistic Producing Director, Bill Bushnell; Producer, Diane White; Consulting Director, Alan Mandell; Design, Timian Alsaker; Sound, Jon Gottlieb; Associate Director/Playwright in Residence, Robert Harders; Set/Lighting, Russell Pyle; Casting, Ronnie Yeskel; Dramaturg, Halldis Hoass; Literary Manager, Mame Hunt; Technical Director, David MacMurtry; Production Supervisor, Donald David Hill; Company Manager, Charles McEwan; Wardrobe, Gina Lucas; General Manager, Carol Baker Tharp; Development, Kathy Pontera; Stage Managers, Lee Alan Byron, Jill Johnson, Maria Schmidt, Joan Toggenburger; Press, Constance Harvey, Kimberly Maxwell, Tom Nixon, Paula Svetlecich.

PRODUCTIONS & CASTS
ALL MY SONS by Arthur Miller; Director, Bill Bushnell; Set, D. Martyn Bookwalter; Lighting, Tom Ruzika; Costumes, Marianna Elliott; Sound, Jon Gottlieb. CAST: Jim Jansen, Philip Baker Hall, Jon Menick, Sheila Shaw, Ruth de Sosa, Bill Pullman, Eric Ratican, Nan Martin, Julie Fulton, Gregory Wagrowski
COMPANY by Samuel Beckett; Director, S. E. Gontarski; Set/Lights/Costume, Timian Alsaker; Sound, Jon Gottlieb. CAST: Alan Mandell (The Figure)
SPAIN '36 by the San Francisco Mime Troupe; Script, Joan Holden; Director, Daniel Chumley; Music/Lyrics, Bruce Barthol/Edward Barnes; Musical Director, Edward Barnes; Choreography, Kimi Okada; Mime/Mask Movement, Leonard Pitt; Set/Lights/Costumes, Timian Alsaker; Production Manager, Stacie Powers. CAST: Wilma Bonet, Charles Degelman, Arthur Holden, Gustave Johnson, Jerry Kerrigan, Ed Levey, Kate Lindsey, Sharon Lockwood, Barrett A. Nelson, Muziki Duane Roberson, Eduardo Robledo, Phillip Ray Rolfe, Joe Romano, Maura Sandoval, Audrey Ann Smith, Leonard L. Thomas, Deanar Ali Young
TARTUFFE by Moliere; Director, Robert W. Goldsby; Set, Karl Eigsti; Costumes/Hair/Makeup, Nicole Morin; Lighting, Toshiro Ogawa; Music, Robert MacDougall. CAST: Rhoda Gemignani, Bonita Friedericy, Jessica Walter, Madge Sinclair, Danny Scheie, Jennifer Tilly, Len Birman, Tom Rosqui, Jeffrey Alan Chandler, Ron Leibman, Basil Langton, Fredric Lehne, Bill Kohne, Matthew Shields
BARABBAS by Michel de Ghelderode; Translated by George Hauger; Director, Stein Winge; Set/Lights/Costumes, Timian Alsaker; Music, Ketil Hvoslef; Assistant Director, Jose Luis Valenzuela. CAST: Bill Pullman, Gerald Hiken, Tim Russ, Cameron Thor, Ron Campbell, Bruce Rodgers-Wright, Anthony Geary, Susan Peretz, Ann Hearn, Stephen Tobolowsky, Kari Faale
EYES OF THE AMERICAN by Samm-Art Williams; Director, Edmund J. Cambridge; Set/Lighting, Russell Pyle; Costumes, Nicole Morin; Sound, Stephen Shaffer. CAST: Carl W. Lumbly, Kashka, Glynn Turman, Henry G. Sanders, Janet MacLachlan, Juanita Jennings
ALPHA by Slawomir Mrozek; Translation, Jacek Laskowski; Director, Robert W. Goldsby; Set/Lights/Costumes, Timian Alsaker. CAST: Aharon Ipale, Franklyn Seales, John Shuman, Carol Rossen, Rhonda Aldrich, Ford Rainey, Mark Rosenblatt
HAPPY DAYS by Samuel Beckett; Director, Alan Mandell; Set/Costume, Timian Alsaker; Lighting, Todd Jared. CAST: Barbara Bain/Angela Paton (Winnie), Martin Beck (Willie)
TAMER OF HORSES by William Mastrosimone; Director, Bill Bushnell; Set/Lighting, D. Martyn Bookwalter; Costumes, Christine Lewis Hover; Assistant Director, M. Neema Barnette. CAST: Joe Morton (Ty Fletcher), Lynn Whitfield (Georgiane), Esai Morales (Hector)
ALFRED AND VICTORIA: A LIFE by Donald Freed; Director, Gerald Hiken; Set, Clifton R. Welch; Lighting, Douglas D. Smith; Costumes, Jill Brousard. CAST: Dinah Manoff (Victoria), Philipa Baker Hall (Alfred)
THE IMPORTANCE OF BEING EARNEST by Oscar Wilde; Director, Charles Marowitz; Set, A. Clark Duncan; Lighting, Martin Aronstein; Costumes, Noel Taylor; Music Arranged by Charles MacKerras. CAST: Jim Piddock, Jonathan Schmock, Gene Ross, Richard Merson, Gary Heilsberg, Diana Chesney, Maria Mayenzet, Jane Windsor, Lucy Lee Flippin
FOOLIN' AROUND WITH INFINITY by Steven Dietz; Director, Bill Bushnell; Set/Lights, Russell Pyle; Costumes, Christine Lewis Hover. CAST: Nick Scarmack, Karen Kondazian, Suzann Calvert, Gregory Wagrowski, Robert Darnell, Budge Threlkeld
COME BACK, LITTLE SHEBA by William Inge; Director, Ray Danton; Set/Lighting, D. Martyn Bookwalter; Costumes, Shigeru Yaji. CAST: Charles Hallahan (Doc), Jami Gertz (Marie), Tyne Daly (Lola), Michael McGrady, Robert Snively, Anne Gee Byrd, Steven Barr, David S. Franklin, Bradley White, Hoke Howell, Al Rossi, Budge Threlkeld

**Right Center: Gerald Hiken, Dinah Manoff
in "Alfred & Victoria" Above: Jessica Walter,
Ron Leibman in "Tartuffe" Top: Philip Baker Hall, Nan Martin,
Bill Pullman, Julie Fulton in "All My Sons"**

THE STICKWIFE by Darrah Cloud; Director, Roberta Levitow; Set/Lights/Costumes, Pavel M. Dobrusky. CAST: Gene Ross, Anne Gee Byrd, Chris Weatherhead, Larry Drake, Camilla Carr, Richard Dean
THE GLASS MENAGERIE by Tennessee Williams; Director, Stein Winge; Set, Timian Alsaker; Lighting, Stephen Bennett; Costumes, Noel Taylor; Original Music, Thomas Pasatieri; Assistant Director, Jose Luis Valenzuela. CAST: Anthony Geary (Son), Joan Hotchkis (Mother), Ann Hearn (Daughter), Stephen Tobolowsky (Gentleman Caller)
THE FILM SOCIETY by Jon Robin Baitz; Director, Robert Egan; Set, D. Martyn Bookwalter; Lighting, Martin Aronstein; Costumes, Robert Blackman; Original Music, Daniel Birnbaum; Stage Manager, James T. McDermott. CAST: Daniel Davis, Anne Twomey, Marrian Walters, William Glover, Henry Woronicz, Alan Mandell
LA VICTIMA by El Teatro de la Esperanza; Director, Jose Luis Valenzuela; Set/Lights/Costumes, Jose de Santiago; Original Music, Marcos Loya; Choreography, Tamara Hurwitz Pullman. CAST: J. Edmundo Araiza, Christine Avila, E. J. Castillo, Evelina Fernandez, Abel Franco, Jacinto Guevara, Marcos Loya, Benita Martinez, Lupe Ontiveros, Jesse J. Rangel, Jr., Peter Schreiner

MARRIOTT'S LINCOLNSHIRE THEATRE

Lincolnshire, Illinois

Producer, Kary M. Walker; Artistic Director, Dyanne K. Earley; Marketing, Peter R. Grigsby; Musical Director, Kevin Stites; Stage Manager, Michael Hendricks; Sound, Randy Allen Johns; Costumes, Nancy Missimi.

PRODUCTIONS & CASTS

THE KING AND I with Music by Richard Rodgers; Book and Lyrics, Oscar Hammerstein II; Director, Dominic Missimi; Choreographer, Michelle Kelly; Set, Thomas M. Ryan; Lighting, John Williams. CAST: Ray Frewen (King), Mary Ernster (Anna), Neil Friedman (Kralahome), Ann Arvia (Lady Thiang), Kurt Johns (Lun Tha), Susan Moniz (Tuptim), Michael Dean Wise (Captain Orton/Sir Edward Ramsay), Todd Schmarak (Louis), Gordon Schmidt (Interpreter), David Lundholm (Chululongkorn), Michelle Nguyen, Michelle Kelly, Tina DeLeone, Peter Anderson, Carol Kuykendall, Michael Bartsch, Randi Stavins, Robyn Peterman, Karen Rahn, Andrew Lupp, Deidre Dolan, Dana Sweeney, Jen Cornelius, Mia Cornelius, Mat Cornelius, John Barry, Paul Barry, Lania Ho, Mary Lisa Rhodes.
THE WIZ Director/Choreographer, David H. Bell; Set, John H. Doepp; Lighting, John Williams. CAST: Susan Moniz (Dorothy), Kenny Ingram (Scarecrow), Michael Lynch (Tinman), Stephen Finch (Lion), Felicia Caldwell (Aunt Em/Glinda), Marshall Titus (Uncle Henry/The Wiz), E. Faye Butler (Addaperle/Evillene), Tim Roberts, Cheridah Best, Charlie Misovye, Andrew Lupp, Everett Gibson, Gregory V. Puckett, Alton White, Tina DeLeone, Michelle Kelly, Marc Robin.
1776 Director, Dominic Missimi; Set, Thomas M. Ryan; Lighting, Diane Ferry Williams. CAST: Roger Mueller (John Adams), Peter Van Wagner, Craig Bennett, Bob Zrna, David Perkovich, Dan Frick, Kurt R. Hanen, Peter Pohlhammer, Richard Henzel, Joe Van Slyke, Art Manke, James Otis, Philip Courington, David Rice, Fred Zimmerman, Don Forston, Tom Galantich, Michael Stevenson, Kurt Johns, Michael Dean Wise, Jim Harms, Ron Keaton, Mary Ernster, Kathy Santen, Rick Boynton.

Tom Maday Photos

Top Right: (L) Mary Ernster (c) in "The King and I"
(R) Susan Moniz in "The Wiz"

Michele Farr, Barry Boys in "Uncle Vanya"
Above: Wanda Bimson, Richard Leighton
in "Napoleon Nightdreams"

McCARTER THEATRE

Princeton, New Jersey

Artistic Director, Nagle Jackson; Managing Director, Alison Harris; Special Programming, W. W. Lockwood, Jr.; Associate Artistic Director, Robert Lanchester; Assistant to the Directors, Megan Miller-Shields; Outreach, Sandra Moskovitz; Business Manager, Timothy J. Shields; Development, Pamela Vevers Sherin; Communications/Graphics, Mary Ellen Schilling; Press, Jamie Saxon; Administrative Director, Laurence Capo; Production Manager, John Herochik; Stage Managers, Jeanne Anich Stives, Peter Cook, C. Townsend Olcott II, Sarah E. Donnelly; Technical Director, David R. York; Sound, Stephen Smith

PRODUCTIONS & CASTS

OUR TOWN by Thornton Wilder; Director, Nagle Jackson; Set, Daniel Boylen; Costumes, Elizabeth Covey; Lighting, F. Mitchell Dana; Choir Director, Janet Peters; Organist, Jean Peters; Dialect Coach, Gordon Jacoby. CAST: George Ede (Stage Manager), Karl Light (Dr. Gibbs), Rick Lawless (Joe Crowell), Greg Thornton (Howie Newsome), Ruth Schudson (Mrs. Gibbs), Liz Fillo (Mrs. Webb), Don Spalding (George Gibbs), Jennifer Rosen (Rebecca Gibbs), Kyle O'Donnell (Wally Webb), Anne Kerry Ford (Emily Webb), Laurence Capo (Prof. Willard), Jay Doyle (Mr. Webb), Deborah Culpin (Woman), Henson Keys (Simon Stimson), Anne Sheldon (Mr. Soames), Jeff Brooks (Constable Warren), Rick Lawless (Si Crowell), Mark A. Brown, Jack Murdock (Joe Stoddard)
LITTLE MURDERS by Jules Feiffer; Director, Paul Weidner; Set, Daniel Boylen; Costumes, Elizabeth Covey; Lighting F. Mitchell Dana; CAST: Ruth Schudson (Marjorie), Rick Lawless (Kenny), Jack Murdock (Carol), Leslie Geraci (Patsy), Michael O'Hare (Alfred Chamberlain), Mark A. Brown, Deborah Culpin, Jay Doyle, Karl Light, Rebecca Rhodes, Anne Sheldon, Don Spalding, Greg Thornton (Wedding Guests), Henson Keys (Rev. Henry Dupas), Jeff Brooks (Lt. Miles Practice)
A CHRISTMAS CAROL by Charles Dickens; Adaptation/Director, Nagle Jackson; Costumes, Elizabeth Covey; Lighting, Richard Moore; Music, Larry Delinger; Choreography, Nancy Thiel; Sound, Rob Gorton; Set, Brian Martin; Wigs, Denise O'Brien. CAST: Robert Lanchester (Scrooge), Greg Thornton, Barry Boys, Michael Early, Don Spalding, Henson Keys, Mary Martello, Mark Brown, Jane Jones, George Ede, Isiah Whitlock, Deborah Jeanne Culpin, Veronique Gusdon, Mark Zaki, Cara MacAdam, Craig O'Donnell, Randy Lilly, Cynthia Martells, Najah T. Mas'udi, Katherine M. Edini, Brian Lanchester, Alexandra Johnston, William Dean, Matthew Chen, Jay Doyle, Margaret Brower, Leonard Elliott, Martin Hilson, Kurt Penney, Rebecca Rhodes
DEBUT by Bruce E. Rodgers; *World Premiere;* Director, Robert Lanchester; Set/Lighting, Don Ehman; Costumes, Barb Taylorr; Scott G. Miller (Jimmy Gray), Basil Wallace (Grunt), Sally Chamberlin (Evelyn Gray), Richard Leighton (Buck Gray), Mary Martello (Rachel)
DON'T TRIFLE WITH LOVE by Alfred de Musset; Translation/Director, Nagle Jackson; *American Professional Premiere;* Costumes, Elizabeth Covey; Lighting, F. Mitchell Dana; Set, Pavel M. Dobrusky; Assistant Director, Colette Berge. CAST: Barry Boys (Chorus), Jay Doyle (Baron), Eric Conger (Perdican), Henson Keys (Master Blazius), Richard Leighton (Master Bridaine), Michelle Farr (Camille), Kimberly King (Dame Pluche), Ann Tsuji (Rosette), Randy Lilly (Messenger), Martin Hilson, Zoran Kovcic
NAPOLEON NIGHTDREAMS by James McLure; *World Premiere;* Director, Nagle Jackson; Costumes, Elizabeth Covey; Lighting, F. Mitchell Dana; Set, Pavel M. Dobrusky; Composer, Robert Sprayberry; Assistant Director, Colette Berge. CAST: Wanda Bimson (Josephine), Barry Boys (Lawyer), Jay Doyle (Architect), Henson Keys (Sleeping Man), Kimberly King (Spider Woman), Rob Lanchester (Francois), Richard Leighton (Napoleon), Randy Lilly (Gascon), Gary Roberts (Duroc), Ann Tsuji (Boy)
UNCLE VANYA by Anton Chekhov; Translation, Michael Henry Heim; Director, Georgi Tovstonogov; Set/Costumes, Eduard Kochergin; Lighting, F. Mitchell Dana. CAST: Ruth Schudson (Marina), Barry Boys (Astrov/Mikhail Lvovich), Robert Lanchester (Voinitsky/Ivan Petrovich:Uncle Vanya), Jay Doyle (Serebryakov/Alexander Vladimirovich), Michele Farr (Yelena Andreevna), Stacy Ray (Sofya Alexandrovna), Edmund Davys (Telegin/Ilya Ilyich), Anne Sheldon (Voinitskaya/Maria Vasilyevna), Mark Brown (Watchman/Laborer)

Andrea Kane Photos

MEADOW BROOK THEATRE

Rochester Michigan

Artistic/General Director, Terence Kilburn; Assistant to General Director/Tour Director, James Spittle; Directors, Terence Kilburn, Charles Nolte, Carl Schurr, Arthur Beer; Sets, Peter W. Hicks, Greg Utech, Barry Griffith; Lighting, Reid Johnson, Daniel Jaffe; Stage Managers, Terry W. Carpenter, Robert Herrle; Technical Directors, Daniel Jaffe, Thomas Kirchner; Scenic Artists, Elaine Sutherland, Judith Irwin; Sound, Tony Vaillancourt; Costume Coordinator, Mary Lynn Bonnell; Wardrobe, Paula Kalevas; Props, Mary Chmelko-Jaffe, Kathleen Holland, William Young; Set Technicians, Bradley Burke, Neil Patterson

PRODUCTIONS & CASTS

RICHARD III with Gregg Almquist, Jeanne Arnold, Loren Bass, Jeff Dolan, David Fox, Thom Haneline, Paul Hopper, Thomas Mahard, Nelson Phillips, Glen Allen Pruett, Juliet Randall, Joseph Reed, Tom Spackman, Peter Gregory Thomson, David Turrentine, Dona Werner, Paul Amadio, Brad Burke, Steven Hendershott, Buckner Gibbs, Duncan Hursley, Dandi Litt, Eric Nelsen, Neil Patterson, Geoff Safron, Tom Suda, Jeanne Taylor, Don Weingust, Tom Whalen, John Swain, Heidi Guthrie
FOXFIRE with Arthur Beer, Mary Fogarty, Paul Hopper, Thomas Mahard, Joseph Reed, Dona Werner
A CHRISTMAS CAROL with Mary Bremer, Bethany Carpenter, Booth Colman, Thom Haneline, Paul Hopper, Phillip Locker, Thomas Mahard, Wayne David Parker, Glen Allen Pruett, Joseph Reed, Mar Riehl, Peter Gregory Thomson, Sandi Litt, Ron Melnik, Melanie Carpenter, Heidi Guthrie, Steve Hendershott, Luke Huber, Sarah Huber, Katie Kenny, Terry Hunt, Chris Kindred, Jim Marino, Dan Montgomery, Eric Nelsen, D. A. Parker, Rebekka Parker, Heather Reed, Kevin Skiles, Mary Rychlewski, Cheryl Zeese
THE ROSE TATTOO with Mary Bremer, Bethany Carpenter, Divina Cook, Roy K. Dennison, Jayne Houdyshell, Henry Jordan, Shirleyann Kaladjian, Phillip Locker, Evelyn Orbach, Mar Riehl, Peggy Thorp, Tyne Turner, David Turrentine, Cheryl Williams, Sandi Litt, Jeanne Taylor
A FLEA IN HER EAR with James Anthony, Brigid Cleary, Paul DeBoy, Jayne Houdyshell, Henry Jordan, Phillip Locker, Wil Love, Joseph Reed, Sherry Skinker, Robert Spencer, Tyne Turner, Cheryl Williams, Ted Moniak, Thomas Suda, Buckner Gibbs, Tracy Gibson, Melanie Hansen, Paula Kalevas, Neil J. Patterson, Michael Warren
PACK OF LIES with Jeanne Arnold, Arthur Beer, Jayne Houdyshell, Shirleyann Kaladjian, Wil Love, Jane Lowry, Carl Schurr, Tyne Turner
PLAY IT AGAIN, SAM with James Anthony, Brigid Cleary, Robert Grossman, Loretta Higgins, Paul Hopper, William Kux, Judi Mann, Leslie Lynn Meeker, Tyne Turner
GO BACK FOR MURDER with Gary Andrews, James Anthony, Bethany Carpenter, Roy K. Dennison, George Gitto, Robert Grossman, Paul Hopper, Jillian Lindig, Peter Gregory Thomson, Tyne Turner, Dona Werner
MASS APPEAL with Arthur Beer, Joey L. Golden

Richard Hunt Photos

Jeanne Arnold, Carl Schurr, Jane Lowry
in "Pack of Lies" Top: Mary Fogarty, Dona
Werner, Paul Hopper, Arthur Beer in "Foxfire"

MERRIMACK REPERTORY THEATRE

Lowell, Massachusetts

Producing Director, Daniel L. Schay; Associate Director, Richard Rose; Administrative Director, Helene Desjarlais; Marketing/Development, Keith E. Stevens; Business Manager, Jacqueline A. Normand; Company Manager, Martha Domine; Stage Managers, Hazel Youngs, Robert Welch, Margaret J. Funk; Costumes, Amanda Aldridge; Costume Design Assistant, Joan St. Germain; Lighting, John Ambrosone; Electrician/Sound, Arlene J. Grabowski; Props, Gregg Watts; Casting, Jay Binder/ Elissa Myers, Mark Teschner

PRODUCTIONS & CASTS

THE FOREIGNER by Larry Shue; Director, Daniel L. Schay; Set, Alison Ford. CAST: Brad Bellamy, Paul Dunn, Leslie Hicks, Lance Lewman, Will Osborne, William Perley, Billie Lou Watt
A CHRISTMAS CAROL by Charles Dickens; Adaptation, Larry Carpenter; Director, Thomas Clewell; Set, Leslie Taylor; Lighting, David "Sparky" Lockner, John Ambrosone. CAST: Robin Chadwick, Pat Dougan, Tim Howard, Gary-Thomas Keating, Richard Maynard, Tammy Richards, Daniel L. Schay, Alice White, Willie Ames, Robert Bryan, Kim Courchaine, Albert Daudelin, Allistair Former, John Griffith, Sonya Halvorsen, Larry Veino, Casandra Wetherbee, Tina Woodland
THE ADDING MACHINE by Elmer L. Rice; Director, Richard Rose; Set, Jeff Schneider; Costumes, Gary English; Lighting, Kendall Smith; Sound, John Bowen. CAST: Dion Anderson, Cynthia Barbak, Aida Berlyn, Matthew Locricchio, Matt Penn
FIRST NIGHT by Jack Neary; Director, Joan Courtney Murray; Set, Leslie Taylor. CAST: John Hickok, Judith Yerby
THE HOSTAGE by Brendan Behan; Director, Daniel L. Schay; Co-Director, Nora Hussey; Set, Gary English; Costumes, Joan St. Germain; Lighting, Sid Bennett. CAST: Kevin Belanger, Leslie Bennett, Maureen Clarke, Leonard Corman, Paul Everett, Kevin Fennessy, Dorothy Gallagher, James Hilbrandt, Katherine Hiler, James Mullen, Mil Nicholson, Ed Peed, Cathy Rand, Timothy Scranton, Christopher Shaw
THE IMPORTANCE OF BEING EARNEST by Oscar Wilde; Director, Richard Rose; Set, Dale F. Jordan. CAST: Kevin Black, Stephanie Clayman, Curzon Dobell, Gary-Thomas Keating, John Milligan, Dee Nelson, M. Lynda Robinson, Alice White

Kevin Harkins Photos

John Hickok, Judith Yerby in "First Night"
Above: Cynthia Babak, Aida Berlyn, Matthew Locricchio
in "The Adding Machine"

MISSOURI REPERTORY THEATRE

Kansas City, Missouri

Executive Director, James D. Costin; Artistic Director, George Keathley; Managing Director, Daniel P. Baker; Production Manager, Ronald Schaeffer; Press, Rendall Himes; Dramaturg, Felicia Hardison Londre; Marketing, Barbara Haviland; Business Manager, Robert L. Thatch; Technical Director, Bruce Bacon; Sets, John Ezell; Costumes, Vincent Scassellati; Lighting, Joseph Appelt; Sound, Tom Mardikes; Stage Managers, Susan Rae Greve, J. F. Mitchell

PRODUCTIONS & CASTS

BRIGHTON BEACH MEMOIRS by Neil Simon; Director, George Keathley; Set, Harry Feiner; Costumes, Baker S. Smith; Music, Larry Bailey. CAST: Doug Hutchison (Eugene), Sonja Lanzener (Blanche), Nicola Sheara (Kate), Lori Andresky (Laurie), Susan Diol (Nora), Dan Eisenhower (Stanley), Richard Halverson (Jack)
EQUUS by Peter Shaffer; Director, George Keathley; Set, Harry Feiner; Lighting, James F. Ingalls; Music, Greg Mackender; Choreographer, Jennifer Martin. CAST: David McCallum (Martin Dysart), Christopher Cull (Alan Strang), Nora Denney (Nurse), Merle Moores (Hester Salomon), Jim Birdsall (Frank Strang), Mary Jane Wells (Dora Strang), Martin Coles (Horseman/Nugget), Gary Neal Johnson (Harry Dalton), Peggy Friesen (Jill Mason), Daryl Champine, Dan Day, Christopher Glaze, Jeffrey Lehr, Craig Oldfather (Horses)
FOOL FOR LOVE by Sam Shepard; Director, Peter Bennett; Set, David Wallace; Costumes, Gwen Walters. CAST: Caryn West (May), Richard McWilliams (Eddie), Timothy Wagner (Martin), Tom Celli (Old Man)
A CHRISTMAS CAROL by Charles Dickens; Adaptation, Barbara Field; Director, Beverly Shatto; Costumes, Baker S. Smith; Musical Director/Arranger, Molly Jessup; Choreographer, Jennifer Martin. CAST: Gary Neal Johnson (Charles Dickens), Jim Birdsall (Scrooge), Mark Robbins, Charles Leader, Brian George Morgan, Richard James-Greene, John Camera, Peter Byger, Andrew Atterbury, Jill Marie Lytton, Bruce Roach, Peggy Friesen, Martin Coles, Jeannine Hutchings, Elizabeth Robbins, Annemarie Potter, Ross Freese, Heidi Schwieterman, David Spatz, Heidi Thomas, George Dulin, Sidonie Garrett, Cammie McKee, Michael Linsley Rapport, Scott Cordes, Terry O'Reagan, Michael Poulin, Eliza Valk, Richard Alan Nichols, Mary Henley Stephenson, Sara Anne Bayer, Randy Joe Stevens
A CLASS "C" TRIAL IN YOKOHAMA by Roger Cornish; Director, George Keathley; Set, Herbert L. Camburn; Music, Allen DeCamp. CAST: Brian Keeler (George Pelham), David Dunard (Art Brown), Mark W. Conklin (Perry Sato), Ernest Abuba (Kinosada Abbe), Daniel Eisenhower (G.I.), Christopher Glaze (Bailiff), Martin English (Court Reporter), Nelson Williams (Shusaku Fukada), Peter Byger (William Johnson), Brian Cutler (Chester Goss), Michael Linsley Rapport (Capt. Berry), Richard Alan Nichols (P. J. Flynn), Jim Ishida (Dr. Yoshita), Keenan Shimizu (Dr. Kase), Erika Honda (Michi-ko), Gerri Igarahsi (Yoshiki Fujino/Mamasan), Sally Frontman (Kyushu Scrub Nurse), Gary Neal Johnson (Capt. Jaegar)
AND MISS REARDON DRINKS A LITTLE by Paul Zindel; Director, George Keathley; Set, James Leonard Joy. CAST: Rosemary DeAngelis (Catherine Reardon), Dodie Brown (Mrs. Pentrano), Dan Day (Delivery Boy), Juliet Randall (Ceil Adams), Nicola Sheara (Anna Reardon), Barbara Houston (Fleur Stein), Peter Byger (Bob Stein)
THE GLASS MENAGERIE by Tennessee Williams; Director, George Keathley; Lighting, Curt Ostermann; Costumes, John Carver Sullivan; Music, Paul Bowles; Arranger, Allen De Camp. CAST: Ann Hillary (Amanda), Bruce Roach (Tom), Tracey Ellis (Laura), Jim Birdsall (Gentleman Caller)

Richard McWilliams, Caryn West in "Fool for Love" Top: Rosemary DeAngelis, Nicola Sheara in "And Miss Reardon Drinks a Little"

NEW AMERICAN THEATER

Rockford, Illinois

Producing Director, J. R. Sullivan; Managing Director, Sharon L. Hensley; Development/Press, Fleur Wright; Production Manager, Cindy Jo Savitski; Technical Director/Assistant Designer, Shawn Carey; Stage Manager, Sarah Wilkinson

PRODUCTIONS & CASTS

LUTHER by John Osborne; Director, J. R. Sullivan; Set/Lights, James Wolk; Costumes, Jon R. Accardo. CAST: Matt K. Miller (Knight), Stephen F. Vrtol III (Martin), Robert Scogin (Prior/Cajetan), Michael Krebs (Lucas), Michael Nash (Tetzel), Gordon Odegard (Staupitz), Martha Terry (Katherine)
INHERIT THE WIND by Jerome Lawrence, Robert E. Lee; Director, J. R. Sullivan; Set/Lights, Chuck Drury; Costumes, Laura Cunningham. CAST: Sandi Massie (Rachel Brown), Michael Krebs (Mertram Cates), Martha Terry (Mrs. Krebs), G. Michael Johnson (Rev. Brown), Daniel Patrick Sullivan (E. K. Hornbeck), Barry B. Nyquist (Matthew Harrison Brady), Rod MacDonald (Henry Drummond)
A CHRISTMAS CAROL by Charles Dickens; Adapted by Amlin Gray; Director, Francis X. Kuhn; Set/Lights, James Wolk; Costumes, Jon R. Accardo. CAST: Peter Aylward/D. C. Anderson (Ebenezer Scrooge), Daniel Patrick Sullivan (Fred), Michael Krebs (Marley's Ghost/Mr. Topper), Sandi Massie (Ghost of Christmas Past/Maria), Colleen Burns (Mrs. Fezziwig), Stephen F. Vrotl III (Young Scrooge/Old Joe), Martha Terry (Belle Wilkins), Michael Nash (Ghost of Christmas Present)
BRIGHTON BEACH MEMOIRS by Neil Simon; Director, J. R. Sullivan; Set/Costumes, Laura Cunningham; Lighting, Daniel Eastman. CAST: Philip Euling (Eugene), Sandi Massie (Blanche), Ellen Lochheed (Kate), Lili Taylor/Katherine Lynch (Laurie), Nathalie Cunningham (Nora), Daniel Patrick Sullivan (Stanley), Michael Krebs (Jack)
THE REAL THING by Tom Stoppard; Director, Tom Mula; Set, Michael S. Philippi; Lights, Miriam Hack; Costumes, Jon R. Accardo. CAST: Thom Sobota (Max), Sandi Massie (Charlotte), David Nisbet (Henry), Amy Wright (Annie), Daniel Patrick Sullivan/Matt K. Miller (Billy)
KINGDOM COME by Amlin Gray; Director, J. R. Sullivan; Set/Costumes, Jon R. Accardo; Lights, David L. Radunsky. CAST: Stephen F. Vrtol III (Ellefstolen Harstad), Matt K. Miller (Paal/Ship Captain), Barry B. Nyquist (Parson/Dockhand), Martha Terry (Gro Endressen), Michael Krebs (Ola Endressen), Daniel Patrick Sullivan (Thomas Ansen), Sandi Massie (Kaja Ansen), David Nisbet (Kal Ansen)
VOICE OF THE PRAIRIE by John Olive; Director, J. R. Sullivan; Set, Michael S. Philippi; Lights, David L. Radunsky; Costumes, Barbara Niederer. CAST: Peter Aylward (Actor 1), Daniel Patrick Sullivan (Actor 2), Sandi Massie (Actor 3)

Chris Welsh Photos

Daniel Patrick Sullivan, Phillip Euling in "Brighton Beach Memoirs"

Matt K. Miller in "Luther"

NORTHLIGHT THEATRE

Evanston, Illinois

Artistic Directors, Michael Maggio, Russell Vandenbroucke; Managing Director, Susan Medak; Stage Managers, Anthony Berg, Rick Berg
PRODUCTIONS & CASTS
ANGELS FALL by Lanford Wilson; Director, Tom Mula; Set, Gary Baugh; Costumes, Kerry Fleming; Lighting, Rita Pietraszek; Technical Director, Greg Murphy. CAST: William J. Norris, Annabel Armour, Chris Karchmar, Jodean Culbert, Tim Gregory, Edgar Meyer
FREE ADVICE FROM PRAGUE (Audience and Unveiling) by Vaclav Havel; Translation, Jan Novak; Director, Kyle Donnelly; Set, Eve Cauley, Costumes, Jessica Hahn; Lighting, Rita Pietraszek; Technical Director, Greg Murphy. CAST: John Cothran, Gary Houston, Kathy Taylor, Tom Amandes
DEALING by June Shellene, Richard Fire; *World Premiere;* Director, Michael Maggio; Set, Linda Buchanan; Costumes, Kaye Nottbusch; Lighting, Robert Shook; Assistant Stage Manager, Dean Bolton; Original Music, Rick Snyder. CAST: Tim Halligan, Ron Dean, Holly Fulger, Kevin Dunn, B. J. Jones, Don Franklin, Gary Houston, Barbara E. Robertson, Terrance Auch, Brian Bakke, Stuart Greenman, Carlton Miller, Kristy Munden, Arthur Pearson, Rick Russo, Michael Sadowski
BENEFACTORS by Michael Frayn; Director, J. R. Sullivan; Set, Gary Baugh; Costumes, Kaye Nottbusch; Lighting, Robert Shook; Technical Director, Greg Murphy. CAST: Brad Armacost, Cynthia Judge, Mark Robbins, Janice St. John
THE PERFECT PARTY by A. R. Gurney, Jr.; Director, Nick Faust; Set, Bill Mikulewicz; Costumes, Virgil Johnson; Lighting, Dan Kotlowitz; Technical Director, Greg Murphy. CAST: Lucy Childs, Barbara Gaines, Camilla Hawk, Jack McLaughlin-Gray, Fredrick Stone

Right: Brad Armacost in "Benefactors"
Top: Ron Dean, Gary Houston, Kevin
Dunn in "Dealing"

ODYSSEY THEATRE ENSEMBLE

Los Angeles, California

Artistic Director, Ron Sossi; Associate Artistic Director, Frank Condon; Literary Manager, Jan Lewis; Production Manager, Lucy Pollak; Technical Director, Duncan Mahoney; Business Manager/Press, Garrett Keller; Development, Janey Potts
PRODUCTIONS & CASTS
JOHNNY JOHNSON (The Biography of Common Man) by Paul Green; Music, Kurt Weill; Director, Ron Sossi; Musical Director, Sue Roberts; Set, Chez Cherry; Lighting, R. Craig Wolf; Costumes, Gayle Susan Baizer; Choreography, Joanne Parmilee; Stage Manager, Karen Hirsch; Assistant Director, Joyce Baldwin; Associate Producer, Mary Meis. CAST: Walt Beaver, Marty Brinton, Matthew and Nathan Brinton, Ralph Bruneau, Marc Cardiff, Michelle Chilton, Don Dexter, Alexander Egan, Joyce E. Greene, Robert Guidi, Brent Hinkley, Bob Kip, Susan Kohler, Janet Lazarus, Sam Loewenberg, Craig McCallister, Thom McCleister, Michael More, Louis R. Plante, Tina Rigali, Mark Simon, Ronnie Sperling, Tim Stadler, Lee E. Stevens, Wayne Wagner, Jill Wakewood, George Woodard, Jack Younger
TOM & VIV by Michael Hastings; Director, Robert W. Goldsby; Set, Ariel; Lighting, Ken Lennon; Costumes, Ruth A. Brown; Sound, Steven Barr; Assistant Director, Danielle Martin; Co-Producer, Lucy Pollak; Associate Producers, Isobel Estorick, Robert Weibezahl. CAST: Cynthia David (Vivienne Haigh-Wood Eliot), Jack Hatcheson (Maurice Haigh-Wood), Beth Hogan (Louise Purdon), Olive Dunbar (Rose Esther Robinson Haigh-Wood), Walt Beaver (Charles Haigh-Wood/William Leonard Janes), Mark Murphey (Thomas Stears Eliot/Charles Marion Todd)
THE WOODS by David Mamet; Director, Frank Condon; Set, Christa Bartels; Costumes, Martha Ferrata; Assistant Director, Marc Figueroa; Lighting, Doc Ballard; Sound, Steven Barr; Props, Betina Appleby; Stage Managers, Christy Gallo, Laurel Koss, Denise Van Wormer. CAST: Sam Anderson (Nick), Susan Heldfond (Ruth)
MASTER CLASS by David Pownall; Director, Ron Sossi; Original Music/Arrangements, John White; Musical Director, Inna Gotman; Set, Susan Lane; Lighting, Dawn Hollingsworth; Costumes, Jackie Dalley; Assistant Director, Joyce Baldwin; Choreography, Tanya Everett; Stage Managers, Ilene Nathan, Terri Thomas, Laurel Koss, Kip Roach. CAST: Randy Dreyfuss (Shostakovich), Gene Dynarski (Stalin), Louis R. Plante (Zhdanov), John Rose (Prokofiev)

Ron Sossi Photos

Randy Dreyfuss, Gene Dynarski, Louis Plante, John Rose in "Master
Class" Above: Mark Murphey, Cynthia David, Olive Dunbar
in "Tom and Viv"

OLD GLOBE THEATRE

San Diego, California
Fifty-first Season

Artistic Director, Jack O'Brien; Executive Producer, Craig Noel; Managing Director, Thomas Hall; Business Manager, Derek Harrison Hurd; Company Manager, Jane Cowgill; Development, Cassie A. Solomon-Hay; Marketing, Joe Kobryner; Press, William B. Eaton, Charlene Baldridge, Mark Hiss; Production Manager, Ken Denison; Technical Director, Loren SchreiberSound, Tony Tait; Props, Tom Hammer, Ruth Long; Costumes, Stacy Sutton; Wardrobe, Roxanne Femling; Wigs/Makeup, Frank O. Bowers

PRODUCTIONS & CASTS

BEYOND THE FRINGE by Alan Bennett, Peter Cook, Jonathan Miller, Dudley Moore; Director, Paxton Whitehead; Set, Alan K. Okazaki; Costumes, Steven Rubin; Lingiting, John B. Forbes; Sound, Corey L. Fayman; Stage Manager, Maria Carrera. CAST: Tom Lacy, Jerry Pavlon, Jim Piddock, Paxton Whitehead

TARTUFFE by Moliere; Director, Craig Noel; Set, Richard Seger; Costumes, Lewis Brown; Lighting, Kent Dorsey; Sound, Mark Sherman; Composer, Larry Delinger; Stage Manager, Diane F. DiVita. CAST: Mitchell Edmonds, Kandis Chappell, William Downe, Harriet Hall, Jo deWinter, Don Took, John Walcutt, Margo Martindale, Jonathan McMurtry (Tartuffe), Ric Oquita, William Anton, Peter Carlton Brown, Ron Richards, Buddy Zimmer

RICHARD II by William Shakespeare; Director, Joseph Hardy; Set, Douglas W. Schmidt; Costumes, Steven Rubin; Lighting, Davie F. Segal; Sound, Michael Holten; Composer, Conrad Susa; Fight Choreographer, Steve Rankin; Stage Manager, Douglas Pagliotti. CAST: Brian Bedford (Richard II), Earle Hyman (Edmund), G Wood (John of Gaunt), Vaughn Armstrong, Erica Yohn, Tom Harrison, Kenneth Gray, Henry J. Jordan, William D. Michie, William Anton, David Anthony Smith, Larry Drake, James Morrison, Robert Hock, Eric Grischkat, Dierk Torsek, Mark Loftis, Steve Rankin, David Toney, Mark Loftis, Monique Fowler, Tim MacDonald, Dorothy Milne, Joyce O'Connor, Ron Richards, John Navarro

JULIUS CAESAR by William Shakespeare; Directors, Anne McNaughton, Dakin Matthews; Set, Fred M. Duer; Costumes, Lewis Brown; Lighting, John Forbes; Stage Manager, Diane DiVita. CAST: Earle Hyman (Julius Caesar), John Vickery (Marcus Brutus), Marc Alaimo, James Morrison, David Toney, Peter Carlton Brown, Eric Grischkat, Ric Oquita, Kandis Chappell (Portia), David Anthony Smith, Erica Yohn (Calpurnia), Tom Harrison (Mark Antony), John Walcutt

MUCH ADO ABOUT NOTHING by William Shakespeare; Director, Brian Bedford; Set, Richard Seger; Costumes, Lewis Brown; Lighting, Kent Dorsey; Composer, Conrad Susa; Choreographer, Ron Cisneros; Stage Manager, Maria Carrera. CAST: Ron Richards, G Wood, Christine Ebersole, Monique Fowler, Vaughn Armstrong, Paxton Whitehead, Kenneth Gray, William D. Michie, William Downe, Dierk Torsek, Don Took, Dan Hendrick, Harriet Hall, Joyce O'Connor, Walter Murray, Tom Lacy, Robert Hock, Buddy Zimmer, Henry J. Jordan, Mark Loftis, Jacqueline Antaramian, Tony Mandle, Dorothy Milne, John Navarro

G Wood, Brian Bedford, Earle Hyman
in "Richard II"

EMILY by Stephen Metcalfe; Director, Jack O'Brien; Set, Douglas W. Schmidt; Costumes, Steven Rubin; Lighting, David F. Segal; Composer, Bob James; Sound, Michael Holten; Stage Manager, Douglas Pagliotti. CAST: Madolyn Smith (Emily), Larry Drake (Fields), Steve Rankin (McCarthy), Jonathan McMurtry (Stein), William Anton (Hill), Mitchell Edmonds (Hugh), Margo Martindale (Hallie), Kenneth Marshall (Jon), Jo deWinter (Dierdre), Mitchell Edmonds (Hugh/Mr. Stone), Keith Devaney, Susan Gosdick, Neil Alan Tadken

INTO THE WOODS (*World Premiere*) Music & Lyrics, Stephen Sondheim; Book/Direction, James Lapine; Musical Directors, Paul Gemignani, Eric Stern; Set, Tony Straiges; Costumes, Ann Hould-Ward, Patricia Zipprodt; Lighting, Richard Nelson; Orchestrator, Jonathan Tunick; Projections, Wendall K. Harrington; Sound, Michael Holten; Production Coordinator, Ira Weitzman; Stage Managers, Johnna Murray, Douglas Pagliotti. CAST: John Cunningham (Narrator/Wolf/Steward), Kim Crosby (Cinderella), Ben Wright (Jack), Chip Zien (Baker), Joanna Gleason (Baker's Wife), Joy Franz (Stepmother/Wolf), Kay McClelland (Florinda/Rapunzel), Lauren Mitchel (Lucinda), Barbara Bryne (Jack's Mother), LuAnne Ponce (Little Red Ridinghood), Ellen Foley (Witch), George Coe (Mysterious Man/Cinderella's Father), Merle Louise (Mother/Grandmother/Wolf/Giant), Chuck Wagner (Rapunzel's Prince), Kenneth Marshall (Cinderella's Prince), Ric Oquita (Footman), Pamela Tomassett (Snow White), Terri Cannicott (Sleeping Beauty)

ORPHANS by Lyle Kessler; Director, Robert Berlinger; Set, Alan K. Okazaki; Costumes, Christina Haatainen; Lighting, John B. Forbes; Fight Choreographer, Steven Pearson; Sound, Corey L. Fayman; Stage Manager, Diane F. DiVita. CAST: Chuck LaFont (Phillip), Dan Shor (Treat), Jonathan McMurtry (Harold)

THE INCREDIBLY FAMOUS WILLY RIVERS by Stephen Metcalfe; Director, Jack O'Brien; Set, Douglas W. Schmidt; Costumes, Robert Blackman; Lighting, David F. Segal; Sound, Michael Holten; Original Music, Denny Markowitz, Denny McCormick; Lyrics, Stephen Metcalfe; Stage Managers, Douglas Pagliotti, Diane F. DiVita. CAST: Brian Kerwin (Willy Rivers), Dann Florek, Pippa Pearthree, Lisa Dunsheath, Sydney Lloyd-Smith, William Anton, James McDaniel, John Bowman, Jonathan McMurtry, Eric Grischkat, Mark Hofflund, Ric Oquita, Pamela Tomassetti

THE PETITION by Brian Clark; Director, David Hay; Set, Fred M. Duer; Costumes, Clare Henkel; Lighting John B. Forbes; Sound, Corey L. Fayman; Stage Managers, Maria Carrera, Robert Drake. CAST: G Wood (Gen. Sir Edmund Milne), Priscilla Morrill (Lady Elizabeth Milne)

INTIMATE EXCHANGES (A Pageant/Affairs in a Tent) by Alan Ayckbourn; Director, Craig Noel; Set, Richard Seger; Costumes, Lewis Brown; Lighting, John B. Forbes; Sound, Michael Holten; Stage Managers, Maria Carrera, Robert Drake. CAST: Kandis Chappell (Celia Teasdale/Sylvie Bell/Irene Pridworthy), William Anton (Toby/Celia's Husband/Lionel Hepplewick/Miles/Rowena's Husband)

ANOTHER ANTIGONE by A. R. Gurney, Jr. Director, John Tillinger; Set/Costumes, Steven Rubin; Lighting, Kent Dorsey; Sound, Corey L. Fayman; Stage Manager, Diane F. DiVita. CAST: George Grizzard (Prof. Henry Harper), Marissa Chibas (Judy/Diana), Debra Mooney (Dean of Humane Studies), Steven Flynn (David)

John Peter Weiss Photos

Joanna Gleason, Chip Zien, Ellen Foley
in "Into the Woods"

176

PENGUIN REPERTORY COMPANY

Stony Point, New York
Tenth Season

Artistic Director/Director of Productions, Joe Brancato; Executive Director, Andrew M. Horn; Designers, Dennis W. Moyes, Alex Polner, Maryann D. Smith, Eiko Yamaguchi; Technical Director, W. Stuart Russell; Stage Managers, April Adams, Kathi Guy, Karen Oberthal

PRODUCTIONS & CASTS

WILD OATS by James McClure; with Riley Austin, John Aaron Beall, Kurt Goldschmidt, Norman Howard, Eden-Lee Jellinek, Bill Perley, Eileen Shea, T. Ryder Smith, Judy Stadt, Jake Turner
SANTA ANITA '42 by Allan Knee; with Nick Affuso, Riley Austin, Tina Chen, David Garcia, Michael Guido, Thomas Ikeda, Koji Okamura, Edward Thom
NOT FOR KEEPS by David Rogers; with David Rogers, Ann Schulman, Judy Stadt
ORPHANS by Lyle Kessler; with Peter DeMaio, Andrew M. Horn, Bruce McDonnell
JANE by S. N. Behrman; Based on story by W. Somerset Maugham; with Kurt Goldschmidt, Bud Gordon, Evelyn Jewell, Bruce McDonnell, Gail Newman, Lisa Onofri, Judy Stadt, Geoff Tarson

Kerwin McCarthy Photos

Right: Eden-Lee Jellinek, Riley Austin, Kurt Goldschmidt, Joan Aaron Beall, Jake Turner, T. Ryder Smith, Norman Howard, Bill Perley, Judy Stadt in "Wild Oats" Top: Tina Chen in "Santa Anita '42"

Susan Greenhill, Rose Stockton, Kymberly Dakin in "More Fun Than Bowling" Above: Hannah Cox, Richard McWilliams in "Cat on a Hot Tin Roof"

PENNSYLVANIA STAGE COMPANY

Allentown, Pennsylvania
Fourth Season

Producing Director, Gregory S. Hurst; General Manager, Dan Fallon; Artistic Associate, Wendy Liscow; Production Manager, Peter Wrenn-Meleck; Technical Director, William Kreider; Costumer, Marianne Faust; Development, Mary Ann Confar; Stage Managers, Thomas M. Kauffman, Elli Agosto; Marketing/Press, Lisa K. Higgins

PRODUCTIONS & CASTS

BRIGHTON BEACH MEMOIRS by Neil Simon; Director, Gregory S. Hurst; Set, Atkin Pace; Costumes, Barbara Forbes; Lighting, Curtis Dretsch. CAST: Jeff Alan-Lee, Katherine Hiler, Julie Huyett, Leland Orser, Joel Rooks, Nicola Sheara, Suzanne Toren
DAMES AT SEA with Book and Lyrics by George Haimsohn, Robin Miller; Music, Jim Wise; Director, Sue Lawless; Choreographer, Edie Cowan; Musical Director, Mark Goodman; Set, Curtis Gretsch; Costumes, Marcy Grace Froehlich; Lighting, Donald Holder. CAST: Matthew Kimbrough, Jana Robbins, Christopher Seppe, Dorothy Stanley, Clark Sterling, Nikki Sahagen
THE HOUSEKEEPER by James Prideaux; Director, Wendy Liscow; Set/Lighting, Linda Sechrist; Costumes, Marianne Faust. CAST: Peter Messaline, Jana Robbins
CAT ON A HOT TIN ROOF by Tennessee Williams; Director, Gregory S. Hurst; Set, Atkin Pace; Costumes, Barbara Forbes; Lighting, Curtis Gretsch; Sound John Clifton. CAST: Hannah Cox, Sally Dunn, Terry Layman, Barbara Lester, Richard McWilliams, John Ramsey, Andrew Cruse, Laura Hansen, Natalie Ann Haubert, Sarah Van Cott, Jeremy Wieand
MORE FUN THAN BOWLING by Steven Dietz; Director, Gregory S. Hurst; Set/Lighting, Clarke Dunham; Costumes, Kathleen Egan. CAST: Kymberly Dakin, Susan Greenhill, Martin LaPlatney, Adam Oliensis, Rose Stockton
A LESSON FROM ALOES by Athol Fugard; Director, Allen R. Belknap; Set/Lighting, Linda Sechrist; Costumes, Marianne Faust. CAST: Charles Antalosky, L. Peter Callender, Ann Ducati
THE FOREIGNER by Larry Shue; Director, Gregory S. Hurst; Set/Lighting, Bennet Averyt; Costumes, Barbara Forbes. CAST: Charles Antalosky, Monique Fowler, Michael French, Larry Golden, Michael Haney, Lucille Patton, Hugh Sinclair, Stephanie Burke, Jim Clausner, Dave DeMaria, Mark Domyan, Tim Gerheart, Wayne Gmitter, Maribeth Mooney, Tom Onushco, Julie Slim, Lisa Smith

Gregory M. Fota Photos

177

PHILADELPHIA DRAMA GUILD

Philadelphia, Pennsylvania

Producing Director, Gregory Poggi; Business Manager, Mark Bernstein, Kathleen Kund Nolan; Marketing, Barbara Konik; Sets, Fred Kolo, Daniel P. Boylen, John Jensen, Neil Peter Jampolis, John Falabella, Edward Worthington, Christopher Nestor; Costumes, Eduardo Sicangco, Frankie Fehr, Karen Roston, Jess Goldstein; Lighting, Fred Kolo, William H. Grant III, James Leitner, Neil Peter Jampolis, Jeff Davis, Jerold R. Forsyth; Musical Director, Ricardo Martin; Stage Managers, Ralph Batman, Donna E. Curci, Katherine Pierce, Marilyn Dampf, William Whelen, Deborah Rader; Press, Eleanore Anderson

PRODUCTIONS & CASTS

A SHAYNA MAIDEL by Barbara Lebow; Director, Robert Kalfin. CAST: Eleanor Reissa, Frank Wittow, Tovah Feldshuh, Ray Dooley, Ann-Sara Matthews, Barbara Spiegel

THE AMEN CORNER by James Baldwin; Director, Edmund J. Cambridge. CAST: Rhetta Greene, Raine D'Jonson, Cynthia Belgrave, Yvonne Talton Kersey, Jeffery V. Thompson, Janeece A. Roderick, Alvin Alexis, Antonio Fargas, Jan Ellis, Miriam Burton, Diane S. Leslie, H. German Wilson, Mel Mathis, Allien Davis, Elizabeth Flax, Zane Holloway, Harvey Hynson, Maurice Owens, Raheen Ballard, Tiffany Johnson, Kaofi N. Lay, Tracey McBeth, Jamar Riggins, Fellowship Choir

THE FOREIGNER by Larry Shue; Director, Art Wolff. CAST: Pat McNamara, Bill Cwikowski, Lynn Cohen, Ben Lemon, Jordan Baker, Bill Fagerbakke, Jim Fyfe, Michael Jordan, Scott Ogan, Stephen Downs, William Thomer

THE CRUCIBLE by Arthur Miller; Director, Michael Murray. CAST: Karla Burns, Tara Carnes, Reno Roop, Margie Hanssens, Megan Bellwoar, Joan Stanley, Harry H. Kunesch, Kathleen L. Warner, Suzanne O'Donnell, Jared Martin, Dolly Wheaton, Charlie Walnut, Richard Bekins, Lizbeth Mackay, Scott Johnson, Douglas Wing, Cyrus Newitt, Allen Fitzpatrick, John Wylie, Robert Sim, Daniel Richards

THE MIDDLE AGES BY A. R. Gurney, Jr.; Director, Charles Karchmer. CAST: Geoffrey Wade, Amanda Carlin, Forrest Compton, Julia Meade

MOTHER (World Premiere) by Chalude Koch; Director, Charles Conwell. CAST: Atticus Fleury, Katherine Conklin, Joseph Daly, Susan Wilder, Tim Moyer, William Cameron

MEAN HARVEST (World Premiere) by John Erlanger; Director, Lon Winston. CAST: Jane Moore, Tom McCarthy, Peter DeLaurier, Denice Hicks

THE VIGIL (World Premiere) by Charles J. Jenkins; Director, Clay Goss. CAST: Johnnie Hobbs, Jr., Donald Jackson, Jr., Mets Suber

Kenneth Kauffman Photos

Forrest Compton, Geoffrey Wade, Amanda Carlin, Julia Meade in "The Middle Ages"
Top: Tovah Feldshuh, Eleanor Reissa in "A Shayna Maidel"

John MacKay, Tom Atkins in "Vikings"
Nancy Nichols, Reed Jones in "She Loves Me"

PITTSBURGH PUBLIC THEATER

Pittsburgh, Pennsylvania
Twelfth Season

Producing Director, William T. Gardner; Casting, Michael Doyle Fender; Development, R. Daniel Shephard, Curt Powell; Technical Director, A. D. Carson; Props, Diana L. Stoughton; Literary Manager, Mary G. Guaraldi; Stage Managers, Marc Field, Jane Rothman, Clayton Phillips; Press, Susanne Ruffner, Cynthia Taylor

PRODUCTIONS & CASTS

SERENADING LOUIE by Lanford Wilson; Director, Lee Sankowich; Set, Ursula Belden; Costumes, Flozanne John; Lighting, Kirk Bookman. CAST: Catherine Butterfield, Helena Ruoti, Thomas Stewart, Peter Webster

SHE LOVES ME by Joe Masteroff; Music, Jerry Boch; Lyrics, Sheldon Harnick; Director, Peter Bennett; Set, Harry Feiner; Costumes, David Toser; Lighting, Kirk Bookman; Music Direction, Ken Gargaro; Choreographer, Judith Ann Contee. CAST: Michael Kell Boone, Ted Brunetti, Risa Brainin, Larro Chelsi, Wynn Harmon, Reed Jones, Ann Kittredge, George McCulloch, Leonore Nemitz, Nancy Nichols, Jeff Paul, Debra Segal, Allan Stevens, Judith Thiergaard, Ron Wisniki

ORPHANS by Lyle Kessler; Director, Mel Shapiro; Set/Costumes, Karl Eigsti; Lighting, Kirk Bookman. CAST: William Jay, Stephen Mailer, James Anthony Shanta

THE PLAY'S THE THING by Ferenc Molnar; Director, George Sherman; Set, Cletus Anderson; Costumes, David Murin; Lighting, Kristine Bick. CAST: Arthur Burns, Tom Celli, Robert Gerringer, Melinda Mullins, Robert Stanton, Greg Vinkler, Time Winters

VIKINGS by Stephen Metcalfe; Director, Lee Sankowich; Set, Eldon Elder; Costumes, Flozanne John; Lighting, Kirk Bookman. CAST: Tom Atkins, Lance Lewman, John MacKay, Marsha Wischusen

PRINCESS GRACE AND THE FAZZARIS (World Premiere) by Marc Alan Zagoren; Director, Peter Bennett; Set, Gary English; Lighting, Phil Monat; Costumes, Laura Crow; Stage Manager, Jane Rothman. CAST: Rosemary DeAngelis (Lucille Fazzari), Colleen Quinn (Rosemary Fazzari), Vera Lockwood (Cabrina Saviola), Sally Prager (Veronica Fazzari), Victor Arnold (Vincent Fazzari), Lorraine Serabian (Joanne Saviola), A. J. Vincent (Sal)

Mark Portland Photos

PLAYMAKERS REPERTORY COMPANY

Chapel Hill, North Carolina

Executive Producer, Milly S. Barranger; Artistic Director, David Hammond; Associate Producer, Margaret Hahn; Marketing/Press, Jon Curtis; Movement, Craig Turner; Voice Coach, Carol Pendergrast; Dialect Coach, Deborah Hecht; Lighting, Robert Wierzel; Sets, Linwood Taylor; Costumes, Bobbi Owen, Laurel Clayson; Stage Managers, Dean Robinson, Becca Symonds
RESIDENT COMPANY: Bernard Addison, Patricia Barnett, Constance Conover, Dede Corvinus, John Feltch, Tom Fitzsimmons, Derek Gagnier, Thom Garvey, Russell Graves, Joe Haj, Kate Haris, Deborah Hecht, Brian Hotaling, Candace Marazita, Robert Murphy, Demetrios Pappageorge, Ilya Parenteau, Melissa Proctor, Suzanna Rinehart, Becket Royce, Teresa Thuman, Paul Tourtillotte, David Whalen, Eben Young
GUEST ARTISTS: Actors: Richard Buck, Mimi Carr, Jenna Cole, Tandy Cronyn, Betsy Friday, Lance Guest, Steven Hendrickson, James Pritchett, Isa Thomas Paul Ukena, Designers: Mark Pirolo, Rusty Smith, Directors: Christian Angerman, Evan Yionoulis
PRODUCTIONS: *Look Homeward, Angel* by Ketti Frings, *Waiting for Godot* by Samuel Beckett, *The Matchmaker* by Thornton Wilder, *A Doll's House* by Henrik Ibsen translated by Eva LeGallienne, *The Human Voice* by Jean Cocteau translated by Anthony Wood, *Lu Ann Hampton Laverty Oberlander* by Preston Jones, *A Midsummer Night's Dream* by William Shakespeare

Kevin Keister, Pam Royal Photos

Top: (L) Tandy Cronyn, John Feltch in "Waiting for Godot" (R) Jenna Cole, David Whalen in "A Doll's House"

Victoria Brasser, Richard Warren Pugh in "The Phantom of the Opera" Above: Howard Witt, Jeff Allin in "All My Sons"

REPERTORY THEATRE OF ST. LOUIS

Saint Louis, Missouri

Artistic Director, Steven Woolf; Managing Director, Mark D. Bernstein; Technical Director, Mac De Volder; Props, John Roslevich, Jr.; Costumes, Holly Poe Durbin; Development, Nancy S. Forsyth; Press, Judy Andrews; Stage Managers, Glenn Dunn, T. R. Martin, Rachael Lindhart, Jane Seiler

PRODUCTIONS & CASTS

ALL MY SONS by Arthur Miller; Director, Timothy Near; Set, Carolyn L. Ross; Costumes, Jeffrey Struckman; Lighting, Max De Volder. CAST: Howard Witt (Joe), Terry Layman (Dr. Bayliss), Tim Snay (Frank), Edith Taylor Hunter (Sue), Marsha Korb (Lydia), Jeff Allin (Chris), Phillip Battaglia (Bert), T-Bob Whitney (Bert), Dorothy Stinette (Kate), Ellen Fiske (Ann), Dennis Predovic (George)
THE RAINMAKER by N. Richard Nash; Director, Jackson Phippin; Set, Tim Jozwick; Costumes, Del W. Risberg; Lighting, Steven Rosen. CAST: Robert Blackburn (H. C.), John Henry Cox (Noah), John Michael Higgins (Jim), Beth Dixon (Lizzie), Christopher Coucill (File), James Paul (Sheriff), Stephen Markle (Starbuck)
THE FOREIGNER by Larry Shue; Director, Edward Stern; Set, John Ezell; Costumes, Dorothy L. Marshall; Lighting, Peter E. Sargent. CAST: Joneal Joplin (Froggy), Bill Kux (Charlie), Trinity Thompson (Betty), Hal Davis (Rev. Lee), Daydrie Hague (Catherine), Edward James Hyland (Owen), Kevin Chamberlin (Ellard)
SIZWE BANSI IS DEAD by Athol Fugard; Director, Jim O'Connor; Set/Costumes, Arthur Ridley; Lighting, Peter E. Sargent. CAST: John Cothran, Jr. (Styles/Buntu), Stephen McKinley Henderson (Sizwe)
THE FLYING KARAMAZOV BROTHERS by and with Howard Jay Patterson, Paul David Magid, Randy Nelson, Sam Williams, Timothy Furst
THE PHANTOM OF THE OPERA (*U.S. Premiere*) by Ken Hill; Director, Peter Farago; Set, Joe Vanek; Costumes, Jim Buff; Lighting, Max De Volder; Musical Direction; Arrangements, Diane Ceccarini; Musical Supervision, Byron Grant; Stage Manager, T. R. Martin. CAST: Crista Moore (Jammes), Stan Rubin (Richard), Bob Amaral (Remy), Stephen Berger (Debienne), Merwin Foard (Raoul), Bob Morissey (Mephistopheles/Persian), Richard Warren Pugh (Faust), Naz Edwards (Mme. Giry), Victoria Brasser (Christine), Kathleen Mahoney-Bennett (Carlotta), Sal Mistretta (The Phantom)
BILLY BISHOP GOES TO WAR by John Gray with Eric Peterson; Director, William Van Keyser; Set, Dorothy L. Marshall; Costumes, Terri McConnell; Lighting, Peter E. Sargent. CAST: Ross Bickell (Billy), Byron Grant (Narrator/Pianist)
LUCKY LINDY by Dick D. Zigun; Director, Russell Vandenbroucke; Set, Richard Tollkuhn; Costumes, Holly Poe Durbin; Lighting, Glenn Dunn. CAST: John Michael Higgins, Cornelia Mills
BEYOND HERE ARE MONSTERS (*U.S. Premiere*) by James Nicholson; Director, Susan Gregg; Set/Lighting, Dale F. Jordon; Costumes, Dorothy L. Marshall; Sound, Brian Poissant. CAST: Boyd Heidenreich (Robin), Susan Pellegrino (Sophie), Naseer El-Kadi (Uncas), Arthur Hanket (Denzil), Jay E. Raphael (Francis), Rohn Thomas (Eleazar DeCarvalho)
IN GREAT ELIZA'S GOLDEN TIME (*World Premiere*) by Tony Kushner; Direction/Set/Costumes, Tony Kushner; Stage Manager, Jane Seiler. CAST: Kari Ely, Jeanne Trevor, Roberta Levine, Priscilla Stampa
THE PROTOZOA REVUE by Tony Kushner; Director, Kari Ely;
GENDERVISION by Kimberly Flynn and Michael Mayer; (*World Premiere*); Director, Wayne Salomon;
TALES OF SOUTH AFRICA by Charles Smith; (*World Premiere*); Director, Wayne Salomon; all three performed by Glynis Brooks, Philip Coffield, Monica Dickens, Bobby Norfolk

Judy Andrews, William Bornefeld Photos

SOUTH COAST REPERTORY

Costa Mesa, California

Producing Artistic Director, David Emmes; Artistic Director, Martin Benson; Business Director, Paula Tomei; Development, Bonnie Brittain Hall; Marketing, John Mouledoux; Production Director, Paul Hammond; Dramaturg, Jerry Patch; Literary Manager, John Glore; Artistic Coordinator, Donna Ruzika; Casting, Martha McFarland; Technical Director, Ted Carlsson; Lighting, Tom Ruzika; Props, Michael Mora; Stage Managers, Julie Haber, Bonnie Lorenger, Andy Tighe, Paul Lockwood; Resident Scenic Designer, Cliff Faulkner; Press, Cristofer Gross
RESIDENT COMPANY: Ron Boussom, Richard Doyle, John Ellington, John-David Keller, Art Koustik, Hal Landon, Jr., Anni Long, Martha McFarland, Don Took, J. Edmundo Araiza, Jack Axelrod, Ivy Bethune, Hal Bokar, Michael Canavan, Ismael Carlo, Craig Carnelia, David Chemel, Jeffrey Combs, Alexander Egan, Geoff Elliott, Elizabeth Faulkner, Lorrayne Fitzgerald, Tom Flynn, Monique Fowler, Marilyn Fox, Scott Freeman, Jane Galloway, Richard Gould, Tom Harrison, Karen Hensel, Mark Herrier, Victoria Hoffman, Gregory Itzin, David Jahns, Dorothy Dorian James, Patti Johns, Hubert Baron Kelly, Jr., Sally Kemp, Virginia Kiser, Hal Landon, Sr., Charley Lang, Heather Lee, Tom Ligon, Patricia Lodholm, Robert Machray, Melora Marshall, Mary Anne McGarry, Ron Michaelson, John C. Moskoff, Nigel Neale, Olivia Negron, Thomas R. Oglesby, Brad O'Hare, Jenifer Parker, Angela Paton, Tony Plana, Dan Priest, Bryan Rasmussen, Carl Reggiardo, Irene Roseen, Manuel Santiago, Socorro Santiago, Ann Siena-Schwartz, Howard Shangraw, Maureen Silliman, French Stewart, Rick D. Telles, Karen Trott, Myriam Tubert, Michael Tulin, James R. Winker.
PRODUCTIONS: *All the Way Home* by Tad Mosel/Director, Martin Benson; *Romeo and Juliet* by William Shakespeare/Director, Edward Payson Call; *The Real Thing* by Tom Stoppard/Director, Lee Shallat; *Charley Bacon and His Family* by Arthur Giron, *(West Coast Premiere)* Director, Martin Benson; *Cloud 9* by Caryl Churchill/Director, Jules Aaron; *Fool for Love* by Sam Shepard/Director, Martin Benson; *Beyond Therapy* by Christopher Durang/Director, Warner Shook; *World Premieres* of *Highest Standard of Living* by Keith Reddin/Director, David Emmes; *Three Postcards* by Craig Lucas and Craig Cornelia; Director, Norman Rene; *Birds* by Lisa Loomer/Director, Ron Lagomarsino; *Cold Sweat* by Neal Bell/Director, David Emmes

Ron Stone Photos

John C. Moskoff, Tony Plana in "Charley Bacon and His Family" Top: Socorro Santiago, Olivia Negron, Heather Lee in "Birds"

STAGEWEST

Springfield, Massachusetts
Twentieth Season

Artistic Director, Gregory Boyd; Managing Director, Marvin E. Weaver; Artistic Administrator, Benita Hofstetter; Production Manager, David Alan Stach; Literary Associate, Catherine Mandel; Business Manager, Val Pori; Development, Pat Ford; Stage Managers, Patricia Noto, Tree O'Halloran; Stage Director, Jean-Bernard Bucky; Sets, Brian Plunkett, Peter David Gould, Jennifer Gallagher, Hugh Landwehr, Rusty Smith; Costumes, Frances Blau, Douglas Fisher, V. Jane Suttell, Sam Fleming; Lighting, Robert Jared, Robert S. Rosentel; Sound, Ann Scibelli; Musical Direction, Martin Erskine; Choreography, Marcia Milgrom Dodge; Press, Mark Auerbach
RESIDENT COMPANY: David Asher, Stephen Berger, Alan Brooks, Dorothy Brooks, Jude Cicollella, Michael Cumpsty, Kathleen Claypool, Maury Cooper, Erick Devine, Lisa Eichhorn, Eric Hill, Chris Helmick, Paul Kandel, Kimberly King, Andrea Koocharian, Ellen Lauren, Kathryn Meisle, Ben Scranton, Nancy Niles Sexton, Noble Shropshire, John Straub, John Leslie Wolfe, Interns: Liz Esquirol, Peri Gilpin, Denise Alessandria Hurd, Brett Penney, Martin Simon, Charles Tuthill
PRODUCTIONS: *The Novelist* (World Premiere) by Howard Fast; *Guys and Dolls* by Frank Loesser, Jo Swerling, Abe Burrows; *The Crucible* by Arthur Miller; *A Midsummer Night's Dream* by William Shakespeare; *Cat's-Paw* by William Mastrosimone; *The Foreigner* by Larry Shue; *Orestes* by Euripedes

Gerry Goodstein Photos

Denise Hurd, Dorothy Brooks, John Leslie Wolfe, Ellen Lauren in "Guys and Dolls" Above: Lisa Eichhorn in "Jane Austen"

STUDIO ARENA THEATRE

Buffalo, New York
Twenty-second Season

Artistic Director, David Frank; Managing Director, Raymond Bonnard; Associate Director/Dramaturg; Controller, James J. Gumulak; Development, Anne E. Hayes; Marketing, Dave Mancuso; Production Manager, Randy Engels; Costumiere, Mary Ann Powell; Sound, Rick Menke; Props, Patricia D. Haines; Technical Director, Ted Zuse; Stage Managers, Christine Michael, Glenn Bruner; Press, Blossom Cohan

PRODUCTION & CASTS

A VIEW FROM THE BRIDGE by Arthur Miller; Director, Tony Giordano; Set, Hugh Landwehr; Costumes, Mary Ann Powell; Lighting, Dennis Parichy. CAST: Joe Aufiery (Marco), Jon Cavaluzzo (Mike), Dominic Chianese (Alfieri), Rafael Ferrer (Rodolpho), Michael Fischetti (Eddie), Joseph Giambra (Officer), Diane Martella (Beatrice), Lawrence Palmisano (Louis), Michael Twain (Officer), Jennifer Van Dyck (Catherine), Shara Alpern, Michael D. Argentieri, Dara Balesteri, Ginger DeCarlo, Dino F. Donati, Helen Guimento, John Kiouses, Dave Mancuso, R. Tony Perri

THE VALUE OF NAMES by Jeffrey Sweet; Director, John Monteith; Set, Michael C. Smith; Costumes, Mary Ann Powell; Lighting, Curt Ostermann. CAST: Allen Swift (Benny), Rebecca Ellens (Norma), Norman Rose (Leo)

QUILTERS by Molly Newman, Barbara Damashek; Director, Kyle Donnelly; Musical Direction, Judy Brown; Movement, Michael Sokoloff; Set, Jeff Bauer; Costumes, Mary Ann Powell; Lighting, Judy Rasmuson; Sound, Rick Menke. CAST: Sylvia Short (Sarah), Jan Leslie Harding, Anne Hills, Kathleen Marsh, Jeanine Morick, Margaret Warncke, Michele-Denise Woods

THE REAL THING by Tom Stoppard; Director, Kathryn Long; Set, Loy Arcenas; Costumes, Robert Morgan; Lighting, Curt Ostermann; Sound, Rick Menke. CAST: Allan Murley (Max), Robin Moseley (Charlotte), Jim Mezon (Henry), Anne Newhall (Annie), William Gonta (Billy), Farryl Lovett (Debbie), David Thornton (Brodie)

A LITTLE NIGHT MUSIC by Stephen Sondheim, Hugh Wheeler; Director, David Frank; Musical Director/Conductor, Judy Brown; Musical Staging, Terry Rieser; Associate Director/Set, Robert Morgan; Costumes, Mary Ann Powell; Lighting, Pat Collins; Sound, Rick Menke. CAST: Beth Barrow-Titus (Mrs. Anderssen), Stephanie Lynn Bax (Fredrika), Liz Callaway (Petra), Suzanne Dawson (Countess Malcolm), Susan Groeschel (Mrs. Nordstrom), Ronald Holgate (Fredrik), Bjorn Johnson (Erlansen/Frid), David King (Mr. Lindquist), Susan Long (Desiree), Hugh Panaro (Henrik), Patricia Ben Peterson (Anne), Vanessa Shaw (Mrs. Segstrom), Jonathan Simmons (Count Malcolm), Joyce Worsley (Madam Armfeldt), Colleen P. Kulikowski (Maid), Lynette O'Connell (Maid), Michael Rees (Bertrand)

T BONE N WEASEL by Jon Klein; Director, Kathryn Long; Set, Rick Dennis; Costumes, Bill Walker; Lighting, Anne Militello; Sound, Rick Menke. CAST: Michael Butler (Weasel), Herb Downer (T Bone), James Hartman (9 characters)

HAY FEVER by Noel Coward; Director, Robert Morgan; Set, Steven Perry; Costumes, Mariann Verheyen; Lighting, Curt Ostermann; Sound, Rick Menke. CAST: Karen Sellon (Sorel), Eric Swanson (Simon) Barbara Lester (Clara), Patricia Fraser (Judith Bliss), John Rainer (David), Laurence Overmire (Sandy), Susan Blommaert (Myra), Steven Crossley (Richard), Mary-Louise Parker (Jackie)

K. C. Kratt Photos

**Top Right: Allen Swift, Rebecca Ellens
in "The Value of Names" Below: Susan
Long, Ronald Holgate in "A Little Night Music"**

STUDIO THEATRE

Washington, D.C.
Ninth Season

Artistic/Managing Director, Joy Zinoman; Associate Artistic Director, Russell Metheny; Associate Managing Director, Virginia Crawford; Assistant Managing Director, Michael Dains; Development, Keith A. Baker; Business Manager, Joy Rankl; Production Manager, Deirdre Finney; Technical Director, A. Dougall Lillie; Dramaturg, Maynard Marshall; Sets, Russell Metheny; Lighting, Daniel MacLean Wagner; Costumes, Ric Thomas Rice; Props, Sandra Fleishman; Stage Manager, Kathi Lee Cochran-Redmond; Press, Marilyn Newton

PRODUCTIONS & CASTS

THE SLAB BOYS TRILOGY:

SLAB BOYS by John Byrne; Director, Joy Zinoman; Music/Sound, David Crandall. CAST: Michael Wells (Phil), Simon Brooking (Spanky), Tomas Kearney (Hector), Isabel Keating (Lucille), Chuck Lippman (Jack), Michael Russotto (Alan), Harry A. Winter (Willie), June Hansen (Sadie)

CUTTIN' A RUG by John Byrne (*U.S. Premiere*); with Michael Wells (Phil), Simon Brooking (Spanky), Tomas Kearney (Hector), Isabel Keating (Lucille), Michael Russotto (Alan), Harry A. Winter (Willie), June Hansen (Sadie), Eileen Russell (Miss Walkinshaw), Jennifer Mendenhall (Bernadette), Robert Carroll (Terry)

STILL LIFE by John Byrne (*U.S. Premiere*); with Michael Wells (Phil), Simon Brooking (Spanky), Isabel Keating (Lucille), Chuck Lippman (Jack), Joseph Scolaro (Workman)

LEMON SKY by Lanford Wilson; Director, Samuel P. Barton; Set, Michael Layton; Original Music, Cornelia J. Post. CAST: Marty Lodge (Alan), Hal Blankenship (Douglas), Suzanne Blakeslee (Ronnie), Kelly Nyks (Jerry), Chad Brian Wain (Jack), Erika Bogren (Penny), Tami Tappan (Carol)

THE ENTERTAINER by John Osborne; Director, Joy Zinoman; Music, John Addison; Costumes, Jane Schloss Phelan; Musical Director, Rob Bowman; Choreography, Anne Day. CAST: Alan Brasington (Archie Rice), Joseph Scolaro (Billy), Muriel Smallwood (Phoebe), Julie Frazer (Jean), James Ream (Frank), Margaret Huffstickler (Gorgeous Gladys), Phil DeSellem (Charlie/Pianist), David Mosedale (Graham), John Ortman (Brother Bill)

AS IS by William Hoffman. Cast and credits not submitted.

Joan Marcus Photos

**Michael Wells, Simon Brooking, Charles
Lippman, Michael Russotto, Tomas Kearney
in "Slab Boys"**

SYRACUSE STAGE

Syracuse, New York
Fourteenth Season

Producing Artistic Director, Arthur Storch; Managing Director, James A. Clark; Business Manager, Diana Coles; Development, Shirley Lockwood; Marketing/Communications, Barbara Beckos; Company Manager, Donna Inglima; Technical Director, William S. Tiesi; Sets, Gary May; Lighting, Sandra Schilling; Sound, Scott David Sanders; Costumer, Maria Marrero; Props, Susan Baker; Stage Managers, Cynthia Poulson, Don Buschmann; Press, Zoe Tolone

PRODUCTIONS & CASTS

LITTLE SHOP OF HORRORS with Music by Alan Menken; Book/Lyrics, Howard Ashman; Director, Carl Schurr; Set, Michael Miller; Lighting, Michael Newton-Brown; Costumes, Patricia M. Risser; Musical Direction, Bobby Hamilton; Musical Staging, Linda Sabo. CAST: Lovette George (Chiffon), Mona Wyatt (Crystal), Tonia Rowe (Ronnette), Irwin Ziff (Mushnik), Eydie Alyson (Audrey), Patrick Brian Collins (Seymour), Michael Dayton (Derelict/Manipulator), Michael Scott (Orin/Bernstein/Luce), Richard Kleber (Audrey II Voice)

A VIEW FROM THE BRIDGE by Arthur Miller; Director, Tony Giordano; Set, Hugh Landwehr; Costumes, Mary Ann Powell; Lighting, Dennis Parichy. CAST: Lawrence Palmisano (Louis), Jon Cavaluzzo (Mike), Dominic Chianese (Alfieri), Michael Fischetti (Eddie), Jennifer Van Dyck (Catherine), Diane Martella (Beatrice), Joe Aufiery (Marco), Rafael Ferrier (Rodolpho), Michael Twain, Len Bilotti (Immigration Officers), Sam Brown, Larry Richards, Anna Clark, Natasha DeFio, Nina DeFio, Joel Ancowitz, Raymond Galuppo

PYGMALION by George Bernard Shaw; Director, John Going; Set, Charles A. Cosler; Costumes, Maria Marrero; Lighting, Marcia Madeira. CAST: Marjorie Miller (Clara), Sally Chamberlin (Mrs. Eynsford-Hill), John R. Little (Freddy), Roma Downey (Eliza), Derek Murcott (Col. Pickering), Richard Poe (Henry Higgins), Myra Carter (Mrs. Pearce), Brendan Burke (Alfred Doolittle), Margaret Hilton (Mrs. Higgins), Lisa Wolff (Maid), Carrie Chantler, Steven Duprey, Dick Harris, Sheila Head, David Hessert, Paul Jackson, Andrea Marshall, Pat O'Connor, Phillip Swender, Roger Truesdell

OF MICE AND MEN by John Steinbeck; Director, Arthur Storch; Set, Victor A. Becker; Costumes, Maria Marrero; Lighting, Judy Rasmuson. CAST: Ron Perkins (George), Matthew Kimbrough (Lennie), Donald Plumley (Candy), Ben Kapen (The Boss), Kevin Eshelman (Curley), Alexandra Neil (Curley's Wife), William Perley (Slim), George Hosmer (Carlson), John Harnagel (Whit), Daryl Edwards (Crooks)

STAGE STRUCK by Simon Gray; Director, Tom Walsh; Costumes, Mary Zihal. CAST: Samuel Maupin (Robert), Jim Abele (Herman), Valerie Von Volz (Anne), John Rainer (Widdecombe)

ON THE VERGE or The Geography of Yearning by Eric Overmyer; Director, Robert Berlinger; Set, Michael Miller; Costumes, Maria Marrero; Lighting, Marc B. Weiss. CAST: Tanny McDonald (Mary), Marceline Hugot (Fanny), Claire Beckman (Alexandra), Jack Kenny (Alphonse/Grover/Troll/Yeti/Mr. Coffee/Mme. Nhu/Gus/Nicky)

Lawrence Mason, Jr.

Top Right: Michael Fischetti, Jennifer Van Dyck, Rafael Ferrer in "A View from the Bridge" Below: Alexandra Neil, Matthew Kimbrough, Ron Perkins in "Of Mice and Men"

Clayton Corzatte, Susan Ludlow-Corzatte
in "The Return of Herbert Bracewell"

TACOMA ACTORS GUILD

Tacoma, Washington

Artistic Director, William Becvar; Managing Director, Kate Haas; Technical Director, Jeff Noyes; Assistant Technical Director, J. Patrick Elmer; Costumes, Wendela K. Jones; Sound, Chuck Hatcher; Lighting/Sound, J. Patrick Elmer; Props, Tim Reda; Stage Managers, Hal Meng, Pamela Guion; Assistant Stage Managers, Diana Rodriguez, Betty Jean Williamson, Lisa Talso; Administrative Director, Nancy Hoadley; Marketing/Press, Connie Lehmen; Press Manager, Greg Monta; Finance/Operations, T. Sue Boyczuk

PRODUCTIONS & CASTS

THE HASTY HEART by John Patrick; Director, Rick Tutor; Set, Judith Cullen; Costumes, Rose Pederson; CAST: David Pichette (Orderly), John Pribyl (Yank), Michael Loggins (Digger), Gregg Loughridge (Kiwi), Ron Blair (Blossom), David H. MacIntyre (Tommy), Laura Ferri (Margaret), Edward Christian (Colonel), Tim Streeter (Lachlen)

WHO'S AFRAID OF VIRGINIA WOOLF? by Edward Albee; Director, William Becvar; Set, Jerry S. Hooker; CAST: Lori Larsen (Martha), Rick Tutor (George), Susan Ronn (Honey), Gregg Loughridge (Nick)

COWARDLY CUSTARD with Words and Music by Noel Coward; Devised by Gerald Frow, Alan Strachan, Wendy Toye; Director, David Ira Goldstein; Music Director, Rose This; Choreographer, Raymond Houle; Set, Bill Forester; Costumes, Frances Kenny; Lighting, Phil Schermer; Musicians, Dan Adams, Janice Bernsten-Mabin. CAST: Mark Anders, Dianne Benjamin Hill, Joanne Klein, Priscilla Hake Lauris, Randy Rogel, Michael Santo, Bill terKuile

THE RETURN OF HERBERT BRACEWELL by Andrew Johns; Director, Robert Robinson; Set, Judith Cullen; Lighting, Richard Devin; Choreographer, Kjelene Scolman. CAST: Clayton Corzatte (Herbert Bracewell), Susan Ludlow-Corzatte (Florence Bracewell)

THE STAR-SPANGLED GIRL by Neil Simon; Director, William Becvar; Set, Jerry S. Hooker; Costumes, Anne Thaxter Watson. CAST: William Downe (Andy Hobart), Eric Ray Anderson (Norman Cornell), Victoria Carver (Sophie Rauschmeyer)

SLEUTH by Anthony Shaffer; Director, Andrew Traister; Set, Everett Chase; Lighting, James Verdery. CAST: Rick Tutor (Andrew Wyke), Frank Corrado (Milo Tindle/Inspector Doppler)

Fred Andrews Photos

THEATRE BY THE SEA

Portsmouth, New Hampshire
Twenty-third Season

Artistic Director, Tom Markus; Management Advisor, Ira Schlosser; Production Manager, John Becker; Stage Manager, Dori Eskenazi; Lighting, Jon Terry; Costumes, Lisa Micheels; Marketing, Michael Reznicek; Development, Tom Birmingham

PRODUCTIONS & CASTS

COLE by Benny Green and Alan Strachan; Director, John Montgomery; Musical Director, Bruce W. Coyle; Set, Richard B. Williams. CAST: Marcy DeGonge, Patricia Kies, Howard Lawrence, Dorothy Stanley, Walter Willison

ISN'T IT ROMANTIC by Wendy Wasserstein; Director, Paul Mroczka; Set, John Falabela; Costumes, Jeffrey Ullman. CAST: Joanne Bayes, Franklin Brown, William Charlton, Jill Holden, Neal Learner, Bob Nixon, James Secrest, Michael Sousa, Maxine Taylor-Morris, Deborah-Jean Templin, Michael Tobin, Bonnie Jean Wilbur

THE GIFT OF THE MAGI by Peter Ekstrom

THE DIARY OF ADAM AND EVE by Jerry Bock and Sheldon Harnick; Director, Darwin Knight; Musical Director, Michael O'Flaherty; Set, Sharon Perlmutter, CAST: Catherine DuPuis, Buck Hobbs, Michael Scott

JOE EGG by Peter Nichols; Director, Tom Markus; Set, Ray Recht. CAST: Briana Campbell, Virginia Downing, Johanna Morrison, Alexandra O'Karma, David Pursley, Ian Stuart

Andy Edgar Photos

Carole Cook, Ronnie Claire Edwards
in "Patio/Porch"

THEATRE THREE

Dallas, Texas
Twenty-fifth Season

Founder/Artistic Director, Norma Young; Executive Producer/Director, Jac Alder; Associate Producer, Charles Howard; Associate Director, Laurence O'Dwyer; Operations, John Briggs; Press, Gary Yawn; Development, John Gunn; Literary Manager, Sharon Bunn; Stage Manager, Jimmy Mullen; Production Manager, Cheryl Denson; Business Manager, Cheryl Thrower; Musical Director, Terry Dobson; Marketing, Marian Rashap, Jack Rakes; Technical Director/Sound, Tristan Wilson

PRODUCTIONS & CASTS

PATIO/PORCH by Jack Heifner; Director, Tom Troupe; Sets, Charles Howard; Costumes, William Ware Theiss; Lighting, Shari Melde. CAST: Carole Cook, Ronnie Claire Edwards

MA RAINEY'S BLACK BOTTOM by August Wilson; Director, Laurence O'Dwyer; Set, Cheryl Denson; Lighting, James Lincoln; Sound Tristan Wilson; Costumes, Susie Thennes. CAST: Jo Livingston, Bill Bolender, Willie H. Minor, Linwood P. Walker III, Cushney Roberts, Tyress Allen, Marilyn Walton, Randy Rakes, Yolonda Williams, Steven Anthony Washington

LIES AND LEGENDS: THE MUSICAL STORIES OF HARRY CHAPIN with Music and Lyrics by Harry Chapin; Director, Bruce R. Coleman; Associate Director, Jac Alder; Sets, Cheryl Denson; Lighting, James Lincoln; Costumes, Susie Thennes. CAST: Keith D. Allgeier, Judy Blue, Scott Bradford, Anita Greene, Philip Hernandez

GRAND PREMIERE; Director, Laurence O'Dwyer; Stage Managers, Beverly Nachimson, Cecilia Flores; Special Direction, Keith Oncale, Bruce R. Coleman, David Stroh; Costumes, Chris Kovarik; Lighting, Jimmy Mullen; Coordinator, Charles Hoard; Designer, Jeff Santino. CAST: Morgan Fairchild, Jac Alder, Sharon Bunn, Camilla Carr, Connie Coit, Leslie Evans Leach, Cathryn Hartt, Doug Jackson, Shirley McFatter, Connie Nelson, Laurence O'Dwyer, Jane Riley, Steve Riley, Sally Soldo, Gary Taggert, Larry Whitcher, Norma Young, Tom Zinn, Keith D. Allgeier, Judy Blue, Scott Bradford, Anita Greene, Pat Ivey, Gary Mead, Keith Oncale, Peggy Pharr Wilson, Kurt Rhoads, Nance Williamson, Tess Campbell, Jim Caruso, Jerry Crow, Laura Yancey, Richard Rollins, Michael Skipper, Donald Snell, Peggy Billo, Jerry Chapa, Amy Mills, Greta Muller, Dwight Sandel, John Rainone, Neil Servetnik

A LITTLE NIGHT MUSIC with Music and Lyrics by Stephen Sondheim; Book, Hugh Wheeler; Director, Jac Alder; Sets, Charles Howard; Costumes, Mary Therese D'Avignon. CAST: Norma Young, Sharon Bunn, Paul Boesing, Natasha Harper, Jennifer Harper, Scott Bradford, Toby Richard, Sally Soldo, Peter Puckett, Shelley Clayton, Peggy Billo, Sonny Franks, Jim Ivey, Amy Mills, Greta Muller, Dianne Brown, Patricia Ivey, Keith Oncale, Tom S. Seay, Cheryl Weaver

THE SHOW-OFF by George Kelly; Director, Laurence O'Dwyer; Sets, Cheryl Denson; Costumes, Chris Kovarik. CAST: Vince Davis, Hugh Feagin, Jim Ivey, Thurman Moss, Connie Nelson, Ray Keith Pond, Michael Skipper, Mary Jane Wells, Nance Williamson

ANIMAL FARM by George Orwell; Adaptation, Peter Hall; Lyrics, Adrian Mitchell; Music, Richard Peaslee; *US Premiere;* Director, Laurence O'Dwyer; Musical Director, Gary C. Mead; Sets, Cheryl Denson; Lighting, Shari Melde; Costumes/Masks, Bruce R. Coleman. CAST: Craig Ames, Sa'mi Chester, Dwain Fail, Lynn Mathis, Kyle McClaran, Beverly Nachimson, Keith Oncale, Kati Porter, Stephanie Rascoe, Kurt Rhoads, Jeff Ricketts, Karen Seal, Ellen Osburn, Quigley Provost, Buckley Sachs, David Stroh

TOP GIRLS by Caryl Churchill; Director, Robin M. Stanton; Set, Tristan Wilson; Lighting, Neale Whitmore; Costumes, Bruce R. Coleman. CAST: Judy Blue, Sharon Bunn, Gail Cronauer, Cheryl Denson, Julie Mayfield, Frankie Wade, Victoria Wright

BLOOD KNOT by Athol Fugard; Director, Charles Howard; Lighting, Robert McVay; Costumes, Bruce R. Coleman. CAST: Hugh Feagin, Leonard Wilson

EL GESTICULADOR by Rodolfo Usigli; a joint venture with Teatro Hispano De Dallas; Director, Cora Cardona; Sets, Jac Alder; Costumes, Bruce R. Coleman; Lighting, Robert McVay; Assistant to Director, Jacky Flynn. CAST: Doug Stewart, Cora Cardona, Chris Carlos, Dolores Godinez, Randolph McKee, Richard Rollin, Carlos Salinas, George Grant, Frank Pena, Rudy Seppy, Everett Sifuentes, Roger Alan Gorton, Darryl Jackson, Danny Wilcox

Susan Kandell Photos

**Left Center: Walter Willison,
Dorothy Stanley in "Cole"**

TRINITY REPERTORY COMPANY

Providence, Rhode Island
Twenty-Third Season

Artistic Director, Adrian Hall; Managing Director, E. Timothy Langan; Assistant to Artistic Director, Marian Simon; Composer, Richard Cumming; New Play Research, Dorothy Cullman; Sets, Eugene Lee, Robert D. Soule; Lighting, John F. Custer; Costumes, William Lane; Production Manager, William Radka; Stage Managers, Wendy Cox, Ruth E. Sternberg; Development, Simone P. Joyaux; Marketing/Press, Anne Marden; Operations, Gene S. Minkow; Press, Jeannie Mac Gregor-Jochim, Jerry O'Brien
GUEST ARTISTS: Spalding Gray (solo performance); Directors, Tony Giordano, Philip Minor, Ken Bryant, David Wheeler, Paul Benedict; Choreographer, Julie Strandberg; Dance, Sharon Jenkins; Music, Randy Newman; Lighting, Natasha Katz; Dramaturg, Marsue Cumming MacNicol
RESIDENT COMPANY: Akin Babatunde, Barbara Blossom, Candy Buckley, James Carruthers, Michael Cobb, Timothy Crowe, William Damkoehler, Margot Dionne, Janice Duclos, Richard Ferrone, Peter Gerety, Ed Hall, Joseph Hindy, Keith Jochim, David C. Jones, Richard Kavanaugh, David Kennett, Richard Kneeland, Becca Lish, Howard London, Jane Loranger, Peter MacNicol, Mina Manente, Brian McEleney, Patricia McGuire, Derek Meader, Barbara Meek, Nicolas Mize, Andrew Mutnick, Richard Oberlin, Barbara Orson, Stella Reed, Anne Scurria, David PB Stephens, Cynthia Strickland, Frederick Sullivan Jr., Patricia Ann Thomas, Jennifer Van Dyck, Daniel Von Bargen, Dan Welch, Laura Ann Worthen
PRODUCTIONS: *Noises Off* by Michael Frayn; *A Funny Thing Happened on the Way to the Forum* by Burt Shevelove, Larry Gelbart, Stephen Sondheim; *Swimming to Cambodia, Terrors of Pleasure, Sex and Death to the Age 14* by Spalding Gray; *The Visit* by Friedrich Durrenmatt; *The Real Thing* by Tom Stoppard; *A Christmas Carol* by Charles Dickens, adapted by Adrian Hall, Richard Cumming; Music & Lyrics by Richard Cumming; *Hurlyburly* by David Rabe; *Our Town* by Thornton Wilder; *Glengarry Glen Ross* by David Mamet; *All the King's Men* by Robert Penn Warren, adapted by Adrian Hall; *Quartermaine's Terms* by Simon Gray; *A Lie of the Mind* by Sam Shepard

Mark Morelli Photos

Peter MacNicol, Peter Gerety in "All the King's Men" Below: Keith Jochim, William Damkoehler, Daniel Von Bargen, Peter Gerety in "Hurlyburly"

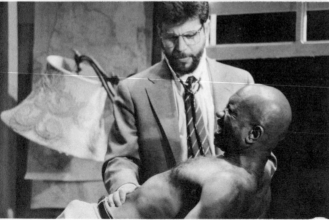

Danton Stone, Lou Myers in "Haut Gout"
Above: Jack Davidson, Michael Garfield
in "Cat on a Hot Tin Roof"

VIRGINIA STAGE COMPANY

Norfolk, Virginia
Eighth Season

Artistic Director, Charles Towers; Managing Director, Dan J. Martin; Associate Artistic Director, Christopher Hanna; Production Manager, Dan Sedgwick; Costumes, Candice Cain; Sound, Dirk Kuyk; Stage Manager, Nancy Kay Uffner; Technical Director, Christopher Fretts; Props, Donna Dickerson; Wigs, Tom Watson; General Manager, Caroline F. Turner; Marketing/Press, Stacey Milcos; Development, Alexis Caswell; Business Manager, Catherine Lake; Company Manager, Marge Prendergast
GUEST ARTISTS: Sets, Marjorie Bradley Kellogg, John Lee Beatty, Nancy Thun; Set/Lighting, Pavel Dobrusky; Lighting, Spencer Mosse, Jackie Manassee; Scenic Artists, Deborah Jasien, Lydia Romero; Music Consultant/Composer, June Cooper
PRODUCTIONS & CASTS
CAT ON A HOT TIN ROOF with Ellen Dolan (Margaret), Michael Garfield (Brick), Mary Chalon (Mae), Mary Hara (Big Mama), Jack Davidson (Big Daddy), John Scanlan (Rev. Tooker), Jude Ciccolella (Cooper), Stephen Lawrence Brown (Dr. Baugh), Rodney Suiter (Lacey), Chantee Davis (Sookey), Aaron Boone, Lindsay Dickon, Kate Rose, Noel Rose, Dawn Scott (Children)
THE FRONTIERS OF FARCE: *The Purging* and *The Singer* with Andreas Burgstaller, Arthur Schmidt, Robert Frisch, Lisa Barnes, Stephen Temperley, Mary Jean Feton, Lauren Thompson, John Scanlan
HAUT GOUT by Allan Havis *(World Premiere)* with Danton Stone (Dr. Jules Gold), Humbert Allen Astredo (Dr. Ludwig Furst), Gordana Rashovich (Jo Anne Gold), Helen Harrelson (Shirley Furst), Lou Myers (LeCroix), Valerie Brandon (Mati), Tom Rolfing (Latch)
THE TEMPEST with Jack Davidson, Laura San Giacomo, Lauren Tom, Richard Elmore, Jim Mohr, Tom Rolfing, Edward Seamon, Nesbitt Blaisdell, Stephen Pelinski, Robert Nelson, Edward D. Allen, Stephen Temperley, Edwin C. Owens, George L. Hasenstab, Scott Forbes Elliott

Mark Atkinson, Cathy Dixson Photos

WALNUT STREET THEATRE COMPANY

Philadelphia, Pennsylvania

Executive Director, Bernard Haver; General Manager, Mary Bensel; Literary Manager, Deborah Baer Quinn; Development, Donald U. Smith III; Marketing, Robin Wray; Production Manager, Ryszard Lukaszewicz; Props, Susan Badger; Wardrobe, Rachel Berkowitz; Stage Managers, Frank Anzalone, Vince Campbell, Kathryn Bauer; Press, Leslie B. Goldstein

PRODUCTIONS & CASTS

THE PRISONER OF SECOND AVENUE by Neil Simon; Director, Tom Markus; Set, Joseph A. Varga; Costumes, Lana Fritz; Lighting, Richard Moore. CAST: Robert Silver (Mel), Judith Granite (Edna), Eleanora Kaye (Jessie), David Berk (Harry), Yvette Edelhart (Pauline), Bette Jerome (Pearl/Lady Upstairs)

A LITTLE NIGHT MUSIC by Stephen Sondheim, Hugh Wheeler; Director, Jack Allison; Musical Director, Elman R. Anderson; Choreography, J. Randall Hugill; Set/Lighting, Fred Kolo; Costumes, Lewis D. Rampino. CAST: Michael Montague (Mr. Lindquist), Lisa Vroman (Mrs. Nordstrom), Susan Lee Daniels (Mrs. Anderson), Jason Opsahl (Mr. Erlanson), Terry Rakov (Mrs. Segstrom), Brad Scott (Mr. Bergman), Johnna Cummings (Fredrika), Paula Laurence (Mme. Armfeldt), Alex Corcoran (Frid), Hugh Panaro (Henrik), Jennifer Lee Andrews (Anne), David Cryer (Fredrik), Kate McCauley (Petra), Barbara Andres (Desiree), Ron Raines (Count Malcolm), Kelly Bishop (Countess Malcolm)

THE BIG KNIFE by Clifford Odets; Director, Malcolm Black; Set/Lighting, Paul Wonsek; Costumes, Kathleen Blake. CAST: Ronal Stepney (Russell), Allen Fitzpatrick (Buddy), Tony Musante (Charlie), Tresa Hughes (Patty), Deborah Strang (Marion), Lionel Croll (Nat), Donald Buka (Marcus), Douglas Wing (Smiley), Lisa Emery (Connie), Geddeth Smith (Hank), Zita Geoffroy (Dixie), Carl Harms (Dr. Frary)

DUMAS by John MacNicholas; Director, Larry Carpenter; Set, John Falabella; Costumes, Lowell Detweiler; Lighting, Marcia Madeira. CAST: Bob Hungerford (Albert/Lord Uppingham), Thomas Carson (Alphonse/Honore de Balzac), Louis Lippa (Gustave Bocage/Baron de Stackelberg), Roger Robinson (Alexander Dumas, pere), Geoffrey Owens (Alexander Dumas, fils), Lynn Chausow (Nicolette), Don Auspitz (Auguste Maquet), Ronal Stepney (Soulouque), Katharine Buffaloe (Susanne), Alex Corcoran (Eugene Dejazet), Judith Hansen (Marie Duplessis), Robin Chadwick (Eugene DeMirecourt), Cynthia Darlow (Lady Uppingham), Mark Capri (Charles, Duc de la Tour Longueville)

TINTYPES by Mary Kyte, Mel Marvin, Gary Pearle; Director, Charles Abbott; Musical Director, Elman R. Anderson; Set, Jeffrey Schneider; Costumes, Barbara Forbes; Lighting, Clarke W. Thornton; Assistant Director, Michael DiFonzo. CAST: Charles Abbott (Charlie), John-Charles Kelly (T.R.), Mary Denise Bentley (Susannah), Lynn Fitzpatrick (Anna), Mary Ellen Ashley (Emma)

ESCOFFIER KING OF CHEFS by Owen S. Rackleff; Director, Laurence Carr; Set, Robert Odorisio; Lighting, Nina Chwast. CAST: Owen S. Rackleff (Georges Auguste Escoffier)

EB & FLO by Blake Walton, Amy Whitman; Director, Jimmy Bohr; Set, Robert Odorisio; Costumes, Lynn A. Fox; Lighting, Nina Chwast. CAST: Ann Morrison (Jesse), Peter Samuel (Michael), Allen Kennedy (Raymond), Jona Harvey (Maggie)

THE NORMAL HEART by Larry Kramer; Director, Charlie Hensley; Set, Robert Odorisio; Costumes, Christine A. Moore; Lighting, Nina Chwast. CAST: Sam Guncler (Craig Donner/Grady/Orderly), Randall Forte (Mickey Marcus), Joel Swetow (Ned Weeks), Edward Gavin (David/Hiram/Doctor/Orderly), Deborah Mayo (Dr. Brookner), David Fuller (Bruce Niles), David McCann (Felix Turner), Robert Michael Kelly (Ben Weeks), Steven McCloskey (Tommy Boatwright)

THREE ONE-ACT PLAYS: Director, Andrew Lichtenberg; Costumes, Christine A. Moore; Lighting, Rebecca R. Klein; Sound, Jeff Chestek. *Applicant* by Harold Pinter; with Janis Dardaris (Miss Piffs), Edward Gavin (Mr. Lamb). *Audience* by Vaclav Havel; with Marty Vale (Head Maltster), Edward Gavin (Ferdinand Vanek). *One for the Road* by Harold Pinter; with Marty Vale (Nicolas), Edward Gavin (Victor), Chris Blake (Nicky), Janis Dardaris (Gila)

NASTY LITTLE SECRETS by Lanie Robertson; Director, Stuart Ross; Set, Robert Odorisio; Costumes, Robert Bevenger; Lighting, George McMahon; Sound, Cathy Ellen Slisky. CAST: Simon Brooking (Joe Orton), Robin Chadwick (Mr. Willoughby), Craig Fols (Kenneth Halliwell), Douglas Wing (Carnes)

David Cryer, Barbara Andres in "A Little Night Music" Below: Tony Musante, Geddeth Smith in "The Big Knife"

THE WHOLE THEATRE

Montclair, New Jersey

Producing Artistic Director, Olympia Dukakis; Associate Artistic Director, Apollo Dukakis; General Manager, Joseph Furnari; Marketing/Press, Bonnie Kramen; Development, David Edelman; Production Manager, Cheryl Soper-Christensen; Stage Managers, Kathleen Cunneen, Travis DeCastro; Sets, Michael Miller, Dale F. Jordan, Lewis Folden, Randy Benjamin, Patricia Woodbridge; Costumes, Karen Gerson, Sigrid Insull, Judy Dearing, Donna M. Larsen; Lighting, Rachel Budin, Ann G. Wrightson, Shirley Prendergast, Jackie Manassee; Directors, Romulus Linney, Suzanne Shepherd, Chris Silva, Billie Allen, Mitchell Ivers; Musical Directors, David Loud, Elena Ruehr

PRODUCTIONS & CASTS

POPS by Romulus Linney *(World Premiere)* with Jane Cronin, William Hardy, Robin Moseley, Adrianne Thompson, Peter Toran, Sam Tsoutsouvas

THE SEA GULL by Anton Chekhov with Alma Cuervo, Apollo Dukakis, Olympia Dukakis, Greg Germann, Mitchell Jason, Keith Reddin, Laila Robins, W. T. Martin, Rebecca Schull, Joseph Warren

WE WON'T PAY! WE WON'T PAY! by Dario Fo, Translated by R. G. Davis, with Apollo Dukakis, Alexandra Gersten, Susie Jordan, Sam Samuels, Joseph Siravo

STEAL AWAY by Ramona King with Patricia Clement, Dorothi Fox, Minnie Gentry, Shawn Judge, Lizan Mitchell, Louise Stubbs

BILLY BISHOP GOES TO WAR Written and Composed by John Gray in Collaboration with Eric Peterson, with Scott Ellis, David Loud

Jeffrey Sestilio Photos

W. T. Martin, Olympia Dukakis in "The Sea Gull" (Fred Mumford)

YALE REPERTORY THEATRE

New Haven, Connecticut

Artistic Director, Lloyd Richards; Managing Director, Benjamin Mordecai; Set Advisor, Ming Cho Lee; Costume Advisor, Jane Greenwood; Lighting Advisor, Jennifer Tipton; Speech Advisor, Barbara Somerville; Movement Advisor, Wesley Fata; Sets, Michael H. Yeargan; Costumes, Dunya Ramicova; Lighting, William B. Warfel; Music Coordinator, Daniel Egan; Assistant to Artistic Director, Tisch Jones; Dramaturgs, Gitta Honegger, Barbara Davenport, Joel Schechter, Mark Lord, Mona Heinze, Walter Bilderback, Margaret E. Glover, Mead Hunter; Business Manager, Patricia Egan; Development, Ann S. Johnson; Press/Marketing, Robert Widman; Production Supervisor, Bronislaw J. Sammler; Stage Managers, Maureen F. Gibson, Margaret Adair; Sound, David Budries, G. Thomas Clark, Susan J. West; Technical Director, Richard J. Loula; Scenic Artists, Kathy Dilkes, Kathryn Sharp; Props, Hunter Nesbitt Spence, J. D. Durst; Casting, Meg Simon/Fran Kumin

PRODUCTIONS & CASTS

HEARTBREAK HOUSE by George Bernard Shaw; Director, Alvin Epstein; Set, Tim Saternow. CAST: Mia Dillon (Ellie Dunn), Bette Henritze (Nurse Guiness), William Swetland (Capt. Shotover), Delphi Harrington (Lady Ariadne Utterword), Jane White (Mrs. Hesione Hushabye), Ralph Williams (Mazzini Dunn), Michael Tolan (Hector Hushabye), Jerome Kilty (Boss Mangan), Michael Lipton (Randall Utterword), Lesley Kahn, Sharon Brady, Bruce Katzman, Susan Gibney, Dana Smith, Patrick Kert, Bill Dawson, Peter Lewis, Pearce Bunting.

NEAPOLITAN GHOSTS (*Questi fantasmi!*) by Eduardo De Filippo; Translation, Marguerita Carra, Louise H. Warner; *World Premiere*; Director, David Chambers; Set, Philip R. Baldwin; Costumes, Ellen V. McCartney; Lighting, Michael R. Chybowski; Stage Manager, Cliff Warner. CAST: Steven Skybell (First Porter), Bruce MacVittie (Raffaele), Cameron M. Smith (Second Porter), Paul Perri (Gastone Califano), Richard Libertini (Pasquale Lojacono), Angela Pietropinto (Carmela), Jossie de Guzman (Maria), Francois Giroday (Alfredo Marigliano), Amy Aquino (Armida), Hebron Simckes-Joffe/Fredric Stolzman (Arturo), Michelle Wordie/Joanna Zahler (Silvia), S. Steven Skybell/Gail Shapiro (Maddalena), Daniel Chace, Cana Smith

THE WINTER'S TALE by William Shakespeare; Director, Gitta Honegger; Costumes, Ann Sheffield; Lighting, Michael Giannitti; Musical Director, Daniel Egan; Choreography, Wesley Fata. CAST: Ben Halley Jr., Robert Black, Denis Holmes, Dwight Bacquie, Mark Capri, Aleta Mitchell, Corey Hobbs, Robert Wise, Susan Knight, Susan Gibney, Paul Milikin, Bruce Katzman, Rob Faber, Priscilla Smith, Kirk Jackson, Babo Harrison, Mary Mara, Brennan Murphy, Anders Bolang, Erik Onate, Nesbitt Blaisdell, David Brisbin, Patrick Kerr, Mark Tankersley, Sharon Washington, Brennan Murphy, Stephanie Nash, Stephen Skybell, Gregory Wallace

WINTERFEST 7 Four New Plays in Repertory: *Apocalyptic Butterflies* by Wendy MacLeod (*World Premiere*); Director, Richard Hamburger; Set, E. David Cosier Jr., Costumes, Philip R. Baldwin; Lighting, Tim Saternow; Stage Manager, Neal Fox. CAST: Steven Skybell (Hank Tater), Tessie Hogan (Muriel), DeAnn Mears (Francine), Frank Hamilton (Dick), Susan Gibney (Trudi), Barbara Coburn Bragg, Colette Kilroy, Frank James Palmer. *Exact Change* by David Epstein (*World Premiere*); Director, Jacques Levy; Set, Marina Draghici; Lighting, Christopher Akerlind; Stage Manager, Maureen C. Donley. CAST: Caris Corfman (Mary), Geoff Pierson (Botts/Ritchie), Kenneth Ryan (Bompkee/Eddie), Jon Korkes (Merola/Ricky), Daniel Chace, Bill Dawson, Peter Lewis, Dana Smith. *The Cemetery Club* by Ivan Menchell (*World Premiere*); Director, William Glenn; Set, Tamara Turchette; Lighting, Michael R. Chybowski; Stage Manager, Tom Aberger. CAST: Patricia Englund (Ida), Sylvia Miles (Lucille), Vera Lockwood (Doris), Rod Colbin (Sam). *The Memento* by Wakako Yamauchi (*World Premiere*); Director, Dennis Scott; Set/Costumes, George Denes Suhayda; Lighting, Michael R. Chybowski; Sound, Ross S. Richards; Stage Manager, Gail A. Burns; Stage Manager, Anne Marie Hobson. CAST: Natsuko Ohama (Marie), Philip Moon (Doug), Ginny Yang (Ruth), Roxanne Chang (Judy), Stanford Egi (Junnichi)

A WALK IN THE WOODS by Lee Blessing; *World Premiere*; Director, Des McAnuff; Set, Bill Clarke; Costumes, Ellen V. McCartney; Lighting, Jennifer Tipton; Music, Michael S. Roth; Sound, Michael S. Roth, G. Thomas Clark. CAST: Josef Sommer (Audrey Botvinnik), Kenneth Welsh (John Honeyman), Bill Dawson, Frank James Palmer (Understudies)

A PLACE WITH THE PIGS Written and Directed by Athol Fugard; *World Premiere*; Set, Ann Sheffield; Costumes, Susan Hilferty; Lighting, Michael R. Chybowski; Sound, David Budries; Stage Manager, Cheryl Mintz. CAST: Athol Fugard (Pavel), Suzanne Shepherd (Praskovya), Colette Kilroy, Steven Skybell (Understudies)

ALMOST BY CHANCE A WOMAN: ELIZABETH by Dario Fo, Translated by Ron Jenkins; *American Premiere*; Director, Anthony Taccone; Set, Tim Saternow; Costumes, Marina Draghici; Lighting, Michael Giannitti. CAST: Joan MacIntosh (Elizabeth), Mary Lou Rosato (Martha), Tom Mardirosian (Egerton), Jim MacLaren, Erick Onate (Guards), Joe Morton (Mama Zaza), Daniel Chace (Boy), Peter Lewis (Assassin), Dwight Bacquie, Marcus Giamatti, Patrick Kerr, Frank James Palmer, Dana Smith

William B. Carter, Paul J. Penders Photos

Top Right: Mia Dillon, Delphi Harrington, Jane White in "Heartbreak House" Below: Mark Capri, Aleta Mitchell, Robert Black in "The Winter's Tale"

Joe Morton, Joan MacIntosh, Mary Lou Rosato in "Elizabeth" Above: Suzanne Shepherd, Athol Fugard in "A Place with the Pigs" (Gerry Goodstein)

PULITZER PRIZE PRODUCTIONS

1918-Why Marry? **1919**-No award, **1920**-Beyond the Horizon, **1921**-Miss Lulu Bett, **1922**-Anna Christie, **1923**-Icebound, **1924**-Hell-Bent fer Heaven, **1925**-They Knew What They Wanted, **1926**-Craig's Wife, **1927**-In Abraham's Bosom, **1928**-Strange Interlude, **1929**-Street Scene, **1930**-The Green Pastures, **1931**-Alison's House, **1932**-Of Thee I Sing, **1933**-Both Your Houses, **1934**-Men in White, **1935**-The Old Maid, **1936**-Idiot's Delight, **1937**-You Can't Take It with You, **1938**-Our Town, **1939**-Abe Lincoln in Illinois, **1940**-The Time of Your Life, **1941**-There Shall Be No Night, **1942**-No award, **1943**-The Skin of Our Teeth, **1944**-No award, **1945**-Harvey, **1946**-State of the Union, **1947**-No award, **1948**-A Streetcar Named Desire, **1949**-Death of a Salesman, **1950**-South Pacific, **1951**-No award, **1952**-The Shrike, **1953**-Picnic, **1954**-The Teahouse of the August Moon, **1955**-Cat on a Hot Tin Roof, **1956**-The Diary of Anne Frank, **1957**-Long Day's Journey into Night, **1958**-Look Homeward, Angel, **1959**-J. B., **1960**-Fiorello!, **1961**-All the Way Home, **1962**-How to Succeed in Business without Really Trying, **1963**-No award, **1964**-No award, **1965**-The Subject Was Roses, **1966**-No award, **1967**-A Delicate Balance, **1968**-No award, **1969**-The Great White Hope, **1970**-No Place to Be Somebody, **1971**-The Effect of Gamma Rays on Man-in-the-Moon Marigolds, **1972**-No award, **1973**-That Championship Season, **1974**-No award, **1975**-Seascape, **1976**-A Chorus Line, **1977**-The Shadow Box, **1978**-The Gin Game, **1979**-Buried Child, **1980**-Talley's Folly, **1981**-Crimes of the Heart, **1982**-A Soldier's Play, **1983**-'night, Mother, **1984**-Glengarry Glen Ross, **1985**-Sunday in the Park with George, **1986**-No award, **1987**-Fences

NEW YORK DRAMA CRITICS CIRCLE AWARDS

1936-Winterset, **1937**-High Tor, **1938**-Of Mice and Men, Shadow and Substance, **1939**-The White Steed, **1940**-The Time of Your Life, **1941**-Watch on the Rhine, The Corn is Green, **1942**-Blithe Spirit, **1943**-The Patriots, **1944**-Jacobowsky and the Colonel, **1945**-The Glass Menagerie, **1946**-Carousel, **1947**-All My Sons, No Exit, Brigadoon, **1948**-A Streetcar Named Desire, The Winslow Boy, **1949**-Death of a Salesman, The Madwoman of Chaillot, South Pacific, **1950**-The Member of the Wedding, The Cocktail Party, The Consul, **1951**-Darkness at Noon, The Lady's Not for Burning, Guys and Dolls, **1952**-I Am a Camera, Venus Observed, Pal Joey, **1953**- Picnic, The Love of Four Colonels, Wonderful Town, **1954**-Teahouse of the August Moon, Ondine, The Golden Apple, **1955**-Cat on a Hot Tin Roof, Witness for the Prosecution, The Saint of Bleecker Street, **1956**-The Diary of Anne Frank, Tiger at the Gates, My Fair Lady, **1957**-Long Day's Journey into Night, The Waltz of the Toreadors, The Most Happy Fella, **1958**-Look Homeward Angel, Look Back in Anger, The Music Man, **1959**-A Raisin in the Sun, The Visit, La Plume de Ma Tante, **1960**-Toys in the Attic, Five Finger Exercise, Fiorello! **1961**-All the Way Home, A Taste of Honey, Carnival, **1962**-Night of the Iguana, A Man for All Seasons, How to Succeed in Business without Really Trying, **1963**-Who's Afraid of Virginia Woolf?, **1964**-Luther, Hello Dolly!, **1965**-The Subject Was Roses, Fiddler on the Roof, **1966**-The Persecution and Assassination of Marat as Performed by the Inmates of the Asylum of Charenton under the Direction of the Marquis de Sade, Man of La Mancha, **1967**-The Homecoming, Cabaret, **1968**-Rosencrantz and Guildenstern Are Dead, Your Own Thing, **1969**-The Great White Hope, 1776, **1970**-The Effect of Gamma Rays on Man-in-the-Moon Marigolds, Borstal Boy, Company, **1971**-Home, Follies, The House of Blue Leaves, **1972**-That Championship Season, Two Gentlemen of Verona, **1973**-The Hot l Baltimore, The Changing Room, A Little Night Music, **1974**-The Contractor, Short Eyes, Candide, **1975**-Equus, The Taking of Miss Janie, A Chorus Line, **1976**-Travesties, Streamers, Pacific Overtures, **1977**-Otherwise Engaged, American Buffalo, Annie, **1978**-Da, Ain't Misbehavin', **1979**-The Elephant Man, Sweeney Todd, **1980**-Talley's Folly, Evita, Betrayal, **1981**-Crimes of the Heart, A Lesson from Aloes, Special Citation to Lena Horne, "The Pirates of Penzance, **1982**-The Life and Adventures of Nicholas Nickleby, A Soldier's Play, (no musical honored), **1983**-Brighton Beach Memoirs, Plenty, Little Shop of Horrors, **1984**-The Real Thing, Glengarry Glen Ross, Sunday in the Park with George, **1985**-Ma Rainey's Black Bottom, (no musical), **1986**-A Lie of the Mind, Benefactors, no musical, Special to Lily Tomlin and Jane Wagner, **1987**-Fences, Les Liaisons Dangereuses, Les Miserables

AMERICAN THEATRE WING ANTOINETTE PERRY (TONY) AWARD PRODUCTIONS

1948-Mister Roberts, **1949**-Death of a Salesman, Kiss Me, Kate, **1950**-The Cocktail Party, South Pacific, **1951**-The Rose Tattoo, Guys and Dolls, **1952**-The Fourposter, The King and I, **1953**-The Crucible, Wonderful Town, **1954**-The Teahouse of the August Moon, Kismet, **1955**-The Desperate Hours, The Pajama Game, **1956**-The Diary of Anne Frank, Damn Yankees, **1957**-Long Day's Journey into Night, My Fair Lady, **1958**-Sunrise at Campobello, The Music Man, **1959**-J. B., Redhead, **1960**-The Miracle Worker, Fiorello! tied with The Sound of Music, **1961**-Becket, Bye Bye Birdie, **1962**-A Man for All Seasons, How to Succeed in Business without Really Trying, **1963**-Who's Afraid of Virginia Woolf?, A Funny Thing Happened on the Way to the Forum, **1964**-Luther, Hello Dolly!, **1965**-The Subject Was Roses, Fiddler on the Roof, **1966**-The Persecution and Assassination of Marat as Performed by the Inmates of the Asylum of Charenton under the Direction of the Marquis de Sade, Man of La Mancha, **1967**-The Homecoming, Cabaret, **1968**-Rosencrantz and Guildenstern Are Dead, Hallelujah Baby!, **1969**-The Great White Hope, 1776, **1970**-Borstal Boy, Applause, **1971**-Sleuth, Company, **1972**-Sticks and Bones, Two Gentlemen of Verona, **1973**-That Championship Season, A Little Night Music, **1974**-The River Niger, Raisin, **1975**-Equus, The Wiz, **1976**-Travesties, A Chorus Line, **1977**-The Shadow Box, Annie, **1978**-Da, Ain't Misbehavin', Dracula, **1979**-The Elephant Man, Sweeney Todd, **1980**-Children of a Lesser God, Evita, Morning's at Seven, **1981**-Amadeus, 42nd Street, The Pirates of Penzance, **1982**-The Life and Adventures of Nicholas Nickleby, Nine, Othello, **1983**-Torch Song Trilogy, Cats, On Your Toes, **1984**-The Real Thing, La Cage aux Folles, **1985**-Biloxi Blues, Big River, Joe Egg, **1986**-I'm Not Rappaport, The Mystery of Edwin Drood, Sweet Charity, **1987**-Fences, Les Miserables, All My Sons

PREVIOUS THEATRE WORLD AWARD WINNERS

1944-45: Betty Comden, Richard Davis, Richard Hart, Judy Holliday, Charles Lang, Bambi Linn, John Lund, Donald Murphy, Nancy Noland, Margaret Phillips, John Raitt

1945-46: Barbara Bel Geddes, Marlon Brando, Bill Callahan, Wendell Corey, Paul Douglas, Mary James, Burt Lancaster, Patricia Marshall, Beatrice Pearson

1946-47: Keith Andes, Marion Bell, Peter Cookson, Ann Crowley, Ellen Hanley, John Jordan, George Keane, Dorothea MacFarland, James Mitchell, Patricia Neal, David Wayne

1947-48: Valerie Bettis, Edward Bryce, Whitfield Connor, Mark Dawson, June Lockhart, Estelle Loring, Peggy Maley, Ralph Meeker, Meg Mundy, Douglass Watson, James Whitmore, Patrice Wymore

1948-49: Tod Andrews, Doe Avedon, Jean Carson, Carol Channing, Richard Derr, Julie Harris, Mary McCarty, Allyn Ann McLerie, Cameron Mitchell, Gene Nelson, Byron Palmer, Bob Scheerer

1949-50: Nancy Andrews, Phil Arthur, Barbara Brady, Lydia Clarke, Priscilla Gillette, Don Hanmer, Marcia Henderson, Charlton Heston, Rick Jason, Grace Kelly, Charles Nolte, Roger Price

1950-51: Barbara Ashley, Isabel Bigley, Martin Brooks, Richard Burton, Pat Crowley, James Daly, Cloris Leachman, Russell Nype, Jack Palance, William Smothers, Maureen Stapleton, Marcia Van Dyke, Eli Wallach

1951-52: Tony Bavaar, Patricia Benoit, Peter Conlow, Virginia de Luce, Ronny Graham, Audrey Hepburn, Diana Herbert, Conrad Janis, Dick Kallman, Charles Proctor, Eric Sinclair, Kim Stanley, Marian Winters, Helen Wood

1952-53: Edie Adams, Rosemary Harris, Eileen Heckart, Peter Kelley, John Kerr, Richard Kiley, Gloria Marlowe, Penelope Munday, Paul Newman, Sheree North, Geraldine Page, John Stewart, Ray Stricklyn, Gwen Verdon

1953-54: Orson Bean, Harry Belafonte, James Dean, Joan Diener, Ben Gazzara, Carol Haney, Jonathan Lucas, Kay Medford, Scott Merrill, Elizabeth Montgomery, Leo Penn, Eva Marie Saint

1954-55: Julie Andrews, Jacqueline Brookes, Shirl Conway, Barbara Cook, David Daniels, Mary Fickett, Page Johnson, Loretta Leversee, Jack Lord, Dennis Patrick, Anthony Perkins, Christopher Plummer

1955-56: Diane Cilento, Dick Davalos, Anthony Franciosa, Andy Griffith, Laurence Harvey, David Hedison, Earle Hyman, Susan Johnson, John Michael King, Jayne Mansfield, Sara Marshall, Gaby Rodgers, Susan Strasberg, Fritz Weaver.

1956-57: Peggy Cass, Sydney Chaplin, Sylvia Daneel, Bradford Dillman, Peter Donat, George Grizzard, Carol Lynley, Peter Palmer, Jason Robards, Cliff Robertson, Pippa Scott, Inga Swenson

1957-58: Anne Bancroft, Warren Berlinger, Colleen Dewhurst, Richard Easton, Tim Everett, Eddie Hodges, Joan Hovis, Carol Lawrence, Jacqueline McKeever, Wynne Miller, Robert Morse, George C. Scott

1958-59: Lou Antonio, Ina Balin, Richard Cross, Tammy Grimes, Larry Hagman, Dolores Hart, Roger Mollien, France Nuyen, Susan Oliver, Ben Piazza, Paul Roebling, William Shatner, Pat Suzuki, Rip Torn

1959-60: Warren Beatty, Eileen Brennan, Carol Burnett, Patty Duke, Jane Fonda, Anita Gillette, Elisa Loti, Donald Madden, George Maharis, John McMartin, Lauri Peters, Dick Van Dyke

1960-61: Joyce Bulifant, Dennis Cooney, Sandy Dennis, Nancy Dussault, Robert Goulet, Joan Hackett, June Harding, Ron Husmann, James MacArthur, Bruce Yarnell

1961-62: Elizabeth Ashley, Keith Baxter, Peter Fonda, Don Galloway, Sean Garrison, Barbara Harris, James Earl Jones, Janet Margolin, Karen Morrow, Robert Redford, John Stride, Brenda Vaccaro

1962-63: Alan Arkin, Stuart Damon, Melinda Dillon, Robert Drivas, Bob Gentry, Dorothy Loudon, Brandon Maggart, Julienne Marie, Liza Minnelli, Estelle Parsons, Diana Sands, Swen Swenson

1963-64: Alan Alda, Gloria Bleezarde, Imelda De Martin, Claude Giraud, Ketty Lester, Barbara Loden, Lawrence Pressman, Gilbert Price, Philip Proctor, John Tracy, Jennifer West.

1964-65: Carolyn Coates, Joyce Jillson, Linda Lavin, Luba Lisa, Michael O'Sullivan, Joanna Pettet, Beah Richards, Jaime Sanchez, Victor Spinetti, Nicolas Surovy, Robert Walker, Clarence Williams III

1965-66: Zoe Caldwell, David Carradine, John Cullum, John Davidson, Faye Dunaway, Gloria Foster, Robert Hooks, Jerry Lanning, Richard Mulligan, April Shawhan, Sandra Smith, Leslie Ann Warren

1966-67: Bonnie Bedelia, Richard Benjamin, Dustin Hoffman, Terry Kiser, Reva Rose, Robert Salvio, Sheila Smith, Connie Stevens, Pamela Tiffin, Leslie Uggams, Jon Voight, Christopher Walken

1967-68: David Birney, Pamela Burrell, Jordan Christopher, Jack Crowder (Thalmus Rasulala), Sandy Duncan, Julie Gregg, Stephen Joyce, Bernadette Peters, Alice Playten, Michael Rupert, Brenda Smiley, Russ Thacker

1968-69: Jane Alexander, David Cryer, Blythe Danner, Ed Evanko, Ken Howard, Lauren Jones, Ron Leibman, Marian Mercer, Jill O'Hara, Ron O'Neal, Al Pacino, Marlene Warfield

1969-70: Susan Browning, Donny Burks, Catherine Burns, Len Cariou, Bonnie Franklin, David Holliday, Katharine Houghton, Melba Moore, David Rounds, Lewis J. Stadlen, Kristoffer Tabori, Fredricka Weber

1970-71: Clifton Davis, Michael Douglas, Julie Garfield, Martha Henry, James Naughton, Tricia O'Neil, Kipp Osborne, Roger Rathburn, Ayn Ruymen, Jennifer Salt, Joan Van Ark, Walter Willison

1971-72: Jonelle Allen, Maureen Anderman, William Atherton, Richard Backus, Adrienne Barbeau, Cara Duff-MacCormick, Robert Foxworth, Elaine Joyce, Jess Richards, Ben Vereen, Beatrice Winde, James Woods

1972-73: D'Jamin Bartlett, Patricia Elliott, James Farentino, Brian Farrell, Victor Garber, Kelly Garrett, Mari Gorman, Laurence Guittard, Trish Hawkins, Monte Markham, John Rubinstein, Jennifer Warren, Alexander H. Cohen (Special Award)

1973-74: Mark Baker, Maureen Brennan, Ralph Carter, Thom Christopher, John Driver, Conchata Ferrell, Ernestine Jackson, Michael Moriarty, Joe Morton, Ann Reinking, Janie Sell, Mary Woronov, Sammy Cahn (Special Award)

1974-75: Peter Burnell, Zan Charisse, Lola Falana, Peter Firth, Dorian Harewood, Joel Higgins, Marcia McClain, Linda Miller, Marti Rolph, John Sheridan, Scott Stevensen, Donna Theodore, Equity Library Theatre (Special Award)

1975-76: Danny Aiello, Christine Andreas, Dixie Carter, Tovah Feldshuh, Chip Garnett, Richard Kelton, Vivian Reed, Charles Repole, Virginia Seidel, Daniel Seltzer, John V. Shea, Meryl Streep, A Chorus Line (Special Award)

1976-77: Trazana Beverley, Michael Cristofer, Joe Fields, Joanna Gleason, Cecilia Hart, John Heard, Gloria Hodes, Juliette Koka, Andrea McArdle, Ken Page, Jonathan Pryce, Chick Vennera, Eva LeGallienne (Special Award)

1977-78: Vasili Bogazianos, Nell Carter, Carlin Glynn, Christopher Goutman, William Hurt, Judy Kaye, Florence Lacy, Armelia McQueen, Gordana Rashovich, Bo Rucker, Richard Seer, Colin Stinton, Joseph Papp (Special Award)

1978-79: Philip Anglim, Lucie Arnaz, Gregory Hines, Ken Jennings, Michael Jeter, Laurie Kennedy, Susan Kingsley, Christine Lahti, Edward James Olmos, Kathleen Quinlan, Sarah Rice, Max Wright, Marshall W. Mason (Special Award)

1979-80: Maxwell Caulfield, Leslie Denniston, Boyd Gaines, Richard Gere, Harry Groener, Stephen James, Susan Kellermann, Dinah Manoff, Lonny Price, Marianne Tatum, Anne Twomey, Dianne Wiest, Mickey Rooney (Special Award)

1980-81: Brian Backer, Lisa Banes, Meg Bussert, Michael Allen Davis, Giancarlo Esposito, Daniel Gerroll, Phyllis Hyman, Cynthia Nixon, Amanda Plummer, Adam Redfield, Wanda Richert, Rex Smith, Elizabeth Taylor (Special Award)

1981-82: Karen Akers, Laurie Beechman, Danny Glover, David Alan Grier, Jennifer Holliday, Anthony Heald, Lizbeth Mackay, Peter MacNicol, Elizabeth McGovern, Ann Morrison, Michael O'Keefe, James Widdoes, Manhatten Theatre Club (Special Award)

1982-83: Karen Allen, Suzanne Bertish, Matthew Broderick, Kate Burton, Joanne Camp, Harvey Fierstein, Peter Gallagher, John Malkovich, Anne Pitoniak, James Russo, Brian Tarantina, Linda Thorson, Natalia Makarova (Special)

1983-84: Martine Allard, Joan Allen, Kathy Whitton Baker, Mark Capri, Laura Dean, Stephen Geoffreys, Todd Graff, Glenne Headly, J. J. Johnston, Bonnie Koloc, Calvin Levels, Robert Westenberg, Ron Moody (Special)

1984-85: Kevin Anderson, Richard Chaves, Patti Cohenour, Charles S. Dutton, Nancy Giles, Whoopi Goldberg, Leilani Jones, John Mahoney, Laurie Metcalf, Barry Miller, John Turturro, Amelia White, Lucille Lortel (Special)

1985-86: Suzy Amis, Alec Baldwin, Aled Davies, Faye Grant, Julie Hagerty, Ed Harris, Mark Jacoby, Donna Kane, Cleo Laine, Howard McGillin, Marisa Tomei, Joe Urla, Ensemble Studio Theatre (Special)

1986-87: Annette Bening, Timothy Daly, Lindsay Madigan, Michael Maguire, Demi Moore, Molly Ringwald, Frances Ruffelle, Courtney B. Vance, Colm Wilkinson, Robert DeNiro (Special)

Elizabeth Ashley

Warren Beatty

Zoe Caldwell

Gregory Hines

Blythe Danner

Richard Gere

1987 THEATRE WORLD AWARD RECIPIENTS
(Outstanding New Talent)

ANNETTE BENING
of "Coastal Disturbances"

TIMOTHY DALY
of "Coastal Disturbances"

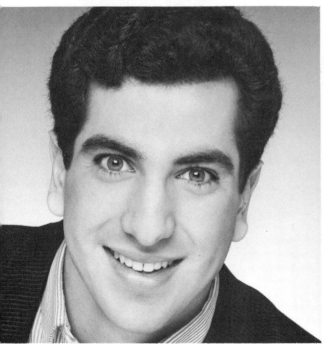

FRANK FERRANTE
of "Groucho: A Life in Revue"

LINDSAY DUNCAN
of "Les Liaisons Dangereuses"

ROBERT LINDSAY
of "Me and My Girl"

AMY MADIGAN
of "The Lucky Spot"

DEMI MOORE
of "The Early Girl"

MICHAEL MAGUIRE
of "Les Miserables"

COURTNEY B. VANCE
of "Fences"

MOLLY RINGWALD
of "Lily Dale"

FRANCES RUFFELLE
of "Les Miserables"

COLM WILKINSON
of "Les Miserables"

THEATRE WORLD AWARDS presentations, Thursday, May 28, 1987. Top (left and right): Laurie Beechman, Andrea McArdle, Walter Willison; James Earl Jones, Maureen Stapleton, Colleen Dewhurst, Page Johnson, Dorothy Loudon, Barbara Cook, John Rubinstein; Below: Christine Lahti, Harvey Fierstein, Linda Lavin, James Earl Jones, Maureen Stapleton, Colleen Dewhurst; Dorothy Loudon, Barbara Cook, John Rubinstein, Melba Moore, Karen Morrow; Bottom: Bill Lewis; John Rubinstein, Melba Moore: Dorothy Loudon, Barbara Cook; Len Cariou, Karen Morrow; Above: Timothy Daly, Caroline Kava, Frank Ferrante, Courtney B. Vance; Annette Bening, Robert Lindsay, Frances Ruffelle, Patricia Elliott, Don Bloomfield
Michael Viade, Van Williams Photos

Top: James Earl Jones, Maureen Stapleton, Colleen Dewhurst, Courtney B. Vance; Michael Maguire, Karen Morrow; Annette Bening, Len Cariou; Lindsay Duncan, Maureen Stapleton; Colleen Dewhurst, Colm Wilkinson; Below: Timothy Daly, Caroline Kava for Demi Moore, Robert Lindsay, Don Bloomfield for Molly Ringwald, Frank Ferrante, Patricia Elliott for Amy Madigan; Bottom: Christine Lahti, Harvey Fierstein, Frances Ruffelle, Karen Morrow, Annette Bening, James Earl Jones, Linda Lavin

Michael Viade, Van Williams Photos

| Jonas Abry | Betsy Aidem | Gerard Alessandrini | Martine Allard | Keith Allen | Christine Andreas |

BIOGRAPHICAL DATA ON THIS SEASON'S CASTS

AARON, CAROLINE. Born Aug. 7, 1954 in Richmond, Va. Graduate Catholic U. Bdwy debut 1982 in "Come Back to the 5 & Dime, Jimmy Dean," followed by "The Iceman Cometh," OB in "Flying Blind," "Last Summer at Bluefish Cove," "Territorial Rites," "Good Bargains," "The House of Bernarda Alba," "Tribute," "Social Security."

ABRAHAM, F. MURRAY. Born Oct. 24, 1939 in Pittsburgh, PA. Attended UTx. Debut OB 1967 in "The Fantasticks," followed by "An Opening in the Trees," "14th Dictator," "Young Abe Lincoln," "Tonight in Living Color," "Adaptation," "Survival of St. Joan," "The Dog Ran Away," "Fables," "Richard III," "Little Murders," "Scuba Duba," "Where Has Tommy Flowers Gone?," "Miracle Play," "Blessing," "Sexual Perversity in Chicago," "Landscape of the Body," "The Master and Margarita," "Biting the Apple," "The Seagull," "Caretaker," "Antigone," "Uncle Vanya," "The Golem," "Madwoman of Chaillot," "Twelfth Night," "Frankie and Johnny in the Claire de Lune," Bdwy in "Man in the Glass Booth"(1968), "6 Rms Riv Vu," "Bad Habits," "The Ritz," "Legend," "Teibele and Her Demon," "Macbeth."

ABRY, JONAS. Born May 12, 1975 in NYC. Debut OB (1986) and Bdwy (1987) in "Coastal Disturbances."

ABUBA, ERNEST. Born Aug. 25, 1947 in Honolulu, HI. Attended Southwestern Col. Bdwy debut 1976 in "Pacific Overtures," followed by "Loose Ends." OB in "Sunrise," "Monkey Music," "Station J.," "Yellow Fever," "Pacific Overtures," "Empress of China," "Man Who Turned into a Stick," "Shogun Macbeth."

ADAMS, MASON. Born Feb. 26, 1919 in NYC. UWisc. graduate. Bdwy credits include "Get Away Old Man," "Public Relations," "Career Angel," "Violet," "Shadow of My Enemy," "Tall Story," "Inquest," "Trial of the Catonsville 9," "The Sign in Sidney Brustein's Window," OB in "Meegan's Game," "Shortchanged Review," "Checking Out," "The Soft Touch," "Paradise Lost," "The Time of Your Life," "Danger: Memory!"

ADAMSON, DAVID. Born May 30, 1940 in Orange, NJ. Graduate Bucknell, Yale. Bdwy debut 1971 in "Unlikely Heroes," followed by "Full Circle," "Hamlet," "Hide and Seek," "Children of a Lesser God," OB in "Isadora Duncan Sleeps with the Russian Navy," "Sister Aimee," "Hamlet," "Happy Birthday Wanda June," "Henry V," "Ice Bridge," "Camp Meeting."

ADLER, BRUCE. Born Nov. 27, 1944 in NYC. Attended NYU. Debut 1957 OB in "It's a Funny World," followed by "Hard to be a Jew," "Big Winner," "The Golden Land," "The Stranger's Return," "The Rise of David Levinsky," Bdwy in "A Teaspoon Every Four Hours" (1971), "Oklahoma" (1979), "Oh, Brother!," "Sunday in the Park with George."

AHEARN, DANIEL. Born Aug. 7, 1948 in Washington, DC. Attended Carnegie-Mellon. Debut 1981 OB in "Woyzek," followed by "Brontosaurus Rex," "Billy Liar," "Second Prize Two Months in Leningrad," "Free Fall."

A'HEARN, PATRICK. Born Sept. 4, 1957 in Cortland, NY. Graduate Syracuse U. Debut 1985 OB in "Pirates of Penzance," followed by "Forbidden Broadway," followed by Bdwy in "Les Miserables" (1987).

AIDEM, BETSY. Born Oct. 28, 1957 in Eastmeadow, NY. Graduate NYU. Debut 1981 OB in "The Trading Post," followed by "A Different Moon," "Balm in Gilead," "Crossing the Bar," "Our Lady of the Tortilla."

AIELLO, DANNY. Born June 20, 1935 in NYC. Bdwy debut 1975 in "Lamppost Reunion" for which he received a Theatre World Award, followed by "Wheelbarrow Closers," "Gemini," "Knockout," "The Floating Light Bulb," "Hurlyburly," "House of Blue Leaves."

ALDREDGE, TOM. Born Feb. 28, 1928 in Dayton, Oh. Attended Dayton U., Goodman Theatre. Bdwy debut 1959 in "The Nervous Set," followed by "UTBU," "Slapstick Tragedy," "Everything in the Garden," "Indians," "Engagement Baby," "How the Other Half Loves," "Sticks and Bones," "Where's Charley?," "Leaf People," "Rex," "Vieux Carre," "St. Joan," "Stages," "On Golden Pond," "The Little Foxes," OB in "The Tempest," "Between Two Thieves," "Henry V," "The Premise," "Love's Labour's Lost," "Troilus and Cressida," "Butter and Egg Man," "Ergo," "Boys in the Band," "Twelfth Night," "Colette," "Hamlet," "The Orphan," "King Lear," "The Iceman Cometh," "Black Angel," "Getting Along Famously," "Fool for Love," "Neon Psalms."

ALESSANDRINI, GERARD. Born Nov. 27, 1953 in Boston, Ma. Graduate Boston Consv. Debut 1982 OB in "Forbidden Broadway."

ALEXANDER, JASON. Born Sept. 23, 1959 in Irvington, NJ. Attended Boston U. Bdwy bow 1981 in "Merrily We Roll Along," followed by "Broadway Bound, OB in "Forbidden Broadway." "Stop the World . . . ," "D.," "Personals."

ALICE, MARY. Born Dec. 3, 1941 in Indianola, Ms. Debut 1967 OB in "Trials of Brother Jero," followed by "The Strong Breed," "Duplex," "Thoughts," "Miss Julie," "House Party," "Terraces," "Heaven and Hell's Agreement," "In the Deepest Part of Sleep," "Cockfight," "Julius Caesar," "Nongogo," "Second Thoughts," "Spell #7," "Zooman and the Sign," "Glasshouse," "The Ditch," "Take Me Along," "Departures," "Marathon 86," Bdwy in "No Place to Be Somebody" (1971), "Fences."

ALLARD, MARTINE. Born Aug. 24, 1970 in Brooklyn, NY. Bdwy debut 1983 in "The Tap Dance Kid" for which she received a Theatre World Award.

ALLEN, DEBBIE (a.k.a. Deborah) Born Jan. 16, 1950 in Houston, Tx. Graduate Howard U. Debut 1972 OB in "Ti-Jean and His Brothers," followed by "Anna Lucasta," "Louis," Bdwy in "Raisin" (1973), "Ain't Misbehavin'," "West Side Story," "Sweet Charity."

ALLEN, ELIZABETH. Born Jan. 25, 1934 in Jersey City, NJ. Attended Rutgers U. Bdwy debut 1957 in "Romanoff and Juliet," followed by "The Gay Life," "Do I Hear a Waltz?," "Sherry!," "42nd Street."

ALLEN, JOAN. Born Aug. 20, 1956 in Rochelle, IL. Attended E. Ill. U., W. ILL. U. Debut 1983 OB in "And a Nightingale Sang" for which she received a Theatre World Award, followed by "The Marriage of Bette and Boo," "Marathon '86," "Burn This!"

ALLEN, KAREN. Born Oct. 5, 1951 in Carrollton, Il. Attended Geo. Wash. U., UMd. Bdwy debut 1982 in "Monday after the Miracle" for which she received a Theatre World Award, OB in "Extremities" followed by "The Miracle Worker."

ALLEN, KEITH. Born Feb. 18, 1964 in Daytona Beach, FL. Bdwy debut 1986 in "La Cage aux Folles."

ALLER, JOHN. Born July 5, 1957 in Cuba. Graduate Hofstra U. Debut 1985 OB in "Pacific Overtures," followed by "Miami," Bdwy in "Rags" (1986).

ALMQUIST, GREGG. Born Dec. 1, 1948 in Minneapolis, Mn. Graduate UMinn. Debut 1974 OB in "Richard III," followed by "A Night at the Black Pig," "Mother Courage," "King Lear," Bdwy in "I'm Not Rappaport" (1986).

ALTON, DAVID. Born May 21, 1949 in Philadelphia, Pa. Graduate LaSalle Col. Debut OB in Propaganda"(1987).

AMENDOLIA, DON. Born Feb. 1, 1945 in Woodbury, NJ. Attended Glassboro State Col., AADA. Debut 1966 OB in "Until the Monkey Comes," followed by "Park," "Cloud 9," Bdwy 1984 in "My One and Only," followed by "Stepping Out."

ANDERMAN, MAUREEN. Born Oct. 26, 1946 in Detroit, Mi. Graduate UMich. Bdwy debut 1970 in "Othello," followed by "Moonchildren" for which she received a Theatre World Award, "An Evening with Richard Nixon . . . ," "The Last of Mrs. Lincoln," "Seascape," "Who's Afraid of Virginia Woolf?," "A History of the American Film," "The Lady from Dubuque," "The Man Who Came to Dinner," "Einstein and the Polar Bear," "You Can't Take It with You," "Macbeth," "Benefactors," "Social Security," OB in "Hamlet," "Elusive Angel," "Out of Our Father's House," "Sunday Runners."

ANDERSON, CHRISTINE. Born Aug. 6 in Utica, NY. Graduate UWi. Bdwy debut in "I Love My Wife" (1980), OB in "I Can't Keep Running in Place," "On the Swing Shift," "Red, Hot and Blue," "A Night at Texas Guinan's," "Nunsense."

ANDERSON, JEAN. Born Dec. 12, 1907 in Eastbourne, Eng. Graduate RADA. Bdwy debut 1987 in the Royal Shakespeare Co.'s "Les Liaisons Dangereuses."

ANDERSON, JOEL. Born Nov. 19, 1955 in San Diego, Ca. Graduate UUtah. Debut 1980 OB in "A Funny Thing Happened on the Way to the Forum," followed by "Joan of Lorraine," "Last of the Knucklemen," "The Widow Claire."

ANDERSON, KEVIN. Born Jan. 13, 1960 in Illinois. Attended Goodman School. Debut 1985 OB in "Orphans" for which he received a Theatre World Award.

ANDERSON, SYDNEY. Born Apr. 4 in Tacoma, WA. Graduate UWa. Debut 1978 OB in "Gay Divorce," Bdwy in "A Broadway Musical" (1978), followed by "Charlie and Algernon," "Oklahoma!," "La Cage aux Folles."

ANDERSON, THOMAS. Born Nov. 28, 1906 in Pasadena, Ca. Attended Pasadena Jr. Col., AmThWing. Bdwy debut 1934 in "4 Saints in 3 Acts," followed by "Roll Sweet Chariot," "Cabin in the Sky," "Native Son," "Set My People Free," "How Long Till Summer," "A Hole in the Head," "The Great White Hope," "70 Girls 70," OB in "Conquering Thursday," "The Peddler," "The Dodo Bird," "Don't Play Us Cheap," "Anna Lucasta," "Willie," "Time out of Time."

ANDREAS, CHRISTINE. Born Oct. 1, 1951 in Camden, NJ. Bdwy debut 1975 in "Angel Street," followed by "My Fair Lady" for which she received a Theatre World Award, "Oklahoma!(1979), "On Your Toes," "Rags," OB in "Disgustingly Rich," "Rhapsody in Gershwin," "Alex Wilder:Clues to a Life."

ANDREWS, DAVID. Born in 1952 in Baton Rouge, La. Attended LSU. Debut 1985 OB in "Fool for Love," followed by "Safe Sex."

ANDREWS, GEORGE LEE. Born Oct. 13, 1942 in Milwaukee, Wi. Debut OB 1970 in "Jacques Brel Is Alive and Well . . .," followed by "Starting Here Starting Now," "Vamps and Rideouts," "The Fantasticks," Bdwy in "A Little Night Music" (1973), "On the 20th Century," "Merlin."

ANGELA, JUNE. Born Aug. 18, 1959 in NYC. Bdwy debut 1970 in "Lovely Ladies, Kind Gentlemen," followed by "The King and I"(1977), OB in "Dream of Kitamura."

ARANAS, RAUL. Born Oct. 1, 1947 in Manilla, PI. Graduate Pace U. Debut 1976 OB in "Savages," followed by "Yellow Is My Favorite Color," "49," "Bullet Headed Birds," "Tooth of Crime," "Teahouse," "Shepard Sets," "Cold Air," "La Chunga," "The Man Who Turned into a Stick," "Twelfth Night," "Shogun Macbeth," Bdwy in "Loose Ends" (1978).

ARANHA, RAY. Born May 1, 1939 in Miami. Fl. Graduate Fl. A&M U., AADA. Bdwy debut 1987 in "Fences." OB in "Zooman and the Sign" (1980).

ARCARO, ROBERT (a.k.a. Bob) Born Aug. 9, 1952 in Brooklyn, NY. Graduate Wesleyan U. Debut 1977 OB in "New York City Street Show," followed by "Working Theatre Festival," "Man with a Raincoat," "Working One-Acts."

ARMSTRONG, MARY. Born in NYC. Graduate Manhattanville Col., Neighborhood Playhouse. Debur 1976 OB in "Uncle Vanya," followed by "The Boor," "Beyond the Horizon," "Riders to the Sea," "China Fish."

AROESTE, JOEL. Born April 10, 1949 in NYC. Graduate SUNY. Bdwy debut 1986 in "Raggedy Ann."

ASBURY, CLEVE. Born Dec. 29, 1958 in Houston, Tx. Attended L.A.Valley Col. Bdwy debut 1979 in "Peter Pan," followed by "West Side Story," "Bring Back Birdie," "Copperfield," "Harrigan 'n' Hart," "Me and My Girl."

ASQUITH, WARD. Born March 21 in Philadelphia, Pa. Graduate UPa., Columbia U. Debut 1979 OB in "After the Rise," followed by "Kind Lady," "Incident at Vichy," "Happy Birthday Wanda June," "Another Part of the Forest," "The Little Foxes."

ASTREDO, HUMBERT ALLEN. Born in San Francisco, Ca. Attended SanFranU. Debut 1967 OB in "Arms and the Man," followed by "Fragments," "Murderous Angels," "Beach Children," "End of Summer," "Knuckle," "Grand Magic," "Big and Little," "Jail Diary of Albie Sachs," "Breakfast Conversations in Miami," "December 7th," "Epic Proportions," Bdwy in "Les Blancs" (1970), "An Evening with Richard Nixon . . .," "The Little Foxes" (1981).

ATKINSON, JAYNE. Born Feb. 18, 1959 in Bournemouth, Eng. Graduate NorthwesternU., Yale. Debut 1986 OB in "Bloody Poetry," followed by "Terminal Bar," "Return of Pinocchio," Bdwy in "All My Sons" (1987).

AUSTIN, BETH. (a.k.a. Elizabeth) Born May 23, 1952 in Philadelphia, Pa. Graduate Point Park Col., Pittsburgh Playhouse. Debut 1977 OB in "Wonderful Town," followed by "The Prevalence of Mrs. Seal," "Engaged," "Pastoral," "Head over Heels," "A Kiss Is Just a Kiss," "Tales of Tinseltown," "Olympus on My Mind," Bdwy in "Sly Fox" (1977), "Whoopee!," "Onward Victoria!," "Raggedy Ann."

AUSTIN, IVY. Born Jan. 19, 1958 in Brooklyn, NY. Graduate Colgate U. Bdwy debut 1986 in "Raggedy Ann," followed by NYCOpera's "Candide," "Sweeney Todd," "The Merry Widow," "South Pacific."

AVRAMOFF, VIVIENNE. Born Oct. 25, 1954. Graduate of Cambridge U. Bdwy debut 1983 with Royal Shakespeare Co. in "All's Well That Ends Well," followed by "Wild Honey," OB in "Henry V."

AYR, MICHAEL. Born Sept. 8, 1953 in Great Falls, MT. Graduate SMU. Debut 1976 OB in "Mrs. Murray's Farm," followed by "The Farm," "Ulysses in Traction," "Lulu" "Cabin 12," "Stargazing," "The Deserter," "Hamlet," "Mary Stuart," "Save Grand Central," "The Beaver Coat," "Richard II," "Great Grandson of Jedediah Kohler," "Domestic Issues," "Time Framed," "The Dining Room," "The Sea Gull," "Love's Labour's Lost," "Rum and Coke," Bdwy in "Hide and Seek" (1980), "Piaf," "The Musical Comedy Murders of 1940."

AZITO, TONY. Born July 18, 1948 in NYC. Attended Juilliard. Debut 1971 OB in "Red White and Black," followed by "Players Project," "Secrets of the Citizens Correction Committee," "Threepenny Opera," "Buskers," "Twelfth Night," Bdwy in "Happy End" (1977), "Pirates of Penzance," "The Mystery of Edwin Drood."

BACKUS, RICHARD. Born Mar. 28, 1945 in Goffstown, NH Harvard graduate. Bdwy debut 1971 in "Butterflies Are Free," followed by "Promenade All," for which he received a Theatre World Award, "Ah, Wilderness!," "Camelot" (1981), OB in "Studs Edsel," "Gimme Shelter," "Sorrows of Stephen," "Missing Persons," "Henry V," "Talley and Son," "Tomorrow's Monday."

BACON, KEVIN. Born July 8, 1958 in Philadelphia, PA. Debut 1978 OB in "Getting Out," followed by "Glad Tidings," "Album," "Flux," "Poor Little Lambs," "Slab Boys," "Men without Dates," "Loot," "Marathon 87."

BAFF, REGINA. Born Mar. 31, 1949 in The Bronx, NY. Attended Western Reserve, Hunter Col. Debut 1969 OB in "The Brownstone Urge," followed by "Patrick Henry Lake Liquors," "The Cherry Orchard," "Domino Courts," "The Rachel Plays," "Donkey's Years," Bdwy in "Story Theatre, "Metamorphosis," "Veronica's Room," "West Side Waltz."

BAGDEN, RONALD. Born Dec. 26, 1953 in Philadelphia, Pa. Graduate Temple U, RADA. Debut 1977 OB in "Oedipus Rex," followed by "Oh! What a Lovely War," "Jack," Bdwy in "Amadeus" (1980).

BAGNERIS, VERNEL. Born July 31, 1949 in New Orleans, La. Graduate Xavier U. Debut 1979 OB in "One Mo' Time" followed by "Staggerlee" both of which he wrote and directed.

BAILA, WENDY. Born April 5, 1961 in NYC. Graduate SUNY/Binghamton. Debut 1986 OB in "Hot Sake," followed by "The Rise of David Levinsky."

BAKER, BLANCHE. Born Dec. 20, 1956 in NYC. Attended Wellesley Col. Bdwy debut 1981 in "Lolita," followed by OB's "Poor Little Lambs," "Hannah," "Steel Magnolias."

BAKER, RAYMOND. Born July 9, 1948 in Omaha, NE. Graduate UDenver. Debut 1972 OB in "The Proposition," followed by "Are You Now or Have You Ever Been . . .," "Character Lines," "Lunch Hour," "Legends of Arthur," "War Babies," "Bathroom Plays," "I'm Not Rappaport," "The Lucky Spot," Bdwy in "Crimes of the Heart," "Division Street," "Is There Life After High School?," "Torch Song Trilogy."

BAKER-JONES, GLORIA. Born May 22 in NYC. Debut OB 1981 in "The Magic Talisman," followed by "Basin Street," "Busting Out of the Boxes," "The Me Nobody Knows," "Back in the Big Time."

BALDINO, MISSY. Born June 13, 1959 in Philadelphia, Pa. Graduate St. Francis Col. Debut 1985 OB in "What's a Nice Country Like You Doing in a State Like This?", followed by "Salon."

BALDWIN, ALEC. Born Apr. 3, 1958 in Massapequa, NY. Attended George Washington U, NYU, Lee Strasberg Inst. Bdwy debut 1986 in "Loot," for which he received a Theatre World Award.

BALIN, INA. Born Nov. 12, 1937 in Brooklyn, NY. Attended NYU. Bdwy debut 1957 in "Compulsion," followed by "A Majority of One" for which she received a Theatre World Award, OB in "Face to Face."

BALOU, BUDDY. Born in 1953 in Seattle, WA. Joined American Ballet Theatre in 1970, rising to soloist. Joined Dancers in 1977. Bdwy debut 1980 in "A Chorus Line," followed by "Song and Dance."

BANES, LISA. Born July 9, 1955 in Chagrin Falls, OH. Juilliard grad. Debut OB 1980 in "Elizabeth I," followed by "A Call from the East," "Look Back in Anger" for which she received a Theatre World Award, "My Sister in This House," "Antigone," "Three Sisters," "The Cradle Will Rock," "Isn't It Romantic," "Fighting International Fat," "Ten by Tennessee," "On the Verge."

BANKSTON, ARNOLD III. Born June 2, 1955 in Los Angeles, Ca. Graduate L.A.City Col. HB Studio. Debut 1985 OB in "A Flash of Lightning," followed by "Mirandolina," "The Journal of Albion Moonlight," Bdwy in "Shakespeare on Broadway"(1987).

BANSAVAGE, LISA. Born Mar. 22, 1953 in Syracuse, NY. Graduate Carnegie-Mellon U, UPittsburgh. Debut 1983 OB in "The Changeling," followed by "As You Like It."

BARAN, EDWARD. Born May 18, 1950 in Minneapolis, Mn. Graduate Williams Col. Debut 1984 OB in "A Fool's Errand," followed by "The Wonder Years," 1951, "The Sneaker Factor."

BARKER, CHRISTINE. Born Nov. 26 in Jacksonville, FL. Attended UCLA. Bdwy debut 1979 in "A Chorus Line."

BARO, REGINA. Born Sept. 7 in NYC. Attended HB Studio. Debut 1987 OB in "Bodega."

BARON, EVALYN. Born Apr. 21, 1948 in Atlanta, GA. Graduate Northwestern., UMinn. Debut 1979 OB in "Scrambled Feet," followed by "Hijinks," "I Can't Keep Running in Place," "Jerry's Girls," "Harvest of Strangers," "Quilters," Bdwy in "Fearless Frank" (1980), "Big River," "Rags." "Social Security."

BARRE, GABRIEL. Born Aug. 26, 1957 in Brattleboro, VT. Graduate AADA. Debut 1977 OB in "Jabberwock," followed by "T.N.T.," "Bodo," "The Baker's Wife," "The Time of Your Life," "Children of the Sun," "Wicked Philanthropy," "Starmites," Bdwy in "Rags" (1986).

BARRETT, BRENT. Born Feb 28, 1957 in Quinter, KS. Graduate Carnegie-Mellon. Bdwy debut 1980 in "West Side Story," followed by "Dance a Little Closer," OB in "March of the Falsettos," "Portrait of Jenny," "The Death of Von Richthofen," "Sweethearts in Concert," "What's a Nice Country like You . . .," "Time of the Cuckoo," "Swan Song."

BARRETT, JOE. Born Nov. 30, 1950 in Webster, NY. Graduate URochester. Debut 1975 OB in "Boy Meets Boy," followed by "The Great American Backstage Musical," "Personals," Bdwy in "Raggedy Ann"(1986).

BARRON, DOUGLAS. Born Oct. 27, 1953 in Topeka, Ks. Attended AzStateU. Debut OB 1985 in "Stud Silo," followed by "Dance of the Mayfly," "Carver Stories."

BART, ROGER. Born Sept. 29, 1962 in Norwalk, Ct. Graduate Rutgers U. Debut 1984 OB in "A Second Wind," followed by "Lessons," Bdwy in "Big River" (1987).

BARTENIEFF, GEORGE. Born Jan. 24, 1933 in Berlin, Ger. Bdwy debut 1947 in "The Whole World Over," followed by "Venus Is," "All's Well That Ends Well," "Quotations from Chairman Mao Tse-Tung," "The Death of Bessie Smith," "Cop-Out," "Room Service," "Unlikely Heroes," OB in "Walking to Waldheim," "Memorandum," "The Increased Difficulty of Concentration," "Trelawny of the Wells," "Charley Chestnut Rides the IRT," "Radio (Wisdom): Sophia Part I," "Images of the Dead," "Dead End Kids," "The Blonde Leading the Blonde," "The Dispossessed," "Growing Up Gothic," "Rosetti's Apologies," "On the Lam," "Samuel Beckett Trilogy," "Quartet," "Help Wanted," "A Matter of Life and Death," "The Heart That Eats Itself."

BARTLETT, ROBIN. Born Apr. 22, 1951 in NYC. Graduate Boston U. Bdwy debut 1975 in "Yentl," followed by "The World of Sholem Aleichem," OB in "Agamemnon," "Fathers and Sons," "No End of Blame," "Living Quarters," "After the Fall," "Cheapside," "The Early Girl."

BARTO, MARY. Born Sept. 27 in Easton, Md. Graduate Peabody Conservatory, Juilliard, Neighborhood Playhouse. Bdwy debut 1980 in "Annie," followed by "The King and I," OB in "A Marriage Proposal," "The Blue Hour," "Hamlet."

BARTON, DANIEL. Born Jan. 23, 1949 in Buffalo, NY. Attended Buffalo State, Albany State. Bdwy debut 1976 in "The Poison Tree," followed by "Timbuktu," OB in "The House of Shadows," "Black Medea," "Legend of Serpents."

BARTON, FRED. Born Oct. 20, 1958 in Camden, NJ. Graduate Harvard. Debut 1982 OB in "Forbidden Broadway."

BASSETT, STEVE. Born June 25, 1952 in Escondido, Ca. Graduate Juilliard. Bdwy debut 1979 in "Deathtrap," followed by OB's "Spring Awakening," "Booth," "Full Hookup," "As Is."

BATES, KATHY. Born June 18, 1948 in Memphis, TN, Graduate S. Methodist U. Debut 1976 OB in "Vanities," followed by "The Art of Dining," "Curse of the Starving Class," "Frankie and Johnny in the Claire de Lune," Bdwy in "Goodbye Fidel" (1980), "5th of July," "Come Back to the 5 & Dime, Jimmy Dean," " 'night, Mother."

BATT, BRYAN. Born March 1, 1963 in New Orleans, La. Graduate Tulane U. Debut 1987 OB in "Too Many Girls."

BATTEN, THOMAS. Born in Oklahoma City, Ok. Graduate USC. Bdwy debut1961 in "How to Succeed in Business . . . ," followed by "Mame," "Gantry," "Mack and Mabel," "She Loves Me," "On the 20th Century," "Can-Can," "Into the Light."

BAVAN, YOLANDE. Born June 1, 1942 in Ceylon. Attended UColombo. Debut 1964 OB in "A Midsummer Night's Dream," followed by "Jonah," "House of Flowers," "Salvation," "Tarot," "Back Bog Beast Bait," "Leaves of Grass," "End of the War," "The Bald Soprano/The Leader," Bdwy in "Heathen," "Snow White."

BAVAN, YOLANDE. Born June 1, 1942 in Ceylon. Attended UColombo. Debut 1964 OB in "A Midsummer Night's Dream," followed by "Jonah," "House of Flowers," "Salvation," "Tarot," "Back Bog Beast Bait," "Leaves of Grass," "The End of the War," "Departures," Bdwy in "Heathen," "Snow White."

BEAN, REATHEL. Born Aug. 24, 1942 in Missouri. Graduate Drake U. OB in "America Hurrah," "San Francisco's Burning," "Love Cure," "Henry IV," "In Circles," "Peace," "Journey of Snow White," "Wanted," "The Faggot," "Lovers," "Not Back with the Elephants," "Art of Coarse Acting," "The Trip Back Down," "Hunting Cockroaches," Bdwy in "Doonesbury" (1983), "Big River."

BECK, CAROLINE. Born Apr. 10, 1966 in Sydney, Australis. Graduate AADA. Debut 1987 OB in "Women Beware Women."

BEDFORD-LLOYD, JOHN. Born Jan. 2, 1956 in New Haven, CT. Graduate Williams Col., Yale. Debut OB 1983 in "Vieux Carre," followed by "She Stoops to Conquer," "The Incredibly Famous Willy Rivers," "Digby," "Rum and Coke," "Trinity Site."

BEECHMAN, LAURIE. Born Apr. 4, 1954 in Philadelphia, Pa. Attended NYU. Bdwy debut 1977 in "Annie," followed by "Pirates of Penzance," "Joseph and the Amazing Technicolor Dreamcoat" for which she received a Theatre World Award, "Some Enchanted Evening" (OB), "Pal Joey in Concert," "Cats."

BELACK, DORIS. Born Feb. 26 in NYC. Attended AADA. Debut 1956 OB in "World of Sholom Aleichem," followed by "P.S. 193," "Letters Home," "Marathon 87," Bdwy in "Middle of the Night," "The Owl and the Pussycat," "The Heroine," "You Know I Can't Hear You . . . ," "90 Day Mistress," "Last of the Red Hot Lovers," "Bad Habits," "The Trip Back Down," "Social Security."

BELMONTE, VICKI. Born Jan. 20, 1947 in U.S.A. Bdwy debut 1960 in "Bye Bye Birdie," followed by "Subways are for Sleeping," "All American," "Annie Get Your Gun" (LC), OB in "Nunsense."

BENEDICT, GAIL K. Born May 7, in Storm Lake, IO. Graduate CalInst of Arts. Bdwy debut 1975 in "Dr. Jazz," followed by "Pal Joey," "Don't Step on My Olive Branch," "Dancin'," "42nd Street," "Raggedy Ann."

BENING, ANNETTE. Born May 29, 1958 in Topeka, Ks. Graduate SanFranStateU. Debut OB 1986 and Bdwy 1987 in "Coastal Disturbances" for which she received a Theatre World Award.

BENSON, CINDY. Born Oct. 2, 1951 in Attleboro, Ma. Graduate St. Leo Col., UIll. Debut 1981 OB in "Some Like It Cole," followed by Bdwy "Les Miserables"(1987).

BENSON, JODI. Born Oct. 10, 1961 in Rockford, Il. Attended Millikin U. Bdwy debut 1983 in "Marilyn: An American Fable," followed by "Smile."

BERNHEIM, SHIRL. Born Sept. 21, 1921 in NYC. Debut 1967 OB in "A Different World," followed by "Stage Movie," "Middle of the Night," "Come Back, Little Sheba," "One-Act Festival."

BERRIDGE, ELIZABETH. Born May 2, 1962 in Westchester, NY. Attended Strasberg Inst. Debut 1984 OB in "The Vampires," followed by "The Incredibly Famous Willy Rivers," "Ground Zero Club," "Outside Waco," "Cruise Control," "Sorrows and Sons," "Crackwalker."

BERTRAND, JACQUELINE. Born June 1, 1939 in Quebec, Ca. Attended Neighborhood Playhouse, Actors Studio,LAMDA. Debut 1978 OB in "Unfinished Women," followed by "Dancing for the Kaiser," "Lulu," "War and Peace," "Nest of the Wood Grouse," "Salon."

BETZ, JANETTA. Born Aug. 7, 1958 in Brockton, Ma. Attended Emerson Col. Debut 1987 OB in "Wish You Were Here."

BEVELANDER, NANNETTE. Born Jan. 19, 1956 in Holland. Graduate Canadian College of Dance. Bdwy debut 1983 in "Oh! Calcutta!"

BEVERLEY, TRAZANA. Born Aug. 9, 1945 in Baltimore, Md. Graduate NYU. Debut 1969 OB in "Rules for Running," followed by "Les Femmes Noires," "Geronimo," "Antigone," "The Brothers," Bdwy in "My Sister, My Sister," "For Colored Girls Who Have Considered Suicide . . ." for which she received a Theatre World Award, "Death and the King's Horseman"(LC).

BIGELOW, SUSAN. Born Apr. 11, 1952 in Abington, Pa. Attended UMd. Bdwy debut 1978 in "Working," followed by "Oklahoma!," "Into the Light," OB in "Diamonds."

BIRNEY, REED. Born Sept. 11, 1954 in Alexandria, Va. Attended Boston U. Bdwy debut 1977 in "Gemini," OB in "The Master and Margarita," "Bella Figura," "Winterplay," "The Flight of the Earls," "Filthy Rich," "Lady Moonsong, Mr. Monsoon," "The Common Pursuit."

BLACK, ROYANA. Born March 1, 1973 in Poughkeepsie, NY. Bdwy debut 1984 in "Brighton Beach Memoirs." OB in "Miami," "Trinity Site."

BLAIR, PAMELA. Born Dec. 5, 1949 in Arlington, Vt. Attended Ntl. Acad. of Ballet. Bdwy debut 1972 in "Promises Promises," followed by "Sugar," "Seesaw," "Of Mice and Men," "Wild and Wonderful," "A Chorus Line," "The Best Little Whorehouse in Texas," "King of Hearts," "The Nerd," OB in "Ballad of Boris K," "Split," "Real Life Funnies," "Double Feature," "Hit Parade."

BLANC, JENNIFER. Born Apr. 21, 1971 in NYC. Attended Professional Children's School. Bdwy debut 1985 in "Brighton Beach Memoirs," OB in "Our Own Family."

BLOCH, SCOTTY. Born Jan. 28 in New Rochelle, NY. Attended AADA. Debut 1945 OB in "Craig's Wife," followed by "Lemon Sky," "Battering Ram," "Richard III," "In Celebration," "An Act of Kindness," "The Price," "Grace," "Neon Psalms," Bdwy in "Children of a Lesser God."

BLOCK, LARRY. Born Oct. 30, 1942 in NYC. Graduate URI. Bdwy bow 1966 in "Hail Scrawdyke," followed by "La Turista," "OB in "Eh?," "Fingernails Blue as Flowers," "Comedy of Errors," "Coming Attractions," "Henry IV Part 2," "Feuhrer Bunker," "Manhattan Love Songs," "Souvenirs," "The Golem," "Responsible Parties," "Hit Parade," "Largo Desolato," "The Square Root of 3," "Young Playwrights Festival," "Hunting Cockroaches."

BLOOMFIELD, DON. Born in Cambridge, Ma. , in 1964. Attended Drew U. Debut 1986 OB in "Lily Dale."

BLUMENFELD, ROBERT. Born Feb. 26, 1943 in NYC. Graduate Rutgers, Columbia U. Bdwy debut 1970 in "Othello," OB in "The Fall and Redemption of Man," "The Tempest," "The Dybbuk," "Count Dracula," "Nature and Purpose of the Universe," "House Music," "The Keymaker," "Epic Proportions," "Tatterdemalion."

BOBBY, ANNE MARIE. Born Dec. 12, 1967 in Paterson, NJ. Attended Oxford U. Debut 1983 OB in "American Passion," followed by "The Human Comedy," "The Real Thing," "Hurlyburly," "Precious Sons," "Smile."

BODLE, JANE. Born Nov 12 in Lawrence, KS. Attended UUtah. Bdwy debut 1983 in "Cats," followed by "Les Miserables."

BOGARDUS, STEPHEN. Born Mar. 11, 1954 in Norfolk, Va. Princeton graduate. Bdwy debut 1980 in "West Side Story," OB in "March of the Falsettos," "Feathertop," "No Way to Treat a Lady."

BOGGS, ELLEN. Born Mar. 23, 1956, in Palo Alto, Ca. Graduate UHi. Debut 1984 OB in "The Holy Terror," followed by "Yellow Is My Favorite Color," "Dr. Korczak and the Children," "Roundheads and Pointheads," "Three Sisters."

BOGOSIAN, ERIC. Born Apr. 24, 1953 in Woburn, Ma. Graduate Oberlin Col. Debut 1982 OB in "Men Inside/Voices of America," followed by "Funhouse," "Drinking in America."

BONAFONS, KEN. Born Mar. 24, 1943 in New Orleans, La. Bdwy debut debut 1977 in "Caesar and Cleopatra," followed by OB's "Count Dracula," "Camp Meeting."

BOOCKVOR, STEVEN. Born Nov. 18 1942 in NYC. Attended Queens Col., Juilliard. Bdwy debut 1966 in "Anya," followed by "A Time for Singing," "Cabaret," "Mardi Gras," "Jimmy," "Billy," "The Rothschilds," "Follies," "Over Here," "The Lieutenant," "Musical Jubilee," "Annie," "Working," "The First," "A Chorus Line."

BOOTH, ERIC. Born Oct. 18, 1950 in NYC. Graduate Emerson, Col., Stanford U. Bdwy debut 1977 in "Caesar and Cleopatra," followed by "Golda," "Whose Life Is It Anyway?," OB in "The Taming of the Shrew," "Episode 26," "Girl's Guide to Chaos."

BOOTHBY, VICTORIA. Born in Chicago, Il. Graduate Barnard Col. Debut 1971 OB in "Jungle of Cities," "Man's a Man," "Coarse Acting Show," "Beethoven/Karl," "False Confessions," "Professor George," Bdwy in "Beethoven's Tenth,"(1984), "Stepping Out."

BORGES, YAMIL. Born June 8, 1958 in San Lorenzo, PR. Attended HB Studio. Bdwy debut 1980 in "West Side Story," OB in "El Bravo," "The Transposed Heads."

BOSCO, PHILIP. Born Sept. 26, 1930 in Jersey City, NJ. Graduate Catholic U. Credits: "Auntie Mame," "Rape of the Belt," "Ticket of Leave Man," "Donnybrook," "Man for All Seasons," "Mrs. Warren's Profession," with LCRep in "The Alchemist," "East Wind," "Galileo," "St. Joan," "Tiger at the Gate," "Cyrano," "King Lear," "A Great Career," "In the Matter of J. Robert Oppenheimer," "The Miser," "The Time of Your Life," "Camino Real," "Operation Sidewinder," "Amphitryon," "Enemy of the People," "Playboy of the Western World," "Good Woman of Setzuan," "Antigone," "Mary Stuart," "Narrow Road to the Deep North," "The Crucible," "Twelfth Night," "Enemies," "Plough and the Stars," "Merchant of Venice," and "A Streetcar Named Desire," "Henry V," "Threepenny Opera," "Streamers," "Stages," "St. Joan," "The Biko Inquest," "Man and Superman," "Whose Life Is It Anyway," "Major Barbara," "A Month in the Country," "Bacchae," "Hedda Gabler," "Don Juan in Hell," "Inadmissible Evidence," "Eminent Domain," "Misalliance," "Learned Ladies," "Some Men Need Help," "Ah, Wilderness!," "The Caine Mutiny Court Martial," "Heartbreak House," "Come Back, Little Sheba," "Love of Anatole," "Be Happy for Me," "Master Class," "You Never Can Tell," "A Man for All Seasons."

BOSNIAK, SLOANE. Born Feb. 18, 1950 in Schenectady, NY. Graduate Goucer Col., Catholic U. Debut 1986 OB in "Annie Wobbler."

BOUCHER, GLORIA. Born Dec. 17, 1954 in Muskegon, Mi. Attended AADA, AMDA. Debut 1982 OB in "Street Scene," followed by "New Girl in Town."

BOVA, JOSEPH. Born May 25 in Cleveland, OH. Graduate Northwestern U. Debut 1959 OB in "On the Town," followed by "Once Upon a Mattress," "House of Blue Leaves," "Comedy," "The Beauty Part," "Taming of the Shrew," "Richard III," "Comedy of Errors," "Invitation to a Beheading," "Merry Wives of Windsor," "Henry V," "Streamers," Bdwy in "Rape of the Belt," "Irma La Douce," "Hot Spot," "The Chinese," "American Millionaire," "St. Joan," "42nd Street."

BOVE, MARK. Born Jan. 9, 1960 in Pittsburgh, Pa. Bdwy debut 1980 in "West Side Story," followed by "Woman of the Year," "A Chorus Line."

BOVSHOW, BUZZ. Born May 14, 1956 in Hollywood, Ca. Graduate UCSanDiego, UInd. Debut 1987 OB in "Second Avenue."

BOWDEN, RICHARD. Born May 21 in Savannah, Ga. Graduate UGa., UBristol/Eng. Bdwy debut 1964 in "Don Carlos" (Schiller Theatre), followed by "Captain Brassbound's Conversion"(1972), OB in "Mlle. Colombe," "Pocahontas," "Freedom Train," "As You Like It."

BOWEN, ROBERT. Born Apr. 8, 1949 in New Haven, Ct. Graduate R.I.School of Design. Debut 1975 OB in "Boy Meets Boy," followed by "A Theatre History."

BOWNE, RICHARD L. Born Nov. 12, 1949 in Bronxville, NY. Graduate UCt. Bdwy debut 1979 in "Snow White and the Seven Dwarfs," followed by "Showboat" (1983), OB in "Moby Dick," "Better Living," "Cowboy."

BRADLEY, HENRY. Born Nov. 23, 1931 in Albany, NY. Attended AmThWing, BlackThWorkshop. Debut 1977 OB in "On-the Lock-in," followed by "Manhattan Story."

BRASINGTON, ALAN. Born in Monticello, NY. Attended RADA. Bdwy debut 1968 in "Pantagleize," followed by "The Misanthrope," "Cock-a-doodle Dandy," "Hamlet," "A Patriot for Me," "Shakespeare's Cabaret," "Merlin," "Into the Light," OB in "Sterling Silver," "Charlotte Sweet."

BRAZDA, DAVID. Born Sept. 28, 1954 in Weisbaden, Ger. Attended UVa., Circle in the Square. Debut 1985 OB in "Onlyman," followed by "Two Gentlemen of Verona," "Pericles."

BREEN, J. PATRICK. Born Oct. 26, 1960 in Brooklyn, NY. Graduate NYU. Debut 1982 OB in "Epiphany," followed by "Little Murders," Bdwy in "Brighton Beach Memoirs" (1983).

BREMER, DEBORAH. Born Aug. 5, 1958 in Augusta, Ga. Graduate UIowa. Bdwy debut 1987 in "Shakespeare on Broadway."

BRENNAN, MAUREEN. Born Oct. 11, 1952 in Washington, DC. Attended UCin. Bdwy debut 1974 in "Candide" for which she received a Theatre World Award, followed by "Going Up," "Knickerbocker Holiday," "Little Johnny Jones," "Stardust," OB in "Shakespeare's Cabaret."

BRENNAN, NORA. Born Dec. 1, 1953 in East Chicago, In. Graduate PurdueU. Bdwy debut 1980 in "Camelot," followed by "Cats."

BRIAN, MICHAEL. Born Nov. 14, 1958 in Utica, NY. Attended Boston Consv. Debut 1979 OB in "Kennedy's Children," followed by "Street Scene," "The Death of Von Richthofen as Witnessed from Earth," "Lenny and the Heartbreakers," "Gift of the Magi," "Next Please!," Bdwy in "Baby" (1983), "Big River."

BRILL, FRAN. Born Sept. 30 in PA. Attended Boston U. Bdwy debut 1969 in "Red, White and Maddox," OB in "What Every Woman Knows," "Scribes," "Naked," "Look Back in Anger," "Knuckle," "Skirmishes," "Baby with the Bathwater," "Holding Patterns," "Festival of One Acts," "Taking Steps," "Young Playwrights Festival," "Claptrap."

BROADHURST, KENT. Born Feb. 4, 1940 in St. Louis, Mo. Graduate UNe. Debut 1968 OB in "The Fourth Wall," followed by "Design for Living," "Marching Song," "Heartbreak House," "Dark of the Moon," "Hunchback of Notre Dame," Bdwy in "The Caine Mutiny Court-Martial"(1983).

BRODERICK, MATTHEW. Born Mar. 21, 1963 in NYC. Debut OB 1981 in "Torch Song Trilogy," followed by "The Widow Claire," Bdwy 1983 in "Brighton Beach Memoirs" for which he received a Theatre World Award, followed by "Biloxi Blues."

BRODY, JONATHAN. Born June 16, 1963 in Englewood, NJ. Debut 1982 OB in "Shulamith," followed by "The Desk Set," Bdwy in "Me and My Girl" (1986).

BROGGER, IVAR. Born Jan. 10, in St. Paul, Mn. Graduate UMn. Debut 1979 OB in "In the Jungle of Cities," followed by "Collected Words of Billy the Kid," "Magic Time," "Cloud 9," "Richard III," "Clarence," "Madwoman of Chaillot," "Seascape with Sharks and Dancer," "Second Man," "Twelfth Night," Bdwy in "Macbeth" (1981), "Pygmalion" (1987).

BROOKS, JEFF. Born Apr. 7, 1950 in Vancouver, Can. Attended Portland State U. Debut 1976 OB in "Titanic," followed by "Fat Chances," "Nature and Purpose of the Universe," "Actor's Nightmare," "Sister Mary Ignatius Explains It All," "Marathon 84," "The Foreigner," Bdwy in "A History of the American Film"(1978).

BROOKS, JEFF. Born Apr. 7, 1950 in Vancouver, Can. Attended Portland State U. Debut 1976 OB in "Titanic," followed by "Fat Chances," "Nature and Purpose of the Universe," "Actor's Nightmare," "Sister Mary Ignatius Explains It All," "Marathon '84," "The Foreigner," Bdwy in "A History of the American Film" (1978).

BROWN, ANN. Born Dec. 1, 1960 in Westwood, NJ. Graduate Trinity Col. Debut 1987 OB in "Shylock."

BROWN, CHUCK. Born Oct. 16, 1959 in Cleveland, OH. Attended Baldwin-Wallace Col. Debut 1984 OB in "Pacific Overtures," followed by "The Shop on Main Street," "Vampire Lesbians of Sodom."

BROWN, ROBIN LESLIE. Born Jan. 18 in Canandaigua, NY. Graduate L.I.U. Debut 1980 OB in "The Mother of Us All," followed by "Yours Truly," "Two Gentlemen of Verona," "The Taming of the Shrew," "The Mollusc," "The Contrast," "Pericles," "Andromache."

BROWN, SULLIVAN. Born Jan. 11, 1952 in Biloela, Australia. Graduate UQueensland. Debut 1986 OB in "Writer's Cramp," Bdwy in "Wild Honey" (1986).

BROWNING, SUSAN. Born Feb. 25, 1941 in Baldwin, NY. Penn State graduate. Bdwy debut 1963 in "Love and Kisses," followed by "Company" for which she received a Theatre World Award, "Shelter," "Goodtime Charley," "Big River," OB in "Jo," "Dime a Dozen," "Seventeen," "Boys from Syracuse," "Collision Course," "Whiskey," "As You Like It," "Removalists," "Africanis Instructus."

BRUNS, PHILIP. Born May 2, 1931 in Pipestone, Mn. Graduate Augustana Col., Yale. Bdwy bow 1964 in "The Deputy," followed by "Lysistrata," OB in "Mr. Simian," "The Cradle Will Rock," "He Who Gets Slapped," "Dr. Willy Nilly," "Come Play with Me," "Listen to the Mocking Bird," "The Bald Soprano," "Jack of the Submission," "Endgame," "Servant of Two Masters," "Pantomania," "Square in the Eye," "Butter and Egg Man," "Spitting Image," "Henry V," "A Dream Out of Time," "Two," "The Electric Man."

BRYAN, DORA. Born July 2, 1924 in Parbold, Lancashire, Eng. Bdwy debut 1987 in "Pygmalion."

BRYANT, DAVID. Born May 26, 1936 in Nashville, Tn. Attended TnStateU. Bdwy debut 1972 in "Don't Play Us Cheap," followed by "Bubbling Brown Sugar," "Amadeus," "Les Miserables," OB in "Up in Central Park," "Elizabeth and Essex," "Appear and Show Cause."

BRYGGMAN, LARRY. Born Dec. 21, 1938 in Concord, Ca. Attended CCSF, AmThWing. Debut 1962 OB in "A Pair of Pairs," followed by "Live Like Pigs," "Stop," "You're Killing Me," "Mod Donna," "Waiting for Godot," "Ballymurphy," "Marco Polo Sings a Solo," "Brownsville Raid," "Two Small Bodies," "Museum," "Winter Dancers," "The Resurrection of Lady Lester," "Royal Bob," "Modern Ladies of Guanabacoa," "Rum and Coke," "Bodies, Rest and Motion," Bdwy in "Ulysses in Nighttown" (1974), "Checking Out," "Basic Training of Pavlo Hummel," "Richard III."

BRYNE, BARBARA. Born Apr. 1, 1929 in London, Eng. Graduate RADA. NY debut 1981 OB in "Entertaining Mr. Sloane," Bdwy in "Sunday in the Park with George" (1984), "Hay Fever."

BUCKLEY, BETTY. Born July 3, 1947 in Big Spring, TX. Graduate TCU. Bdwy debut 1969 in "1776," followed by "Pippin," "Cats," OB in "Ballad of Johnny Pot," "What's a Nice Country Like You . . .," "Circle of Sound," "I'm Getting My Act Together . . .", "Juno's Swans," "The Mystery of Edwin Drood (OB and Bdwy), "Song and Dance."

BUCKLEY, MELINDA. Born Apr. 17, 1954 in Attleboro, MA. Graduate UMa. Bdwy debut 1983 in "A Chorus Line," followed by "Raggedy Ann," OB in "Damn Yankees," "Pal Joey."

BUELL, BILL. Born Sept. 21, 1952 in Paipai, Taiwan. Attended Portland State U. Debut 1972 OB in "Crazy Now," followed by "Declassee," "Lorenzaccio," "Promenade," "The Common Pursuit," Bdwy in "Once a Catholic"(1979), "The First."

BULLOCK, OSMUND. Born July 25, 1951 in London. Attended Webber-Douglas Academy. Bdwy debut 1987 in "Pygmalion."

BULOS, YUSEF. Born Sept. 14, 1940 in Jerusalem. Attended Beirut Am. U., AADA. Debut 1965 OB with American Savoyards in repertory, followed by "Saints," "The Trouble with Europe," "The Penultimate Problem of Sherlock Holmes," "In the Jungle of Cities," "Hernani," "Bertrano," "Duck Variations," "Insignificance," "Panache," Bdwy in "Indians"(1970), "Capt. Brassbound's Conversion."

BURK, TERENCE. Born Aug. 11, 1947 in Lebanon, IL. Graduate S.Ill.U. Bdwy debut 1976 in "Equus," OB in "Religion," "The Future," "Sacred and Profane Love," "Crime and Punishment."

BURKE, MAGGIE. Born May 2, 1936 in Bay Shore, NY. Graduate Sarah Lawrence Col. OB in "Today Is Independence Day," "Lovers and Other Strangers," "Jules Feiffer's Cartoons," "Fog," "Home Is the Hero," "King John," "Rusty & Rico & Lena & Louie," "Friends," "Butterfaces," "Old Times," "Man with a Raincoat," Bdwy debut 1985 in "Brighton Beach Memoirs."

BURKS, DONNY. Born in Martinsville, VA. Graduate St. John's U. Debut 1964 OB in "Dutchman," followed by "Billy Noname" for which he received a Theatre World Award, "Miracle Play," Bdwy in "Hair" (1968), "The American Clock," "The Tap Dance Kid."

BURNETT, ROBERT. Born Feb. 28, 1960 in Goshen, NY. Attended HB Studio. Bdwy debut 1985 in "Cats."

BURNS, CATHERINE. Born Sept. 25, 1945 in NYC. Attended AADA. Bdwy 1968 in "The Prime of Miss Jean Brodie," OB in "Dream of a Blacklisted Actor," "The Disintegration of James Cherry," "Operation Sidewinder," "Dear Janet Rosenberg, Dear Mr. Kooning" for which she received a Theatre World Award, "Two Small Bodies," "Voices," "Jungle of Cities," "One Wedding," "Metamorphosis," "Within the Year," "Twelfth Night."

BURRELL, FRED. Born Sept. 18, 1936. Graduate UNC, RADA. Bdwy debut 1964 in "Never Too Late," followed by "Illya Darling," OB in "The Memorandum," "Throckmorton," "Texas," "Voices in the Head," "Chili Queen."

BURRELL, PAMELA. Born Aug. 4, 1945 in Tacoma, WA. Bdwy debut 1966 in "Funny Girl," followed by "Where's Charley?," "Strider," "Sunday in the Park with George," OB in "Arms and the Man" for which she received a Theatre World Award, "Berkeley Square," "The Boss," "Biography: A Game," "Strider: Story of a Horse," "A Little Madness."

BURRELL, TERESA (formerly Terry). Born Feb. 8, 1952 in Trinidad, WI. Attended Pace U. Bdwy debut 1977 in "Eubie!," followed by "Dreamgirls," "Honky Tonk Nights," OB in "That Uptown Feeling," "They Say It's Wonderful," "George White's Scandals," "Just So."

BURTON, IRVING. Born Aug. 5, 1923 in NYC. Bdwy debut 1951 in "Peer Gynt," OB in "Three Unnatural Acts," 24 years with Paper Bag Players, "Pal Joey," "Keegan & Lloyd Again," "One-Act Festival."

BURTON, KATE. Born Sept. 10, 1957 in Geneva, Switz. Graduate Brown U., Yale. Bdwy debut 1982 in "Present Laughter," followed by "Alice in Wonderland," "Doonesbury," "Wild Honey," OB in "Winners" for which she received a Theatre World Award, "Romeo and Juliet," "The Accrington Pals," "Playboy of the Western World."

BUTLER, GREGORY. Born Mar. 2, 1962 in Detroit, Mi. Attended Juilliard. Bdwy debut 1986 in "Raggedy Ann."

BUTT, JENNIFER. Born May 17, 1958 in Valparaiso, In. Stephens Col. graduate. Debut 1983 OB in "The Robber Bridegroom," Bdwy in "Les Miserables" (1987).

BUTTRAM, JAN. Born June 19, 1946 in Clarkesville, Tx. Graduate NTxState. Debut 1974 OB in "Fashion," followed by "Startup," "Camp Meeting," Bdwy in "The Best Little Whorehouse in Texas"(1978).

BYERS, RALPH. Born Jan. 10, 1950 in Washington, DC. Graduate William & Mary Col., Catholic U. Debut 1975 OB in "Hamlet," followed by "Julius Caesar," "Rebel Women," "No End of Blame," "Henry IV Part I," "Sunday in the Park with George," Bdwy in "Herzl" (1976), "Goodbye Fidel," "Big River."

CAIN, WILLIAM B. Born May 27, 1931 in Tuscaloosa, Al. Graduate UWash, Catholic U. Debut 1962 OB in "Red Roses for Me," followed by "Jericho Jim Crow," "Henry V," "Antigone," "Relatively Speaking," "I Married an Angel in Concert," "Buddha," "Copperhead," Bdwy in "Wilson in the Promise Land" (1970), "Of the Fields Lately," "You Can't Take It with You," "Wild Honey."

CALLANDER, BARBARA. Born Mar. 3, 1950 in Washington, D.C. Graduate Oberlin Col. Debut 1980 OB in "The Betrothal," followed by "Period of Adjustment," "Playboy of the Western World," "Spider's Web," "War Games," "Mrs. Warren's Profession," "Midsummer Night's Dream."

CAMACHO, BLANCA. Born Nov. 19, 1956 in NYC. Graduate NYU. Debut 1984 OB in "Sarita," followed by "Maggie Magalita," "Salon."

CAMP, JOANNE. Born Apr. 4, 1951 in Atlanta, GA. Graduate FlAtlanticU, Geo WashU. Debut 1981 OB in "The Dry Martini," followed by "Geniuses," for which she received a Theatre World Award, "June Moon," "Painting Churches," "Merchant of Venice," "Lady from the Sea," "The Contrast," "Coastal Disturbances," "The Rivals," "Andromache."

CAMPBELL, JENNIFER. Born Nov. 29, 1955 in Highland Park, Il. Amherst Col. graduate. Debut 1987 OB in "Wicked Philanthropy."

CANNON, CATHERINE. Born Apr. 18, 1957 in Boston, Ma. Graduate Sarah Lawrence Col. Debut 1980 OB in "Friend of the Family," followed by "8X10 Glossy," "Women at the Wheel," "Vatzlav."

CAPRI, MARK. Born July 19, 1951 in Washington, DC. Graduate Stanford U, RADA. Debut 1984 OB in "On Approval" for which he received a Theatre World Award, followed by "An Enemy of the People."

CAREW, PETER. Born Nov. 8, 1922 in Old Forge, Pa. Graduate NYU. Debut 1948 OB in "Coffee House," followed by "Street Scene," "Ah, Wilderness," "Antigone," "Waiting for Lefty," "12 Angry Men," "Falling from Heaven," "Go Show Me a Dragon," "A Stage Affair," "King of the Whole Damn World," "Purple Canary," "Kiss Mama," "A View from the Bridge," "He Who Gets Slapped," "Istanboul," "Thunder Rock," "Monsters," "Dazy," Bdwy in "The Great White Hope"(1969).

CARHART, PAMELA CUMING. Born April 17 in Plainfield, NJ. Attended Brookdale Col., Neighborhood Playhouse. Debut 1987 OB in "Child's Play."

CARHART, TIMOTHY. Born Dec. 24, 1953 in Washington, DC. UIll. graduate. Debut 1984 OB in "The Harvesting," followed by "The Ballad of Soapy Smith," "Hitch-hikers," "Highest Standard of Living."

CARIOU, LEN. Born Sept. 30, 1939 in Winnipeg, Can. Bdwy debut 1968 in "House of Atreus," followed by "Henry V" and "Applause" for which he received a Theatre World Award, "Night Watch," "A Little Night Music," "Cold Storage," "Sweeney Todd," "Dance a Little Closer," OB in "A Sorrow Beyond Dreams," "Up from Paradise," "Master Class," "Day Six."

CARLIN, AMANDA. Born Dec. 12 in Queens, NY. Graduate Tufts U. Bdwy debut 1980 in "Major Barbara," followed by "The Man Who Came to Dinner," "The Front Page," OB in "The Dining Room," "Twelfth Night," "The Accrington Pals," "Comedy of Errors," "Playboy of the Western World," "Waltz of the Toreadors," "The Maderati."

CARLIN, CHET. Born Feb. 23, 1940 in Malverne, NY. Graduate Ithaca Col., Catholic U. Bdwy debut 1972 in "An Evening with Richard Nixon . . .," OB in "Under Gaslight," "Lou Gehrig Did Not Die of Cancer," "Graffiti!," "Crystal and Fox," "Golden Honeymoon," "Arms and the Man," "Arsenic and Old Lace," "The Father," "Comedy of Errors," "Never the Sinner."

CARLING, P. L. Born Mar. 31. Graduate Stanford, UCLA. Debut 1955 OB in "The Chairs," followed by "In Good King Charles' Golden Days," "Magistrate," "Picture of Dorian Gray," "The Vise," "Lady from the Sea," "Booth Is Back in Town," "Ring Round the Moon," "Philadelphia Here I Come," "Sorrows of Frederick," "Biography," "Murder on the Nile," "3 Lost Plays of O'Neill," "Verdict," "The Dispute," "Relative Values," Bdwy in "The Devils" (1965), "Scratch," "Shenandoah."

CARMINE, MICHAEL. Born Mar. 6, 1959 in Brooklyn, NY. Attended Cal.Inst.of Arts. Debut 1984 OB in "Sarita," followed by "Cuba and His Teddy Bear."

CARNELIA, CRAIG. Born Aug. 13, 1949 in Queens, NY. Attended Hofstra U. Debut 1969 OB in "The Fantasticks," followed by "Lend an Ear, "Three Postcards."

CARPENTER, CARLETON. Born July 10, 1926 in Bennington, Vt. Attended Northwestern U. Bdwy debut 1944 in "Bright Boy," followed by "Career Angel," "Three to Make Ready," "Magic Touch," "John Murray Anderson's Almanac," "Hotel Paradiso," "Box of Watercolors," "Hello, Dolly!," OB in "Stage Affair," "Boys in the Band," "Dylan," "The Greatest Fairy Story Ever Told," "A Good Old Fashioned Revue," "Miss Stanwyck Is Still in Hiding," "Rocky Road," "Apollo of Bellac," "Light Up the Sky," "Murder at Rutherford House."

CARPENTER, WILLIE C. Born Aug. 9, 1945 in Eutaw, Al. Graduate OhioStateU. Debut 1985 OB in "Rude Times," Bdwy in "The Musical Comedy Murders of 1940"(1987).

CARROLL, ALISA. Born Sept. 16, 1971 in Connecticut. Debut 1987 OB in "Take Me Along."

CARROLL, DANNY. Born May 30, 1940 in Maspeth, NY. Bdwy bow in 1957 "The Music Man," followed by "Flora the Red Menace," "Funny Girl," "George M!," "Billy," "Ballroom," "42nd Street," OB in "Boys from Syracuse," "Babes in the Woods."

CARRUBBA, PHILIP. Born May 3, 1951 in San Francisco, Ca. Graduate SFStateU. Bdwy debut 1981 in "Joseph and the Amazing Technicolor Dreamcoat," followed by OB in "They're Playing Our Song," "Take Me Along," "Dazy," "The Wonderful Ice Cream Suit."

CARSON, THOMAS. Born May 27, 1939 in Iowa City, Io. Graduate UIo. Debut 1981 OB in "The Feuhrer Bunker," followed by "Breakfast Conversations in Miami," "Sullivan and Gilbert," "The Tempest."

CASS, PEGGY. Born May 21, 1926 in Boston, MA. Attended Wyndham Sch. Credits include "Touch and Go," "Live Wire," "Bernardine," "Othello," "Henry V," "Auntie Mame" for which she received a Theatre World Award, "A Thurber Carnival," "Children from Their Games," "Don't Drink the Water," "Front Page" (1969), "Plaza Suite," "Once a Catholic," "42nd Street," "The Octette Bridge Club," OB in "Phoenix '55," "Are You Now or Have You Ever Been," "One Touch of Venus," "George White's Scandals."

CASSERLY, KERRY. Born Oct. 26, 1953 in Minneapolis, MN. Attended UMinn. Bdwy debut 1980 in "One Night Stand," followed by "A Chorus Line," "My One and Only."

CASSESE, ANDREW. Born Feb. 12, 1972 in Patchogue, NY. Bdwy debut 1982 in "Nine," followed by "Smile," OB in "Christopher Blake."

CASSIDY, TIM. Born March 22, 1952 in Alliance, OH. Attended UCincinnati. Bdwy debut 1974 in "Good News," followed by "A Chorus Line."

CASTAY, LESLIE. Born Dec. 11, 1963 in New Orleans, La. Graduate Tulane U. Debut 1985 OB in "The Second Hurricane," followed by "Too Many Girls."

CASTLE, DIANA. Born Aug. 18, 1957 in NYC. Graduate FlaStateU. Debut 1981 OB in "Seesaw," followed by "A . . . My Name is Alice," "What's a Nice Country Like You Still Doing in a State Like This?," "Holy Ghosts."

CATLIN, JODY. Born July 6, 1946 in Nebraska. Graduate William & Mary Col. Debut 1977 OB in "Porno Stars at Home," followed by "Colonomos," "The Price of Genius," "A Chaste Maid in Cheapside."

CATTRALL, KIM. Born Aug. 21, 1956 in Liverpool, Eng. Graduate AADA. Bdwy debut 1986 in "Wild Honey."

CAULFIELD, MAXWELL. Born Nov. 23, 1959 in Glasgow, Scot. Debut 1979 OB in "Class Enemy" for which he received a Theatre World Award, followed by "Crimes and Dreams," "Entertaining Mr. Sloane," "The Inheritors," "Paradise Lost," "Salonika."

CAVISE, JOE ANTONY. Born Jan. 7, 1958 in Syracuse, NY. Graduate Clark U. Debut 1981 OB in "Street Scene," followed by Bdwy 1984 in "Cats."

CECIL, PAMELA. Born Dec. 20 in Newport, RI. Attended Midland Lutheran Col., IowaStateU. Bdwy debut 1981 in "Can-Can," followed by "42nd Street," "La Cage aux Folles."

CELLARIO, MARIA. Born June 19, 1948 in Buenos Aires, Arg. Graduate Ithaca Col. Bdwy debut 1975 in "The Royal Family," followed by OB in "Fugue in a Nursery," "Declassee," "Equinox," "Flatbush Faithful," "Our Lady of the Tortilla."

CHAMBERLAIN, Richard. Born Mar. 31, 1935 in Beverly Hills, Ca. Attended Pomona Col. Bdwy debut 1976 in "Night of the Iguana," followed by "Blithe Spirit," OB in "Fathers and Sons."

CHANDLER, DAVID. Born Feb. 3, 1950 in Danbury, Ct. Graduate Oberlin Col. Bdwy debut 1980 in "The American Clock," followed by "Death of a Salesman," OB in "Made in Heaven," "Black Sea Follies."

CHANNING, CARISSA. Born Nov. 7, 1963 in Hollywood, Ca. Graduate NYU. Debut 1985 OB in "The Fickle Fiddle," followed by "Rhinoceros," "The Last Laugh," "The Red Corvette," "Bliss."

CHAPMAN, ROGER. Born Jan. 1, 1947 in Cheverly, Md. Graduate Rollins Col. Debut 1976 OB in "Who Killed Richard Corey?," followed by "My Life," "Hamlet," "Innocent Thoughts," "Harmless Intentions," "Richard II," "The Great Grandson of Jedediah Kohler," "Threads," "Time Framed," "Nuclear Follies."

CHARLES, WALTER. Born Apr. 4, 1945 in East Stroudsburg, PA. Graduate Boston U Bdwy debut 1973 in "Grease," followed by "1600 Pennsylvania Avenue," "Knickerbocker Holiday," "Sweeney Todd," "Cats," "La Cage aux Folles."

CHARNAY, LYNNE. Born April 1 in NYC. Attended UWis., Columbia, AADA. Debut 1950 OB in "Came the Dawn," followed by "A Ram's Head," "In a Cold Hotel," "Amata," "Yerma, "Ballad of Winter Soldiers," "Intimate Relations," "Play Me Zoltan," "Grand Magic," "The Time of Your Life," "Nymph Errant," "Nude with Violin," "American Power Play," "Salon," Bdwy in "Julia, Jake and Uncle Joe"(1961), "A Family Affair," "Broadway," "Inspector General," "Grand Tour."

CHINN, SANDRA. Born in 1961 in Berkeley, Ca. Appeared with Dennis Wayne Dancers, Chamber Ballet U.S.A. before 1987 debut OB in "Funny Feet."

CHRYST, GARY. Born in 1959 in LaJolla, Ca. Joined Joffrey Ballet in 1968, Bdwy debut in "Dancin' " (1979), followed by "A Chorus Line," OB in "One More Song, One More Dance," "Music Moves Me."

CIOFFI, CHARLES. Born Oct. 31, 1935 in NYC. UMinn graduate. OB in "A Cry of Players," "King Lear," "In the Matter of J. Robert Oppenheimer," "Antigone," "Whistle in the Dark," "Hamlet"(LC), "Self Defense."

CLARK, CHERYL. Born Dec. 7, 1950 in Boston, MA. Attended Ind. U., NYU. Bdwy debut 1972 in "Pippin," followed by "Chicago," "A Chorus Line."

CLEMM, SUSANNA. Born Sept. 24 in Berlin, W. Germany. Attended HB Studio. Bdwy debut 1971 in "Follies," followed by OB in "Sports Czar," "Lovers and Liars," "1984."

COCCIOLETTI, PHILIP. Born June 26, 1953 in Greensburg, Pa. Graduate Appalachian State U. Debut 1987 OB in "The Maderati."

COHEN, BILL. Born Jan. 12, 1953 in Brooklyn, NY. Yale graduate. OB debut 1984 in "Child's Play," followed by "The Man Who Killed the Buddha," "One-Act Festival."

COHEN, MARK. Born Apr. 2, 1949 in Boston, Ma. Graduate Yale, London's Guildhall. Debut 1977 OB in "The Days of the Turbins," followed by "Nightmare Alley," "A Midsummer Night's Dream," Bdwy in "Romeo and Juliet" (1977).

COHENOUR, PATTI. Born Oct. 17, 1952 in Albuquerque, NMx. Attended UNMx. Bdwy debut 1982 in "A Doll's Life," followed by "Pirates of Penzance," "Big River," "The Mystery of Edwin Drood." OB in "La Boheme" for which she received a Theatre World Award.

COLE, DEBRA. Born Oct. 27, 1962 in Buffalo, NY. Graduate NYU. Debut 1984 OB in "Fables for Friends," followed by "Daughters," "Bunker Reveries," Bdwy in "House of Blue Leaves" (1986).

COLE, KAY. Born Jan. 13, 1948 in Miami, FL. Bdwy debut 1961 in "Bye Bye Birdie," followed by "Stop the World I Want to Get Off," "Roar of the Greasepaint . . .," "Hair," "Jesus Christ Superstar," "Words and Music," "Chorus Line," OB in "The Cradle Will Rock," "Two If By Sea," "Rainbow," "White Nights," "Sgt. Pepper's Lonely Hearts Club Band," "On the Swing Shift," "Snoopy," "Road to Hollywood," "One-man Band."

COLEMAN, JACK. Born in 1958 in Easton, Pa. Graduate Duke U. Debut 1987 OB in "The Common Pursuit."

COLKER, JERRY. Born Mar. 16, 1955 in Los Angeles, CA. Attended Harvard U. Debut 1975 OB in "Tenderloin," followed by "Pal Joey," "3 Guys Naked from the Waist Down," Bdwy in "West Side Story," "Pippin," "A Chorus Line."

COLL, IVONNE. Born Nov. 4 in Fajardo, PR. Attended UPR, LACC, HB Studio. Debut 1980 OB in "Spain 1980," followed by "Animals," "Wonderful Ice Cream Suit," "Cold Air," "Fabiola," Bdwy in "Goodbye Fidel" (1980). "Shakespeare on Broadway."

COLLINS, PAUL. Born July 25, 1937 in London. Attended LACC. OB in "Say Nothing," "Cambridge Circus," "The Devils," "Rear Column," "Jail Diary of Albie Sachs," "The Feuhrer Bunker," "Great Days," "Courage," "State of the Union," "China Fish," "The Maderati," "As It Is in Heaven," Bdwy in "The Royal Hunt of the Sun"(1965), "A Minor Adjustment," "A Meeting by the River," "Eminent Domain."

COLLINS, RAY. Born July 20, 1949 in London, Eng. Attended LAMDA. Debut 1985 OB in "Roundheads and Peakheads," followed by "The Constant Wife," "Ragged Trousered Philanthropists."

COLTON, CHEVI. Born Dec. 21 in NYC. Attended Hunter Col. OB in "Time of Storm," "Insect Comedy," "The Adding Machine," "O Marry Me," "Penny Change," "The Mad Show," "Jacques Brel Is Alive . . .," "Bits and Pieces," "Spelling Bee," "Uncle Money," "Miami," Bdwy in "Cabaret," "Grand Tour," "Torch Song Trilogy."

CONE, MICHAEL. Born Oct. 7, 1952 in Fresno, Ca. Graduate UWash. Bdwy debut 1980 in "Brigadoon," followed by "Rags."

CONNELL, DAVID. Born Nov. 24, 1935 in Cleveland, Oh. Bdwy debut 1968 in "The Great White Hope," followed by "Don't Play Us Cheap," OB in "Ballet Behind the Bridge," "Miracle Play," "Time Out of Time," "Champeen!," "One Flew over the Cuckoo's Nest," "In the House of the Blues."

CONNELL, GORDON. Born Mar. 19, 1923 in Berkeley, CA. Graduate UCal, NYU. Bdwy debut 1961 in "Subways Are for Sleeping," followed by "Hello, Dolly!," "Lysistrata," "The Human Comedy," "Big River," OB in "Beggar's Opera," "The Butler Did It," "With Love and Laughter."

CONNELL, JANE. Born Oct. 27, 1925 in Berkeley, CA. Attended UCal. Bdwy debut in "New Faces of 1956," followed by "Drat! The Cat!," "Mame" (1966/'83), "Dear World," "Lysistrata," "Me and My Girl," OB in "Shoestring Revue," "Threepenny Opera," "Pieces of Eight," "Demi-Dozen," "She Stoops to Conquer," "Drat!," "The Real Inspector Hound," "The Rivals," "The Rise and Rise of Daniel Rocket," "Laughing Stock," "The Singular Dorothy Parker," "No No Nanette in Concert."

CONNELL, KELLY. Born June 9, 1956 in Seneca Falls, NY. Attended Cayuga Com.Col. Debut 1982 OB in "The Butter and Egg Man," followed by "Neon Psalms," "Love's Labour's Lost," "Quiet in the Land," "The Musical Comedy Murders of 1940."

CONNOLLY, JOHN P. Born Sept. 1, 1950 in Philadelphia, PA. Graduate Temple U. Debut 1973 OB in "Paradise Lost," followed by "The Wizard of Oz," "Fighting Bob," "For the Use of the Hall," "The Golem," "A Step Out of Line," "For Sale," "Filthy Rich," "Colette in Love," Bdwy in "Big River."

CONOLLY, PATRICIA. Born Aug. 29, 1933 in Tabora, EAfrica. Attended USydney. With APA in "You Can't Take It with You," "War and Peace," "School for Scandal," "The Wild Duck," "Right You Are," "We Comrades Three," "Pantagleize," "Exit the King," "The Cherry Orchard," "The Misanthrope," "The Cocktail Party," and "Cock-a-Doodle Dandy," followed by "A Streetcar Named Desire," "The Importance of Being Earnest," "Blithe Spirit."

CONTRERAS, RAY. Born Apr. 14, 1960 in Jersey City, NJ. Attended Strasberg Inst. Debut 1977 OB in "Runaways," followed by "Dispatches," "Street Dreams," "Pacific Overtures," "The Architect and the Emperor," Bdwy in "Runaways"(1978), "West Side Story"(1980).

COOK, BARBARA. Born Oct. 25, 1927 in Atlanta, Ga. Bdwy debut 1951 in "Flahooley," followed by "Plain and Fancy" for which she received a Theatre World Award, "Candide," "Music Man," CC's "Carousel" and "The King and I," "She Loves Me," "Something More," "Any Wednesday," "Show Boat"(LC), "Little Murders," "Man of La Mancha," "Grass Harp," "Enemies"(LC), "A Concert for the Theatre."

COOK, RODERICK. Born in 1932 in London, Eng. Attended Cambridge U. Bdwy debut 1961 in "Kean," followed by "Roar Like a Dove," "The Girl Who Came to Supper," "Noel Coward's Sweet Potato," "The Man Who Came to Dinner," "Woman of the Year," "Eileen," "Oh Coward!," OB in "A Scent of Flowers," "Oh, Coward!," "Sweethearts in Concert," "Jubilee in Concert."

COOPER, FAY. Born Nov. 3, 1947 in NYC. Attended WayneStateU. Debut 1987 OB in "Taster's Choice."

COOPER, MARILYN. Born Dec. 14, 1936 in NYC. Attended NYU. Appeared in "Mr. Wonderful," "West Side Story," "Brigadoon," "Gypsy," "I Can Get It for You Wholesale," "Hallelujah Baby!," "Golden Rainbow," "Mame," "A Teaspoon Every 4 Hours," "Two by Two," "On the Town," "Ballroom," "Woman of the Year," "The Odd Couple" (1985), OB in "The Mad Show," "Look Me Up," "The Perfect Party."

COPELAND, JOAN. Born June 1, 1922 in NYC. Attended Brooklyn Col, AADA. Debut 1945 OB in "Romeo and Juliet," followed by "Othello," "Conversation Piece," "Delightful Season," "End of Summer," "American Clock," "The Double Game," "Isn't It Romantic?," "Hunting Cockroaches," Bdwy in "Sundown Beach," "Detective Story," "Not for Children," "Hatful of Fire," "Something More," "The Price," "Two by Two," "Pal Joey," "Checking Out," "The American Clock."

CORBIN, PRISCILLA. Born May 9, 1959 in Huntington, WVa. Graduate Princeton, Columbia U. Debut 1986 OB in "Hitler's Childhood," followed by "Modigliani."

COUNCIL, RICHARD. Born Oct. 1, 1947 in Tampa, Fl. Graduate UFl. Debut 1973 OB in "Merchant of Venice," followed by "Ghost Dance," "Look, We've Come Through," "Arms and the Man," "Isadora Duncan Sleeps with the Russian Navy," "Arthur," "The Winter Dancer," "The Prevalence of Mrs. Seal," "Jane Avril," Bdwy in "The Royal Family"(1975), "Philadelphia Story," "I'm Not Rappaport."

Vernel
Bagneris

Wendy
Baila

Alec
Baldwin

Lisa
Banes

Arnold
Bankston

Regina
Baro

Evalyn
Baron

Gabriel
Barre

Mary
Barto

Tom
Batten

Caroline
Beck

Reed
Birney

Larry
Block

Anne Marie
Bobby

Ken
Bonafons

Victoria
Boothby

Mark
Bove

Deborah
Bremer

Fran
Brill

Chuck
Brown

Dora
Bryant

Terence
Burk

Catherine
Burns

Ralph
Byers

William
Cain

Blanca
Camacho

Mark
Capri

Alisa
Carroll

Joe Antony
Cavise

Joan
Copeland

COUNTRYMAN, MICHAEL. Born Sept. 15, 1955 in St. Paul, Mn. Graduate Trinity Col., AADA. Debut 1983 OB in "Changing Palettes," followed by "June Moon," "Terra Nova," "Out!," "Claptrap," "The Common Pursuit."

COUSINS, BRIAN. Born May 9, 1959 in Portland, Me. Graduate Tulane, UWash. Debut 1987 OB in "Death of a Buick."

COVER, FRANKLIN. Born Nov. 20, 1928 in Cleveland, Oh. Graduate Denison, Western ReserveU. OB in "Julius Caesar," "Henry IV," "She Stoops to Conquer," "The Plough and the Stars," "The Octoroon," "Hamlet," "Macbeth," "Kildeer," Bdwy in "Giants, Sons of Giants"(1962), "Calculated Risk," "Abraham Cochrane," Any Wednesday," "The Investigation," "40 Carats," "A Warm Body," "Applause," "Wild Honey."

COX, CATHERINE. Born Dec. 13, 1950 in Toledo, OH. Wittenberg U. graduate. Bdwy debut 1976 in "Music Is," followed by "Whoopee!" "Oklahoma!," "Shakespeare's Cabaret," "Barnum," "Baby," "Oh Coward!," OB in "By Strouse," "It's Better With a Band," "In Trousers," "Crazy Arnold."

CRABTREE, DON. Born Aug. 21, 1928 in Borger, TX. Attended Actors Studio. Bdwy bow 1959 in "Destry Rides Again," followed by "Happiest Girl in the World," "Family Affair," "Unsinkable Molly Brown," "Sophie," "110 In the Shade," "Golden Boy," "Pousse Cafe," "Mahagonny" (OB), "The Best Little Whorehouse in Texas," "42nd Street."

CRAFTON, KELLY. Born Apr. 8, 1960 in Washington, DC. Attended UMd. Debut 1987 OB in "Too Many Girls."

CRAIG, BETSY. Born Jan. 5, 1952 in Hopewell, VA. Attended Berry Col. Bdwy debut 1972 in "Ambassador," followed by "Smith," "Brigadoon," "La Cage aux Folles."

CRAIG, NOEL. Born Jan. 4 in St. Louis, MO. Attended Northwestern U., Goodman Theatre, London Guildhall. Bdwy debut 1967 in "Rosencrantz and Guildenstern Are Dead," followed by "A Patriot for Me," "Conduct Unbecoming," "Vivat! Vivat Regina!," "Going Up," "Dance a Little Closer," "A Chorus Line," OB in "Pygmalion," "Promenade," "Family House," "Inn at Lydda."

CRAIG, PHYLLIS. Born Aug. 5, 1936 in London. Debut 1968 OB in "Scuba Duba," followed by "The Actors," Bdwy in "Borstal Boy"(1970).

CRAVEN, MATT. Born Nov. 10, 1956 in Port Colborne, Can. Debut 1984 OB in "Blue Windows," followed by "Crackwalker."

CRISP, QUENTIN. Born Dec. 25, 1908 in Carshalton, Eng. Debut 1978 OB in "An Evening with Quentin Crisp," followed by "The Importance of Being Earnest," "Lord Alfred's Lover," "Murder at Rutherford House."

CRISWELL, KIM. Born July 19, 1957 in Hampton, Va. Graduate UCin. Bdwy debut 1981 in "The First," followed by "Nine," "Baby," "Stardust."

CRIVELLO, ANTHONY. Born Aug. 2, 1955 in Milwaukee, Wi. Bdwy debut 1982 in "Evita," followed by "The News," "Les Miserables," OB in "The Juniper Tree,"

CROFT, PADDY. Born in Worthing, Eng. Attended Avondale Col. Debut 1961 OB in "The Hostage," followed by "Billy Liar," "Live Like Pigs," "Hogan's Goat," "Long Day's Journey into Night," "Shadow of a Gunman," "Pygmalion," "The Plough and the Stars"(LC), "Kill," Bdwy in "The Killing of Sister George," "The Prime of Miss Jean Brodie," "Crown Matrimonial," "Major Barbara."

CROMWELL, DAVID. Born Feb. 16, 1946 in Cornwall, NY. Graduate Ithaca Col. Debut 1968 OB in "Up Eden," followed by "In the Boom Boom Room," "Hamlet," Bdwy in "A History of the American Film" (1978), "The Mystery of Edwin Drood."

CROOKS, KITTY. Born Feb. 23, 1958 in Doylestown, Pa. Yale graduate. Bdwy debut 1986 in "Wild Honey."

CRYER, GRETCHEN. Born Oct. 17, 1935 in Indianapolis, In. Graduate DePauw U. Bdwy debut 1962 in "Little Me," followed by "110 in the Shade," OB in "Now Is the Time for All Good Men," "Gallery," "Circle of Sound," "I'm Getting My Act Together . . .," "Blue Plate Special," "To Whom It May Concern," "Alterations."

CRYER, JON. Born Apr. 16, 1965 in NYC. Attended RADA. Bdwy debut 1983 in "Torch Song Trilogy," followed by "Brighton Beach Memoirs."

CUERVO, ALMA. Born Aug 13 1951 in Tampa, FL. Graduate Tulane U, Yale U. Debut 1977 in "Uncommon Women and Others," followed by "A Foot in the Door," "Put Them All Together," "Isn't It Romantic," "Miss Julie," "Quilters," Bdwy in "Once in a Lifetime," "Bedroom Farce," "Censored Scenes from King Kong," "Is There Life after High School?," "The Sneaker Factor," "Songs on a Shipwrecked Sofa."

CUKA, FRANCES. Born in London; graduate Guildhall School. Bdwy debut 1961 in "A Taste of Honey," followed by "Travesties," "Oliver!," "The Life and Adventures of Nicholas Nickleby," OB in "The Entertainer," "It's Only a Play," "Quartermaine's Terms," "Not Waving."

CULLEY, JANE. Born Dec. 3, 1943 in Lawrenceburg, Tn. Attended Reed Col. Debut 1964 OB in "Of Mice and Men," followed by "Scuba Duba," "Night of the Iguana," "A Phantasmagoria Historia . . . ," "Til Jason Comes," "Holy Junkie."

CULLITON, JOSEPH. Born Jan. 25, 1948 in Boston, Ma. Attended CalStateU. Debut 1982 OB in "Francis," followed by "Flirtations," "South Pacific"(LC).

CULLIVER, KAREN. Born Dec. 30, 1959 in Florida. Attended Stetson U. Bdwy debut 1983 in "Show Boat," followed by "The Mystery of Edwin Drood," OB in "The Fantasticks."

CULLUM, JOHN. Born Mar. 2, 1930 in Knoxville, Tn. Graduate UTn. Bdwy debut 1960 in "Camelot," followed by "Infidel Caesar," "The Rehearsal," "Hamlet," "On a Clear Day You Can See Forever" for which he received a Theatre World Award, "Man of La Mancha," "1776," "Vivat! Vivat Regina!," "Shenandoah," "Kings," "The Trip Back Down," "On the 20th Century," "Deathtrap," "Doubles," "You Never Can Tell," "The Boys in Autumn," OB in "Three Hand Reel," "The Elizabethans," "Carousel," "In the Voodoo Parlor of Marie Leveau," "The King and I"(JB), "Whistler."

CULP, STEVEN. Born Dec. 3, 1955 in LaJolla,Ca. Graduate Wm & Mary, Brandeis U. Debut 1983 OB in "Richard III," followed by "The Lisbon Traviata," "Highest Standard of Living."

CURRY, CHRISTOPHER. Born Oct. 22, 1948 in Grand Rapids, Mi. Graduate UMi. Debut 1974 OB in "When You Comin' Back Red Ryder?," followed by "The Cherry Orchard," "Spelling Bee," "Ballymurphy," "Isadora Duncan Sleeps with the Russian Navy," "The Promise," "Mecca," "Soul of the White Ant," "Strange Snow," "Love Letters on Blue Paper," "Kennedy at Colonus," "The Foreigner," Bdwy in "Crucifer of Blood" (1978), "All My Sons" (1987).

CURTIS, KEENE. Born Feb. 15, 1925 in Salt Lake City, UT. Graduate UUtah. Bdwy bow 1949 in "Shop at Sly Corner," with APA in "School for Scandal," "The Tavern," "Anatole," "Scapin," "Right You Are," "Importance of Being Earnest," "Twelfth Night," "King Lear," "Seagull," "Lower Depths," "Man and Superman," "Judith," "War and Peace," "You Can't Take It With You," "Pantagleize," "Cherry Orchard," "Misanthrope," "Cocktail Party," "Cock-a-Doodle Dandy," and "Hamlet," "A Patriot for Me," "The Rothschilds," "Night Watch," "Via Galactica," "Annie," "Division Street," "La Cage aux Folles," OB in "Colette," "Ride Across Lake Constance."

DACIUK, MARY. Born July 7, 1951 in Toronto, Can. Graduate York U. Debut 1984 OB in "The Undefeated Rhumba Champ," followed by "Crown Cork Cafeteria," "The Person I Once Was," "A Flight of Angels," "Man with a Raincoat," "Working One-Acts."

DAHLIA, RICHARD. Born May 22 in Peekskill, NY. Attended Westchester Com.Col. Debut 1984 OB in "Sacraments," followed by "Trumpets and Drums," "Night Watch," "The Jew of Malta."

DALE, JIM. Born Aug 15, 1935 in Rothwell, Eng. Debut 1974 OB with Young Vic Co. in "Taming of the Shrew," "Scapino" that moved to Bdwy, followed by "Barnum," "Joe Egg," "Me and My Girl."

DALY, TIMOTHY. Born Mar. 1, 1956 in NYC. Graduate Bennington Col. Debut 1984 OB in "Fables for Friends," followed by "Oliver Oliver," Bdwy in "Coastal Disturbances"(1987) for which he received a Theatre World Award.

DANEK, MICHAEL. Born May 5, 1955 in Oxford, Pa. Graduate Columbia Col. Bdwy debut 1978 in "Hello, Dolly!" followed by "A Chorus Line," "Copperfield," "Woman of the Year," OB in "Big Bad Burlesque", "Dreams."

DANETTE, LEILA. Born Aug. 23, 1909 in Jacksonville, Fl. Graduate Morgan State Col., UMd. Bdwy debut 1968 in "The Great White Hope," OB in "Don't Let It Go to Your Head," "Amen Corner," "The Long Black Block," "The Brothers," "Strivers Row," "The Actress."

DANIELLE, MARLENE. Born Aug. 16 in NYC. Bdwy debut 1979 in "Sarava," followed by "West Side Story," "Marlowe," "Damn Yankees" (JB), "Cats," OB in "Little Shop of Horrors."

DANIELLE, SUSAN. Born Jan. 30, 1949 in Englewood, NJ. Graduate Wm. Patterson Col. Debut 1979 OB in "Tip-Toes," Bdwy in "A Chorus Line" (1985).

DANIS, AMY. Born Jan. 20 in Dayton, Oh. Member of Joffrey Ballet before Bdwy debut (1980) in "Brigadoon," followed by OB's "Fire in the Basement."

DANNER, BLYTHE. Born in Philadelphia. Graduate Bard Col. Debut 1966 OB in "The Infantry," followed by "Collision Course," "Summertree," "Up Eden," "Someone's Comin' Hungry," "Cyrano," "The Miser" for which she received a Theatre World Award, "Twelfth Night," "The New York Idea," Bdwy in "Butterflies Are Free," "Betrayal," "The Philadelphia Story," "Blithe Spirit."

DANNER, BRADEN. Born in 1976 in Indianapolis, In. Bdwy debut 1984 in "Nine," followed by "Oliver!," "Starlight Express," "Les Miserables."

DANZIGER, MAIA. Born Apr. 12, 1950. Attended NYU. Bdwy debut 1973 in "Waltz of the Toreadors," OB in "Total Eclipse," "Milk of Paradise," "The Rachel Plays," "Kill."

DARIN, TRACY. Born Feb. 28, 1961 in Springfield, Mo. Graduate Drury Col. Debut 1987 OB in "Wish You Were Here."

DAVIES, JAMES. Born Oct. 29, 1960 in Cambridge, Ma. Graduate Catholic U. Debut 1987 OB in "Taster's Choice," followed by "The Little Foxes."

DAVIS, BRUCE ANTHONY. Born Mar. 4, 1959 in Dayton, Oh. Attended Juilliard. Bdwy debut 1979 in "Dancin'," followed by "Big Deal," "A Chorus Line."

DAVIS, OSSIE. Born Dec. 18, 1917 in Cogdell, Ga. Attended Howard U. Bdwy debut 1946 in "Jeb," followed by "Anna Lucasta," "Leading Lady," "Smile of the World," "The Wisteria Trees," "The Royal Family"(CC), "Green Pastures," "Remains to Be Seen," "Touchstone," "No Time for Sergeants," "Jamaica," "Raisin in theSun," "Purlie Victorious," "The Zulu and the Zayda," "Ain't Supposed to Die a Natural Death," "I'm Not Rappaport," OB in "Ballad of Bimshire," "Take It from the Top."

DAVIS, SHEILA KAY. Born May 30, 1956 in Daytona, FL. Graduate Spelman Col. Debut 1982 OB in "Little Shop of Horrors."

DAY, CONNIE. Born Dec. 26, 1940 in NYC. Debut 1971 OB in "Look Me Up," followed by "Antigone," "Walking Papers," Bdwy in "Molly"(1973), "The Magic Show," "42nd Street."

DEAKINS, LUCY. Born in NYC in 1971. Debut 1986 OB in "The Hands of It's Enemy."

DeALMEIDA, JOAQUIN. Born Mar. 15, 1957 in Portugal. Attended Lisbon Consv. Has appeared OB in "The Marriage Proposal," "The Sign in Sidney Brustein's Window," "A Christmas Carol," "Talk to Me Like Rain," "What Would Jeanne Moreau Do?," "Roosters."

DEAYTON, ANGUS. Born Jan. 6, 1956 in London. Graduate Oxford U. Bdwy debut 1986 in "Rowan Atkinson at the Atkinson."

de GANON, CAMILLE. Born in Springfield, Oh. Appeared with several dance companies before making her Bdwy debut in 1986 in "The Mystery of Edwin Drood."

DeKOVEN, ROGER. Born Oct. 22, 1907 in Chicago, Il. Attended UChicago, Northwestern, Columbia. Bdwy debut 1926 in "Juarez and Maximilian," followed by "Mystery Man," "Once in a Lifetime," "Counselor-at-law," "Murder in the Cathedral," "The Eternal Road," "Brooklyn U.S.A.," "The Assassin," "Joan of Lorraine," "Abie's Irish Rose," "The Lark," "Hidden River," "Compulsion," "Miracle Worker," "Fighting Cock," "Herzl," "Strider," OB in "Deadly Game," "Steal the Old Man's Bundle," "St. Joan," "Tiger at the Gates," "Walking to Waldheim," "Cyrano de Bergerac," "An Enemy of the People," "Ice Age," "Prince of Homburg," "Biography: A Game," "Strider," "Ivanov," "13," "Roots."

DeLAURENTIS, SEMINA. Born Jan. 21 in Waterbury, Ct. Graduate Southern Ct. State Col. Debut 1985 OB in "Nunsense," followed by "Have I Got a Girl for You."

DEL POZO, EMILIO. Born Aug 6, 1948 in Havana, Cuba. Attended AMDA. Debut 1983 OB in "Union City Thanksgiving," followed by "El Grande de Coca Cola," "Senorita from Tacna," "Twelfth Night," "The Wonderful Ice Cream Suit."

DELLA PIAZZA, DIANE. Born Sept. 3, 1962 in Pittsburgh, Pa. Graduate Cincinnati Consv. Bdwy debut 1987 in "Les Miserables."

DeLUCA, JOHN. Born Sept. 6 in Orange, NJ. Graduate Boston U. Bdwy debut 1980 in "Dancin'," followed by "The Mystery of Edwin Drood," OB in "The Boogie Woogie Rumble of a Dream Deferred."

DeMIRJIAN, DENISE. Born July 8, 1952 in Los Angeles, Ca. Graduate CalInst of Arts. Debut 1978 OB in "Cartoons," followed by "No Strings," "Oh," "Baby!," "To Feed Their Hopes."

DEMPSEY, JEROME. Born Mar. 1, 1929 in St. Paul, Mn. Graduate Toledo U. Bdwy debut 1959 in "West Side Story," followed by "The Deputy," "Spofford," "Room Service," "Love Suicide at Schofield Barracks," "Dracula," "Whodunit," "You Can't Take It with You," "The Mystery of Edwin Drood," "The Front Page" (LC), OB in "Cry of Players," "The Year Boston Won the Pennant," "The Crucible," "Justice Box," "Trelawny of the Wells," "Old Glory," "Six Characters in Search of an Author," "Threepenny Opera," "Johnny on the Spot," "The Barbarians," "he and she," "A Midsummer Night's Dream," "The Recruiting Officer," "Oedipus the King," "The Wild Duck," "The Fuehrer Bunker," "Entertaining Mr. Sloane," "The Clownmaker."

DeMUNN, JEFFREY. Born Apr. 15, 1947 in Buffalo, NY. Graduate Union Col. Debut 1975 OB in "Augusta," followed by "A Prayer for My Daughter," "Modigliani," "Chekhov Sketchbook," "A Midsummer Night's Dream," "Total Abandon," "The Country Girl," "Hands of Its Enemy," Bdwy in "Comedians"(1976), "Bent," "K2," "Sleight of Hand."

DENGEL, JAKE. Born June 19, 1933 in Oshkosh, Wi. Graduate Northwestern U. Debut OB in "The Fantasticks," followed by "Red Eye of Love," "Fortuna," "Abe Lincoln in Illinois," "Dr. Faustus," "An Evening with Garcia Lorca," "The Shrinking Bride," "Where Do We Go from Here?," "Woyzeck," "Endgame," "Measure for Measure," "Ulysses in Traction," "Twelfth Night," "The Beaver Coat," "The Great Grandson of Jedediah Kohler," "Caligula," "The Mound Builders," "Quiet in the Land," Bdwy in "The Royal Hunt of the Sun," "Cock-a-Doodle Dandy," "Hamlet," "The Changing Room."

DeNIRO, ROBERT. Born Aug. 17, 1943 in NYC. Studied with Stella Adler. Debut 1970 OB in "One Night Stands of a Noisy Passenger," followed by "Kool Aid (LC)," "Cuba and His Teddy Bear."

DENNIS, RONALD. Born Oct. 2, 1944 in Dayton, Oh. Debut 1966 OB in "Show Boat," followed by "Of Thee I Sing," "Moon Walk," "Please Don't Cry," Bdwy in "A Chorus Line"(1975), "My One and Only," "La Cage aux Folles."

DeRAEY, DANIEL. Born April 2, 1946 in NYC. Fordham U. graduate. Debut 1979 OB in "Class Enemy," followed by "The Return of Pinocchio."

DeSALVO, ANNE. Born April 3 in Philadelphia, Pa. OB in "Iphigenia in Aulis," "Lovers and Other Strangers," "First Warning," "Warringham Roof," "God Bless You, Mr. Rosewater," "Girls Girls Girls," "Thin Ice," Bdwy in "Gemini" (1977), "Safe Sex."

DeSHIELDS, ANDRE. Born Jan. 12, 1946 in Baltimore, MD. Graduate UWi. Bdwy debut 1973 in "Warp," followed by "Rachel Lily Rosenbloom," "The Wiz," "Ain't Misbehavin'," "Haarlem Nocturne," "Just So.," "Stardust," OB in "2008½," "Jazzbo Brown," "The Soldier's Tale," "The Little Prince," "Haarlem Nocturne," "Sovereign State of Boogedy Boogedy."

DESMOND, DAN. Born July 4, 1944 in Racine, Wi. Graduate UWi, Yale. Bdwy debut 1981 in "Morning's at Seven," followed by "Othello," "All My Sons," OB in "A Perfect Diamond," "The Bear," "Vienna Notes," "On Mt. Chimborazo," "Table Settings."

DEVINE, LORETTA. Born Aug. 21 in Houston, TX. Graduate UHouston, Brandeis U. Bdwy debut 1977 in "Hair," followed by "A Broadway Musical," "Dreamgirls," "Big Deal," OB in "Godsong," "Lion and the Jewel," "Karma," "The Blacks," "Mahalia," "Long Time Since Yesterday," "The Colored Museum."

DeVRIES, JON. Born Mar. 26, 1947 in NYC. Graduate Bennington Col., Pasadena Playhouse. Debut 1977 OB in "The Cherry Orchard," followed by "Agamemnon," "The Ballad of Soapy Smith," Bdwy in "The Inspector General," "Devour the Snow," "Major Barbara," "Execution of Justice,""the dreamer examines his pillow."

DeVRIES, MICHAEL. Born Jan. 15, 1951 in Grand Rapids, Mi. Graduate UWash. Debut 1987 OB in "Ready or Not."

DEWAR, JOHN. Born Jan. 24, 1953 in Evanston, Il. Graduate UMinn. Bdwy debut 1987 in "Les Miserables."

DEWHURST, COLLEEN. Born June 3, 1926 in Montreal, Can. Attended Downer Col., AADA. Bdwy debut 1952 in "Desire under the Elms," followed by "Tamburlaine the Great," "The Country Wife," "Caligula," "All the Way Home," "Great Day in the Morning," "Ballad of the Sad Cafe," "More Stately Mansions," "All Over," "Mourning Becomes Electra," "Moon for the Misbegotten," "Who's Afraid of Virginia Woolf?," "An Almost Perfect Person," "The Queen and the Rebels," "You Can't Take It with You," OB in "The Taming of the Shrew," "The Eagle Has Two Heads," "Camille," "Macbeth," "Children of Darkness" for which she received a 1958 Theatre World Award, "Antony and Cleopatra," "Hello and Goodbye," "Good Woman of Setzuan," "Hamlet," "Are You Now or Have You Ever . . .?, "Taken in Marriage," "My Gene."

DICKERSON, GEORGE. Born in Topeka, Ks. Yale graduate. Debut OB 1986 in "Shots at Fate."

DIDAWICK, DAWN. Born July 30 in Woodstock, Va. Attended American U. Debut 1976 OB in "A Night at the Black Pig," followed by "The Laundermat," "Romeo and Juliet," "Night Must Fall," "The Contrast," "The Rainman," Bdwy in "All My Sons" (1987).

DIEKMANN, MARK. Born Aug. 10, 1953 in Springfield, Ma. Attended Clark U., HB Studio. Debut 1987 OB in "Misalliance."

DIERSON, MARY A. Born Sept. 26 in Brooklyn, NY. Attended L.I.U. Bdwy debut 1979 in "Dracula," followed by "The Elephant Man," "Amadeus," OB in "The Common Pursuit."

DIETRICH, DENA. Born Dec. 4, 1928 in Pittsburgh, Pa. Attended AADA. Debut 1962 OB in "Out of This World," followed by "Cindy," "Rimers of Eldritch," "Mortally Fine," "Six Women on a Stage," Bdwy in "Funny Girl," "Here's Where I Belong," "Freaking Out of Stephanie Blake," "Prisoner of Second Avenue."

DILLEY, CAROL. Born Mar. 12, 1955 in Mt. Vernon, Il. Graduate IllStateU. Debut 1985 OB in "In Trousers," followed by "Too Many Girls."

DILLION, MIA. Born July 9, 1955 in Colorado Springs, CO. Graduate Penn State U. Bdwy debut 1977 in "Equus," followed by "Da," "Once a Catholic," "Crimes of the Heart," "The Corn Is Green," "Hay Fever," OB in "The Crucible," "Summer," "Waiting for the Parade," "Crimes of the Heart," "Fables for Friends," "Scenes from La Vie de Boheme," "Three Sisters." "Wednesday," "Roberta in Concert," "Come Back, Little Sheba," "Vienna Notes," "George White's Scandals," "Lady Moonsong, Mr. Monsoon."

DiPASQUALE, FRANK J. Born July 15, 1955 in Whitestone, NY. Graduate USC. Bdwy debut 1983 in "La Cage aux Folles."

DIXON, ED. Born Sept. 2, 1948 in Oklahoma. Attended OkU. Bdwy in "The Student Prince," followed by "No, No, Nanette," "Rosalie in Concert," "The Three Musketeers," OB in "By Bernstein," "King of the Schnorrers," "Rabboni," "Moby Dick," "Shylock."

DIXON, MacINTYRE. Born Dec. 22, 1931 in Everett, Ma. Graduate Emerson Col. Bdwy debut 1965 in "Xmas in Las Vegas," followed by "Cop-Out," "Story Theatre," "Metamorphosis," "Twigs," "Over Here!," "Once in a Lifetime," "Alice in Wonderland," OB in "Quare Fellow," "Plays for Bleecker Street," "Stewed Prunes," "Cat's Pajamas," "Three Sisters," "3 X 3," "Second City," "Mad Show," "Meow!," "Lotta," "Rubbers," "Conjuring an Event," "His Majesty the Devil," "Tomfoolery," "A Christmas Carol," "Times and Appetites of Toulouse-Lautrec," "Room Service," "Sills and Company," "Little Murders."

DONAHOE, JIM. Born Feb. 13, 1939 in Pittsburgh, Pa. Graduate UFla. Debut 1984 OB in "Up in Central Park," followed by "Hot Sake."

DONAHOE, JOHN. Born June 17, 1948 in Norfolk, Va. Graduate UVa. Debut 1985 OB in "Deathtrap," followed by "The Flower Palace."

DOOLEY, PAUL. Born Feb. 22, 1928 in Parkersburg, WVa. Graduate UWVa. Bdwy debut in "The Odd Couple," OB in "Threepenny Opera," "Toinette," "Fallout," "Dr. Willy Nilly," "Second City," "Adaptation," "White House Murder Case," "Jules Feiffer's Hold Me," "The Amazin' Casey Stengel," "Sills & Company."

DORAN, JESSE. Born June 23; attended AMDA. Bdwy debut 1976 in "The Runner Stumbles," OB in "Goose and Tom Tom," "Fool for Love," "Spookhouse," "Snowman," "My Papa's Wine."

DORFMAN, ROBERT. Born Oct. 8, 1950 in Brooklyn, NY. Attended CUNY, HB Studio. Debut 1979 OB in "Say Goodnight, Gracie," followed by "America Kicks," "Winterplay," "The Normal Heart," "Waving Goodbye," Bdwy in "Social Security"(1987).

DORFMAN, ROBERT. Born Oct. 8, 1950 in Brooklyn, NY. Attended CUNY, HB Studio. Debut 1979 OB in "Say Goodnight, Gracie," followed by "America Kicks," "Winterplay," "The Normal Heart."

DOUGHERTY, J. P. Born July 25, 1953 in Lincoln, Ill. Attended S.Ill.U. Debut 1982 OB in "The Frances Farmer Story," followed by "The Little Prince," "The Sound of Music," "The Trojan Women," "Tropical Fever in Key West," "Have I Got a Girl For You," Bdwy in "The Three Musketeers"(1984).

DOUGLASS, PI. Born in Sharon, CT. Attended Boston Consv. Bdwy debut 1969 in "Fig Leaves Are Falling," followed by "Hello, Dolly!," "Georgy," "Purlie," "Ari," "Jesus Christ Superstar," "Selling of the President," "The Wiz," "La Cage aux Folles," OB in "Of Thee I Sing," "Under Fire," "The Ritz," "Blackberries," "Dementos."

DRAKE, DONNA. Born May 21, 1953 in Columbia, SC. Attended USC, Columbia. Bdwy debut 1975 in "A Chorus Line," followed by "It's So Nice to Be Civilized," "1940's Radio Hour," "Woman of the Year," "Sophisticated Ladies," "Wind in the Willows," OB in "Memories of Riding with Joe Cool."

DRAPER, JASE. Born Sept. 26, 1962 in Bronxville, NY. Attended Northwestern U. Debut 1987 OB in "Take Me Along."

DRILLINGER, BRIAN. Born June 27, 1960 in Brooklyn, NY. Graduate SUNY/Purchase. Bdwy debut 1985 in "Brighton Beach Memoirs," followed by OB's "Square Root of Three," "Roots."

DUDLEY, CRAIG. Born Jan. 22, 1945 in Sheepshead Bay, NY. Graduate AADA, AmThWing. Debut 1970 OB in "Macbeth," followed by "Zou," "I Have Always Believed in Ghosts," "Othello," "War and Peace," "Dial 'M' for Murder," "Misalliance."

DUFF-MacCORMICK, CARA. Born Dec. 12 in Woodstock, Can. Attended AADA. Debut 1969 OB in "Love Your Crooked Neighbor," followed by "The Wager," "Macbeth," "A Musical Merchant of Venice," "Ladyhouse Blues," "The Philanderer," "Bonjour, La, Bonjour," "Journey to Gdansk," "The Dining Room," "All the Nice People," "Faulkner's Bicycle," "Earthworms," "The Acting Lesson," "Craig's Wife," "The Wager," "Neon Psalms," Bdwy in "Moonchildren" (1972) for which she received a Theatre World Award, "Out Cry," "Animals."

DUKAKIS, OLYMPIA. Born in Lowell, MA. Debut 1960 OB in "The Breaking Wall," followed by "Nourish the Beast," "Curse of the Starving Class," "Snow Orchid," "The Marriage of Bette and Boo," Bdwy in "The Aspern Papers" (1962), "Abraham Cochrane," "Who's Who in Hell," "Social Security."

DUNCAN, LINDSAY. Born Nov. 7, 1950 in Edinburgh, Scotland. Attended Central School of Speech/Drama, London. Debut OB 1982 in "Top Girls," Bdwy in "Les Liaisons Dangereuses" for which she received a 1987 Theatre World Award.

DUNDAS, JENNIFER. Born Jan. 14, 1971 in Boston, Ma. Bdwy debut 1981 in "Grownups," OB in "Before the Dawn," "I Love You, I Love You Not."

DURAN, MICHAEL. Born Nov. 25, 1953 in Denver, Co. Graduate UCol. Debut 1981 OB in "Godspell," followed by "Anonymous," "Dragons," Bdwy in "Into the Light"(1986).

DUTTON, CHARLES S. Born Jan. 30, 1951 in Baltimore, MD. Graduate Yale U. Debut 1983 OB in "Richard III," followed by "Pantomime," "Fried Chicken and Invisibility," Bdwy in "Ma Rainey's Black Bottom" (1984) for which he received a Theatre World Award.

DuVAL, HERBERT. Born May 4, 1941 in Schenectady, NY. Graduate UMich. Debut 1977 OB in "Arsenic and Old Lace," followed by "Prairie Avenue," "Once More with Feeling," "The Devil's Disciple," "The Green Bay Tree," "A Definite Maybe," "Two Orphans," "Night Watch," Bdwy in "Hide and Seek" (1980).

DWYER, FRANK. Born Feb. 1, 1945 in Kansas City, Mo. Graduate NYU, SUNY. Debut 1970 OB in "Moby Dick," followed by "Hamlet," "Bacchai," "A Streetcar Named Desire," "Darkness at Noon," "Vatzlav," "Brand," "Frankenstein."

EASTON, EDWARD. Born Oct. 21, 1942 in Moline, Il. Graduate Lincoln Col., UIll., Neighborhood Playhouse. Debut 1967 OB in "Party on Greenwich Avenue," followed by "Middle of the Night," "Summer Brave," "Sunday Afternoon," "The Education of Miss February," "The Little Foxes."

EBERT, JOYCE. Born June 26, 1933 in Homestead, Pa. Graduate Carnegie Tech. U. Debut 1956 OB in "Liliom," followed by "Sing of Winter," "Asmodee," "King Lear," "Hamlet," "Under Milk Wood," "Trojan Women," "White Devil," "Tartuffe," Bdwy in "Solitaire/Double Solitaire"(1971), "The Shadow Box," "Watch on the Rhine," "Requiem for a Heavyweight," "All My Sons."

ECHOLS, ANGELES. Born in Memphis, Tn. Graduate Cornell U. Debut 1982 OB in "The Fabulous '50's," followed by "Staggerlee."

EDDLEMAN, JACK. Born Sept. 7, 1944 in Chicago, Il. Attended UOk, UMo, Northwestern. Bdwy debut 1957 in "Shinbone Alley," followed by "Carousel"(CC), "Oh, Captain!," "Camelot," "Hot Spot," "The Girl Who Came to Supper," "Oh, What a Lovely War!," "My Fair Lady"(CC), OB in "Diversions," "Lend an Ear," "Great Scott!," "Jacques Brel Is Alive . . . ," "Swan Song."

EDELMAN, GREGG. Born Sept. 12, 1958 in Chicago, Il. Graduate Northwestern U. Bdwy debut 1982 in "Evita," followed by "Oliver!," "Cats," OB in "Weekend," "Shop on Main Street," "Forbidden Broadway."

EDENFIELD, DENNIS. Born July 23, 1946 in New Orleans, LA. Debut 1970 OB in "The Evil That Men Do," followed by "I Have Always Believed in Ghosts," "Nevertheless They Laugh," "Cowboy," Bdwy in "Irene" ('73), "A Chorus Line."

EDMEAD, WENDY. Born July 6, 1956 in NYC. Graduate NYCU. Bdwy debut 1974 in "The Wiz," followed by "Stop the World . . .," "America," "Dancin'," "Encore," "Cats."

EDWARDS, ALISON. Born Aug. 7, 1953 in Jackson, Ms. Graduate Boston U. Debut 1986 OB in "Night Watch."

EDWARDS, BRANDT. Born Mar. 22, 1947 in Holly Springs, MS. Graduate UMiss. NY debut off and on Bdwy 1975 in "A Chorus Line," followed by "42nd Street."

EDWARDS, DAVID. Born Dec. 13, 1957 in NYC. Graduate NYU. Bdwy debut 1972 in "The Rothschilds," followed by "The Best Little Whorehouse in Texas," "42nd Street," "A Chorus Line," OB in "Wish You Were Here."

EDWARDS, NAZ (formerly Nazig). Born Feb. 2, 1952 in Philadelphia, Pa. Debut 1981 OB in "Oh, Johnny!," followed by "Olympus on My Mind," Bdwy in "Zorba."

EICHHORN, LISA. Born in Reading, Pa. in 1952. Attended Queens Ontario U., RADA. Debut 1987 OB in "The Common Pursuit."

EILBER, JANET. Born July 27, 1951 in Detroit, Mi. Attended Juilliard. Appeared with Martha Graham Dance Co. before Bdwy debut (1980) in "Dancin'," followed by "Swing," "The Little Prince and the Aviator," "Stepping Out."

EISENBERG, NED. Born Jan. 13, 1957 in NYC. Attended Cal. Inst. of Arts. Debut 1980 OB in "The Time of the Cuckoo," followed by "Our Lord of Lynchville," "Dream of a Blacklisted Actor," "Second Avenue."

ELDREDGE, LYNN. Born July 25, 1953 in Holden, Ma. Graduate SanFranStateU. Debut 1982 OB in "Charlotte Sweet," followed by "Hollywood Opera," "Etiquette."

ELIO, DONNA MARIE. Born Oct. 30, 1962 in Paterson, NJ. Bdwy debut 1974 in "Gypsy," followed by "Merrily We Roll Along," "Smile."

ELIOT, DREW. Born in Newark, NJ. Graduate Columbia, RADA. OB in "The Fairy Garden," "Dr. Faustus," "Servant of Two Masters," "Henry V," "Stephen D," "Sjt. Musgrave's Dance," "Deadly Game," "Taming of the Shrew," "Appear and Show Cause," Bdwy in "Elizabeth the Queen," "The Physicists," "Romulus."

ELLIOTT, PATRICIA. Born July 21, in Gunnison, Co. Graduate UCo., London Academy. Debut 1968 with LCRep in "King Lear" and "A Cry of Players," followed by OB's "Henry V," "The Persians," "A Doll's House," "Hedda Gabler," "In Case of Accident," "Water Hen," "Polly," "But Not for Me," "By Bernstein," "Prince of Homburg," "Artichokes," "Wine Untouched," "Misalliance," "Virginia," "Sung and Unsung Sondheim," "Voice of the Turtle," "Lillian Wald," "Bunker Reveries," Bdwy debut 1973 in "A Little Night Music" for which she received a Theatre World Award, followed by "The Shadow Box," "Tartuffe," "13 Rue d L'Amour," "The Elephant Man," "A Month of Sundays."

ELLIS, FRASER. Born May 1, 1957 in Boulder, CO. Graduate UCo. Bdwy debut 1982 in "A Chorus Line."

ELMORE, STEVE. Born July 12, 1936 in Niangua, MO. Debut 1961 in "Madame Aphrodite," followed by "Golden Apple," "Enclave," Bdwy in "Camelot," "Jenny," "Fade in Fade Out," "Kelly," "Company," "Nash at 9," "Chicago," "42nd St."

EMMET, ROBERT. Born Oct. 3, 1952 in Denver, CO. Graduate UWash. Debut 1976 OB in "The Mousetrap," followed by "The Seagull," "Blue Hotel," "Miss Jairus," "Hamlet," "Deathwatch," "Much Ado About Nothing," "Songs and Ceremonies," "Mass Appeal," "Macbeth," "Bell, Book and Candle," "Comes the Happy Hour," "The Gift." "Merchant of Venice," "Arms and the Man," "The Lady from the Sea," "Two Gentlemen from Verona," "Andromache."

ENGEL, DAVID. Born Oct. 19, 1959 in Orange, CA. Attended UCal/Irvine. Bdwy debut 1983 in "La Cage aux Folles."

ERDE, SARA. Born Mar. 18, 1970 in NYC. Debut 1987 OB in "Roosters," followed by "Dancing Feet."

ERICKSON, CLARIS. Born Dec. 13, 1940 in Aurora, Il. Graduate Northwestern U., Edinburgh U. Debut 1962 OB in "Little Eyolf," followed by "A Tribute to Lili Lamont," "As Is," Bdwy in "As Is"(1985).

ETJEN, JEFF. Born June 12, 1953 in Chicago, Il. Graduate Rollins Col. Debut 1983 OB in "Forbidden Broadway," followed by "Romantic Arrangements," "Mandrake," "Gifts of the Magi."

EVANS, DILLON. Born Jan. 2, 1921 in London, Eng. Attended RADA. Bdwy debut 1950 in "The Lady's Not for Burning," followed by "School for Scandal," "Streamers," "Hamlet," "Ivanov," "Vivat! Vivat Regina!," "Jockey Club Stakes," "Dracula," "Death and the King's Horseman"(LC), OB in "Druid's Rest," "Rondelay," "The Little Foxes," "Playing with Fire."

EVERS, BRIAN. Born Feb. 14, 1942 in Miami, FL. Graduate Capital U, UMiami. Debut 1979 OB in "How's the House?," followed by "Details of the 16th Frame," "Divine Fire," "Silent Night, Lonely Night," "Uncommon Holidays," "The Tamer Tamed," "Death of a Buick," Bdwy in "House of Blue Leaves" (1986).

EWING, GEOFFREY C. Born Aug. 10, 1951 in Minneapolis, Mn. Graduate UMn. Bdwy debut 1983 in "Guys in the Truck," followed by "Cork," "The Leader/The Bald Soprano."

FAIRMAN, DeNICA. Born May 24, 1962 in Victoria, B.C., Can. Attended RADA. Bdwy debut 1986 with Royal Shakespeare Co. in "The Life and Adventures of Nicholas Nickleby."

FAITH, MICHELLE M. Born July 16, 1945 in Kittanning, Pa. Graduate Seton Hill Col., UMass. Debut 1986 OB in "North Shore Fish."

FALKENHAIN, PATRICIA. Born Dec. 3, 1926 in Atlanta, GA. Graduate Carnegie-Mellon, NYU. Debut 1946 OB in "Juno and the Paycock," followed by "Hamlet," "She Stoops to Conquer," "Peer Gynt," "Henry IV," "The Plough and the Stars," "Lysistrata," "Beaux Stratagem," "The Power and the Glory," "M. Amilcar," "Home," "The Marriage of Bette and Boo," Bdwy in "Waltz of the Toreadors," "The Utter Glory of Morrissey Hall," "Once a Catholic," "House of Blue Leaves."

FANCY, RICHARD. Born Aug. 2, 1943 in Evanston, Il. Attended LAMDA. Debut 1973 OB in "The Creeps," followed by "Kind Lady," "Rites of Passage," "A Limb of Snow," "The Meeting," "Child's Play," "Our Own Family."

FARER, RHONDA (a.k.a. Ronnie). Born Oct. 19, 1951 in Colonia, NJ. Graduate Rider Col. Debut 1973 in "Rachel Lily Rosenbloom," followed by "They're Playing Our Song," OB in "The Dog beneath the Skin" (1974), "Sally and Marsha," "The Deep End."

FARINA, MARILYN J. Born Apr. 9, 1947 in NYC. Graduate Sacred Heart Col. Debut 1985 OB in "Nunsense."

FARO, LYNN. Born June 30, 1951 in Los Angeles, Ca. Graduate UCal/Irvine. Bdwy debut 1985 in "La Cage aux Folles."

FARONE, FELICIA. Born Mar. 5, 1961 in Orange, NJ. Graduate Montclair State Col. Debut 1985 OB in "Rabboni," followed by "The Pajama Game."

FARR, KIMBERLY. Born Oct. 16, 1948 in Chicago, Il. Graduate UCLA. Bdwy debut 1972 in "Mother Earth," followed by "The Lady from the Sea," "Going Up," "Happy New Year," OB in "More Than You Deserve," "The S. S. Benchley," "At Sea with Benchley," "Suffragett," "Brownstone," "The Golden Windows," "Brownstone."

FEINSTEIN, ALAN. Born Sept. 10, 1948 in NYC. Attended LACC. Bdwy debut 1966 in "Malcolm," followed by "Zelda," "A Streetcar Named Desire" (1973), "A View from the Bridge" (1983), OB in "Iphigenia in Aulis," "Come Back, Little Sheba," "Light Up the Sky," "Seahorse," "Papers," "Shoot Anything with Hair That Moves," "The Sandcastle," "As Is."

FERRANTE, FRANK. Born Apr. 26, 1963 in Los Angeles, Ca. Graduate USCal. Debut 1986 OB in "Groucho: A Life in Revue" for which he received a Theatre World Award.

FIEDLER, JOHN. Born Feb. 3, 1925 in Plateville, Wi. Attended Neighborhood Playhouse. OB in "The Seagull," "Sing Me No Lullaby," "The Terrible Swift Sword," "The Raspberry Picker," "The Frog Prince," "Raisin in the Sun," Bdwy in "One Eye Closed" (1954), "Howie," "Raisin in the Sun," "Harold," "The Odd Couple," "Our Town."

FIELD, CRYSTAL. Born Dec. 10, 1942 in NYC. Attended Juilliard, Graduate Hunter Col. Debut OB in "A Country Scandal (1960)," and most recent appearance was in "A Matter of Life and Death," followed by "The Heart That Eats Itself."

FIERSTEIN, HARVEY. Born June 6, 1954 in Brooklyn, NY. Graduate Pratt Inst. Debut 1971 OB in "Pork," followed by "International Stud," "Figure In a Nursery," Bdwy 1982 in "Torch Song Trilogy," for which he received a Theatre World Award, "Safe Sex."

FINKEL, BARRY. Born July 21, 1960 in Philadelphia, Pa. Attended Temple U., AMDA. Debut 1986 OB in "Have I Got a Girl for You," followed by "Cowboy."

FINKEL, FYVUSH. Born Oct. 9, 1922 in Brooklyn, NY. Bdwy debut 1970 in "Fiddler On the Roof" (also 1981 revival), OB in "Gorky," "Little Shop of Horrors."

FINLAY-McLENNAN, STEWART. Born Sept. 7, 1957 in Broken Hill, Australia. Debut 1987 OB in "Down an Alley Filled with Cats."

FIORDELLISI, ANGELINA. Born Mar. 15, 1955 in Detroit, MI. Graduate UDetroit. Bdwy debut 1983 in "Zorba," OB in "An Ounce of Prevention," "Have I Got a Girl for You."

FIRE, NORMA. Born June 9, 1937 in Brooklyn, NY. Graduate Bklyn.Col. Debut 1982 OB in "3 Acts of Recognition," followed by "Merry Wives of Windsor," "Henry V," "It's All Talk," "Macbeth."

FIRE, NORMA. Born June 9, 1937 in Brooklyn, NY. Graduate Bklyn Col. Debut 1982 OB in "3 Acts of Recognition," followed by "Merry Wives of Windsor," "Henry V," "It's All Talk," "Macbeth."

FITZGERALD, FERN. Born Jan. 7, 1947 in Valley Stream, NY. Bdwy debut 1976 in "Chicago," followed by "A Chorus Line."

FITZGERALD, GERALDINE. Born Nov. 24, 1914 in Dublin, Ire. Bdwy debut 1938 in "Heartbreak House," followed by "Sons and Soldiers," "Doctor's Dilemma," "King Lear," "Hide and Seek," "Ah, Wilderness," "The Shadow Box," "A Touch of the Poet," OB in "Cave Dwellers," "Pigeons," "Long Day's Journey into Night," "Everyman and Roach," "Streetsongs," "Danger: Memory!" (LC)

FLAGG, TOM. Born March 30 in Canton, Oh. Attended KentStateU., AADA. Debut 1975 OB in "The Fantasticks," followed by "Give Me Liberty," "The Subject Was Roses," "Lola," "Red, Hot and Blue," "Episode 26," "Dazy," Bdwy in "Legend (1976)," "Shenandoah," "Players."

FLANAGAN, KIT. Born July 6 in Pittsburgh, PA. Graduate Northwestern U. Debut 1979 OB in "The Diary of Anne Frank," followed by "An Evening with Dorothy Parker," "Still Life," "Cloud 9," "Alto Part," "A Step Out of Line," "Goodbye Freddy," Bdwy in "All My Sons" (1987).

FLANINGAM, LOUISA. Born May 5, 1945 in Chester, SC. Graduate UMd. Debut 1971 OB in "The Shrinking Bridge," followed by "Pigeons on the Walk," "Etiquette," "The Knife," Bdwy in "Magic Show," "Most Happy Fella" (1979), "Play Me a Country Song."

FLEISS, JANE. Born Jan. 28 in NYC. Graduate NYU. Debut 1979 OB in "Say Goodnight, Gracie," followed by "Grace," "The Beaver Coat," "The Harvesting," "D.," "Second Man," Bdwy in "5th of July" (1981), "Crimes of the Heart," "I'm Not Rappaport."

FLODEN, LEA. Born Feb. 13, 1958 in Rockford, Il. Graduate IndianaU. Debut 1980 OB in "The Ladder," followed by "Cherokee County," "Short Change," "Murder in the Mummy's Tomb."

FLOOD, AMY. Born May 7, 1963 in Sharon, Ct. Was with Ballet Hispanico before 1987 OB debut in "Funny Feet."

FLOREK, DAVE. Born May 19, 1953 in Dearborn, MI. Graduate Eastern MiU. Debut 1976 OB in "The Collection," followed by "Richard III," "Much Ado About Nothing," "Young Bucks," "Big Apple Messenger," "Death of a Miner," "Marvelous Gray," "Journey to Gdansk," "The Last of Hitler," "Thin Ice," "The Incredibly Famous Willy Rivers," "Responsible Parties," "For Sale," "The Foreigner," "Copperhead," Bdwy 1980 in "Nuts."

FOGARTY, MARY. Born in Manchester, NH. Debut 1959 OB in "The Well of Saints," followed by "Shadow and Substance," "Nathan the Wise," "Bonjour La Bonjour," "Family Comedy," "Steel Magnolias," Bdwy in "The National Health," "Watch on the Rhine" (1980), "Of the Fields Lately."

FOLEY, BRENDA. Born Apr. 19, 1960 in Jacksonville, Fl. Graduate USantaClara, CalifInst. of Arts. Debut 1985 OB in "Playboy of the Western World," followed by "Edward II."

FOLLANSBEE, JULIE. Born in Sept. 1919 in Chicago, Il. Bryn Mawr Graduate. Debut 1949 OB in "The Fifth Horseman," followed by "Luminosity without Radiance," "Johnny Doesn't Live Here Anymore," "Epitaph for George Dillon," "Maromichaelis," "Brothers Karamazov," "Excelsior," "In the Summer House," "Road to the Graveyard," "Day of the Dolphin," "Bell, Book and Candle," "Crime and Punishment," "Pas de Deux."

FONTAINE, LUTHER. Born Apr. 14, 1947 in Kansas City, Ks. Graduate UMo, NYU. Bdwy debut 1973 in "Two Gentlemen of Verona," followed by "Timbuktu," "The First," OB in "All Night Strut," "Feeling Good," "Dream on Monkey Mountain," "Bojangles," "Back in the Big Time."

FORBES, BRENDA. Born Jan. 14, 1909 in London, Eng. Bdwy debut 1931 in "The Barretts of Wimpole Street," followed by "Candida," "Lucrece," "Flowers of the Forest," "Pride and Prejudice," "Storm over Patsy," "Heartbreak House," "One for the Money," "Two for the Show," "Three to Make Ready," "Yesterday's Magic," "Morning Star," "Suds in Your Eyes," "Quadrille," "The Reluctant Debutante," "Loves of Cass McGuire," "Darling of the Day," "The Constant Wife," "My Fair Lady," "Aren't We All?," OB in "Busybody," "Pygmalion in Concert."

FORD, SPENCE. Born Feb. 25, 1954 in Richmond, VA. Attended UVa. Debut 1976 OB in "Follies," followed by "Pal Joey," Bdwy in "King of Hearts," "Carmelina," "Peter Pan," "Copperfield," "Dancin'," "Merlin," "La Cage aux Folles."

FORLOW, TED. Born Apr. 29, 1931 in Independence, Mo. Attended Baker U. Bdwy debut 1957 in "New Girl in Town," followed by "Juno," "Destry Rides Again," "Subways Are for Sleeping," "Can-Can," "Wonderful Town," "A Funny Thing Happened on the Way . . .," "Milk and Honey," "Carnival" (CC), "Man of La Mancha" (1965/1977), "Into the Light," OB in "A Night at the Black Pig," "Glory in the Flower," "Perfect Analysis Given by a Parrot," "Cat and the Fiddle," "One Cannot Think of Everything," "Man of Destiny."

FORTGANG, AMY. Born Sept. 5, 1960 on Long Island, NY. Graduate Bucknell U. Debut 1987 OB in "Too Many Girls."

FOSTER, FRANCES. Born June 11 in Yonkers, NY. Bdwy debut 1955 in "The Wisteria Trees," followed by "Nobody Loves an Albatross," "Raisin in the Sun," "The River Niger," "First Breeze of Summer," OB in "Take a Giant Step," "Edge of the City," "Tammy and the Doctor," "The Crucible," "Happy Ending," "Day of Absence," "An Evening of One Acts," "Man Better Man," "Brotherhood," "Akokawe," "Rosalee Pritchett," "Sty of the Blind Pig," "Ballet Behind the Bridge," "Good Woman of Setzuan" (LC), "Behold! Cometh the Vanderkellans," "Origin," "Boesman and Lena," "Do Lord Remember Me," "Henrietta," "Welcome to Black River," "House of Shadows," "The Miracle Worker."

FOSTER, HERBERT. Born May 14, 1936 in Winnipeg, Can. Debut 1967 OB in "The Imaginary Invalid," followed by "A Touch of the Poet," "Tonight at 8:30," "Papers," "Henry V," "Playboy of the Western World," "Good Woman of Setzuan," "Scenes from American Life," "Mary Stuart," "Twelfth Night."

FOWLER, CLEMENT. Born Dec. 27, 1924 in Detroit, MI. Graduate Wayne State U. Bdwy debut 1951 in "Legend of Lovers," followed by "The Cold Wind and the Warm," "Fragile Fox," "The Sunshine Boys," "Hamlet (1964), OB in "The Eagle Has Two Heads," "House Music," "Transfiguration of Benno Blimpie," "The Inheritors," "Paradise Lost," "The Time of Your Life," "Children of the Sun," "Highest Standard of Living."

FRANCER, LARRY. Born Oct. 27, 1956 in Boston, Ma. Graduate Wesleyan U. Debut 1987 OB in "Wish You Were Here."

FRANZ, JOY. Born in 1944 in Modesto, Ca. Graduate UMo. Debut 1969 OB in "Of Thee I Sing," followed by "Jacques Brel Is Alive . . .," "Out of This World," "Curtains," "I Can't Keep Running in Place," "Tomfoolery," "Penelope," "Bittersuite," Bdwy in "Sweet Charity," "Lysistrata," "A Little Night Music," "Pippin," "Musical Chairs."

FRASER, ALISON. Born July 8, 1955 in Natick, Ma. Attended Carnegie-Mellon U., Boston Conservatory. Debut 1979 OB in "In Trousers," followed by "March of the Falsettos," "Beehive," "Four One-Act Musicals," "Tales of Tinseltown," "Next Please!," Bdwy in "The Mystery of Edwin Drood" (1986).

FRATANTONI, DIANE. Born Mar. 29, 1956 in Wilmington, DE. Bdwy debut 1979 in "A Chorus Line," followed by "Cats."

FREDERICKS, CONNIE. Born Aug. 30, 1948 in Springfield, Ma. Attended Fashion Inst. Debut 1984 OB in "Oh, Baby!," followed by "Forever, My Darlin'," "Abyssinia."

FREDRICKSON, JOEL. Born May 11, 1959 in Bethesda, Md. Yale graduate. Debut 1982 OB in "Scenes Dedicated to My Brother," followed by "The Miser," "Shylock."

FREEMAN, MORGAN. Born June 1, 1937 in Memphis, Tn. Attended LACC. Bdwy debut 1967 in "Hello, Dolly!," followed by "The Mighty Gents," OB in "Ostrich Feathers," "Niggerlovers," "Exhibition," "Black Visions," "Cockfight," "White Pelicans," "Julius Caesar," "Coriolanus," "Mother Courage," "The Connection," "The World of Ben Caldwell," "Buck," "The Gospel at Colonus," "Medea and the Doll," "Driving Miss Daisy."

FRELICH, PHYLLIS. Born Feb. 29, 1944 in North Dakota. Graduate Gallaudet Col. Bdwy debut 1970 in National Theatre of the Deaf's "Songs from Milkwood," followed by "Children of a Lesser God," OB in "Poets from the Inside," "Hands of Its Enemy."

FREULON, ALAIN. Born Oct. 10, 1958 in Paris, France. Debut 1986 OB in "Have I Got a Girl for You."

FRID, JONATHAN. Born Dec. 1924 in Hamilton, Ont., Can. Graduate McMaster U., Yale, RADA. Debut 1959 OB in "The Golem," followed by "Henry IV, Parts I & II," "The Moon in the Yellow River," "The Burning," "Murder in the Cathedral," Bdwy in "Roar Like a Dove" (1964), "Arsenic and Old Lace" (1986).

FRIED, JONATHAN. Born Mar. 3, 1959 in Los Angeles, Ca. Graduate Brown U, UCalSan-Diego. Debut 1986 OB in "1951," followed by "Dispatches from Hell."

FRIEDMAN, PETER. Born Apr. 24, 1949 in NYC. Debut 1971 OB in "James Joyce Memorial Liquid Theatre," followed by "Big and Little," "A Soldier's Play," "Mr. and Mrs.," "And a Nightingale Sang," "Dennis," "The Common Pursuit," Bdwy in "The Visit," "Chemin de Fer," "Love for Love," "Rules of the Game," "Piaf!," "Execution of Justice."

FRISCH, RICHARD. Born May 9, 1933 in NYC. Graduate Juilliard. Bdwy debut 1964 in "The Passion of Josef D," followed by "Fade Out-Fade In," "Rags," OB in "Jonah," "Antigone," "The Mother of Us All," "Up from Paradise," "Pere Goriot," "Pearls."

FRUGE, ROMAIN. Born Mar. 4, 1959 in Los Angeles, Ca. Graduate Allentown Col. Bdwy debut 1986 in "Big River."

FURS, EDDIE L. Born July 23, 1957 in Brooklyn, NY. Graduate NYU. Debut 1986 OB in "Dance of Death," followed by "Night Must Fall," "Squaring the Circle," "The Miser," "Harpo," "Family Portrait," "Queen Christina," "Chaste Maide in Cheapside."

GABLE, JUNE. Born June 5, 1945 in NYC. Graduate Carnegie Tech. OB in "Macbird," "Jacques Brel Is Alive and Well . . .," "A Day in the Life of Just About Everyone," "Mod Donna," "Wanted," "Lady Audley's Secret," "Comedy of Errors," "Chinchilla," "Beggar's Opera," "Shoe Palace Murray," "Star Treatment," "Coming Attractions," "Times and Appetites of Toulouse-Lautrec," "The Perfect Party," "No Way to Treat a Lady," Bdwy in "Candide" (1974),

GAINES, BOYD. Born May 11, 1953 in Atlanta, Ga. Graduate Juilliard. Debut 1978 OB in "Spring Awakening," followed by "A Month in the Country" for which he received a Theatre World Award, BAM Theatre Co.'s "Winter's Tale," "The Barbarians" and "Johnny on a Spot," "Vikings," "Double Bass," "The Maderati."

GALE, ANDY. Born in NYC; graduate Antioch Col. Debut 1981 OB in "The Eternal Love," Bdwy in "The World of Sholom Aleichem" (1982), followed by "Rags."

GALLAGHER, HELEN. Born in 1926 in Brooklyn, NY. Bdwy debut 1947 in "Seven Lively Arts," followed by "Mr. Strauss Goes to Boston," "Billion Dollar Baby," "Brigadoon," "High Button Shoes," "Touch and Go," "Make a Wish," "Pal Joey," "Guys and Dolls," "Finian's Rainbow," "Oklahoma!," "Pajama Game," "Bus Stop," "Portofino," "Sweet Charity," "Mame," "Cry for Us All," "No, No, Nanette," "A Broadway Musical," "Sugar Babies," OB in "Hothouse," "Tickles by Tucholsky," "The Misanthrope," "I Can't Keep Running in Place," "Red Rover," "Tallulah," "The Flower Palace."

GALLAGHER, PETER. Born Aug. 19, 1955 in Armonk, NY. Bdwy debut 1977 in "Hair," followed by "Grease," "A Doll's Life" for which he received a Theatre World Award, "The Corn Is Green," "The Real Thing," "Long Day's Journey into Night."

GALLOWAY, JANE. Born Feb. 27, 1950 in St. Louis, Mo. Attended Webster Col. Debut 1976 OB in "Vanities," followed by "Domino Courts," "Comanche Cafe," "Dementos," "Three Postcards," Bdwy in "Little Johnny Jones" (1982).

GALLUP, BONNIE LEE. Born Nov. 17, 1945 in Long Beach, Ca. Attended CalStateU., Juilliard. Bdwy debut 1972 in "The Great God Brown," followed by "Don Juan," "The Visit," "Chemin de Fer," "Holiday," OB in "Roots," "Square Root of Three."

GAMACHE, LAURIE. Born Sept. 25, 1959 in Mayville, ND. Graduate Stephens Col. Bdwy debut 1982 in "A Chorus Line."

GARBER, VICTOR. Born Mar. 16, 1949 in London, Can. Debut 1973 OB in "Ghosts" for which he received a Theatre World Award, followed by "Joe's Opera," "Cracks," Bdwy in "Tartuffe," "Deathtrap," "Sweeney Todd," "They're Playing Our Song," "Little Me," "Noises Off," "You Never Can Tell."

GARDNER, LAURA. Born Mar. 17, 1951 in Flushing, NY. Graduate Boston U., Rutgers U. Debut 1979 OB in "The Office Murders," followed by "Welded," "Living Quarters," "Beggar's Opera," "Office Murders," "Kids and Dogs," Bdwy in "Smile" (1986).

GARFIELD, JULIE. Born Jan. 10, 1946 in Los Angeles, Ca. Attended UWi, Neighborhood Playhouse. Debut 1969 OB in "Honest-to-God-Schnozzola," followed by "East Lynne," "The Sea," "Uncle Vanya" for which she received a Theatre World Award, "Me and Molly," "Chekhov Sketchbook," "Rosario and the Gypsies," "Occupations," "Modern Ladies of Guanabacoa," "Broken Eggs," "Passover," "Cleveland and Half Way Back," "Second Avenue," Bdwy in "The Good Doctor," "Death of a Salesman," "The Merchant."

GARRICK, BARBARA. Born Feb. 3, 1962 in NYC. Debut 1986 OB in "Today I Am a Fountain Pen," followed by "A Midsummer Night's Dream," "Rosencrantz and Guildenstern Are Dead."

GARSIDE, BRAD. Born June 2, 1958 in Boston, MA. Graduate NorthTexState U. Debut 1983 OB in "Forbidden Broadway."

GARZA, TROY. Born Aug. 20, 1954 in Hollywood, Ca. Attended RADA. Bdwy debut 1977 in "A Chorus Line," followed by "Got Tu Go Disco," OB in "Fourtune," "Paris Lights."

GAUDET, CHRISTIE. Born Mar. 28, 1957 in New Orleans, La. Attended Tulane U. Debut 1987 OB in "Staggerlee."

GAVON, IGORS. Born Nov. 14, 1937 in Latvia. Bdwy bow 1961 in "Carnival," followed by "Hello, Dolly!" "Marat/deSade," "Billy," "Sugar," "Mack and Mabel," "Musical Jubilee," "Strider," "42 St," OB in "Your Own Thing," "Promenade," "Exchange," "Nevertheless They Laugh," "Polly," "The Boss," "Biography: A Game," "Murder in the Cathedral."

GEBEL, DAVID. Born June 17, 1957 in Milwaukee, Wi. Graduate UMn. Debut 1981 OB in "Fourtune," followed by "The Fantasticks," "Too Many Girls."

GEE, KEVIN JOHN. Born Mar. 19, 1962 in San Francisco, Ca. Attended Chabot Col. Debut 1977 OB in "Helen," followed by "Boticelli," "Tropical Tree," "Prime Time."

GEESON, JUDY. Born Sept. 10, 1948 in Arunel, Sussex, Eng. Debut 1986 OB in "The Common Pursuit."

GEFFNER, DEBORAH. Born Aug. 26, 1952 in Pittsburgh, PA. Attended Juilliard, HB Studio. Debut 1978 OB in "Tenderloin," Bdwy in "Pal Joey," "A Chorus Line."

GELB, JODY. Born March 11 in Cincinnati, Oh. Graduate Boston U. Debut 1983 OB in "Wild Life," followed by "36 Dramatic Situations," "Love Suicides," "Baal," "Past Lives."

GELFER, STEVEN. Born Feb. 21, 1949 in Brooklyn, NY. Graduate NYU, IndU. Debut 1968 OB and Bdwy in "The Best Little Whorehouse in Texas," followed by "Cats."

GELLAR, SARAH MICHELLE. Born Apr. 14, 1977 in NYC. Debut 1986 OB in "The Widow Claire."

GENEST, EDMOND. Born Oct. 27, 1943 in Boston, Ma. Attended Suffolk U. Debut 1972 OB in "The Real Inspector Hound," followed by "Second Prize: Two Months in Leningrad," "Maneuvers," "Pantomime," Bdwy in "Dirty Linen/New Found Land" (1977), "Whose Life Is It Anyway?"

GENTLES, AVRIL. Born Apr. 2, 1929 in Upper Montclair, NJ. Graduate UNC. Bdwy debut 1955 in "The Great Sebastians," followed by "Nude with Violin," "Present Laughter," "My Mother, My Father and Me," "Jimmy Shine," "Grin and Bare It," "Lysistrata," "Texas Trilogy," "Show Boat" (1983), "Musical Comedy Murders of 1940," OB in "Dinny and the Witches," "The Wives," "Now Is the Time," "Man with a Load of Mischief," "Shay," "A Winter's Tale," "Johnny on a Spot," "The Barbarians," "The Wedding," "Nymph Errant," "A Little Night Music."

GEOFFREYS, STEPHEN. Born Nov. 22, 1964 in Cincinnati, Oh. Attended NYU. Bdwy debut 1984 in "The Human Comedy" for which he received a Theatre World Award, OB in "Maggie Magalita," "Songs on a Shipwrecked Sofa."

GERACI, FRANK. Born Sept. 8, 1939 in Brooklyn, NY. Attended Yale. Debut 1961 OB in "Color of Darkness," followed by "Mr. Grossman," "Balm in Gilead," "The Fantasticks," "Tom Paine," "End of All Things Natural," "Union Street," "Uncle Vanya," "Success Story," "Hughie," "Merchant of Venice," "The Three Zeks," "Taming of the Shrew," "The Lady from the Sea," "Rivals," "Deep Swimmer," Bdwy in "The Love Suicide at Schofield Barracks" (1972).

GERARD, TOM. Born Oct. 10, 1947 in Newark, NJ. Graduate Syracuse U. Debut 1970 OB in "The Drunkard," followed by "Better Living," Bdwy in "Grease" (1974).

GERROLL, DANIEL. Born Oct. 16, 1951 in London, Eng. Attended Central Sch. of Speech. Debut 1980 OB in "The Slab Boys," followed by "Knuckle" and "Translations" for which he received a Theatre World Award, "The Caretaker," "Scenes from La Vie de Boheme," "The Knack," "Terra Nova," "Dr. Faustus," "Second Man," "Cheapside," "Bloody Poetry," "The Common Pursuit," Bdwy in "Plenty" (1982).

GIANNINI, CHERYL. Born June 15 in Monessen, PA. Bdwy debut 1980 in "The Suicide," followed by "Grownups," OB in "Elm Circle," "I'm Not Rappaport."

GIBSON, TERI. Born Dec. 23, 1959 in Mahopac, NY. Graduate Adelphi U. Bdwy debut 1981 in "Marlowe," followed by OB in "Too Many Girls."

GIBSON, THOMAS. Born July 3, 1962 in Charleston, SC. Graduate Juilliard. Debut 1985 OB in "Map of the World," followed by "Twelfth Night," "Bloody Poetry," "Marathon 87," "Two Gentlemen of Verona." Bdwy in "Hay Fever (1985)."

GIDEON, DAVID. Born May 18, 1945 in NYC. Graduate Franklin & Marshall Col. Debut 1972 OB in "Rose Bernd," followed by "Richard III," "Streamers," "Day Game," "Modigliani," "Cowards."

GIESENSCHLAG, RUSSELL. Born July 8, 1959 in San Diego, Ca. Attended SanDiegoStateU. Bdwy debut 1982 in "Seven Brides for Seven Brothers," OB in "Girl Crazy," followed by "Pageant."

GIFFIN, NORMA JEAN. Born Oct. 31, 1956 in Haverhill, Ma. Graduate Barat Col., AADA. Debut 1980 OB in "Last Stop Blue Jay Lane" followed by "On Extended Wings."

GILBORN, STEVEN. Born in New Rochelle, NY. Graduate Swarthmore, Col., Stanford U. Bdwy debut 1973 in "Creeps," followed by "Basic Training of Pavlo Hummel," "Tartuffe," OB in "Rosmersholm," "Henry V," "Measure for Measure," "Ashes," "The Dybbuk," "Museum," "Shadow of a Gunman," "It's Hard to Be a Jew," "Isn't It Romantic," "Principia Scriptoriae," "Panache!"

GILES, LEE ROY. Born Dec. 3, 1936 in Witchita, Ks. Attended Fordham, Adelphi, L.I.U. Bdwy debut 1971 in "No Place to Be Somebody," OB in "Deep Swimmer," "Big City Breakdown."

GILES, NANCY. Born July 17, 1960 in Queens, NYC. Graduate Oberlin Col. Debut 1985 OB in "Mayor" for which she received a Theatre World Award, followed by "The Sneaker Factor."

GILL, RAY. Born Aug. 1, 1950 in Bayonne, NJ. Attended Rider Col. Bdwy debut 1978 in "On the 20th Century" followed by "Pirates of Penzance," "The First," "They're Playing Our Song," "Sunday in the Park with George," OB in "A Bundle of Nerves," "Driving Miss Daisy."

GILLETTE, ANITA. Born Aug. 16, 1938 in Baltimore, MD. Debut 1960 OB in "Russell Patterson's Sketchbook" for which she received a Theatre World Award, followed by "Rich and Famous," "Dead Wrong," "Road Show," Bdwy in "Carnival," "All American," "Mr. President," "Guys and Dolls," "Don't Drink the Water," "Cabaret," "Jimmy," "Chapter Two," "They're Playing Our Song," "Brighton Beach Memoirs."

GINTY, ROBERT. Born Nov. 14, 1948 in Brooklyn, NY. Attended CUNY. Debut 1970 OB in "Three in One," followed by "Silent Partner," "Bring It All Back Home," Bdwy in "The Great God Brown" (1972), "Don Juan."

GIOMBETTI, KAREN. Born May 24, 1955 in Scranton, PA. Graduate NYU. Bdwy debut 1978 in "Stop the World, I Want to Get Off," followed by "The Most Happy Fella," "Woman of the Year," "Zorba" (1983), "The Mystery of Edwin Drood."

GIONSON, MEL. Born Feb. 23, 1954 in Honolulu, HI. Graduate UHi. Debut 1979 OB in "Richard II," followed by "Sunrise," "Monkey Music," "Behind Enemy Lines," "Station J," "Teahouse," "A Midsummer Night's Dream," "Empress of China," "Chip Shot," "Manoa Valley," "Ghashiram," "Shogun Macbeth," "Life of the Land."

GIORDANO, GREG. Born Dec. 8, 1959 in Brooklyn, NY. Attended Rockland Com. Col. Debut 1986 OB in "Crown Cork Cafeteria," followed by "Golden Boy," "Man with a Raincoat," "Great Labor Day Classic," "Working One-Acts."

GLAZE, SUSAN. Born Oct. 9, 1956 in Murfreesboro, Tn. Graduate UTn., AADA. Debut 1982 OB in "The Broken Heart," followed by "Le Grande Cafe," "Tribute to Jerome Kern," "Pippin," Bdwy in "Big River" (1985).

GLEASON, JOANNA. Born June 2, 1950 in Toronto, CAN. Graduate UCLA. Bdwy debut 1977 in "I Love My Wife" for which she received a Theatre World Award, followed by "The Real Thing," "Social Security," OB in "A Hell of a Town." "Joe Egg," "It's Only a Play."

GLUSHAK, JOANNA. Born May 27, 1958 in NYC. Attended NYU. Debut 1983 OB in "Lenny and the Heartbreakers," followed by "Lies and Legends," "Miami," Bdwy in "Sunday in the Park with George" (1984), "Rags" "Les Miserables."

GOETZ, PETER MICHAEL. Born Dec. 10, 1941 in Buffalo, NY. Graduate SUNY/Fredonia, Southern ILU. Debut 1980 OB in "Jail Diary of Albie Sachs," "Before the Dawn," followed by Bdwy in "Ned and Jack" (1981), "Beyond Therapy," "The Queen and the Rebels," "Brighton Beach Memoirs."

GOLDSMITH, MERWIN. Born Aug. 7, 1937 in Detroit, Mi. Graduate UCLA, Old Vic. Bdwy debut 1970 in "Minnie's Boys," followed by "The Visit," "Chemin de Fer," "Rex," "Dirty Linen/New Found Land," "The 1940's Radio Hour," "Slab Boys," OB in "Hamlet as a Happening" (1967), "Leda Had a Little Swan," "Chickencoop Chinamen," "Wanted," "Comedy," "Rubbers," "Yankees 3 Detroit 0," "Trelawny of the Wells," "Chinchilla," "Real Life Funnies," "Big Apple Messenger," "La Boheme," "Yours, Anne."

GOLDSTEIN, BERT. Born Jan. 23, 1955 in Michigan City, In. Graduate MacAlester Col. Debut OB 1987 in "Fire in the Basement."

GOLER, LAUREN. Born Nov. 10, 1961 in Washington, DC. Bdwy debut 1980 in "Happy New Year," followed by "Onward Victoria!," "Smile," OB in "Joseph."

GOODMAN, LORRAINE. Born Feb. 11, 1962 in The Bronx, NY. Graduate Princeton U. Debut 1985 OB in "Very Warm for May," Bdwy 1987 in "The Mystery of Edwin Drood."

GOODMAN, MARGARET. Born Oct. 10, 1936 in Knoxville, Tn. Graduate Bryn Mawr, New Eng. Consv. Debut 1976 OB in "Follies," followed by "Louisiana Summer," "Camp Meeting."

GOODROW, GARRY. Born Nov. 5, 1938 in Malone, NY. Debut 1960 OB in "Many Loves," followed by "The Connection," "Tonight We Improvise," "In the Jungle of Cities," "National Lampoon's Lemmings," "Taming of the Shrew," "Sills & Company," Bdwy in "The Committee," "Story Theatre."

GORDON, CLARKE. Born in Detroit, Mi. Graduate WayneStateU. Debut 1949 OB in "The Son," followed by "The Philistines," "The Truth," "Porch," "China Fish," Bdwy in "Night Music" (1951), "Pal Joey" (1952), "The Vamp."

GORDON-CLARK, SUSAN. Born Dec. 31, 1947 in Jackson, Ms. Graduate Purdue U. Debut 1984 OB in "The Nunsense Story," followed by "Chip Shot," "Nunsense."

GORMAN, CLIFF. Born Oct. 13, 1936 in NYC. Attended UCLA. Debut 1965 OB in "Hogan's Goat," followed by "Boys in the Band," "Ergo," "Angelo's Wedding," Bdwy in "Lenny" (1971), "Chapter Two," "Doubles," "Social Security."

GOSSETT, ROBERT. Born Mar. 3, 1954 in The Bronx, NY. Attended AADA. Debut 1973 OB in "One Flew over the Cuckoo's Nest," followed by "The Amen Corner," "Weep Not for Me," "Colored People's Time," "A Soldier's Play," "Sons and Fathers of Sons," "Manhattan Made Me," "A Visitor to the Veldt."

GOULD, GORDON. Born May 4, 1930 in Chicago, Ill. Graduate Yale, Cambridge (Eng.). Bdwy debut 1965 in "You Can't Take It with You," followed by "War and Peace," "Right You Are," "The Wild Duck," "Pantagleize," "Exit the King," "The Show-Off," "School for Wives," "Freedom of the City," "Strider," "Amadeus," OB in "Man and Superman," "Scapin," "Impromptu at Versailles," "The Lower Depths," "The Tavern," "Judith," "Naked," "Tatyana Rapina," "The Middle Ages," "On Approval," "Swan Song."

GOULD, MURIEL. Born Oct. 12, 1928 in Brooklyn, NY. Graduate Bklyn. Col., Columbia U. Debut 1975 OB in "A Little Night Music," followed by "Pelicans Please Mute," "Tronzini Ristorante Murders."

GOUTMAN, CHRISTOPHER. Born Dec. 19, 1952 in Bryn Mawr, PA. Graduate Haverford Col., Carnegie-Mellon U. Debut 1978 OB in "The Promise" for which he received a Theatre World Award, followed by "Grand Magic," "The Skirmishers," "Imaginary Lovers," "Balm in Gilead," "Love's Labour's Lost."

GRAAE, JASON. Born May 15, 1958 in Chicago, IL. Graduate Cincinnati Consv. Debut 1981 OB in "Godspell," followed by "Snoopy," "Heaven on Earth," "Promenade," "Feathertop," "Tales of Tinseltown," "Living Color," "Just So," "Olympus on My Mind," Bdwy 1982 in "Do Black Patent Leather Shoes Really Reflect Up?," "Stardust."

GRAFF, RANDY. Born May 23, 1955 in Brooklyn, NY. Graduate Wagner Col. Debut 1978 OB in "Pins and Needles," followed by "Station Joy," "A . . . My Name Is Alice," "Once on a Summer's Day," Bdwy in "Sarava," "Grease," "Les Miserables."

GRANT, FAYE. Born July 16, in Detroit, Mi. Bdwy debut 1985 in "Singin' in the Rain" for which she received a Theatre World Award, followed by "House of Blue Leaves."

GRANT, JOAN. Born May 30, 1946 in San Francisco, Ca. Graduate San FranStateU. Debut 1986 OB in "House of Shadows," followed by "Hidden Parts."

GRAY, DOLORES. Born June 7, 1924 in Hollywood, Ca. Bdwy debut 1944 in "Seven Lively Arts," followed by "Are You with It?," "Annie Get Your Gun," "Two on the Aisle," "Carnival in Flanders," "Destry Rides Again," "Sherry!," "42nd Street."

GRAY, KEVIN. Born Feb. 25, 1958 in Westport, Ct. Graduate Duke U. Debut 1982 OB in "Lola," followed by "Pacific Overtures," "Family Snapshots," "The Baker's Wife," "The Knife."

GRAY, SAM. Born July 18, 1923 in Chicago, IL. Graduate Columbia U. Bdwy debut 1955 in "Deadfall," followed by "Six Fingers in a Five Finger Glove," "Saturday, Sunday, Monday," "Golda," "A View from the Bridge," OB in "Ascent of F-6," "Family Portrait," "One Tiger on a Hill," "Shadow of Heroes," "The Recruiting Officer," "The Wild Duck," "Jungle of Cities," "3 Acts of Recognition," "Returnings," "A Little Madness," "The Danube," "Dr. Cook's Garden," "Child's Play," "Kafka Father and Son," "D," "Dennis," "Panache!"

GREENBERG, HELEN. Born Sept. 28, 1961 on Long Island, NY. Graduate NYU. Debut 1987 OB in "Words Words Words."

GREENBERG, MITCHELL. Born Sept. 19, 1950 in Brooklyn, NY. Graduate Harpur Col., Neighborhood Playhouse. Debut 1979 OB in "Two Grown Men," followed by "Scrambled Feet," "A Christmas Carol," "A Thurber Carnival," "Isn't It Romantic," "Crazy Arnold," Bdwy in "A Day in Hollywood/A Night in the Ukraine" (1980), "Can-Can" (1981), "Marilyn," "Into the Light."

GREENE, JAMES. Born Dec. 1, 1926 in Lawrence, MA. Graduate Emerson Col. OB in "The Iceman Cometh," "American Gothic," "The King and the Duke," "The Hostage," "Plays for Bleecker Street," "Moon in the Yellow River," "Misalliance," "Government Inspector," "Baba Goya," LCRep 2 years, "You Can't Take It With You," "School for Scandal," "Wild Duck," "Right You Are," "The Show-Off," "Pantagleize," "Festival of Short Plays," "Nourish the Beast," "One Crack Out," "Artichoke," "Othello," "Salt Lake City Skyline," "Summer," "The Rope Dancers," "Frugal Repast," "Bella Figura," "The Freak," "Park Your Car in the Harvard Yard," "Pigeons on the Walk," "Endgame," "Great Days," "Playboy of the Western World," Bdwy in "Romeo and Juliet," "Girl on the Via Flaminia," "Compulsion," "Inherit the Wind," "Shadow of a Gunman," "Andersonville Trial," "Night Life," "School for Wives," "Ring Round the Bathtub," "Great God Brown," "Don Juan," "Foxfire," "Play Memory," "The Iceman Cometh."

GREENHILL, SUSAN. Born Mar. 19 in NYC. Graduate UPa., Catholic U. Bdwy debut 1982 in "Crimes of the Heart," followed OB by "Hooters," "Our Lord of Lynchville," "September in the Rain," "Seascape with Sharks and Dancer," "Young Playwrights Festival," "Festival of One-Acts."

GREGORIO, ROSE. Born in Chicago, Ill. Graduate Northwestern, Yale. Debut 1962 OB in "The Days and Nights of Beebee Fenstermaker," followed by "Kiss Mama," "The Balcony," "Bivouac at Lucca," "Journey to the Day," "Diary of Anne Frank," "Weekends Like Other People," "Curse of the Starving Class," "Dream of a Blacklisted Actor," Bdwy in "The Owl and the Pussycat," "Daphne in Cottage D," "Jimmy Shine," "The Cuban Thing," "The Shadow Box," "A View from the Bridge."

GREGORY, MICHAEL SCOTT. Born Mar. 13, 1962 in Ft. Lauderdale, Fl. Attended Atlantic Foundation. Bdwy debut 1981 in "Sophisticated Ladies," followed by "Starlight Express."

GREY, JOEL. Born Apr. 11, 1932 in Cleveland, Oh. Attended Cleveland Play House. Bdwy debut 1951 in "Borscht Capades," followed by "Come Blow Your Horn," "Stop the World—I Want to Get Off," "Half a Sixpence," "Cabaret," "George M!," "Goodtime Charley," "Grand Tour," OB in "The Littlest Revue," "Harry Noon and Night," "Marco Polo Sings a Solo," "The Normal Heart."

GRIFFITH, KRISTIN. Born Sept. 7, 1953 in Odessa, Tx. Juilliard Graduate. Bdwy debut 1976 in "A Texas Trilogy," OB in "Rib Cage," "Character Lines," "3 Friends/2 Rooms," "A Month in the Country," "Fables for Friends," "The Trading Post," "Marching to Georgia," "American Garage," "A Midsummer Night's Dream," "Marathon 87."

GRIFFITH, LISA. Born June 18 in Honolulu, Hi. Graduate Brandeis U, Trinity U. Debut 1977 OB in "The Homesickness of Capt. Rappaport," followed by "The Kennedy Play," "Chalkdust," "Murder at the Vicarage," "Ah, Wilderness!," "Stud Silo," "The Miser."

GROENENDAAL, CRIS. Born Feb. 17, 1948 in Erie, PA. Attended Allegheny Col, Exeter U, HB Studio. Bdwy debut 1979 in "Sweeney Todd," followed by "Sunday in the Park with George," "Brigadoon" (LC), OB in "Francis," "Sweethearts in Concert," "Oh, Boy " "No No Nanette in Concert," LC's "South Pacific" and "Sweeney Tood."

GROENER, HARRY. Born Sept. 10, 1951 in Augsburg, Ger. Graduate UWash. Bdwy debut 1979 in "Oklahoma!," for which he received a Theatre World Award, followed by "Oh, Brother!," "Is There Life after High School," "Cats," "Harrigan 'n Hart," "Sunday in the Park with George," "Sleight of Hand," OB in "Beside the Seaside."

GROH, DAVID. Born May 21, 1939 in NYC. Graduate Brown U., LAMDA. Debut 1963 OB in "The Importance of Being Earnest," followed by "Elizabeth the Queen" (CC), "The Hot l Baltimore," "Be Happy for Me," "Dead Wrong," "Face to Face," "Road Show," Bdwy in "Chapter Two" (1978).

Phyllis Craig	David Cromwell	Frances Cuka	Richard Dahlia	Leila Danette	Joaquim De Almeida
Emilio Del Pozo	Dawn Didawick	Frank J. DiPasquale	Donna Drake	Craig Dudley	Jennifer Dundas
Wendy Edmead	Ned Eisenberg	Sara Erde	Alan Feinstein	Norma Fire	Luther Fontaine
Jonathan Frid	June Gable	Peter Gallagher	Laura Gardner	Kevin John Gee	Avril Gentles

Teri Gibson	David Gideon	Norma Jean Giffin	Mel Gionson	Margaret Goodman	Michael Scott Gregory

GUIDALL, GEORGE. Born June 7, 1938 in Plainfield, NJ. Attended UBuffalo, AADA. Bdwy debut 1969 in "Wrong Way Light Bulb," followed by "Cold Storage," OB in "Counsellor-at-Law," "Taming of the Shrew," "All's Well That Ends Well," "The Art of Dining," "Biography," "After All," "Henry V," "Time of the Cuckoo," "Yours Anne," "The Perfect Party," "A Man for All Seasons."

GULACK, MAX. Born May 19, 1928 in NYC. Graduate CCNY, Columbia U. Debut 1952 OB in "Bonds of Interest," followed by "The Warrior's Husband," "Worm in the Horseradish," "Marcus in the High Grass," "Country Scandal," "Song for the First of May," "Threepenny Opera," "Taming of the Shrew," "Misalliance."

GUNN, NICHOLAS. Born Aug. 28, 1947 in Brooklyn, NY. Appeared with Paul Taylor Dance Co. before Bdwy debut in "The Mystery of Edwin Drood" (1985).

GUNTON, BOB. Born Nov. 15, 1945 in Santa Monica, CA. Attended UCal. Debut 1971 OB in "Who Am I?," followed by "The Kid," "Desperate Hours," "Tip-Toes," "How I Got That Story," "Hamlet," "Death of Von Richthofen," "The Man Who Could See Through Time," Bdwy in "Happy End" (1977), "Working," "King of Hearts," "Evita," "Passion," "Big River."

GUTTMAN, RONALD. Born Aug. 12, 1952 in Brussels, Belg. Graduate Brussels U. Debut OB (1986) and Bdwy (1987) in "Coastal Disturbances."

HABERSHAM, RICHARD. Born Apr. 28, 1974 in NYC. Debut 1986 OB in "A Raisin in the Sun."

HACK, STEVEN. Born Apr. 20, 1958 in St. Louis, MO. Attended CalArts, AADA, Debut 1978 OB in "The Coolest Cat in Town," followed by Bdwy in "Cats" (1982).

HADARY, JONATHAN. Born Oct. 11, 1948 in Chicago, IL. Attended Tufts U. Debut 1974 OB in "White Nights," followed by "El Grande de Coca-Cola," "Songs from Pins and Needles," "God Bless You, Mr. Rosewater," "Pushing 30," "Scrambled Feet," "Coming Attractions," "Tom-foolery," "Charley Bacon and Family," "Road Show," Bdwy in "Gemini," (1977/also OB), "Torch Song Trilogy, "As Is."

HAFNER, JULIE J. Born June 4, 1952 in Dover, Oh. Graduate KentStateU. Debut 1976 OB in "The Club," followed by "Nunsense," Bdwy in "Nine."

HAGEN, UTA. Born June 11, 1919 in Goettingen, Ger. Bdwy debut 1938 in "The Seagull," followed by "The Happiest Years," "Key Largo," "Vickie," "Othello," "A Streetcar Named Desire," "Country Girl," "St. Joan," "The Whole World Over," "In Any Language," "The Magic and the Loss," CC's "Angel Street" and "Tovarich," "Who's Afraid of Virginia Woolf?," "The Cherry Orchard," "Charlotte," "You Never Can Tell," OB in "A Month in the Country," "Good Woman of Setzuan," "Mrs. Warren's Profession."

HAGERTY, JULIE. Born June 15, 1955 in Cincinnati, Oh. Attended Juilliard. Debut 1979 OB in "Mutual Benefit Life," followed by "Wild Life," "House of Blue Leaves" (1979), Bdwy in "House of Blue Leaves" (1986) for which she received a Theatre World Award, "Front Page."

HALL, DAVIS. Born Apr. 10, 1946 in Atlanta, Ga. Graduate Northwestern U. Bdwy debut 1973 in "Butley," followed by "Dogg's Hamlet and Cahoot's Macbeth," OB in "The Promise," "Dream-boats," "The Taming of the Shrew," "Donkey's Years."

HALL, GEORGE. Born Nov. 19, 1916 in Toronto, Can. Attended Neighborhood Playhouse. Bdwy bow 1946 in "Call Me Mister," followed by "Lend an Ear," "Touch and Go," "Live Wire," "The Boy Friend," "There's a Girl in My Soup," "An Evening with Richard Nixon .," "We Interrupt This Program," "Man and Superman," "Bent," "Noises Off," "Wild Honey," OB in "The Balcony," "Ernest in Love," "A Round with Rings," "Family Pieces," "Carousel," "The Case Against Roberta Guardino," "Marry Me!" "Arms and the Man," "The Old Glory," "Dancing for the Kaiser," "Casualties," "The Seagull," "A Stitch in Time," "Mary Stuart," "No End of Blame," "Hamlet," "Colette Collage," "The Homecoming," "And a Nightingale Sang," "The Bone Ring."

HALLEY, BEN, JR. Born Aug. 6, 1951 in Harlen, NY. Graduate CCNY, Yale. Bdwy debut 1978 in "A History of the American Film," OB in "A Day in the Life of the Czar," "A Midsummer Night's Dream," "The Recruiting Officer," "The Wild Duck," "Oedipus the King," "Death and the King's Horseman" (LC).

HALLIDAY, ANDY. Born Mar. 31, 1953 in Orange, Ct. Attended USIU/San Diego. Debut OB 1985 in "Vampire Lesbians of Sodom," followed by "Times Square Angel."

HALLOW, JOHN. Born Nov. 28, 1924 in NYC. Attended Neighborhood Playhouse. Bdwy debut 1954 in "Anastasia," followed by "Ross," "Visit to a Small Planet," "Foxy," "Oh, Dad, Poor Dad . . .," "Ben Franklin in Paris," "Three Bags Full," "Don't Drink the Water," "Hadrian VII," "Tough to Get Help," "Ballroom," "A New York Summer," "The Man Who Came to Dinner," OB in "Hamlet," "Do I Hear a Waltz?," "Kind Lady," "The Butler Did It," "Festival of One Acts," "Sorrows and Sons," "Second Avenue."

HAMILL, MARK. Born Sept. 25, 1952 in Oakland, CA. Attended LACC. Bdwy debut 1981 in "The Elephant Man," followed by "Amadeus," "Harrigan 'n Hart," "The Nerd," OB in "Room Service."

HAMILTON, RICHARD. Born Dec. 31, 1920 in Chicago, Il. Attended Pasadena Jr. Col. Bdwy debut 1952 in "First Lady," followed by "Cloud 7," "Blood, Sweat and Stanley Poole," "Scratch," "Anna Christie" (1977), "A Touch of the Poet," "Morning's at 7," OB in "The Exception and the Rule," "The Bench," "Siamese Connections," "Cream Cheese," "Buried Child," "Fool for Love," "Husbandry," "Kill."

HAMMOND, MICHAEL. Born Apr. 30, 1951 in Clinton, Ia. Graduate UIa, LAMDA. Debut 1974 OB in "Pericles," followed by "The Merry Wives of Windsor," "A Winter's Tale," "Barbarians," "The Purging," "Romeo and Juliet," "The Merchant of Venice."

HANAN, STEPHEN. Born Jan 7, 1947 in Washington, DC. Graduate Harvard, LAMDA. Debut 1978 OB in "All's Well That Ends Well," followed by "Taming of the Shrew," "Rabboni," Bdwy in "Pirates of Penzance" (1978),"Cats."

HANDLER, EVAN. Born Jan. 10, 1961 in NYC. Attended Juilliard. Debut 1979 OB in "Biography: A Game," followed by "Strider," "Final Orders," "Marathon 84," "Found a Peanut," "What's Wrong with This Picture?" "Bloodletters," "Young Playwrights Festival," Bdwy in "Solomon's Child" (1982), "Biloxi Blues," "Brighton Beach Memoirs," "Broadway Bound."

HANSEN, LARRY. Born Mar. 11, 1952 in Anacortes, WVa. Graduate Western Wash.U. Debut 1978 OB in "Can-Can," Bdwy in "Show Boat" (1983).

HA'O, WILLIAM. Born Aug. 10, 1953 in Honolulu, Hi. Attended Chaminade Col., Leeward Col. Debut 1981 OB in "The Shining House," followed by "Gaugin in Tahiti," "Teahouse," "A Midsummer Night's Dream," "Rain," "Dream of Kitamura," "Sleepless City."

HARALDSON, MARIAN. Born Sept. 5, 1933 in Northwood, ND. Graduate St. Olaf Col. Bdwy debut 1959 in "First Impressions," followed by "The Unsinkable Molly Brown," "Mr. President," "The Girl Who Came to Supper," "The Merry Widow," "Walking Happy," "Dear World," "No, No, Nanette," "Lorelei," "Woman of the Year," OB in "Peace," "A Book of Etiquette."

HARMAN, PAUL. Born July 29, 1952 in Mineola, NY. Graduate Tufts U. Bdwy debut 1980 in "It's So Nice to Be Civilized," followed by "Les Miserables," OB in "City Suite."

HARNEY, BEN. Born Aug. 29, 1952 in Brooklyn, NY. Bdwy debut 1971 in "Purlie," followed by "Pajama Game," "Tree-Monisha," "Pippin," "Dreamgirls," OB in "Don't Bother Me I Can't Cope," "The Derby," "The More You Get," "Williams & Walker," "Brownstone."

HARPER, JAMES. Born Oct. 8, 1948 in Bell, Ca. Attended Marin Col., Juilliard. Bdwy debut 1973 in "King Lear," followed by "The Robber Bridegroom," "The Time of Your Life," "Mother Courage," "Edward II," OB in "A Midsummer Night's Dream," "Recruiting Officer," "The Wild Duck," "The Jungle of Cities," "The Cradle Will Rock," "All the Nice People," "Cruelties of Mrs. Schnayd," "Territorial Rites."

HARRINGTON, DELPHI. Born Aug. 26 in Chicago, Ill. Graduate Northwestern U. Debut 1960 OB in "A Country Scandal," followed by "Moon for the Misbegotten," "A Baker's Dozen," "The Zykovs," "Character Lines," "Richie," "American Garage," "After the Fall," "Rosencrantz and Guildenstern Are Dead," Bdwy in "Thieves" (1974), "Everything in the Garden," "Romeo and Juliet," "Chapter Two."

HARRINGTON, DON. Born June 27, 1944 in Washington, DC. Graduate American U. Debut 1978 OB in "All's Well That Ends Well," followed by "A Midsummer Night's Dream," "Street Scene," "Carmilla," "Etiquette," "The Heart That Eats Itself."

HARRIS, BAXTER. Born Nov. 18, 1940 in Columbus, KS. Attended UKan. Debut 1967 OB in "America Hurrah," followed by "The Reckoning," "Wicked Women Revue," "More than You Deserve," "Pericles," "him," "Battle of Angels," "Down by the River," "Selma," "Ferocious Kisses," "Three Sisters," "Gradual Clearing," "Dolphin Position," "Paradise Lost," "Ghosts," "Madwoman of Chaillot," "The Time of Your Life," "Children of the Sun."

HARRIS, VIOLA. Born Sept. 14, 1928 in NYC. Graduate Hunter Col., Northwestern U. Bdwy debut 1948 in "On the Town," followed by "Zelda," OB in "Three Steps Down," "Berkeley Square," "Ivanov," "Waving Goodbye."

HARRISON, STANLEY EARL. Born Sept. 17, 1955 in Cheverly, Md. Graduate MorganStateU. Debut 1978 OB in "The Phantom," followed by "The Boogie-Woogie Rumble of a Dream Deferred," "The Medium," "Mud," "The Mighty Gents," "Abyssinia," "A Matter of Conscience," Bdwy in "The King and I" (1985).

HART, CECILIA. Born June 6 in Cheyenne, Wy. Graduate Emerson Col. Debut 1974 OB in "Macbeth," followed by "Emperor of Late Night Radio," "The Good Parts," "Division Street," Bdwy in "The Heiress" (1976), "Dirty Linen" for which she received a Theatre World Award, "Othello" (1982), "Design for Living."

HART, PAUL E. Born July 20, 1939 in Lawrence, Ma. Graduate Merrimack Col. Debut 1977 OB in "Turandot," followed by "Darkness at Noon," "Light Shines in the Darkness," "Pictures at an Exhibition," "Blessed Event," "Cork," Bdwy in "Fiddler on the Roof" (1981).

HARTSOUGH, EEVIN. Born June 4, 1976 in Ridgewood, NJ. Debut 1987 OB in "The Miracle Worker."

HARUM, EIVIND. Born May 24, 1944 in Stavanger, Norway. Attended Utah State U. Credits include "Sophie," "Foxy," "Baker Street," "West Side Story" ('68),"A Chorus Line," "Woman of the Year."

HASTINGS, BILL. Born July 30, 1952 in Vinita, Ok. Graduate LSU. Bdwy debut 1979 in "The Most Happy Fella," followed by "Rags," OB in "Anyonè Can Whistle."

HATCHER, ROBYN. Born Sept. 8, 1956 in Philadelphia, Pa. Graduate Adelphi U. Debut 1983 OB in "Macbeth," followed by "Edward II," "Deep Sleep," "Flatbush Faithful," "Pardon/Permission."

HAUSMAN, ELAINE. Born June 8, 1949 in Sacramento, Ca. Graduate UCal., Juilliard. Bdwy debut 1975 in "The Robber Bridegroom," followed by "Edward II," "The Time of Your Life," "Three Sisters," "Brigadoon," OB in "Top Girls," "Photographer," "The Merchant of Venice."

HAWKINS, TRISH. Born Oct. 30, 1945 in Hartford, CT. Attended Radcliffe, Neighborhood Playhouse. Debut OB 1970 in "Oh! Calcutta!" followed by "Iphigenia," "The Hot l Baltmore" for which she received a Theatre World Award, "him," "Come Back, Little Sheba," "Battle of Angels," "Mound Builders," "The Farm," "Ulysses in Traction," "Lulu," "Hogan's Folly," "Twelfth Night," "A Tale Told," "Great Grandson of Jedediah Kohler," "Time Framed," "Levitations." "Love's Labour's Lost," "Talley & Son," "Tomorrow's Monday," "Caligula," "Quiet in the Land," "Road Show," Bdwy (1977) in "Some of My Best Friends," "Talley's Folly" (1979).

HAYNES, ROBIN. Born July 20, 1953 in Lincoln, Ne. Graduate UWash. Debut 1976 OB in "A Touch of the Poet," followed by "She Loves Me," "Romeo and Juliet," "Twelfth Night," "Billy Bishop Goes to War," "The Comedy of Errors" (LC), Bdwy in "The Best Little Whorehouse in Texas" (1978).

HAYNES, TIGER. Born Dec. 13, 1907 in St. Croix, VI. Bdwy bow 1956 in "New Faces," followed by "Finian's Rainbow," "Fade Out-Fade In," "Pajama Game," "The Wiz," "A Broadway Musical," "Comin' Uptown," "My One and Only," OB in "Turns," "Bags," "Louis," "Taking My Turn."

HAYS, REX. Born June 17, 1946 in Hollywood, Ca. Graduate SanJoseStateU, Brandeis U. Bdwy debut 1975 in "Dance with Me," followed by "Angel," "King of Hearts," "Evita," "Onward Victoria," "Woman of the Year," "La Cage aux Folles," OB in "Charley's Tale."

HEALD, ANTHONY. Born Aug. 25, 1944 in New Rochelle, NY. Graduate MiStateU. Debut 1980 OB in "The Glass Menagerie," followed by "Misalliance" for which he received a Theatre World Award, "The Caretaker," "The Fox," "Quartermaine's Terms," "The Philanthropist," "Henry V," "Digby," "Principia Scriptoriae," Bdwy in "The Wake of Jamey Foster" (1982), "Marriage of Figaro."

HEARD, CELESTINE. Born Dec. 21 in Cleveland, Oh. Graduate AADA. Debut 1972 OB in "Voices of the Third World," followed by "Things of the Heart," "Death and the King's Horseman" (LC).

HEATH, D. MICHAEL. Born Sept. 22, 1953 in Cincinnati, Oh. Graduate UCin. Bdwy debut 1979 in "The Most Happy Fella," followed by "Starlight Express," OB in "Chanticler," "Street Scene."

HEFFERNAN, JOHN. Born May 30, 1934 in NYC. Attended CCNY, Columbia, Boston U. Bdwy debut 1963 in "Luther," followed by "Tiny Alice," "Postmark Zero," "Woman Is My Idea," "Morning Noon and Night," "Purlie," "Bad Habits," "Lady from the Sea," "Knock Knock," "Sly Fox," "The Suicide," "Alice in Wonderland," OB in "The Judge," "Julius Caesar," "The Great God Brown," "Lysistrata," "Peer Gynt," "Henry IV," "Taming of the Shrew," "She Stoops to Conquer," "The Plough and the Stars," "Octoroon," "Hamlet," "Androcles and the Lion," "A Man's a Man," "Winter's Tale," "Arms and the Man," "St. Joan," "Memorandum," "Invitation to a Beheading," "The Sea," "Shadow of a Gunman," "Johnny on a Spot," "Barbarians," "Women Beware Women."

HEIKEN, NANCY. Born Nov. 28, 1948 in Philadelphia, Pa. Graduate Sarah Lawrence Col. Bdwy debut 1981 in "Pirates of Penzance," followed by OB's "La Boheme," "Carmilla."

HEMPLEMAN, TERRY. Born Dec. 6, 1960 in Asheville, NC. Graduate UNC. Debut 1986 OB in "Out!" followed by "After Sarah."

HENIG, ANDI. Born May 6 in Washington, DC. Attended Yale. Debut 1978 OB in "One and One," followed by "Kind Lady," "Downriver," Bdwy in "Oliver!" (1984), "Big River."

HENNER, MARILU. Born Apr. 4, 1952 in Chicago, Il. Bdwy debut 1987 in "Social Security."

HERNDON, JAN LEIGH. Born Apr. 9, 1955 in Raleigh, NC. Graduate ValntermontCol. Bdwy debut 1982 in "A Chorus Line," followed by "La Cage aux Folles," "The Mystery of Edwin Drood," OB in "Joan and the Devil."

HERRERA, JOHN. Born Sept. 21, 1955 in Havana, Cuba. Graduate Loyola U. Bdwy debut 1979 in "Grease," followed by "Evita," "Camelot," "The Mystery of Edwin Drood," OB in "La Boheme," "Lies and Legends."

HETTINGER, CHARLES D. Born July 8, 1950 in Norman, Ok. Graduate UOk. Debut 1987 OB in "Ready or Not."

HICKS, LAURA. Born Nov. 17, 1956 in NYC. Graduate Juilliard. Debut 1978 OB in "Spring Awakening," followed by "Talking With," "The Cradle Will Rock," "Paducah," "10 by Tennessee," "On the Verge."

HIGGINS, MICHAEL. Born Jan. 20, 1926 in Brooklyn, NY. Attended AmThWing. Bdwy debut 1946 in "Antigone," followed by "Our Lan'," "Romeo and Juliet," "The Crucible," "The Lark," "Equus," "Whose Life Is It Anyway?," OB in "White Devil," "Carefree Tree," "Easter," "The Queen and the Rebels," "Sally, George and Martha," "L'Ete," "Uncle Vanya," "The Iceman Cometh," "Molly," "Artichoke," "Reunion," "Chieftans," "A Tale Told," "Richard II," "The Seagull," "Levitations," "Love's Labour's Lost," "In This Fallen City."

HILBOLDT, LISE. Born Jan. 7, 1954 in Racine, Wil Attended UWi., Webber-Douglas Academy. Bdwy debut 1981 in "To Grandmother's House We Go," followed by "You Never Can Tell," OB in "Top Girls," "Maneuvers."

HILLNER, NANCY. Born June 7, 1949 in Wakefield, RI. Graduate ULowell. Bdwy debut 1975 in "Dance with Me," followed by OB in "Nite Club Confidential," "Trading Places," "Nunsense."

HINNANT, SKIP. Born Sept. 12, 1940 in Chincoteague Island, Va. Yale graduate. Debut 1964 OB in "The Knack," followed by "You're a Good Man, Charlie Brown," "Two," "Taking Steps."

HIRSCH, JUDD. Born Mar. 15, 1935 in NYC. Attended AADA. Bdwy debut 1966 in "Barefoot in the Park," followed by "Chapter Two," "Talley's Folly," OB in "On the Necessity of Being Polygamous," "Scuba Duba," "Mystery Play," "Hot 1 Baltimore," "Prodigal," "Knock Knock," "Life and/or Death," "Talley's Folly," "The Sea Gull," "I'm Not Rappaport."

HODES, GLORIA. Born Aug. 20 in Norwich, Ct. Bdwy debut in "Gantry" (1969), followed by "Me and My Girl," OB in "The Club" for which she received a Theatre World Award, "Cycles of Fancy," "The Heroine," "Pearls."

HODES, RYN. Born Dec. 28, 1956 in NYC. Graduate NYU. Debut 1979 OB in "Mirandolina", followed by "Boy Meets Swan," "A Collier's Friday Night," "Suicide in B Flat," "Kaspar," "Fanshen," "Holy Terrors," "The Hungry Man," "Colonomos," "Jack."

HODGES, PATRICIA. Born in Puyallup, Wa. Graduate UWa. Debut 1985 OB in "The Normal Heart," followed by "On the Verge."

HOFFMAN, AVI. Born Mar. 3, 1958 in The Bronx, NY. Graduate UMiami. Debut 1983 OB in "The Rise of David Levinsky," followed by "It's Hard to Be a Jew," "A Rendezvous with God," "The Golden Land."

HOFFMAN, JANE. Born July 24 in Seattle, Wa. Graduate UCal. Bdwy debut 1940 in "Tis of Thee," followed by "Crazy with the Heat," "Something for the Boys," "One Touch of Venus," "Calico Wedding," "Mermaids Singing," "Temporary Island," "Story for Strangers," "Two Blind Mice," "The Rose Tattoo," "The Crucible," "Witness for the Prosecution," "Third Best Sport," "Rhinoceros," "Mother Courage and Her Children," Fair Game for Lovers," "A Murderer among Us," "Murder among Friends," OB in "American Dream," "Sandbox," "Picnic on the Battlefield," "Theatre of the Absurd," "Child Buyer," "A Corner of the Bed," "Slow Memories," "Last Analysis," "Dear Oscar," "Hocus Pocus," "Lessons," "The Art of Dining," "Second Avenue Rag," "One Tiger to a Hill," "Isn't It Romantic?," "Alto Part," "Marathon 84," "The Frog Prince," "Alterations."

HOFMAIER, MARK. Born July 4, 1950 in Philadelphia, Pa. Graduate UAz. Debut 1978 OB in "A Midsummer Night's Dream," followed by "Marvelous Gray," "Modern Romance," "Relative Values."

HOFVENDAHL, STEVE. Born Sept. 1, 1956 in San Jose, Ca. Graduate USantaClara, Brandeis U. Debut 1986 OB in "A Lie of the Mind," followed by "Ragged Trousered Philanthropists," "The Miser."

HOGAN, JONATHAN. Born June 13, 1951 in Chicago, Il. Graduate Goodman Theatre. Debut 1972 OB in "The Hot 1 Baltimore," followed by "The Mound Builders," "Harry Outside," "Cabin 12," "5th of July," "Glorious Morning," "Innocent Thoughts, Harmless Intentions," "Sunday Runners," "Threads," "Time Framed," "Balm in Gilead," "Burn This!," Bdwy in "Comedians" (1976), "Otherwise Engaged," "5th of July," "The Caine Mutiny Court-Martial," "As Is."

HOLBROOK, RUBY. Born Aug. 28, 1930 in St. John's, Nfd. Attended Denison U. Debut 1963 OB in "Abe Lincoln in Illinois," followed by "Hamlet," "James Joyce's Dubliners," "Measure for Measure," "The Farm," "Do You Still Believe the Rumor?," "The Killing of Sister George," "An Enemy of the People," Bdwy in "Da" (1979), "5th of July," "Musical Comedy Murders of 1940."

HOLGATE, RONALD. Born May 26, 1937 in Aberdeen, SD. Attended Northwestern U., NewEngConserv. Debut 1961 OB in "Hobo," followed by "Hooray, It's a Glorious Day," "Blue Plate Special," Bdwy in "A Funny Thing Happened on the Way. . ," "Milk and Honey," "1776," "Saturday Sunday Monday," "The Grand Tour," "Musical Chairs," "42nd Street."

HOLLAND, ANTHONY. Born Oct. 17, 1933 in Brooklyn, NY. Graduate UChicago. OB in "Venice Preserved," "Second City," "Victim of Duty," "New Tenant," "Dynamite Tonight," "Quare Fellow," "White House Murder Case," "Waiting for Godot," "Tales of the Hasidim," "Taming of the Shrew," "Diary of Anne Frank," "The Hunger Artist," Bdwy in "My Mother, My Father and Me," "We Bombed in New Haven," "Dreyfus in Rehearsal," "Leaf People," "Division Street."

HOLLIS, TOMMY. Born Mar. 27, 1954 in Jacksonville, TX. Graduate UHouston. Debut 1985 OB in "Diamonds," followed by "Secrets of the Lava Lamp," "Paradise," "Africanus Instructus," "The Colored Museum."

HOLMES, GEORGE. Born June 3, 1935 in London, Eng. Graduate ULondon. Debut 1978 OB in "The Changeling," followed by "Love from a Stranger," "The Hollow," "The Story of the Gadsbys," "Learned Ladies," "The Land Is Bright," "Something Old, Something New," "Oscar Wilde Solitaire," "Like Them That Dream."

HOLMES, SUSAN DAVIS. Born Sept. 19, 1960 in Santa Barbara, Ca. Graduate Manhattan Sch. of Music. Debut 1984 OB with L.O.O.M. in "Yeomen of the Guard," followed by "Sweethearts," "The Drunkard," "The Mikado," "The Gondoliers," "The Merry Widow," "The New Moon," "Pirates of Penzance," "Give My Regards to Broadway."

HOMBERG, TERRI. Born Jan. 5, 1959 in Jacksonville, Fl. Attended SanJoseStateU, Neighborhood Playhouse. Bdwy debut 1982 in "Joseph and the Amazing Technicolor Dreamcoat," followed by "Jerry's Girls," "Into the Light."

HONDA, CAROL A. Born Nov. 20 in Kealakekua, HI. Graduate UHi. Debut 1983 OB in "Yellow Fever," followed by "Empress of China," "Manoa Valley," "Once Is Never Enough," "Life of the Land."

HORWITZ, MURRAY. Born Sept. 28, 1949 in Dayton, Oh. Graduate Kenyon Col. Debut 1976 OB in "An Evening with Sholom Aleichem" (also 1983 and 1986 revivals), "Hard Sell."

HOUGHTON, KATHARINE. Born Mar 10, 1945 in Hartford, CT. Graduate Sarah Lawrence Col. Bdwy debut 1965 in "A Very Rich Woman," followed by "The Front Page" (1969), OB in "A Scent of Flowers" for which she received a Theatre World Award, "To Heaven in a Swing," "Madwoman of Chaillot," "Vivat! Vivat Regina!" "The Time of Your Life," "Children of the Sun," "Buddha," "On the Shady Side," "The Right Number."

HOWARD, ARTHUR. Born Jan. 26 in NYC. Graduate Reed Col. Debut 1974 OB in "Decades," followed by "That's It, Folks!," "The Rise of David Levinsky," Bdwy in "The Magic Show" (1979).

HOWARD, DAVID. Born Sept. 10, 1928 in Mr. Kisco, NY. Graduate Cornell U. Debut 1964 OB in "Cindy," followed by "Hamp," "Hamlet," "Nude with Violin," "Man Enough," "Passover."

HOYT, LON. Born Apr. 6, 1958 in Roslyn, NY. Graduate Cornell U. Bdwy debut 1982 in "Rock 'n' Roll," followed by "Baby," "Leader of the Pack," "Starlight Express."

HUBER, KATHLEEN. Born Mar. 3, 1947 in NYC. Graduate UCal. Debut 1969 OB in "A Scent of Flowers," followed by "The Virgin and the Unicorn," "The Constant Wife," "Milestones."

HUDSON, TRAVIS. Born Feb. 2 in Amarillo, Tx. UTx graduate. Bdwy debut in "New Faces of 1962," followed by "Pousse Cafe," "Very Good Eddie," "The Grand Tour," OB in "Triad," "Tattooed Countess," "Young Abe Lincoln," "Get Thee to Canterbury," "The Golden Apple," "Annie Get Your Gun," "Nunsense."

HUDSON, WALTER. Born Sept. 8, 1953 in Philadelphia, Pa. Attended Temple U. Bdwy debut 1982 in "Pirates of Penzance," followed by "The Human Comedy," OB in "The Confidence Man," "The Three Cuckolds," "Little Shop of Horrors," "Have I Got a Girl for You!"

HUFFMAN, CADY. Born Feb. 2, 1965 in Santa Barbara, Ca. Debut 1983 OB in "They're Playing Our Song," Bdwy 1985 in "La Cage aux Folles," followed by "Big Deal."

HUGHES, MICHAELA. Born Mar. 31, 1935 in Morristown, NJ. Danced with Houston, Feld and ABT companies before Bdwy 1983 Bdwy debut in "On Your Toes," followed by "Mame," "Raggedy Ann."

HUGHES, TRESA. Born Sept. 17, 1929 in Washington, DC. Attended Wayne U. OB in "Electra," "The Crucible," "Hogan's Goat," "Party on Greenwich Avenue," "Fragments," "Passing Through from Exotic Places," "Beggar on Horseback," "Early Morning," "The Old Ones," "Holy Places," "Awake and Sing," "Standing on My Knees," "Modern Ladies of Guanabacoa," "After the Fall," "Claptrap," Bdwy in "The Miracle Worker," "The Devil's Advocate," "Dear Me, the Sky Is Falling," "The Last Analysis," "Spofford," "Man in the Glass Booth," "Prisoner of Second Avenue," "Tribute," "A View from the Bridge."

HULL, BRYAN. Born Sept. 12, 1937 in Amarillo, TX. Attended UNMx, Wayne State U. Bdwy debut 1976 in "Somethin's Afoot," OB in "The Fantasticks."

HUNT, NEIL. Born Dec. 12, 1942 in Bangor, North Wales. Attended RADA. Debut 1973 OB in "The Beggar's Opera," followed by "Donkey's Years."

HUNT, W. M. Born Oct. 9 in St. Petersburg, Fl. Graduate UMi. Debut 1973 OB in "The Proposition," followed by "The Glorious Age," "Mary," "Forty-deuce," "The Rise of David Levinsky."

HURST, LILLIAN. Born Aug. 13, 1949 in San Juan, PR. Attended UPR. Debut 1983 OB in "The Great Confession," followed by "The Cuban Swimmer/Dog Lady," "The Birds Fly Out with Death," "Our Lady of the Tortilla," Bdwy in "The Cuban Thing" (1968).

HURT, WILLIAM. Born Mar. 20, 1950 in Washington, D.C. Graduate Tufts U., Juilliard. Debut 1976 OB in "Henry V," followed by "My Life," "Ulysses in Traction," "Lulu," "5th of July," "The Runner Stumbles." He received a 1978 Theatre World Award for his performances with Circle Repertory Theatre, followed by "Hamlet," "Mary Stuart," "Childe Byron," "The Diviners," "Richard II," "The Great Grandson of Jedediah Kohler," "A Midsummer Night's Dream," "Hurlyburly," "Joan of Arc at the Stake," Bdwy in "5th of July," "Hurlyburly."

HYACINTH, ROMMEL. Born May 27, 1958 in Port-au-Prince, Haiti. Graduate Brooklyn Col. Debut 1983 OB in "Throw Down," followed by "Dessalines," "Prime Time."

HYMAN, EARLE. Born Oct. 11, 1926 in Rocky Mount, NC. Attended New School, AmThWing. Bdwy debut 1943 in "Run Little Chillun," followed by "Anna Lucasta," "Climate of Eden," "Merchant of Venice," "Othello," "Julius Caesar," "The Tempest," "No Time for Sergeants," "Mr. Johnson" for which he received a Theatre World Award, "St. Joan," "Hamlet," "Waiting for Godot," "The Duchess of Malfi," "Les Blancs," "The Lady from Dubuque," "Execution of Justice," "Death of the King's Horseman," OB in "The White Rose and the Red," "Worlds of Shakespeare," "Jonah," "Life and Times of J. Walter Smintheus," "Orrin," "The Cherry Orchard," "House Party," "Carnival Dreams," "Agamemnon," "Othello," "Julius Caesar," "Coriolanus," "Remembrance," "Long Day's Journey into Night," "Sleep Beauty."

INGE, MATTHEW. Born May 29, 1950 in Fitchburg, MA. Attended Boston U., Harvard. Bdwy debut 1976 in "Fiddler on the Roof," followed by "A Chorus Line."

INNES, LAURA. Born Aug. 16, 1957 in Pontiac, MI. Graduate Northwestern U. Debut 1982 OB in "Edmond," followed by "My Uncle Sam," "Life is a Dream," "Alice and Fred," "A Country Doctor," "Vienna Lusthaus."

IRVING, GEORGE S. Born Nov. 1, 1922 in Springfield, Ma. Attended Leland Powers Sch. Bdwy debut 1943 in "Oklahoma!," followed by "Call Me Mister," "Along 5th Avenue," "Two's Company," "Me and Juliet," "Can-Can," "Shinbone Alley," "Bells Are Ringing," "The Good Soup," "Tovarich," "A Murderer Among Us," "Alfie," "Anya," "Galileo," "4 on a Garden," "An Evening with Richard Nixon . . . ," "Irene," "Whos Who in Hell," "All Over Town," "So Long 174th Street," "Once in a Lifetime," "I Remember Mama," "Copperfield," "Pirates of Penzance," "On Your Toes," "Rosalie in Concert," "Pal Joey in Concert," "Me and My Girl."

IRWIN, BILL. Born Apr. 11, 1950 in California. Attended UCLA, Oberlin, Clown Col. Debut 1982 OB in "The Regard of Flight," followed by "The Courtroom," Bdwy in "5–6–7–8 Dance" (1983), "Accidental Death of an Anarchist," "The Regard of Flight" (LC).

IRWIN, MICHAEL. Born Aug. 31, 1953 in Baltimore, Md. Graduate VaComU. Debut 1985 OB in "A Flash of Lightning," followed by "A New York Summer," "Borders," "Into Evening."

ISHEE, SUZANNE. Born Oct. 15 in High Point, NC. Graduate UNC, Manhattan Sch. of Music. Bdwy debut 1983 in "Show Boat," followed by "Mame," "La Cage aux Folles."

IVEY, DANA. Born Aug. 12, in Atlanta, GA. Graduate Rollins Col. LAMDA. Bdwy debut 1981 in "Macbeth" (LC), followed by "Present Laughter," "Heartbreak House," "Sunday in the Park with George," "Pack of Lies," "Marriage of Figaro," OB in "A Call from the East," "Vivien," "Candida in Concert," "Major Barbara in Concert," "Quartermaine's Terms," "Baby with the Bathwater," "Driving Miss Daisy."

IVEY, JUDITH. Born Sept. 4, 1951 in El Paso, Tx. Bdwy debut 1979 in "Bedroom Farce," followed by "Steaming," "Hurlyburly," "Blithe Spirit," OB in "Dulsa, Fish, Stas and Vi," "Sunday Runners," "Second Lady," "Hurlyburly."

JABLONS, KAREN. Born July 19, 1951 in Trenton, NJ. Juilliard graduate. Debut 1969 OB in "The Student Prince," followed by "Sound of Music," "Funny Girl," "Boys from Syracuse," "Sterling Silver," "People in Show Business Make Long Goodbyes," "In Trousers," Bdwy in "Ari," "Two Gentlemen of Verona," "Lorelei," "Where's Charley?," "A Chorus Line."

JACKS, SUSAN J. Born Nov. 5, 1953 in Brooklyn, NY. Graduate SUNY. Debut 1983 OB in "Forbidden Broadway."

JACKSON, ANNE. Born Sept. 3, 1926 in Allegheny, PA. Attended Neighborhood Playhouse. Bdwy debut 1945 in "Signature," followed by "Yellow Jack," "John Gabriel Borkman," "The Last Dance," "Summer and Smoke," "Magnolia Alley," "Love Me Long," "Lady from the Sea," "Never Say Never," "Oh, Men! Oh, Women!," "Rhinoceros," "Luv," "The Exercise," "Inquest," "Promenade All," "Waltz of the Toreadors," "Twice around the Park," OB in "The Tiger," "The Typist," "Marco Polo Sings a Solo," "Diary of Anne Frank," "Nest of the Wood Grouse," "Madwoman of Chaillot."

JACKSON, DAVID. Born Dec. 4, 1948 in Philadelphia, Pa. Bdwy debut 1980 in "Eubie!," followed by "My One and Only," "La Cage aux Folles."

JACKSON, ERNESTINE. Born Sept. 18 in Corpus Christi, TX. Graduate Del Mar Col., Juilliard. Debut 1966 in "Show Boat" (LC), followed by "Finian's Rainbow," "Hello Dolly!," "Applause," "Jesus Christ Superstar," "Tricks," "Raisin" for which she received a Theatre World Award, "Guys and Dolls," "Bacchae," OB in "Louis," "Some Enchanted Evening," "Money Notes," "Jack and Jill," "Black Girl," "Brownstone."

JACKSON, JULIE. Born Feb. 18, 1964 in Kingsport, Tn. Graduate UTn. Debut 1986 OB in "Cafe au Go Go," followed by "Southern Lights," "Hypothetic."

JACOBS, MAX. Born Apr. 28, 1937 in Buffalo, NY. Graduate UAz. Bdwy debut 1965 in "The Zulu and the Zayda," OB in "Full Circle," "The Working Man," "Hallowed Halls," "The Man in the Glass Booth," "Different People, Different Rooms," "Second Avenue."

JACOBY, MARK. Born May 21, 1947 in Johnson City, Tn. Graduate GaStateU, FlaStateU, St. John's U. Debut 1984 OB in "Bells Are Ringing," Bdwy 1986 in "Sweet Charity" for which he received a Theatre World Award.

JAMES, ELMORE. Born May 3, 1954 in NYC. Graduate SUNY/Purchase. Debut 1970 OB in "Moon on a Rainbow Shawl," followed by "The Ups and Downs of Theopholus Maitland," "Carnival," "Until the Real Thing Comes Along," "A Midsummer Night's Dream," "The Tempest," Bdwy in "But Never Jam Today" (1979), "Your Arms Too Short to Box with God," "Big River."

JAMES, KRICKER. Born May 17, 1939 in Cleveland, Oh. Graduate Denison U. Debut 1966 OB in "Winterset," followed by "Out of Control," "Rainbows for Sale," "The Firebugs," "Darkness at Noon," "The Hunting Man," "Sacraments," "Trifles."

JANSEN, CHRISTINE. Born July 7, 1950 in Cincinnati, Oh. Graduate UCin. Debut 1980 OB in "Father Dreams," followed by "American Garage," "Mine," "How to Say Goodbye."

JARCHOW, BRUCE A. Born May 19, 1948 in Evanston, Il. Graduate Amherst Col. Debut 1982 OB in "Edmond," followed by "True West," "Sills & Company."

JAROSLOW, RUTH. Born May 22 in Brooklyn, NY. Attended HB Studio. Debut 1964 OB in "That 5 A.M. Jazz," followed by "Jonah," "Fighting International Fat," "Kvetch," Bdwy in "Mame," "Fiddler on the Roof" (1964/77/81), "The Ritz."

JBARA, GREGORY. Born Sept. 28, 1961 in Wayne, Mi. Graduate UMi, Juilliard. Debut 1986 OB in "Have I Got a Girl for You!"

JENKINS, KEN. Born in Kentucky in 1940. Bdwy debut 1986 in "Big River."

JENNER, JAMES. Born Mar. 5, 1953 in Houston, Tx. Attended UTx, LAMDA. Debut 1980 OB in "Kind Lady," followed by "Station J," "Yellow Fever," "Comedy of Errors," "Taster's Choice."

JENNINGS, KEN. Born Oct. 10, 1947 in Jersey City, NJ. Graduate St. Peter's Col. Bdwy debut 1975 in "All God's Chillun Got Wings," followed by "Sweeney Todd" for which he received a Theatre World Award, "Present Laughter," OB in "Once on a Summer's Day," "Mayor," "Rabboni," "Gifts of the Magi," "Carmilla."

JENRETTE, RITA. Born Nov. 25, 1949 in San Antonio, Tx. Graduate UTx. Debut 1986 OB in "Girl's Guide to Chaos."

JEROME, TIMOTHY. Born Dec. 29, 1943 in Los Angeles, CA. Graduate Ithaca Col. Bdwy debut 1969 in "Man of La Mancha," followed by "The Rothschilds," "Creation of the World . . . ," "Moony Shapiro Songbook," "Cats," "Me and My Girl," OB in "Beggar's Opera," "Pretzels," "Civilization and Its Discontents," "The Little Prince," "Colette Collage," "Room Service."

JETER, MICHAEL. Born Aug. 26, 1952 in Lawrenceburg, TN. Graduate Memphis State U. Bdwy debut 1978 in "Once in a Lifetime," OB in "The Master and Margarita," "G. R. Point" for which he received a Theatre World Award, "Alice in Concert," "El Bravo," "Cloud 9," "Greater Tuna."

JOHANSON, DON. Born Oct. 19, 1952 in Rock Hill, SC. Graduate USC. Bdwy debut 1976 in "Rex," followed by "Cats," OB in "The American Dance Machine."

JOHL, PETER. Born Aug. 16, 1927 in NYC. Juilliard graduate. Debut 1959 OB in "The Matchmaker," followed by "Diary of Anne Frank," "Modigliani," Bdwy in "Luther" (1965), "Baker Street," "Pousse Cafe."

JOHNSON, MARLA. Born Mar. 21, 1956 in NYC. Graduate Georgian Court Col. Debut 1979 OB in "The Miracle Worker," followed by "Relative Values."

JOHNSON, MELISSA. Born Sept. 14, 1960 in Savannah, Ga. Debut 1987 OB in "Take Me Along."

JOHNSON, ONNI. Born Mar. 16, 1949 in NYC. Graduate Brandeis U. Debut 1964 in "Unfinished Business," followed by "She Stoops to Conquer," "22 Years," "The Master and Margarita," "Haggedah," "Fragments of a Greek Trilogy," Bdwy in "Oh, Calcutta!"

JOHNSON, PAGE. Born Aug. 25, 1930 in Welch, WV. Graduate Ithaca Col. Bdwy bow 1951 in "Romeo and Juliet," followed by "Electra," "Oedipus," "Camino Real," "In April Once," for which he received a Theatre World Award, "Red Roses for Me," "The Lovers," "Equus," "You Can't Take It With You," OB in "The Enchanted," "Guitar," "4 in 1," "Journey of the Fifth Horse," APA's "School for Scandal," "The Tavern," and "The Seagull," "Odd Couple," "Boys In The Band," "Medea," "Deathtrap," "Best Little Whorehouse in Texas," "Fool for Love."

JOHNSON, TINA. Born Oct. 27, 1951 in Wharton, Tx. Graduate NTxStateU. Debut 1979 OB in "Festival," followed by "Blue Plate Special," "Just So," Bdwy in "The Best Little Whorehouse in Texas," "South Pacific" (NYCOpera).

JOHNSTON, J. J. Born Oct. 24, 1933 in Chicago, IL. Debut 1981 OB in "American Buffalo," and Bdwy 1983 in "American Buffalo" for which he received a Theatre World Award, followed by "Glengarry Glen Ross," "Arsenic and Old Lace."

JOHNSTON, JUSTINE. Born June 13 in Evanston, Il. Debut 1959 OB in "Little Mary Sunshine," followed by "The Time of Your Life" (CC), "The Dubliners," "The New York Idea," Bdwy in "Pajama Game," "Milk and Honey," "Follies," "Irene," "Molly," "Angel," "Me and My Girl."

JOLLY, RUSS. Born Sept. 23, 1961 in Bossier City, La. Graduate NCSchool of Arts. Bdwy debut 1986 in "Big River."

JONES, CHERRY. Born Nov. 21, 1956 in Paris, Tn. Graduate Carnegie-Mellon U. Debut 1983 OB in "The Philanthropist," followed by "He and She," "The Ballad of Soapy Smith," "The Importance of Being Earnest," "I Am a Camera," "Claptrap," Bdwy in "Stepping Out" (1987).

JONES, DEAN. Born Jan. 25, 1930 in Decatur, Al. Attended Ashburn Col., UCLA. Bdwy debut 1960 in "There Was a Little Girl," followed by "Under the Yum-Yum Tree," "Company," "Into the Light."

JONES, EDDIE. Born in Washington, PA. Debut 1960 OB in "Dead End," followed by "Curse of the Starving Class," "The Ruffian on the Stairs," "An Act of Kindness," "Big Apple Messenger," "The Skirmishers," "Maiden Stakes," "The Freak," "Knights Errant," "Slacks and Tops," "Burkie," "Curse of the Starving Class" (1985), "Sorrows and Sons," "Bigfoot Stole My Wife," Bdwy in "That Championship Season" (1974), "Devour the Snow."

JONES, FRANZ. Born Nov. 11, 1951 in Washington, DC. Graduate TxChristianU. Debut 1974 OB in "Holocaust," followed by "Trade-Offs," "Brainwashed," "Pepperwine," "Things of the Heart," Bdwy in "Big River" (1985).

JONES, GORDON G. Born Nov. 1, 1941 in Urania, La. Graduate LaTech, UAk. Debut 1980 OB in "Room Service," followed by "The Front Page," "The Caine Mutiny Court-Martial," "Panhandle," "Caveat Emptor," "Progress," "The Italian Straw Hat," "The Fantasticks," "June Moon," "The Little Foxes," "In the Matter of J. Robert Oppenheimer."

JONES, JAMES EARL. Born Jan. 17, 1931 in Arktabula, Ms. Graduate UMi. OB debut 1957 in "Wedding in Japan," followed by "The Pretender," "The Blacks," "Clandestine on the Morning Line," "The Apple," "A Midsummer Night's Dream," "Moon on a Rainbow Shawl" for which he received a Theatre World Award, "Henry V," "Measure for Measure," "Richard II," "The Tempest," "Merchant of Venice," "Macbeth," "P.S. 193," "The Last Minstrel," "Love Nest," "Bloodknot," "Othello," "Baal," "Danton's Death," "Boesman and Lena," "Hamlet," "The Cherry Orchard," Bdwy in "The Egghead" (1957), "Sunrise at Campobello," "The Cool World," "Infidel Caesar," "Next Time I'll Sing to You," "Coriolanus," "Troilus and Cressida," "A Hand Is on the Gate," "The Great White Hope," "Les Blancs," "King Lear," "The Iceman Cometh," "Of Mice and Men," "Paul Robeson," "A Lesson from Aloes," "Othello," "Master Harold..and the boys," "Fences."

JONES, JAY AUBREY. Born Mar. 30, 1954 in Atlantic City, NJ. Graduate Syracuse U. Debut 1981 OB in "Sea Dream," followed by "Divine Hysteria," "Inacent Black and the Brothers," "La Belle Helene," Bdwy in "Cats" (1986).

JONES, JEN. Born Mar. 23, 1927 in Salt Lake City, Ut. Attended UUt. Debut 1960 OB in "Drums under the Window," followed by "The Long Voyage Home," "Diff'rent," "Creditors," "Look at Any Man," "I Knock at the Door," "Pictures in the Hallway," "Grab Bag," "Bo Bo," "Oh, Dad, Poor Dad...," "Henhouse," Bdwy in "Dr. Cook's Garden," "But Seriously," "Ecentricities of a Nightingale," "The Music Man" (1980), "The Octette Bridge Club."

JONES, LEILANI. Born May 14, in Honolulu, HI. Graduate UHi. Debut 1981 OB in "El Bravo," followed by "The Little Shop of Horrors," Bdwy (1985) in "Grind" for which she received a Theatre World Award.

JONES, REED. Born June 30, 1953 in Portland, OR. Graduate USIU. Bdwy debut 1979 in "Peter Pan," followed by "West Side Story," "America," "Play Me a Country Song," "Cats," "Loves of Anatole," OB in "Music Moves Me," "Jubilee in Concert."

JONES, SHANNON LEE. Born Dec. 9, 1960 in Louisville, Ky. Attended Kennasaw Col. Debut 1983 OB in "Skyline," Bdwy in "La Cage aux Folles" (1986).

JOSEPH, STEPHEN. Born Aug. 27, 1952 in Shaker Heights, Oh. Graduate Carnegie-Mellon U., FlaStateU. Debut 1978 OB in "Oklahoma!," followed by "Is Paris Flaming?," "Innuendo."

JOY, ROBERT. Born Aug. 17, 1951 in Montreal, Can. Graduate Nfd. Memorial U. Oxford U. Debut 1978 OB in "The Diary of Anne Frank," followed by "Fables for Friends," "Lydie Breeze," "Sister Mary Ignatius Explains It All," "Actor's Nightmare," "What I Did Last Summer," "The Death of Von Richthofen," "Lenny and the Heartbreakers," "Found a Peanut," "Field Day," "Life and Limb," Bdwy in "Hay Fever" (1985), "The Nerd."

JOYCE, HEIDI. Born Sept. 12, 1960 in Cleveland, Oh. Graduate IndU. Debut 1986 OB in "Girl Crazy," followed by "The Shop on Main Street," "Have I Got a Girl for You."

JOYCE, STEPHEN. Born Mar 7, 1933 in NYC. Attended Fordham U. Bdwy debut 1966 in "Those That Play the Clowns," followed by "The Exercise," "The Runner Stumbles," "Devour the Snow," "The Caine Mutiny Court-Martial," OB in "Three Hand Reel," "Galileo," "St. Joan," "Stephen D" for which he received a Theatre World Award, "Fireworks," "School for Wives," "Savages," "Scribes," "Daisy," "Maneuvers."

KAEL, DAN. Born July 1, 1962 in Los Angeles, Ca. Yale graduate. Debut 1987 OB in "Take Me Along."

KALEMBER, PATRICIA. Born Dec. 30, 1956 in Schenectady, NY. Graduate IndU. Debut 1981 OB in "The Butler Did It," followed by "Sheepskin," "Playboy of the Western World," Bdwy in "The Nerd" (1987).

KAMPF, JAMES EDWARD. Born Oct. 24, 1962 in Chicago, Il. Attended Ball State U. Debut 1986 OB in "The Mikado," followed by "Funny Girl."

KAN, LILAH. Born Sept. 4, 1931 in Chicago, Il. Attended UCBerkeley, NYU. Debut 1974 OB in "Year of the Dragon," followed by "Pursuit of Happiness," "G.R. Point," "Primary English Class," "The Blind Young Man," "Paper Angels," "Liberty Call," "Sleepless City."

KANE, DONNA. Born Aug. 12, 1962 in Beacon, NY. Graduate Mt. Holyoke Col. Debut 1985 OB in "Dames at Sea" for which she received a Theatre World Award.

KANE, MARY. Born March 21, 1961 in Scranton, Pa. Graduate Mt. Holyoke Col. Debut 1986 OB in "Alterations."

KANSAS, JERI. Born Mar. 10, 1955 in Jersey City, NJ. Debut 1978 OB in "Gay Divorce," Bdwy 1979 in "Sugar Babies," followed by "42nd Street."

KARIN, RITA. Born Oct. 24, 1919 in Warsaw, Poland. Bdwy debut 1960 in "The Wall," followed by "A Call on Kuprin," "Penny Wars," "Yentl," OB in "Pocket Watch," "Scuba Duba," "House of Blue Leaves," "Yentl the Yeshiva Boy," "Poets from the Inside," "Sharon Shashanovah," "I Love You, I Love You Not."

KAUFFMAN, JEAN. Born Feb. 5, 1957 in NYC. Attended CalStateU/Northridge. Debut 1979 OB in "The Beggar's Soap Opera," followed by "Before the Flood," "She Loves Me," "The Rise of David Levinsky."

KAUFMAN, MICHAEL. Born July 28, 1950 in Washington, DC. Graduate UWi. Debut 1978 OB in "Hooters," followed by "First Thirty," "Warriors from a Long Childhood," "Scenes from La Vie de Boheme," "Man Overboard," "Marathon '86," "Dream of a Blacklisted Actor," Bdwy in "Gemini" (1980).

KAYE, JUDY. Born Oct. 11, 1948 in Phoenix, AZ. Attended UCLA, Ariz. State U. Bdwy debut 1977 in "Grease," followed by "On the 20th Century" for which she received a Theatre World Award, "Moony Shapiro Songbook," "Oh, Brother!," OB in "Eileen in Concert," "Can't Help Singing," "Four to Make Two," "Sweethearts in Concert," "Love," "No No Nanette in Concert."

KEAL, ANITA. Born in Philadelphia, Pa. Syracuse U. Graduate. Debut 1956 OB in "Private Life of the Master Race," followed by "Brothers Karamazov," "Hedda Gabler," "Witches Sabbath," "Six Characters in Search of an Author," "Yes, My Darling Daughter," "Speed Gets the Poppy," "You Didn't Have to Tell Me," "Val Christie and Others," "Do You Still Believe the Rumor?," "Farmyard," "Merry Wives of Scarsdale," "Exiles," "Fish Riding Bikes," "Haven," "The Affair."

KEATING, CHARLES. Born Oct. 22, 1941 in London, Eng. Bdwy debut 1969 in "Arturo Ui," followed by "The House of Atreus," "Loot," OB in "An Ounce of Prevention," "A Man For All Seasons."

KEELER, DANA. Born Oct. 30, 1953 in Attleboro, Ma. Graduate UWi. Debut 1986 OB in "Today I Am a Fountain Pen."

KEHR, DON. Born Sept. 18, 1963 in Washington, DC. Bdwy debut 1976 in "Legend," followed by "The Human Comedy," "The Mystery of Edwin Drood," OB in "American Passion," "She Loves Me."

KELLERMANN, SUSAN. Born July 4. Attended Neighborhood Playhouse. Bdwy debut 1979 in "Last Licks" for which she received a Theatre World Award, followed by "Whose Life Is It Anyway?," "Lunch Hour," OB in "Wine Untouched," "Crab Quadrille," "Country Club," "Cinque and the Jones Man," "Rich Relatives."

KELLY, K. C. Born Nov. 12, 1952 in Baraboo, Wi. Attended UWis. Debut 1976 OB in "The Chicken Ranch," followed by "Last of the Knucklemen," "Young Bucks," "Writer's Cramp," Bdwy in "Romeo and Juliet" (1977), "The Best Little Whorehouse in Texas."

KELLY, MARGUERITE. Born Dec. 7, 1959 in Washington, DC. Attended Catholic U. Debut 1986 OB in "Taking Steps."

KELLY, RITAMARIE. Born Sept. 18, 1959 in Camden, NJ. Attended Adelphi U. Debut 1986 OB in "Have I Got a Girl for You."

KEMLER, ESTELLE. Born March 8 in NYC. Attended Carnegie-Mellon U. Debut 1981 OB in "Amidst the Gladiolas," followed by "Goodnight, Grandpa," "Made in Heaven," "My Three Angels," "Night Watch."

KEMP, ELIZABETH. Born Nov. 5, 1954 in Key West, Fl. Attended AADA. Debut 1974 OB in "Heat," followed by "The Best Little Whorehouse in Texas," "Playing with Fire," "Full Moon and High Tide in the Ladies Room," "North Shore Fish," Bdwy in "Once in a Lifetime" (1978).

KENER, DAVID. Born May 21, 1959 in Brooklyn, NY. Graduate NYU. Debut 1987 OB in "The Rise of David Levinsky."

KENNEDY, LAURIE. Born Feb. 14, 1948 in Hollywood, Ca. Graduate Sarah Lawrence Col. Debut 1974 OB in "End of Summer," followed by "A Day in the Death of Joe Egg," "Ladyhouse Blues," "He and She," "The Recruiting Officer," "Isn't It Romantic?," "After the Fall," "The Miracle Worker," Bdwy in "Man and Superman" (1978) for which she received a Theatre World Award, "Major Barbara."

KENNY, JACK. Born Mar. 9, 1958 in Chicago, Il. Attended Juilliard. Debut 1983 OB in "Pericles," followed by "Tartuffe," "Play and Other Plays," "A Normal Heart," "The Rise of David Levinsky."

KENYON, LAURA. Born Nov. 23, 1948 in Chicago, Il. Attended USCal. Debut 1970 OB in "Peace," followed by "Carnival," "Dementos," "The Trojan Women," "Have I Got a Girl for You," Bdwy in "Man of La Mancha" (1971), "On the Town," "Nine."

KERNS, LINDA. Born June 2, 1953 in Columbus, Oh. Attended Temple U, AADA, Debut 1981 OB in "Crisp," Bdwy in "Nine" (1982), "Big River."

KERSEY, BILLYE. Born Oct. 15, 1955 in Norfolk, VA. Bdwy debut 1981 in "42nd Street."

KERSHAW, WHITNEY. Born Apr. 10, 1962 in Orlando, FL. Attended Harkness/Joffrey Ballet Schools. Debut 1981 OB in "Francis," Bdwy in "Cats."

KERT, LARRY. Born Dec. 5, 1934 in Los Angeles, Ca. Attended LACC. Bdwy debut 1953 in "John Murray Anderson's Almanac," followed by "Ziegfeld Follies," "Mr. Wonderful," "Walk Tall," "Look, Ma, I'm Dancin'," "Tickets Please," "West Side Story," "A Family Affair," "Breakfast at Tiffany's," "Cabaret!," "La Strada," "Company," "Two Gentlemen of Verona," "Music! Music!," "Musical Jubilee," "Side by Side by Sondheim," "Rags," OB in "Changes," "From Rodgers and Hart with Love," "They Say It's Wonderful," "The Rise of David Levinsky."

KHEEL, LEE. Born Oct. 24, 1918 in Springfield, Ma. Graduate Ithaca Col, URochester. Debut 1980 OB in "The Time of the Cuckoo," followed by "One Act Festival."

KHOURY, PAMELA. Born May 17, 1954 in Beirut, Lebanon. Graduate UTx. Bdwy debut 1980 in "West Side Story," followed by "Oh, Brother!," OB in "Too Many Girls."

KILEY, RICHARD. Born Mar. 31, 1922 in Chicago, Il. Attended Loyola U. Bdwy debut 1953 in "Misalliance" for which he received a Theatre World Award, followed by "Kismet," "Sing Me No Lullaby," "Time Limit!," "Redhead," "Advise and Consent," "No Strings," "Here's Love," "I Had a Ball," "Man of La Mancha" (also LC and 1977 revivals), "Her First Roman," "The Incomparable Max," "Voices," "Absurd Person Singular," "The Heiress," "Knickerbocker Holiday," "All My Sons" (1987).

KILLINGER, MARION. Born July 12, 1941 in Corbin, Ky. Bdwy debut 1972 in "Via Galactica," followed by OB in "Queen Christina."

KIMBALL, WENDY. Born July 4 in NYC. Attended Hofstra U, Neighborhood Playhouse. Bdwy debut 1980 in "The Music Man," followed by "Annie," "Rags," OB in "Louisiana Summer."

KING, GINNY. Born May 12, 1957 in Atlanta, GA. Attended NCSch of Arts. Bdwy debut 1980 in "42nd Street."

KING, RON. Born Sept. 26, 1958 in Ann Arbor, Mi. Graduate Carnegie-Mellon U. Debut 1978 OB in "Tis a Pity She's a Whore," followed by "Danton's Death," "Hamlet," "Savage/Love," "Edward II," "The Three Sisters."

KING, W. McGREGOR. Born Apr. 1, 1952 in Fitchburg, Ma. Graduate Bryant & Stratton Col. Debut 1976 OB in "Lysistrata," followed by "The Lower Depths," "Maid to Marry," "Times Square," "The Ugly Truckling," "The Lunch Girls," "Creeps," "Cork," "Timbuktu," "Perfect Crime."

KINGSLEY-WEIHE, GRETCHEN. Born Oct. 6, 1961 in Washington, DC. Attended Tulane U. Debut 1985 OB in "Mowgli," followed by "This Could Be the Start," Bdwy in "Les Miserables" (1987).

KIRKHAM, WILLI. Born Dec. 14, 1929 in Ponca City, Ok. Attended OkCol. for Women. Debut 1978 OB in "The Countess of Mulberry St.," followed by "The Courting."

KIRKLAND, SALLY. Born Oct. 31, 1944. Bdwy debut 1961 in "Step on a Crack," followed by "Bicycle Ride to Nevada," "Marathon '33," OB in "A Midsummer Night's Dream," "Fitz," "Bitch of Waverly Place," "Tom Paine," "Futz," "Sweet Eros," "Witness," "One Night Stands of a Noisy Passenger," "Justice Box," "Delicate Champions," "Where Has Tommy Flowers Gone?," "Chickencoop Chinaman," "Largo Desolato," "Women Beware Women."

KIRSCH, CAROLYN. Born May 24, 1942 in Shreveport, LA. Bdwy debut 1963 in "How to Succeed . . . ," followed by "Follies Bergere," "La Grosse Valise," "Skyscraper," "Breakfast at Tiffany's," "Sweet Charity," "Hallelujah, Baby!," "Dear World," "Promises, Promises," "Coco," "Ulysses in Nighttown," "A Chorus Line," OB in "Silk Stockings," "Telecast."

KLATT, DAVID. Born July 15, 1958 in Martins Ferry, OH. Attended West Liberty State Col. Bdwy debut 1984 in "La Cage aux Folles."

KLEIN, ROBERT. Born Feb. 8, 1942 in NYC. Graduate Alfred U., Yale. OB in "Six Characters in Search of an Author," "Second City Returns," "Upstairs at the Downstairs," Bdwy in "The Apple Tree," "New Faces of 1968," "Morning Noon and Night," "They're Playing Our Song," "The Robert Klein Show," "Robert Klein on Broadway."

KLEMPERER, WERNER. Born in Germany; graduate Pasadena Playhouse. Bdwy debut 1947 in "Heads or Tails," followed by "Galileo," "The Insect Comedy," "20th Century," "Dear Charles," "Night of the Tribades," and OB in "Master Class."

KLUGMAN, JACK. Born Apr. 17, 1925 in Philadelphia, Pa. Attended Carnegie Tech, AmThWing. Bdwy debut 1952 in "Golden Boy," followed by "A Very Special Baby," "Gypsy," "Tchin-Tchin," "The Odd Couple," "The Sudden and Accidental Re-Education of Horse Johnson," "I'm Not Rappaport," OB in "Coriolanus," "Stevedore," "St. Joan," "Bury the Dead."

KNIGHT, LILY. Born Nov. 30, 1949 in Jersey City, NJ. Graduate NYU. Debut 1980 OB in "After the Revolution," followed by "The Wonder Years," "The Early Girl," "Musical Comedy Murders of 1940," Bdwy in "Agnes of God" (1983).

KNIGHT, SHIRLEY. Born July 5, 1936 in Goessel, Ks. Attended Phillips U, Wichita U. Bdwy debut 1964 in "The Three Sisters," followed by "We Have Always Lived in a Castle," "The Watering Place," "Kennedy's Children," OB in "Journey to the Day," "Rooms," "Happy End," "Landscape of the Body," "A Lovely Sunday for Creve Coeur," "Losing Time," "Come Back Little Sheba," "Women Heroes," "The Depot."

KNOWLES, CHRISTOPHER. Born May 4, 1959 in Brooklyn, NY. Debut 1973 OB in "The Life and Times of Joseph Stalin," followed by "A Mad Man, A Mad Giant, A Mad Dog," "Buffalo Dreams," Bdwy in "A Letter for Queen Victoria" (1975).

KNUDSON, KURT. Born Sept. 7, 1936 in Fargo, ND. Attended NDStateU, UMiami. Debut 1976 OB in "The Cherry Orchard," followed by "Geniuses," "Room Service," Bdwy in "Curse of an Aching Heart" (1982), "Sunday in the Park with George," "Take Me Along."

KOKA, JULIETTE. Born Apr. 4, 1930 in Finland. Attended Helsinki School of Dramatic Arts. Debut 1977 OB in "Piaf . . . A Remembrance" for which she received a Theatre World Award, followed by "Ladies and Gentlemen Jerome Kern," "Salon."

KOLBER, LYNNE. Born in Montreal, Can. Graduate Vassar Col. Debut OB 1983 in "Robin Hood," followed by "Nightingale," "Senor Discretion," "Charley's Tale," "Too Many Girls."

KOLINSKI, JOSEPH. Born June 26, 1953 in Detroit, Mi. Attended UDetroit. Bdwy debut 1980 in "Brigadoon," followed by "Dance a Little Closer," "The Three Musketeers," "Les Miserables," OB in "Hijinks!," "The Human Comedy" (also Bdwy).

KOMOROWSKA, LILIANA. Born Apr. 11, 1956 in Gdansk, Poland. Graduate Warsaw State Col. Debut 1986 OB in "Shots of Fate."

KOSTROFF, MICHAEL. Born May 22, 1961 in NYC. Attended HB Studio. Debut 1986 OB in "Sh-Boom," followed by "The American Boys."

KOTLER, JILL. Born Oct. 3, 1952 in Chicago, Il. Graduate USCal. OB in "The Piaglies," "Goatman," "Willie," "Play with an Ending," "Sh-Boom!," "Etiquette," "The Heart That Eats Itself."

KUHN, JUDY. Born May 20, 1958 in NYC. Graduate Oberlin Col. Debut 1985 OB in "Pearls," followed by "The Mystery of Edwin Drood (OB & Bdwy)," "Rags," "Les Miserables."

KUROWSKI, RON. Born Mar. 14, 1953 in Philadelphia, Pa. Attended Temple U., RADA. Bdwy debut 1977 in "A Chorus Line."

KURSHAL, RAYMOND. Born in NYC; Hunter Col. graduate. Bdwy debut 1985 in "Singin' in the Rain," OB in "The Garden of Earthly Delights."

KURTH, JULIETTE E. Born July 22, 1960 in Madison, Wi. Graduate SUNY/Purchase. Debut 1984 OB in "The Miser," followed by Bdwy in "La Cage aux Folles" (1986).

KURTZ, MARCIA JEAN. Born in The Bronx, NY. Juilliard graduate. Debut 1966 OB in "Jonah," followed by "America Hurrah," "Red Cross," "Muzeeka," "The Effects of Gamma Rays . . . ," "The Year Boston Won the Pennant," "The Mirror," "The Orphan," "Action," "The Dybbuk," "Ivanov," "What's Wrong with This Picture?," "Today I Am a Fountain Pen," "The Chopin Playoffs," Bdwy in "The Chinese and Dr. Fish," "Thieves," "Execution of Justice."

KURTZ, SWOOSIE. Born Sept. 6 in Omaha, Ne. Attended USCal, LAMDA. Debut 1968 OB in "The Firebugs," followed by "The Effect of Gamma Rays . . . ," "Enter a Free Man," "Children," "Museum," "Uncommon Women and Others," "Wine Untouched," "Summer," "The Beach House," Bdwy in "Ah, Wilderness!" (1975), "Tartuffe," "A History of the American Film," "5th of July," " House of Blue Leaves."

LACHOW, STAN. Born Dec. 20, 1931 in Brooklyn, NY. Graduate Roger Williams U. Debut 1977 OB in "Come Back, Little Sheba," followed by "Diary of Ann Frank," "Time of the Cuckoo," "Angelus," "The Middleman," "Charley Bacon and Family," "Crossing the Bar," "Today I Am a Fountain Pen," Bdwy in "On Golden Pond" (1979).

LACONI, ROBERT. Born Apr. 23, 1954 in Akron, Oh. Graduate KentStateU. Debut 1978 OB in "Gulliver's Travels," followed by "A Book of Etiquette," "cummings and goings," "Let's Face It," "Julius Caesar," "Comedy of Errors," "New Girl in Town."

LaDUCA, PHIL. Born Dec. 10, 1954 in Chicago, Il. Attended DePaul U., Goodman School. Bdwy debut 1980 in "Brigadoon," followed by "Pirates of Penzance," "Singin' in the Rain," OB in "Buskers," "Pajama Game."

LaGRECA, PAUL. Born June 23, 1962 in The Bronx, NY. Graduate AADA. Debut 1983 OB in "Barnum's Last Life," followed by "Really Rosie."

LAHTI, CHRISTINE. Born Apr. 4, 1950 in Detroit, MI. Graduate UMich, HB Studio. Debut 1979 OB in 'The Wood" for which she received a Theatre World Award followed by "Landscape of the Body," "The Country Girl," "Little Murders," Bdwy in "Loose Ends" (1980), "Division Street," "Scenes and Revelations," "Present Laughter."

LAINE, CLEO. Born Oct. 28, 1927 in Southall, Eng. Bdwy debut 1985 in "The Mystery of Edwin Drood" for which she received a Theatre World Award.

LALLY, JAMES. Born Oct. 2, 1956 in Cleveland, Oh. Attended Sarah Lawrence Col. Debut 1977 OB in "The Mandrake," followed by "The Taming of the Shrew," "All's Well That Ends Well," "As You Like It," "Murder in the Mummy's Tomb."

LAMB, MARY ANN. Born July 4, 1959 in Seattle, Wa. Attended Neighborhood Playhouse. Bdwy debut 1985 in "Song and Dance," followed by "Starlight Express."

LAMPERT, ZOHRA. Born May 13, 1936 in NYC. Attended UChicago. Bdwy debut 1956 in "Major Barbara," followed by "Maybe Tuesday," "Look, We've Come Through," "First Love," "Mother Courage," "Nathan Weinstein, Mystic, Conn.," "Lovers and Other Strangers," "The Sign in Sidney Brustein's Window," "Unexpected Guests," OB in "Venus Observed," "Diary of a Scoundrel," "After the Fall," "Marco Millions," "Drinks before Dinner," "Gifted Children," "My Papa's Wine."

LANDES, FRANCINE. Born July 30, 1953 in San Francisco, Ca. Graduate Juilliard, Columbia U. Bdwy debut 1985 in "The Mystery of Edwin Drood."

LANDFIELD, TIMOTHY. Born Aug. 22, 1950 in Palo Alto, Ca. Graduate Hampshire Col. Bdwy debut 1977 in "Tartuffe," followed by "Crucifer of Blood," "Wild Honey," OB in "Actors Nightmare," "Sister Mary Ignatius Explains It All," "Charlotte Sweet," "Flight of the Earls."

LANE, NANCY. Born June 16, 1951 in Passaic, NJ. Attended Va. CommonwealthU., AADA. Debut 1975 OB and Broadway in A Chorus Line.

LANE, NATHAN. Born Feb. 3, 1956 in Jersey City, NJ. Debut 1978 OB in "A Midsummer Night's Dream," followed by "Love," "Measure for Measure," Bdwy in "Present Laughter" (1982), "Merlin," "Wind in the Willows," "Claptrap," "The Common Pursuit."

LANG, STEPHEN. Born July 11, 1952 in NYC. Graduate Sworthmore Col. Debut 1975 OB in "Hamlet," followed by "Henry V," "Shadow of a Gunman," "A Winter's Tale," "Johnny on a Spot," "Barbarians," "Ah, Men," "Clownmaker," "Hannah," "Rosencrantz and Guildenstern Are Dead," Bdwy in "St. Joan" (1977), "Death of a Salesman" (1984).

LARRETA, ANNA. Born July 26, 1960 in Brazil. Debut 1986 OB in "The Red Madonna."

LARSEN, LIZ. Born Jan. 16, 1959 in Philadelphia, PA. Attended Hofstra U, SUNY/Purchase. Bdwy debut 1981 in "Fiddler on the Roof," OB in "Kuni Leml," "Hamlin," "Personals," "Starmites."

LARSON, JILL. Born Oct. 7, 1947 in Minneapolis, Mn. Graduate Hunter Col. Debut 1980 OB in "These Men," followed by "Peep," "Serious Bizness," "It's Only a Play," "Red Rover," "Enter a Freeman," Bdwy in "Romantic Comedy" (1980), "Death and the King's Horseman" (LC).

LASKY, ZANE. Born Apr. 23, 1953 in NYC. Attended Manhattan Col. HB Studio. Debut 1973 OB in "The Hot 1 Baltimore," followed by "The Prodigal," "Innocent Thoughts, Harmless Intentions," "Time Framed," "Balm in Gilead," "Shlemiel the First," "Caligula," "The Mound Builders," "Quiet in the Land," Bdwy in "All Over Town" (1974).

LAUB, SANDRA. Born Dec. 15, 1956 in Bryn Mawr, Pa. Graduate Northwestern U. Debut 1983 OB in "Richard III," followed by "Young Playwrights Festival," "Domestic Issues," "Say Goodnight Gracie," "Les Mouches," "Three Sisters," "Edward II."

LAVIN, LINDA. Born Oct. 15, 1939 in Portland, Me. Graduate William & Mary Col. Bdwy debut 1962 in "A Family Affair," followed by "Riot Act," "The Game Is Up," "Hotel Passionato," "It's a Bird . . . It's Superman!," "On a Clear Day You Can See Forever," "Something Different," "Cop-Out," "Last of the Red Hot Lovers," "Story Theatre," "The Enemy Is Dead," "Broadway Bound," OB in "Wet Paint" for which she received a Theatre World Award, "Comedy of Errors."

LAWLESS, RICK. Born Dec. 31, 1960 in Bridgeport, Ct. Graduate Fairfield U. Debut 1985 OB in "Dr. Faustus," followed by "The Foreigner," "Camp Meeting," "Lady Moonsong, Mr. Monsoon."

LAWRENCE, HOWARD. Born Dec. 20 in Brooklyn, NY. Graduate SUNY/Oneonta. Debut 1981 OB in "The Fantasticks."

LEE, ANN MARIE. Born Feb. 21 in Bridgeport, Ct. Graduate Catholic U. Debut 1981 OB in "Rimers of Eldritch," followed by "Swan Song."

LEE, JENNIFER. Born July 19, 1967 in Chicago, Il. Attended UTx. Debut 1985 OB in "The Fantasticks."

LEE-ARANAS, MARY. Born Sept. 23, 1959 in Taipei, Taiwan. Graduate UOttawa. Debut 1984 OB in "Empress of China," followed by "A State without Grace," "Return of the Phoenix," "Yellow Is My Favorite Color," "The Man Who Turned into a Stick," "The Impostor."

LEFFERT, JOEL. Born Dec. 8, 1951 in NYC. Graduate Brown U. Debut 1976 OB in "Orphee," followed by "Heroes," "The Last Burning," "Relatively Speaking," "The Bachelor," "Scaramouche," "Macbeth," "Don Juan in Hell," "Village Wooing," "The Long Smouldering," "Love-play."

LEIGH-SMITH, ANDREA. Born Dec. 21, 1962 in Louisville, Ky. Attended SUNY/Purchase. Bdwy debut 1986 in "Smile."

LeMASSENA, WILLIAM. Born May 23, 1916 in Glen Ridge, NJ. Attended NYU. Bdwy debut 1940 in "Taming of the Shrew," followed by "There Shall Be No Night," "The Pirate," "Hamlet," "Call Me Mister," "Inside U.S.A.," "I Know My Love," "Dream Girl," "Nina," "Ondine," "Fallen Angels," "Redhead," "Conquering Hero," "Beauty Part," "Come Summer," "Grin and Bare It," "All Over Town," "A Texas Trilogy," "Deathtrap," "Blithe Spirit," OB in "The Coop," "Brigadoon," "Life with Father," "F. Jasmine Addams," "The Dodge Boys," "Ivanov."

LENOX, ADRIANE. Born Sept. 11, 1956 in Memphis, TN. Graduate Lambuth Col. Bdwy debut 1979 in "Ain't Misbehavin'," followed by "Dreamgirls," OB in "Beehive."

LEO, MELISSA. Born Sept. 14, 1960 in NYC. Attended SUNY/Purchase. Debut 1984 OB in "Cinders," followed by "Out of Gas on Lover's Leap," "Today I Am a Fountain Pen."

LeSTRANGE, PHILIP. Born May 9, 1942 in The Bronx, NY. Graduate Catholic U., Fordham U. Debut 1970 OB in "Getting Married," followed by "Erogenous Zones," "The Quilling of Prue," "The Front Page" (LC).

LEVELS, CALVIN. Born Sept. 30, 1954 in Cleveland, OH. Graduate CCC. Bdwy debut 1984 in "Open Admissions" for which he received a Theatre World Award, OB in "Prairie du Chien," "The Shawl," "Common Ground."

LEVINE, ANNA. Born Sept. 18, in NYC. Debut 1975 OB in "Kid Champion," followed by "Uncommon Women and Others," "City Sugar," "A Winter's Tale," "Johnny-on-the-Spot," "The Wedding," "American Days," "The Singular Life of Albert Nobbs," "Cinders," "Rose Cottages," "School of Giorgione," "The Maderati."

LEWIS, MARCIA. Born Aug. 18, 1938 in Melrose, Ma. Attended UCin. OB in "The Impudent Wolf," "Who's Who, Baby," "God Bless Coney," "Let Yourself Go," "Romance Language," Bdwy in "The Time of Your Life," "Hello, Dolly!," "Annie," "Rags."

LEWIS, MATTHEW. Born Jan. 12, 1937 in Elizabeth, NJ. Graduate Harvard U. Debut 1970 OB in "Chicago '70," followed by "Fathers and Sons," "The Freak," "Happy Days Are Here Again," "Levitations," "The Seagull," "My Papa's Wine," Bdwy in "Angels Fall" (1983).

LEWIS, TODD. Born May 26, 1952 in Chicago, Il. Graduate Lewis U. Debut 1989 OB in "Flying Blind," followed by "Willie and Sahara," "Sawney Bean," "A Perfect Diamond," "Soup du Soir," "Blood."

LEWIS, VICKI. Born Mar. 17, 1960 in Cincinnati, Oh. Graduate CinConsv. Bdwy debut 1982 in "Do Black Patent Leather Shoes Really Reflect Up?," followed by "Wind in the Willows," OB in "Snoopy," "A Bundle of Nerves," "Angry Housewives."

LEYDEN, LEO. Born Jan. 28, 1929 in Dublin, Ire. Attended Abbey ThSch. Bdwy debut 1960 in "Love and Libel," followed by "Darling of the Day," "Mundy Scheme," "The Rothschilds," "Capt. Brassbound's Conversion," "The Plough and the Stars" (LC), "Habeas Corpus," "Me and My Girl."

LIBERATORE, LOU. Born Aug. 4, 1959 in Jersey City, NJ. Graduate Fordham U. Debut 1982 OB in "The Great Grandson of Jedediah Kohler," followed by "Threads," "Black Angel," "Richard II," "Thymus Vulgaris," "As Is," "Burn This!," Bdwy "As Is" (1985).

LICATO, FRANK. Born Apr. 20, 1952 in Brooklyn, NY. Attended Emerson Col. Debut 1974 OB in "Deathwatch," followed by "Fever," "American Music," "Angel City," "Killer's Head," "Haunted Lives."

LIN, BEN. Born Sept. 28, 1934 in Shanghai, China. Graduate UPa, Temple U. Debut 1986 OB in "The Impostor."

LIND, JANE. Born Nov. 6, 1950 in Hump Back Bay, Perryville, Ak. Attended NYU. Debut 1981 OB in "Black Elk Lives," followed by "Very Warm for May," "Fragments of a Greek Trilogy."

LIND, KIRSTEN. Born Feb. 12, in Delft, Holland. Graduate NYU. Debut 1982 OB in "Deep in the Heart," followed by "Very Warm for May," "Girl Crazy."

LINDEN, HAL. Born Mar. 20, 1931 in NYC. Attended CCNY, AmThWing. Bdwy debut 1956 in "Strip for Action," followed by "Bells Are Ringing," "Wildcat," "Subways Are for Sleeping," "Something More," "Anything Goes" (OB), "The Apple Tree," "The Education of Hyman Kaplan," "The Rothschilds," "The Sign in Sidney Brustein's Window," "Pajama Game," "I'm Not Rappaport."

LINDSAY, ROBERT. Born Dec. 13, 1951 in Ilkeston, Derbyshire, Eng. Attended RADA. Bdwy debut 1986 in "Me and My Girl" for which he received a Theatre World Award.

LIPMAN, DAVID. Born May 12, 1938 in Brooklyn, NY. Graduate LIU, Brooklyn Col. Debut 1973 OB in "Moonchildren," followed by "The Devil's Disciple," "Don Juan in Hell," "Isn't It Romantic," "Second Avenue," Bdwy in "Fools" (1981).

LIPNER, NANCY. Born Aug. 6, 1947 in Colfax, Wa. Graduate UCal/Berkeley. Debut 1978 OB in "Rosa," followed by "The Cherry Orchard," "Iolanthe," "Hay Fever," "Misalliance," "Richard III," "The Trojan Women," "A Chaste Maid in Cheapside."

LITHGOW, JOHN. Born Oct. 19, 1945 in Rochester, NY. Graduate HarvardU. Bdwy debut 1973 in "The Changing Room," followed by "My Fat Friend," "Comedians," "Anna Christie," "Once in a Lifetime," "Spokesong," "Bedroom Farce," "Division Street," "Beyond Therapy," "Requiem for a Heavyweight," "The Front Page" (LC), OB in "Hamlet," "Trelawny of the Wells," "A Memory of Two Mondays," "Secret Service," "Boy Meets Girl," "Salt Lake City Skyline," "Kaufman at Large."

LITTLE, CLEAVON. Born June 1, 1939 in Chickasha, OK. Attended San Diego State U., AADA. Debut 1967 OB in "Macbird," followed by "Hamlet," "Someone's Coming Hungry," "Ofay Watcher," "Scuba Duba," "Narrow Road to the Deep North," "Great MacDaddy," "Joseph and the Amazing Technicolor Dreamcoat," "Resurrection of Lady Lester," "Keyboard," "I'm Not Rappaport," Bdwy in "Jimmy Shine," "Purlie," "All over Town," "The Poison Tree."

George
Guidall

Julie J.
Hafner

Davis
Hall

Marian
Haraldson

D. Michael
Heath

Andi
Henig

Lise
Hilboldt

Avi
Hoffman

Susan Davis
Holmes

David S.
Howard

Kathleen
Huber

Rommel
Hyacinth

Matthew
Inge

Suzanne
Ishee

David
Jackson

Christine
Jansen

Page
Johnson

Shannon Lee
Jones

Lilah
Kan

Michael
Kaufman

Dana
Keeler

David
Kener

Liliana
Komorowska

Raymond
Kurshal

Robert
Laconi

Mary Ann
Lamb

Timothy
Landfield

Mary
Lee-Aranas

Calvin
Levels

Nancy
Lipner

LOFTUS, ELIZABETH. Born Mar. 27, 1956 in Takoma Park, Md. Graduate UMd, SMU. Debut 1987 OB in "Misalliance."

LOGAN, JEFFERY. Born Aug. 18, 1956 in Victorville, Ca. Graduate UCBerkeley. Bdwy debut 1986 in "Shakespeare on Broadway."

LONDON, BECKY. Born Feb. 11, 1958 in Philadelphia, Pa. Graduate Yale U. Debut 1985 OB in "Isn't It Romantic," followed by "Vampire Lesbians of Sodom."

LONDON, CHET. Born Apr. 8, 1931 in Boston, Ma. Attended St. Alselm's Col. Bdwy debut 1961 in "First Love," followed by "Calculated Risk," OB in "The Shoemaker and the Peddler," "Romeo and Juliet," "A Midsummer Night's Dream," "Hamlet," "The Deadly Game," "Macbeth," "Women Beware Women."

LONG, JODI. Born in NYC; graduate SUNY/Purchase. Bdwy debut 1963 in "Nowhere to Go but Up," followed by "Loose Ends," "Bacchae," OB in "Fathers and Sons," "Family Devotions," "Rohwer," "Tooth of Crime," "Dream of Kitamura," "A Midsummer Night's Dream."

LOOZE, KAREN. Born Feb. 19, 1938 in Chicago, Il. Graduate IndU. Debut 1964 OB in "Streets of New York," followed by "The Wide Open Cage," "Grace," Bdwy in "Big River" (1986).

LOR, DENISE. Born May 3, 1929 in Los Angeles, Ca. Debut 1968 OB in "To Be or Not to Be," Bdwy in "42nd Street" (1987).

LOTI, ELISA. Born Aug. 26 in Guayaquil, Ecuador. Vassar graduate. Bdwy debut 1961 in "Rhinoceros," OB in "Come Share My House" (1960) for which she received a Theatre World Award, "The Laundry," "Lucky Rita," "A Murder Is Announced," "Enter Laughing," "Before the Dawn."

LOTT, LAWRENCE. Born Apr. 13, 1950 in Greeley, CO. Graduate UCal/Irvine, UPittsburgh. Debut 1976 OB in "Bingo," followed by "Heartbreak House," "Two Noble Kinsmen," "The Normal Heart."

LOUDON, DOROTHY. Born Sept. 17, 1933 in Boston, MA. Attended Emerson Col., Syracuse U. Debut 1961 in "World of Jules Feiffer," Bdwy 1963 in "Nowhere to Go but Up" for which she received a Theatre World Award followed by "Noel Coward's Sweet Potato," "Fig Leaves Are Falling," "Three Men on a Horse," "The Women," "Annie," "Ballroom," "West Side Waltz," "Noises Off," "Jerry's Girls."

LUCAS, ROXIE. Born Aug. 25, 1951 in Memphis, TN. Attended UHouston. Bdwy debut 1981 in "The Best Little Whorehouse in Texas," followed by "Harrigan 'n Hart," OB in "Forbidden Broadway."

LUDWIG, SALEM. Born July 31, 1915 in Brooklyn, NY. Attended Brooklyn Col. Bdwy debut 1946 in "Miracle in the Mountains," followed by "Camino Real," "Enemy of the People," "All You Need Is One Good Break," "Inherit the Wind," "Disenchanted," "Rhinoceros," "Three Sisters," "The Zulu and the Zayda," "Moonchildren," "American Clock," "A Month of Sundays," OB in "The Brothers Karamazov," "Victim," "Troublemaker," "Man of Destiny," "Night of the Dunce," "Corner of the Bed," "Awake and Sing," "Prodigal," "Babylon," "Burnt Flower Bed," "American Clock," "Friends Too Numerous to Mention," "What's Wrong with this Picture?," "After the Fall."

LUM, ALVIN. Born May 28, 1931 in Honolulu, Hi. Attended UHi. Debut 1969 OB in "In the Bar of a Tokyo Hotel," followed by "Pursuit of Happiness," "Monkey Music," "Flowers and Household Gods," "Station J," "Double Dutch," "Teahouse," "Song for a Nisei Fisherman," "Empress of China," "Manos Valley," "Hot Sake," Bdwy in "Lovely Ladies, Kind Gentlemen," "Two Gentlemen of Verona."

LUM, MARY. Born July 26, 1948 in NYC. Graduate Hunter Col. Debut 1982 OB in "Hibakusha: Stories from Hiroshima," followed by "Plaid on Both Sides," "Full-Time Active," "Autumn Dusk," "Afternoon Shower," "Food," "Sister Sister," "Daughters," "Electra Speaks," "Caucasian Chalk Circle," "Julius Caesar," "Eat a Bowl of Tea," "The Impostor," "Wha . . . I, Whai, A long Time Ago."

LUPINO, RICHARD. Born Oct. 29, 1929 in Hollywood, Ca. Attended LACC, RADA. Bdwy debut 1956 in "Major Barbara," followed by "Conduct Unbecoming," "Sherlock Holmes," OB in "The Tantalus," "Swan Song."

LuPONE, ROBERT. Born July 29, 1956 in Brooklyn, NY. Juilliard graduate. Bdwy debut 1970 in "Minnie's Boys," followed by "Jesus Christ Superstar," "The Rothschilds," "Magic Show," "A Chorus Line," "St. Joan," OB in "Charlie Was Here," "Twelfth Night," "In Connecticut," "Snow Orchid," "Lennon," "Black Angel," "The Quilling of Prue," "Time Framed," "Class 1 Acts."

LUSTIG, AARON. Born Sept. 17, 1956 in Rochester, NY. Graduate Ithaca Col. Debut 1979 OB in "The Second Man," followed by "Lone Star," "White Boys," "Story of the Gadsbys," "Well of the Saints," "Death Knocks," "Misalliance."

LUSTIK, MARLENA. Born Aug. 22, 1944 in Milwaukee, Wi. Attended Marquette U. Bdwy debut 1966 in "Pousse Cafe," followed by "Days in the Trees," OB in "The Effect of Gamma Rays . . .," "Billy Liar," "One Flew over the Cuckoo's Nest," "Night Watch."

LUTSKY, MARC. Born Apr. 15 in NYC. Attended Lehman Col. OB in "The Misanthrope," "The Investigation," "Twelfth Night," "And Baby Makes Four," "The Lunch Girls," "Between Time and Timbuktu," "Perfect Crime."

LYND, BETTY. Born In Los Angeles, CA. Debut 1968 OB in "Rondelay," followed by "Love Me, Love My Children," Bdwy in "The Skin of Our Teeth" (1975), "A Chorus Line."

LYNDECK, EDMUND. Born Oct. 4, 1925 in Baton Rouge, La. Graduate Montclair State Col., Fordham U. Bdwy debut 1969 in "1776," followed by "Sweeney Todd," "A Doll's Life," "Merlin," OB in "The King and I" (JB), "Mandragola," "A Safe Place," "Amoureuse," "Piaf, A Remembrance," "Children of Darkness," "Kill."

LYNG, NORA MAE. Born Jan. 27, 1951 in Jersey City, NJ. Debut 1981 OB in "Anything Goes," followed by "Forbidden Broadway," "Road to Hollywood," "Tales of Tinseltown," Bdwy in "Wind in the Willows" (1985).

MACCHIO, RALPH. Born in Huntington, NY in 1962. Debut 1986 OB in "Cuba and His Teddy Bear," and Bdwy debut in same play and year.

MacDONALD, PIRIE. Born Mar. 24, 1932 in NYC. Graduate Harvard U. Debut 1957 OB in "Under Milk Wood," followed by "The Zoo Story," "Innocent Pleasure," "Romance," "Marathon 87," Bdwy in "Shadow and Substance," "Golden Fleecing," "Big Fish, Little Fish," "Death of a Salesman," "But Not for Me."

MacINTOSH, JOAN E. Born Nov. 25, 1945 in NJ. Graduate Beaver Col., NYU. Debut OB 1969 in "Dionysus in '69," followed by "Makbeth," "The Beard," "Tooth of Crime," "Mother Courage," "Marilyn Project," "Seneca's Oedipus," "St. Joan of the Stockyards," "Wonderland in Concert," "Dispatches," "Endgame," "Killings on the Last Line," "Request Concert," "3 Acts of Recognition," "Consequence," "Whispers."

MacNICOL, PETER. Born April 10 in Dallas, TX. Attended UMn. Bdwy debut 1981 in "Crimes of the Heart" for which he received a Theatre World Award, OB in "Found a Peanut," "Rum and Coke," "Twelfth Night," "Richard II."

MacRAE, HEATHER. Born in NYC. Attended Colo. Women's Col. Bdwy debut 1968 in "Here's Where I Belong," followed by "Hair," "Coastal Disturbances." OB in "Hot l Baltimore," "Coastal Disturbances."

MacVITTIE, BRUCE. Born Oct. 14, 1956 in Providence, RI. Graduate Boston U. Bdwy debut 1983 in "American Buffalo," followed OB in "California Dog Fight," "The Worker's Life," "Cleveland and Half Way Back," "Marathon 87."

MACY, W. H. Born Mar. 13, 1950 in Miami, Fl. Graduate Goddard Col. Debut 1980 OB in "The Man in 605," followed by "Twelfth Night," "The Beaver Coat," "A Call from the East," "Sittin'," "Sunshine," "The Dining Room," "Speakeasy," "Wild Life," "Flirtations," "Baby with the Bathwater," "Prairie/Shawl," "The Nice and the Nasty," "Bodies," "Rest and Motion."

MADIGAN, AMY. Born Sept. 11, 1950 in Chicago, Il. Graduate Marquette U. Debut 1987 OB in "The Lucky Spot" for which she received a Theatre World Award.

MAGRADEY, JACK. Born May 18, 1952 in Philadelphia, Pa. Graduate Penn State U. Bdwy debut 1976 in "So Long 174th Street," followed by "A Chorus Line," "Peter Pan," "Gotta Go Disco," "A Day in Hollywood/A Night in the Ukraine," "Cats."

MAGUIRE, MICHAEL. Born Feb. 20, 1955 in Newport News, Va. Graduate Oberlin Col., UMi. Bdwy debut 1987 in "Les Miserables" for which he received a Theatre World Award.

MAHONEY, JOHN. Born June 20, 1940 in Manchester, Eng. Attended Quincy Col., W.Ill.U. Debut 1985 OB in "Orphans" for which he received a Theatre World Award, Bdwy in "House of Blue Leaves" (1986).

MAJOR, CHARLES. Born Mar. 19 in NYC. Attended Bates Col., Adelphi U, Neighborhood Playhouse. Bdwy debut 1967 in "Spofford," followed by "Sly Fox," OB in "Gloria & Esperanza," "The Elizabethans," "Sports Czar," "The Iceman Cometh," "Othello," "Six Characters in Search of an Author," "An Ordinary Man," "Tribute," "Better Living."

MALCOLM, GRAEME. Born July 31, 1951 in Dunfermline, Scot. Graduate Central School of Speech and Drama. Debut 1985 OB in "Scapin," followed by "Pantalone," Bdwy in "Benefactors" (1986), "Death and the King's Horseman" (LC).

MALKOVICH, JOHN. Born Dec. 9, 1953 in Christopher, IL. Attended EastIllU, IllStateU. Debut 1982 OB in "True West" for which he received a Theatre World Award, followed by "Burn This!," Bdwy in "Death of a Salesman" (1984).

MALM, MIA. Born Oct. 18, 1962 in Ann Arbor, Mi. Graduate SanFranSchool of Arts. Bdwy debut 1986 in "42nd Street," followed by "Smile."

MANCINELLI, CELESTE. Born Mar. 6, 1953 in Paterson, NJ. Graduate Rutgers U. Paterson Col. Debut 1986 OB in "A Girl's Guide to Chaos."

MANDRACCHIA, CHARLES. Born Mar. 29, 1962 in Brooklyn, NY. Graduate Brooklyn Col. Debut 1987 in NYC Opera's "South Pacific," OB in "Wish You Were Here."

MANTELL, PAUL. Born Nov. 21, 1953 in Brooklyn, NY. Graduate Carnegie-Mellon U. Debut 1975 OB in "The Mikado," followed by "Don Juan," "Little Malcolm," "Richard II," "Line," "Moving Day," "Merchant of Venice," "The Key and the Wall," "Lush Life," "Pushcart Peddlers," "Dreamboats," "Beagelman and Brackett," "Walk the Dog, Willie," "The Affair," "A Chaste Maid In Cheapside."

MANTELLO, JOE. Born Dec. 27, 1962 in Rockford, Il. Attended NC School of Arts. Debut 1987 OB in "Crackwalker."

MANZI, WARREN. Born July 1, 1955 in Laurence, Ma. Graduate Holy Cross, Yale. Bdwy debut 1980 in "Amadeus."

MARADEN, FRANK. Born Aug. 9, 1944 in Norfolk, Va. Graduate UMn., MiStateU. Debut 1980 OB in "A Winter's Tale," followed by "Johnny on a Spot," "Barbarians," "The Wedding," "A Midsummer Night's Dream," "The Recruiting Officer," "The Wild Duck," "Jungle of Cities," "Three Acts of Recognition," "Don Juan," "The Workroom," "Egyptology," "Photographer," "Landscape of the Body," "Pantomime," "Romance Language," "Rum and Coke," Bdwy in "Wild Honey" (1986).

MARBLE, CAROLYN. Born June 7, 1955 in Schenectady, NY. Graduate SUNY/Purchase. Bdwy debut 1986 in "Raggedy Ann."

MARCUM, KEVIN. Born Nov. 7, 1955 in Danville, Il. Attended UIl. Bdwy debut 1976 in "My Fair Lady," followed by "I Remember Mama," "Cats," "Sunday in the Park with George," "Les Miserables."

MARCUS, DANIEL. Born May 26, 1955 in Redwood City, CA. Graduate Boston U. Bdwy debut 1981 in "The Pirates of Penzance," followed OB in "La Boheme," "Kuni Leml," "A Flash of Lightning," "Pajama Game."

MARCY, HELEN. Born June 3, 1920 in Worcester, MA. Attended Yale U. Bdwy in "Twelfth Night," "In Bed We Cry," "Dream Girl," "Love and Let Love," OB in "Lady Windermere's Fan," "Relative Values." "Verdict," "Hound of the Baskervilles," "Appointment with Death," "Ladies in Retirement," "Dr. Cook's Garden," "Murder in the Vicarage," "Black Coffee."

MARDIROSIAN, TOM. Born Dec. 14, 1947 in Buffalo, NY. Graduate UBuffalo. Debut 1976 OB in "Gemini," followed by "Grand Magic," "Losing Time," "Passione," "Success and Succession," "Ground Zero Club," "Cliffhanger," "Cap and Bells," "The Normal Heart," "Measure for Measure," "Largo Desolato," Bdwy in "Happy End," "Magic Show."

MARGOLIS, LAURA. Born Sept. 17, 1951 in Kansas City, MO. Graduate Catholic U. Debut 1978 OB in "Laura," followed by "Getting Ready," "Mantikee," "Arms and the Man," "Merchant of Venice," "Her Great Match," "The Contrast," "Pericles," "Deep Swimmer."

MARKELL, JODIE. Born Apr. 13, 1959 in Memphis, Tn. Attended Northwestern U. Debut 1984 OB in "Balm in Gilead," followed by "Carrying School Children."

MARKHAM, MARCELLA. Born Aug. 1, 1928 in NYC. Graduate AADA, RADA. Debut 1953 OB in "Threepenny Opera," followed by "Are You Now or Have You Ever Been . . ., Dispatches from Hell," Bdwy in "The Iceman Cometh" (1946), "Cry Havoc," "Flamingo Road."

MARKS, KENNETH. Born Feb. 17, 1954 in Harwick, Pa. Graduate UPa., LeHigh U. Debut 1978 OB in "Clara Bow Loves Gary Cooper," followed by "Canadian Gothic," "Time and the Conways," "Savoury Meringue," "Thrombo," "Class 1 Acts."

MARLOWE, THERESA. Born Aug. 20, 1958 in Monroe, Mi. Debut 1985 OB in "Vampire Lesbians of Sodom," followed by "Times Square Angel," "Psycho Beach Party."

MARONA, EDWARD. Born May 13, 1961 in Chattanooga, Tn. Graduate Berry Col., Brandeis U. Debut 1986 OB in "Pageant."

MARSDEN, LES. Born Feb. 26, 1957 in Fresno, Ca. Graduate CalStateU/Fresno. Debut 1986 OB in "Groucho: A Life in Revue."

MARSHALL, PETER. Born Mar. 30, 1930 in Clarksburg, WVa. Bdwy debut 1961 in "How to Make a Man," followed by "Skyscraper," "Les Cage aux Folles."

MARSHALL, ROB. Born Oct. 17, 1960 in Madison, Wi. Graduate Carnegie-Mellon U. Debut 1982 OB in "Boogie-Woogie Rumble of a Dream Deferred," Bdwy in "The Mystery of Edwin Drood" (1985).

MARTENS, RICA. Born Jan. 8, 1925 in Eliasville, Tx. Graduate NTxU. Bdwy debut 1947 in "Laura," followed by "The Shrike," OB in "Assent of F6," "The Bird the Bear and the Actress," "Edward My Son," "Oedipus and Jocasta," "Beckett," "My Great Dead Sister," "Tied by the Leg," "Saved," "Ah, Wilderness!," "Naomi Court," "Gods in Summer," "Manners," "Waiting for the Parade," "Rule of Three."

MARTIN, GEORGE N. Born Aug. 15, 1929 in NYC. Bdwy debut 1970 in "Wilson in the Promise Land," followed by "The Hothouse," "Plenty," "Total Abandon," "Pack of Lies," "The Mystery of Edwin Drood," OB in "Painting Churches," "Henry V," "Springtime for Henry."

MARTIN, LUCY. Born Feb. 8, 1942 in NYC. Graduate Sweet Briar Col. Debut 1962 OB in "Electra," followed by "Happy as Larry," "The Trojan Women," "Iphigenia in Aulis," "Wives," "The Cost of Living," Bdwy in "Shelter" (1973), "Children of a Lesser God," "Pygmalion."

MARTIN, MILLICENT. Born June 8, 1934 in Romford, Eng. Attended Atalia Conti Sch. Bdwy debut 1954 in "The Boy Friend," followed by "Side by Side by Sondheim," "King of Hearts," "42nd Street."

MARTIN, W. T. Born Jan. 17, 1947 in Providence, RI. Attended Lafayette Col. Debut 1972 OB in "The Basic Training of Pavlo Hummel," followed by "Ghosts," "The Caretaker," "Are You Now or Have You Ever . . .," "Fairy Tales of New York," "We Won't Pay," "Black Elk Lives," "The End of the War," "A Little Madness," "All the Nice People," "Enter a Free Man," "The Other Side of Newark," "Not Showing."

MARTIN, YVONNE. Born in Los Angeles, Ca. Attended CalStateU. Debut 1987 OB in "The Wonderful Ice Cream Suit."

MARTINO, MARK. Born Aug. 26, 1953 in Indianapolis, In. Graduate Wm and Mary Col. Bdwy debut 1981 in "Broadway Follies," followed by "Oh, Brother!," OB in "Forbidden Broadway."

MASTERSON, MARY STUART. Born in 1967 in NYC. Debut 1987 OB in "Lily Dale," followed by "The Lucky Spot."

MASTRANTONIO, MARY ELIZABETH. Born Nov. 17, 1958 in Chicago, IL. Attended UIll. Bdwy debut 1980 in "West Side Story," followed by "Copperfield," "Oh, Brother!," "The Marriage of Figaro," OB in "Henry V," "A Christmas Carol," "Measure for Measure," "The Knife."

MATANKY, GARY J. Born Feb. 2, 1958 in Los Angeles, Ca. Attended UCLA, SanFranStateU. Debut 1986 OB in "Tigers Wild."

MATHERS, JAMES. Born Oct. 31, 1936 in Seattle, WA. Graduate UWA., Beverly Col. Debut 1983 OB in "Happy Birthday, Wanda June," followed by "Uncommon Holidays," "Harvest of Strangers," "Crime and Punishment," "Class 1 Acts."

MATHIEU, RACHEL. Born Aug. 31, 1977 in Brooklyn, NY. Debut 1987 OB in "Coastal Disturbances."

MATSUSAKA, TOM. Born Aug. 8 in Wahiawa, Hi. Graduate MiStageU. Bdwy debut 1968 in "Mame," followed by "Ride the Winds," "Pacific Overtures," "South Pacific" (NYC Opera), OB in "Agamemnon," "Chu Chem," "Jungle of Cities," "Santa Anita '42," "Extenuating Circumstances," "Rohwer," "Teahouse," "Song of a Nisei Fisherman," "Empress of China," "Pacific Overtures" (1984), "Eat a Bowl of Tea," "Shogun Macbeth," "The Impostor."

MATTHEWS, ANDERSON. Born Oct. 21, 1950 in Springfield, Oh. Graduate Carnegie-Mellon U. Bdwy debut 1975 in "The Robber Bridegroom," followed by "Edward II," "The Time of Your Life," "Ten by Tennessee," "Beef," "The Sneaker Factor."

MATZ, JERRY. Born Nov. 15, 1935 in NYC. Graduate Syracuse U. Debut 1965 OB in "The Old Glory," followed by "Hefetz," "A Day out of Time," "A Mad World My Masters," "The Rise of David Levinsky," "The Last Danceman," "Madrid Madrid."

MAY, BEVERLY. Born Aug. 11, 1927 in East Wellington, BC, Can. Yale graduate. Debut 1976 OB in "Female Transport," followed by "Bonjour La Bonjour," "My Sister in This House," "Slab Boys," "And a Nightingale Sang," Bdwy in "Equus" (1977), "Once in a Lifetime," "Whose Life Is It Anyway?," "Rose," "Curse of an Aching Heart," "The Front Page" (LC).

MAYHEW, CAROL. Born Dec. 25, in New Jersey. Graduate Pace U, AADA. Debut 1986 OB in "Perfect for Blue," followed by "Ring Round the Moon," "Oedipus the Human Being."

MAZZIE, MARIN. Born Oct. 9, 1960 in Rockford, Il. Graduate WMiU. Debut 1983 OB in "Where's Charley?," Bdwy in "Big River" (1986).

McARDLE, ANDREA. Born Nov. 5, 1963 in Philadelphia, Pa. Bdwy debut 1977 in "Annie" for which she received a Theatre World Award, followed by "Starlight Express," OB in "They Say It's Wonderful."

McATEER, KATHRYN. Born Sept. 4, 1949 in Englewood, NJ. Graduate Montclair State Col. Debut 1983 OB in "Upstairs at O'Neal's," followed by "Mayor," "Take Me Along," Bdwy in "Mayor," (1985), "Into the Light."

McBRIDE, BILLIE. Born Nov. 13, 1945 in LeRoy, Il. Graduate Ill Wesleyan U. Debut 1971 OB in "Honky Tonk Trash," followed by "Safe Sex," Bdwy 1987 in "Safe Sex."

McCALL, KATHLEEN S. Born Jan. 11 in Denver, Co. Graduate Moorhead Stat U., LAMDA. Debut 1986 OB in "Thanksgiving," followed by "Acapella Hardcore," "Class 1 Acts."

McCANN, CHRISTOPHER. Born Sept. 29, 1952 in NYC. Graduate NYU. Debut 1975 OB in "The Measures Taken," followed by "Ghosts," "Woyzzeck," "St. Joan of the Stockyards," "Buried Child," "Dwelling in Milk," "Tongues," "3 Acts of Recognition," "Don Juan," "Michi's Blood," "Five of Us," "Richard III," "The Golem," "Kafka Father and Son," "Flatbush Faithful."

McCARTHY, ANDREW. Born in 1963 in NYC. Bdwy debut 1985 in "Boys of Winter," followed by OB in "Bodies, Rest and Motion."

McCARTHY, JEFF. Born Oct. 16, 1954 in Los Angeles, CA. Graduate American Consv. Theatre. Bdwy debut 1982 in "Pirates of Penzance," followed by "Zorba" (1983), OB in "Gifts of the Magi," "On the 20th Century.

McCARTY, MICHAEL. Born Sept. 7, 1946 in Evansville, In. Graduate IndU, MiStateU. Debut 1976 OB in "Fiorello!," followed by "The Robber Bridegroom," Bdwy in "Dirty Linen," "King of Hearts," "Amadeus," "Oliver!," "Big River."

McCAULEY, WILLIAM. Born Nov. 20, 1947 in Wayne, Pa. Graduate Northwestern U, Goodman Theatre. Bdwy debut 1974 in "Saturday, Sunday, Monday," OB in "Everybody's Gettin' into the Act," "Can-Can," "Scrambled Feet," "Take Me Along."

McCLURE, SPARTAN. Born May 17, 1959 in Yoakum, Tx. Debut 1986 OB in "The Widow Claire."

McCONNELL, C. LYNDA. Born July 2, 1957 in Milford, De. Graduate Hawthorne Col. Debut 1980 OB in "Mama, I Want to Sing," Bdwy 1987 in "Dreamgirls."

McCORRY, MARION. Born Oct. 10, 1945 in The Bronx, NY. Hunter Col. graduate. Debut 1974 OB in "Ionescapade," followed by "Cappella," "The Flower Palace."

McDONALD, BETH. Born May 25, 1954 in Chicago, Il. Juilliard graduate. Debut 1981 OB in "A Midsummer Night's Dream," followed by "The Recruiting Officer," "Jungle of Cities," "Kennedy at Colonus," "Our Own Family."

McDONALD, CHRISSIE. Born Oct. 11, 1977 in Baton Rouge, La. Bdwy debut 1987 in "Les Miserables."

McFARLAND, ROBERT. Born May 7, 1931 in Omaha, Ne. Graduate UMi, ColumbiaU. Debut 1978 OB in "The Taming of the Shrew," followed by "When the War Was Over," "Divine Fire," "Ten Little Indians," "The Male Animal," "Comedy of Errors," "Appointment with Death," "The Education of One Miss February," "Rule of Three."

McGILLIN, HOWARD. Born Nov. 5, 1953 in Los Angeles, Ca. Graduate UCal/Santa Barbara. Debut 1984 OB in "La Boheme," followed by Bdwy in "Sunday in the Park with George," "The Mystery of Edwin Drood" for which he received a Theatre World Award.

McGOVERN, ELIZABETH. Born July 18, 1961 in Evanston, IL. Attended Juilliard. Debut 1981 OB in "To Be Young, Gifted and Black," followed by "Hotel Play," "My Sister in This House" for which she received a Theatre World Award, "Painting Churches," "Hitch-Hikers," "Map of the World," "Two Gentlemen of Verona."

McGUINNESS, MICHAEL JOHN. Born May 13, 1961 in Corning, NY. Graduate NYU. Debut 1985 OB in "Brand," followed by "Frankenstein," "Wakefield/Chester Mystery Play Cycle," "The Real Inspector Hound," "Richard II," "Andromache."

McHATTIE, STEPHEN. Born Feb. 3 in Antigonish, NS. Graduate Arcadia U, AADA. Bdwy debut 1968 in "The American Dream," followed by "The Misanthrope," "Heartbreak House," "You Never Can Tell," OB in "Henry IV," "Richard III," "The Persians," "Pictures in the Hallway," "Now There's Just the Three of Us," "Anna K," "Twelfth Night," "Mourning Becomes Electra," "Alive and Well in Argentina," "The Iceman Cometh," "Winter Dancers," "Casualties," "Three Sisters," "Mensch Meier," "Haven."

McINERNEY, BERNIE. Born Dec. 4, 1936 in Wilmington, De. Graduate UDe, Catholic U. Bdwy debut 1972 in "That Championship Season," followed by "Curse of an Aching Heart," "The Front Page" (LC), OB in "Life of Galileo," "Losing Time," "Three Friends," "American Clock," "Father Dreams," "Winners," "Digby."

McKECHNIE, DONNA. Born Nov. 1944 in Detroit, Mi. Bdwy debut 1961 in "How to Succeed in Business . . .," followed by "Promises Promises," "Company," "On the Gown," "Music! Music!" (CC), "A Chorus Line," OB in "Wine Untouched."

McKELLEN, IAN. Born May 25, 1939 in Burnley, Eng. Attended St. Catherine's Col. Bdwy debut 1967 in "The Promise," followed by "Amadeus," "Wild Honey."

McKENNA, CHRISTIANE. Born Mar. 14, 1952 in San Francisco, Ca. Attended Juilliard, Pacific Consv. Debut 1980 OB in "Merton of the Movies," followed by "Madwoman of Chaillot," "A Midsummer Night's Dream," "Sjt. Musgrave's Dance," "Boys in the Backroom," "Lust and the Unicorn."

McLACHLAN, RODERICK. Born Sept. 9, 1960 in Detroit, Mi. Graduate Northwestern U. Debut 1987 in "Death and the King's Horseman" (LC).

McLAUGHLIN, JACK. Born Sept. 3, 1938 in Arlington, Ma. Graduate Boston Col., Harvard, NYU. Debut 1972 OB in "A God and a Machine," followed by "The Prophets," "Dancers on My Ceiling," "Tale without Title," "Evening Song."

McLERNON, PAMELA. Born March 1 in Lynn, Ma. Graduate Lowell State Col. Debut 1975 OB in "Tenderloin," followed by "Ready or Not," Bdwy in "Sweeney Todd," "Copperfield."

McMILLAN, KENNETH. Born July 2, 1934 in Brooklyn, NY. Bdwy debut 1970 in "Borstal Boy," followed by "American Buffalo," OB in "Red Eye of Love," "King of the Whole Damn World," "Little Mary Sunshine," "Babes in the Wood," "Moonchildren," "Merry Wives of Windsor," "Where Do We Go from Here?," "Kid Champion," "Streamers," "Henry IV Part II," "Weekends Like Other People," "Danger: Memory!" (LC).

McMORROW, TOM, JR. Born Jan. 8, 1956 in NYC. Attended Queens Col., Neighborhood Playhouse. Debut 1987 OB in "Taster's Choice."

McNAMARA, DERMOT. Born Aug. 24, 1925 in Dublin, Ire. Bdwy debut 1959 in "A Touch of the Poet," followed by "Philadelphia, Here I Come," "Donnybrook," "Taming of the Shrew," OB in "The Wise Have Not Spoken," "3 by Synge," "Playboy of the Western World," "Shadow and Substance," "Happy as Larry," "Sharon's Grave," "A Whistle in the Dark," "Red Roses for Me," "The Plough and the Stars," "Shadow of a Gunman," "No Exit," "Stephen D," "Hothouse," "Home Is the Hero," "Sunday Morning Bright and Early," "The Birthday Party," "All the Nice People," "Roots."

McROBBIE, PETER. Born Jan. 31, 1943 in Hawick, Scot. Graduate Yale U. Debut 1976 OB in "The Wobblies," followed by "The Devil's Disciple," "Cinders," "The Ballad of Soapy Smith," Bdwy in "Whose Life Is It Anyway?" (1979), "Macbeth" (1981) "The Mystery of Edwin Drood."

McTIGUE, MARY. Born Sept. 5, in Webster City, Ia. Graduate Clarke Col. Debut 1979 OB in "Vanities," followed by "Who's Happy Now," "Disintegration of James Cherry," "Marriage of Bette and Boo," "Seven Scenes from American Life," "Richard III," "Long Voyage Home," "Night Watch," "Transformational Country Dancers."

MEDINA, HAZEL J. Born Oct. 8 in Colon, Panama. Attended LACC. Debut 1982 OB in "Brixton Recovery," followed by "Time out of Time," "Street Sounds," "The Beautiful LaSalles," "State of the Union," "Two Can Play," "Time Out of Time."

MEEHAN, JOHN. Born May 1, 1950 in Brisbane, Australia. Appeared with Australian Ballet, Am Ballet Theatre before Bdwy debut in "Song and Dance" (1986).

MEISTER, FREDERIKKE. Born Aug. 18, 1951 in San Francisco, Ca. Graduate NYU. Debut 1978 OB in "Museum," followed by "Dolphin Position," "Waiting for the Parade," "Dream of a Blacklisted Actor," "No Damn Good."

MELEDANDRI, WAYNE. Born Oct. 8, 1959 in New Kensington, Pa. Graduate Carnegie-Mellon U. Bdwy debut 1985 in "A Chorus Line."

MELLOR, STEPHEN. Born Oct. 17, 1954 in New Haven, CT. Graduate Boston U. Debut 1980 OB in "Paris Lights," followed by "Coming Attractions," "Plenty," "Tooth of Crime," "Shepard Sets," "A Country Doctor," "Harm's Way," Bdwy in "Big River."

MELOCHE, KATHERINE. Born June 1, 1952 in Detroit, MI. Bdwy debut 1976 in "Grease," followed by "Dancin'," OB in "Street Scene," "Little Shop of Horrors."

MENDILLO, STEPHEN. Born Oct. 9, 1942 in New Haven, Ct. Graduate Colo. Col., Yale U. Debut 1973 OB in "Nourish the Beast," followed by "Gorky," "Time Steps," "The Marriage," "Loot," "Subject to Fits," "Wedding Band," "As You Like It," "Fool for Love," Bdwy in "National Health" (1974), "Ah, Wilderness," "A View from the Bridge," "Wild Honey."

MERKERSON, S. EPATHA. Born Nov. 28, 1952 in Saganaw, Mi. Graduate Wayne State U. Debut 1979 OB in "Spell #7," followed by "Home," "Puppetplay," "Tintypes," "Every Goodbye Ain't Gone," "Hospice," "The Harvesting," "Moms," "Lady Day at Emerson's Bar and Grill," Bdwy in "Tintypes" (1982).

MERRITT, GEORGE. Born July 10, 1942 in Raleigh, NC. Graduate CatholicU. Bdwy debut 1976 in "Porgy and Bess," followed by its 1983 revival, "Ain't Misbehavin'," "Big River."

METCALF, LAURIE. Born June 16, 1955 in Edwardsville, IL. IllStateU graduate. Debut 1984 OB in "Balm in Gilead" for which she received a Theatre World Award, followed by "Bodies, Rest and Motion," "Educating Rita."

METCALF, MARK. Born Mar. 11 in Findlay, OH. Attended UMi. Debut 1973 OB in "Creeps," followed by "The Tempest," "Beach Children," "Hamlet," "Patrick Henry Lake Liquors," "Streamers," "Salt Lake City Skyline," "Mr. & Mrs.," "Romeo and Juliet," "Blue Window," "A Midsummer Night's Dream," "Trinity Site."

MICHAELS, DEVON. Born Oct. 22, 1973 in NYC. Bdwy debut 1986 in "Rags," followed by OB in "Passover," "The Knife."

MILES, JOANNA. Born Mar. 6, 1940 in Nice, France. Attended Actors Studio. Bdwy debut 1963 in "Marathon 33," followed by "Lorenzo," OB in "Walk-Up," "Cave Dwellers," "Once in a Lifetime," "Home Free," "Drums in the Night," "Dylan," "Dancing for the Kaiser," "The Wakefield Plays," "Private Opening," "Ski Bum," "Having Fun in the Bathroom," "Niagara Falls."

MILLER, ALICIA. Born Nov. 17, 1963 in NYC. Graduate Wash. U. Debut 1987 OB in "Wish You Were Here."

MILLER, ROGER. Born Jan. 2, 1936 in Ft. Worth, Tx. Bdwy debut 1986 in "Big River" for which he wrote the music and lyrics.

MILLS, JOHN. Born Feb. 22, 1908 in North Elmham, Eng. Bdwy debut 1961 in "Ross," followed by "Pygmalion" (1987).

MILWARD, KRISTIN. Born in Kent, Eng. Graduate U.East Anglia, RADA. Bdwy debut 1987 in "Les Liaisons Dangereuses."

MINOT, ANNA. Born in Boston, Ma. Attended Vassar Col. Bdwy debut 1942 in "The Strings, My Lord, Are False," followed by "The Russian People," "The Visitor," "The Iceman Cometh," "An Enemy of the People," "Love of Four Colonels," "Trip to Bountiful," "Tunnel of Love," "Ivanov," OB in "Sands of the Niger," "Getting Out," "Vieux Carre," "State of the Union," "Her Great Match," "Rivals."

MIRABAL, JEANNETTE. Born Dec. 5, 1958 in Havana, Cuba. Graduate NYU. Debut 1984 OB in "Cuban Swimmer/Dog Lady," followed by "The Bitter Tears of Petra Von Kant," "A Little Something to Ease the Pain."

MITCHELL, MARK. Born July 10, 1953 in Nashville, Tn. Graduate George Peabody Col. Debut 1985 OB in "Forbidden Broadway."

MITZMAN, MARCIA. Born Feb. 28, 1959 in NYC. Attended SUNY/Purchase, Neighborhood Playhouse. Debut 1978 OB in "Promises Promises," followed by "Taming of the Shrew," "Around the Corner from the White House," Bdwy in "Grease" (1979), "Oliver!," "South Pacific" (LC).

MOE, ELAINE. Born Dec. 8, 1944 in Houston, Tx. Graduate UAz. Debut 1986 OB in "To Feed Their Hopes."

MOHLER, BETSY. Born Nov. 18, 1959 in Washington, DC. Graduate Yale. Debut 1987 OB in "Wicked Philanthropy."

MOLINA-TOBIN, OLGA. Born Oct. 26, 1934 in NYC. Attended Hunter Col., Brooklyn Col. Debut 1974 OB in "Scribbles," followed by "The Guest," "Bodega."

MOOR, BILL. Born July 13, 1931 in Toledo, OH. Attended Northwestern, Denison U. Bdwy debut 1964 in "Blues for Mr. Charlie," followed by "Great God Brown," "Don Juan," "The Visit," "Chemin de Fer," "Holiday," "P.S. Your Cat Is Dead," "Night of the Tribades," "Water Engine," "Plenty," "Heartbreak House," "The Iceman Cometh," OB in "Dandy Dick," "Love Nest," "Days and Nights of Beebee Fenstermaker," "The Collection," "The Owl Answers," "Long Christmas Dinner," "Fortune and Men's Eyes," "King Lear," "Cry of Players," "Boys in the Band," "Alive and Well in Argentina," "Rosmersholm." "The Biko Inquest," "A Winter's Tale," "Johnny on a Spot," "Barbarians," "The Purging," "Potsdam Quartet," "Zones of the Spirit," "The Marriage of Bette and Boo."

MOORE, BENJAMIN. Born Jan. 2, 1960 in Syracuse, NY. Graduate Hamilton Col. Debut 1987 OB in "Take Me Along."

MOORE, CHARLOTTE. Born July 7, 1939 in Herrin, Il. Attended Smith Col. Bdwy debut 1972 in "The Great God Brown," followed by "Don Juan," "The Visit," "Chemin de Fer," "Holiday," "Love for Love," "A Member of the Wedding," "Morning's at 7," OB in "Out of Our Father's House," "A Lovely Sunday for Creve Coeur," "Summer," "Beside the Seaside," "The Perfect Party."

MOORE, DEMI. Born Nov. 11, 1962 in Roswell, NMx. Debut 1986 OB in "The Early Girl" for which she received a Theatre World Award.

MOORE, JONATHAN. Born Mar. 24, 1923 in New Orleans, La. Attended Piscator School. Debut 1961 OB in "After the Angels," followed by "Berkeley Square," "Checking Out," "The Biko Inquest," "Sullivan and Gilbert," Bdwy in "Dylan," "1776," "Amadeus," "Wild Honey."

MOORE, JUDITH. Born Feb. 12, 1944 in Princeton, WVa. Graduate UInd. Debut 1971 OB in "The Drunkard," followed by "Ten by Six," "Boys from Syracuse," "The Evangelist," "Miracle of the Month," Bdwy in "Sunday in the Park with George" (1984).

MOORE, KIM. Born Jan. 11, 1956 in Wheaton, Mn. Graduate MoorheadStateU, LAMDA. Debut 1985 OB in "The Fantasticks."

MOORE, MAUREEN. Born Aug. 12, 1951 in Wallingford, Ct. Bdwy debut 1974 in Gypsy, followed by "Do Black Patent Leather Shoes Really Reflect Up?," "Amadeus," "Song and Dance," OB in "Unsung Cole," "By Strouse."

MORAN, DANIEL. Born July 31, 1953 in Corcoran, CA. Graduate NYU. Debut 1980 OB in "True West," followed by "The Vampires," "Tongues and Savage Love," "Life Is a Dream," "The Filthy Rich," "The Return of Pinocchio," "Merchant of Venice."

MORAN, LIZZIE. Born Sept. 3, 1951 in Baltimore, Md. Graduate UMd. Bdwy debut 1981 in "42nd Street."

MORAN, MARTIN. Born Dec. 29, 1959 in Denver, Co. Attended Stanford U., AmConsvTh. Debut 1983 OB in "Spring Awakening," followed by "Once on a Summer's Day," Bdwy in "Oliver!" (1984), "Big River."

MORANZ, BRAD. Born Aug. 29, 1952 in Houston, TX. Bdwy debut in "A Day in Hollywood/A Night in the Ukraine" (1981), OB in "Little Shop of Horrors."

MORANZ, JANNET. (formerly Horsley) Born Oct. 13, 1954 in Los Angeles, CA. Attended CaStateU. Bdwy debut 1980 in "A Chorus Line."

MORATH, KATHRYN (a.k.a Kathy) Born Mar. 23, 1955 in Colorado Springs, Co. Graduate Brown U. Debut 1980 OB in "The Fantasticks," followed by "Dulcy," "Snapshot," "Alice in Concert," "A Little Night Music," "The Little Prince," "Professionally Speaking," "The Apple Tree,"Bdwy in "Pirates of Penzance" (1982)."

MORATH, MAX. Born in 1927 in Colorado Springs, Co. Attended Colo. Col. OB debut 1969 in "An Evening with Max Morath at the Turn of the Century," followed by "Living a Ragtime Life."

MORENO, RENE. Born May 25, 1959 in Dallas, Tx. Graduate SMU. Bdwy debut 1982 in "Amadeus," followed by "Shakespeare on Broadway," OB in "Bits and Pieces," "The Man of Destiny," "And That's the Way It Is."

MORGAN, RON. Born Dec. 13, 1958 in Indianapolis, In. Attended Ball State, Butler U. Bdwy debut 1987 in "Starlight Express."

MOROZ, BARBARA. Born Feb. 9, 1958 in Dearborn, Mi. Bdwy debut 1984 in "Oliver!," followed by "Harrigan 'n' Hart," "Me and My Girl."

MORRISEY, BOB. Born Aug. 15, 1946 in Somervill, Ma. Attended UWi. Debut 1974 OB in "Ionescapade," followed by "Company," "Anything Goes," "Philistines," Bdwy in "The First" (1981), "Cats," "Raggedy Ann."

MORROW, KAREN. Born Dec. 15, 1936 in Chicago, Il. Attended Clarke Col. Debut 1961 OB in "Sing, Muse!" for which she received a Theatre World Award, followed by "The Boys from Syracuse," CC's "Oklahoma!," "Most Happy Fella," "Brigadoon," "Carnival" and "Music! Music!," Bdwy in "I Had a Ball," "Joyful Noise," "I'm Solomon," "The Grass Harp," "Selling of the President," "The Mystery of Edwin Drood."

MORTON, JOE. Born Oct. 18, 1947 in NYC. Attended Hofstra U. Debut 1968 OB in "A Month of Sundays," followed by "Salvation," "Charlie Was Here and Now He's Gone," "G. R. Point," "Crazy Horse," "A Winter's Tale" "Johnny on a Spot," "Midsummer Night's Drean," "The Recruiting Officer," "Oedipus the King," "The Wild Duck," "Rhinestone," "Souvenirs," "Cheapside," Bdwy in "Hair," "Two Gentlemen of Verona," "Tricks," "Raisin" for which he received a Theatre World Award, "Oh, Brother!,""Honky Tonk Nights."

MOSIEJ, JAMES E. Born Dec. 14, 1965 in Chicago, IL. Graduate IllWesternU. Debut 1983 OB in "Water Music," Bdwy in "Oh! Calcutta!" (1984).

MOZER, ELIZABETH. Born Nov. 17, 1960 in Jamaica, NY. Graduate SUNY/Brockport. Debut 1986 OB in "Funny Girl."

MULKEEN, JOHN. Born Aug. 31, 1956 in Detroit, Mi. Graduate UMi, UWi. Debut 1987 OB and Bdwy in "Safe Sex."

MURPHY, DONNA. Born Mar. 7, 1959 in Corona, NY. Attended NYU. Bdwy debut 1979 in "They're Playing Our Song," followed by "The Human Comedy," "The Mystery of Edwin Drood," OB in "Francis," "Portable Pioneer and Prairie Show," "Little Shop of Horrors," "A . . . My Name Is Alice."

MURPHY, ROSEMARY. Born Jan. 13, 1927 in Munich, Ger. Attended Neighborhood Playhouse, Actors Studio. Bdwy debut 1950 in "Tower Beyond Tragedy," followed by "Look Homeward, Angel," "Period of Adjustment," "Any Wednesday," "Delicate Balance," "Weekend," "Death of Bessie Smith," "Butterflies Are Free," "Ladies at the Alamo," "Cheaters," "John Gabriel Borkman," "Coastal Disturbances," OB in "Are You Now or Have You Ever Been," "Learned Ladies," "Coastal Disturbances."

MURRAY, MARY GORDON. Born Nov. 13, 1953 in Ridgewood, NJ. Attended Ramapo Col., Juilliard. Bdwy debut 1976 in "The Robber Bridegroom," followed by "Grease," "I Love My Wife," "Little Me," "Play Me a Country Song," OB in "A . . . My Name Is Alice," "Blue Plate Special," "The Knife."

MURTAUGH, JAMES. Born Oct. 28, 1942 in Chicago, Il. Debut OB in "The Firebugs," followed by "Highest Standard of Living," "Marathon 87."

MYERS, PAULENE. Born Nov. 9 in Ocilla, Ga. Attended New Theatre School. Bdwy debut 1933 in "Growin' Pains," followed by "Plumes in the Dust," "The Willow and I," "The Naked Genius," "Dear Ruth," "Take a Giant Step," "Anniversary Waltz," OB in "Goodnight Ms. Calabash," "Mama."

NAHRWOLD, THOMAS. Born June 25, 1954 in Ft. Wayne, In. Attended U.S.Intl.U., AmConsTh. Bdwy debut 1982 in "84 Charing Cross Road," followed by OB "A Midsummer Night's Dream," "Bigfoot Stole My Wife."

NAKAHARA, RON. Born July 20, 1947 in Honolulu, HI. Attended UHI. Tenri U. Debut 1981 OB in "Danton's Death," followed by "Flowers and Household Gods," "A Few Good Men," "Rohwer," "A Midsummer Night's Dream," "Teahouse," "Song for Nisei Fisherman," "Eat a Bowl of Tea," "Once Is Never Enough," "Shogun Macbeth," "Life of the Land."

NATALE, PATRICIA. Born Mar. 17, 1937 in Newark, NJ. Debut 1987 OB in "Wicked Philanthropy."

NEIL, ROGER. Born Nov. 19, 1948 in Galesburg, IL. Graduate Northwestern U. Debut 1974 OB in "The Boy Friend," followed by "Scrambled Feet," "The Fantasticks."

NEILSON, RICHARD. Born Nov. 30, 1924 in London, Eng. Debut 1959 OB in "Heloise," followed by "O Say Can You See," "Tea Party," "Pygmalion in Concert," Bdwy in "Pickwick" (1964), "Wise Child," "My Fair Lady," "Equus," "Pygmalion" (1987).

NELSON, BARRY. Born in 1920 in Oakland, Ca. Bdwy debut 1943 in "Winged Victory," followed by "Light Up the Sky," "The Moon Is Blue," "Wake Up Darling," "Rat Race," "Mary Mary," "Nobody Loves an Albatross," "The Cactus Flower," "Everything in the Garden," "Only Game in Town," "Fig Leaves Are Falling," "Engagement Baby," "Seascape," "The Norman Conquests," "The Act," "42nd Street."

NELSON, MARK. Born Sept. 26, 1955 in Hackensack, NJ. Graduate Princeton U. Debut 1977 OB in "The Dybbuk," followed by "Green Fields," "The Keymaker," "The Common Pursuit," Bdwy in "Amadeus" (1981), "Brighton Beach Memoirs," "Biloxi Blues."

NELSON, P. J. Born Nov. 17, 1952 in NYC. Attended Manhattan School of Music. Bdwy debut 1978 in "Hello, Dolly!," followed by "The Music Man," OB in "Something for the Boys," "New Girl in Town."

NEUBERGER, JAN. Born Jan. 21, 1953 in Amityville, NY. Attended NYU. Bdwy debut 1975 in "Gypsy," OB in "Silk Stockings," "Chase a Rainbow," "Anything Goes," "A Little Madness," "Forbidden Broadway."

NEWMAN, ANDREW HILL. Born Oct. 23, 1959 in Scarsdale, NY. Graduate UVt., Brandeis U. Bdwy debut 1982 in "Merlin," followed by "Big River," OB in "Little Shop of Horrors."

NEWMAN, PHYLLIS. Born Mar. 19, 1935 in Jersey City, NJ. Attended Western Reserve U. Bdwy debut 1953 in "Wish You Were Here," followed by "Bells Are Ringing," "First Impressions," "Subways are for Sleeping," "The Apple Tree," "On the Town," "Prisoner of Second Avenue," "Madwoman of Central Park West," "Miami," "I Married an Angel in Concert," "Broadway Bound," OB in "I Feel Wonderful," "Make Someone Happy," "I'm Getting My Act Together," "Red River," "The New Yorkers."

NEWMAN, STEPHEN D. Born Jan. 20, 1943 in Seattle, Wa. Graduate Stanford U. Debut 1971 OB in "Hamlet," followed by "School for Wives," "Beggar's Opera," "Pygmalion," "In the Voodoo Parlor," "Richard III," "Santa Anita '42," "Polly," "Rosencrantz and Guildenstern Are Dead," Bdwy in "An Evening with Richard Nixon," "Emperor Henry IV," "Habeas Corpus," "Rex," "Dirty Linen," "Dogg's Hamlet, Cahoot's Macbeth," "The Misanthrope."

NEWMAN, WILLIAM. Born June 15, 1934 in Chicago, Il. Graduate UWVa, Columbia U. Debut 1972 OB in "Beggar's Opera," followed by "Are You Now . . .?," "Conflict of Interest," "Mr. Runaway," "Uncle Vanya," "One Act Play Festival," "Routed," "The Great Divide," "Come Back Little Sheba," "Hit Parade," "Women Beware Women," Bdwy in "Over Here" (1974), "Rocky Horror Show," "Strangers."

NICHOLSON, CASEY. Born Oct. 6, 1962 in Santa Monica, Ca. Attended UCLA. Debut 1986 OB in "Pajama Game."

NICOLAISEN, KARI. Born Feb. 16, 1961 in San Francisco, Ca. Debut 1987 OB in "Wish You Were Here," followed by "Something for the Boys," Bdwy in "A Chorus Line" (1987).

NIELSEN, TOM. Born Jan. 30, 1955 in Milwaukee, Wi. Attended UWi. Debut 1987 OB in "Pas de Deux."

NIESPOLO, JOHN. Born Feb. 5, 1944 in Brooklyn, NY. Graduate Loyola U, Oxford U. Debut 1984 OB in "Jack Came Tumbling Down," followed by "The Wood Demon," "The Miracle Worker."

NIXON, CYNTHIA. Born Apr. 9, 1966 in NYC. Debut 1980 in "The Philadelphia Story"(LC) for which she received a Theatre World Award, OB in "Lydie Breeze," "Hurlyburly," "Sally's Gone, She Left Her Name," "Lemon Sky," "Cleveland and Half-Way Back," "Alterations." Bdwy in "The Real Thing" (1983), "Hurlyburly."

NOLAN, KATHLEEN. Born Sept. 27, 1933 in St. Louis, Mo. Attended Neighborhood Playhouse. Bdwy debut 1954 in "Peter Pan," followed by "Love in E-Flat," OB in "Accounts," "Copperhead."

NORCIA, PATRIZIA. Born Apr. 6, 1954 in Rome, Italy. Graduate Hofstra U., Yale. Debut 1978 OB in "Sganarelle," followed by "The Master and Margarita," "The Loves of Cass McGuire," "Fanshen," "The Price of Genius," "The Taming of the Shrew," "Epic Proportions."

NORMAN, DARA. Born Aug. 8 in NYC. Attended UCin., UMiami. Bdwy debut 1975 in "The Magic Show," followed by "Oh! Calcutta!," OB in "Dr. Selavy's Magic Theatre," "Beggar's Opera," "The Boys in the Live Country Band," "Talking Dirty," "Between Time and Timbuktu."

NORMAN, JOHN. Born May 13, 1961 in Detroit, Mi. Graduate Cincinnati Conservatory. Bdwy debut 1987 in "Les Miserables."

NORMAN, RENDE RAE. Born Apr. 1, 1958 in Pryor, Ok. Graduate Emporia State U, Southwest MoStateU. Debut 1985 OB in "Rabboni," followed by "Nuclear Follies," "The Rise of David Levinsky."

NOTO, LORE. Born June 9, 1923 in NYC. Attended AADA. Debut 1940 OB in "The Master Builder," followed by "Chee Chee," "Time Predicted," "Bomb Shelter," "Armor of Light," "Truce of the Bear," "Shake Hands with the Devil," "The Italian Straw Hat," "The Failures," "The Fantasticks" (continuously since 1972).

NUGENT, JAMES. Born June 22, 1940 in The Bronx, NY. Graduate UFla. Debut 1984 OB in "Air Rights," followed by "The Merchant of Venice," "Arms and the Man," "Mme. Colombe," "Two Gentlemen of Verona," "Days to Come," "The Good Doctor," "Pericles," "The Rivals," "Lady from the Sea," "Deep Swimmer."

NUGENT, JAMES. Born June 22, 1940 in The Bronx, NY. Graduate UFla. Debut 1984 OB in "Air Rights," followed by "The Merchant of Venus," "Arms and the Man," "Mme. Colombe," "Two Gentlemen of Verona," "Days to Come," "The Good Doctor," "Lady from the Sea," "Two Gentlemen from Verona."

NUSSBAUM, MIKE. Born Dec. 29, 1923 in Chicago, Il. Attended UWisc. Bdwy debut 1984 in "Glengarry Glen Ross," followed by "House of Blue Leaves," OB in "The Shawl," "Principia Scriptoriae," "Marathon '86," "Little Murders."

NUTE, DON. Born Mar. 13, in Connellsville, PA. Attended Denver U. Debut OB 1965 in "The Trojan Women" followed by "Boys in the Band," "Mad Theatre for Madmen," "The Eleventh Dynasty," "About Time," "The Urban Crisis," "Christmas Rappings," "The Life of a Man," "A Look at the Fifties."

NYGREN, CARRIE. Born Nov. 26, 1961 in Sweden. Attended Lee Strasberg Inst. Bdwy debut 1986 in "Sweet Charity."

OAKES, CINDY. Born Mar. 25, 1959 in Homestead, Pa. Graduate UPittsburgh. Bdwy debut 1986 in "Me and My Girl," followed by "Smile."

O'CONNELL, IAN. Born Nov. 10, 1945 in Sligo, Ire. Graduate UNC. Debut 1976 OB in "Maggie Flynn," followed by "Twelfth Night," "Triangles."

O'CONNELL, PATRICK. Born July 7, 1957 in Westport, Ct. Graduate Juilliard. Bdwy debut 1983 in "Amadeus," OB in "A Man for All Seasons" (1987).

O'CONNOR, KEVIN. Born May 7, 1938 in Honolulu, HI. Attended UHi., Neighborhood Playhouse. Debut 1964 OB in "Up to Thursday," followed by "Six from La Mama," "Rimers of Eldritch," "Tom Paine," "Boy on the Straightback Chair," "Dear Janet Rosenberg," "Eyes of Chalk," "Alive and Well in Argentina," "Duet," "Trio," "The Contractor," "Kool Aid," "The Frequency," "Chucky's Hutch," "Birdbath," "The Breakers," "Crossing the Crab Nebula," "Jane Avril," "Inserts," "3 by Beckett," "The Dicks," "A Kiss Is Just a Kiss," "Last of the Knucklemen," "Thrombo," "The Dark and Mr. Stone," "The Miser," Bdwy in "Gloria and Esperanza," "The Morning after Optimism," "Figures in the Sand," "Devour the Snow," "The Lady from Dubuque."

O'HARA, PAIGE. Born May 10, 1956 in Ft. Lauderdale, FL. Debut 1975 OB in "The Gift of the Magi," followed by "Company," "The Great American Backstage Musical," "Oh, Boy!," "Rabboni," Bdwy in "Show Boat" (1983), "The Mystery of Edwin Drood."

O'HERN, JOHN. Born Jan. 2, 1953 in Albany, NY. Graduate St. Michael's Col. Debut 1986 OB in "Out!"

O'KEEFE, MICHAEL. Born Apr. 24, 1955 in Westchester, NY. Attended NYU. Debut 1974 OB in "The Killdeer," followed by "Christmas on Mars," "Short Eyes," Bdwy in "5th of July," "Mass Appeal" for which he received a Theatre World Award.

OLIVER, ROCHELLE. Born Apr. 15, 1937 in NYC. Attended Brooklyn Col. Bdwy debut 1960 in "Toys in the Attic," followed by "Harold," "Who's Afraid of Virginia Woolf?," "Happily Never After," OB in "Brothers Karamazov," "Jack Knife," "Vincent," "Stop, You're Killing Me," "Enclave," "Bits and Pieces," "Roads to Home," "A Flower Palace."

OLSON, MARCUS. Born Sept. 21, 1955 in Missoula, Mt. Graduate Amherst Col. Debut 1986 in "Personals," followed by "Where the Cookie Crumbles."

O'ROURKE, KEVIN. Born Jan. 25, 1956 in Portland, OR. Graduate Williams Col. Debut 1981 OB in "Declassee," followed by "Sister Mary Ignatius . . .," "Submariners," "A Midsummer Night's Dream," "Visions of Kerouac," "Self Defense," Bdwy in "Alone Together" (1984).

O'SHEA, MILO. Born June 2, 1926 in Dublin, Ire. Bdwy debut 1968 in "Staircase," followed by "Dear World," "Mrs. Warren's Profession," "Comedians," "A Touch of the Poet," "Mass Appeal," "Corpse," OB in "Waiting for Godot," "Mass Appeal," "The Return of Herbert Bracewell," "Educating Rita."

O'SULLIVAN, ANNE. Born Feb. 6, 1952 in Limerick City, Ire. Debut 1977 OB in "Kid Champion," followed by "Hello Out There," "Fly Away Home," "The Drunkard," "Dennis," "The Three Sisters," "Another Paradise," "Living Quarters," "Welcome to the Moon," "the dreamer examines his pillow," "Mama Drama," "Free Fall."

O'TOOLE, PETER. Born Aug. 2, 1932 in Connemara, Ire. Attended RADA. Bdwy debut 1987 in "Pygmalion."

OWENS, ELIZABETH. Born Feb. 26, 1938 in NYC. Attended New School, Neighborhood Playhouse. Debut 1955 OB in "Dr. Faustus Lights the Lights," followed by "Chit Chat on a Rat," "The Miser," "The Father", "The Importance of Being Earnest," "Candida," "Trumpets and Drums," "Oedipus," "Macbeth," "Uncle Vanya," "Misalliance," "The Play's the Thing," "The Rivals," "Death Story," "The Rehearsal," "Dance on a Country Grave," "Othello," "Little Eyolf," "The Winslow Boy," "Playing with Fire," "The Chalk Garden," "The Entertainer," "The Killing of Sister George," "Waltz of the Toreadors," "The Miracle Worker," Bdwy in "The Lovers," "Not Now Darling," "The Play's the Thing."

OWSLEY, STEVE. Born Aug. 2, 1957 in Michigan City, In. Graduate Western Mi.U. Debut 1984 OB in "Red, Hot and Blue," Bdwy in "Grind" (1985), followed by "Raggedy Ann."

PAIS, JOSH. Born June 21, 1958 in Princeton, NJ. Graduate Syracuse U., LAMDA. Debut 1985 OB in "Short Change," followed by "I'm Not Rappaport," "The Lower Depths," "The Survivor," "Untitled Play," Bdwy in "I'm Not Rapport" (1987).

PALANCE, BROOKE. Born Feb. 7, 1954 in NYC. Attended CalInst of Arts. Debut 1986 OB in "The Fox," followed by "Bedroom Farce."

PALEY, PETRONIA. Born May 31, in Albany, Ga. Graduate Howard U. Debut 1972 OB in "Us vs Nobody," followed by "The Cherry Orchard," "The Corner," "Three Sisters," "Frost of Renaissance," "Long Time Since Yesterday," Bdwy in "The First Breeze of Summer" (1975).

PALMER, JEANETTE. Born Sept. 15, 1955 in Salem, Ma. Attended Boston Consv. Debut 1987 OB in "Take Me Along."

PARLATO, DENNIS. Born Mar. 30, 1947 in Los Angeles, Ca. Graduate Loyola U. Bdwy debut 1979 in "A Chorus Line," followed by "The First," OB in "Beckett," "Elizabeth and Essex," "The Fantasticks," "Moby Dick," "The Knife," "Shylock," "Have I Got A Girl for You."

PARRY, WILLIAM. Born Oct. 7, 1947 in Steubenville, Oh. Graduate Mt. Union Col. Bdwy debut 1971 in "Jesus Christ Superstar," followed by "Rockabye Hamlet," "The Leaf People," "Camelot" (1980), "Sunday in the Park with George," "Into the Light," OB in "Sgt. Pepper's Lonely Hearts Club Band," "The Conjurer," "Noah," "The Misanthrope," "Joseph and the Amazing Technicolor Dreamcoat," "Agamemnon," "Coolest Cat in Town," "Dispatches," "The Derby," "The Knife."

PASSELTINER, BERNIE. Born Nov. 21, 1931 in NYC. Graduate Catholic U. OB in "Square in the Eye," "Sourball," "As Virtuously Given," "Now Is the Time for All Good Men," "Rain," "Kaddish," "Against the Sun," "End of Summer," "Yentl, the Yeshiva Boy," "Heartbreak House," "Every Place Is Newark," "Isn't It Romantic," "Buck," "Pigeons on the Walk," "Waving Goodbye," Bdwy in "The Office," "The Jar," "Yentl."

PATINKIN, MANDY. Born Nov. 30, 1952 in Chicago, Il. Attended Juilliard. OB in "Henry IV," followed by "Leave It to Beaver Is Dead," "Rebel Women," "Hamlet," "Trelawny of the Wells," "Savages," "The Split," "The Knife," Bdwy in "Evita" (1979), "Sunday in the Park with George."

PATTERSON, DICK. Born in Clear Lake, Ia. Graduate UCLA. Bdwy debut in "Vintage 1960," followed by "The Billy Barnes People," "Bye Bye Birdie," "Fade-Out, Fade-In," "Something Old, Something New," "Smile."

PATTON, LUCILLE. Born in NYC; attended Neighborhood Playhouse. Bdwy debut 1946 in "A Winter's Tale," followed by "Topaze," "Arms and the Man," "Joy to the World," "All You Need Is One Good Break," "Fifth Season," "Heavenly Twins," "Rhinoceros," "Marathon 33," "The Last Analysis," "Dinner at 8," "La Strada," "Unlikely Heroes," "Love Suicide at Schofield Barracks," OB in "Ulysses in Nighttown," "Failures," "Three Sisters," "Yes Yes No No," "Tango," "Mme. de Sade," "Apple Pie," "Follies," "Yesterday Is Over," "My Prince, My King," "I Am Who I Am," "Double Game," "Love in a Village," "1984."

Jeffery
Logan

Denise
Lor

Marc
Lutsky

Mia
Malm

Charles
Mandracchia

Laura
Margolis

Rica
Martens

Tom
Matsusaka

Marin
Mazzie

Jeff
McCarthy

Lynda
McConnell

Dermot
McNamara

Wayne
Meledandri

Jeannette
Mirabal

Bill
Moor

Kari
Nicolaisen

Don
Nute

Cindy
Oakes

Rochelle
Oliver

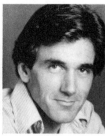
Dennis
Parlato

Lucille
Patton

Stephen
Pearlman

Gail
Pennington

Luis
Perez

Kurt
Peterson

Lenka
Peterson

Dennis
Pfister

Katell
Pleven

David
Purdham

Bernadette
Quigley

216

PAYAN, ILKA TANYA. Born Jan. 7, 1943 in Santo Domingo, DR. Attended Peoples Col. of Law. Debut 1969 OB in "The Respectful Prostitute," followed by "Francesco Cenci," "The Effect of Gamma Rays . . .," "Blood Wedding," "Miss Margarida's Way," "The Bitter Tears of Petra Von Kant," "The Servant."

PEACH, MARY. Born in Durban, S. Africa in 1934. Bdwy debut 1987 in "Pygmalion."

PEACOCK, CHIARA. Born Sept. 19, 1962 in Ann Arbor, Mi. Graduate Sarah Lawrence Col. Debut 1985 OB in "Yours, Anne," followed by "Maggie Magalita."

PEARCE, EVE. Born Apr. 17, 1929 in Aberdeen, Scot. Graduate RADA. Bdwy debut 1986 in "The Life and Adventures of Nicholas Nickleby."

PEARLMAN, STEPHEN. Born Feb. 26, 1935 in NYC. Graduate Dartmouth Col. Bdwy bow 1964 in "Barefoot in the Park," followed by "La Strada," OB in "Threepenny Opera," "Time of the Key," "Pimpernel," "In White America," "Viet Rock," "Chocolates," "Bloomers," "Richie," "Isn't It Romantic," "Bloodletters," "Light Up the Sky," "The Perfect Party."

PEARSON, SCOTT. Born Dec. 13, 1941 in Milwaukee, WI. Attended Valparaiso U, UWisc. Bdwy debut 1966 in "A Joyful Noise," followed by "Promises, Promises," "A Chorus Line."

PELZER, BETTY. Born in Berkeley, Ca. Graduate Stanford U. Bdwy debut 1979 in "Wings," OB in "Suddenly Last Summer," "Henhouse."

PENDLETON, AUSTIN. Born Mar. 27, 1940 in Warren, Oh. Attended Yale U. Debut 1962 OB in "Oh, Dad, Poor Dad . . .," followed by "The Last Sweet Days of Isaac," "The Three Sisters," "Say Goodnight, Gracie," "The Office Murders," "Up from Paradise," "The Overcoat," "Two Character Play," "Master Class," "Educating Rita," Bdwy in "Fiddler on the Roof," "Hail Scrawdyke," "The Little Foxes," "American Millionaire," "The Runner Stumbles," "Doubles."

PENNINGTON, GAIL. Born Oct. 2, 1957 in Kansas City, MO. Graduate SMU. Bdwy debut 1980 in "The Music Man," followed by "Can-Can," "America," "Little Me" (1982), "42nd Street," OB in "The Baker's Wife."

PERCASSI, DON. Born Jan. 11 in Amsterdam, NY. Bdwy debut 1964 in "High Spirits," followed by "Walking Happy," "Coco," "Sugar," "Molly," "Mack and Mabel," "A Chorus Line," "42nd Street."

PEREZ, LUIS. Born July 28, 1959 in Atlanta, Ga. With Joffrey Ballet before 1986 debut in "Brigadoon" (LC), OB in "The Wonderful Ice Cream Suit."

PEREZ, MERCEDES. Born Oct. 25, 1961 in Arlington, Va. Debut 1983 OB in "Skyline," followed by Bdwy in "Take Me Along" (1985), "A Chorus Line."

PERKINS, JOHN. Born May 7, 1927 in Boston, Ma. Attended Irvine Studio. Bdwy debut 1951 in "Romeo and Juliet," followed by "Wish You Were Here," "The Physicists," OB in "The Balcony," "Felix," "The Art of War."

PERLEY, WILLIAM. Born Nov. 24, 1942 in NYC. Graduate UFla. Debut 1975 OB in "Tenderloin," followed by "Housewives, Cantata," "Count of Monte Cristo," "The Marquise," "Camp Meeting," Bdwy in "Vieux Carre" (1977).

PERRY, ELIZABETH. Born Oct. 18, 1937 in Pawtuxet, RI. Attended RISU, AmThWing. Bdwy debut 1956 in "Inherit the Wind," followed by "The Women," with APA in "The Misanthrope," "Hamlet," "Exit the King," "Beckett" and "Macbeth," OB in "Royal Gambit," "Here Be Dragons," "Lady from the Sea," "Heartbreak House," "him," "All the Way Home," "The Frequency," "Fefu and Her Friends," "Out of the Broomcloset," "Ruby Ruby Sam Sam," "Did You See the Elephant?," "Last Stop Blue Jay Lane," "A Difficult Borning," "Presque Isle," "Isn't It Romantic."

PESATURO, GEORGE. Born July 29, 1949 in Winthrop, MA. Graduate Manhattan Col. Bdwy debut 1976 in "A Chorus Line," OB in "The Music Man" (JB).

PETER, FRANCES. Born June 27 in Chicago, Il. Attended U Chicago, AmThWing. Debut 1949 OB in "Lady from the Sea," followed by "Eccentricites of a Nightingale," "Fanny's First Play," "I Am a Camera," "Tartuffe," "Sold to the Movies," "Count Dracula," "Misbegotten Angels," "The Jew of Malta," "Postcards," "The Underlings."

PETERS, BERNADETTE. Born Feb. 28, 1948 in Jamaica, NY. Bdwy debut in "Girl in the Freudian Slip," followed by "Johnny No-Trump," "George M!" for which she received a Theatre World Award, "La Strada," "On the Town," "Mack and Mabel," "Sunday in the Park with George," "Song and Dance," OB in "Curley McDimple," "Penny Friend," "Most Happy Fella," "Dames at Sea," "Nevertheless They Laugh," "Sally and Marsha."

PETERS, JANNE. Born Nov. 2, 1949 in Minneapolis, Mn. Graduate MankatoStateU. Debut OB in "The Bitter Tears of Petra Von Kant" (1986).

PETERSEN, ERIKA. Born Mar. 24, 1949 in NYC. Attended NYU. Debut 1963 OB in "One Is a Lonely Number," followed by "I Dreamt I Dwelt in Bloomingdale's," "F. Jasmine Addams," "The Dubliners," "P.S. Your Cat Is Dead," "The Possessed," "Murder in the Cathedral," "The Further Inquiry," "State of the Union," "Brand," "Frankenstein," "Death and the King's Horseman."

PETERSON, KURT. Born Feb. 12, 1948 in Stevens Point, Wi. Attended AMDA. Bdwy debut 1969 in "Dear World," followed by "Follies," "Knickerbocker Holiday," OB in "An Ordinary Miracle," "West Side Story" (LC), "Dames at Sea," "By Bernstein," "I Married an Angel in Concert."

PETERSON, RICHARD. Born Apr. 25, 1945 in Palo Alto, Ca. Graduate Boston U. Debut 1972 OB in "Antony and Cleopatra," followed by "Titanic," "Twelfth Night," "Looking Glass," "The Front Page" (LC).

PFISTER, DENNIS. Born Sept. 27, 1951 in Detroit, Mi. Debut 1980 OB in "Romeo and Juliet," followed by "Two Gentlemen of Verona," "Relative Values."

PHELAN, DEBORAH. Born Apr. 15 in New Haven, CT. Graduate Point Park Col. Bdwy debut in "Pippin" (1973), followed by "King of Hearts," "A Chorus Line," "Dancin'," "Encore," "La Cage aux Folles," "Jerry's Girls."

PHILLIPS, RANDY. Born Jan. 22, 1926 in NYC. Attended Juilliard. Bdwy debut in "How to Succeed in Business . . .," followed by "Hello, Dolly!," "Mame," OB in "Pinafore," "Riverwind," "Mink Sonata."

PICARD, NICOLE. Born Oct. 19, 1960 in Rhode Island. Graduate Sarah Lawrence Col. Debut 1984 OB in "A View from the Bridge," followed by "Cry of Angels," Bdwy in "Starlight Express" (1987).

PICKLES, CHRISTINA. Born Feb. 17, 1938 in Eng. Attended RADA. Bdwy in APA's "School for Scandal," "War and Peace," "The Wild Duck," "Pantagleize," "You Can't Take It with You," "The Seagull" and "The Misanthrope," "Inadmissible Evidence," "Who's Who in Hell," "Sherlock Holmes," OB in "Chez Nous," "Death of a Buick."

PIERCE, DAVID. Born Apr. 3, 1959 in Albany, NY. Graduate Yale U. Debut 1982 on Bdwy in "Beyond Therapy," followed by OB in "Summer," "That's It, Folks!," "The Three Zeks," "Donuts," "Hamlet," "The Maderati," "Marathon 87."

PIETROPINTO, ANGELA. Born Feb. 5, in NYC. Graduate NYU. OB credits include "Henry IV," "Alice in Wonderland," "Endgame," "Our Late Night," "The Sea Gull," "Jinx Bridge," "The Mandrake," "Marie and Bruce," "Green Card Blues," "3 by Pirandello," "The Broken Pitcher," "A Midsummer Night's Dream," "The Rivals," "Cap and Bells," "Thrombo," "Lies My Father Told Me," "Twelfth Night," Bdwy in "The Suicide" (1980).

PIKSER, ROBERTA. Born in Chicago, Il. Graduate U Chicago. Debut 1986 OB in "The War Party."

PITONIAK, ANNE. Born Mar. 30, 1922 in Westfield, MA. Attended UNC Women's Col. Debut 1982 OB in "Talking With," followed by "Young Playwrights Festival," Bdwy in "'night, Mother" (1983) for which she received a Theatre World Award, "The Octette Bridge Club."

PLANK, SCOTT. Born Nov. 11, 1958 in Washington, DC. Attended NCSch of Arts. Bdwy debut 1981 in "Dreamgirls," followed by "A Chorus Line," OB in "Death of a Buick."

PLAYTEN, ALICE. Born Aug. 28, 1947 in NYC. Attended NYU. Bdwy debut 1960 in "Gypsy" followed by "Oliver," "Hello, Dolly!," "Henry Sweet Henry," for which she received a Theatre World Award, "George M!," OB in "Promenade," "The Last Sweet Days of Isaac," "National Lampoon's Lemmings," "Valentine's Day," "Pirates of Penzance," "Up from Paradise," "A Visit," "Sister Mary Ignatius Explains It All," "An Actor's Nightmare," "That's It, Folks."

PLEVEN, KATELL. Born Apr. 9, 1962 in Brooklyn, NY. Graduate Hampshire Col. Debut 1987 OB in "Women Beware Women."

PLUMMER, AMANDA. Born Mar. 23, 1957 in NYC. Attended Middlebury Col., Neighborhood Playhouse. Debut 1978 OB in "Artichoke," followed by "A Month in the Country," "A Taste of Honey" for which she received a Theatre World Award, "Alice in Concert," "A Stitch in Time," "Life under Water," "A Lie of the Mind," Bdwy in "A Taste of Honey," "Agnes of God," "The Glass Menagerie," "You Never Can Tell," "Pygmalion" (1987).

PLUNKETT, MARYANN. Born In 1953 in Lowell, Ma. Attended UNH. Bdwy debut 1983 in "Agnes of God," followed by "Sunday in the Park with George," "Me and My Girl."

POE, RICHARD. Born Jan. 25, 1946 In Portola, Ca. Graduate USanFrancisco, UCal/Davis. Debut 1971 OB in "Hamlet," followed by "Seasons Greetings," "Twelfth Night."

POGGI, JACK. Born June 14, 1928 in Oakland, Ca. Graduate Harvard, Columbia U. Debut 1962 OB in "This Side of Paradise," followed by "The Tavern," "Dear Janet Rosenberg," "House Music," "The Closed Door," "Ghosts," "Uncle Vanya," "Tiger at the Gates," "Wars of Roses," "Pajama Game."

POLIS, JOEL. Born Oct. 3, 1951 in Philadelphia, Pa. Graduate USC, Yale. Debut 1976 OB in "Marco Polo," followed by "Family Business," "Just Like the Night," "Claptrap."

POLLACK, DANIEL. Born July 25, 1927 in NYC. Graduate CCNY, Adelphi, NYU. Debut 1949 OB in "An American Tragedy," followed by "Goodnight, Grandpa," "Victory Bonds," "Imaginary Invalid," "Six Candles," Bdwy in "The Price" (1979).

PONAZECKI, JOE. Born Jan. 7, 1934 in Rochester, NY. Attended Rochester U, Columbia U. Bdwy debut 1959 in "Much Ado about Nothing," followed by "Send Me No Flowers," "A Call on Kuprin," "Take Her She's Mine," "Fiddler on the Roof," "Xmas in Las Vegas," "3 Bags Full," "Love in E-Flat," "90 Day Mistress," "Harvey," "Trial of the Catonsville 9," "The Country Girl," "Freedom of the City," "Summer Brave," "Music Is," "The Little Foxes," OB in "The Dragon," "Muzeeka," "Witness," "All Is Bright," "The Dog Ran Away," "Dream of a Blacklisted Actor," "Innocent Pleasures," "Dark at the Top of the Stairs," "36," "After the Revolution," "The Raspberry Picker," "Raisin' in the Sun," "Light Up the Sky," "Marathon '86."

PORTER, RICK. Born Jan. 21, 1951 in Fall River, Ma. Graduate Bates Col., Brandeis U. Debut OB 1981 in "Catch 22," followed by "Philco Blues," "Tallulah," "Silverlake," "She Loves Me," "Chili Queen," "Pajama Game."

POTTER, DON. Born Aug. 15, 1932 in Philadelphia, Pa. Debut 1961 OB in "What a Killing," followed by "Sunset," "You're a Good Man, Charlie Brown," "One Cent Plain," "The Ritz," Bdwy in "Gypsy" (1974), "Snow White," "Moose Murders," "42nd Street."

PRICE, LONNY. Born Mar. 9, 1959 in NYC. Attended Juilliard. Debut 1979 OB in "Class Enemy" for which he received a Theatre World Award, followed by "Up from Paradise," "Rommel's Garden," "Times and Appetites of Toulouse-Lautrec," "Room Service," Bdwy 1980 in "The Survivor," followed by "Merrily We Roll Along," "Master Harold and the boys," "The Time of Your Life," "Children of the Sun," "Rags."

PRIMUS, BARRY. Born Feb. 16, 1938 in NYC. Attended CCNY. Bdwy debut 1960 in "The Nervous Set," followed by "Oh, Dad, Poor Dad . . .," "Creation of the World and Other Business," "Teibele and Her Demon," OB in "Henry IV," "Huui, Huui," "The Criminals," "Diary of a Scoundrel," "Jesse and the Bandit Queen," "Dream of a Blacklisted Actor."

PRUITT, RICHARD. Born Jan. 20, 1950 in New Albany, In. Graduate IndU. Debut 1987 OB in "Wicked Philanthropy."

PULLIAM, ZELDA. Born Oct. 18 in Chicago, Il. Attended Roosevelt U. Bdwy debut 1969 in "Hello, Dolly!," followed by "Purlie," "Raisin," "Pippin," "Dancin'," OB in "Croesus and the Witch," "Abyssinia."

PURDHAM, DAVID. Born June 3, 1951 in San Antonio, TX. Graduate UMd., UWa. Debut 1980 OB in "Journey's End," followed by "Souvenirs," "Once on a Summer's Day," "Twelfth Night," "Maneuvers," "The Times and Appetites of Toulouse-Lautrec," "The Winter's Tale," "Rosencrantz and Guildenstern Are Dead," Bdwy in "Piaf" (1981).

PURI, RAJIKA. Born Sept. 14, 1945 in Daves-salaam, Tanzania. Graduate Delhi U. NYU. Debut 1986 OB in "The Transposed Heads" (LC).

QUIGLEY, BERNADETTE. Born Nov. 10, 1960 in Coldspring, NY. Debut 1983 OB in "Ah, Wilderness!," followed by "Relative Values."

QUINN, HENRY J. Born Aug. 6, 1928 in Boston, Ma. Graduate Catholic U. Debut 1979 OB in "The Sound of Music," followed by "Mrs. Warren's Profession," "Towards Zero," "Among the Fallen," "Misalliance."

QUINN, PATRICK. Born Feb. 12, 1950 in Philadelphia, PA. Graduate Temple U. Bdwy debut 1976 in "Fiddler on the Roof," followed by "A Day in Hollywood/A Night in the Ukraine," "Oh Coward!," OB in "It's Better with a Band," "By Strouse," "Forbidden Broadway," "A Little Night Music."

RACKLEFF, OWEN S. Born July 16, 1934 in NYC. Graduate Columbia U, London U. Bdwy debut 1977 in "Piaf," OB in "The Lesson" (1978), "Catsplay," "Arms and the Man," "Escoffier: King of Chefs," "New Way to Pay Old Debts," "Samson Agonistes," "Enter Laughing," "The Jew of Malta."

RAEBECK, LOIS. Born in West Chicago, Il. Graduate Columbia U. Debut 1986 OB in "Rule of Three," followed by "Cork," "Between Time and Timbuktu."

RAGNO, JOSEPH. Born Mar. 11, 1936 in Brooklyn, NY. Attended Allegheny Col. Debut 1960 OB in "Worm in the Horseradish," followed by "Elizabeth the Queen," "A Country Scandal," "The Shrike," "Cymbeline," "Love Me, Love My Children," "Interrogation of Havana," "The Birds," "Armenians," "Feedlot," "Every Place Is Newark," "Modern Romance," "Hunting Cockroaches," Bdwy in "Indians," "The Iceman Cometh."

RAIDER-WEXLER, VICTOR. Born Dec. 31, 1943 in Toledo, Oh. Attended UToledo. Debut 1976 OB in "The Prince of Homburg," followed by "The Passion of Dracula," "Ivanov," "Brandy before Breakfast," "The Country Girl," "Dream of a Blacklisted Actor," "One Act Festival," "Loveplay," "Our Own Family," Bdwy in "Best Friend" (1976).

RAIKEN, LAWRENCE/LARRY. Born Feb. 5, 1949 on Long Island, NY. Graduate William & Mary Col., UNC. Debut 1979 OB in "Wake Up, It's Time to Go to Bed," "The Rise of David Levinsky," "Bells Are Ringing," "Pageant," Bdwy in "Woman of the Year" (1981).

RAINES, ROGER. Born Nov. 25, 1965 in New York City; Attended NYU. Bdwy debut 1983 in "Brighton Beach Memoirs."

RAMAKER, JULIANNE. (a.k.a. Julie) Born Aug. 16, 1952 in LaCross, Wi. Graduate Drake U. OB in "The Real Inspector Hound," "Doctor in the House," "Hay Fever," "Shakespeare Panache," "Arms and the Man," "Uncle Vanya," "Twelfth Night," "A Midsummer Night's Dream," "Transformational Country Dances."

RANDEL, MELISSA. Born June 16, 1955 in Portland, ME. Graduate UCal/Irvine. Bdwy debut 1980 in "A Chorus Line."

RANDELL, RON. Born Oct. 8. 1920 in Sydney, Aust. Attended St. Mary's Col. Bdwy debut 1949 in "The Browning Version," followed by "Harlequinade," "Candida," "World of Suzie Wong," "Sherlock Holmes," "Mrs. Warren's Profession," "Measure for Measure," "Bent," "The Troll Palace," OB in "Holy Places," "After You've Gone," "Patrick Pearse Motel," "Maneuvers," "Swan Song," "A Man for All Season," "Rosencrantz and Guildenstern Are Dead."

RANDOLPH, JOHN. Born June 1, 1915 in The Bronx, NY. Attended CCNY, Actors Studio. Bdwy debut 1937 in "Revolt of the Beavers," followed by "The Emperor's New Clothes," "Capt. Jinks," "No More Peace," "Coriolanus," "Medicine Show," "Hold on to Your Hats," "Native Son," "Command Decision," "Come Back, Little Sheba," "Golden State," "Peer Gynt," "Paint Your Wagon," "Seagulls over Sorrento," "Grey-Eyed People," "Room Service," "All Summer Long," "House of Flowers," "The Visit," "Mother Courage," "Sound of Music," "Case of Libel," "Conversation at Midnight," "My Sweet Charlie," "The American Clock," "Broadway Bound," OB in "An Evening's Frost," "The Peddler and the Dodo Bird," "Our Town," "Line," "Baba Goya," "Nourish the Beast," "Back in the Race," "The American Clock."

RASHOVICH, GORDANA. Born Sept. 18 in Chicago, Il. Graduate Roosevelt U., RADA. Debut 1977 OB in "Fefu and Her Friends" for which she received a Theatre World Award, followed by "Selma," "Couple of the Year," "Mink Sonata."

RAVELO, HENRY. Born Aug. 14, 1958 in Manila, Phil. Attended UWis. Debut 1984 OB in "Pacific Overtures," followed by "Ghashiram," "South Pacific" (NYCOpera).

REAMS, LEE ROY. Born Aug. 23, 1942 in Covington, KY. Graduate U. Cinn. Cons. Bdwy debut 1966 in "Sweet Charity," followed by "Oklahoma!" (LC), "Applause," "Lorelei" "Show Boat" (JB), "Hello, Dolly!" (1978), "42nd Street," "La Cage aux Folles," OB in "Sterling Silver," "Potholes," "The Firefly in Concert."

REBHORN, JAMES. Born Sept. 1, 1948 in Philadelphia, PA. Graduate Wittenberg U, Columbia U. Debut 1972 OB in "Blue Boys," "Are You Now Or Have You Ever Been," "Trouble with Europe," "Othello," "Hunchback of Notre Dame," "Period of Adjustment," "The Freak," "Half a Lifetime," "Touch Black," "To Gillian on Her 37th Birthday," "Rain," "The Hasty Heart," "Husbandry," "Isn't It Romantic," "Blind Date," Bdwy in "I'm Not Rappaport."

REBICH, CISSY. Born May 20, 1952 in Aliquippa, Pa. Graduate Duquesne U. Debut 1980 OB in "Annie Get Your Gun," followed by "Bugout," "Gifts of the Magi," Bdwy in "Mame" (1983), "Rags.".

REDFIELD, ADAM. Born Nov. 4, 1959 in NYC. Attended NYU. Debut 1977 OB in "Hamlet," followed by "Androcles and the Lion," "Twelfth Night," "Reflected Glory," "Movin' Up," "The Unicorn," "Young Playwrights Festival," "Swan Song," Bdwy 1980 in "A Life" for which he received a Theatre World Award, followed by "Beethoven's Tenth," "Execution of Justice."

REDMAN, JOYCE. Born in 1918 in County Mayo, Ire. Attended RADA. Bdwy debut 1946 with the Old Vic Company "Henry IV Part II," "Uncle Vanya" and "Oedipus," followed by "Duet for Two Hands," "Anne of the Thousand Days," "Pygmalion" (1987).

REED, MAGGI-MEG. Born in Columbus, Oh. Graduate Harvard U. Debut 1984 OB in "She Stoops to Conquer," followed by "Playboy of the Western World," "Triangles."

REEHLING, JOYCE. Born Mar. 5, 1949 in Baltimore, Md. Graduate NCSchool of Arts. Debut 1976 OB in "Hot 1 Baltimore," followed by "Who Killed Richard Cory?," "Lulu," "5th of July," "The Runner Stumbles," "Life and/or Death," "Back in the Race," "Time Framed," "Extremities," "Hands of Its Enemy," Bdwy in "A Matter of Gravity" (1976), "5th of July."

REGION, DANIEL. Born Nov. 11, 1948 in Sandwich, IL. Debut 1981 OB in "Cowboy Mouth," followed by "Widows and Children First," "A Midsummer Night's Dream," "Beyond Therapy," "Taming of the Shrew," "Her Great Match," "Pericles," Bdwy in "Torch Song Trilogy" (1982).

REID, KATE. Born Nov. 4, 1930 in London, Eng. Attended Toronto U. Bdwy debut 1962 in "Who's Afraid of Virginia Woolf?," followed by "Dylan," "Slapstick Tragedy," "The Price," "Freedom of the City," "Cat on a Hot Tin Roof," "Bosoms and Neglect," "Morning's at 7," "Death of a Salesman," OB in "The Flower Palace."

REINGOLD, JACKIE. Born Mar. 13, 1959 in NYC. Graduate Oberlin Col. Debut 1978 OB in "A Wrinkle in Time," followed by "Marat/Sade," "Unfettered Letters," "Working One-Acts."

REINKING, ANN. Born Nov. 10, 1949 in Seattle, Wa. Attended Joffrey School, HB Studio. Bdwy debut 1969 in "Cabaret," followed by "Coco," "Pippin," "Over Here" for which she received a Theatre World Award, "Goodtime Charley," "A Chorus Line," "Chicago," "Dancin'," "Sweet Charity" (1986), OB in "One More Song/One More Dance," "Music Moves Me."

REISSA, ELEANOR. Born May 11 in Brooklyn, NY. Graduate Brooklyn Col. Debut 1979 OB in "Rebecca the Rabbi's Daughter," followed by "That's Not Funny That's Sick," "The Rise of David Levinsky," "Match Made in Heaven."

RENDERER, SCOTT. Born in Palo Alto, Ca. Graduate Whitman Col. Bdwy debut 1983 in "Teaneck Tanzi," OB in "And Things That Go Bump in the Night," "Crossfire," "Just Like the Lions," "the dreamer examines his pillow."

REPOLE, CHARLES. Born May 24, 1945 in Brooklyn, NY. Graduate Hofstra U. Bdwy debut 1975 in "Very Good Eddie," for which he received a Theatre World Award, followed by "Finian's Rainbow," "Whoopee!," "Doubles," OB in "Make Someone Happy," "George White's Scandals," "Olympus on My Mind."

REYNOLDS, BILL. Born June 25, 1927 in Cotulla, Tx. Graduate UTx. Bdwy debut 1957 in "Most Happy Fella," followed by "Carousel" (CC), OB in "Stud Silo," "Too Many Girls."

REYNOLDS, JEFFREY. Born Apr. 1, 1932 in El Paso, Tx. Bdwy debut 1973 in "Irene," followed by "The Debbie Reynolds Show," "Woman of the Year," OB in "Cowboy."

REYNOLDS, VICKILYN. Born June 2, 1955 in Philadelphia, Pa. Debut 1986 OB in "The Colored Museum."

RICE, REVA. Born in Toledo, Ohio, in 1961. Attended Boston Cons. of Music. Bdwy debut 1987 in "Starlight Express."

RICE, SARAH. Born Mar. 5, 1955 in Okinawa. Attended AzStateU. Debut 1974 OB in "The Fantasticks," followed by "The Enchantress," "The Music Man," "Swan Song," Bdwy 1979 in "Sweeney Todd" for which she received a Theatre World Award.

RICHARDS, CAROL. Born Dec. 26 in Aurora, IL. Graduate Northwestern U, Columbia U. Bdwy debut 1965 in "Half a Sixpence," followed by "Mame," "Last of the Red Hot Lovers," "Company," "Cats."

RICHARDS, JESS. Born Jan. 23, 1943 in Seattle, WA. Attended UWash. Bdwy debut 1966 in "Walking Happy," followed by "South Pacific" (LC) "Two by Two," "On the Town" for which he received a Theatre World Award, "Mack and Mabel," "Musical Chairs," "A Reel American Hero," "Barnum," OB in "One for the Money," "Lovesong," "A Musical Evening with Josh Logan," "The Lullaby of Broadway," "All Night Strut!, ""Station Joy."

RICHARDSON, LaTANYA. Born Oct. 21, 1949 in Atlanta, Ga. Graduate Spelman Col. Debut 1976 OB in "Perdido," followed by "Unfinished Women Cry in No Man's Land," "Spell #7," "The Trial of Dr. Beck," "Charlotte's Web," "Nonsectarian Conversations with the Dead," "An Organdy Falsetto," "Boogie Woogie and Booker T."

RICHARDSON, PATRICIA. Born Feb. 23 in Bethesda, MD. Graduate SMU. Bdwy debut 1974 in "Gypsy," followed by "Loose Ends," "The Wake of Jamey Foster," OB in "Coroner's Plot," "Vanities," "Hooters," "The Frequency," "Fables for Friends," "The Miss Firecracker Contest," "Cruise Control," "Trinity Site."

RICHERT, WANDA. Born Apr. 18, 1958 in Chicago, IL. Bdwy debut 1980 in "42nd Street" for which she received a Theatre World Award, followed by "Nine," "A Chorus Line."

RIDDLE, SAM. Born Aug. 4, 1980 in Missoula, Mt. Debut 1987 OB in "Wicked Philanthropy."

RIEBLING, TIA. Born July 21, 1964 in Pittsburgh, Pa. Attended NYU, Carnegie-Mellon U. Debut OB 1983 in "American Passion," followed by "Preppies," "Hamelin," "Wish You Were Here," Bdwy in "Smile" (1986).

RIEGELMAN, RUSTY. Born Sept. 9, 1948 in Kansas City, Mo. Attended UCin. Bdwy debut 1981 in "This Was Burlesque," followed by OB in "Not Now Darling," "Pal Joey," "Olympus on My Mind."

RIEGERT, PETER. Born Apr. 11, 1947 in NYC. Graduate UBuffalo. Debut 1975 OB in "Dance with Me," followed by "Sexual Perversity in Chicago," "Sunday Runners," "Isn't It Romantic," "La Brea Tarpits," "A Hell of a Town," "Festival of One Acts," "A Rosen by Any Other Name," Bdwy in "The Nerd" (1987).

RIGNACK, ROGER. Born Sept. 24, 1962 in NYC. Graduate Emerson Col. Debut 1985 OB in "Dead! A Love Story," followed by "Disappearing Acts," "The Red Madonna," "Our Lady of the Tortilla."

RILEY, LARRY. Born June 21, 1952 in Memphis, TN. Graduate Memphis State U. Bdwy debut 1978 in "A Broadway Musical," followed by "I Love My Wife," "Night and Day," "Shakespeare's Cabaret," "Big River," OB in "Street Songs," "Amerika," "Plane Down," "Sidewalkin'," "Frimbo," "A Soldier's Play," "Maybe I'm Doing It Wrong," "Diamonds," "The Leader."

RINEHART, ELAINE. Born Aug. 16 in San Antonio, Tx. Graduate NC School of Arts. Debut 1975 OB in "Tenderloin," followed by "Native Son," "Joan of Lorraine," "Dumping Ground," "Fairweather Friends," "Roots," "Bachelor Flats," Bdwy in "The Best Little Whorehouse in Texas."

RINGWALD, MOLLY. Born in 1968 in Sacramento, Ca. Debut 1986 OB in "Lily Dale" for which she received a Theatre World Award.

RISEMAN, NAOMI. Born Oct. 6, 1930 in Boston, Ma. Graduate NYU, Columbia U. Debut 1959 OB in "Boo Hoo East Lynn," followed by "Merry Wives of Windsor," "The Lady's Not for Burning," "Romeo and Juliet," "Ernest in Love," "Will the Mail Train Run Tonight?," "Once in a Lifetime," "Promenade," "Heartbreak House," "About Heaven and Earth," "The Closed Door," "Relative Values," Bdwy in "Status Quo Vadis" (1973), "How to Be a Jewish Mother," "Fiddler on the Roof."

RIVERA, MICHAEL. Born Jan. 21, 1949 in NYC. Attended Richmond Col. Bdwy debut 1979 in "Carmelina," followed by "West Side Story," "Marilyn, An American Fable," "Shakespeare on Broadway."

ROBARDS, JASON. Born July 26, 1922 in Chicago, Il. Attended AADA. Bdwy debut 1947 with D'Oyly Carte, followed by "Stalag 17," "The Chase," "Long Day's Journey into Night" for which he received a Theatre World Award, "The Disenchanted," "Toys in the Attic," "Big Fish Little Fish," "A Thousand Clowns," "Hughie," "The Devils," "We Bombed in New Haven," "The Country Girl," "Moon for the Misbegotten," "A Touch of the Poet," "You Can't Take It with You," "The Iceman Cometh," "A Month of Sundays," OB in "American Gothic," "The Iceman Cometh," "After the Fall," "But For Whom Charlie," "Long Day's Journey into Night."

ROBB, R. D. Born Mar. 31, 1972 in Philadelphia, Pa. Bdwy debut 1980 in "Charlie and Algernon," followed by "Oliver!," "Les Miserables."

ROBERTS, TONY. Born Oct. 22, 1939 in NYC. Graduate Northwestern U. Bdwy debut 1962 in "Something about a Soldier," followed by "Take Her, She's Mine," "Last Analysis," "Never Too Late," "Barefoot in the Park," "Don't Drink the Water," "How Now, Dow Jones," "Play It Again, Sam," "Promises Promises," "Sugar," "Absurd Person Singular," "Murder at the Howard Johnson's," "They're Playing Our Song," "Doubles," "Brigadoon" (LC), "South Pacific" (LC), OB in "The Cradle Will Rock," "Losing Time," "The Good Parts," "Time Framed."

ROBERTSON, DEBORAH (formerly Bauers). Born July 19, 1953 in Nashville, TN. Graduate UCol., Smith Col. Bdwy debut 1982 in "Oh! Calcutta!"

ROBINS, LAILA. Born Mar. 14, 1959 in St. Paul, Mn. Graduate UWis, Yale. Bdwy debut 1984 in "The Real Thing," followed by OB in "Bloody Poetry."

ROBINSON, MARTIN P. Born Mar. 9, 1954 in Dearborn, MI. Graduate WiStateU, AADA. Debut 1980 OB in "The Haggadah," followed by "Yellow Wallpaper," "The Lady's Not for Burning," "Little Shop of Horrors."

ROBINSON, MEGHAN. Born Aug. 11, 1955 in Wilton, Ct. Graduate Bennington Col. Debut 1982 OB in' "The Dubliners," followed by "The Habits of Rabbits," "Episode 26," "Macbeth," "King Lear," "Sleeping Beauty or Coma," "Vampire Lesbians of Sodom," "Psycho Beach Party."

ROCCO, MARY. Born Sept. 12, 1933 in Brooklyn, NY. Graduate Queens Col., CCNY. Debut 1976 OB in "Fiorello!," followed by "The Constant Wife," "Archy and Mehitabel," "Sweethearts," "Hot Sake," "Funny Girl", Bdwy in "Show Boat" (1983).

ROCKAFELLOW, MARILYN. Born Jan. 22, 1939 in Middletown, NJ. Graduate Rutgers U. Debut 1976 OB in "La Ronde," followed by "The Art of Dining," "One Act Play Festival," "Open Admissions," "Bathroom Plays," "Marathon 87," Bdwy in "Clothes for a Summer Hotel," "Open Admission," "Play Memory."

RODD, MARCIA. Born July 8, in Lyons, Ks. Attended Northwestern U, Yale U. Bdwy debut 1964 in "Love in E-Flat," followed by "Last of the Red Hot Lovers," "Shelter," "I'm Not Rappaport," OB in "O Say Can You See L.A.," "Cambridge Circus," "Mad Show," "Merry Wives of Windsor," "I Can't Keep Running in Place," "Daughters."

RODRIGUEZ, EDWARD. Born Mar. 11, 1946 in Bayamon, PR. AMDA graduate. Debut 1974 OB in "How to Get Rid of It," followed by "Lady with a View."

ROGERS, ANNE. Born July 29, 1933 in Liverpool, Eng. Attended St. John's Col. Bdwy debut 1957 in "My Fair Lady," followed by "Zenda," "Half a Sixpence," "42nd Street."

ROGERS, DAVID. Born in NYC. Attended AmThWing. Bdwy debut 1985 in "Doubles," followed by "Broadway."

ROMAN, ARLENE. Born Mar. 21, 1959 in The Bronx, NY. Attended NYU. Debut 1986 OB in "The Bitter Tears of Petra Von Kant," followed by "Birth Rites."

ROOS, CASPER. Born Mar. 21, 1925 in The Bronx, NY. Attended Manhattan School of Music. Bdwy debut 1959 in "First Impressions," followed by "How to Succeed in Business . . . ," "Mame," "Brigadoon," "Shenandoah," "My One and Only," "Into the Light," OB in "Street Scene," "Another Part of the Forest."

ROSE, GEORGE. Born Feb. 19, 1920 in Bicester, Eng. Bdwy debut with Old Vic 1946 in "Henry IV," followed by "Much Ado About Nothing," "A Man for All Seasons," "Hamlet," "Royal Hunt of the Sun," "Walking Happy," "Loot," "My Fair Lady," (CC'68), "Canterbury Tales," "Coco," "Wise Child," "Sleuth," "My Fat Friend," "My Fair Lady" (1976), "She Loves Me," "Peter Pan," BAM's "The Play's the Thing," "The Devil's Disciple," and "Julius Caesar," "The Kingfisher," "Pirates of Penzance," "Dance a Little Closer," "You Can't Take It with You," "Beethoven's Tenth," "Aren't We All?" "The Mystery of Edwin Drood."

ROSENBAUM, DAVID. Born in NYC. Debut OB 1968 in "America Hurrah," followed by "The Cave Dwellers," "Evenings with Chekhov," "Out of the Death Cart," "After Miriam," "The Indian Wants the Bronx," "Allergy," "Family Business," "Beagleman and Brackett," Bdwy in "Oh! Calcutta!"

ROSENBLATT, SELMA. Born Jan. 21, 1926 in NYC. Hunter Col. graduate. Debut 1982 OB in "Primal Time," followed by "The Coarse Acting Show," "Gertie's Gone," "The Return of Pinocchio," "Stepping Out!

ROSIN, JAMES (a.k.a. Jim). Born Oct. 20, 1946 in Philadelphia, Pa. Attended Temple U. Debut 1979 OB in "A Yank in Beverley Hills," followed by "A Force of Nature," "A Boy in New York, Calls His Mom in L. A."

ROSS, JAMIE. Born May 4, 1939 in Markinch, Scot. Attended RADA. Bdwy debut 1962 in "Little Moon of Alban," followed by "Moon Beseiged," "Ari," "Different Times," "Woman of the Year," "La Cage aux Folles," "42nd Street," OB in "Penny Friend," "Oh, Coward!"

ROSS, JUSTIN. Born Dec. 15, 1954 in Brooklyn, NY. Debut 1974 OB in "More Than You Deserve," followed by "Fourtune," "Ready for More?," "Weekend," "Party Mix," Bdwy in "Pippin" (1975), "A Chorus Line," "Got to Go Disco."

ROSSETTER, KATHY. Born July 31 in Abington, Pa. Graduate Gettsburg Col. Debut 1982 OB in "After the Fall," followed by "The Incredibly Famous Willy Rivers," "A Midsummer Night's Dream," "How to Say Goodbye," Bdwy in "Death of a Salesman" (1984).

ROSWELL, MAGGIE. Born Nov. 14 in Los Angeles, Ca. Attended LACC. Debut 1986 OB in "Sills & Co."

ROTH, MARY ROBIN. Born Mar. 5, 1955 in Grand Rapids, Mn. Graduate Col. of St. Catherine. Bdwy debut 1986 in "The Mystery of Edwin Drood."

ROTH, TISHA. Born Feb. 28, 1961 in Norristown, Pa. Graduate NC School of Arts. Debut 1986 OB in "Movie Queens," followed by "The Age of Pie," "The Early Girl."

ROTHHAAR, MICHAEL. Born June 22, 1953 in Pittsburgh, Pa. Graduate Catholic U. Debut 1982 OB in "Who'll Save the Plowboy?," followed by "Dispatches from Hell," "Frankenstein," Bdwy in "The Corn Is Green" (1983), "The Front Page" (LC).

ROTHMAN, NANCY, Born Oct. 13, 1950 in Boston, Ma. Graduate Emerson Col. Debut 1983 OB in "Small Help," followed by "Action," "Haunted Lives," "American Music."

ROWE, HANSFORD. Born May 12, 1924 in Richmond, Va. Graduate URichmond. Bdwy debut 1968 in "We Bombed in New Haven," followed by "Porgy and Bess," "Mourning Becomes Electra," "Da," "Nuts," "Singin' in the Rain," OB in "Curley McDimple," "The Fantasticks," "Last Analysis," "God Says There Is No Peter Ott," "Bus Stop," "Secret Service," "Boy Meets Girl," "Getting Out," "The Unicorn," "The Incredibly Famous Willy Rivers," "The Knife," "Bigfoot Stole My Wife."

ROWE, STEPHEN. Born June 3, 1948 in Johnstown, PA. Graduate Emerson Col., Yale. Debut 1979 OB in "Jungle Coup," followed by "A Private View," "Cinders," "Coming of Age in SoHo," "The Normal Heart," "Whispers."

ROZSA, J. DAVID. Born May 20, 1973 in Montreal, Can. Debut 1985 OB in "Life and Limb," followed by "One Act Festival."

RUBIN, STAN. Born Jan. 7, 1938 in The Bronx, NYC. Attended Fashion Inst. Debut 1974 OB in "You Can't Take It With You," followed by "The Sign in Sidney Brustein's Window," "A Slight Case of Murder," "Witness for the Prosecution," "Damn Yankees," "Kiss Me Kate," "Gingerbread Lady," "Pearls," Bdwy in "Rags" (1986).

RUBINSTEIN, JOHN. Born Dec. 8, 1946 in Los Angeles, CA. Attended UCLA. Bdwy debut 1972 in "Pippin" for which he received a Theatre World Award, followed by "Children of a Lesser God," "Fools," "The Soldier's Tale." "The Caine Mutiny Court-Martial," "Hurlyburly," OB in "Rosencrantz and Guildenstern Are Dead."

RUCK, PATRICIA. Born Sept. 11, 1963 in Washington, DC. Attended Goucher Col. Bdwy debut 1986 in "Cats."

RUCKER, BO. Born Aug. 17, 1948 in Tampa, FL. Debut 1978 OB in "Native Son" for which he received a Theatre World Award, followed by "Blues for Mr. Charlie," "Streamers," "Forty Deuce," "Dustoff."

RUFFELLE, FRANCES. Born in 1966 in London, Eng. Bdwy debut 1987 in "Les Miserables" for which she received a Theatre World Award.

RUGGIERO, JASON. Born Sept. 19, 1978 in Santa Monica, Ca. Debut 1986 OB in "How to Say Goodbye."

RUIZ, ANTHONY. Born Oct. 17, 1956 in NYC. Attended NYCity Col. Debut 1987 OB in "The Wonderful Ice Cream Suit."

RUIZ, ELIZABETH. Born May 21, 1958 in NYC. Graduate Hunter Col. Debut 1986 OB in "The Red Madonna."

RUSSELL, ANNE. Born Mar. 22 in Raleigh, NC. Attended St. Mary Col. Bdwy debut 1965 in "Flora, The Red Menace," followed by "The Best Little Whorehouse in Texas," OB in "Very Warm for May."

RUSSELL, CATHY. Born Aug. 6, 1955 in New Canaan, CT. Graduate Cornell U. Debut 1980 OB in "City Sugar," followed by "Miss Schuman's Quartet," "A Resounding Tinkle," "Right to Life," "Collective Choices," "The Lunch Girls," "Home on the Range," "Perfect Crime."

RUSSELL, TOM. Born Oct. 6, 1953 in Niagara Falls, NY. Graduate Stamford U. Debut 1985 OB in "The Merry Widow," followed by "Naughty Marietta," "The Pajama Game."

RUSSO, WILLIAM. Born Apr. 15, 1966 in Brooklyn, NY. Attended NYU. Debut 1987 OB in "Rosencrantz and Guildenstern Are Dead."

RUSSOM, LEON. Born Dec. 6, 1941 in Little Rock, Ar. Attended Southwestern U. Debut 1968 OB in "Futz," followed by "Cyrano de Bergerac," "Boys in the Band," "Oh! Calcutta!," "Trial of the Catonsville 9," "Henry VI," "Richard III," "Shadow of a Gunman," "The New York Idea," "Three Sisters," "Old Flames," "Loving Reno," "Ruffian on the Stair," "Royal Bob," "Our Lord of Lynchville," "Laughing Stock," "State of the Union," "China Fish," "Hidden Parts."

RYALL, WILLIAM. Born Sept. 18, 1954 in Binghamton, NY. Graduate AADA. Debut 1979 OB in "Canterbury Tales," followed by "Elizabeth and Essex," "He Who Gets Slapped," "The Seagull," "Tartuffe," Bdwy in "Me and My Girl" (1986).

RYAN, STEVEN. Born June 19, 1947 in NYC. Graduate Boston U., UMn. Debut 1978 OB in "Winning Isn't Everything," followed by "The Beethoven," "September in the Rain," "Romance Language," Bdwy in I'm Not Rappaport," (1986).

RYDER, RICHARD. Born Aug. 20, 1942 in Rochester, NY. Attended Colgate U., Pratt Inst. Bdwy debut 1972 in "Oh! Calcutta!," followed by "Via Galactica," "Raggedy Ann," OB in "Rain," "Oh, Pshaw!," "The Dog beneath the Skin," "Polly," "Lovers," "Green Pond," "Piano Bar," "She Loves Me," "Upstairs at O'Neal's," "Rap Master Ronnie," "Misalliance," "Marvin's Garden," "Brothers."

RYLAND, JACK. Born July 2, 1935 in Lancaster, Pa. Attended AADA. Bdwy debut 1958 in "The World of Suzie Wong," followed by "A Very Rich Woman," "Henry V," OB in "A Palm Tree in a Rose Garden," "Lysistrata," "The White Rose and the Red," "Old Glory," "Cyrano de Bergerac," "Mourning Becomes Electra," "Beside the Seaside," "Quartermaine's Terms," "The Miracle Worker."

SACHS, ANN. Born Jan. 23, 1948 in Boston, Ma. Graduate Carnegie Tech U. Bdwy debut 1970 in' "Wilson in the Promise Land," followed by "Dracula," "Man and Superman," OB in "Tug of War," "Sweetshoppe Miriam," "Festival of American Plays," "The Clownmaker," "A Think Piece," "Panache!," "Mama Drama."

SADLER, WILLIAM (BILL). Born Apr. 13, 1950 in Buffalo, NY. Graduate SUNY/Genesco, Cornell U. Debut 1975 OB in "Ivanov," followed by "Limbo Tales," "Chinese Viewing Pavilion," "Lennon," "Necessary Ends," "Hannah," Bdwy in "Biloxi Blues" (1985).

St. JOHN, MARCO. Born May 7, 1939 in New Orleans, La. Graduate Fordham U. Bdwy debut 1964 in "Poor Bitos," followed by "And Things That Go Bump in the Night," "The Unknown Soldier and His Wife," "Weekend," "40 Carats," "We Comrades Three," "War and Peace," OB in "Angels of Anadarko," "Man of Destiny," "Timon of Athens," "Richard III," "Awake and Sing," "Desire under the Elms," "Hamlet," "Twelfth Night."

SAIRE, REBECCA. Born Apr. 16, 1963 in Hertfordshire, Eng. Attended Guildhall School. Bdwy debut 1986 in "The Life and Adventures of Nicholas Nickleby."

SALAMONE, NICK. Born Nov. 25, 1954 in Conshohocken, Pa. Graduate Tufts U. Debut OB 1979 in "Nightshift," followed by "The Sea Gull," "Design for Living," "Preggin and Liss," "The Open Meeting," "Kennedy's Children," "We Bombed in New Haven," "Lorca, A Shadow of Cypress."

SALLOWS, TRACY. Born Apr. 27, 1963 in Valley Stream, NY. Graduate SUNY/Purchase. Bdwy debut 1986 in "You Never Can Tell."

SALVATORE, JOHN. Born Nov. 3, 1961 in Rockville Center, NY. Attended Adelphi U. Bdwy debut 1986 in "A Chorus Line," followed by OB in "Pageant."

SAMUEL, PETER. Born Aug. 15, 1958 in Pana, Il. Graduate East Ill.U. Bdwy debut 1981 in "The First," followed by "The Three Musketeers," "Rags," OB in "Little Eyolf," "The Road to Hollywood," "Elizabeth and Essex."

SANDERS, FRED. Born Feb. 24, 1955 in Philadelphia, PA. Yale graduate. Debut 1981 OB in "Coming Attractions," followed by "The Tempest," "Responsible Parties," "An Evening with Lenny Bruce," "Green Fields," "Incident at Vichy," "The Wonder Years," "Festival of One Acts," "Roots," "The Miser."

SANDY, GARY. "Born Dec. 25, 1945 in Dayton, Oh. Attended Wilmington Col., AADA. Debut 1973 OB in "The Children's Mass," followed by "Romeo and Juliet," Bdwy in "Saturday, Sunday, Monday," (1974), "Pirates of Penzance," "Arsenic and Old Lace."

SANTARELLI, GENE. Born Feb. 20, 1946 in Kingston, Pa. Graduate Wilkes Col., Bloomsbury State Col. Debut 1983 OB in "George by George by George," followed by "The Taming of the Shrew," "Holy Heist."

SANTELL, MARIE. Born July 8 in Brooklyn, NY. Bdwy debut 1957 in "Music Man," followed by "A Funny Thing Happened on the Way . . . ," "Flora, the Red Menace," "Pajama Game," "Mack and Mabel," "La Cage aux Folles," OB in "Hi, Paisano!," "Boys from Syracuse," "Peace," "Promenade," "The Drunkard," "Sensations," "The Castaways," "Fathers and Sons."

SANTORIELLO, ALEX. Born Dec. 30, 1956 in Newark, NJ. Attended Ks. State, Kean State. Debut 1986 OB in "La Belle Helene," followed by "A Romantic Detachment," Bdwy in "Les Miserables" (1987).

SANTORO, MICHAEL. Born Nov. 23, 1957 in Brooklyn, NYC. Attended Lee Strasberg Inst. Debut 1985 OB in "The Normal Heart."

SAUNDERS, MARY. Born Dec. 14, 1945 in Morristown, NJ. Graduate Mt. Holyoke, Middlebury Col. Debut 1975 OB in "The Gifts of the Magi," followed by "The Hunchback of Notre Dame," Bdwy in "The Utter Glory of Morrissey Hall" (1979).

SAUNDERS, NICHOLAS. Born June 2, 1914 in Kiev, Russia. Bdwy debut 1942 in "Lady in the Dark," followed by "A New Life," "Highland Fling," "Happily Ever After," "The Magnificent Yankee," "Anastasia," "Take Her, She's Mine," "A Call on Kuprin," "Passion of Josef D," OB in "An Enemy of the People," "End of All Things Natural," "The Unicorn in Captivity," "After the Rise," "All My Sons," "My Great Dead Sister," "The Investigation," "Past Tense," "Scenes and Revelations," "Zeks," "Blood Moon," "Family Comedy," "American Power Play," "Take Me Along."

SAUNDERS, SHEILA. Born July 9, 1934 in London, Eng. Graduate Brown U., RADA. Debut 1987 OB in "The World Is Made of Glass."

SAVIN, RON LEE. Born July 20, 1947 in Norfolk, Va. Graduate Wm. & Mary Col. Debut 1981 OB in "Francis," followed by "Greater Tuna," "Road to Hollywood," "Streetheat," "One Act Festival."

SAVIOLA, CAMILLE. Born July 16, 1950 in The Bronx, NY. Debut 1970 OB in "Touch," followed by "Rainbow," "Godspell," "Starmites," "Battle of the Giants," "Dementos," "Spookhouse," "A Vaudeville," "Road to Hollywood," "Hollywood Opera," "Secrets of the Lava Lamp," "Angry Housewives," "South Pacific" (NYC Opera), Bdwy in "Nine" (1982).

SCARFE, ALAN. Born June 8, 1946 in London, Eng. Attended UBritColumbia, LAMDA. Debut 1986 OB in "Africanis Instructus," followed by "Black Sea Follies," "As It Is in Heaven."

SCARPONE, JUDITH. Born Nov. 6, 1942 in Jersey City, NJ. Graduate Douglass Col. Debut 1984 OB in "Sacraments," followed by "Postcards," "Rule of Three."

SCHACHTER, DAVID. Born Sept. 15, 1961 in Levittown, NY. Graduate NYU. Debut 1984 OB in "Uncommon Holidays," followed by "She Stoops to Conquer," "The Aquatic Chinese," "The Wager," "The American Boys."

SCHACT, SAM. Born Apr. 19, 1936 in The Bronx, NY. Graduate CCNY. OB in "Fortune and Men's Eyes," "Cannibals," "I Met a Man," "The Increased Difficulty of Concentration," "One Night Stands of a Noisy Passenger," "Owners," "Jack Gelber's New Play," "The Master and Margarita," "Was It Good for You?," "True West," "Today I Am a Fountain Pen," "The Chopin Playoffs," "Dream of a Blacklisted Actor," "Marathon 87," Bdwy in "The Magic Show," "Golda."

SCHAFER, SCOTT. Born Aug. 26, 1958 in Chicago, Il. Graduate DePauw U. Debut 1980 OB in "Aphrodite, The Witch Play," followed by "Babes in Toyland," "Sally,"Bdwy in "Raggedy Ann" (1986).

SCHAUT, ANN LOUISE. Born Nov. 21, 1956 in Minneapolis, MN. Attended UMn. Bdwy debut 1981 in "A Chorus Line."

SCHERER, JOHN. Born May 16, 1961 in Buffalo, NY. Graduate Carnegie-Mellon U. Debut 1983 OB in "Preppies," followed by "Jass," "Downriver," "Ladies and Gentlemen, Jerome Kern," "Olympus on My Mind."

SCHLARTH, SHARON. Born Jan. 19 in Buffalo, NY. Graduate SUNY/Fredonia. Debut 1983 OB in "Full Hookup," followed by "Fool for Love," "Love's Labour's Lost," "Caligula," "The Mound Builders," "Quiet in the Land," "The Early Girl," Bdwy in "Sleight of Hand" (1987).

SCHNABEL, STEFAN. Born Feb. 2, 1912 in Berlin, Ger. Attended UBonn, Old Vic. Bdwy debut 1937 in "Julius Caesar," followed by "Shoemaker's Holiday," "Glamour Preferred," "Land of Fame," "The Cherry Orchard," "Around the World in 80 Days," "Now I Lay Me Down to Sleep," "Idiot's Delight," "Love of Four Colonels," "Plain and Fancy," "Small War on Murray Hill," "A Very Rich Woman," "A Patriot for Me," "Teibele and Her Demon," "Social Security," OB in "Tango," "In the Matter of J. Robert Oppenheimer," "Older People," "Enemies," "Little Black Sheep," "Rosmersholm," "Passion of Dracula," "Biography," "The Firebugs," "Twelve Dreams."

SCHNEIDER, JANA. Born Oct. 24, 1951 in McFarland, Wi. Graduate UWis. Debut 1976 OB in "Women Behind Bars," followed by "Telecast," "Just Like the Lions," Bdwy in "The Robber Bridegroom," "The Mystery of Edwin Drood."

SCHOCH, CARLOTTA. Born June 12, 1954 in Dickinson, ND. Graduate Ft. Wright Col. Debut 1985 OB in "Curse of the Starving Class," followed by "A Scent of Almonds," Bdwy in "Execution of Justice." (1986).

SCHRAMM, DAVID. Born Aug. 14, 1946 in Louisville, Ky. Attended Western Ky.U, Juilliard. Debut 1972 OB in "School for Scandal," followed by "Lower Depths," "Women Beware Women," "Mother Courage," "King Lear," "Duck Variations," "The Cradle Will Rock," "Twelfth Night," Bdwy in "Three Sisters," "Next Time I'll Sing to You," "Edward II," "Measure for Measure," "The Robber Bridegroom," "Bedroom Farce," "Goodbye, Fidel," "The Misanthrope."

SCHULL, REBECCA. Born Feb. 22 in NYC. Graduate NYU. Bdwy debut 1976 in "Herzl," followed by "Golda," OB in "Mother's Day," "Fefu and Her Friends," "On Mt. Chimborazo," "Mary Stuart," "Balzamov's Wedding," "Before She Is Ever Born," "Exiles," "Nest of the Wood Grouse," "Green Fields," "Panache!"

SCHWARTZ, LAURENCE. Born Sept. 7, 1961 in NYC. Graduate Boston U. Debut 1985 OB in "Max's Millions," followed by "Edward II," "The Three Sisters," "The Quare Fellow," "Objective Case," "Allegro," "The Brick and the Rose."

SCOTT, ANNA. Born Apr. 9, 1957 in Sydney, Australia, Attended RADA. Debut 1987 OB in "Taster's Choice."

SCOTT, SERET. Born Sept. 1, 1949 in Washington, DC. Attended NYU. Debut 1969 OB in "Slave Ship," followed by "Ceremonies in Dark Old Men," "Black Terror," "Dream," "One Last Look," "My Sister My Sister," "Weep Not for Me," "Meetings," "The Brothers," "Eyes of the American," "Remembrances/Mojo."

SEFF, RICHARD. Born Sept. 23, 1927 in NYC. Attended NYU. Bdwy debut 1951 in "Darkness at Noon," followed by "Herzl," "Musical Comedy Murders of 1940," (also OB), OB in "Big Fish, Little Fish," "Modigliani," "Childe Byron," "Richard II," "Time Framed," "The Sea Gull."

SEGAL, KATHRIN KING. Born Dec. 8, 1947 in Washington, DC. Attended HB Studio. Debut 1969 OB in "Oh! Calcutta!," followed by "The Drunkard," "Alice in Wonderland," "Pirates of Penzance," "Portfolio Revue," "Philomen," "Butter and Egg Man," "Art of Self-Defense," "Festival of One Acts," "Camp Meeting."

SELBY, JAMES. Born Aug. 29, 1948 in San Francisco, CA. Graduate UWash. Debut 1978 OB in "The Rivals," followed by "Caligula," "L'Ete," "A Prayer for My Daughter," "Amidst the Gladiolas," "Delusion of Angels."

SELDES, MARIAN. Born Aug. 23, 1928 in NYC. Attended Neighborhood Playhouse. Bdwy debut 1947 in "Medea," followed by "Crime and Punishment," "That Lady," "Tower Beyond Tragedy," "Ondine," "On High Ground," "Come of Age," "The Chalk Garden," "The Milk Train Doesn't Stop Here Anymore," "The Wall," "A Gift of Time," "A Delicate Balance," "Before You Go," "Father's Day," "Equus," "The Merchant," "Deathtrap," OB in "Different," "Ginger Man," "Mercy Street," "Isadora Duncan Sleeps with the Russian Navy," "Painting Churches," "Gertrude Stein and Companion."

SENTER, EVELYN. Born July 20 in Freeport, Tx. Graduate USMs, Memphis StateU. Debut 1987 OB in "A Man for All Seasons."

SERRA, RAYMOND. Born Aug. 13, 1937 in NYC. Attended Rutgers U., Wagner Col. Debut 1975 OB in "The Shark," followed by "Mama's Little Angels," "Manny," "The Front Page" (LC), Bdwy in "The Wheelbarrow Closers," "Marlowe," "Accidental Death of an Anarchist."

SERRANO, NESTOR. Born Nov. 5, 1955 in The Bronx, NYC. Attended Queens Col. Debut 1983 OB in "Union City Thanksgiving," followed by "Diamonds," "Cuba and His Teddy Bear."

SERRECCHIA, MICHAEL. Born Mar. 26, 1951 in Brooklyn, NY. Attended Brockport State U. Teachers Col. Bdwy debut 1972 in "The Selling of the President," followed by "Heathen!," "Seesaw," "A Chorus Line," OB in "Lady Audley's Secret."

SESMA, THOM. Born June 1, 1955 in Sasebo, Japan. Graduate UCal. Bdwy debut 1983 in "La Cage aux Folles."

SHAKAR, MARTIN. Born Jan. 1, 1940 in Detroit, Mi. Attended Wayne State U. Bdwy bow 1969 in "Our Town," OB in "Lorenzaccio," "Macbeth," "The Infantry," "American Pastoral," "No Place to Be Somebody," "World of Mrs. Solomon," "And Whose Little Boy Are You," "Investigation of Havana," "Night Watch," "Owners," "Actors," "Richard III," "Transfiguration of Benno Blimpie," "Jack Gelber's New Play," "Biko Inquest," "Second Story Sunlight," "Secret Thighs of New England Women," "After the Fall," "Faith Healer," "Hunting Cockroaches."

SHALHOUB, TONY. Born Oct. 9, 1953 in Green Bay, Wi. Graduate Yale U. Bdwy debut 1985 in "The Odd Couple," OB in "Richard II," "Henry IV Part I."

SHAW, MARCIE. Born June 19, 1954 in Franklin Square, NY. Attended UIll. Bdwy debut 1980 in "Pirates of Penzance," followed by "Les Miserables," OB in "A Midsummer Night's Dream," "Non Pasquale," "Promenade," "La Boheme."

SHEARA, NICOLA. Born May 23 in NYC. Graduate USyracuse. Debut 1975 OB in "Another Language," followed by "Sananda Sez," "All the Way Home," "Inadmissible Evidence," "Another Part of the Forest," "Working One-Acts."

SHELL, CLAUDIA. Born Sept. 11, 1959 in Passaic, NJ. Debut 1980 OB in "Jam," Bdwy in "Merlin," followed by "Cats."

SHELLEY, CAROLE. Born Aug. 16, 1939 in London, Eng. Bdwy debut 1965 in "The Odd Couple," followed by "The Astrakhan Coat," "Loot," "Noel Coward's Sweet Potato," "Hay Fever," "Absurd Person Singular," "The Norman Conquests," "The Elephant Man," "The Misanthrope," "Noises Off," "Stepping Out," OB in "Little Murders," "The Devil's Disciple," "The Play's the Thing," "Double Feature," "Twelve Dreams," "Pygmalion in Concert," "A Christmas Carol," "Jubilee in Concert," "Waltz of the Toreadors."

SHELTON, SLOANE. Born Mar. 17, 1934 in Asheville, NC. Attended Bates Col., RADA. Bdwy debut 1967 in "The Imaginary Invalid," followed by "A Touch of the Poet," "Tonight at 8:30," "I Never Sang for My Father," "Sticks and Bones," "The Runner Stumbles," "Shadow Box," "Passione," "Open Admission," OB in "Androcles and the Lion," "The Maids," "Basic Training of Pavlo Hummel," "Play and Other Plays," "Julius Caesar," "Chieftans," "Passione," "The Chinese Viewing Pavilion," "Blood Relations," "The Great Divide," "Highest Standard of Living," "The Flower Palace."

SHEPARD, JOAN. Born Jan. 7 in NYC. Graduate RADA. Bdwy debut 1940 in "Romeo and Juliet," followed by "Sunny River," "The Strings, My Lord, Are False," "This Rock," "Foolish Notion," "A Young Man's Fancy," "My Romance," "Member of the Wedding," OB in "Othello," "Plot against the Chase Manhattan Bank," "Philosophy in the Boudoir," "Knitters in the Sun," "School for Wives," "The Importance of Being Earnest," "Enter Laughing," "World War Won," "Misalliance."

SHEPARD, KATHERINE. Born Oct. 15, 1932 in Newark, NJ. Attended Vassar, UMo. Debut 1983 OB in "The King Trilogy," followed by "Blood," "The Maids."

SHEPARD, MARY BETH. Born Sept. 25, 1965 in Tonawanda, NY. Graduate Niagara, U. Debut 1987 OB in "Take Me Along."

SHERWOOD, MADELEINE. Born Nov. 13, 1926 in Montreal, Can. Attended Yale U. OB in "Brecht on Brecht," "Medea," "Hey, You, Light Man," "Friends and Relations," "Older People," "O Glorious Tintinnabulation," "Getting Out," "Secret Thighs of New England Women," "Rain," "Ghosts," "Paradise Lost," "Madwoman of Chaillot," Bdwy in "The Chase" (1952), "The Crucible," "Cat on a Hot Tin Roof," "Invitation to a March," "Camelot," "Arturo Ui," "Do I Hear a Waltz?," "Inadmissible Evidence," "All Over!"

SHEW, TIMOTHY. Born Feb. 7, 1959 in Grand Forks, ND. Graduate Millikin U., UMi. Debut 1987 OB in "The Knife."

SHIMIZU, KEENAN. Born Oct. 22, 1956 in NYC. Debut 1965 in CC's "South Pacific" and "The King and I," OB in "The Year of the Dragon," "The Catch," "Peking Man," "Flowers and Household Gods," "Behind Enemy Lines," "Station J," "The Impostor."

Owen S. Rackleff	Lois Raebeck	Henry Ravelo	Cissy Rebich	Charles Repole	Vickilyn Reynolds
Sarah Rice	Jess Richards	LaTanya Richardson	Sam Riddle	Tia Rieblin	Michael Rivera
Martin Robinson	Mary Rocco	David Rogers	Arlene Roman	David Rosenbaum	Selma Rosenblatt
Kathryn Rossetter	Anthony Ruiz	Ann Sachs	Marco St. John	Marie Santell	Michael Santoro
Ron Lee Savin	Judith Scarpone	John Scherer	Seret Scott	Tony Shalhoub	Katherine Shepard

SHULL, RICHARD B. Born Feb. 24, 1929 in Evanston, Il. Graduate State U. Io. Debut 1953 OB in "Coriolanus," followed by "Purple Dust," "Journey to the Day," "American Hamburger League," "Frimbo," "Fade the Game," "Desire under the Elms," "The Marriage of Bette and Boo," "The Front Page" (LC), Bdwy in "Black-Eyed Susan" (1954), "Wake Up, Darling," "Red Roses for Me," "I Knock at the Door," "Pictures in the Hallway," "Have I Got a Girl for You," "Minnie's Boys," "Goodtime Charley," "Fools," "Oh, Brother!"

SHULMAN, CONSTANCE (a.k.a. Connie). Born Apr. 4, 1958 in Johnson City, Tn. Graduate UTn. Debut 1985 OB in "Walking Through," followed by "Windfall," "Pas de Deux," "Steel Magnolias."

SILLIMAN, MAUREEN. Born Dec. 3 in NYC. Attended Hofstra U. Bdwy debut 1975 in "Shenandoah," followed by "I Remember Mama," "Is There Life after High School?," OB in "Umbrellas of Cherbourg," "Two Rooms," "Macbeth," "Blue Window," "Three Postcards."

SILVA, DONALD. Born Feb. 7, 1949 in Gloucester, Ma. Graduate Brandeis U. Debut 1985 OB in "Loose Connections," followed by "Bodega."

SILVER, DEBBIE. Born Nov. 2, 1956 in New Haven, Ct. Graduate Boston U. Bdwy debut 1985 in "Home Front," OB in "Close Enough for Jazz," "The War at Home," "The Soldier's Tale," "Waving Goodbye."

SILVER, RON. Born July 2, 1946 in NYC. Graduate SUNY, St. John's U. Debut OB in "El Grande de Coca Cola," followed by "Lotta," "Kaspar," "More Than You Deserve," "Emperor of Late Night Radio," "Friends," "Hunting Cockroaches," Bdwy in "Hurlyburly" (1984), "Social Security."

SILVERMAN, JONATHAN. Born Aug. 5, 1966 in Los Angeles, CA. Attended USCal. Bdwy debut 1983 in "Brighton Beach Memoirs," followed by "Broadway Bound."

SIMES, DOUGLAS. Born Apr. 21, 1949 in New Salem, NY. Graduate Lehigh U., Yale U. Debut 1974 OB in "The Lady's Not for Burning," followed by "The Dumb Waiter," "The Revenger's Tragedy," "The Lady from the Sea," "Between Time and Timbuktu," "A Chaste Maid and Cheapside."

SIMONS, LESLIE A. Born Aug. 8, 1957 in Hatboro, PA. Graduate Beaver Col. Bdwy debut 1983 in "La Cage aux Folles."

SINGER, MARLA. Born Aug. 2, 1957 in Oklahoma City, OK. Graduate OkCityU. Debut 1981 OB in "Seesaw," followed by Bdwy's "42nd Street" (1985).

SINKYS, ALBERT. Born July 10, 1940 in Boston, Ma. Attended Boston U., UCLA. Debut 1981 OB in "In the Matter of J. Robert Oppenheimer," followed by "The Caine Mutiny Court-Martial," "Man in the Glass Booth," "Six Candles."

SISTO, ROCCO. Born Feb. 8, 1953 in Bari, Italy. Graduate UIll., NYU. Debut 1982 OB in "Hamlet," followed by "The Country Doctor," "The Times and Appetites of Toulouse-Lautrec," "Merchant of Venice."

SKOUSEN, KEVIN. Born Oct. 8, 1959 in Long Beach, Ca. Graduate Claremont Col., UCal/Irvine. Debut 1986 OB in "Highest Standard of Living."

SLATER, HELEN. Born Dec. 14, 1963 in NYC. Debut 1987 OB in "One Act Festival," followed by "Almost Romance."

SLEZAK, VICTOR. Born July 7, 1957 in Youngstown, Oh. Debut 1979 OB in "The Electra Myth," followed by "The Hasty Heart," "Ghosts," "Alice and Fred," "The Widow Claire," "The Miracle Worker."

SLOMAN, JOHN. Born June 23, 1954 in Rochester, NY. Graduate SUNY/Genasco. Debut 1977 OB in "Unsung Cole," followed by "The Apple Tree," Bdwy in "Whoopee!," "The 1940's Radio Show," "A Day in Hollywood/A Night in the Ukraine," "Mayor."

SLUTSKER, PETER. Born Apr. 17, 1958 in NYC. Graduate UMi. Bdwy debut 1983 in "On Your Toes," followed by OB in "No Way to Treat a Lady."

SMALL, LARRY. Born Oct. 6, 1947 in Kansas City, MO. Attended Manhattan School of Music. Bdwy debut 1971 in "1776," followed by "La Strada," "Wild and Wonderful," "A Doll's Life," OB in "Plain and Fancy," "Forbidden Broadway."

SMITH, JENNIFER. Born Mar. 9, 1956 in Lubbock, TX. Graduate TxTechU. Debut 1981 OB in "Seesaw," followed by "Suffragette," Bdwy in "La Cage aux Folles" (1983).

SMITH, LOIS. Born Nov. 3, 1930 in Topeka, Ks. Attended UWVa. Bdwy debut 1952 in "Time Out for Ginger," followed by "The Young and the Beautiful," "Wisteria Trees," "The Glass Menagerie," "Orpheus Descending," "Stages," OB in "A Midsummer Night's Dream," "Non Pasquale," "Promenade," "La Boheme," "Bodies, Rest and Motion," "Marathon 87."

SMITH, LOUISE. Born Feb. 8, 1955 in NYC. Graduate Antioch Col. Debut 1981 OB in "The Haggadah," followed by "Salt Speaks," "The Tempest," "Betty and the Blenders," "Life Simulated."

SMITH, NICK. Born Jan. 13, 1932 in Philadelphia, Pa. Attended Boston U. Debut 1963 OB in "The Blacks," followed by "Man Is Man," "The Connection," "Blood Knot," "No Place to Be Somebody," "Androcles and the Lion," "So Nice They Named It Twice," "In the Recovery Lounge," "Liberty Call," "Raisin in the Sun," "Boogie Woogie and Booker T."

SMITH, REX. Born Sept. 19, 1955 in Jacksonville, Fl. Bdwy debut 1978 in "Grease," followed by "The Pirates of Penzance" for which he received a Theatre World Award, "The Human Comedy," OB in "Brownstone."

SMITH, SHEILA. Born Apr. 3, 1933 in Coneaut, OH. Attended Kent State U., Cleveland Play House. Bdwy debut 1963 in "Hot Spot," followed by "Mame" for which she received a Theatre World Award, "Follies," "Company," "Sugar," "Five O'Clock Girl," "42nd Street," OB in "Taboo Revue," "Anything Goes," "Best Foot Forward," "Sweet Miami," "Florello," "Taking My Turn," "Jack and Jill."

SMITH-CAMERON, J. Born Sept. 7 in Louisville, KY. Attended FlaStateU. Bdwy debut 1982 in "Crimes of the Heart," followed by "Wild Honey," OB in "Asian Shade," "The Knack," "Second Prize: 2 Weeks in Leningrad," "The Great Divide," "The Voice of the Turtle," "Women of Manhattan," "Alice and Fred."

SNOW, DONNA. Born March 23 in Philadelphia, Pa. Graduate UWash. Debut 1985 OB in "Private Scenes," followed by "Shots at Fate."

SOD, TED. Born May 12, 1951 in Wilkes-Barre, Pa. Graduate King's Col. Debut 1976 OB in "Henry V," followed by "Savages," "City Junket," "A Midsummer Night's Dream," "Recruiting Officer," "Jungle of Cities," "The Wild Duck," "Buck," "Landscape of the Body," "Young Playwrights Festival."

SOUHRADA, TOM. Born May 27, 1962 in Bay Shore, NY. Graduate NYU. Debut 1985 OB in "The Second Hurricane," followed by "Bugout," "Take Me Along."

SOUTHERN, DANIEL. Born in Los Angeles, Ca. Graduate UCal/Berkeley. Bdwy debut 1985 in "The Loves of Anatol," OB in "Rosencrantz and Guildenstern Are Dead" (1987).

SPACEY, KEVIN. Born July 26, 1959 in South Orange, NJ. Attended LACC, Juilliard. Debut 1981 OB in "Henry IV Part I," followed by "Barbarians," "Uncle Vanya," "The Robbers," "Life and Limb," "As It Is in Heaven," Bdwy in "Ghosts" (1982), "Hurlyburly," "Long Day's Journey into Night."

SPAISMAN, ZIPORA. Born Jan. 2, 1920 in Lublin, Poland. Debut 1955 OB in "Lonesome Ship," followed by "In My Father's Court," "Thousand and One Nights," "Eleventh Inheritor," "Enchanting Melody," "Fifth Commandment," "Bronx Express," "The Melody Lingers On," "Yoshke Muzikant," "Stempenyu," "Generations of Green Fields," "Shop," "A Play for the Devil," "Broome Street America," "Flowering Peach."

SPANO, NEALLA. Born Sept. 26, 1958 in NYC. Graduate Northwestern U. Debut 1981 OB in "Lady Windermere's Fan," followed by "The Night Is Young," "The Coarse Acting Show," "Serious Bizness," "Found a Peanut," "I Shaw," "Roots," "As It Is in Heaven," "Carrying School."

SPERBERG, FRITZ. Born July 20 in Borger, Tx. Graduate Trinity U. Debut 1979 OB in "Getting Out," followed by "Battery," "The Sea Gull," Bdwy in "Loose Ends" (1979), "Macbeth" (LC).

STADLEN, LEWIS J. Born Mar. 7, 1947 in Brooklyn, NY. Attended Stella Adler Studio. Bdwy debut 1970 in "Minnie's Boys" for which he received a Theatre World Award, followed by "The Sunshine Boys," "Candide," "The Odd Couple," OB in "The Happiness Cage," "Heaven on Earth," "Barb-A-Que," "Don Juan and Non Don Juan," "Olympus on My Mind."

STANLEY, DOROTHY. Born Nov. 18 in Hartford Ct. Graduate Ithaca Col., Carnegie-Mellon U. Debut 1978 OB in "Gay Divorce," followed by "Dames at Sea," Bdwy in "Sugar Babies" (1980), "Annie," "42nd Street."

STANLEY, GORDON. Born Dec. 20, 1951 in Boston, Ma. Graduate Brown U., Temple U. Debut 1977 OB in "Lyrical and Satirical," followed by "Allegro," "Elizabeth and Essex," "Red Hot and Blue," "Two on the Isles," "Moby Dick," Bdwy in "Onward Victoria," (1980), "Joseph and the Amazing Technicolor Dreamcoat," "Into the Light."

STANTON, ROBERT. Born Mar. 8, 1963 in San Antonio, Tx. Graduate George Mason U, NYU. Debut OB 1985 in "Measure for Measure," followed by "Rum and Coke," "Cheapside," "Highest Standard of Living."

STATTEL, ROBERT. Born Nov. 20, 1937 in Floral Park, NY. Graduate Manhattan Col. Debut 1958 OB in "Heloise," followed by "When I Was a Child," "Man and Superman," "The Storm," "Don Carlos," "Taming of the Shrew," "Titus Andronicus," "Henry IV," "Peer Gynt," "Hamlet," LCRep's "Danton's Death," "The Country Wife," "The Caucasian Chalk Circle," and "King Lear," "Iphigenia in Aulis," "Ergo," "The Persians," "Blue Boys," "The Minister's Black Veil," "Four Friends," "Two Character Play," "The Merchant of Venice," "Cuchulain," "Oedipus Cycle," "Gilles de Rais," "Woyzeck," "King Lear," "The Fuehrer Bunker," "Learned Ladies," "Domestic Issues," "Great Days," "The Tempest," "Brand," "A Man for All Seasons."

STAVRAKIS, TASO. Born July 12, 1957 in Canton, Oh. Graduate Carnegie-Mellon U. Debut 1983 OB in "Etched in Stone," followed by "The Jew of Malta."

STEIN, JUNE. Born June 13, 1950 in NYC. Debut 1979 OB in "The Runner Stumbles," followed by "Confluence," "Am I Blue," "Balm in Gilead," "Danny and the Deep Blue Sea," "The Miss Firecracker Contest," "As Is."

STEINBERG, ROY. Born Mar. 24, 1951 in NYC. Graduate Tufts U, Yale U. Debut 1974 OB in "A Midsummer Night's Dream," followed by "The Firebugs," "The Doctor in Spite of Himself," "Romeo and Juliet," "After the Rise," "Our Father," "Zeks," "In Agony," "Merchant of Venice," "Macbeth," Bdwy in "Wings" (1979).

STEINER, STEVE. Born Nov. 30, 1951 in Chicago, Il. Graduate Webster U. Debut 1986 OB in "Two Blind Mice," followed by "Hot Sake."

STEPHENSON, DENISE. Born Mar. 22, 1959 in Aberdeen, Scot. Attended LAMDA. Debut 1982 OB in "No End of Blame," followed by "The Philanthropist," "The Accrington Pals," "The Circle," "Children of the Sun," "Bloody Poetry."

STEPHENSON, DON. Born Sept. 10, 1964 in Chattanooga, Tn. Graduate UTn. Debut 1986 OB in "Southern Lights," followed by "Hypothetic."

STERLING, PHILIP. Born Oct. 9, 1922 in NYC. Graduate UPa. Bdwy debut 1955 in "Silk Stockings," followed by "Interlock," "An Evening with Richard Nixon . . .," "Broadway Bound," OB in "Victims of Duty," "Opening of a Window," "Trojan Women," "Party for Divorce," "Party on Greenwich Avenue," "Peddler," "Summertree," "Older People."

STERNHAGEN, FRANCES. Born Jan. 13, 1932 in Washington, DC. Graduate Vassar Col. OB in "Admirable Bashful," "Thieves' Carnival," "Country Wife," "Ulysses in Nighttown," "Saintliness of Margery Kemp," "The Room," "A Slight Ache," "Displaced Person," "Playboy of the Western World," "The Prevalence of Mrs. Seal," "Summer," "Laughing Stock," "The Return of Herbert Bracewell," "Little Murders," Bdwy in "Great Day in the Morning," "The Right Honourable Gentleman," with APA in "The Cocktail Party," and "Cock-a-Doodle Dandy," "The Sign in Sidney Brustein's Window," "Enemies" (LC), "The Good Doctor," "Equus," "Angel," "On Golden Pond," "The Father," "Grownups," "You Can't Take It With You."

STEVENS, ALLAN. Born Nov. 30, 1949 in Los Angeles, Ca. Attended LAMDA. Bdwy debut 1975 in "Shenandoah," followed by "Kings," OB in "It's Wilde!," "Frozen Assets," "Rule of Three," "Donkey's Years."

STEVENS, FISHER. Born Nov. 27, 1963 in Chicago, IL. Attended NYU. Bdwy debut 1982 in "Torch Song Trilogy," followed by "Brighton Beach Memoirs," OB in "Out of Gas on Lover's Leap," "Miami," "Little Murders," "Terminal Bar," "One-Act Festival," "Carrying School Children."

STOECKLE, ROBERT. Born Sept. 21, 1947 in Port Chester, NY. Graduate Hartt Col. Bdwy debut 1980 in "Canterbury Tales," OB in "110 in the Shade," "A Midsummer Night's Dream," "Camp Meeting."

STOLARSKY, PAUL. Born Feb. 18, 1933 in Detroit, Mi. Graduate WayneStateU., UMich. Debut 1972 OB in "Bluebeard," followed by "Let Yourself Go," "Rocket to the Moon," "D.," "My Mother, My Father and Me," "Me and Molly," "Shlemiel the First," "The Rachel Plays," "The Front Page" (LC), Bdwy in "Nuts" (1980).

STOLTZ, ERIC. Born in 1961 in California. Attended USCal. Debut 1987 OB in "The Widow Claire."

STONE, DANTON. Born in Queens, NYC. Debut OB 1976 in "Mrs. Murray's Farm," followed by "In This Fallen City," "Say Goodnight, Gracie," "Angels Fall," "Balm in Gilead," Bdwy in "5th of July" (1980).

STORCH, LARRY. Born Jan. 8, 1923 in NYC. Bdwy debut 1958 in "Who Was That Lady I Saw You With?," followed by "Porgy and Bess" (1983), "Arsenic and Old Lace" (1986), OB in "The Littlest Revue" (1956).

STRANSKY, CHARLES. Born Jan. 31, 1946 in Boston, Ma. Graduate S.Ill.U., Brandeis U. Bdwy debut 1984 in "Glengarry Glen Ross," followed by "The Front Page" (LC), OB in "Pantomime."

SULKA, ELAINE. Born in NYC; graduate Queens Col., Brown U. Debut 1962 OB in "Hop, Signor!," followed by "Brotherhood," "Brothers," "The Last Prostitute," "The Courting," Bdwy in "The Passion of Josef D.," "Medea."

SUMMERHAYS, JANE. Born Oct. 11, in Salt Lake City, Ut. Graduate UUt., Catholic U. Debut 1980 OB in "Paris Lights," followed by "On Approval," Bdwy in "Sugar Babies" (1980), "A Chorus Line," "Me and My Girl."

SUNG, ELIZABETH. Born Oct. 14, 1954 in Hong Kong. Juilliard graduate. Debut 1982 OB in "Station J," followed by "A Midsummer Night's Dream," "Sound and Beauty," "Eat a Bowl of Tea," "Wha . . . Whai, A Long Time Ago."

SUTTON, DOLORES. Born in NYC; graduate NYU. Bdwy debut 1962 in "Rhinoceros," followed by "General Seeger," OB in "Man with the Golden Arm," "Machinal," "Career," "Brecht on Brecht," "To Be Young, Gifted and Black," "The Web and the Rock," "My Prince My King," "Our Own Family."

SWARBRICK, CAROL. Born Mar. 20, 1948 in Inglewood CA. Graduate UCLA, NYU. Debut 1971 OB in "Drat!," followed by "The Glorious Age," Bdwy in "Side by Side by Sondheim," "Whoopee!," "42nd Street."

SWIFT, CHERYL. Born Sept. 28, 1959 in Milwaukee, WS. Attended UWisc. Debut 1985 OB in "Very Warm for May."

SZYMANSKI, WILLIAM. Born May 16, 1949 in Omaha, Ne. Attended UNe. Debut 1979 OB in "Big Bad Burlesque," followed by "Little Shop of Horrors."

TABOR, RICHARD. Born Aug. 4, 1951 in Southington, Ct. Graduate Central Ct.St.U. Debut 1986 OB in "Out!"

TABORI, KRISTOFFER. Born Aug. 4, 1952 in Cal. Bdwy debut 1969 in "The Penny Wars," followed by "Henry V," "Habeas Corpus," OB in "Emile and the Detectives," "Suns of Carrar," "A Cry of Players," "Dream of a Blacklisted Actor," "How Much, How Much?" for which he received a Theatre World Award, "The Wager," "Scribes," "The Trouble with Europe," "The Common Pursuit."

TALBOT, JOHN C. Born Sept. 18, 1950 in NYC. Graduate NYU. Debut 1983 OB in "Richard III," followed by "Romeo and Juliet," "A Midsummer Night's Dream," "Ball Boys," "Misalliance."

TALMAN, ANN. Born Sept. 13, 1957 in Welch, WVa. Graduate PaStateU. Debut 1980 OB in "What's So Beautiful about a Sunset over Prairie Avenue?," followed by "Louisiana Summer," "Winterplay," "Prairie Avenue," "Broken Eggs," "Octoberfest," "We're Home," "Yours Anne," "Songs on a Shipwrecked Sofa," Bdwy in "The Little Foxes" (1981), "House of Blue Leaves."

TANNER, MELINDA. Born Oct. 5, 1946 in Los Angeles, Ca. Attended LACC. Debut 1975 OB in "The Sea," followed by "Godspell," "I Can't Keep Running," "Ready or Not," Bdwy in "The Robber Bridegroom" (1976).

TARLETON, DIANE. Born Oct. 25, in Baltimore, MD. Graduate UMd. Bdwy debut 1965 in "Anya," followed by "A Joyful Noise," "Elmer Gantry," "Yentl," "Torch Song Trilogy," OB in "A Time for the Gentle People," "Spoon River Anthology," "International Stud," "Too Much Johnson," "To Bury a Cousin," "A Dream Play," "Crime and Punishment," "Miss Julie."

TARTEL, MICHAEL. Born Mar. 21, 1936 in Newark, NJ. Attended Manhattan Col. Debut 1969 OB in "The Fantasticks," followed by "Swan Song," Bdwy in "Billy" (1969), followed by "Going Up."

TATE, MARZETTA. Born March 11 in Brooklyn, NY. Graduate Manhattan Sch. of Music. Bdwy debut 1978 in "Timbuktu," OB in "La Belle Helene," "Hot Sake," "Tate to Tate," "The Mystery of Phyllis Wheatley," "Sancocho."

TATUM, MARIANNE. Born Feb. 18, 1951 in Houston, TX. Attended Manhattan School of Music. Debut 1971 OB in "Ruddigore," followed by "The Sound of Music," "The Gilded Cage," "Charley's Tale," Bdwy in "Barnum" (1980), for which she received a Theatre World Award, "The Three Musketeers."

TAYLOR, CYNDY. Born Jan. 21, 1960 in Champaign, Il. Graduate Ithaca Col. Debut 1987 OB in "Take Me Along."

TAYLOR, GEORGE. Born Sept. 18, 1930 in London, Eng. Attended AADA. Debut 1972 OB in "Hamlet," followed by "Enemies," "The Contractor," "Scribes," "Says I, Says He," "Teeth 'n' Smiles," "Viaduct," "Translations," "Last of the Knucklemen," "The Accrington Pals," "Ragged Trousered Philanthropists," Bdwy in "Emperor Henry IV" (1973), "The National Health."

TAYLOR, REGINA. Born Aug. 22, 1960 in Dallas, Tx. Graduate SMU. Debut 1983 OB in "Young Playwrights Festival," followed by "As You Like It," "Macbeth," "Map of the World," "The Box," Bdwy in "Shakespeare on Broadway" (1987).

TAYLOR, ROBIN. Born May 28 in Tacoma, Wa. Graduate UCLA. Debut 1979 OB in "Festival," followed by "On the 20th Century," Bdwy in "A Chorus Line" (1985).

TAYLOR, SCOTT. Born June 29, 1962 in Milan, Tn. Attended Ms.State U. Bdwy in "Wind in the Willows" (1985), followed by "Cats."

TERRY, W. BENSON. Born Aug. 10, 1927 in Chicago, Il. Attended Columbia U. Bdwy debut in "The Death of Bessie Smith" (1968), OB in "The Bedbug," "A Midsummer Night's Dream," "The Strong Breed," "Trials of Brother Jero," "Someone's Comin' Hungry," "Deep Swimmer."

TESTA, MARY. Born June 4, 1955 in Philadelphia, Pa. Attended URI. Debut 1979 OB in "In Trousers," followed by "Company," "Life Is Not a Doris Day Movie," "Not-So-New Faces of '82," "American Princess," "Mandrake," "4 One-act Musicals," "Next Please!," "Daughters," "One Act Festival," "The Knife," Bdwy in "Barnum" (1980), "Marilyn," "The Rink."

THACKER, RUSS. Born June 23, 1946 in Washington, DC. Attended Montgomery Col. Bdwy debut 1967 in "Life with Father" followed by "Music! Music!," "The Grass Harp," "Heathen," "Home Sweet Homer," "Me Jack, You Jill," "Do Black Patent Leather Shoes Really Reflect Up?," OB in "Your Own Thing" for which he received a Theatre World Award, "Dear Oscar," "Once I Saw a Boy Laughing," "Tip-Toes," "Oh, Coward!," "New Moon in Concert," "The Firefly in Concert," "Rosalie in Concert," "Some Enchanted Evening," "Roberta in Concert," "Olio."

THELEN, JODI. Born June 12, 1962 in St. Cloud, Mn. Bdwy debut 1983 in "Brighton Beach Memoirs," OB in "Before the Dawn," "Springtime for Henry," "Largo Desolato," "The Nice and the Nasty," "Dream of a Blacklisted Actor."

THEODORE, LAURA. Born Dec. 11, 1957 in Cleveland, Oh. Attended OhU. Debut 1986 OB in "Beehive."

THOLE, CYNTHIA. Born Sept. 21, 1957 in Silver Spring, Md. Graduate Butler U. Debut 1982 OB in "Nymph Errant," followed by Bdwy in "42nd Street" (1985), "Me and My Girl."

THOMAS, RAYMOND ANTHONY. Born Dec. 19, 1956 in Kentwood, La. Graduate UTx/El Paso. Debut 1981 OB in "Escape to Freedom" followed by "The Sun Gets Blue," "Blues for Mr. Charlie," "The Huchback of Notre Dame."

THOMAS, RICHARD. Born June 13, 1951 in NYC. Bdwy debut 1958 in "Sunrise at Campobello," followed by "A Member of the Wedding," "Strange Interlude," "The Playroom," "Richard III," "Everything in the Garden," "5th of July," OB in "The Seagull," "The Front Page" (LC).

THOMAS, WILLIAM, JR. Born Nov. 8 in Columbus, OH. Graduate OhStateU. Debut 1972 OB in "Touch," followed by "Natural," "Godspell," "Poor Little Lambs," "Loose Joints," "Not-So-New Faces of '81," Bdwy in "Your Arms Too Short to Box with God" (1976), "La Cage aux Folles."

THOMPSON, OWEN. Born Sept. 16, 1962 in Los Angeles, Ca. Debut 1974 OB in "The Trojan Women," followed by "The Importance of Being Earnest," "She Loves Me," "The Browning Version," "King John," "Richard III," "Enter Laughing," "Misalliance."

THORNTON, ANGELA. Born in Leeds, Eng. Attended Webber-Douglas School. Bdwy debut 1956 in "Little Glass Clock," followed by "Nude with Violin," "Present Laughter," "Hostile Witness," "Pygmalion" (1987), OB in "The Mousetrap," "Big Broadcast," "Mary Barnes."

THORSON, LINDA. Born June 18, 1947 in Toronto, Can. Graduate RADA. Bdwy debut 1982 in "Steaming" for which she received a Theatre World Award, followed by "Noises Off."

TILLMAN, JUDITH. Born Apr. 25, 1934 in Cleveland, Oh. Graduate Case Western Reserve U. Debut 1963 OB in "The Darker Flower," followed by "Do I Hear a Waltz?," "Ten Little Indians," "Patrick Pearse Motel," "Deathtrap," "Cowboy."

TIPPIT, WAYNE. Born Dec. 19, 1932 in Lubbock, TX. Graduate UIowa. Bdwy debut 1959 in "Tall Story," followed by "Only in America," "Gantry," "The Nerd," OB in "Dr. Faustus," "Under the Sycamore Tree," "Misalliance," "The Alchemist," "MacBird," "Trainor, Dean Liepolt & Co.," "Young Master Dante," "Boys in the Band," "Wayside Motor Inn," "For Sale," "Lemon Sky," "Alterations."

TIRELLI, JAIME. Born Mar. 4, 1945 in NYC. Attended UMundial, AADA. Debut 1975 OB in "Rubbers/Yanks 3 Detroit 0," followed by "The Sun Always Shines on the Cool," "Body Bags," "Bodega."

TOMEI, MARISA. Born Dec. 4, 1964 in Brooklyn, NY. Attended Boston U., NYU. Debut 1986 OB in "Daughters" for which she received a Theatre World Award, followed by "Class 1 Acts."

TOMLINSON, ROBERT MICHAEL. Born Aug. 29, 1953 in Brooklyn, NYC. Graduate Temple U. Debut 1984 OB in "Delirious," followed by "Mirandolina," "Hedda Gabler," "Gravity Shoes," "Murder in the Mummy's Tomb."

TONER, THOMAS. Born May 25, 1928 in Homestead, Pa. Graduate UCLA. Bdwy debut 1973 in "Tricks," followed by "The Good Doctor," "All Over Town," "The Elephant Man," "California Suite," "A Texas Trilogy," "The Inspector General," "Me and My Girl," OB in "Pericles," "The Merry Wives of Windsor," "A Midsummer Night's Dream," "Richard III," "My Early Years," "Life and Limb," "Measure for Measure," "Little Footsteps."

TORO, PULI. Born in San Juan, PR. Attended NewEngConsv. Debut 1974 OB in "The Merry Widow," followed by "Union City Thanksgiving," "Festival Latino '86," "Bodega."

TORREN, FRANK. Born Jan. 5, 1939 in Tampa, FL. Attended UTampa, AADA. Debut 1964 OB in "Jo," followed by "No Corner in Heaven," "Treasure Island," "Open Season for Butterflies," "The Brownstone Urge," "The Meehans," "Where's Charley?," "Ladies and Gentlemen, Jerome Kern," "Funny Girl," "The Red Madonna."

TOVATT, PATRICK. Born Dec. 11, 1940 in Garrett Ridge, Co. Attended Antioch, Harvard Cols. Debut 1984 OB in "Husbandry," followed by "The Right Number."

TRACY, STAN. Born Dec. 2, 1950 in Oceanside, Ca. Graduate San Diego State. Debut 1976 OB in "Love's Labor's Lost," followed by "King of the Castle," "Yesterday Continued," "Henhouse."

TRAVERS, JOSEPH. Born Jan. 2, 1960 in NYC. Graduate SUNY/Albany. Debut 1987 OB in "The Jew of Malta."

TREBOR, ROBERT. Born June 7, 1953 in Philadelphia, Pa. Graduate Northwestern U. Debut 1980 OB in "City Junket," followed by "The Changeling," "The New Living Newspaper," "One Act Play Festival."

TROY, LOUISE. Born Nov. 9 in NYC. Attended AADA. Debut 1955 OB in "The Infernal Machine," followed by "Merchant of Venice," "Conversation Piece," "Salad Days," "O, Oysters!," "A Doll's House," "Last Analysis," "Judy and Jane," "Heartbreak House," "Rich Girls," Bdwy in "Pipe Dream" (1955), "A Shot in the Dark," "Tovarich," "High Spirits," "Walking Happy," "Equus," "Woman of the Year," "Design for Living," "42nd St."

TSOUTSOUVAS, SAM. Born Aug. 20, 1948 in Santa Barbara, Ca. Attended UCal, Juilliard. Debut 1969 OB in "Peer Gynt," followed by "Twelfth Night," "Timon of Athens," "Cymbeline," "School for Scandal," "The Hostage," "Women Beware Women," "Lower Depths," "Emigre," "Hello Dali," "The Merchant of Venice," "The Leader," "The Bald Soprano," Bdwy in "The Three Sisters," "Measure for Measure," "Beggar's Opera," "Scapin," "Dracula."

TUBB, BARRY. Born in 1963 in Snyder, Tx. Attended AmConsTheatre. Bdwy debut 1986 in "Sweet Sue."

TUCCI, MARIA. Born June 19, 1941 in Florence, It. Attended Actors Studio. Bdwy debut 1963 in "The Milk Train Doesn't Stop Here Anymore," followed by "The Rose Tattoo," "The Little Foxes," "The Cuban Thing," "The Great White Hope," "School for Wives," "Lesson from Aloes," "Kingdoms," "Requiem for a Heavyweight," OB in "Corruption in the Palace of Justice," "Five Evenings," "Trojan Women," "White Devil," "Horseman, Pass By," "Yerma," "Shepherd of Avenue B," "The Gathering," "Man for All Seasons."

TUNE, TOMMY. Born Feb. 28, 1939 in Wichita Falls, TX. Graduate UTX. Bdwy debut 1965 in "Baker Street," followed by "A Joyful Noise," "How Now Dow Jones," "Seesaw," "My One and Only," OB in "Ichabod."

TURNER, PATRICK. Born Dec. 2, 1952 in Seattle, WA. Attended UWash., AmConsTheatre. Debut 1984 OB in "The Merchant of Venice," followed by "Double Inconstancy," "The Taming of the Shrew," "Lady from the Sea," "Two Gentlemen of Verona," "The Contrast," "Pericles," "The Rivals."

TURTURRO, JOHN. Born Feb. 28, 1957 in Brooklyn, NYC. Graduate SUNY/New Paltz, Yale U. Debut 1984 OB in "Danny and the Deep Blue Sea" for which he received a Theatre World Award, followed by "Men without Dates," "Chaos and Hard Times," "Steel on Steel," "Tooth of Crime," "Of Mice and Men," "Jamie's Gang," "Marathon '86," "The Bald Soprano/The Leader," Bdwy in "Death of a Salesman" (1984).

TYLER, EDWINA LEE. Born Jan. 29, 1944 in NYC. Debut 1975 OB in "Three Marias," followed by "Sappho and Aphrodite," "Death of the King's Horseman" (LC).

UHLER, ERIC. Born Feb. 25, 1949 in Youngstown, Oh. Graduate Ohio U. Bdwy debut 1978 in "Once in a Lifetime," OB in "Show Me a Hero," "Love and Junk," "Henhouse."

ULISSEY, CATHERINE. Born Aug. 4, 1961 in NYC. Attended Ntl. Acad. of Arts. Bdwy debut 1986 in "Rags," followed by "The Mystery of Edwin Drood."

ULLETT, NICK. Born Mar. 5, 1947 in London, Eng. Graduate Cambridge U. Debut 1967 OB in "Love and Let Love," followed by "The Importance of Being Earnest," Bdwy in "Loot" (1986), "Me and My Girl."

UNDERWOOD, ERIC. Born Apr. 27, 1959 in Coral Gables, Fl. Attended UUtah. Bdwy debut 1985 in "La Cage aux Folles."

URICH, TOM. Born Mar. 26 in Toronto, Oh. Attended CinConsvMusic. Bdwy debut 1970 in "Applause," followed by "Musical Chairs," "La Cage aux Folles," OB in "Streets of NY," "The Fantasticks," "Shoemaker's Holiday."

URLA, JOE. Born Dec. 25, 1958 in Pontiac, Mi. Graduate UMi, Yale U. Debut 1985 OB in "Measure for Measure," followed by "Henry V," "Principia Scriptoriae" for which he received a Theatre World Award, " Our Own Family," "Return of Pinocchio."

UTLEY, BYRON. Born Nov. 4, 1954 in Indianapolis, In. Attended UDC. Bdwy debut 1977 in "Hair," followed by "Reggae," "Big Deal," OB in "Bones," "The Trojan Women," "Sweet Will Shakespeare," "Transposed Heads," "Death and the King's Horseman" (LC).

VALE, MICHAEL. Born June 28, 1922 in Brooklyn, NY. Attended New School. Bdwy debut 1961 in "The Egg" followed by "Cafe Crown," "Last Analysis," "The Impossible Years," "Saturday Sunday Monday," "Unexpected Guests," "California Suite," OB in "Autograph Hound," "Moths," "Now There's the Three of Us," "Tall and Rex," "Kaddish," "42 Seconds from Broadway," "Sunset," "Little Shop of Horrors."

VALLEE, GREG (a.k.a. Gregory Paul Jackson). Born Mar. 22, 1955 in NJ. Graduate Boston U. Debut 1980 OB in "Times Square," followed by "A Loss of Roses," "Ladies of the Odeon," "Initiation Rites."

VAN GRIETHUYSEN, TED. Born Nov. 7, 1934 in Ponca City, Ok. Graduate UTx., RADA. Bdwy debut 1962 in "Romulus," followed by "Moon Besieged," "Inadmissible Evidence," OB in "Failures," "Lute Song," "O Marry Me," "Red Roses for Me," "Basement," "Hedda Gabler," "Othello," "First Time Anywhere!," "Man for All Seasons."

VANCE, COURTNEY B. Born Mar. 12, 1960 in Detroit, Mi. Harvard graduate. Bdwy debut 1987 in "Fences" for which he received a Theatre World Award.

VARON, SUSAN. Born May 5, 1952 in The Bronx, NY. Attended Hofstra U. Debut 1977 OB in "The Madwoman of Chaillot," followed by "The Way of the World," "The Anniversary," "The Seahorse," "The Cabbagehead," "Red Cross," "Remember the Sun," "A Flash of Lightning," "No Damn Good."

VAUGHAN, MELANIE. Born Sept. 18 in Yazoo City, Ms. Graduate LaStateU. Bdwy debut 1976 in "Rex," followed by "Sunday in the Park with George," "On the 20th Century," "Music Is," "Starlight Express," OB in "Canterbury Tales."

VENORA, DIANE. Born in 1952 in Hartford, CT. Graduate Juilliard. Debut 1981 OB in "Penguin Touquet," followed by "A Midsummer Night's Dream," "Hamlet," "Uncle Vanya," "Messiah," "Tomorrow's Monday," "Largo Desolato," "A Man for All Seasons."

VIDNOVIC, MARTIN. Born Jan. 22, 1945 in Peoria, Il. Graduate UIll, UCLA, Juilliard. Debut 1974 OB in "Robber Bridegroom," followed by "King John," "Father Uxbridge Wants to Marry," "Hard Sell," "Ross," "Double Feature," "Tender Places," "A Private View," "Love," "Poker Session," "Olympus on My Mind," Bdwy in "Robber Bridegroom." (1976), "The Magic Show," "The Grand Tour," "Loose Ends," "A Midsummer Night's Dream."

VINCENT, ED. Born Oct. 9, 1943 in Rochester, NY. Graduate SyracuseU., IndU. Debut 1976 OB in "The Misunderstanding," followed by "The 20 Second Day," "Beyond Illusion," "Stones of Venice," "The Wise Woman."

VITELLA, SEL. Born July 7, 1934 in Boston, Ma. Graduate San Francisco Inst. of Music. Debut 1975 OB in "The Merchant of Venice," followed by "Gorey Stories," "Jane Eyre," "Preppies," "Professionally Speaking," "Dazy," Bdwy in "Something's Afoot" (1976), "Gorey Stories."

VOET, DOUG. Born Mar. 1, 1951 in Los Angeles, CA. Graduate BYU. Bdwy debut in "Joseph and the Amazing Technicolor Dreamcoat" (1982), OB in "Forbidden Broadway."

VOIGTS, RICHARD. Born Nov. 25, 1934 in Streator, IL. Graduate InU, Columbia U. Debut 1979 OB in "The Constant Wife," followed by "Company," "The Investigation," "Dune Road," "The Collection," "Miracle Man," "As Time Goes By," "Silence," "Station J," "Frozen Assets," "Happy Birthday, Wanda June," "My Three Angels," "Child's Play," "Once Is Never Enough," "Black Coffee," "Take Me Along."

VON DOHLEN, LENNY. Born Dec. 22, 1958 in Augusta, Ga. Graduate Loretto Heights Col. Debut 1982 OB in "Cloud 9," followed by "Twister," "Asian Shade," "Desire under the Elms," "Marathon '86," "The Maderati."

VON SCHERLER, SASHA. Born Dec. 12 in NYC. Bdwy debut 1959 in "Look after Lulu," followed by "Rape of the Belt," "The Good Soup," "Great God Brown," "First Love," "Alfie," "Harold," "Bad Habits," "Musical Comedy Murders of 1940," OB in "Admirable Bashful," "The Comedian," "Conversation Piece," "Good King Charles' Golden Days," "Under Milk Wood," "Plays, for Bleecker Street," "Ludlow Fair," "Twelfth Night," "Sondra," "Cyrano de Bergerac," "Crimes of Passion," "Henry VI," "Trelawny of the Wells," "Screens," "Soon Jack November," "Pericles," "Kid Champion," "Henry V," "Comanche Cafe," "Museum," "Grand Magic," "The Penultimate Problem of Sherlock Holmes," "Keymaker," "Hunting Scenes from Lower Bavaria," "Slacks and Tops."

VOSBURGH, DAVID. Born Mar. 14, 1938 in Coventry, RI. Attended Boston U. Bdwy debut 1968 in "Maggie Flynn," followed by "1776," "A Little Night Music," "Evita," "A Doll's Life," OB in "Smith," "The Rise of David Levinsky."

WADE, ADAM. Born Mar. 17, 1935 in Pittsburgh, Pa. Attended VaStateU. Debut 1976 OB in "My Sister My Sister," followed by "Shades of Harlem," "Falling Apart," "The War Party," "Staggerlee."

WAHL, KIRBY. Born Mar. 9, 1957 in Monticello, Ia. Graduate Webster U. Debut 1986 OB in "Hot Sake."

WAITES, THOMAS G. Born in 1954; attended Juilliard. OB in "American Buffalo," "Awake and Sing," "Forty Deuce," "Extremities," "North Shore Fish," Bdwy in "Richard III" (1979), "Teaneck Tanzie."

WALDROP, MARK. Born July 30, 1954 in Washington, DC. Graduate Cincinnati Consv. Debut 1977 OB in "Movie Buff," Bdwy in "Hello, Dolly!" (1978), "The Grand Tour," "Evita," "La Cage aux Folles."

WALKER, KATHRYN. Born in Jan. in Philadelphia, Pa. Graduate Wells Col., Harvard, LAMDA. Debut 1971 OB in "Slag," followed by "Alpha Beta," "Kid Champion," "Rebel Women," Bdwy in "The Good Doctor" (1973), "Mourning Pictures," "A Touch of the Poet," "Wild Honey."

WALKER, PETER. Born July 24, 1927 in Mineola, NY. Bdwy debut 1955 in "Little Glass Clock," followed by "Dear World," "Where's Charley?," "Follies," "Into the Light," OB in "Dancing for the Kaiser," "My Old Friends," "Do You Still Believe the Rumor."

WALLACH, ROBERTA. Born July 13, 1938 in NYC. Attended Sarah Lawrence Col., Neighborhood Playhouse. Debut 1978 OB in "The Diary of Anne Frank," followed by "Second Avenue," "One Act Festival."

WALLER, KENNETH. Born Apr. 12, 1945 in Atlanta, Ga. Graduate Piedmont Col. Debut 1976 OB in "Boys from Syracuse," Bdwy in "Sarava" (1979), "Onward Victoria," "Me and My Girl."

WALSH, BARBARA. Born June 3, 1955 in Washington, DC. Attended Montgomery Col. Bdwy debut 1982 in "Rock 'n' Roll: The First 5000 Years," followed by "Nine," OB in "Forbidden Broadway."

WALSH, JUANITA. Born May 3, 1951 in Milwaukee, Wi. Graduate Stephens Col. Debut 1980 OB in "Mo' Tea Miss Ann," followed by "The Land Is Bright," "Modern Statuary," "All on Her Own," "The Bookworm," "Another Part of the Forest," "The Little Foxes."

WALTERS, FREDERICK. Born July 19, 1930 in Schenectady, NY. Graduate Centenary Col., Rutgers U. Debut 1979 OB in "Biography: A Game," followed by "A Midsummer Night's Dream," "Not Now, Darling," "Desire under the Elms," "Man for All Seasons," "Bless Me, Father," "Strictly Dishonorable," "The Little Foxes."

WALTON, JIM. Born July 31, 1955 in Tachikawa, Japan. Graduate UCincinnati. Debut 1979 OB in "Big Bad Burlesque," followed by "Scrambled Feet," "Stardust," Bdwy in "Perfectly Frank" (1980), "Merrily We Roll Along," "42nd Street," "Stardust."

WARD, DOUGLAS TURNER. Born May 5, 1930 in Burnside, LA. Attended UMi. Bdwy debut 1959 in "A Raisin in the Sun," followed by "One Flew over the Cuckoo's Nest," "Last Breeze of Summer," OB in "The Iceman Cometh," "The Blacks," "Pullman Car Hiawatha," "Bloodknot," "Happy Ending," "Day of Absence," "Kongi's Harvest," "Ceremonies in Dark Old Men," "The Harangues," "The Reckoning," "Frederick Douglass through His Own Words," "River Niger," "Brownsville Raid," "The Offering," "Old Phantoms," "The Michigan," "About Heaven and Earth," "Louie and Ophelia."

WARING, RICHARD. Born May 27, 1912 in Buckinghamshire, Eng. Appeared with Civic Rep. Co. and in "Romeo and Juliet," "Camille," "Cradle Song," "Boy Meets Girl," "The Corn Is Green," "Henry VIII," "Androcles and the Lion," "What Every Woman Knows," "Alice in Wonderland," "Gramercy Ghost," "Measure for Measure," "Edwin Booth," "Portrait of a Queen," OB in "The Cherry Orchard," "The Actors."

WARING, WENDY. Born Dec. 7, 1960 in Melrose, Ma. Attended Emerson Col., NYU. Debut 1987 OB in "Wish You were Here."

WARREN, DIANE. Born Apr. 6 in Fall River, Ma. Graduate R.I.Col. Debut 1980 OB in "Biography," followed by "Private Ear/Public Eye," "Triangles."

WARREN, JENNIFER LEIGH. Born Aug. 29 in Dallas TX. Graduate Dartmouth Col. Debut 1982 OB in "Little Shop of Horrors," followed by "Next, Please!" "Abyssinia," Bdwy in "Big River" (1985).

WARREN, JOSEPH. Born June 5, 1916 in Boston, MA. Graduate UDenver. Bdwy debut 1951 in "Barefoot in Athens," followed by "One Bright Day," "Love of Four Colonels," "Hidden River," "The Advocate," "Philadelphia, Here I Come," "Borstal Boy," "Lincoln Mask," OB in "Brecht on Brecht," "Jonah," "Little Black Sheep," "Black Tuesday," "The Show-Off," "Big Apple Messenger," "The Ballad of Soapy Smith," "Her Great Match," "Measure for Measure," "Hamlet," "The Rivals."

WATERBURY, MARSHA (formerly Marsha Skaggs). Born Aug. 23, 1949 in Bedford, Oh. Attended Purdue U., AADA. Bdwy debut 1981 in "They're Playing Our Song," followed by "Einstein and the Polar Bear," "Smile," OB in "Little Shop of Horrors."

WEAVER, ANTHONY B. Born Feb. 17, 1960 in NYC. Attended Central School of Speech/Drama. Debut 1985 OB in "The Crows," followed by "The Widow Claire."

WEAVER, LYNN. Born May 17 in Paris, Tn. Graduate UTn, Neighborhood Playhouse. Debut 1981 in "The Italian Straw Hat," followed by "Tiger at the Gates," "The Cherry Orchard," "Murder on the Nile," "A Midsummer Night's Dream," "Milestones."

WEAVER, SIGOURNEY. Born in 1949 in NYC. Attended Yale, Stanford U. Debut 1976 OB in "Titanic," followed by "Das Lusitania Songspiel," "Merchant of Venice," "Beyond Therapy," Bdwy in "Hurlyburly" (1984).

WEINER, JOHN. Born Dec. 17, 1954 in Newark, NJ. Graduate Wm. & Mary Col. Bdwy debut 1983 in "La Cage aux Folles."

WEISS, GORDON J. Born June 16, 1949 in Bismarck, ND. Attended Moorhead State Col. Bdwy debut 1974 in "Junipers," followed by "Goodtime Charley," "King of Hearts," "Raggedy Ann."

WEISS, JEFF. Born in 1940 in Allentown, Pa. Debut 1986 OB in "Hamlet," followed by "The Front Page" (LC).

WELLS, CRAIG. Born July 2, 1955 in Newark, NJ. Graduate Albion Col. Debut 1985 OB in "Forbidden Broadway."

WELLS, DEANNA. Born Aug. 7, 1962 in Milwaukee, Wi. Graduate Northwestern U. Debut 1985 OB in "On the 20th Century," Bdwy in "Smile," "South Pacific" (LC).

WENDSCHUH, RONALD. Born Apr. 19, 1939 in Minnesota. Graduate Luther Col., UMn. Debut 1977 OB in "The Crucible," followed by "Relative Values."

WENTWORTH, PHILIP. Born Dec. 6, 1925 in Rockland, Me. Attended NYU, AmThWing. Debut 1956 in CC's "The King and I" and "Kiss Me, Kate," OB in "Interlock," "You Never Can Tell," "Tronzini Ristorante Murders."

Maureen Silliman	Douglas Simes	Lois Smith	Nick Smith	Donna Snow	Tom Souhrada
Daniel Southern	Dorothy Stanley	Don Stephenson	Elaine Sulka	Richard Tabor	Marzetta Tate
Marianne Tatum	W. Benson Terry	Laura Theodore	Wayne Tippit	Edwina Lee Tyler	Nick Ulett
Greg Vallee	Roberta Wallach	Ken Waller	Juanita Walsh	Richard Waring	Lynn Weaver
Deanna Wells	William Wise	Wendy Worth	John Wylie	Christina Youngman	Christopher Zunner

WEST, MATT. Born Oct. 2, 1958 in Downey, CA. Attended Pfiffer-Smith School. Bdwy debut in "A Chorus Line" (1980).

WESTFALL, RALPH DAVID. Born July 2, 1934 in North Lewisburg, Oh. Graduate OhWesleyanU, SUNY/New Paltz. Debut 1977 OB in "Richard III," followed by "The Importance of Being Earnest," "Anyone Can Whistle," "A Midsummer Night's Dream," "Macbeth," "Gifts of the Magi," "A Theatre History."

WESTPHAL, ROBIN. Born Nov. 24, 1953 in Salt Lake City, UT. Graduate UUtah. Debut 1983 OB in "June Moon," followed by "Taming of the Shrew," "Merchant of Venice," "Somewheres Better," "Lady from the Sea," "Her Great Match," "Antigone," "Pericles," "The Rivals," "Murder in the Mummy's Tomb."

WHALEY, FRANK. Born July 20, 1963 in Syracuse, NY. Graduate SUNY/Albany. Debut 1986 OB in "Tigers Wild."

WHITE, DAVID A. Born June 26, 1960 in West Va. Graduate Ashland Col. Debut 1986 OB in "Olympus on My Mind."

WHITE, RICHARD. Born Aug. 4, 1953 in Oak Ridge, Tn. Graduate Oberlin Col. Bdwy debut 1979 in "The Most Happy Fella," followed by "Brigadoon" (LC), OB in "Elizabeth and Essex," "South Pacific" (LC).

WIEST, DIANNE. Born Mar. 28, 1948 in Kansas City, Mo. Attended UMd. Debut 1976 OB in "Ashes," followed by "Leave It to Beaver Is Dead," "The Art of Dining" for which she received a Theatre World Award, "Bonjour La Bonjour," "The Three Sisters," "Serenading Louie," "Other Places," "Hunting Cockroaches," "After the Fall," Bdwy in "Frankenstein" (1981), "Othello," "Beyond Therapy."

WIKES, MICHAEL. Born June 22, 1955 in Brackenridge, Pa. Graduate Boston U. OB in "Talk to Me Like the Rain," "Old Business," "Self Defense."

WILDING, MICHAEL. Born Jan. 6, 1955 in Los Angeles, Ca. Debut 1986 OB in "Dead Wrong," followed by "Dispatches from Hell," "Bedroom Farce."

WILHOITE, KATHLEEN. Born June 29, 1964 in Santa Barbara, Ca. Attended USCa. Debut 1987 OB in "Division Street."

WILKINSON, COLM. Born June 5, 1944 in Dublin, Ire. Bdwy debut 1987 in "Les Miserables" for which he received a Theatre World Award.

WILKINSON, KATE. Born Oct. 25 in San Francisco, Ca. Attended San Jose State Col. Bdwy debut 1967 in "Little Murders," followed by "Johnny No Trump," "Watercolor," "Postcards," "Ring Round the Bathtub," "The Last of Mrs. Lincoln," "Man and Superman," "Frankenstein," "The Man Who Came to Dinner," OB in "La Madre," "Ernest in Love," "Story of Mary Surratt," "Bring Me a Warm Body," "Child Buyer," "Rimers of Eldritch," "A Doll's House," "Hedda Gabler," "The Real Inspector Hound," "The Contractor," "When the Old Man Died," "The Overcoat," "Villager," "Good Help Is Hard to Find," "Lumiere," "Rude Times," "Steel Magnolias."

WILKOF, LEE. Born June 25, 1951 in Canton, OH. Graduate UCincinnati. Debut 1977 OB in "Present Tense," followed by "Little Shop of Horrors," "Holding Patterns," "Angry Housewives," Bdwy in "Sweet Charity" (1986), "The Front Page" (LC).

WILLIAMS, KEITH. Born Oct. 2, 1954 in Scranton, PA. Graduate Mansfield Col., Catholic U. Debut 1983 OB in "Lady Windermere's Fan," followed by "Verdict," "My Three Angels," "Something Old, Something New," "Murder at the Vicarage," "Rule of Three."

WILLIAMSON, RUTH. Born Jan. 25, 1954 in Baltimore, Md. Graduate UMd. Bdwy debut 1981 in "Annie," followed by "Smile," OB in "Preppies," "Bodo."

WILLISON, WALTER. Born June 24, 1947 in Monterey Park, Ca. Bdwy debut 1970 in "Norman, Is That You?," followed by "Two by Two" for which he received a Theatre World Award, "Wild and Wonderful," "A Celebration of Richard Rodgers," "Pippin," "A Tribute to Joshua Logan," "A Tribute to George Abbott," OB in "They Say It's Wonderful," "Broadway Scandals of 1928," and "Options," both of which he wrote.

WILLOUGHBY, RONALD. Born June 3, 1937 in Boss, MS. Graduate Millsaps Col., Northwestern U. Debut 1963 OB in "Walk in Darkness," followed by "Little Eyolf," "Antony and Cleopatra," "Balm in Gilead," "Dracula. Sabbat.," "The Faggot," "King of the U.S.," "Twelfth Night," "Black People's Party," "Mrs. Warren's Profession," "Why Marry?" "The Green Bay Tree," "Julius Caesar," "A Man's World," "The Sound of Murder," "Milestones," "Sailor, Beware!"

WILSON, K. C. Born Aug. 10, 1945 in Miami, Fl. Attended AADA. Debut 1973 OB in "Little Mahagonny," followed by "The Tempest," "Richard III," "Macbeth," "Threepenny Opera," "The Passion of Dracula," "Francis," "Robin Hood," "Tatterdemalion," "Beef," "The Art of War," Bdwy in "Smile" (1986).

WILSON, MARY LOUISE. Born Nov. 12, 1936 in New Haven, CT. Graduate Northwestern U. Bdwy debut 1963 in "Hot Spot," followed by "Flora the Red Menace," "Criss-Crossing," "Promises, Promises," "The Women," "The Gypsy," "The Royal Family," "Importance of Being Earnest," "Philadelphia Story," "Fools," "Alice in Wonderland," "The Odd Couple," OB in "Our Town," "Upstairs at the Downstairs," "Threepenny Opera," "A Great Career," "Whispers on the Wind," "Beggar's Opera," "Buried Child," "Sister Mary Ignatius Explains It All," "Actor's Nightmare," "Baby with the Bathwater," "Musical Comedy Murders of 1940."

WILSON, TREY. Born Jan. 21, 1948 in Houston, Tx. Bdwy debut 1979 in "Peter Pan," followed by "Tintypes," "The First," "Foxfire," OB in "Personals," "Custom of the Country," "The Front Page" (LC).

WINDE, BEATRICE. Born Jan. 6 in Chicago, Il. Debut 1966 OB in "In White America," followed by "June Bug Graduates Tonight," "Strike Heaven on the Face," "Divine Comedy," "Crazy Horse," "My Mother My Father and Me," "Steal Away," "The Actress," Bdwy in "Ain't Supposed to Die a Natural Death" (1971) for which she received a Theatre World Award.

WINSON, SUZI. Born Feb. 28, 1962 in NYC. Bdwy debut 1980 in "Brigadoon," followed by OB in "Moondance," "Nunsense."

WINTERS, TIME. Born Feb. 3, 1956 in Lebanon, Or. Graduate Stephens Col. Debut 1981 OB in "Nathan the Wise," followed by "Round and Round the Garden," "Fanshen," "Henry V," "Taming of the Shrew," "Ragged Trousered Philanthropists," Bdwy in "Amadeus" (1983).

WINTERSTELLER, LYNNE. Born Sept. 18, 1955 in Sandusky, OH. Graduate UMd. Bdwy debut 1982 in "Annie," OB in "Gifts of the Magi" (1984), "The Rise of David Levinsky."

WISE, WILLIAM. Born May 11 in Chicago, Il. Attended Bradley U., NorthwesternU. Debut 1970 OB in "Adaptation/Next," followed by "Him," "The Hot l Baltimore," "Just the Immediate Family," "36," "For the Use of the Hall," "Orphans," "Working Theatre Festival," "Copperhead."

WOJDA, JOHN. Born Feb. 19, 1957 in Detroit, Mi. Attended UMi. Bdwy debut 1982 in "Macbeth," followed by OB in "Merchant of Venice," "Natural Disasters," "The Coming of Mr. Pine."

WOLF, KELLY. Born Jan. 9, 1964 in Nashville, Tn. Graduate Interlochen Arts Acad. Debut 1983 OB in "Ah, Wilderness!," followed by "Marathon 86," "Young Playwrights Festival," "Bloody Poetry."

WOLPE, LENNY. Born Mar. 25, 1951 in Newburgh, NY. Graduate Geo. Wash. U, UMn. Debut 1978 OB in "Company," followed by "Brownstone," "Mayor," Bdwy in "Onward Victoria" (1980), "Copperfield," "Mayor," "Into the Light."

WOOD, JOHN. Born in 1931 in Derbyshire, Eng. Attended Oxford. Bdwy debut 1967 in "Rosencrantz and Guildenstern Are Dead," followed by "Sherlock Holmes," "Travesties," "Tartuffe," "Deathtrap," "Amadeus," OB in "Rosencrantz and Guildenstern Are Dead."

WOODS, CAROL. Born Nov. 13, 1943 in Jamaica, NY. Graduate Ithaca Col. Debut 1980 OB in "One Mo' Time," followed by "Stepping Out," Bdwy in "Grind" (1985), "Big River."

WOODS, RICHARD. Born May 9, 1923 in Buffalo, NY. Graduate Ithaca Col. Bdwy in "Beg, Borrow or Steal," "Capt. Brassbound's Conversion," "Sail Away," "Coco," "Last of Mrs. Lincoln," "Gigi," "Sherlock Holmes," "Murder among Friends," "The Royal Family," "Deathtrap," "Man and Superman," "The Man Who Came to Dinner," "The Father," "Present Laughter," "Alice in Wonderland," "You Can't Take It with You," "Design for Living," "Smile," OB in "The Crucible," "Summer and Smoke," "American Gothic," "Four-in-One," "My Heart's in the Highlands," "Eastward in Eden," "The Long Gallery," "The Year Boston Won the Pennant," "In the Matter of J. Robert Oppenheimer," "with APA in "You Can't Take It with You," "War and Peace," "School for Scandal," "Right You Are," "The Wild Duck," "Pantagleize," "Exit the King," "The Cherry Orchard," "Cock-a-Doodle Dandy," and "Hamlet," "Crimes and Dreams," "Marathon 84."

WOPAT, TOM. Born in 1950 in Lodi, Wi. Attended UWi. Debut 1978 OB in "A Bistro Car on the CNR," followed by "Oklahoma!," "The Robber Bridegroom," "Olympus on My Mind," Bdwy in "I Love My Wife" (1979).

WORTH, WENDY. Born Jan. 12 in Morristown, NJ. Attended Pima Col. Bdwy debut 1974 in "Irene," OB in "Dazy" (1987).

WRIGHT, AMY. Born Apr. 15, 1950 in Chicago, Il. Graduate Beloit Col. Debut 1977 OB in "The Stronger," followed by "Nightshift," "Hamlet," "Miss Julie," "Slacks and Tops," "Terrible Jim Fitch," "Village Wooing," "The Stronger," "Time Framed," "Trifles," Bdwy in "5th of July" (1980), "Noises Off."

WRIGHT, ANDREA. Born Nov. 19, 1954 in Hartford, Ct. Attended Sarah Lawrence Col. Bdwy debut 1981 in "Barnum," followed by "America," "Raggedy Ann," OB in "KaBoom," "Blackberries."

WRIGHT, MARY CATHERINE. Born Mar. 19, 1948 in San Francisco, Ca. Attended CCSF, SFState Col. Bdwy debut 1970 in "Othello," followed by "A History of American Film," "Tintypes," "The Front Page" (LC), OB in "East Lynne," "Mimi Lights the Candle," "Marvin's Gardens," "The Tempest," "The Doctor in spite of Himself," "Love's Labour's Lost," "Pushcart Peddlers," "Sister Mary Ignatius Explains It All," "Actor's Nightmare," "Marathon 84," "The Dining Room," "Rimes of Passion."

WYLIE, JOHN. Born Dec. 14, 1925 in Peacock, Tx. Graduate North Tx.State U. Debut 1987 OB in "The Lucky Spot."

WYMAN, NICHOLAS. Born May 18, 1950 in Portland, Me. Graduate Harvard U. Bdwy debut 1975 in "Very Good Eddie," followed by "Grease," "The Magic Show," "On the 20th Century," "Whoopee!," "My Fair Lady" (1981), "Doubles," "Musical Comedy Murders of 1940," OB in "Paris Lights," "When We Dead Awaken," "Charlotte Sweet," "Kennedy at Colonus," "Once on a Summer's Day," "Angry Housewives."

YANCEY, KIM. Born Sept. 25, 1959 in NYC. Graduate CCNY. Debut 1978 OB in "Why Lillie Won't Spin," followed by "Escape to Freedom," "Dacha," "Blues for Mr. Charlie," "American Dreams," "Ties That Bind," "Walking Through," "Raisin in the Sun."

YANG, GINNY. Born Apr. 22, 1952 in Korea. Graduate Catawba Col. Debut 1980 OB in "F.O.B.," followed by "Peking Man," "Extenuating Circumstances," "Wha . . . Wha, Along Time Ago," Bdwy in "Plenty" (1982).

YOSHIDA, PETER. Born May 28, 1945 in Chicago, Il. Graduate UIll, Princeton, AADA. Debut 1965 OB in "Coriolanus," followed by "Troilus and Cressida," "Santa Anita '42," "Pursuit of Happiness," "Servant of Two Masters," "The Peking Man," "Monkey Music," "Station J," "Double Dutch," "Prime Time."

YOUNG, DAVID. Born July 14, 1947 in Kansas City, Mo. Graduate UKs. Debut 1973 OB in "The Raree Show," followed by "Inexhaustible Banquet," "Times Like These," "The Night Boat," "Rabboni," "Madison Avenue," Bdwy in "Into the Light" (1986).

YOUNGMAN, CHRISTINA. Born Sept. 14, 1963 in Philadelphia, Pa. Attended Point Park Col. Debut 1983 OB in "Emperor of My Baby's Heart," followed by "Carouselle des Folles," Bdwy in "Starlight Express" (1987).

YOUSE, DAVID J. Born Jan. 19, 1966 in Philadelphia, Pa. Attended AADA. Debut 1986 OB in "Lonely Streets," followed by "My Papa's Wine."

YULIN, HARRIS. Born Nov. 5, 1937 in Calif. Attended USCal. Debut 1963 OB in "Next Time I'll Sing to You," followed by "A Midsummer Night's Dream," "Troubled Waters," "Richard III," "King John," "The Cannibals," "Lesson from Aloes," "Hedda Gabler," "Barnum's Last Life," "Hamlet," "Mrs. Warren's Profession," "Marathon '86," "Marathon 87," Bdwy in "Watch on the Rhine" (1980).

ZACHARIAS, EMILY. Born July 27, 1953 in Memphis, Tn. Graduate Northwestern U. Debut 1980 OB in "March of the Falsettos," followed by "America Kicks Up Its Heels," "Crazy He Calls Me," "Olympus on My Mind," Bdwy in "Perfectly Frank" (1980).

ZAPP, PETER. Born Oct. 2, 1951 in Cleveland, Oh. Graduate Baldwin Wallace Col. Debut 1983 OB in "Half a Lifetime," followed by "Strange Behavior," "Plainsong," "Brass Bell Superette," "State of the Union," "Hitch-Hikers," "Tigers Wild," Bdwy in "End of the World . . ." (1984).

ZIEN, CHIP. Born in 1947 in Milwaukee, WI. Attended UPa. OB in "You're a Good Man, Charlie Brown," followed by "Kadish," "How to Succeed . . .," "Dear Mr. G," "Tuscaloosa's Calling," "Hot l Baltimore," "El Grande de Coca Cola," "Split," "Real Life Funnies," "March of the Falsettos," "Isn't It Romantic," "Diamonds," Bdwy in "All Over Town" (1974), "The Suicide."

ZUNNER, CHRISTOPHER. Born Nov. 30, 1960 in Kenmore, NY. Graduate Niagara U. Debut 1985 OB in "The Merry Widow," followed by "Naughty Marietta," "Babes in Toyland," "The Gondoliers," "The Mikado," "Take Me Along."

Walter Abel

Seth Allen

Hermione Baddeley

Bil Baird

Michael Baseleon

Louis Beachner

OBITUARIES

TOM ABBOTT, 53, Texas-born dancer known for his stagings of Jerome Robbins's musicals and ballets, was found dead in his Manhattan home, April, 8, 1987. He made his Broadway debut in *West Side Story* in 1957, followed by *Fiddler on the Roof,* assisting Robbins on both, as well as the film of *West Side,* in which he also appeared. He reproduced Robbins' choreography for the film of *Fiddler,* the 1976 and 1981 Broadway revivals of that show, and the 1964 City Center and 1980 Broadway revivals of *West Side.* He also staged productions of *Fiddler* in Tel Aviv, London, Amsterdam, Hamburg, West Germany, and Vienna, and for the Australian Opera. He is survived by a brother and two sisters.

WALTER ABEL, 88, Minnesota-born stage, film, radio and TV character actor, died March 26, 1987 in Essex, CT. He made is Broadway debut in *Forbidden* in 1919, followed by *Back to Methuselah, As You Like It, Love for Love, The Enemy, The Seagull, First Mortgage, At the Bottom, I Love an Actress, The Mermaids Singing, Parlor Story, The Biggest Thief in Town, The Wisteria Trees, The Pleasure of His Company, Night Life, The Ninety-Day Mistress, Saturday, Sunday, Monday,* and *Trelawny of the Wells* (LC, 1975). He is survived by two sons.

SETH ALLEN, 45, Brooklyn-born actor, writer, and director, died of cryptococcal meningitis Aug. 14, 1986, at his home in Manhattan. He won an Obie as best actor in 1966–67 for *Futz,* and also appeared Off-Broadway in *Viet Rock, Hair, Candaules Commissioner, Mary Stuart, Narrow Road to the Deep North, More Than You Deserve, Split Lip, The Misanthrope, Hard Sell, The Wild Duck, Jungle of Cities, Egyptology, The Lisbon Traviata,* and on Broadway in *Jesus Christ Superstar* and *Accidental Death of an Anarchist.* His plays include *Sissy,* and his directorial credits include *A Rat's Mass* and *Blonde Roots,* which he also wrote. He is survived by a brother and three sisters.

HERMIONE BADDELEY, 79, British-born stage, film, and TV actress and comedienne, died of complications from a stroke, August 19, 1986 in Los Angeles, CA. Perhaps best known to TV audiences as Mrs. Naugatuck, the spry housekeeper on *Maude,* she made her stage debut at age six and starred in many London successes before making her Broadway bow in *A Taste of Honey* in 1960, followed by *The Milk Train Doesn't Stop Here Anymore, Canterbury Tales, Whodunnit,* and *I Only Want an Answer* Off-Broadway. She is survived by her daughter, son and sister.

BIL BAIRD (William Britton Baird), 82, Nebraska-born stage and TV puppeteer, died March 18, 1987 of pneumonia after a struggle with bone marrow cancer, at his home in Manhattan. Considered the man who brought puppeteering into the 20th Century, his creations starred on Broadway in *The Ziegfeld Follies of 1941, Flahooley, Baker Street, Ali Baba and the Forty Thieves, The Man in the Moon,* and *Davy Jones's Locker,* Off-Broadway in *The Wizard of Oz* and *The Whistling Wizard* among others, at Radio City Music Hall, and in the film *The Sound of Music.* In 1936 he created puppets for Orson Welles' W.P.A. Federal Theatre Project of *Dr. Faustus,* where he met actress Cora Burlar, who became his wife and partner. The Bairds received the Outer Circle Award in 1967 for having founded a permanent puppet theatre Off-Broadway. He is survived by his daughter, son and brother.

MICHAEL BASELEON, 61, Missouri-born stage, film, and TV actor, died Oct. 9, 1986 in Lenox, Mass., where he was appearing in *Antony and Cleopatra.* His Broadway credits include *Caligula, Night Life, Dear Me, The Sky is Falling, Venus Is,* and Off-Broadway in *Hamlet, Henry IV, Richard II, Romeo and Juliet, The Tempest, Journey to the Day, Harold and Sondra,* and *Peer Gynt* (CP). He is survived by several sisters.

HOWARD BAY, 74, stage designer, considered by many to be "the dean of American designers," died Nov. 21, 1986 of a heart attack at his home in Manhattan. His more than 170 productions began in 1933 with *There's a Moon Tonight,* followed by *One Third of a Nation, The Merry Wives of Windsor, The Little Foxes, The Moon Is Down, Count Me In, The Children's Hour, Magdalena, Chalk Dust, Battle Hymn, Finian's Rainbow, The Wall, The Cool World, Look Back in Anger, Night of the Auk, One Touch of Venus, Come Back Little Sheba,* and *As the Girls Go* (which he also directed). He won Tony Awards for *Toys in the Attic* and *Man of LaMancha,* and Donaldson Awards for *Carmen Jones* and *Up in Central Park.* He is survived by a son and a daughter.

LOUIS BEACHNER, 63, New Jersey-born actor, died of cancer September 19, 1986 in NYC. He made his Broadway debut in *Junior Miss,* followed by *No Time for Sergeants, Georgy, The Changing Room, National Health, Where's Charley?, Passion, Oliver,* and Off-Broadway in *Time to Burn, The Hostage, Savages,* and *The Overcoat.* He is survived by a brother.

JOHN C. BECHER, 71, Milwaukee-born stage, film, and TV actor, died Sept. 20, 1986 of cancer in Hollywood, CA. He made his Broadway bow in 1946 with American Rep. Theatre, followed by *Skipper Next to God, Idiot's Delight, Picnic, Brigadoon* (CC), *No Time for Sergeants, Ballad of the Sad Cafe, Mame* (1966, '83), *Harvey, Gypsy,* and Off-Broadway in *American Dream, Death of Bessie Smith, Happy Days, Dumbwaiter, Child Buyer,* and *That Thing at the Cherry Lane.* He is survived by his widow Margaret, two sisters and a brother.

RAY BOLGER (Raymond Wallace Bolger) Dorchester, Mass-born song-and-dance-man of stage, screen, and TV, forever remembered as the Scarecrow in the film *The Wizard of Oz,* died of cancer January 15, 1987, one week after his 83rd Birthday in Los Angeles. His many credits include *The Merry World* (1926), *A Night in Paris, Ritz-Carlton Nights, Heads Up, George White's Scandals of 1931,* the inaugural program dedicating Radio City Music Hall (1932), *Life Begins at 8:40, On Your Toes, Keep Off the Grass, By Jupiter* (1943 Page One Award), *Three to Make Ready* (two 1946 Donaldson Awards, won Variety NY Drama Critics Poll), *Where's Charley?* (1949 Tony Award), *All American,* and *Come Summer.* Surviving is his widow.

WALTER BROOKE, 71, New York-born stage, screen, radio, and TV actor, died Aug. 20, 1986 of emphysema in Los Angeles. He made his Broadway debut in Gielgud's *Hamlet,* followed by *Romeo and Juliet, The Barber Had Two Sons, The Eagle Has Two Heads, Two Blind Mice, Twilight Walk, Seagulls Over Sorrento, The Second Man,* and *Hide and Seek.* He is survived by his wife, a son and a daughter.

PETER BURNELL, New York-born stage, film, and TV actor, died of unreported causes in Chicago, on Jan. 5, 1987. He appeared Off-Broadway in *Henry IV, Antony and Cleopatra, The Tempest, Macbeth, Olathe Response, Ubu Roi/Ubu Bound, Dancing for the Kaiser, The Prince of Homburg, Flying Blind,* and on Broadway in *In Praise of Love* for which he received a 1974 Theatre World Award. He is survived by his parents, two sisters and a brother.

DAVID CAHN, 29, actor-dancer, died Jan. 22, 1987 in New York after a long illness. His Broadway credits include *Jesus Christ Superstar, Little Me,* and *La Cage aux Folles,* and he toured in the international company of *A Chorus Line.* He is survived by his mother and brother.

ROGER C. CARMEL, 53, stage, film, and TV character actor, was found dead of an apparent drug overdose at his Hollywood condominium on Nov. 11. 1986. His Broadway credits include *A Man for All Seasons, Half a Sixpence, Rhinoceros, Caligula,* and *Once There Was a Russian.* No reported survivors.

ALLEN CASE, 51, Texas-born stage, film, and TV actor, died of a heart attack Aug. 25, 1986 while on vacation in Truckee, CA. He appeared on Broadway in *Damn Yankees, South Pacific* (CC), *Once Upon a Mattress,* and *Hallelujah, Baby!,* and Off-Broadway in *Pleasure Dome, The Carefree Heart,* and *Once Upon a Mattress.* He is survived by his daughter, mother and sister.

JAMES COCO, 56, New York-born stage, film, and TV character actor, died Feb. 25, 1987 of a heart attack in New York City. He made his debut Off-Broadway in *Salome,* followed by *Moon in the Yellow River, Squat Betty/The Sponge Room, That 5 a.m. Jazz, Lovey, The Basement, Fragments, Witness, Next, Monsters/The Transfiguration of Benno Blimpie, It's Only a Play,* and was on Broadway in *Hotel Paradiso* (debut 1956), *Everybody Loves Opal, Passage to India, Arturo Ui, The Devils, Man of LaMancha, The Astrakhan Coat, Here's Where I Belong, Last of the Red Hot Lovers, Wally's Cafe, Little Me* (1981), and *You Can't Take It with You.* There are no immediate survivors.

227

LADY DIANA COOPER (Diana Manners), 93, the dowager Viscountess Norwich, stage and screen actress, legendary beauty, and quintessential English eccentric, died June 16, 1986 at the London home where she had been bedridden for two years. She had a brief but spectacular career in the 20's in Max Reinhardt's pageant *The Miracle,* touring from London, to Europe, to Broadway, and across the U.S. on and off for 12 years. She is survived by her son, John Julius Cooper, the second Viscount Norwich.

PETER COE, 58, London-born stage and film director, and former stage actor, was killed with his mother May 25, 1987 in an automobile accident in Byfleet, south of London. His vast international directing credits include the Broadway successes *Oliver!* (1965 & 1984), *On a Clear Day You Can See Forever, Mister Lincoln, A Life* (1981 Tony nomination), and *Othello* (1982 Tony Award). Survived by a son and two daughters.

HELEN CRAIG, 74, Texas-born stage, film, radio, and TV actress, died July 20, 1986 in New York of cardiac arrest. Best remembered as the deaf-mute in *Johnny Belinda,* she made her Broadway debut in *Russet Mantle* (1936), followed by *New Faces of 1936, Julius Caesar* (Orson Welles' Mercury Theater), *Soliloquy, Family Portrait, The Unconquered, As You Like It, Lute Song, Land's End, The House of Bernarda Alba, Maya, Diamond Orchid, Medea, To Clothe the Naked,* and Off-Broadway in *More Stately Mansions.* She is survived by her husband of 52 years, actor John Beal, two daughters, a brother, and a sister.

PEGGY CORNELL BENLINE, Kansas-city born former dancer, Ziegfeld girl, and co-president of the Ziegfeld Club, died of pneumonia in New York City August 30, 1986, after having had an operation for cancer. Broadway appearances include *Dilly Dally, Rio Rita* (1927), *Show Boat* (1934), and *As Thousands Cheer* (replacing an ailing Marilyn Miller). She retired from the stage in 1951. Survived by her husband and a sister.

CHERYL CRAWFORD, 84, Ohio-born theatrical producer, and co-founder of the Group Theatre and the Actors Studio, died Oct. 7, 1986 in New York City of complications resulting from a severe fall. One of the first and most successful female producers, made her Broadway debut as assistant stage manager and bit player in *Juarez and Maximilian* in 1926, and was casting director for the Theatre Guild before producing such shows as *Men in White, Waiting for Lefty, Awake and Sing, Golden Boy,* and *Bury the Dead* (all for the Group Theatre), *Porgy and Bess* (1942), *One Touch of Venus, Brigadoon, Skipper Next to God, Love Life, The Rose Tattoo, Camino Real, Sweet Bird of Youth, Period of Adjustment, Flahooley, Paint Your Wagon, Oh, Men! Oh, Women!, Comes a Day,* and *Blues for Mr. Charlie, Baby Want a Kiss,* and *The Three Sisters* (exec producer for the Actors Studio). In 1986 she produced *So Long on Lonely Street* in New York, and *Legends,* on tour with Mary Martin and Carol Channing. She is survived by a brother.

CATHRYN DAMON, 56, Seattle-born stage and film actress, died May 4, 1987 of cancer in Los Angeles. Best known as Mary Campbell on the TV series SOAP, for which she received an Emmy Award in 1980, she made her Broadway debut in 1954 in *By the Beautiful Sea,* followed by *The Vamp, Shinbone Alley, A Family Affair, Foxy, Flora the Red Menace, UTBU, Come Summer, Criss-Crossing, A Place for Polly, Last of the Red Hot Lovers, Passion,* and Off-Broadway in *Boys from Syracuse, The Secret Life of Walter Mitty, Show Me Where the Good Times Are, Effect of Gamma Rays on Man-in-the-Moon Marigolds, Siamese Connections, Prodigal, Down by the River . . ., Sweet Bird of Youth,* and *The Cherry Orchard.* Survivors include her mother and a sister.

ALFRED deLIAGRE, JR., 82, New Jersey-born producer and director for 50 years, died March 5, 1987 of lung cancer in his Manhattan apartment. He produced and directed his first Broadway show, *Three-Cornered Moon* in 1933, followed by *By Your Leave, Pure in Heart, Petticoat Fever, Fresh Fields, Yes, My Darling Daughter, The Walrus and the Carpenter, Mr. and Mrs. North* (also directed) *Voice of the Turtle, The Mermaids Singing, The Druid Circle, The Madwoman of Chaillot* (made a Chevalier of the French Legion of Honor as a result of this production), *Second Threshold, The Deep Blue Sea, The Golden Apple, Janus, The Girls in 509, J. B., Kwamina, The Irregular Verb to Love, Photo Finish, Love in E-Flat, Deathtrap,* and *On Your Toes* (1983). He was a first v.p. of the Actors Fund of America, a governor emeritus of the League of American Theaters and Producers, and elected to the Theatre Hall of Fame. He is survived by his wife, a son and a daughter.

HUGH DEMPSTER, 86, London-born stage and film actor, died of heart failure in Chicago. He made his Broadway debut in 1929 in *Rope's End,* followed by shows including *Baker Street,* and was best known for Pickering in *My Fair Lady* on national tour for more than 2,500 performances. He is survived by his wife and brother.

ROBERT DRIVAS, 50, Florida-born director, stage, screen and TV actor, died June 29, 1986 in New York City. He made his Broadway debut in 1958 in *The Firstborn,* followed by *One More River, The Wall, Lorenzo, The Irregular Verb to Love,* Off-Broadway in *Diff'rent,* and *Mrs. Dally has a Lover* (1963) for which he received a Theatre World Award. He directed such productions as *Bad Habits* (1974 Obie Award), *The Ritz, Legend, It Had to Be You, Little Me* (1981), directed and co-starred in *Monsters/Side Show/Transfiguration of Benno Blimpie.* His last stage appearance was in 1985 in *Jacques and His Master* at Harvard's American Repertory Theater. He is survived by his mother, a sister and two brothers.

KENN DUNCAN, 56, prominent photographer of dance and theatre, died July 26, 1986 in New York City of tocoplasmosis. Among his published books are *Red Shoes* and *View of the Theatre from Behind,* a backstage view of Broadway. He is survived by a sister and a brother.

VIVIAN DUNCAN, 84, who with her sister Rosetta performed as the Duncan Sisters, died Sept. 19, 1986 in Los Angeles, after suffering from Alzheimer's disease for several years. Their Broadway appearances include *Doing Our Bit* in 1918, followed by *Tip-Top, The Ziegfeld Follies.* They toured the U.S. in *Topsy and Eva* from 1923 to 1926, and in 1931 and 1934. She is survived by her daughter, and a brother, former tennis pro Harold Duncan.

WILBUR W. EVANS, 81, Philadelphia-born actor-singer of stage, film, and radio died May 31, 1987 in Elmer, N.J. His Broadway appearances include *Up in Central Park, Mexican Hayride, Desert Song, By the Beautiful Sea, The Merry Widow The New Moon* (Carnegie Hall), and he replaced Ezio Pinza in the London cast of *South Pacific.* He is survived by his wife and a son.

HUGH FRANKLIN, 70, Oklahoma-born retired stage, screen, and TV actor, died of cancer Sept. 26, 1986 in Torrington, CT. He made his Broadway bow in 1938 in *Gloriana,* followed by *Harriet, Alice in Wonderland, Medea, The Best Man, Luther, A Shot in the Dark, Arturo Ui, The Devils, What Did We Do Wrong?,* and Off-Broadway in *How Much, How Much?, Misalliance,* and *The Play's the Thing.* He is survived by his wife, writer Madeleine L'Engle, a son, and two daughters.

TILDA GETZ (Tilda Stoneburn), 68, stage actress and dancer, and later secretary to Richard Rodgers, died in her sleep of natural causes Nov. 25, 1985 in her New York City apartment. Discovered by Rodgers and Hart, she made her Broadway debut in 1935 in *Jumbo,* followed by such shows as *Pal Joey* and *Between the Devil.* She is survived by a son and daughter.

WYNNE GIBSON, 82, New York-born stage, film, radio, and TV actress, chairwoman of the Equity Library Theatre and an Actors Equity board member, died May 15, 1987 of a stroke in Laguna Niguel, CA. She made her Broadway bow in *Little Jessie James,* followed by *Jarnegan* in 1929, before moving to Hollywood to appear in more than 40 films. There are no survivors.

MARGALO GILLMORE, 89, London-born stage and film actress, died June 30, 1986 in New York City. She made her Broadway debut in 1917 in *The Scrap of Paper,* followed by *The Famous Mrs. Fair, The Straw, He Who Gets Slapped, Outward Bound, The Green Hat, Berkeley Square, The Barretts of Wimpole Street, Flowers of the Forest, Valley Forge, The Women, No Time for Comedy, State of the Union, Diary of Anne Frank, Little Eyolf, Juarez and Maximilian, Ned McCobb's Daughter, The Silver Cord, The Second Man, Marco Millions, No Time for Comedy, Kind Sir, Peter Pan,* and *Sail Away* (1961). There are no immediate survivors.

HERMIONE GINGOLD, 89, London-born stage, film, and TV actress, died May 24, 1987, of pneumonia complicated by heart disease in New York City. The comedienne whose tart, quick-witted repartee became her trademark, is perhaps best known for her portrayal of the lovable retired courtesan, Mamita, in the film *Gigi,* in which she sang the duet *I Remember It Well* with Maurice Chevalier. She made her Broadway bow in 1953 in *John Murray Anderson's Almanac* (1954 Donaldson Award), followed by *Sleeping Prince, First Impressions, From A to Z, Milk and Honey, Oh, Dad, Poor Dad, Mama's Hung You . . .,* and *A Little Night Music.* Among her survivors are two sons, including director Stephen Joseph, and a sister.

MURRAY HAMILTON, 63, stage, film, and TV actor, died Sept. 1, 1986 of cancer in his native Washington, NC. He made his Broadway debut in 1945 in *Strange Fruit,* followed by *Mister Roberts, The Chase, Stockade* (Off-Broadway), *Critic's Choice, The Heroine, Absence of a Cello* (1964 Tony Award), and *Forty Carats.* He is survived by his wife, Terry, who was one of the DeMarco sisters, and son David, an actor-singer.

ROBERT HELPMANN, 77, Australian dancer who became an international ballet star and choreographer, stage and film actor/director, died Sept. 28, 1986 in Sydney after a long illness. He appeared on Broadway in 1951 in Laurence Olivier's productions of *Caesar and Cleopatra* and *Antony and Cleopatra: Two on the Nile.* He was knighted in 1968. No reported survivors.

ALAN HEWITT, 71, New York City-born stage, film, and TV actor, died Nov. 7, 1986 of cancer in New York. He made his Broadway bow in 1935 in *The Taming of the Shrew,* followed by more than 20 plays including *Idiot's Delight, The Masque of Kings, Amphitryon 38, The Sea Gull, The American Way, Love's Old Sweet Song, The Moon Is Down, The Gentleman from Athens, Death of a Salesman, Call Me Madam, Ondine,* and *Inherit the Wind.* He is survived by his mother and a brother.

ABRAM HILL (Ab Hill), 76, Georgia-born stage director/playwright, and a major figure in the development of black theatre, died at his home in Harlem on Oct. 6, 1986. The founder of the American Negro Theatre in Harlem in 1940, his 1944 adaptation of Philip Yordan's play *Anna Lucasta* became one of Broadway's longest running plays (900 performances). While with the Federal Theatre Project in 1938, he wrote such plays as *On Strivers' Row, Walk Hard, Hell's Half Acre,* and *Liberty Deferred.* He is survived by his wife, a sister and a brother.

JOYCE JAMESON, about 55, stage, film, and TV actress, died of undetermined causes Jan. 16, 1987 in Burbank, CA. She made her Broadway bow in 1959 in *The Billy Barnes Revue,* followed by *The Billy Barnes People* and *Venus at Large.* She is survived by a son, musician Tyler Barnes.

BEATRICE KAY, 79, New York-born singer and actress of stage, screen, radio and TV, who gained fame as "The Gay 90's Girl," died Nov. 8, 1986 as the result of a stroke. Her Broadway appearances include *Secrets* (1922), *Sweet Adeline, Jarnegan, The Provincetown Follies, Behind the Red Lights,* and *Tell Me Pretty Maiden* (1937). She leaves no survivors.

DANNY KAYE, (David Daniel Kominski), 74, Brooklyn-born stage, film, and TV actor, comedian, singer, dancer, and conductor who became Good Will Ambassador to the World, died March 3, 1987 In Los Angeles of a heart attack. He appeared in vaudeville before his 1939 Broadway bow in *Left of Broadway,* followed by *The Straw Hat Revue* (written by Sylvia Fine, who became his wife, collaborator, and coach for the next 47 years), *Lady in the Dark, Let's Face It,* and his 1970 return in *Two By Two.* UNICEF'S ambassador-at-large for 34 years, his many honors include a special Tony Award (1953), a special Academy Award (1954), a 1963 Emmy Award, a Peabody Award, the Sam S. Shubert Award (1970–71) the Jean Hersholt Humanitarian Award (1982), and the Kennedy Center Honors (1984). He is survived by his wife, and a daughter, Dena Kaye.

NORA KAYE, (Nora Koreff) New York City-born, leading American ballerina, and later a film producer, died Feb. 28, 1987 in her Los Angeles home after a long illness. The international star first appeared on Broadway in *Virginia* (1937), followed by *Great Lady, Stars in Your Eyes,* and *Two's Company.* She is survived by her husband, producer-director-choreographer Herbert Ross.

BETTY KEAN, 69, Hartford-born stage, film, TV, and nightclub actress and comedienne, died of cancer Sept. 29, 1986 in her Hollywood home. She began her Broadway career in *George White's Scandals,* followed by *It's All Yours, Early to Bed, The Girl From Nantucket, Ankles Aweigh* (co-starring her sister Jane Kean), *The Pajama Game, Hit the Deck, Show Boat,* and *No, No, Nanette.* In addition to her sister, she is survived by a daughter.

RICHARD KENDRICK, early 80's, South Dakota-born retired stage actor, died in NYC Feb. 10, 1987 after suffering a stroke. He made his Broadway debut in 1933 in *Double Door,* followed by *Personal Appearance, A Room in Red and White, Spring Dance, Stage Door, Excursion, Stars in Your Eyes, Claudia,* and *Two Blind Mice.* There are no immediate survivors.

DENNIS KING, JR., 64, English-born stage, screen, and TV singer-actor, died Aug. 24, 1986 of a heart attack in Las Vegas. He appeared in 24 Broadway shows including his debut in *Lower North,* followed by *The Trojan Horse, Kiss Them for Me, The Playboy of the Western World, Parlor Story, The Cradle Will Rock,* and *The Vigil.* No reported survivors.

GLENN B. KEZER, 63, Oklahoma-born stage, film, and TV actor, died March 26, 1987 of cancer in Okemah, OK. He appeared on Broadway in *My Fair Lady, Camelot, Fade Out-Fade In, Little Murders, The Trial of Lee Harvey Oswald, Threepenny Opera* and Off-Broadway in *Promenade, Oh Say Can You See LA, Brigadoon, Walk in Darkness,* and *You Never Can Tell.* He is survived by his wife and two daughters.

TONY KRABER, 81, retired actor, director, singer, and playwright, died of emphysema Sept. 9, 1986 at his home in Brooklyn. Seen on and Off-Broadway since 1927, he produced the Pulitzer Prize-winning *My Heart's in the Highland's* and *Waiting for Lefty* for the Group Theatre in the 30's and last appeared on Broadway in *Nobody Heard the Lions Roar* (1977). Survived by his wife, and a son.

ELSA LANCHESTER, 84, British-born stage and film actress, best known for eccentric and comic roles such as the monster's wife in the film *Bride of Frankenstein,* died Dec. 26, 1986 in Woodland Hills, CA. She had been incapacitated since suffering a stroke in 1983. A successful London stage actress with more than 50 films to her credit, she appeared on Broadway in *Payment Deferred* (1931), *The Tempest, They Walk Alone, No Strings, The Party, A Zany Evening with Elsa Lanchester,* and *Elsa Lanchester-Herself* (1961). There are no survivors. She was the widow of the late actor Charles Laughton.

PHILIP LAWRENCE, 66, Arkansas-born stage actor and director, died Feb. 19, 1987 in NYC of complications resulting from diabetes. He won an Obie Award as Best Actor in 1954–55 for *Twelfth Night.* Other appearances include *Hamlet* (1956), *Twelfth Night* (director, 1957), *King Lear* (director, 1959), *Royal Gambit,* and *The Jackass.* He left no immediate survivors.

STANLEY LEBOWSKY, 59, Broadway conductor, musical director, and composer, died Oct. 19, 1986 after a heart attack in his NYC home. He conducted more than two dozen musicals, including *Pippin, Chicago, The Act, Half a Sixpence, The 1940's Radio Hour, Jesus Christ Superstar, Irma La Douce, Cats,* and *Me and My Girl.* He was musical supervisor for *Singin' in the Rain,* and composed the music for *Gantry.* He is survived by his daughter and son.

ALAN JAY LERNER, 67, New York City-born lyricist, playwright and producer, died of lung cancer June 14, 1986 in New York, after toasting his family and close friends with champagne in his hospital room the preceding night. With composer Frederick Lowe he formed one of the legendary partnerships of the American musical theatre, beginning with their collaboration on *What's Up* (1943), and continuing with *The Day Before Spring, Brigadoon, Paint Your Wagon, My Fair Lady, Camelot,* the stage version of their film hit *Gigi,* and *Carmelina* (1979). He also collaborated on *Love Life* (music by Kurt Weill), *On a Clear Day You Can See Forever* (Burton Lane), *Coco* (Andre Previn), *1600 Pennsylvania Avenue* (Leonard Bernstein), and *Dance a Little Closer* (Charles Strouse). He is survived by his eighth wife, actress Liz Robertson, his son, and three daughters.

VIVIAN MARTIN, 95, actress, died March 16, 1987 after a long illness. She made her debut in 1901 in *Cyrano de Bergerac,* at age 12 played *Little Lord Fauntleroy,* and also appeared on Broadway in shows including *Just Married, the Wild Westcotts, Puppy Love, Hearts Are Trumps!, Half a Widow, Caste, Mrs Dane's Defense, Sherlock Holmes* (1928), and *Marry the Man!* (1929). No survivors reported.

HARRIET MacGIBBON, 81, Chicago-born stage, screen, and TV actress forever remembered as Mrs. Drysdale on TV's *The Beverly Hillbillies,* died Feb. 8, 1987 in Beverly Hills, CA, after having suffered from pulmonary and cardiac problems for several years. She made her Broadway debut in 1923 in *Beggar on Horseback,* followed by such productions as *Howdy King, Ringside, The Marriage Bed, Houseparty, Midnight, The Inside Story, Shooting Star, Our Betters, Lightnin', Two on an Island, The Ladies of the Corridor,* and *Cloud 7* (1958). She is survived by a grandson.

SCOTT McKAY (Carl Gose), 71, Iowa-born stage, film, radio, and TV actor, died of kidney failure March 1, 1987 in New York. Among his many Broadway appearances that began in 1938 with *Good Hunting,* are *Swan Song, Another Part of the Forest, Mr. Barry's Etchings, The Live Wire, Bell, Book and Candle, First Lady, Sabrina Fair, Nature's Way, Requiem for a Nun, Once for the Asking, Brigadoon* (1957 & '64), *The Little Foxes, Eve of St. Mark, The Moon Is Down,* and *Mary, Mary.* He is survived by his wife, a sister, two sons, and three step-children.

SIOBHAN McKENNA, 63 or 64, North Ireland-born stage and film actress, died Nov. 16, 1986 of a heart attack following surgery for lung cancer in Dublin. Considered one of Ireland's greatest actresses, she made her Broadway bow in 1955 in *The Chalk Garden,* followed by *Saint Joan* (perhaps her most acclaimed performance), as *Hamlet* (Off-Broadway), *Twelfth Night* (1957 & '59), *The Rope Dancers, Macbeth, St. Joan of the Stockyards, Juno and the Paycock, Best of Friends,* and *Here are the Ladies* (Off-Broadway, 1970). She is survived by her son, to the late actor Denis O'Dea, and a sister.

VINCENTE MINNELLI, 83, Chicago-born stage and film director, designer, and playwright, and Academy Award winner, died July 25, 1986 in his sleep at his Beverly Hills home. One of the foremost cinematic stylists of his era while under contract to MGM for nearly 26 years he began his career on Broadway as a set and costume designer for Earl Carroll's *Vanities* in 1932, followed by *DuBarry,* and at Radio City Music Hall staging ballets and producing a new show every month from 1933–35. He continued to design his own productions with his Broadway directing debut in 1935 with *At Home Abroad,* followed by *Ziegfeld Follies* (1935–'36), *The Show Is On, Hooray for What!,* and *Very Warm for May* (1939), and he wrote *Dance Me a Song* (1950). Surviving are his fourth wife, and his two daughters, actress Liza Minnelli (by former wife Judy Garland) and Christiana Nina Minnelli, from his second marriage.

EARL MONTGOMERY, 65, Memphis-born stage, screen, film, and TV actor, died March 4, 1987 of a heart attack in Los Angeles. He made his Broadway debut in 1947 in *Galileo,* followed by *Summer and Smoke, The Relapse, Mr. Pickwick, Love's Labour's Lost, Merchant of Venice, The Strong Are Lonely, Heavenly Twins, Visit to a Small Planet, Look after Lulu, Lady of the Camellias, Tovarich, Rehearsal, Her First Roman, Waltz of the Toreadors,* at LC in *Caucasian Chalk Circle, The Alchemist, East Wind, Galileo, St. Joan, Tiger at the Gates,* and *Cyrano.* He is survived by his stepmother and two stepbrothers.

ELIZABETH MORGAN, 84, stage. film, radio, TV, and nightclub actress, and longtime officer and board member of AFTRA, died May 31, 1987 at her Manhattan home as the result of a stroke. Her Broadway credits include *The Mimic World of 1921* (1921), *Elsie Janis and Her Gang, Americana, New Faces,* and *American Holiday* (1936). She is survived by a stepdaughter.

GRETA MOSHEIM, 81, a leading German stage actress, died of cancer Dec. 29, 1986 at her home in Manhattan. She appeared on Broadway in *Baby Mine* (1927), *This Was a Man, Burlesque Artiste, Street Scene, Phaedra, Die Fee: The Fairy, Kommt ein Vogel Geflogen, Waterloo Bridge, Faust* (1932), *Two Share a Dwelling, Letters to Lucerne, Calico Wedding,* and succeeded Lotte Lenya Off-Broadway in *The Threepenny Opera.* Survivors include two nieces.

DAME ANNA NEAGLE (Florence Marjorie Robertson), 81, British-born stage and screen actress, producer, and one of England's greatest stars, died June 3, 1986 at a nursing home in Surrey. She made her London stage debut in 1917 in *The Wonder Tales,* followed by *Charlot's Revue, Rose Marie, Bubly, The Charlot Show of 1926, The Desert Song, This Year of Grace, Wake Up and Dream* (in which she made her Broadway debut in 1929), *Stand Up and Sing, Twelfth Night* (1936), *As You Like It, Peter Pan* (1937), her greatest stage success as Lady Hadwell in *Charley Girl* (1965) for 2,047 performances, *No, No Nanette* (1973), *The Dame Sark, Maggie,* and *My Fair Lady* (revival). She appeared in 36 films, all but four of which were produced and directed by Herbert Wilcox, her husband. There are no survivors.

JOAN NEUMAN, 60, New York City-born stage and film actress, died Jan. 14 1987. She made her debut Off-Broadway in *A Woman of No Importance,* followed by *Arsenic and Old Lace, Camino Real, All the King's Men, Happy Sunset Inc.,* and *Triptych.* No other information.

VIRGINIA O'BRIEN, 90, stage actress who appeared in the *I Remember Mama* TV series from 1949–57, died May 2, 1987 in Weymouth, Mass. She appeared on Broadway with her husband, the late Donald Brian, in *The Chocolate Soldier* (1921), *The Merry Widow, Buddies,* and *The Man Behind the Gun,* and was in such productions as *Jack and Jill, The Rise of Rosie O'Reilly, Princess Ida, How's Your Health?, Sabrina Fair,* and *Keep Off the Grass* (1940). Surviving is her daughter.

ELAINE PERRY, 64, New York City-born actress, producer and director, died Jan. 30, 1987 at her home in Buena Vista, Colo. The daughter of Antoinette Perry (also an actress and producer for whom the "Tony" Awards were named), began her career as understudy to Ingrid Bergman in *Liliom* and appeared in *Glamour Preferred, No For An Answer,* and *The Trojan Women,* stage managed *The Barretts of Wimpole Street,* and produced *Touchstone, Anastasia, King of Hearts,* and *The Late Christopher Bean.* She is survived by a sister.

John C.
Becher

Ray
Bolger

Peter
Burnell

Allen
Case

James
Coco

Helen
Craig

Cathryn
Damon

Robert
Drivas

Wilbur
Evans

Hugh
Franklin

Wynne
Gibson

Margalo
Gillmore

Hermione
Gingold

Murray
Hamilton

Danny
Kaye

Glenn
Kezer

Elsa
Lanchester

Scott
McKay

Anna
Neagle

Joan
Neuman

Roy
Poole

Robert
Preston

John D.
Seymour

Dick
Shawn

Kate
Smith

RON PLACZEK (Ronald A. Placzek), 36, set designer for theatre and TV in the US and Europe and Emmy Award winning art director of CBS TV's *The Guiding Light*, died of pneumonia Nov. 27, 1986 in Manhattan. His many credits include the Off-Broadway productions of *Broadway Scandals of 1928, Wednesday, Blood Relations* (Villager Award), *The Singular Life of Alberta Nobbs, An Evening of Sholom Aleichem, The Inheritors, Paradise Lost, Rain, Ghosts, The Hasty Heart,* and *Options.* He is survived by his parents.

ROY POOLE, 62, San Bernardino, CA-born stage, film, and TV actor, died July 5, 1986 in Mount Kisco, NY. He made his Broadway bow in 1950 in *Now I Lay Me Down to Sleep*, followed by *St. Joan, The Bad Seed, I Knock at the Door, Long Day's Journey into Night, Face of a Hero, Moby Dick, Poor Bitos, 1776, Scratch, Once a Catholic,* and Off-Broadway in *27 Wagons Full of Cotton, A Memory of Two Mondays, Secret Service, Boy Meets Girl, Villager,* and *Quartermaine's Terms.* He is survived by his wife.

ABLE PORKAS, 68, Philadelphia-born dancer, director, and choreographer, died April 22, 1987 in Los Angeles of unreported causes. His Broadway appearances include *Something for the Boys, Lady in the Dark, Lute Song, Annie Get Your Gun, How to Succeed in Business Without Really Trying, Fade Out-Fade In, The Rothschilds, Sugar, No, No, Nanette,* and *Irene.* He is survived by a brother.

ROBERT PRESTON (Robert Preston Meservey), 68, Massachusetts-born stage, screen, and TV actor, immortalized by his brilliant Tony-Award-winning portrayal of Prof. Harold Hill in *The Music Man* on Broadway and in the film version, died March 21, 1987 of lung cancer in Santa Barbara, CA. After a lengthy film career, he made his Broadway debut in 1951 in *Twentieth Century*, followed by *The Male Animal, Men of Distinction, His and Hers, The Magic and the Loss, Tender Trap, Janus, Hidden River, The Music Man, Too True to Be Good, Nobody Loves an Albatross, Ben Franklin in Paris, The Lion in Winter, I Do! I Do!* (Tony Award), *Mack and Mabel,* and *Sly Fox* (1977). He is survived by his wife, former actress Catherine Feltus, and his father.

BROTHER JONATHAN RINGKAMP, 57, Brooklyn-born Franciscan brother and playwright, died Sept. 19, 1986 of pneumonia in Manhattan. In 1967 he and actress Geraldine Fitzgerald founded the Everyman Theater of Brooklyn. His plays include *Everyman and Roach, The Zinger* (a musical co-authored by Harry Chapin, 1976), *Bella Figura* (1982), and *Poisoner of the Wells* (1983). He is survived by a brother.

BENNY RUBIN, 87, comedian and tap dancer, died July 15, 1986 in Los Angeles. Prior to an almost 50 year film career, he appeared on Broadway in *Half a Window* (1927), *Radio Carnival* (1932), and in *Vaudeville* at the Palace (1927, '30, '32). He is survived by two brothers and two daughters.

BRUCE SAVAN, 59, Oregon-born agent, died April 13, 1987 in New York of AIDS. After an early career as a singer and performer, he stage managed *Time Out for Ginger* (1952) and *The Girl in Pink Tights* (1954) on Broadway, before shifting to talent management in 1954. As vice-president and head of the legit department of APA for the past 23 years his clients included many prominent artists. He is survived by a sister.

ALBERT WIGGIN SELDEN, 64, New York-born producer, composer, lyricist, and managing director of the Goodspeed Opera House in East Haddam, CT since 1963, died of cancer June 6, 1987 at his home in Santa Fe, NM. He made his Broadway debut as a composer with *Small Wonder* (1948), followed by *Month of Sundays*, and he produced shows including *The Grey-Eyed People* (1952), *The Body Beautiful, The Girls Against the Boys*, and co-produced *Irene* and *Man of La Mancha.* He is survived by his wife, three daughters, four sons, two stepchildren, and two sisters.

JOHN D. SEYMOUR, 88, Boston-born stage, screen, radio, and TV actor, died of heart failure July 10, 1986 in New York City. Representing the sixth generation of an acting family, he appeared in some 70 Broadway productions, beginning with his debut in 1918 in *Out There*, followed by *Richard III, Dearest Enemy, Blood Money, Barretts of Wimpole Street, Sweet Adeline, Cyrano de Bergerac, Pride and Prejudice, Susan and God, Here Today, The Moon Is Down, Eastward in Eden, The Vigil, Light up the Sky, Sacred Flame, The Father, Pal Joey* (CC), *The King and I, Life with Father, We Interrupt This Program,* and Off-Broadway in *12 Angry Men.* He is survived by his wife, actress Abby Lewis, a son, and a daughter.

DICK SHAWN, 63 (elsewhere reported to be 57 or 58), Buffalo, NY-born stage, film, TV actor and comedian, died April 17, 1987 of an apparent heart attack, falling on stage while performing his standup act at U. of CA, San Diego. He made his Broadway debut in 1948 in *For Heaven's Sake, Mother*, followed by *A Funny Thing Happened on the Way . . ., The Egg, Peterpat, Fade Out-Fade In, I'm Solomon, Musical Jubilee,* and Off-Broadway in *Rebirth Celebration of the Human Race*, and his one-man show *The Second Greatest Entertainer in the Whole Wide World.* He is survived by a son, three daughters, and a brother.

KATE SMITH, 79, Virginia-born stage, screen, radio, and TV entertainer and one of the most popular singers of the century died June 17, 1986 at Raleigh (NC) Community Hospital. She had been in poor health since 1976, when she suffered brain damage as a result of a diabetic coma. The vibrant-voiced singer who is immortalized by her memorable rendition of "*God Bless America*" appeared on Broadway in *Honeymoon Lane* (1926), *Flying High* (1930), and in *Vaudeville* at the Palace in 1929, '31, and '32. She never married, and is survived by her sister and two nieces.

HARVEY STEPHENS, 85, stage and film character actor, died Dec. 22, 1986 in Laguna Hills, CA. His Broadway credits include *South Pacific, Dishonored Lady, The Animal Kingdom, Tomorrow and Tomorrow,* and *Over 21.* He is survived by his wife and three children.

PAUL STEVENS, 65, stage, screen, and TV actor, died June 4, 1986 of pneumonia in New York. He made his Broadway bow in 1957 in *Compulsion*, followed by *Girls of Summer, General Seegar, Andorra, The Advocate,* and Off-Broadway in *The Crucible, Romeo and Juliet, Two Gentlemen of Verona, As You Like It, Much Ado about Nothing, Ivanov, The White Devil,* and *The Memorandum.* He is survived by a sister and two brothers.

ROY K. STEVENS, 40, Philadelphia-born stage and TV actor, dancer, and singer, died April 12, 1987 in New York of unreported causes. He appeared on Broadway in *Amadeus, Macbeth, Herzl,* and *Fire,* and Off-Broadway in *She Loves Me.* He is survived by his parents and two brothers.

MAXINE SULLIVAN (Marietta Williams), 75, jazz singer with a stage, nightclub, and recording career that spanned 50 years, died April 7, 1987 in the Bronx, NY of a seizure brought on by pneumonia. She received a 1979 Tony Award nomination for her Broadway performance in *My Old Flame.* A daughter and a son survive.

DAVID SUSSKIND, 66, New York City-born prolific stage, screen, and TV producer, was found dead of an apparent heart attack Feb. 22, 1987 in his hotel suite in Manhattan. The host of a syndicated TV talkshow for 28 years, his producing credits on Broadway include *Rashomon, Mr. Lincoln, A Very Special Baby, All In Good Time, Kelly,* and *Brief Lives.* His many award-winning TV productions include *Look Homeward, Angel, Eleanor and Franklin, The Crucible, The Diary of Anne Frank, The Glass Menagerie, The Price, Death of a Salesman,* and most recently *Lyndon Johnson.* He is survived by a son, three daughters, a sister and a brother.

BLANCHE SWEET, 90, Chicago-born stage and pioneer screen star, died of a stroke Sept. 6, 1986 at her home in Manhattan. She began her stage career at age four and her film career at 12, becoming a D. W. Griffith star (124 movies, all but three silent), and she appeared on Broadway in *The Petrified Forest* (1934), *There's Always a Breeze, Aries is Rising,* and *Those Endearing Young Charms* (1943). There are no immediate survivors.

DWIGHT TAYLOR, 84, New York City-born playwright, screenwriter, and author, died of a heart attack Dec. 31, 1986 in Woodland Hills, CA. The son of playwright Charles A. Taylor and actress Laurette Taylor, his first produced play on Broadway was *Don't Tell George* in 1928, followed by *Lipstick, The Gay Divorce,* and *Out of This World,* and he produced *Where Do We Go From Here?* (1938). He is survived by two daughters, a son, and a sister.

VERREE TEASDALE, 80, Washington-born stage and screen actress and the widow of actor Adolphe Menjou, died Feb. 17, 1987 of unreported causes. She made her Broadway bow in 1924 in *The Youngest*, followed by such productions as *The Morning After, The Master of the Inn, Buy, Buy Baby, The Constant Wife, By Request, Precious, Nice Women, Soldiers and Women, Elizabeth and Essex, The Royal Virgin, The Greeks Had a Word for It, Marriage for Three,* and *Experience Unneccessary.* No immediate survivors reported.

CAROL TEITEL, 62, New York City-born stage, radio, and TV actress, died July 27, 1986 in Camden, NJ of complications following an automobile accident in Pensacola, FL. She made her Broadway debut in 1957 in *The Country Wife*, followed by *The Entertainer, Hamlet, Marat/de Sade, A Flea in Her Ear, Crown Matrimonial, All Over Town, The Little Foxes, The Marriage of Figaro* (1985), and Off-Broadway in *Way of the World, Juana La Loca, An Evening with Ring Lardner, The Misanthrope, Shaw Festival, A Country Scandal* (Obie Award), *The Bench, Colombe, Under Milk Wood* (Obie Award), *7 Days of Mourning, Long Day's Journey into Night, The Old Ones, Figures in the Sand, The World of Sholom Aleichem, Big and Little, Duet, Trio, Every Good Boy Deserves Favor* (LC), *Fallen Angels, A Stitch in Time, Faces of Love, The Keymaker, Learned Ladies, Major Barbara in Concert, Baseball Wives,* and *Flight of the Earls.* She is survived by her husband, playwright Nathan Teitel, and her mother.

ROBERT LEEMING THIRKIELD, 49, actor, director, and a founder of the Circle Repertory Company Off-Broadway, jumped to his death from his Manhattan apartment July 9, 1986. He created roles in *Futz, Tom Paine, Balm in Gilead, The Mound Builders, Hot L Baltimore,* and *Rimers of Eldritch.* He is survived by a son, a daughter, a stepson, and a sister.

TEMPLE TEXAS, 63, Texas-born former actress and theatrical press agent, died June 18, 1986 in Newport Beach, CA of natural causes. The widow of agent Joe Shribman, she appeared on Broadway in shows including *Seven Lively Arts, It Takes Two, The Girl from Nantucket,* and *Pipe Dream.* She is survived by a son and daughter.

| Blanche Sweet | Carol Teitel | Antony Tudor | Forrest Tucker | Bill Tynes | Keenan Wynn |

FORREST TUCKER, 71, Indiana-born veteran stage, screen, and TV actor, died of cancer Oct. 25, 1986 in Woodland Hills, CA. Perhaps best known for his portrayal of Sgt. Morgan O'Rourke in the 1960's TV series *F Troop*, and for his appearances in over 50 films, he made his Broadway bow in 1964 in *Fair Game For Lovers*, and toured for three-and-a-half years as Prof. Harold Hill in *The Music Man*. He is survived by his wife, two daughters, a son, sister, and his mother.

LORENZO TUCKER, 79, Philadelphia-born stage and screen actor known as "the colored Valentino" in all-black films of the 20's and 30's, died Aug. 19, 1986 of cancer in Hollywood, CA. He made his Broadway debut in 1929 in *Make Me Know It*, followed by *The Constant Sinner, Ol' Man Satan*, and *Hummin' Sam* (1933). He is survived by his wife.

ANTONY TUDOR, 78 or 79, London-born, one of the foremost ballet choreographers of the century, died April 19, 1987 of a heart attack at his home in Manhattan. For Broadway he choreographed *Hollywood Pinafore* (1945) and *The Day Before Spring*. His honors include New York City's Handel Medallion, the Kennedy Center Honors, the Capezio Award, and the first Dance/USA National Honors (in tandem with Martha Graham). There are no immediate survivors.

BILL TYNES, 30, California-born actor and founder and artistic director of the New Amsterdam Theater Company, died Jan. 9, 1987 at his parents' home in Placentia, CA, of complications from AIDS. He made his debut Off-Broadway in 1977 in *The Three Sisters*, followed by *Can-Can, Strider*, and on Broadway in *Strider* in 1979. He produced the concert versions of *The New Moon, Sweet Adeline, One Touch of Venus, Jubilee*, and *I Married an Angel*, all at Town Hall. He is survived by his parents, two sisters and two brothers.

RUDY VALLEE, 84, Vermont-born stage, screen, radio, TV actor and crooning idol of the 30's and 40's famed for his hand-held megaphone, died of a heart attack July 3, 1986 at his home in North Hollywood, CA while watching the Statue of Liberty centennial salute on TV. He appeared in *Vaudeville* at the Palace (1929) and made his legit debut in 1931 in *George White's Scandals*, followed by *George White's Scandals of 1935, The Man in Possession* (1939), and the comeback that rejuvenated his career in *How To Succeed in Business* . . . . in 1961 in his best known role as J. B. Biggley, which he subsequently recreated in the film of the play. He was married four times and had no children.

LILI VALENTY, 86, Polish-born stage, film, radio, and TV actress, died March 11, 1987 in Hollywood, CA. She appeared in 20 Broadway plays, including *Bitter Stream* (1936), *Cue for Passion, The Land Is Bright, Pick-Up Girl, Sky Drift*, and *Now I Lay Me Down to Sleep* (1950). There are no survivors.

HERBURT VIGRAN, 76, veteran character actor on stage, screen, and TV, died of complications from cancer Nov. 29, 1986 in Los Angeles. His appearances on Broadway include *Achilles Had a Heel* (1935), *Cyrano de Bergerac* (1936), *Happy Valley, Limited, Having a Wonderful Time*, and *Boy Meets Girl*. No survivors reported.

MARIA VON TRAPP, 82, the extraordinary woman whose life-story inspired Rodgers and Hammerstein's immortal classic *The Sound of Music*, died March 28, 1987 of congestive heart failure in Morrisville, VT. Baroness von Trapp had been living in Stowe, VT, where the family settled in 1942 after fleeing to the US in 1938 to escape Nazi rule. The Trapp family played its first US concert at New York's Town Hall in 1938 and continued to tour internationally until the mid-50's. Baron Georg von Trapp died in 1947 at age 57. She is survived by a son, two daughters, two stepsons, and three stepdaughters.

PATRICK WADDINGTON, 86, stage and film character actor, died Feb. 4, 1987 in his native York, England. His Broadway appearances include *First Episode* (1934), *The Magnificent Hugo, Kean, Rosmersholm, The Affair*, and *A Darker Flower*, and he played Col Pickering in more than 1,000 performances of *My Fair Lady* on tour in Britain. No survivors reported.

EARL WILSON, 79, Ohio-born, last of the legendary Broadway columnists who chronicled the foibles and fancies of the entertainment world, died Jan. 16, 1987 of Parkinson's Disease in New York. His syndicated column *It Happened Last Night* originated in The New York Post and was carried in newspapers across the country. He is survived by his son, playwright and composer Earl Wilson, Jr.

KEENAN WYNN, 70, New York-born stage, screen, and TV actor, perhaps best known as one of the clowning thugs in the film version of *Kiss Me Kate*, died of cancer Oct. 14, 1986 at his home in Brentwood, CA. He appeared in more than 220 films, 250 TV shows (including *Requiem for a Heavyweight*, in which he co-starred with his father, the late Ed Wynn), 100 stage productions, and 21 Broadway productions, including *Ten Minute Alibi* (1935), *Remember the Day, Hey Diddle Diddle, Room Service, Star Wagon, Blind Alley, Jason, The Stag at Bay, The Little Inn, Feather in the Breeze, Hitch Your Wagon!, One for the Money, Two for the Show, The More the Merrier, Johnny on the Spot*, and *Strip for Action* (1942). He is survived by his wife, two daughters, and two sons.

INDEX

233